CONTEMPORARY LESBIAN WRITERS OF THE UNITED STATES

CONTEMPORARY LESBIAN WRITERS OF THE UNITED STATES

A Bio-Bibliographical Critical Sourcebook

EDITED BY
Sandra Pollack
AND
Denise D. Knight

GREENWOOD PRESS
Westport, Connecticut • London

Library of Congress Cataloging-in-Publication Data

Contemporary lesbian writers of the United States : a bio-
　　bibliographical critical sourcebook / edited by Sandra Pollack and
　　Denise D. Knight.
　　　p.　cm.
　　Includes bibliographical references and index.
　　ISBN 0-313-28215-3
　　　1. Lesbians' writings, American—Bio-bibliography.　2. American
　　literature—Women authors—Bio-bibliography.　3. American
　　literature—Women authors—Dictionaries.　4. Women authors,
　　American—Biography—Dictionaries.　5. Lesbians—United States—
　　Biography—Dictionaries.　6. Lesbians' writings, American—
　　Dictionaries.　I. Pollack, Sandra.　II. Knight, Denise D.
　　PS153.L46C65　1993
　　810.9'9206643—dc20　　　　92-39468

British Library Cataloguing in Publication Data is available.

Library of Congress Catalog Card Number: 92-39468
ISBN: 0-313-28215-3

First published in 1993

Greenwood Press, 88 Post Road West, Westport, CT 06881
An imprint of Greenwood Publishing Group, Inc.

Printed in the United States of America

The paper used in this book complies with the
Permanent Paper Standard issued by the National
Information Standards Organization (Z39.48–1984).

10 9 8 7 6 5 4 3 2 1

In 1982, I asked Audre Lorde if she'd let me interview her for the film *Before Stonewall: The Making of a Gay and Lesbian Community*. She agreed, but not before asking, "I won't be the only black lesbian in it, will I?" The question did not surprise me. Audre was always deeply aware of the various communities—black, women, lesbian, artist—that gave her sustenance throughout her extraordinary lifetime. She refused to allow herself to be quick-frozen into the position of "Black Lesbian Spokesperson." Her roots were too wide and too deep for that to happen. Her 58 years of life were spent creating the exquisite poetry and asking the provocative questions engendered by those roots.

When Senator Jesse Helms pointed to her work as an example of obscenity that should not be supported by public arts funding I understood immediately that it was her provocative questions and her wide reach that terrified him and the religious right. Fortunately there were as many people inspired by her insistent expectations as there were those frightened by them. Her blunt question made me examine the Stonewall film project and my role in it, as well as my role in the political and professional worlds. It is an examination I will never suspend. It is a rigor that will keep me growing.

In a naming ceremony on St. Croix shortly before she died, Audre took on the name Gamba Adisa, meaning Warrior: She Who Makes Her Meaning Clear. It is a name Audre Lorde never carried lightly in any of her communities whether acting as Poet Laureate of the State of New York or lesbian activist or supporter of black women in South Africa or creative writing teacher. This volume is dedicated to Audre Lorde—her writing will keep asking the important questions, keep making her meaning clear.

Jewelle L. Gomez
December 15, 1992

CONTENTS

PREFACE

In January of 1991, when Denise called and asked if I'd be interested in co-editing a book on contemporary lesbian writers, I experienced many thoughts and feelings. I was intrigued. It felt important to do. I was hesitant about taking on another project. But the underlying thought was, who is this woman and why is she asking me? As we spoke, it was clear that Denise had already given much thought to what this book would look like and that she already had a probable publisher. Why then did she want someone else involved? I asked if she was a lesbian. She wasn't. I became cynical. Did she need an out lesbian to give the project credibility? Did I want to work with a straight woman on this project? Why does she even want to do this? We met for lunch; I shared my concerns, and I listened. I realized I was hesitant, but I was impressed. Denise was smart, well organized, energetic, and enthusiastic. I checked with friends—lesbian faculty she had worked with in graduate school. I got high recommendations, and I began to be more open to the idea of working with an ally. I decided to go ahead. I have not been disappointed. It has been a pleasure to work with someone so conscientious, so meticulous, so committed to this project.

In the process of making the decision to work on this book, I had to examine my initial skepticism about a straight woman's sensitivity and willingness to work with lesbian literature. I recalled the blunders white women have made in writing about women of color. I recalled my anger at the recognition men are now getting for their work in women's studies when for so long women's writing went largely unacknowledged by the academy. I got in touch, once again, with my own internalized homophobia. No matter that I am out as a lesbian writer; on my own campus, I still rarely mention my lesbian writing. Even today, I find that I grit my teeth when I leave work of obviously lesbian content for typing or duplicating. I know that there will be negative comments and snide remarks made behind my back. I recalled that when I was married, it was easier for me to include lesbian and gay materials in my classes. I was being a ''liberal'' and an "aware" professor. Now I have to be wary that some student doesn't complain that I'm "pushing my lifestyle" on the class when we discuss a lesbian or gay poem, story, or author. I lost that heterosexual privilege over fifteen years ago and have been struggling with ways to legitimize lesbian literature in the classroom ever since. Denise had that safety, and I had to deal with feelings of resentment that the recognition of that privilege brought up for me.

But the more I looked at the bigger picture, the more I began to appreciate the value of our working together. I don't want lesbian writing to be something that is circulated only in the lesbian community. I do want others to know about and to appreciate our lives. Lesbian literature can help make that happen. This means that our literature has to be taught in our classrooms. It means that lesbian *and* straight faculty will have to become more familiar with and feel more comfortable teaching lesbian literature. It is my hope that this book and the work of over one hundred contributors to this book will be part of that process.

Sandra Pollack

When I first began contemplating this project, I discussed the possible ramifications with a number of friends and colleagues. Several asked why, as a straight woman, I would want to edit a sourcebook on American lesbian writers. Inquiries ranged from polite curiosity to exaggerated concern. For the most part, however, reaction was positive and people supportive. And the question that I kept being asked—*why* do you want to do this?—was a legitimate one that deserved an honest answer.

Initially, I was approached by a colleague, Emmanuel S. Nelson, who knew that I was working on the private diaries of Charlotte Perkins Gilman and that I was struggling to define her ambiguous sexuality. In particular, I was attempting to decode some of the enigmatic language through which she characterized her very intense relationships with other women. Professor Nelson was, at the time, in the process of editing a volume of essays for Greenwood Press, *Contemporary Gay American Novelists: A Bio-Bibliographical Critical Sourcebook*, and he suggested that I edit a companion volume on American lesbian writers. I knew that the project would be an important one: no one had ever compiled a sourcebook on American lesbian writers, so the proposed edition would fill an existing gap in American literary and cultural studies. At the same time, however, I was well aware that lesbian literature was not exactly my area of expertise. But I strongly believed that this was a worthwhile project and one that *should* be undertaken. I just wasn't at all sure that it was I who should be undertaking it.

When I first started teaching literature courses as a graduate student in 1985, I made a conscious decision to select readings that would be more "representative" than those that I was typically assigned as an undergraduate literature major. I had always made an effort to construct a syllabus with reading selections that carefully balanced gender, ethnicity, and geography, and incorporated as many non-canonical writers as possible. Through all my attempts to balance the reading selections, however, not once had I ever consciously given thought to sexual self-identity. Quite frankly, for all my efforts at making my reading list "representative," issues of sexual preference in the selection of writers and works had simply never occurred to me. Then, during my first semester at the State University of New York College at Cortland, a most disturbing incident in my Introduction to Literature course caused me to reassess my reading selections and to realize that sexual identity is, indeed, an important consideration that must be factored into the equation.

It was during the fall of 1990 that I had assigned David Leavitt's short story "Territory," which centers on a gay man in his early twenties who brings his lover home to meet his mother for the first time. The story actually focuses more on the relationship between the protagonist, Neil, and his mother than between Neil and his partner, Wayne. In essence, the story deals with the process by which Neil learns to let go of his guilt. There are no sexually explicit scenes in the story.

In the five years that I had been teaching, nothing had prepared me for what occurred in class that day. At the State University of New York at Albany, where I taught before moving to Cortland, I had assigned D. H. Lawrence's *The Fox*, which deals with lesbian love, and Alice Munro's short story "Privilege," which focuses on an adolescent crush that one girl has on another. Whether or not the students' receptiveness to these works was the result of what could be construed as non-threatening or "acceptable" endings (the death of Jill Banford in *The Fox*, and the failure to act on the fantasy in "Privilege"), I do not know. What I do know is that the discussions of these works were fruitful, illuminating, and open-minded. When I began discussion of Leavitt's "Territory," however, that autumn afternoon, I was stunned by the students' reactions. "Why do we have to read about homos?" some of them asked. "This story is disgusting," others remarked.

I had frequently encountered opinions in the classroom that betrayed evidence of misogyny, racism, religious intolerance, and classism; I had never, until that day, encountered homophobia. For fifty minutes, the students and I talked about their feelings, their opinions, their perceptions, their fears. That incident ended my vacillation; I left class that day fully committed to undertake the project.

Still, I knew that I lacked the expertise, the experience, and the connections necessary to see the project through. I wrote to a former colleague, a prominent lesbian scholar, asking if she knew of other lesbian scholars who might be interested in co-editing the project. She phoned a few days later with several names. Among them was Sandra Pollack, who had considerable experience as the editor of two anthologies and who happened to live close by. Sandy was cautious when I introduced myself by phone, but she agreed to meet me to discuss my proposal. I was delighted when, after thoughtful consideration, she agreed to co-edit the book, and, in truth, I literally could not have done it without her; nor would I have wanted to. She has been a superb co-editor in every respect: she is bright, hardworking, committed, and energetic. She is also fun to work with.

The project has entailed an enormous amount of work, but it has been a great experience and one that has allowed me to grow. I have learned much about the contributions of lesbian writers, about the importance of lesbian literature, and about the need to continue to expand my own course readings to make them truly representative.

Denise D. Knight

* * * * *

As we began this book, we struggled with how exactly to define the content and scope of the project. We wanted to focus on American writers, since we both specialized in American literature and knew that we had a rich and diverse core of writers around whom we could construct a comprehensive volume. But a more difficult decision was where, historically, to begin. We weighed the benefits of going back to the nineteenth century against those of focusing on a briefer period of time. We decided to limit our study to contemporary writers, particularly since the number of self-identified lesbian writers has grown dramatically within the last twenty years. Although the 1969 Stonewall riots are often seen as a turning point in the formation of the contemporary gay movement, many lesbian writers, particularly white women, found their voices during the women's movement of the 1970s. The diversity of lesbian voices is articulated as the growing numbers of Asian, Black, Chicana, Latina, Native, and other liberation movements continue to grow. Slowly the voices are reflecting the wide range of lesbian lives—sexualities, physical conditions, ages.

In terms of genres, we restricted our selection to women who have primarily written poetry, fiction, and drama, even though one of the strengths of contemporary lesbian writing has been the breaking down of genres—the essays, the autobiographies, the anthologies that nourished our lives as we became stronger in our visible lesbian consciousness (see the Bibliography for a sample of some of these non-fiction works).

Another decision revolved around the question of nationality. Specifically, we needed to decide how to define writers "*of* the United States." Many of our writers have immigrated to the United States and now consider the United States a part of their identity. Except for Jane Rule, we chose not to include lesbians who are no longer living in the United States. Rule, born in Plainfield, New Jersey, now lives in Canada, has had a significant impact on the development of U.S. lesbian literature, and her writing continues to have a strong U.S. following.

The term *lesbian* was, of course, harder to define. Several questions complicated the issue. Should we, for example, include writers who we had heard through the grapevine were now sexually involved with men? Or, what if they had publicly declared that they were involved sexually with men? Many of the women included began writing when they were involved in heterosexual relationships; most, however, found an authentic voice when they claimed their lesbian identity. We decided that we would include authors who, at some point during the 1970–1992 period, had written as self-identified lesbians. We also decided that we would not include women who have not been open about their lesbianism even if we knew them to be in lesbian relationships. When we were uncertain about how public any woman was, we contacted her for her permission to be included.

Readers will note that there are a few prominent names that are conspicuously missing: some well-known and highly respected lesbian writers have specifically requested that they *not* be included. In some cases, writers did not wish to foreground their lesbian identity in favor of their professional or racial identities; in other cases, there was clear discomfort at being "labeled." We have respected their wishes.

After our parameters had been decided, we drew up a tentative list of well-known lesbian writers, which we circulated to scholars, editors, bookstores, and organizations, asking for feedback and additional names. We placed ads in a number of journals and newsletters announcing the project and asking for contributors and ideas about how to expand the list to make it as inclusive as possible. The feedback we received was encouraging. Our initial list of just over fifty writers quickly doubled. Space restrictions, however, forced us to cap the list at one hundred writers. Certainly there are many more writers who could have been included. As late as a month before our deadline, we were still receiving suggestions.

Each of the one hundred essays in this volume follows a specific five-part format: a biography containing information about the writer's personal history; a discussion of the author's major works and themes; an overview of critical studies examining the writer's work; and a two-part bibliography, featuring works by the author and studies of the author.

For many of these writers—indeed, for the entire field of lesbian literature—"critical studies" are not yet found in the scholarly academic format that we traditionally expect. Many of the featured writers, for example, have not yet enjoyed a critical reception of their work, but rather, their recognition has come primarily in the form of reviews. For emerging writers in particular, the paucity of critical material is typical. As Adrienne Lauby notes in her essay on Martha Courtot, included in this edition, many of the bibliographical references "remain dispersed in the newspapers and magazines of the U.S. women's movement. The fact that even the most consistent and respected of these publications are rarely collected by libraries or indexed by standard reference sources makes a thorough research of her and other lesbian writers difficult." Complicating efforts to collect source references is the fact that many of the early journals in which much of the material first appeared were sporadically published and often appeared without dates or page numbers. Another factor making the collection of complete bibliographical information difficult was that some of the material originally appeared in small pamphlets, newsletters, and programs, which may no longer be extant. In many cases, too, our contributors worked from old photocopies or from clippings containing only partial information in scrapbooks and personal collections of the authors about whom they were writing. But despite the occasional absence of traditional academic criticism in some of the essays, this volume contributes to the ongoing attempt to recover material that may be lost or forgotten. Along with the groundbreaking efforts by the Lesbian Herstory Archives in New York City, the Center for Gay and Lesbian Studies (CGALS) at the City University of New York, and the San Francisco Main Library Center (to open in 1995), which will contain the extensive collection of books and monographs dating back to 1860 donated by Barbara Grier and Donna McBride, we are optimistic that the research engendered on the writers included in this volume will continue to yield a more complete record of their literary accomplishments.

The work of lesbian writers has, historically, found recognition primarily in book reviews and articles within the lesbian community. Readers will note, for example, that many of the women whose entries we have included have themselves written entries on other writers. Lesbian writers generally feel a sense of community in supporting other lesbian writers, and a reality, at present, is that it is primarily other lesbians who are most familiar with lesbian writings and who are in the position, therefore, to write about this material. As we widen the community exposed to lesbian authors, more people will feel comfortable using and writing seriously about lesbian literature in the future.

In addition to the bibliographies for the individual writers, this volume includes an extensive bibliography of non-fiction resources focusing on lesbian issues—including works in psychology, sexuality, parenting, health, history, and theory that may be of interest to the reader. A glance at the publication dates will reveal the increasing visibility of lesbian writers in recent years. Two appendices feature, respectively, a list of publishers of lesbian writers and a list of periodicals and journals featuring lesbian writers.

There are many people who have contributed time and energy to the production of *Contemporary Lesbian Writers of the United States: A Bio-Bibliographical Critical Sourcebook.* We would like to give special thanks to the women who reviewed our initial list and who offered suggestions of writers to be included: Nancy Bereano, SDiane Bogus, Tucker Farley, Judith Fetterley, Nelly Furman, Linda Gardiner, Jewelle Gomez, Biddy Martin, Marilyn Murphy, Mona Oikawa, Minnie Bruce Pratt, Mariana Romo-Carmona, Catharine Stimpson, and Elaine Upton. We also wish to express our gratitude to those who wrote essays but were unable to secure the permission necessary for inclusion: Terry Brown, Elisa Davila, Ann Gebhard, Larry Harred, and Stacey Sheridan. To those who had to turn their essays over to others for completion—Ayofemi Folayan because of the Los Angeles riots, Maria Gonzales because of differences in interpretation with the author, and Dori Steele because of an automobile accident—we owe special thanks. Our thanks to Tucker Farley for writing the introduction, which places contemporary lesbian writers of the United States in a historical and theoretical framework. Ellen Kline also deserves thanks for compiling the bibliography of non-fiction lesbian writings. And particular thanks go to all of the contributors who made this volume possible by devoting their time and energy.

Sandy's special thanks go to Ba Stopha, her partner of twelve years, for her continuous reminder that this project, like others before it, would get completed. Denise thanks her husband, Michael Barylski, for his support and encouragement. She also thanks the English Department at the State University of New York at Cortland for granting a course reduction during the spring 1992 semester so that she could devote more time to the project. We both thank Emmanuel S. Nelson for his numerous insights and suggestions, and his good humor and generosity, and Marilyn Brownstein and Julie Cullen, our editors at Greenwood Press, for their support of this project. Finally, we thank Carol Roberts, our indexer, for lending her expertise and professionalism in the final stages of this project.

INTRODUCTION: DECONSTRUCTING THE ABSOLUTE—REALITY AND DIFFERENCE

Tucker Pamella Farley

The silence appeared absolute

When I fell in love with BJ, a girl a year ahead of me in high school, I had no way of understanding what that might be about. She gave me a book of golden leaves full of quotes from famous people about friendship: mostly Greek men who spoke about their love for each other in the highest terms. I had never heard of homosexuals or lesbians. I had no way of understanding what impelled me to sneak out of my parents' house at midnight and steal the family car to go meet BJ. Maybe if I hadn't gotten caught in the act, the car snagged on a metal post in the turnaround while I was trying to push it noiselessly and steer at the same time, I might have made the connection that night.

As it was, I wrote an essay on the ennobling love I felt for BJ and tried to read it aloud in English class. Sylvia Plath had won a contest a few years before in the same English class, and ever since, Mr. Crockett had insisted that all his honors students submit three pieces to the ladies' magazine that sponsored the contest. That year I had written a poem about looking at life through reflections in a mud puddle, a story I have forgotten but whose title might have been (my favorite at the time) "Shorn." And the other was this essay quoting all those famous Greeks on what the book called friendship and which they called love.

When it was my turn to stand up and read one of my entries, Mr. Crockett suggested I read my poem. I preferred to read my essay. He declined to hear the essay and suggested the story. I declined to read the story and declared I would read my essay. In his soft-spoken voice he warned me once again away from the essay, but I stood up and marched to the podium filled with the idealized passion and commitment of young love.

I began my reading bravely and enthusiastically; it took a while for me to notice the quality of the silence in the room. This silence felt to me like a wall—

not boredom, not a leaning forward to listen. As I read, some unnamed heaviness filled the air and slowed me down. I looked up at my audience, and faltered. Fighting to continue, I read more slowly, my enthusiasm out of place and draining away, to be replaced by nameless dread. Their listening was turning my wonderful essay into something awful.

The atmosphere was nearly suffocating; I didn't understand; didn't they want to know, learn, or be touched by the spirit of love? I struggled to keep going, despite the way the silence grew louder and louder. I wanted to share this beauty; to be true to everything I knew at once: I felt torn. I read more softly, haltingly. Something was reaching out and wrapping itself around my tongue.

Finally, I couldn't speak. Dazed, I searched for a clue in the faces of my silent classmates. Nothing. I turned my gaze toward the teacher's desk; hunched there, hands folded, without a word, he stared back. No one said a word. I stood there, paralyzed. The silence appeared absolute. Carrying my half-read essay, I made my way back to my seat. Still, no one said a word.

No one ever said a word.

Even today I ask myself exactly how a roomful of rather sheltered young students could have so actively participated in making that silence so loud. Yet most were upwardly mobile honor students, and these were the suburbs of the mid-fifties, one of the most repressive periods in our social history. Without knowing it at the time, I became committed to understanding the activity of listening space, within and without, and to making change, so that no one would ever have to suffer that silencing again. This, then, is a step on that road.

INVISIBILITY: THE BOUNDS OF CONSENSUS REALITY

In my high school classroom, I suspect none of us could have articulated what was happening, so unconscious and apparently invisible were the dynamics of how reality gets constructed; in the fifties the guiding lights of the cold war, and the scientific method that justified the rightness of "our" side, it was assumed at Gamaliel Bradford Senior High School that there was an objectively perceivable reality out there. The experts knew what it was, and anything different, anything that didn't fit in, had no reality. Difference was ignored, denied, suppressed, rendered invisible. Hadn't the adults around us learned this process, and modeled it for the children, unconsciously, trying to teach us properly? And hadn't we learned, some better than others, to modify or give up our sense of what "was" when it differed from theirs? To some extent, hadn't education been an instruction in distrusting the idiosyncratic? And doesn't every community provide examples by which children learn how to treat the *idios*?

In this case, we had studied Greek philosophers in class; but we did not know we read expurgated texts, where the homosexual love had been excised. The quotes I read were laundered, taken out of context and published in a list of "quotable quotes." Nonetheless, they had given me a sense that this new experience of mine could be connected to the prevailing discourse by which judgments were made concerning what was considered good. As a teenager hoping her enthusiasm would convey something special to her classmates, I had transgressed the bounds of consensus reality about love relationships. I did not see that my classmates had no way of fitting my essay into the "reality" I was by 1978 able to call "compulsory heterosexuality."[1]

We were led to think, in the Age of Sputnik, that a dictionary definition supplied a yardstick whereby language measured an already existing "thing" waiting out there to be matched up with its descriptive word(s). Hence, a neutral scientific yardstick could be applied to human affairs. So strong has been this underlying assumption in the modern period, so valorized by the credibility and authority granted to "the scientific method" and the assumption that experts are scientific, that in Western culture people tend automatically to maintain the idea that there is one reality. Traditionally, what is different gets treated as unreal or perverse, not as an indication that the prevailing reality is too narrow. Rather than change the terms of reality, the prevailing dominant ethos prefers to change the idiosyncratic—to deny, punish, cure, treat, or redeem her. The pressure to repress or deny a lesbian perspective that challenges hegemonic authority has been a driving force in maintaining heterosexual/patriarchal culture.

It has taken me three to four decades to realize that there may be different ways of construing what can be counted on as "real." For me and for others in this culture whose realities were constructed by not being "white," male, or rich, the torturous journey to save sanity and the imperative to survive and find a means of living together on the planet without the necessity for war have led us to challenge basic modernist structures for determining what is real. Decades of thinking that what I saw in a text or life was "right" and being smashed for being considered "wrong," decades of still trying to speak and be heard, forced me to figure out that these differences may not be matters of what already exists out there prepackaged on the shelf of life, as modernist scientific objectivity would have it, but may be socially constructed, and language might be a constitutive shaping force. "Homosexual" and "straight" are but two of the many discourses by which different understandings of what is deemed "natural," possible, and desirable may be produced as narratives of what "is."

AUTOMATICITY AND DISCOURSE

How many aspects of our daily lives go into making the fabric, the ordinary background of our days! Most of what is "obvious" in a community actually seems to disappear into the patterns of the fabric, and is assumed; the shared and the assumed constitute what appears as natural and real. What stands out then are the variations, interruptions, and breakdowns that call attention to what has been broken, as I found that day in my high school English class.

These ways of understanding are absorbed very young, almost by osmosis, and they become part of our automaticity. Versions of what is possible, desirable, acceptable, alien, or frightening shape our feelings and hopes, ideas and reactions, just as our resistances, imaginations, and creativity do. So inbuilt are these social processes that construct our automaticity, so much a part of the way the heart pounds, the stomach contracts, the shoulders tense, the glands sweat, that we operate always already out of what we have absorbed. The process becomes invisible; our culture tells us that the mind and the body are separate and what we see is "out there." We barely notice that what we see as "out there" is a function of the way discourses "out there" have become part of what is "in here." Discourse doesn't live just on paper or in the practice of groups; it lives also in the automaticity of flesh and blood.

In my high school classroom that day, all this learning had already taken place in invisible ways, as we had learned to speak. The others, who may not have had the context I had in knowing BJ, had already been silenced, and their silence silenced me. If there were other students there that day who loved someone of the same sex, could they have spoken up into the listening space of that classroom? Or even of that period in the history of this country? I doubt it.

SOCIAL DYNAMICS AND LISTENING SPACE: "NATURAL" SELECTION

Most voices of difference are lost, hidden, or coded in the effort to negotiate a way to speak and be heard in public space. Those who survive may be judged worthwhile by those who have allowed them space, without noticing that their own listening constructed the judgment and then attributed it as a characteristic to what was judged. "He is intelligent" and "her writing is good" are judgments that reveal more about the evaluators and their discourse than about the ones evaluated. The unnatural has been treated as sinful, sick, or criminal, as the prevailing discourses change. The selection process becomes invisible as the activity of making judgments is called "description." If the context shifts, this selection process may produce different assessments. Shifts may occur from one historical period to the next or from one community to another, or both, and may themselves be the subject of controversy. For example, what race means or how "it" functions continually changes and the changes shift listening spaces.

By the nature of the phenomenon, then, activity of the listening space functions on many levels. Social listening space operates within the commonalities of gender, community, culture, language and discourse, family, epoch, or education (and as many other domains as appear relevant). Individual listening space functions within the automaticity, allowing for variations, resistances to the predominant ways of construing "reality," and for conflicting interpretations that vie for attention. Linguistic listening space simultaneously shapes articulation and obscures the constructed nature of the shaping process.

LITERATURE AND THE CONSTRUCTION OF REALITIES

Part of the popularity of literature is that writing which is "creative" allows us to negotiate these interpretive terrains of difference in fictional, poetic, or dramatic worlds. Readers think, maybe there *are* different versions, different views, depending on where you are standing. In this sense literature can be subversive of the totalitarian notion that only one reality "exists." While literature is "made up," there is something "realistic" about it too. Readers enter different worlds. Different worlds are about life, are like life, create the narrative or sense of what life is. This opens the possibility that maybe life, like literature, is composed of different worlds constructed and interpreted variously, depending on a myriad of factors.

In the postmodern period we are beginning to understand that a biography or a history is an account made up by somebody with a certain perspective that influenced what they saw and that what they said was real. More and more we are coming to understand that it is practically impossible to pin down one so-called objective version of events. It is also becoming increasingly difficult to command the authority to declare that narrative the correct one, in "literature," in "history," or in daily "life."

Like the telling of a historical narrative, even in science what may have appeared as essentially natural, solid, and scientifically verifiable in the modernist discourse of objectivity has come to be seen as constructed by particular yardsticks. Science lays claim to the ultimate discourse of universal truth; the scientific method is the tool for establishing the facts. Science narratives eliminate diverse discourses. Physicists have scientifically proven that light is composed of waves; yet others of their colleagues, conversely, have also scientifically proven the opposite, that light is composed of chaotic, unwavelike particles. If one insists upon a belief in universal truth, then these contradictory proofs cannot possibly coexist. Yet they are both adduced by the scientific method. These two groups of physicists prove that the only common truth they have found is that seemingly incompatible realities coexist. The story of universality has broken down in the face of the realization that the instruments used to "see" always affect what is "seen."

Assumptions about "Man" believed to be true and obvious in the modernist discourses by which I was educated no longer hold up as universal truths, but now appear as generalizations of particular historical epochs. In our era, what has made the scaffolding of these constructions apparent is the growth of movements struggling in the names of the dispossessed to become visible in the spaces that had rendered them invisible: women, people of color, Jews, those differently abled, homosexuals, and others who didn't "fit" as representative "western man."

NEGOTIATING IN THE LISTENING SPACE

The journey from experiencing a wall of silence in my fifties classroom to introducing a book designed to facilitate more inclusiveness in classrooms has chronicled a shift in sensibility made possible by participation in movements that have helped change the listening space. These movements have contributed to laying the groundwork for what is known today as postmodern theory. But theory need not be some rarified practice isolated from our day-to-day practices. Most of us will recognize that there have been moments in our own lives when it seemed we couldn't be heard no matter how hard we tried, or, conversely, when we felt that we were entirely heard. Learning to understand the components that function in such everyday occurrences is similar to reading literature and participating in the construction of its meaning and the determination of its place in our culture. Some of the most important activity in liberating listening space takes place in classrooms, libraries, and discussion groups as people participate in deciding what a work of literature is good for.

Despite the existence of many-faceted pressures to bleach and blend popular and professional thinking into a monolithic, homogeneous culture of the fifties, we have again seen the stirrings of a democratic spirit. Most of us who find our versions of reality labeled different, biased, subjective, colored, distorted, un-American, or unnatural can now find some support for understanding that we are not crazy if we think we see reality differently. Movements get built around the effort to present into public listening space a view that has not been consensually "heard." As these movements make themselves heard, they shift the listening space, and make possible and available understandings that had been "invisible," denied, or unauthorized. As a result, different views have to be negotiated in taking account of "the public good" or even in defining who or what "the public" is.

While those who point out problems are often considered problematic and are punished for being troublemakers that disturb the status quo, they are often the ones who make visible the energies that generate a paradigm shift. In our culture, we are in the throes of such a paradigmatic shift, where an assumption of absolutes and universals is being challenged by the emergence of voices of difference fighting for the right to speak and be heard and still survive. The voices of this book are an important part of this shift. There is no one right way to read them. This possibility for different interpretations of what might appear on the surface to be "the same thing" is an everyday phenomenon of communication. That we can legitimately read "the same" texts differently opens up a new world of literary critical possibilities. Herein lie richness, and a possibilty for participating in reconstructing the values of our time.

SPEAKING/WRITING OUT OF AND INTO LISTENING SPACE: STYLE AND STRATEGY

Speaking into hostile listening space is costly and affects style. Lesbian culture and writing have moved from closets and coding to clarity. When I was discovering my love for women, we had no language for distinguishing; I didn't learn "queer" or "funny" until I went to college, and didn't learn "lesbian" until after that. I was engaging in what we now call "coming out" before there was a term for it; ordinary signs became signals for something else. Words, gestures with a commonly accepted meaning in the community or culture became suggestive, layered with possible illicit interpretations; anything could be eroticized or coded for special significance. At the same time, we didn't speak at first, for we would have been considered perverse: criminal or sick. Electroshock and surgery were correctives for the *idios* in the 1950s. From movements for liberation we learned to speak out, organize, and re-present ourselves. What distinguishes the writers in this volume is a breaking through those walls of silencing, an emerging clarity with which it has been possible to speak and write and act.

The literature we have recovered from the periods before the second wave of feminism and the concomitant growth of lesbian and gay liberations reflects the effort of trying to speak into listening spaces not yet conditioned to hear that version fully. Teaching lesbian literature the last twenty years has given me an acute sense of how a writer's style is bound up intimately with her strategies for speaking, being published/heard at least by some—or not—and surviving in her listening space(s). Style in literary theory is becoming as much a matter of these textual negotiations of speaking and listening as a matter of what has been called aesthetics. Yet aesthetics, or what appears beautiful, is also shaped by these same considerations that I have been suggesting are in some basic way political and social concerns. In part, what is considered beautiful or great is a judgment about what is to be handed down in a tradition. It must be contended with. In part what is considered beautiful or great is a matter of what conforms to predominant ideals and standards, and sells in literary and educational marketplaces. In part it is shaped by cultural values about innovation, uniqueness, difference, and the function and power of art.

This matter of judging style or aesthetics is in some measure a matter of how writers, publishers, and readers negotiate the terrain of what can be said and heard, under what circumstances, and how. As communities of readers and writers we are learning to be respectful of difference, and to deconstruct universals and value the differences they hide. A politics of identity has grown up in the process of building platforms for different voices to be heard. It becomes clear that the particular historical conditions under which any specific assessment is asserted make all the difference to our understanding, and that these understandings are a function of those times. Even more startling perhaps, they function to make up what is called identity. If what I am calling listening space permeates conscious and unconscious activity in the body and constructs personal automaticity as well as social forces, then our bodies, like our stories, invent—and are invented by—living in the world(s) we inhabit. There is no one essential nature or sex drive absolutely given and fixed. How we think about, label, understand "lesbian" changes over time. Writing about the historical background and context of this book has helped me to realize that the language used for description and explanation shifts, so that what is "lesbian," what is "sexual," what is "political," and even what is "literature" changes during the course of this narrative.

Contemporary Lesbian Writers of the United States: A Bio-Bibliographical Critical Sourcebook may appear to have a certain defining authority. Yet it is at the same time a result of multiple negotiations at the historical moment of its composition, and is a reflection of diverse political realities for many writers in many communities. There is no agreement about what single set of meanings this historical moment represents. Other writers would—and, hopefully, will— call up other reflections, share other ways of understanding and teaching, and construct different narratives.

TEACHING TO EMPOWER DIFFERENT VOICES: READING AND WRITING

Each of us speaks, and some of us write, into listening space; the strategies we use to be heard will vary. Rather than focusing on "finding" the meaning buried "in" the text, I ask students to focus on the processes by which interpretation is produced: to look at what may be happening in the writing, revising, editing, publishing process; what may be happening in the reading process for various readers; what may appear to be happening via interacting dynamics of the text; what standards of evaluation are most meaningful to themselves and other groups, and why. I ask them to write. Thinking about writing, we may ask, of all my potential listeners, which one(s) (living in my imagination as I write) are akin to me, and already understand perfectly what I mean? Who needs to be cleverly drawn in so they can see something a new way? Which listeners threaten the production entirely? Who silences me? Which listeners can be dismissed, rendered unimportant, or ignored? What do our answers reveal about the social dynamics of the listening space? These questions are helpful in classroom discussions of canonical and non-canonical literature as ways of understanding how a text/style may be read as a dynamic site of negotiation among the many voices—those we find reverberating in the text, what we make up as that of "the author," and the myriad possibilities of interpretive modes by readers of different epochs, classes, races, sexual identities, and cultures with all their various stances.

TELLING IT SLANT: RECOVERING LESBIAN LITERATURE

As a teacher I have found these critical notions extremely useful. They help me to understand the context for the flowering of lesbian writing in the second wave of feminism on which we have focused in this book, and why Emily Dickinson, for example, a century before, kept most of her poetry in a drawer.

Wild Nights—Wild Nights!
Were I with thee

Wild Nights should be
Our luxury!

Futile—the Winds—
To a Heart in port—
Done with the Compass—
Done with the Chart!

Rowing in Eden—
Ah, the Sea!
Might I but moor—Tonight—
In Thee!

Written for Sue Gilbert, the ecstatic abandon and erotic longing of the poem could be expressed for her ears and eyes, but not for others'. Married to Emily's brother, Sue lived next door to Emily, who wrote much of her best poetry as communications to Sue. The poetry and correspondence suggest a passion interrupted between the two women. Love, separation, and loss inspire the body of Dickinson's poetic work, which she showed to Sue or wrote in the absence of Sue, publishing only seven poems in her lifetime. The mid-nineteenth century saw many women break the taboos against a writing career for females, but had Dickinson to worry about publishing her poetry, as her correspondence with T. W. Higginson demonstrates, she would have had to develop very different strategies: metaphors, posture, tone, subject; everything, in short.

The letters from Dickinson in her isolated New England town to the abolitionist supporter of women's rights and literary light of the period, T. W. Higginson, reveal how ironically Dickinson could use the conventions of slavish submission in penning a revolt that might not be read as such at the time, except to "a discerning eye." She resolved to "Tell all the Truth but tell it slant"; still, relatives jealous of the family reputation laundered her journals, letters, and the poems themselves, heterosexualizing her life and work for posthumous publication at a time when both the general acceptance of women's romantic friendships and women's friendships themselves were beginning to become suspect.

While love between women was common in the nineteenth century, and was contained by the institution of marriage and the heterosexual presumption that sex was phallic and women's lovemaking could result neither in babies nor in alternatives to male-headed households—indeed, it was not considered "sex"—this fine distinction began to break down after the turn of the century. Freud granted everyone including women a sexual nature, and labeled the common practice of clitoral stimulation an immature phase that all girls went through. He invented the notion of a different, vaginal, orgasm as the hallmark of mature sexuality, and theorized that women who didn't emerge from their immature pleasures in clitoral orgasms were arrested in their development; not much could be done to cure them, an opinion disregarded by the burgeoning psychiatric profession in the twentieth century, when Dickinson's identity and reputation were made.

When I first read Dickinson, most of the love poetry was either omitted or interpreted as heterosexual; the most liberal editors commented that she had her pronouns or imagery confused. The most conservative simply "corrected" her work. Everything that was printed was expurgated, and her diaries and letters to Sue, mutilated after her death by anxious relatives and editors, were not available. Respectable scholars performed acrobatic feats of scholarship to avoid any hint at the nature of their relationship in biographical accounts and, in critical studies, any interpretation of the work in the light of it. Even today readers, teachers, and critics must contend with the most labored accumulation of biographical nonsense and wade through an erudite marsh of critical denial to participate in scholarly conversation about our foremost nineteenth-century woman poet.

Thanks to contemporary scholarship, readers today may enjoy letters and journals by Angelina Weld Grimké, Margaret Fuller, Sarah Edgerton and Luella B. Case, Charlotte Perkins Gilman, and others. Critics and historians have hesitated to attribute sexual activity to "longtime companions" or to "Boston marriages" among women who themselves did not use "sex" in their language. The defining yardstick has been that there was an activity labeled by a word and that the matter was objectively representable; if they didn't use the word, the activity didn't happen. However, now it is possible to see that the language and listening spaces have changed. A century ago the term *lesbian* didn't exist. In the nineteenth century "sex" was used to refer to phallic activity, particularly penetration. In the universal terms of twentieth-century psychoanalytic theory, *sexual* came to mean heterosexual, thereby calling forth heterosexual woman as opposed to lesbian other. The norm, defined in opposition to perversion, labeled as characteristic what before had been activity anyone could engage in. Now a person could be identified as deviant. Female eroticism, at first ignored, came to be considered "foreplay" or presexual activity; since the second wave of feminism, it has come to be regarded as sexual activity whether a penis or its substitute is present. Where earlier lesbians may not have spoken of themselves as "sexual" because they did not engage in phallic penetration, we would regard what the women themselves referred to as "lovemaking" to be "sexual." Their expressions of passion, endearment, and physical intimacy need not be explained away as conventional and meaningless expressions. We think via the language of our listening space, and they thought through theirs.

In this time of transition around the turn of the century, when women were demanding and winning higher education, occupations in the professions and public employment, and, finally in 1920, the vote, the possibility that they might lead lives independent of men threatened patriarchal institutions of male supremacy and occasioned a sweeping backlash that included much of what appeared "new" and for that listening space progressive, including psychology. Gertrude Stein was one of the women caught up in conflicting ways of viewing lesbian love relationships; tracing her work is tracing some of the shifts she went through.

Stein, whose narratives and writing style were shaped by a necessity for coding, wrote and rewrote her own experience, putting the early drafts away in a trunk. When Alice B. Toklas discovered a manuscript that had been buried and asked Stein about it, Stein replied that she had "forgotten" it. What she had done was remake her journal into the story of yet another triangle, rehearsing her own story under the guise of telling the story of a pair of women at a woman's college who find themselves in a triangle when one of them succumbs to a male colleague—a narrative based on the experience of M. Carey Thomas at Bryn Mawr before she found her "life-time companion." After writing these two versions, Stein reconstructed the story again, casting her part in the role of a young male doctor who falls in love with a woman who has learned "wisdom" and "power" and how to "really" love from another woman, thus making him suspicious of her love. In the published version Stein utilized a private lexicon that amounted to a code for lesbian love. She further distanced the autobiographical material and sheltered the lesbian elements of the plot by setting the story in the Black community, thus situating her/Jeff's concern about respectable love as one about race. Readers now can trace these developments by reading *QED, Fernhurst and Other Writings* as background for the story of "Melanctha" in *Three Lives*.

For women of color as well as white women, especially those in the working classes who were not themselves writers, the languages of dress codes spoke volumes. In Native American cultures there had been a place for women whose visions led them to positions as peacemakers or homemakers with other women, but colonial policies worked to suppress such possibilities, and they have remained largely invisible outside the work of contemporary gay and lesbian historians both in and outside Native communities. Cora Anderson (Ralph Kerwinieo) passed for many years. Many cross-dressing women passed as men to accomplish a mission, like Sojourner Truth working on the underground railroad, or as a way of life that need not conform to the confines of women's roles, like stagecoach driver Mary Fields, who had been born into slavery but who worked freely as a man. Murray Hall married and lived for some time as a Tammany Hall politician. Unlike Mary MacLane, who published her autobiography in 1902, few wrote their own stories.

Reading biographical, historical, and medical accounts of lesbian lives brings sharply into focus the ways the discourse of the teller of the tale constructs the "reality" of those lives. Some told their stories in journalistic accounts. A few were apprehended and incarcerated in hospitals or jails. But thousands of women up to and even after the turn of the century lived publicly as men. Willa Cather, who when young and living in the West dressed as a man, told her stories about the West when she came east, casting some of her characters as males in ways that have given rise to complex readings.

Several women writers were able during this period to form relationships with other women that sustained them spiritually and professionally; despite the increasing difficulty of openly acknowledging what we think of as lesbian relationships, some writers included these themes, images, and struggles in their works. Angelina Weld Grimké and Sarah Orne Jewett were among those who wrote with subtlety and, as with Agnes Smedley, varying degrees of elision. Amy Lowell, claiming women poets were "a queer lot," wrote in "Sisters" a poignant query about her place in the tradition of women poets, noting how each in turn accommodated herself in the dilemma of speaking and living in her particular listening space; as a more openly woman-centered spirit, Lowell was left rather exposed. H.D. took on the patriarchy and developed a woman's poetics in her work. Ma Rainey and Bessie Smith sang openly about their affairs with women, though this aspect of the blues has been downplayed until recently. Ruth Said/Jo Sinclair came to be considered a writer for young adults, chronicling those tender years when it was still acceptable for girls to bond.

The first quarter of the century nurtured enclaves of women, from women's colleges to settlement house communities to Parisian salons like Natalie Barney's where Reneé Vivien wrote; these communities were able to nurture same-sex lovers to some extent. For those outside the enclaves the medicalization of erotic relationships between women pushed all but the extraordinary woman into silence—or into cross-dressing and masquerade, which made economic, social, and political opportunities available: even marriage. Tension between increased freedom for women and increased pressure to liberalize women's positions in heterosexual ways, even for liberals, radicals, and bohemians expected by their comrades to live in companionate marriages with men, affected writers like Edna St. Vincent Millay, whose bisexual lifestyle came to be inscribed by erasure of its lesbian aspects. A "too obvious" drama opening in New York might threaten the cultural acceptance of female companions in an established relationship in a woman's college in Philadelphia.

The silence and apparent silence or privacy, ambivalence, and coding or masquerade of the first quarter of the century was itself exploded within a decade of women's getting the vote. The influence of Virginia Woolf's work in this country is difficult to estimate, so great has it been. Having made herself ill over the necessity to heterosexualize her first novel, suffering enforced rest cures and emerging guarded but supported in her sapphism and feminism by Vita Sackville West, Woolf published several volumes in the 1920s which had an impact in both opening up the field for books such as Rosamund Lehman's *Dusty Answer* (1927) and occasioning a repressive backlash.

The carefully crafted ambiguity of style of Woolf's *Mrs. Dalloway* (1925) revealed and concealed the repressed homosexual sides of both Septimus Smith and Clarissa Dalloway and focused on "the twin forces of Conformity and Conversion"—in particular on their repressive operations in the medical profession, which Woolf herself knew from her own experience. Although often characterized as a modernist, she has consistently portrayed the different listening spaces operating simultaneously. What appeared to some as cultural progress, such as the development of fields like eugenics and psychology, proved for others a tyrannical system of repression and control. Woolf extended Gilman's ("The Yellow Wallpaper") exposé of rest cures as forms of social control over women who manifested symptoms of discontent over their assigned gender roles. Woolf showed how medical practices were the domestic basis for British imperialism. It must be noted, however, that the interpretive strategies of some readers still yield less radical readings of ''the same'' novel.

Women were going to college, working in the world as workers and professionals, and feminism had made electoral gains for women. Alternatives to marriage were becoming possible, and lesbian love was becoming visible as such. Margaret Anderson and Jane Heap edited *The Little Review*, publishing most of the early modernists writing in English. By 1928 an explosion occurred; in the same year Woolf published *Orlando*, a fabulous journey through the styles of English literature featuring a persona who changes sex while retaining her identity; Djuna Barnes published the fantastical *Ladies Almanack*; Radclyffe Hall published *The Well of Loneliness*, and then called on other writers to help her defend in the courts its right to public life against charges of obscenity. Based in a calculated way on the theories of sexologists, and arguing that the ''mannish'' lesbian was a congenital invert made by God and thus entitled to live, the novel had probably a wider impact than any other single artifact of culture in shaping versions of what a lesbian ''was'' for generations to come.

The strict adherence to heterosexual roles and the explanation by genetics both contributed, as much as the appeal from God's creation, to an essentialist defense of homosexuality at the beginnings of homophile organizing in the following decade of repression. Since then, self-narratives told or written by lesbians reveal that they have often read such accounts and felt the need to understand their choices as determined by God or genetic predisposition. They rarely defied the weight of such explanatory power before the second wave of feminism, which opened up the possibility of a different type of reasoning in the culture. Many of these feminists have felt empowered by their choices to build a lesbian culture in defiance of patriarchal mores and norms, and they have fueled the theoretical shifts to social constructionist defenses of recent lesbian and gay liberation struggles.

But the court battles of the late twenties constituted a warning, and published accounts of lesbian life began to be structured by the obligatory morbidity that allowed lesbian existence to appear at all. Gale Wilhelm's 1938 *We Too Are Drifting* and 1938 *Torchlight to Valhalla*, and Djuna Barnes's 1937 *Nightwood* show two different routes lesbian writing took in the listening spaces of the 1930s. Wilhelm's works came out in the genre of sleaze and made way for pornography to accommodate most of the published lesbian writing for the following decades of the cold war at home and abroad.

Barnes's work was deemed high literature by virtue of the obscurity and ornateness of its style, much praised by T. S. Eliot, who himself cherished the notion of an elite poetic imagination. So dense is the wrought-iron prose of the novel, it is practically impossible to discern that the novel concerns not only a transvestite doctor but a lesbian triangle dominated by alcoholism, exoticizing lesbians whose passionate and sordid lives deteriorate elaborately in the course of the narrative. But how was Barnes to speak of such a topic, except through such an obscurative stylistic strategy? The listening space of the literati, dominated by the male modernists with a credo to institute new virile writing and banish the "sentimental," had effectively shifted the listening space in literary circles so that romantic friendships and women "scribblers" inspired and sustained by the love of other women were no longer possible themes or viable authors.

In the wake of the stock market crash and the Great Depression, censors and watchdog agencies were established in the 1930s to "uphold standards" of "decency and normality." Lillian Hellman's 1934 play *The Children's Hour* was heterosexualized only two years later in the film *Let These Three*. Even in less elite literary circles the effects of backlash were felt; Anna Weirauch's lesbian character (from an earlier novel, *The Scorpion*) in 1933's *The Outcast* goes straight. Autobiographies by Elizabeth Craigin, Diana Frederic, and Vida Scudder reveal attitudes ranging from the claim that lesbian sex was healthy to ambivalence about sexuality to rejection of Freudian notions of sexuality.

The walls of silence were being reinforced. Relaxed briefly to encourage the war economy, and incidentally bringing women together in cities and military sites where a lesbian subculture could become established, they were erected again higher than ever after the war. This time the backlash was highly institutionalized; the anonymity of witch-hunters in government, the military, and places of employment allowed no legal recourse. Homosexuals were hounded, dismissed, jailed, operated on, and treated for their disease. Faceless accusers led to denial and secrecy; lesbian writing was forced into the pulps. The postwar lesbian paper *Vice Versa* was short-lived, and the story "Sappho Remembered," published in 1954 by the homophile magazine *One*, was censored by the Los Angeles postmaster general, a verdict upheld by the Federal District Court. While Kinsey reported that 28 percent of American women had homosexual tendencies, witch-hunting was the national mood.

From the 1920s through the 1940s many middle- and upper-class women, Black and white, retreated into more or less flagrant bisexuality, which kept some form of lesbian life and a little writing afloat on the modernist sea for those who could flee abroad and lead the expatriate life. Margaret Anderson's three-volume autobiography—*My Thirty Year's War* (1951), *The Fiery Fountains* (1960), and *The Strange Necessity* (1969)—speaks of her work and highlights her great loves in the United States and France during this period. Anaïs Nin's heterosexual alliances and the bawdy rebellions of her male counterparts provided some space for her excursions into lesbiana in such works as the 1946 *Ladders to Fire* in the guise of autobiographical writing, considered a stepchild to "literature." Mabel Dodge Luhan used the form in *Intimate Memories* (1932) to detail her lesbian relationships. But the repressive epoch effectively poisoned the wellsprings of lesbian literary creativity. The 1950s, while driving many lesbians into the closet and forcing a respectable drag onto working women who passed as straight, also fostered the development of a public bar culture characterized by the opposite, a drag of queer (and, in the cities, nearly compulsory) butch-femme roles. The literature available in the 1950s, such as Claire Morgan's *The Price of Salt* (1958), and most of the 1960s, such as Elizabeth Craigin's 1963 *Either Is Love*, was published as pornography, with its obligatory pulp morbidity about lesbianism. However, the anti-communism, anti-feminism, anti-black activism, and anti-homosexuality that characterized the postwar 1940s and the 1950s spurred resistance, which was to help shift that listening space. The Mattachine Society was founded in 1948 and the Daughters of Bilitis in 1955. Jeannette Foster self-published *Sex Variant Women in Literature* in 1956. The lesbian periodical *The Ladder* came out from 1956 to 1972, when feminism transformed the voice from the closet that had paved the way for the founding of Naiad Press, the first of several lesbian publishing houses.

As a small group of radicals and liberals, civil rights activists and student freedom organizers, anti-war activists and homophiles began in the early and mid-1960s to crack the ice of the McCarthyite cold war, an established writer broke the "literary" silence. The period out of which a liberation movement came as a reaction must be understood as the context for May Sarton's *Mrs. Stevens Hears the Mermaids Singing* (1965). For the time it was an extraordinarily courageous portrait of the variant woman, the lesbian whose inspiration has primarily been a female muse, and whose poetic genius justified her odd proclivities; she goes out of her way to assure her young male poet protégé that a homosexual experience need not define him and exclude him from the natural happiness a normal man would want. Highly structured and rather formalistic, the novel nonetheless is written in clear language and constitutes a claim to a limited but powerful legitimacy: that of the writer.

The danger for most lesbian writing was that the subject matter would relegate the work to a "subliterary" genre. Han Suyin's *Two Loves* (1962) was republished as *Winterlove* in 1970, the same year she came out with *Cast But One Shadow*. Historical fiction had provided women writers like Mary Renault, interested in portraying homosexual themes, with a means of publishing even a series of novels. Elizabeth Mavor published her narrative of two eighteenth-century lesbians as a combination popular paperback and scholarly study, *The Ladies of Llangollen* (1970), shortly after the feminist movement had begun to sweep the nation. Poets such as Muriel Rukeyser and Elizabeth Bishop continued to publish in the ambiguities of a form already suited for layered meanings. But the most consistent domain for openly lesbian work was publication as pornography where the "twilight" world of "unnatural love" constituted the novelistic counterpart of urban lesbian bar culture. This listening space began to shift with the emergence of feminism in the mid-1960s.

Isabel Miller's work reflected the beginnings of a feminist analysis of roles. Published as *A Place for Us* in 1969 in what I recall as a hot pink cover, the novel was renamed *Patience and Sarah* (1972) in the first flush of lesbian feminism. Its author had had to hawk the novel and self-publish to keep it alive before a publisher could be convinced to bring it out, and it stands as one of the early benchmarks of the contemporary lesbian-feminist literary movement.

The early 1970s saw publications as varied as the New York Radicalesbians "Women Identified Women" (1973); the commercial success, Rita Mae Brown's *Rubyfruit Jungle* (1973); and Monique Wittig's radical *Les Guerilleres* (1971), which depicted a revolution of women with all the symbols and cultural practices of a revolutionary society including gay men against the patriarchy, and simultaneously decried the need for a separatist culture, given the winning power of the women. The Furies critiqued heterosexuality as an institution. Lesbians were organizing "everywhere," and poetry nourished and was nourished by the growth of "women's culture" even as women's culture exploded into diversity. Ann Allen Schockley published *Loving Her*, a lesbian interracial love story (1974), and Dolores Klaitch published *Woman Plus Woman*. In 1975 Joan Larkin and Elly Bulkin edited a pathbreaking anthology, *Amazon Poetry*, Gene Damon (Barbara Grier) published *The Lesbian in Literature: A Bibliography*, Beth Hedges edited a lesbian issue of *Margains*, Catherine Nicholson and Harriet Desmoines founded *Sinister Wisdom*, and Jane Rule published *Lesbian Images*. Then in 1976 Rosa Guy published *Ruby*, her novel of lesbian love between a West Indian girl and a North American Black girl living in Harlem, the same year that Adrienne Rich published her prose work on the institution of motherhood from a lesbian-feminist perspective. Jane Chambers, a New York playwright and novelist, depicted a contemporary relationship of two women as being taken over by the spirits of two lesbians from the past thought to be witches (*Burning*, 1977). The Berkshire Women's History Conference held its first lesbian theory session. Jane Rule's *Desert of the Heart* (1978) openly explored a lesbian relationship between a nightclub worker and a teacher, popular in both novel and subsequently film form.

By this time the stunning collections of poetry by writers such as Adrienne Rich, Audre Lorde, and Olga Broumas were to become classics not only in this country but internationally, and book after book was to explode upon the scene; book readings became major events in communities around the country. Poets like June Jordan were to publish lesbian poetry; journals, reviews, and presses sprang into existence; and songwriters and musicians made lesbian music. The decade had given birth to a new, visionary lesbian culture, and the listening space of silence began to become rapidly transformed in the discourses, the automaticity, and the living spaces of lesbians in both city and countryside.

Out of the civil rights and anti–Vietnam War movements, the explosion of women's liberation in the 1960s gave birth to the movements for lesbian and gay liberation in the 1970s, and for twenty years feminism provided a vital energy to these and other movements, which themselves contributed transformative changes to feminism. The heady days of consciousness-raising, acting politically on behalf of women and their needs, identifying systemic as well as local sources of oppression—naming them, and developing autonomy as women all fostered the growth of "women's culture": poetry, art, theater, music and songs, women's studies courses, newspapers and small reviews, criticism, manifestos, position papers, journal entries, rituals, conferences, groups and organizations, dances, caucuses, collectives, living and working spaces, advocacy and services for women. The National Women's Studies Association was organizing lesbian writers, teachers, students, staff, and community women nationally, and lesbians were coming out in organizations as varied as the National Organization for Women (NOW), the Combahee River Collective, and various Marxist Feminist groups. In practice, much of "women's" music, cultural space, and literature was predominantly lesbian.

CONTEMPORARY LESBIAN WRITING

In this new listening space lesbian literature broke into stylistic and thematic clarity. The work documented in this book emerged out of this listening space and helped invent it. The atmosphere encouraged creative innovation and experimentation, and critiques of old forms seen as oppressive. The new feminist culture invented new lesbians who invented new feminisms; people's automaticity was shifting with these new discourses, and lesbians "came out" of closets, came out by choice, came out publicly. The literature of this period was functional; it didn't sit on the shelf; poetry, for example, was used to begin and end political meetings. Traditional literary genres too broke down. Alice Walker wrote a literary critical essay in which she put a character, her mother, in a scene. The Women's Experimental Theater did "research"; Roberta Sklar and Sondra Siegal conducted workshops for women employing a variety of exercises and art forms in which participating women remembered their experience as females, and as artistic directors worked this collectivity of voice and experience into the theater's dramatic productions.

Some of the earliest lesbian "literature" in the second wave of feminism was song. Non-fiction magazines like *Sinister Wisdom* published notes so theoretically radical the authors could barely get them written, like Catherine Nicholson's questions after studying Jane Ellen Harrison's feminist anthropological challenges to patriarchal accounts of the classical period. Each had been practically silenced by the listening spaces of academe; and not only did editors Harriet Desmoines and Catherine Nicholson not censor such "unfinished fragments" for not being scholarly or professional enough, but they developed a critique of the repressive pressures of academia. Teachers of early women's studies courses were nurtured by the movement; often they came from "the community" and generally were better equipped than non-activist academics to teach the new courses with their emphasis on learning from women's lives and developing theory from practice. "Literature" was as likely to be a pamphlet like Ann Koedt's *Myth of the Vaginal Orgasm* as Toni Morrison's *Sula*, which Barbara Smith read as a lesbian, a reading she used in developing notes toward a Black feminist criticism, articulating a stance born of the Combahee River Collective politics. The non-traditional, the new, the spirit of change, and the promise of liberation infused the lesbian literature documented in this book.

The expansion of the listening space for lesbians made room for many new voices, the breakdown of silences, the emergence of new visions and new communities where everyone was encouraged to write, to participate in the making of "our bodies, our selves," and to remake the world. "I wanted her as very few people have wanted me" Judy Grahn wrote; "I wanted her and me to own and control and run the world we lived in" (*A Woman is Talking to Death* 1978). Much of the leadership and energy of the movement came from lesbians who began to articulate a woman-centered politics and perspective that challenged heterosexual paradigms. Defending themselves from the early attacks of straight women, the Furies founded a separate collectivity, published theoretical forays against the patriarchy, and championed the advanced role lesbians were playing in enacting feminist practice. Jill Johnston developed "lesbian nation" in newspaper articles devoid of traditional punctuation and sentence structure. The poetry, essays, and plays of writers like Susan Griffin were made into posters. Betty Powell and Ginny Appuzo ran an openly lesbian political campaign for a state assembly seat. Lesbian Barnard College students conducted their own search for a professor who could and would teach a lesbian studies course and fought for it; much of the early research I did in lesbian studies was shared in classrooms there, at Brooklyn College, and community spaces such as Maidenrock Women's Learning Institute and Gay Women's Alternative. The Lesbian Herstory Archives provided a space for the breaking of silences and the preservation of lesbian culture.

Inventing the Other became the invention of Others. Debates ensued about whether lesbianism "skewed the women's movement" or whether it was committed praxis of feminism; about whether women could be a class and patriarchy a structure, as the radical feminists claimed, or whether women were a subordinate part of every class as defined by working-class perspectives on capitalist class structures; about whether women's spaces were safe against male violence and oppression or exclusive of women of color engaged with their brothers in the ongoing struggle against racism; about whether roles were oppressive remnants of patriarchal institutions demeaning women or cultural norms of lesbian community; about whether sadomasochism, bondage, leather were radical sex practices based on consent or were the fetishized erotics of a degenerate and dehumanizing capitalist patriarchy.

These debates were waged not only in meetings but at cultural events and in art forms that fed the movements even as they fractured into identity groups to define their own voices and perspectives. Was holding a public dance for women an apolitical activity that drained the energy of the movement, or was it a political activity that challenged the practices of compulsory heterosexuality? Early on, the forms of activism in the liberation movements of women, lesbians, and people of color constituted a challenge both to hegemonic culture and to what was considered "political" in progressive communities; regrounded authority in the everyday experience of large numbers of people empowered to speak in their own voices; and construed the variety of "realities" with which we had to contend as a valuable contribution to decentering the universalism that masked white male imperialist power.

Asian, Native, Chicana, and Latina lesbians often led the way in articulating the colonial pressures and practices of mainstream society and too often of the movements as well. The issues were explored in poetry and art, in music and at meetings, in classrooms and theaters, in philosophical and academic treatises, in photographs and clothing, in fiction and autobiography, and in bed. Styles of lovemaking and dress were debated. Science fiction became an arena for envisioning "other" realities from a lesbian perspective. For many years literature and movement culture were more important than mainstream press accounts in shaping our sense of where the many we(s) were in the movements in which we participated. Lesbians explored who could say what to whom and under what conditions, survive and be heard; and lesbians founded presses that nurtured a fledgling lesbian literature emerging finally into a receptive listening space.

In such a context it is easy to see that traditional notions of what constitutes "literature" had been radically challenged. What had formally been subgenres or literary stepchildren, like autobiography and utopian fiction, had become important vehicles in the lesbian and feminist culture(s). What constituted theory might just as easily be found in the pages of lesbian science fiction and fantasy novels as in an anthology of the now popular type of women's studies textbook collections that were to be found on practically every campus in the country. Similarly, what constituted a lesbian was not a simple matter, either. As research conducted both in and outside academia turned up more and more historical, biographical, and textual material and feminists began writing and teaching it in lesbian and gay studies, queer theory, women's studies, ethnic studies, and gender studies courses, thousands of people began participating in discussions of what defined whom under what conditions and in whose name.

Can you go back before the word *lesbian* was used and call the eighteenth-century ladies of Llangollen, for example, lesbians? What kind of lesbians were they if both of them wore men's suits? Eleanor Roosevelt was married; did living in the White House with her female lover make her a lesbian? If Lillian Hellman slept with a woman, did that make her a lesbian? Is a woman who identifies as a straight woman but writes a series of popular sleazy lesbian pulp stories about a working-class dyke in the village writing lesbian literature? Is a woman who eschews a public identity like lesbian but who writes a best-selling novel about two women who love each other sexually as well as spiritually writing lesbian literature? How do the languages of different communities and periods translate? Is a bulldyke or bulldagger the same as a Top? Is every dyke a butch? Does a woman who participates in women's events with her lesbian lover and writes poetry with lesbian content and publishes these works even in a lesbian and gay anthology but declines to be included in an anthology of lesbian writers not a lesbian writer? Who gets to say? Questions of representation, authorization, appropriation, and self-definition, as well as the ways different audiences and communities participate in determining "meaning" for a text, all have become vital and hotly debated matters constructing the conditions of literary production and publication.

It is not surprising that such issues should flourish in a space that is committed to respect for difference as well as equity and rights concerns, in a time when the very initial successes of lesbian and gay liberation and the flourishing of lesbian and gay literature and art have also generated a vicious backlash, repression, and censorship. The writing, energy and activism, the thinking and forms of social and political organizing generated by movements articulating politics of difference provided, in the context of global challenges to the hegemony of "first world" authority, the groundwork for what became known in theoretical circles as postmodernism. Much of what is recognized as "theory" of postmodern thought articulated by academics once again makes invisible the lesbian, gay, feminist, and even sometimes the "third world" activity that played such a crucial role in constructing postmodern listening spaces. But for most of us "in the movement" what was said in an academic treatise was much less important than Gloria Anzaldúa's early promise, as a radical Chicana bilingual lesbian refusing to repress any of her identities to accommodate any of the others, to "brew and forge" a revolution.

Nonetheless, the work covered by *Contemporary Lesbian Writers of the United States: A Bio-Bibliographical Critical Sourcebook* offers an important chronicle of what in postmodern theory may be called the politics of representation. It springs from the multiple perspectives of people as well situated as any others to explore the shaping power of language and to use its creative force to unmask authoritarian claims to reality/power/knowledge on every level from the symbolic to the erotic. Yes, here is to be found material on the ways discourse subversive to oppressive gender systems has emerged in the United States in the second wave of feminism; for this difference can stir the blood, shapeshift in dreams and loves, disrupt traditional practices of power and authority in the automaticity of the nervous system, and become energy for changing the world.

Let us hope that classrooms can become sites of transformation that echo and reverberate rather than silence voices of difference. This book is dedicated to expanding the listening spaces for lesbian writings, in all their variety and in all their many voices, a commitment that walls of silence never again appear absolute, and a promise to keep speaking and listening anew.

NOTE

1. (Tucker) Pamella Farley, "Power, Oppression and the Politics of Culture: Beyond Marx and Freud," paper presented at the first lesbian theory session of the Berkshire Women's History Conference, Mt. Holyoke, 1978; also presenting were Audre Lorde, "Power of the Erotic"; Emily Jensen, "The Suiciding Heroine"; Barbara Smith, "Notes Toward a Black Feminist Criticism."

CONTEMPORARY LESBIAN WRITERS OF THE UNITED STATES

DONNA ALLEGRA (1953–   )
Luvenia Pinson

BIOGRAPHY

For Black lesbians wanting and needing to write, life has many necessities. Some are mundane, often routine, occasionally extraordinary, but always reflecting resistance to the Freudian interpretations of Black life in the popular culture. There are no trust funds, few grants, and no wealthy sponsors allowing for secluded vacations, productive writing retreats, or time out for inspirational gatherings. Therefore, since 1981, Donna Allegra has trained and worked as an electrician in construction. She is also an African and a jazz dancer, a teacher of Yoga, and a woman who moves through the maze of New York city traffic most often on her bicycle, pausing periodically to meditate in quiet places, a song heard by all that will listen. She smiles readily, bright eyes twinkle, and tomorrow, she will talk to you in poetry, essay, or short prose.

In the thirty-ninth year of her life, Donna Allegra, kissed by the sun in the land of her ancestors, floats in a sea of verbal imprints. She records daily impressions in her journal, and has since the age of thirteen, that translate into poetry, essays, and short prose. Her writings and performances span a sixteen-year publication and communication herstory in both the electronic and print media.

She was born in Brooklyn, New York, and graduated from its public school system during a resurgence of the current civil rights movement. The philosophy of this movement can be seen in her writing. Her poems, essays, and short prose usually relate to various types of oppression, a lack of choices, racism, and class perceptions. Her higher education sojourn began at Bennington College; she graduated, however, from New York University in 1977 with a B.A. in dramatic literature, theater history and cinema.

Today, Donna Allegra lives in New York City's East Village. She describes herself in "Dance of the Cranes" as a "spiritual woman rebel, pagan, holy, often possessed by my demons. Yes, I'm still mad. Richly blessed to have incarnated as a Writer, Dancer, and Drummer. Lover of the literary and performing arts. Live in New York City, lay claim to the world.'' She credits Jemima, the first self-acknowledged Black lesbian writers group, as the entity that helped her find her voice in poetry and as being the most helpful to her writing career.

Allegra won the 1992 Pat Parker Memorial Poetry Prize.

MAJOR WORKS AND THEMES

Donna Allegra's writing is usually about women or about the impact events and experiences have on her consciousness and the way they affect her aesthetically. Her poetry has a conversational, often intimate tone. At times, she attempts to reconcile inner anxieties with outer realities. In her short story "The Electrician's Girl,'' Allegra gives the reader a perspective on what it's like to work in an all-male environment, particularly as a woman in a non-traditional job, and how some women respond to sexism. The narrative is from a male point of view. In this world, we come to realize that the smartest behavior mode is close attention to one's work and personal aloofness. However, there are always a smile and conversation for other sisters. The reader is brought into the inner thoughts of a young girl learning the moves and rituals in a West African dance class, and her concern and appreciation for the older woman dancers, in ''Dance of the Cranes.'' ''A Toast of Babatine'' reflects Allegra's appreciation for the culture of her ancestors and the role of women in that culture. It projects the role of music and dance, while extolling the beauty and sensuousness of a particular woman and the feelings she inspires.

Poetry is the mirror to Donna Allegra's inner world. In ''26 Going On,'' she journeys across the breadth of life, finding that life is its own necessity for going on. ''Last Minute Woman'' addresses the demands of time, persons, and events and the challenge of prioritizing anticipation, while waiting for the woman of your choice. Like all of Allegra's poetry, it has a rhythm of its own, a cadence determined by Black culture, which on occasion will identify as it creates a standard or value. ''Pretty in the Dark Morning'' spreads over the reader like warm Caribbean water kissing the beach, and in ''From the Temple of the Goddess,'' we hear a song of praise to women divinity figures that Allegra believes are influenced by cosmic energy signs.

Donna Allegra holds on to African culture and values through her poetry and prose. ''When People Ask'' is her poem about the spectrum of skin color, herstory, and the things that come to pass and questions that will be asked forever about Blacks by people who don't want to know. ''Recipes'' gives us insight into her thoughts on feminism and on the right to make our own choices: the choice to be a vegetarian, to do non-traditional work, to move at our own pace, and most importantly, to be aware of things that can hurt.

CRITICAL RECEPTION

Donna Allegra has written for, and published in, several feminist and lesbian/
gay magazines, newspapers, newsletters, journals, periodicals and non-lesbian/
gay magazines including *Jemima*, *The Salsa Soul Gayzette*, *Azalea*, *Heresies*,
Sinister Wisdom, *Conditions*, and *Essence*. Her writings have never been col-
lectively published by any publishing house large or small, in spite of her
popularity and the abundance of material she has created. She also produced
radio programs for Station WBAI FM in New York City from 1975 to 1981,
and has written theater, book, film, and dance reviews for *Majority Report
Newspaper*, *New York City News*, *Sappho's Isle Newspaper*, *Womanews*, and
Sojourner. She participated in the Gap Tooth Girlfriends Writers Workshop and
performed with NAPS, a Black lesbian theater group, and with Edwina Lee
Tyler and A Piece of the World as a percussionist.

Although Allegra has never received individual acclaim from the literary
world, she remains a favorite poet and essayist in the New York City gay
community. For over sixteen years, she has received favorable receptions from
lesbian and gay audiences as a performing poet and essayist. She has read her
works during Gay Pride Week celebrations, at local schools, cafes, and other
gay/lesbian spaces.

At any gathering of words spoken, recited, repeated, or sung, the bystander
will often see a comfortably attired, short dredlocked, slim Black woman standing
by herself. She will smile, and Donna Allegra will emerge. She will recite
poetry, read an essay, and if it is your lucky day, she will also dance.

BIBLIOGRAPHY

Works by Donna Allegra

Poems

"Looking All Sweet and Casual." *From the Heart*. New York: Jemina, 1976. 21–23.
"A Prayer for my Soul." *Essence* (September 1978): 24.
"Up In the Sky." *Conditions* 5 (1979): 101–2.
"A Rape Poem for Men" and "When People Ask." *Lesbian Poetry*. Ed. Joan Larkin
    and Elly Bulkin. Watertown, MA: Persephone Press, 1981. 255–59.
"Recipies" and "A Small Rape." *Lesbians Rising* (Winter 1981): 10–11.
"She Knew Ways." *Sinister Wisdom* 17 (Summer 1981): 15–19.
"A Black Woman's Welcome: A Warning" and "Liverwish and Tumblesauce." *Lesbians
    Rising* (Winter/Spring 1982): 6–7.
"Before I Dress and Soar Again." *Home Girls: Black Feminist Anthology*. Ed. Barbara
    Smith. Lathan, NY: Kitchen Table Press, 1983. 166–67.
"On drums, dance and love: The eye of a hurricane." *Ache: A Journal for Lesbians of
    African Descent* 4:3 (July/August 1992): 22.

Short Stories and Essays

"On Her Knees Before the Machine Pleading Mercy." *Azalea* 3:3 (Fall 1980): 19–20.
"Butch on the Streets." *Fight Back! Feminist Resistance to Male Violence*. Ed. Frédérique
    Delacoste and Felice Newman. Pittsburgh: Cleis Press, 1981. 44–45.
"Buddies." *Sinister Wisdom* 20 (Spring 1982): 24–28.
"Some Personal Notes on Racism among Women." *Heresies* 5 (1982): 33.
"Dance of the Cranes." *Common Lives: Lesbian Lives* 23 (1987): 27–35.
"The Electrician's Girl." *Sinister Wisdom* 32 (Summer 1987): 33–36.
"Thoughts on Love and Romance." *Lesbian Ethics* 2 (Summer 1987): 79–84.
"A Toast of Babatine." *Sinister Wisdom* 34 (Spring 1988): 59–64.
"Coming Out." *The Original Coming Out Stories*. Ed. Julia Penelope and Susan J.
    Wolfe. Freedom, CA: The Crossing Press, 1989. 211–15.
"One Mirror, Three Reflections." *Finding the Lesbians: Personal Accounts from Around
    the World*. Ed. Julia Penelope and Sarah Valentine. Freedom, CA: The Crossing
    Press, 1990. 217–24.
"Brownstones." *Sinister Wisdom* 46 (Spring 1992): 89–97.
"Navigating by Stars." *Common Lives: Lesbian Lives* 42 (Spring 1992): 25–31.
"Tango." *Quickies: Lesbian Short Stories*. Ed. Irene Zahava. Ithaca, NY: Violet Ink,
    1992. 31–32.
"Time and Love." *At the Crossroads: A Journal for Women Artists of African Descent*
    (Spring 1992): 38–44.

PAULA GUNN ALLEN (1939–   )
Annette Van Dyke

BIOGRAPHY

Born in Albuquerque, New Mexico, Paula Gunn Allen describes herself as a "multicultural event" (Coltelli 17). She is Laguna Pueblo/Sioux/Lebanese/ Scotch-American and grew up in Cubero, New Mexico, a Spanish-Mexican land grant village that abuts the Laguna reservation, the Acoma reservation, and the Cibola National Forest. Raised as a Catholic, Allen had family members who were "heathen, Catholic, Protestant, Jewish" and Maronite ("The Autobiography" 144). For Allen, all of these influences have combined to make her who she is—someone who can relate to the world as a multicultural event, as "a rainbow, . . . reflect[ing] light." Allen believes if "it's possible for me to stay alive, then it's possible for the whole world to stay alive. If I can communicate, then all the different people in the world can communicate with one another" (Coltelli 17).

Allen's Laguna heritage comes to her from her mother's side and is the perspective out of which she writes. Allen says that her "mother's Laguna people are Keres Indian, reputed to be the last extreme mother-right people on earth" (*Sacred Hoop* 48). In this woman-centered culture, descent was matrilineal, the ownership of houses was held by women, and the major deities were female. A major focus of Allen's work is to delineate the worldview of this female-centered culture.

Allen's father, E. Lee Francis, who owned a store, Cubero Trading Company, was born of Lebanese parents at Seboyeta, Spanish-Mexican land grant village north of Laguna Pueblo. He spoke only Spanish and Arabic until he was about ten and was raised Roman Catholic since there was not a Maronite rite in the area. He was lieutenant governor of New Mexico from 1967 through 1970. Allen's mother, Ethel, who was Laguna and Scotch, converted from Presbyterianism to Catholicism when she married. Allen's great-grandmother, Meta Atseye, had married a Scotchman named Kenneth Gunn, who had immigrated into the area—hence the Gunn in Allen's name.

Allen attended mission schools in Cubero and then in nearby San Fidel. When she was seven, she was sent to boarding school with the Sisters of Charity in Albuquerque; she attended the same school until she graduated, but lived with her paternal grandfather in Albuquerque. Allen attended Colorado Women's College but received her B.A. in English (1966) and M.F.A. in creative writing (1968) from the University of Oregon. She also married, had three children, and divorced. She earned a Ph.D. in American studies with an emphasis on Native American literature from the University of New Mexico (1975).

In addition to being a poet and a novelist, Allen is recognized as a major scholar, literary critic, and teacher of Native American literature. She has taught at San Francisco State University, the University of New Mexico, Fort Lewis College in Durango, Colorado, and the University of California at Berkeley; currently, she is professor of English at the University of California, Los Angeles. Allen's edited collection of essays on teaching Native American literature, *Studies in American Indian Literature* (1983), is an important text in the field, containing an extensive bibliography and course designs.

Allen received an NEA (National Endowment for the Arts) Fellowship for Writing in 1978, and a postdoctoral fellowship research grant from the Ford Foundation–National Research Council in 1984–85. She was associate fellow at Stanford Humanities Institute for 1984–85. During this time she coordinated the Gynosophic Gathering, A Woman Identified Worship Service, in Berkeley. She is also active in the anti-nuclear movement. Her *Spider Woman's Granddaughters* won an American Book Award in 1990. In addition to her novel in progress, *Raven's Road*, Allen is also working on a book on the Lebanese Maronite tradition.

MAJOR WORKS AND THEMES

Allen's poetry chapbooks include *The Blind Lion* (1975), *Coyote's Daylight Trip* (1978), *Star Child* (1981), and *A Cannon Between My Knees* (1981). She has published three books of poetry: *Shadow Country* (1982), *Wyrds* (1987), and *Skins and Bones* (1988). She is also widely anthologized and has published poems in numerous literary magazines including those which feature lesbian writers such as *Sinister Wisdom*.

Allen's poetry, and her fiction as well, often seeks out the wild places in urban environments, the sense that everything is infused with spirit not necessarily controllable by humans, particularly not by Euro-Americans, the creators of the technology. She writes about the layers of shadows, of spirits, civilization upon civilizations, blending across time, fading in and out, and the inner personal shadows. For Allen, one task of the poet is to bridge, to articulate the shadows. Her poetry is finely detailed, resonating with sense of place, whether it be the city, the reservation, or the interior. Tricksters such as coyote appear frequently in conjunction with the images of technology, urban sprawl, and colonization.

The articulation of goddess-centered culture appears frequently in her poetry as well as the difficulty of reconciling that worldview in contemporary society. Allen's later work becomes more feminist and more focused upon women. Love poems infuse human relationships with the sacred aspects of the landscape. For instance, in "Arousing" (*Skins and Bones* 50), the goddess of water, of spring, intermingles with the lesbian lovers, blessing them and they her. In such poems as "The Beautiful Woman Who Sings" (*Cannon* n.p.), the mythic dimensions of women's relationship to the sacred are delineated. Themes of healing, rebirth, and transformatory magic are also frequent. Underlying all of Allen's writing is the belief in the power of the oral tradition, now particularly embodied in poetry or "fiction," to promote healing, rebirth, transformatory magic, survival, and continuance.

Allen's poetry also explores the plight of the contemporary and traditional Native American women. A section in *A Cannon Between My Knees* looks at a number of contemporary women, while a section in *Skins and Bones* is devoted to such historical/mythical personas as Eve, La Malinchi, Pocahontas, Molly Brant, and Sacagawea. The poem "Some Like Indians Endure," in *Living the Spirit*, compares lesbians/dykes to Native Americans.

Allen's poetry can also be characterized by her varying structures and rhythms. Because of her multicultural background, she responds to and incorporates rhythms that come from listening and participating in such disparate events as Pueblo corn dances, Plains' fancy dances, Arabic chanting, singing ten different masses, Mozart, and Western music. Allen cites Gertrude Stein as a major influence on her writing, because of the way Stein "dislocated . . . linearity of language" (Ballinger and Swann 21)—an important element to a person writing out of a non-linear storytelling tradition in a language (English) which does not express that concept well.

Allen's critical essays have been extremely important to the literary field and also reflect her changing emphasis of woman-centered concerns. Her 1975 germinal essay, "The Sacred Hoop: A Contemporary Perspective," now part of her collected essays, *The Sacred Hoop: Recovering the Feminine in American Indian Traditions* (1986), was one of the first to speak to the ritual function of Native American literature as opposed to Euro-American literature but made no mention of women's participation in this ritual tradition. Indeed, the essay even uses the generic *he* as a pronoun, but this is redone in the later version. Allen's later essays focus on such concepts as the difference between women's and men's ritual experiences, the concept that little has been recorded about Native American women's spiritual or daily lives, and the destruction of women's traditional power because of the patriarchal influence of Western culture. Woman-centeredness becomes the core and is reflected in the three sister creators who create without what Western culture might see as the male principle until Christianity enters the stories and changes one sister to a male.

Allen's "Who Is Your Mother? Red Roots of White Feminism" (1984), which came out in *Sinister Wisdom*, was a startling and brilliant articulation of Native American contributions to democracy and feminism, especially elaborating on the roles and power of Native American women. Allen's work counters the idea held, especially by some feminist anthropologists, that there never were any societies in which women's power was equal to men's as she points to Native American societies within recent memory in which women held such power.

In a ground-breaking essay, first published in *Conditions*, "Beloved Women: Lesbians in American Indian Cultures" (1981) and then reworked for *The Sacred Hoop*, Allen brings forth her ideas about the roles of Native American lesbians in traditional cultures, explaining the "medicine dyke" or "ceremonial lesbian" as one who follows the way of a particular Spirit Guide, who possesses spiritual power used for the good of the community, and who is respected by the community for following that spiritual path. She notes that respect for gays and lesbians in Native American culture was eroded along with women's central position by the Western patriarchal culture.

In *Spider Woman's Granddaughters: Traditional Tales and Contemporary Writing by Native American Women* (1989), Allen attempts to correct the invisibility of Native American women in the literature collections. She pulls together a wide variety of stories—from those of major female deities to contemporary stories about Native American women's lives, including her own "Deep Purple," which has a lesbian protagonist. Allen divides the collection into stories of "Warriors," "The Casualties," and "The Resistance." She introduces each selection, giving the reader some sense of how it fits into the geographically various oral traditions.

In *Grandmothers of the Light: A Medicine Woman's Sourcebook* (1991), Allen carries further her interest in the ritual experience of women as exhibited in the traditional stories. Rather than just recording the stories as she did in *Spider Woman's Granddaughters*, Allen retells them, acting in her own capacity as storyteller. Traditionally, Native American storytellers drew the story out of the audience, and Allen attempts to tailor the stories to a contemporary, mostly Euro-American, female readership. This collection of stories is meant to serve as models for walking in the sacred way, and Allen delineates the stages that every woman can traverse on her spiritual path—the way of the daughter, the householder, the mother, the gatherer and the ritualist, the teacher, and the wise woman. This collection also follows another of Allen's interests—that of exploring how one goes from one stage of life to another. She notes that she is in a "middle passage" of consciousness, one taking ten or twelve years (Coltelli 39).

Allen's novel, *The Woman Who Owned the Shadows* (1983), is a ritual journey of the protagonist to recover the woman-centeredness of her culture and to recover her own particular spiritual way, which is to follow the path of the medicine women, or, as Allen has called them elsewhere, "the medicine dykes." The novel is Allen's delineation of the idea of a separate women's ritual tradition and the way that tradition might be recovered in an age when so much has been destroyed. It was the first Native American novel to focus on this separate women's ritual tradition. True to her multicultural background, Allen creates a protagonist who uses traditional Laguna Pueblo healing ceremonies on her journey as well as psychotherapy, the story of Sky Woman (Iroquois), and the aid of a psychic Euro-American woman. A central trauma of the novel is the protagonist's separation from her female childhood friend and lover and her being forced into heterosexuality. Another trauma is her betrayal and rape by a trusted male cousin. Many readers have found the novel difficult to follow because of its multicultural allusions, which draw, however, on the Native American ritual tradition, and its setting in the mind of the psychically and spiritually ill protagonist.

CRITICAL RECEPTION

Allen makes no secret in her work that she is lesbian, but lesbianism inseparable from her vision of Native American culture as being woman-centered, and thus many critics have missed or ignored this aspect of her work. Much of the explicitly lesbian work first appeared in feminist publications and, therefore, did not reach a mainstream audience. These poems and essays were incorporated into her collections but have not received much notice there. For instance, Elizabeth Hanson's fifty-page biography of Allen for Boise State University's Western Writers Series (1990) only briefly mentions that Allen is lesbian, and just as briefly mentions her lesbian themes, even though she addresses Allen's feminist content at more length. Allen's interest in gay and lesbian issues is mentioned in a reference to Allen's idea that gays and lesbians were accorded honor in traditional Native American cultures and in Hanson's discussion of *The Woman Who Owned the Shadows*. The *MELUS* interview (Ballinger and Swann 1983) is one of the few that mention that Allen is lesbian.

Allen's *Woman Who Owned the Shadows* was reviewed by *New York Times Book Review*, *New Women's Times*, and *Hurricane Alice*, among others, but only Annette Van Dyke's review in *Hurricane Alice* noted the lesbian content, while all noted the feminist and Native American content. Bonnie Zimmerman's 1990 *The Safe Sea of Women: Lesbian Fiction 1969–1989* and Van Dyke's essay in *Lesbian Texts and Contexts* give two of the few accounts of the novel as lesbian. A. LaVonne Ruoff's 1990 *American Indian Literatures: An Introduction, Bibliographic Review, and Selected Bibliography* gives a synopsis of the novel, but omits the lesbian content. These omissions certainly seem to indicate a homophobic reaction and, perhaps, a heterosexual blindness to Allen's work, even though at the time of the novel's publication, Allen's then partner, well-known lesbian writer Judy Grahn, wrote a piece for the back cover. Grahn went on to feature Allen in her *Another Mother Tongue* (1984), and Allen's influence can also be seen in Grahn's novel *Mundane's World* (1988), in which Grahn creates a European-based, woman-centered tribal culture. Even the title seems to refer to Allen's idea that there is a fine line between the "mundane" and the "arcane" (*Grandmothers* 5).

Although the critical reaction to Allen has been good if one counts how many times she is quoted by scholars writing especially on Native American women writers, justice has not been done to her as the foremost Native American lesbian-feminist theorist. More work needs to be done that recognizes the breadth and the depth of her contributions. Allen's ideas challenge many dearly held feminist beliefs and corroborate others, writing in the best radical lesbian tradition. Despite the lack of recognition of her lesbian content, Allen continues to work on lesbian themes. She has a "medicine-dyke" novel in progress. Excerpts from *Raven's Road* have appeared in Will Roscoe's *Living the Spirit: A Gay American Indian Anthology* and elsewhere. Allen says that she is "trying to pose two communities, Indian and lesbian, with characters that bridge both communities. So it's really a bridge novel" (Coltelli 37). On the path of the medicine woman, as one who communicates with and for her multicultural world, Allen includes lesbian culture. As she says in an interview: "It all has to do with spirit, with restoring an awareness of our spirituality as gay people" (quoted in Walter Williams, *The Spirit and the Flesh* 251).

BIBLIOGRAPHY

Works by Paula Gunn Allen

"Symbol and Structure in Native American Literature: Some Basic Considerations." *College Composition and Communication* 24:3 (October 1973): 267–70.

"The Mythopoetic Vision in Native American Literature." *American Indian Culture and Research Journal* 1:1 (1974): 3–13.

The Blind Lion. Berkeley, CA: Thorpe Springs Press, 1975.

"The Sacred Hoop: A Contemporary Indian Perspective on American Indian Literature." *Literature of the American Indians: Views and Interpretations.* Ed. Abraham Chapman. New York: New American, 1975.

"Sipapu: A Cultural Perspective." Diss., University of New Mexico, 1975.

Coyote's Daylight Trip. Albuquerque: La Confluencia, 1978.

Guest Editorial. *A Journal of Contemporary Literature* (Special Issue: Native Women of New Mexico) 3:2 (Fall 1978): 1.

"Iyani: It Goes This Way." *The Remembered Earth: An Anthology of Contemporary Native American Literature.* Ed. Gary Hobson. Albuquerque: Red Earth, 1979. 191–93.

"A Stranger in My Own Life: Alienation in American Indian Prose and Poetry." *MELUS* 7:2 (Summer 1980): 3–19.

"Beloved Women: The Lesbians in American Indian Cultures." *Conditions* 7 (1981): 65–87.

A Cannon Between My Knees. New York: Strawberry, 1981.

Foreword to "Song of the Sky." *Greenfield Review* (Special Issue: American Indian Writings) 9:3–4 (1981): 116–21.

"The Grace That Remains—American Indian Women's Literature." *Book Forum* 5:3 (1981): 376–88.

Review of *What Moon Drove Me to This?* by Joy Harjo. *Greenfield Review* (Special Issue: American Indian Writings) 8:3–4 (1981): 12–14.

Star Child. Marvin, SD: Blue Cloud Quarterly, 1981.

"Answering the Deer." *American Indian Culture and Research Journal* 6:3 (1982): 35–45.

Shadow Country. Los Angeles: University of California American Indian Studies Center, 1982.

"Judy Grahn: 'Gathering the Tribe.' " *Contact II* (Special issue on Women Poets) 5:27–29 (1982–83): 7–9.

Studies in American Indian Literature: Critical Essays and Course Designs. Ed. Paula Gunn Allen. New York: Modern Language Association of America, 1983.

The Woman Who Owned the Shadows. San Francisco: Spinsters Ink, 1983.

"The Feminine Landscape of Leslie Marmon Silko's *Ceremony.*" *Studies in American Indian Literature: Critical Essays and Course Designs.* Ed. Paula Gunn Allen. New York: Modern Language Association of America, 1984. 127–33.

"Who Is Your Mother? Red Roots of White Feminism." *Sinister Wisdom* 25 (Winter 1984): 34–46.

"Haggles." *Trivia: A Journal of Ideas* 8 (Winter 1986): 61–73.

From *Raven's Road. The New Native American Novel, Works in Progress.* Ed. Mary Dougherty Bartlett. Albuquerque: University of New Mexico Press, 1986. 51–63.

The Sacred Hoop: Recovering the Feminine in American Indian Traditions. Boston: Beacon Press, 1986. 111–35.

"The Autobiography of a Confluence." *I Tell You Now: Autobiographical Essays by Native American Writers.* Ed. Brian Swann and Arnold Krupat. Lincoln and London: University of Nebraska Press, 1987. 141–54.

Wyrds. San Francisco: Taurean Horn, 1987.

Selections from *Raven's Road. Living the Spirit: A Gay American Indian Anthology.* Ed. Will Roscoe. New York: St. Martin's Press, 1988. 134–52.

Skins and Bones. Albuquerque: West End, 1988.

"Some Like Indians Endure." *Living the Spirit: A Gay American Indian Anthology.* Ed. Will Roscoe. New York: St. Martin's Press, 1988. 9–13.

"Where I Come from God Is a Grandmother." *Sojourner: The Women's Forum* (August 1988): 16–18.

Spider Woman's Granddaughters: Traditional Tales and Contemporary Writing by Native American Women. Boston: Beacon Press, 1989.

"The Woman I Love Is a Planet: The Planet I Love Is a Tree." *Woman of Power* 18 (Fall 1990): 5–7.

Studies of Paula Gunn Allen

Ballinger, Franchot, and Brian Swann. "A *MELUS* Interview: Paula Gunn Allen." *MELUS* 10:2 (Summer 1983): 3–25.

Bannon, Helen. "Spider Woman's Web: Mothers and Daughters in Southwestern Native American Literature." *The Lost Tradition: Mothers and Daughters in South-*

western Native American Literature. Ed. Cathy N. Davidson and E. M. Broner. New York: Frederick Ungar, 1980. 286–79.

Bataille, Gretchen M., and Kathleen Mullen Sands. *American Indian Women: Telling Their Lives*. Lincoln: University of Nebraska Press, 1984.

Cliff, Michelle. "Journey of the Spirit" (Review of *The Woman Who Owned the Shadows*.) *Woman's Review of Books* 1:6 (March 1984): 8.

Coltelli, Laura. Interview with Paula Gunn Allen. *Winged Words: American Writers Speak*. Lincoln: University of Nebraska Press, 1990. 11–39.

Grahn, Judy. *Another Mother Tongue: Gay Words, Gay Worlds*. Boston: Beacon, 1984.

Hanson, Elizabeth J. *Paula Gunn Allen*. Western Writers Series. Boise, Idaho: Boise State University Press, 1990.

Hoffman, Alice. "Ephanie's Ghosts" (Review of *The Woman Who Owned the Shadows*). *New York Times Book Review* 89 (June 3, 1984), Sect. 7: 18.

Jahner, Elaine. "A Laddered, Rain-bearing Rug: Paula Gunn Allen's Poetry." *Women and Western American Literature*. Ed. Helen Winter Stauffer and Susan Rosowski. Troy, NY: Whitson, 1982. 311–26.

————. Review of *Shadow Country*. *American Indian Quarterly: A Journal of Anthropology, History, and Literature* (Summer 1983): 84–86.

Ruoff, A. LaVonne. *American Indian Literatures: An Introduction, Bibliographic Review, and Selected Bibliography*. New York: Modern Language Association, 1990. 92–94.

Ruppert, James. "Paula Gunn Allen and Joy Harjo: Closing the Distance between Personal and Mythic Space." *American Indian Quarterly* 7:1 (1983): 27–40.

Scarberry, Susan J. "Grandmother Spider's Lifeline." *Studies in American Indian Literature: Critical Essays and Course Designs*. Ed. Paula Gunn Allen. New York: Modern Language Association, 1983. 100–107.

Swallow, Jean. Review of *The Woman Who Owned the Shadows*. *New Women's Times Feminist Review* 9:35 (September–October 1984): 7.

Van Dyke, Annette. "Balancing" (Review of *The Woman Who Owned the Shadows*). *Hurricane Alice* 1:4 (Spring/Summer 1984): 9.

————. "The Journey Back to Female Roots: A Laguna Pueblo Model." *Lesbian Texts and Contexts: Radical Revisions*. Ed. Karla Jay and Joanne Glasgow. New York: New York University Press, 1990. 339–54.

————. Review of *The Woman Who Owned the Shadows*. *Explorations in Sights and Sounds* 5 (Summer 1985): 3–4.

————. *The Search for a Woman-Centered Spirituality*. New York: New York University Press, 1992. 12–40.

Williams, Walter. *The Spirit and the Flesh: Sexual Diversity in American Indian Culture*. Boston: Beacon Press, 1986.

Zimmerman, Bonnie. *The Safe Sea of Women: Lesbian Fiction, 1969–1989*. Boston: Beacon, 1990.

DOROTHY ALLISON (1949–   )
Lisa Moore

BIOGRAPHY

Because Dorothy Allison's writing is "very autobiographical, but not autobiography" (unless otherwise noted, all quotes are from personal communication with the author), readers of her fiction, poetry, and essays are already familiar with the emotional texture and some of the major events of her life. She was born on April 11, 1949, in Greenville, South Carolina. Of her family background, she says, "I'm many generations trash. . . . We're the caricatures of the society—the laundry workers and whores of America. . . . I feel like I came out of a world nobody knows about, that maybe doesn't exist anymore" (Huston 70). Like Bone, the protagonist in Allison's novel *Bastard Out of Carolina*, Allison's origins became a family story: "My mother was unconscious for the first three days of my life, and my aunts named me and took care of me. I was registered a bastard in the state of South Carolina because the aunts didn't get the facts straight with the hospital" (70).

When Allison was a teenager, her family planned a clandestine overnight move to Florida to avoid crippling debt. She recalls: "My parents worked out a scheme so that it appeared my stepfather had abandoned us, but instead he went down to Florida, got a new job and rented us a house" ("A Question of Class"). She graduated from Maynard High School in Orlando, "the only one of my one hundred or so cousins to have acquired a diploma" ("A Question of Class"). Assisted by a National Merit Scholarship, she received a B.A. in anthropology from Florida Presbyterian College in 1971, a fact she calls "nothing short of astonishing. . . . I never doubted that if we had remained in South Carolina, I would have been trapped by my family's heritage of poverty, jail, and illegitimate children" ("Class"). Instead, she took graduate classes in anthropology at Florida State University in 1973, and in 1987 received an M.A. in urban anthropology from the New School of Social Research in New York City.

Throughout this period of intense intellectual and political work, she also honed her craft as a writer, studying with such teachers as Bertha Harris, Blanche Boyd, and Rita Mae Brown at the Sagaris Institute in Lyndonville, Vermont (1975), and with Susan Shreve and John Gardner at the Ginny Moore Writing Contest Workshop at George Washington University (1978).

Despite being touted as "one of the highest-paid lesbian authors in the country" (Huston 71) after receiving a $37,000 advance for her novel, *Bastard Out of Carolina* (1992), Allison insists that the "hardest thing about being a writer is the astonishing poverty in which you must live," saying that she, like other lesbian writers, can only "marginally survive" by doing other kinds of work when she can get it. "Teaching is one of the main ways I survive," she says. Since 1988, Allison has taught an ongoing writing class at A Different Light Bookstore, a gay and lesbian bookstore in San Francisco. She has taught writing, literature, feminist theory, and/or anthropology at universities, colleges, and art institutes. She has also worked for many years as a journalist and editor for such publications as *Out/Look Magazine* (a national gay and lesbian quarterly), *New York Native* (a gay and lesbian magazine), *Conditions* (a feminist journal she helped found in New York), *Quest: A Feminist Quarterly*, and *Amazing Grace*, a Florida feminist magazine. She has been a frequent contributor to the *Village Voice* and the *Voice Literary Supplement*, writing book reviews as well as literary essays.

Like her writing, Allison's activism is notable for its challenge to lesbian-feminist orthodoxies of both the "pro-sex" and "anti-violence" varieties. She claims, "I never found a doctrinaire theory that satisfied my life." From 1984 to 1986, she worked on the Board of New York Women Against Rape; during that same period, she was active in the Lesbian Sex Mafia, a consciousness-raising group for women who identify as perverts, which she helped found in 1981. She currently lives in San Francisco with her lover, Alix Layman and their son Wolf Michael.

MAJOR WORKS AND THEMES

Although she is best known for her fiction, Allison's first book was a collection of poems entitled *The Women Who Hate Me*. The language of her poetry shares many of the best qualities of her prose: specific and often surprising images, sardonic humor, and a ruthless attention to what she calls "the real events" of women's lives. In these poems, as in her fiction, food is often a powerful metaphor for the conjunction of raw emotion and physical need that motivates many of these characters. Characters often experience sex acts as if they were enjoying beloved foods. But food, like sex in Allison's world, can also be dangerously powerful, monstrous, and even slightly ridiculous. The poems insist on the necessity of words—names, lists, stories—for survival. Like her stories, the poems struggle against the invisibility of the people and events Allison knows best, against their silencing by a dominant culture that just doesn't want to know.

In *Trash*, her collection of linked short stories, Allison moves to a more explicit single narrative point of view, that of a woman like herself, "a cross-eyed working-class lesbian, addicted to violence, language, and hope, who has made the decision to live, is determined to live, on the page and on the street, for me and mine" (12). The first story, "River of Names," includes brutal details about each of the family members she wants to remember. "We were so many we were without number and, like tadpoles, if there was one less from time to time, who counted" (14). This series of brief anecdotes performs that work of counting—of remembering the victims of rape, suicide, murder, ordinary violence, remembering them as names and stories. "The Meanest Woman Ever Left T...nessee," about the narrator's great-grandmother, "Mama," about a little girl learning rage from her father and survival from her mother, and "Don't Tell Me You Don't Know," in which the narrator finally reveals the family secret by telling her aunt about having been raped by her stepfather, all examine the legacy women leave to the girls of the next generation. This mixed heritage of protection and willed ignorance, unconditional love and inevitable betrayal, shapes the narrator's relation to feminism, explored in the later stories in the volume. "Violence Against Women Begins at Home," for example, describes how violence is committed in the name of feminism on a lesbian artist whose drawings are deemed "pornographic" by her community. The political investments of Allison's writing, then, span both sides of the so-called lesbian sex wars—she fiercely analyzes and condemns child sexual abuse and male violence, but just as fiercely argues for women's right to all kinds of artistic and sexual expressions, including violent ones.

Bastard Out of Carolina, Allison's first novel, draws heavily from the characters and plots of the first half of *Trash*. The story opens with the birth of the protagonist, Bone, in a car accident. Such unpredictable violence is to become the hallmark of her family's relationships as her mother moves through several lovers and ends up marrying Daddy Glen, whose jealousy of Bone and her little sister, Reese, gradually escalates into beatings and sexual abuse. Although readers may want to identify Bone as the child who grows up to be one of the lesbian protagonists of *Trash*, there is really only one lesbian character in the novel: Bone's Aunt Raylene, with whom she finds refuge after a particularly brutal beating. The story focuses on how the women of the family cope with such violence and attempt to protect their children, and on the betrayal the children feel when this protection fails. In the novel's final scene, Bone's perspective shifts to an augmented understanding of the constraints under which women like her mother live. At thirteen, she realizes that the constraints of womanhood are hers as well:

[Mama's] life had folded into mine. What would I be like when I was fifteen, twenty, thirty? Would I be as strong as she had been, as hungry for love, as desperate, determined, and ashamed? . . . I was who I was going to be, someone like her, like Mama, a Boatwright woman. (309)

Such a reframing exemplifies one of the greatest risks Allison's fiction takes: the risk of understanding what leads mothers to fail their children in this way, without forgiving such failure in any easy way.

Allison's non-fiction prose will appear from Firebrand Books in a collection entitled *Skin: Talking about Sex, Class and Literature*. Her best known essay is "Private Silence, Public Terror," in which she places feminist debates over pornography and sadomasochism in the context of the fear that circumscribes women's sexual experience and imagination. She calls on feminism to work against that fear rather than promote it through "self-righteous hatred" ("Private Silence" 106). She calls for fewer taboos and more sexual honesty among women: "as women we don't know enough about each other, our fears, our desires or the many ways that this society has acted upon us" ("Private Silence" 108). In the unpublished manuscript cited above, "A Question of Class" (to appear in *Sisters, Sexperts and Queers*, ed. Arlene Stein), Allison signals a theoretical shift that her fiction has already made, to the consideration of "the absolute intrinsic impact of being born in a condition of poverty that this society finds shameful, contemptible, and somehow deservedly entrenched." The essay is an autobiographical consideration of the failures of feminist theory and lesbian communities to take class seriously as an axis of the oppression of women. Allison's insights on this crucial absence mark hers as one of the clearest and most uncompromising political voices not only in lesbian literature, but in feminist theory as well.

CRITICAL RECEPTION

There have been no scholarly or critical examinations of Allison's work to date. *The Women Who Hate Me* and *Trash* were both favorably reviewed in the women's and alternative presses. *Bastard Out of Carolina* has already been widely reviewed, due in part to its publication by Dutton, a major New York publishing house. Mainstream reviewers have tended to classify it with Southern regionalist fiction, like that of William Faulkner, Margaret Mitchell, and Flannery O'Connor rather than with a tradition of lesbian or feminist fiction. Many of these reviews praise Allison's command of folk idiom ("Allison can make an ordinary moment transcendent with her sensuous mix of kitchen-sink realism and down-home drawl"; Kaufman 21), perhaps as a way of avoiding talking about the book's lesbian and feminist themes. However, Charles Wilmoth, who reviewed the novel both for the gay/lesbian journal *NYQ* and the mainstream *American Book Review*, tackles the novel's status as a "troubling and original fiction about incest and rape" in both pieces. He notes the complexity of Allison's treatment of this theme in the representation of Bone's sexual fantasies: "This detailed eroticism, along with Bone's dogged struggle for autonomy, her hickory switch tough personality, and the pursuit of her own interests, such as reading, all resist a representation of Bone as a helpless victim" (*NYQ* 40). Reviewers have been uniformly enthusiastic about the novel, but when they do question its merits, they focus on problems in structure and plotting: "*Bastard* has a tendency to bog down in its own heat, speech and atmosphere . . . the book seems more often to meander than to move, lending its conclusion an air of inconclusiveness" (*Washington Post*). This same reviewer, however, calls the writer "abundantly gifted"; clearly, Dorothy Allison has achieved a visibility in the mainstream of American literature with her depictions of violence against women, feminism, and lesbian sexuality.

BIBLIOGRAPHY

Works by Dorothy Allison

"Demon Lover." *off our backs* Fiction/Poetry Supplement (July 1979).

"I'm Working on my Charm." *Conditions* 6 (Spring 1980): 15–20.

"Boston, Massachusetts." *The Lesbian Poetry Anthology*. Ed. Elly Bulkin and Joan Larkin. Watertown, MA: Persephone Press, 1982. 202–3.

"River of Names" and "I'm Working on My Charm." *The Lesbian Fiction Anthology*. Ed. Elly Bulkin. Watertown, MA: Persephone Press, 1982. 175–82.

"My Career as a Thief." *Conditions* 9 (Spring 1983): 32–35.

The Women Who Hate Me [poems]. New York: Long Haul Press, 1983.

"Anonymous Letters." *On Our Backs* 1: 2 (Fall 1984): 18.

"Public Silence, Private Terror." *Pleasure and Danger*. Ed. Carol Vance. Boston and London: Routledge and Kegan Paul, 1984. 103–14.

"Tomato Song." *Southern Exposure* 12: 3 (July 1984): 38.

"A Bastard Out of Carolina." *Village Voice Literary Supplement* (October 1986): 5–7.

"Demon." *Coming to Power*. Ed. Samois Collective. Boston: Alyson Publications, 1987. 114–15.

"Not Speaking, Screaming" and other poems. *Naming the Waves: Contemporary Lesbian Poetry*. Ed. Christian McEwen. London: Virago Press, 1988. 1–4.

"A River of Names." *Southern Exposure* 16: 3 (Fall 1988): 51–54.

"To the Bone" and other poems. *Open Lines: Gay and Lesbian Poetry in Our Time*. Ed. Joan Larkin and Carl Morse. New York: St. Martin's Press, 1988. 1–7.

Trash: Short Stories. Ithaca, New York: Firebrand Books, 1988.

"The Future Is Female: Octavia Butler's Mother Lode" [critical essay]. *Reading Black, Reading Feminist*. Ed. Henry Louis Gates, Jr. New York: New American Library, 1990. 471–78.

"A Lesbian Appetite." *Women on Women*. Ed. Joan Nestle and Naomi Holach. New York: New American Library, 1990. 281–99.

"Mama." *Calling Home: Working Class Women's Writings*. Ed. Janet Zandy. New Brunswick, NJ: Rutgers University Press, 1990. 138–49.

"Private Rituals." *High Risk*. Ed. Ira Silverberg and Amy Scholder. New York: New American Library, 1991. 169–86.

The Women Who Hate Me. Poetry: 1980–1990. Ithaca, New York: Firebrand Books, 1991.

Bastard Out of Carolina. New York: Dutton, 1992.

"A Question of Class." *Sisters, Sexperts and Queers*. Ed. Arlene Stein. New York: New American Library (forthcoming).
Skin: Talking about Sex, Class and Literature. Ithaca, NY: Firebrand, 1993.

Studies of Dorothy Allison

Reviews of Bastard Out of Carolina

Advocate April 7, 1992: 70 + .
Aletti, Vince. *Village Voice Literary Supplement* (June 1992): 1.
Book Review July 5, 1992: 126.
Barnes, Noreen C. *Bay Area Reporter* 11: 16 (April 16, 1992): 20.
Cooper, Jackie. *Lambda Book Report* (May 1992): 42.
Garrett, George. *New York Times Book Review* July 5, 1992: 3.
Karpen, Lynn. "Truth is Meaner than Fiction." *New York Times Book Review* July 5, 1992: 3.
Kaufman, K. *San Francisco Chronicle* (April 19, 1992).
Kirkus Review 60 (Fall 1992): 126.
Picker, Lauren. *Newsday* April 19, 1992: 21.
Publisher's Weekly 239 (January 27, 1992): 88.
San Francisco Review of Books 16 (April 1992): 21 + .
Voice Literary Supplement (June 1992): 7.
Washington Post, May 3, 1992.
Wilmoth, Charles. *American Book Review* (June 1992).
———. *NYQ*, April 26, 1992: 40

Reviews of Trash

Belles Lettres 4 (Spring 1989), 18.
Galst, Liz. *Women's Review of Books* 6 (July 1989): 14–15.
McEwen, Christian. *Village Voice*, March 7, 1989.
———. *Voice Literary Supplement* 73: 6 (April 1989): 28.
Publisher's Weekly 234 (November 18, 1988): 74.
Women's Review of Books 6 (July 1989): 14.

Reviews of The Women Who Hate Me

Annas, Pamela. *Women's Review of Books* 1 (September 1984): 5–6.
Brook, Donna. *Voice Literary Supplement* 19: 3 (September 1983): 21.
Kulp, Denise. *off our backs* 13 (December 1983): 21.

Interviews with Dorothy Allison

Huston, Bo. *Advocate* (April 7, 1992): 70–72.
Stamps, Wickie. *Gay Community News* 19: 33–34 (March 22–April 4, 1992): 7–12.
Wieners, Brad. *City* (San Francisco), April 1992.
Wilmoth, Charles. *NYQ*, April 26, 1992: 36–37.

GLORIA E. ANZALDÚA (1942–)
Juanita Ramos

BIOGRAPHY

Gloria E. Anzaldúa was born on September 26, 1942, on a ranch settlement called Jesus Maria y Los Vergeles in the Rio Grande Valley of South Texas. When she was eleven her family moved to Hargill, "that triangular piece of land wedged between the river y el golfo which serves as the Texas–U.S./Mexican border" (*Borderlands* 35). The daughter of a sharecropper and a field worker, she was raised on farms and ranches, her parents making barely enough to feed the family. After the death of her father, when she was fourteen, Anzaldúa worked in the fields every weekend and summer until she finished her undergraduate studies. She spent her spare time reading, writing, and drawing.

Anzaldúa received a B.A. in English, art, and secondary education from Pan American University in 1969. In 1972 she received an M.A. in English and education from the University of Texas at Austin. She is currently pursuing her Ph.D. in the Literature Program at the University of California at Santa Cruz with a focus on feminist theory and cultural studies.

Anzaldúa began her teaching career in 1969 in the Bilingual Pre-school program in San Juan, Texas. She also taught special education to emotionally and mentally retarded students, English at the high school level, and advised teachers and administrators on curriculum and methods of teaching migrant Mexican-American students. These experiences and her own rural upbringing allowed her to become acquainted early on with the problems encountered by rural and urban students of color in the United States, especially those whose first language is not English.

At the university level, Anzaldúa has taught feminist studies, Chicano studies, and creative writing (University of Texas at Austin, San Francisco State University, Vermont College of Norwich University). She has been a writer-in-residence (The Loft, Minneapolis), artist-in-residence (Chicano studies, Panoma

College), contributing editor to *Sinister Wisdom* since 1984, and serves on various editorial boards.

MAJOR WORKS AND THEMES

In 1981, Anzaldúa co-edited with Cherrìe Moraga the anthology *This Bridge Called My Back: Writings by Radical Women of Color. This Bridge* is a collection of "prose, poetry, personal narrative and analysis" by twenty-nine Afro-American, Asian American, Latina, and Native American women and was intended "to reflect an uncompromised definition of feminism by women of color in the U.S." (*This Bridge* xxiii). The anthology's main themes—the invisibility of women of color within the movements they are part of, racism within the white-dominated women's movement, divisions among women of color, writing as a tool of radical change, the emergence of a feminist theory among Third World women in the United States, and Third World feminist visions for the future—were identified by the editors as the major areas of concern for Third World women seeking to build a "broad-based political movement."

One of the main accomplishments of *This Bridge* was that it brought together lesbians and heterosexual feminists of color. Lesbians of color who read the book precisely because it was edited by two Chicana lesbians can relish the voices that speak about the pain of living in a country where all aspects of self are considered inferior and about the courage it takes to come out within one's own culture.

In the autobiographical essay, "La Prieta" (*This Bridge* 198–209), Anzaldúa lays out some of the major themes that she will continue to develop in her later work: homophobia in Chicano (a)/Latino(a) culture, the impact of the European conquest on indigenous peoples, people of color as accomplices in their own oppression, the fear that the criticism she makes of people of color will be seen as a "betrayal," and the need for oppressed peoples to unite in order to transform life on the planet. In "La Prieta," Anzaldúa also addresses the double messages about womanhood she received from her mother:

"Machona—india ladin" (masculine—wild indian), she would call me because I did not act like a nice little Chicanita is supposed to act: later, in the same breath she would praise and blame me, often for the same thing—being a tomboy and wearing boots, being unafraid of snakes or knives, showing my contempt for women's roles, leaving home to go to college, not settling down and getting married, being a politica, siding with the Farmworkers. (*This Bridge* 201)

Pressured by her family and various political movements to prioritize her different identities, Anzaldúa responds to the question "What am I?" with "A third world lesbian feminist with Marxist and mystic leanings." For Anzaldúa, her lesbian identity cannot be separated from her other identities. Her concept of "queer" and the world she envisions include much more than lesbian and gay people:

The rational, the patriarchal, and the heterosexual have held sway and legal tender for too long. Third World women, lesbians, feminists, and feminist-oriented men of all colors are banding and bonding together to right that balance. . . . We are the queer groups, the people that don't belong anywhere, not in the dominant world nor completely within our own respective cultures. (*This Bridge* 209)

In 1987, Anzaldúa published *Borderlands/La Frontera: The New Mestiza*, where she explores the socioeconomic, political, and spiritual impact of the European conquest as well as the ways in which people of color oppress one another. In "La conciencia de la mestiza" (77–98), Anzaldúa describes how heterosexism and homophobia are experienced in Chicana(o) culture and calls on mestizas to "support each other in changing the sexist elements in the Mexican-Indian culture" (*Borderlands* 84).

For Anzaldúa, oppressed people can survive, thrive, and change the conditions of their oppression by developing a tolerance for "ambiguity." This ambiguity is expressed by Anzaldúa's concept of mestiza:

As a mestiza I have no country, my homeland cast me out; yet all countries are mine because I am every woman's sister or potential lover. (As a lesbian I have no race, my own people disclaim me; but I am all races because there is the queer of me in all races.) I am cultureless because, as a feminist, I challenge the collective cultural/religious male-derived beliefs of the Indo-Hispanics and Anglos; yet I am cultured because I am participating in the creation of yet another culture. (80–81)

Anzaldúa's strength as a visionary lies in her ability to see the potential for unity when others cannot. This potential for unity defies gender boundaries; "I, like other queer people, am two in one body, both male and female. I am the embodiment of the hieros granos: the coming together of opposite qualities within" (19).

Lesbian sexuality, according to Anzaldúa, plays a radical role in cultures of color: "For the lesbian of color, the ultimate rebellion she can make against her native culture is through her sexual behavior. She goes against two moral prohibitions: sexuality and homosexuality" ("Movimientos de rebeldia y las culturas que traicionan" 19). By coming out of the closet, lesbians and gays contribute to "overcoming a tradition of silence" ("How to Tame a Wild Tongue" 54) about the positive historical role they have played and the repression they have faced.

We come from all colors, all classes, all races, all time periods. Our role is to link people with each other. . . . Colored homosexuals have more knowledge of other cultures; have always been at the forefront (although sometimes in the closet) of all liberation struggles in this country; have suffered more injustices and have survived them despite all odds. (*Borderlands* 84–85)

Anzaldúa's "convergence" of identities, represented by the mestiza, also extends to the languages used in her text. Although primarily writing in standard

English, Anzaldúa weaves into the text words and sentences in Chicano Spanish, Tex-Mex, Nahuatl, and Pachoco, thus seeking to create a new language. Anzaldúa's use of different languages throughout the text allows her to deepen the emotional impact of her message by using those words and phrases in each language that best describes what she wants us to feel and envision. Moreover, *Borderlands* defies genre; it is a combination of autobiography, historical documentation, and poetry. Half of the text is devoted to poetry.

Anzaldúa's poems can be sensual as in "Companera, cuando amabamos," deeply sad as in "En el nombre de todas las madres que han perdido hijos en la guerra," or anger provoking as in "We Call Them Greasers." Anzaldúa's poems tend to be short and narrative. Although they are "deeply political" as Melanie Kaye/Kantrowitz notes, "these poems mostly manage to steer clear of rhetoric" (60). Anzaldúa frequently interrupts her prose with lines taken from poems and popular songs written by others as well as by herself.

Anzaldúa's talents as a short story writer parallel her talents as an essayist and a poet. It is in her short stories that Anzaldúa speaks more intimately about the conflicts created by having to choose between cultural traditions that demand she become a wife and mother and those reaffirming her lesbian identity. In "El Paisano is a Bird of Good Omen" (*Cuentos* 153–175), Andrea, the main character, resolves the conflict by reaffirming that she is "queer": "I am that I am" (175). In "La Historia de Una Marimacho" (*Third Woman* 64–68), a complement to "El Paisano," the main character takes her lover far away from her father only to have him catch up with them later on. The conflict is resolved when the narrator of the story cuts off the father's fingers and one of his ears thus forcing him to accept her relationship with his daughter.

In 1990, Anzaldúa published *Making Face, Making Soul/Haciendo Caras*. A collection of works by sixty-one lesbian and heterosexual women of color, its main themes sought to pick up where *This Bridge* left off: the impact of racism and heterosexism on women of color, ridding oneself of internalized racism and violence, learning to be true to ourselves, women of color as writer and intellectuals, and the continuing need for women of color to build alliances and coalitions with one another across race, ethnicity, class, sexual orientation, etc.

In the essay "En rapport, In Opposition: Cobrando cuentas a las nuestras," Anzaldúa speaks about women of color: "Like fighting cocks, razor blades strapped to our fingers, we slash out at each other. We have turned our anger against ourselves." This internalized anger leads women of color to find themselves in a constant state of civil war, "entreguerras" (*Making Face* 143). This is the result, for Anzaldúa, of continuing to keep the white, the male, the heterosexual as the frame of reference. The solution she proposes is for women of color to develop their own frame of reference from their own experiences of oppression and to develop an "understanding and acceptance of the spirituality of our root ethnic cultures" (147). The combination of spiritual and material is a necessary step in the process of healing and changing.

CRITICAL RECEPTION

The reviews of Anzaldúa's work have been overwhelmingly positive. The more negative responses, however, have been conditioned by the fact that Anzaldúa refuses to deny any aspect of who she is or to change her writing style to meet conventional standards. She is shunned by some Anglos for calling them on their racism and classism. She is rejected by some heterosexual Chicanos(as) because she refuses to deny her lesbianism. And she has been criticized by lesbians such as Cherrìe Moraga (*Third Woman* 152) and Melanie Kaye/Kantrowitz (*Village Voice* 60), who feel that Anzaldúa's mixing of genres sometimes has the effect of fragmenting the text and leaving ideas undeveloped. Anzaldúa's response to the latter criticism is, "The first rule that I break is the rule that says that there is a cohesive, coherent, self-directed self" (*Borderlands/La Frontera* 6).

Anzaldúa's genius for communicating the contradictions inherent in human affairs is recognized by the anonymous reviewer of *Borderlands/La Frontera* for *Publishers Weekly*: "With exceptional insight, she creates a mosaic of the marginal person: a person like herself, who exists in a state of transition, of ambivalence, of conflict" (72).

Some critics such as Debra D. Andrist respond to Anzaldúa's open lesbianism by downplaying it. In the essay "La semiotica de la Chicana: La escritura de Gloria Anzaldúa," Andrist describes Anzaldúa as a leading Chicana writer who seeks to reach an equilibrium between her main identities of woman, Chicana, and writer. However, in one or two passing references to Anzaldúa's lesbianism, she merely states that Anzaldúa's attempts to reach an equilibrium between her three identities is complicated by the fact that she has a fourth identity, that of being a lesbian.

Shelley Fishkin, on the other hand, recognizes that Anzaldúa's value lies precisely in the fact that she, like the other writers discussed in the essay, represent the "stories of people who were dismissed and devalued because they had the 'wrong' race, class, gender, ethnicity, or sexual preference" (133).

Discussing Anzaldúa's poetry in *Borderlands*, Arthur Ramirez concludes, "Ultimately she is an excellent storyteller in verse, with a fine command of tempo and narrative development" (186). Margaret Randall's review of *Borderlands* recognizes Anzaldúa's work as "major writing" (9). After rereading some of Anzaldúa's poems she declares, "I will walk through again and again, discovering with each passage further demands upon my own cultural myopia, racism, and conformity" (9).

Commenting on *Making Face, Making Soul*, an anonymous reviewer writes for *Publishers Weekly* (439), "From this perspective, reading this book is a cathartic and, potentially, individuating experience." Cheryl Clarke's impression of *Making Face, Making Soul* is that it is "an hospitable and generous altar, filled with engaging, seductive, new and familiar gifts" (129).

HONORS AND AWARDS

This Bridge Called My Back received the Before Columbus Foundation American Book Award. *Borderlands/La Frontera* was selected as one of the 38 Best Books by *Library Journal*. In 1990, *Making Face, Making Soul/Haciendo Caras* was winner of the Lambda Lesbian Small Press Book Award. In 1991, Gloria E. Anzaldúa received a National Endowment for the Arts Award in Fiction. During the fall of 1982, she was the recipient of a MacDowell Artist Colony Fellowship.

BIBLIOGRAPHY

Works by Gloria Anzaldúa

This Bridge Called My Back: Writings by Radical Women of Color [edited jointly with Cherrìe Moraga.] Watertown, MA: Persephone Press, 1981. Rpt. New York: Kitchen Table Women of Color Press, 1983. In 1988, *This Bridge Called My Back* was published in Spanish as *Esta Puenta Mi Espalda* (San Francisco: Ism Press, 1988). Anzaldúa's role as one of its editors was omitted from the translation by Cherrìe Moraga and Ana Castillo.
"El Paisano is a Bird of Good Omen." *Cuentos: Stories by Latinas*. Ed. Alma Gómez, Cherrìe Moraga, and Mariana Romo-Carmona. New York: Kitchen Table Press, 1983. 153–75.
Borderlands/La Frontera: The New Mestiza. San Francisco: Spinsters/Aunt Lute, 1987.
"La Historia de Una Marimacho." *Third Woman*, (1989): 64–68.
Making Face, Making Soul/Haciendo Caras: Creative and Critical Perspectives by Feminists of Color. [ed.] San Francisco: Aunt Lute Foundation Books, 1990.
Anzaldúa's work has also appeared in *Third Woman, A Literary Journal, Cuentos: Stories by Latinas, IKON, Bilingual Review, Conditions, Trivia*, and *Lesbian Philosophies and Cultures*. She has also been a contributing editor to *Sinister Wisdom* since 1984.

Studies of Gloria Anzaldúa

Alarcon, Norma. "The Theoretical Subject(s) of *This Bridge Called My Back* and Anglo American Feminism." *Making Face, Making Soul/Haciendo Caras: Creative and Critical Perspectives by Feminists of Color*. Ed. Gloria Anzaldúa. San Francisco: Aunt Lute Foundation Books, 1990. 356–69.
Andrist, Debra D. "La semiotica de la Chicana: La escritura de Gloria Anzaldúa." *Mujer y Literatura Mexicana y Chicana Culturas en contacto*. Ed. Aralia Lopez Gonzalez, Amelia Malagamba, and Elena Urrutia. Mexico D.F., Mexico: El Colegio de Mexico, 1990. 243–47.
Bader, Elenor J. "Alive and Well and Living en la Frontera." *Belles Lettres* 3 (May 1988): 13.
Baldwin, Elizabeth. "Interview with Gloria Anzaldúa." *Matrix* (May 1988): 1–33.
Caron, Andrea. Review of *Borderlands/La Frontera: The New Mestiza*. *Library Journal* 112 (September 1, 1987): 171.

Clarke, Cheryl. Review of *Making Face, Making Soul/Haciendo Caras*. *Bridges* 2, no. 1 (Spring 1991): 128–33.

De la Peña, Terri. "On the Borderlands with Gloria Anzaldúa." *off our backs* 21, no. 7 (July 1991): 1–4.

Fennell, Rose. *Lambda Book Report* 2 (August 1990): 44.

Fishkin, Shelley. "Borderlands of Culture: Writing by W.E.B. Du Bois, James Agee, Tillie Olsen, and Gloria Anzaldúa." *Literary Journalism in the Twentieth Century*. Ed. Norman Sims. New York: Oxford University Press, 1991. 133–82.

Freedman, Diane. "Living in the Borderlands: The Poetic Prose of Anzaldúa and Susan Griffin." *Women and Language* 12, no. 1 (Spring 1989): 1–4.

Kaye/Kantrowitz, Melanie. "Crossing Dreams." *Village Voice* 33 (June 28, 1988): 60, 62.

Mandelbaum, Sara. Review of *This Bridge Called My Back*. *Ms.* 10 (March 1982): 39.

Mennis, Bernice. Review of *Making Face, Making Soul/Haciendo Caras*. *Bridges: A Journal of Jewish Feminists and Our Friends* 2, no. 1 (Spring 1991): 133–38.

Molina, I. Review of *Borderlands/La Frontera: The New Mestiza*. *Choice* 25 (April 1988): 1279.

Moraga, Cherrìe. " 'Algo secretamente amado': A Review of Gloria Anzaldúa's *Borderlands/La frontera: The New Mestiza*." *Third Woman* 4 (Fall 1989): 151–56.

Nelson, Susan. Review of *Making Face, Making Soul/Haciendo Caras: Creative and Critical Perspectives by Feminists of Color*. *Booklist* 87 (October 1, 1990): 247.

Ramirez, Arthur. Review of *Borderlands/La Frontera: The New Mestiza*. *Americas Review* 17, nos. 3–4 (Fall 1989): 185–87.

Randall, Margaret. "Una conciencia de mujer." *Women's Review of Books* 5 (December 1987): 8–9.

Review of *Borderlands/La Frontera: The New Mestiza*. *Library Journal* 113 (April 1988): 40.

Review of *Borderlands/La Frontera: The New Mestiza*. *Library Journal* 113 (January 1988): 40.

Review of *Borderlands/La Frontera: The New Mestiza*. *Publishers Weekly* 232 (July 31, 1987): 72.

Review of *Making Face, Making Soul/Haciendo Caras*. *Publishers Weekly* 237 (August 10, 1990): 438–39.

Review of *This Bridge Called My Back: Writings by Radical Women of Color*. *Choice* 19 (October 1981): 244.

Review of *This Bridge Called My Back: Writings by Radical Women of Color*. *Reference Service Review* 12 (Summer 1984): 85.

Saldivar-Hull, Sonia. "Feminism on the Border: From Gender Politics to Geopolitics." *Criticism in the Borderlands: Studies in Chicano Literature, Culture and Ideology*. Ed. Hector Calderon and Jose Saldivar. Durham, NC: Duke University Press, 1991. 203–20.

Woodward, Carolyn. Review of Gloria Anzaldúa's *Borderlands/La Frontera: The New Mestiza*. *National Women's Studies Association Journal* 1, no. 3 (Spring 1988): 530–32.

NUALA ARCHER (1955–   )
Robin Becker

BIOGRAPHY

Nuala Archer was born on June 21, 1955, in Rochester, New York, to immigrant Irish parents. Her family moved briefly to Windsor, Ontario, before spending two years in Costa Rica and another two years in Equador. At the age of four and a half, she moved with her family to Panama for nine and a half years. In the late 1960s, the Archers returned to the United States, spending about a year in Salamanca, New York, before moving to Corpus Christi, Texas, where Archer completed high school. She attended Wheaton College in Illinois and received, in three years, a B.A. in British and American literature. After earning her degree, she moved to Ireland for a year (1977–1978) where she studied Anglo-Irish literature at Trinity College of the University of Dublin. This year was a decisive one, as Archer established important personal and professional relationships in that country. For the next six years, she considered Ireland her base, purchasing a house there in 1981, the year in which she won the distinguished Irish Distillers/Patrick Kavanagh Award for her book of poems entitled *Whale on the Line*.

Archer says of herself the following:

My continuity is discontinuity and fragmentation. Although I fought against these forces for a long time, in recent years I've come to accept the pieces, to see how they form a crazy quilt. In some ways, the fragmentation helps me identify with people all over the world. I have no single, solid place to stand. But who does? The Second World War disrupted history in Europe, changed the way people thought of history; when I travel there, I never feel out of place. Here in the United States, where people cling to the notion of the ground beneath their feet, I feel most aware of my fragmentation. What grounds me is my connection to language and a community of women friends. (personal communication, June 1992)

In 1983, Archer received a Ph.D. in English literature and creative writing from the University of Wisconsin at Milwaukee. The following year, she accepted a position as a visiting assistant professor at Oklahoma State University and became an assistant professor in 1985. For the next five years, she traveled frequently to Ireland, maintaining her contacts with Irish poets and writers. After four years at Oklahoma State University, she was invited to Yale University as a visiting assistant professor. In 1989, she received tenure at Oklahoma State University. In 1991, she was offered and accepted the position of director of the Cleveland State University Poetry Center, where she was tenured at the level of associate professor of English and where she teaches today. Archer has been instrumental in shaping the curriculum, and in 1992, she taught a seminar on the work of Audre Lorde, Muriel Rukeyser, and Gertrude Stein. She currently lives in Cleveland and frequently travels to Ireland.

MAJOR WORKS AND THEMES

Nuala Archer's first collection, *Whale on the Line,* published in 1981 by the Gallery Press in Dublin, won the Patrick Kavanagh Award in Ireland. In 1989, the New Poets Series in Baltimore, Maryland, joined with Salmon Publishing (Galway, Ireland) to print *Two Women, Two Shores*, a collection containing poems by Nuala Archer and the Irish poet Medbh McGuckian. *Pan/ama*, a chapbook, was published by Red Dust Press, New York, in 1992. The simultaneous publication of *From a Mobile Home* and *The Hour of Pan/ama* (Salmon Publishing, Galway Ireland, 1992) established Nuala Archer as an important contemporary lesbian poet.

Few contemporary lesbian writers take as their major theme what Nuala Archer calls ''the brutality of immigrant dreams.'' From her earliest collection to the 1992 publications, Archer has been developing a poetics to examine displacement—geographical, social, and sexual. She destabilizes the notion of a single, fixed identity with her claim to multiple selves and speaks in many voices. Archer uses the word ''voices'' strategically: to evoke the many personae within the poet; to extend the metaphorical ''reach'' of her poems, bringing in material from astronomy, natural history, psychology. In ''Pastures of First Permission,'' she tells us that voices ''roam through the house.'' The verb ''roam'' is key to Archer's project, a part of her ongoing engagement with literal and metaphorical movement. In ''Wild Turkeys at Vinson,'' she looks to the natural world to mirror her own internal state and finds in the seasons a chorus of ''voices.'' This poem ends with the bold declaration that the poet is descending ''into the Africa of my own returning flesh.'' The body is a central trope in Archer's work. Fearlessly, she explores the sense of exile that results from physical trauma. For example, in ''The Deviant Mantis'' (from *Whale on the Line*) she assumes the persona of a praying mantis decapitated by a mate: ''I found I can function / without a brain. I have / other nerve centres. / Stories come to me / through my toes. / My wings are transparent antennae.'' At the end of the poem, the mantis declares, ''I hear strange news / from all over the world.'' With this brilliant shift, Archer transforms the mantis's apparent ''handicap'' into a gift for insight and communication. Having lived in Panama, Ireland, and in many regions of North, Central, and South America, Archer, like the mantis, is attuned to many countries and communities. Her poems reflect this ''internationalist'' perspective as well as her struggle to feel grounded in the world. Just as the mantis must adapt to its new state, so must the poet tell her stories despite social interdictions against rootlessness and sexual deviance.

Her first important North American publication appeared in *The Irish Women's Anthology*, a special issue of the *Midland Review Journal*, published in 1985. The publication of *Two Women, Two Shores* in 1989 made explicit Archer's continued connection to Ireland and broadened her themes by including poems set in the American Southwest. Several of these poems, such as ''Here in Oklahoma,'' reappear in *From a Mobile Home* and serve as a bridge to Archer's new work. In ''Here in Oklahoma,'' Archer invites her readers to explore our relationships to landscapes. She playfully deconstructs our experiences of geographic places by taking apart the syllables of the state. ''Did I say I was so low and la? / So low and la? Did I say / so Lola and here in Oklahoma? / O. Mama mia, Mama mia! / Oklahoma? Oklahoma?''

The poet Minnie Bruce Pratt has this to say about Archer's work: ''In *From a Mobile Home*, Nuala Archer is migrant, immigrant, wanderer poet. In these poems, we move between Oklahoma, Ireland, Swilly and Sewanee, Munster, and Ponca City. Archer takes us with her on an exhilarating search for a place and a language to convey the lonely company, the dark sweetness of her experience'' (jacket notes).

While Archer often uses specific place-names in her poems, she continually reminds us of our membership in a larger, global sisterhood. She considers the illegal aliens who are ''chancing their cunning in the Rio Grande's flow'' (''She Had Licked Her Name,'' *From a Mobile Home*). In a poem entitled ''Emigrant,'' from the same collection, Archer illustrates the interconnectedness of women's lives and names this feeling ''a community of presences.'' In a long persona poem from the same collection, Archer speaks in the voice of the Statue of Liberty explaining Liberty's decision to leave her watery post. The voice conveys bitterness and irony, as the silent female figure of freedom catalogues her disappointments and imagines how the population will respond to her absence. *From a Mobile Home* ends with the disappearance of this well-known symbol, leaving readers to ponder Liberty's refusal to stand, mute, forever.

One of Archer's gifts is her ability to ''relocate'' cultural and sexual marginality, forging a poetic language that privileges lesbianism and makes sexuality a source of strength and meaning. Within the harsh and violent landscape of the American Southwest, one woman asks another, ''what do you want of me? / Less than a lesbian / landscape and lingo? The dusty bread / of legitimacy?''

This poem, entitled "Pastures of First Permission," is filled with evidence that survival, for these women, will not be easy. The patriarchial cowboy culture and the extreme terrain force the speaker to demand, "hadn't our courage /better be / as mind-boggling / as cunt-crazy?" Archer wrests the word "cunt" from its culturally overdetermined meaning, creating a phrase signifying female empowerment.

Archer weaves memories of childhood incest throughout the first section of *The Hour Of Pan/Ama*; in the second section, she offers strategies for healing. A poem called "Weird Little Wordless Words" describes the speaker's experience at a mineral bath in Saratoga Springs. Archer depicts lesbian sexuality as vital to the speaker's recovery. The physical release of the curative waters permits the poet to remember, to claim her experience and transform debris to living flesh. Despite damaging childhood experiences, Archer fills *The Hour Of Pan/ Ama* with healing female figures: Gertrude, the attendant at Saratoga Springs; Olga, her Panamanian nurse; a childhood friend named Leigh; Janis Joplin. She combines figures from popular culture with historical facts and personal history, weaving images together in an experimental fashion. She makes use of the graphics of the page—breaking lines unexpectedly, shaping stanzas, using the prose poem to create a stream-of-consciousness narrative.

The appropriation and transformation of language is, for Archer, both a subject and a method. In a poem entitled "Splashie Sweeping," she creates a textured meditation in many voices. Each line (there are ninety-two) is an independent stanza and begins with a lowercase letter preceded by a comma. Coming at the beginning of the line, the comma startles and surprises. In the poem, Archer juxtaposes familiar clichés and regional colloquialisms in a non-linear fashion; the ungendered voices spin off in many directions, the way thoughts interrupt and supersede one another. What emerges is a portrait of a rural community with its loyalties and customs, its language and history.

Archer's linguistic flexibility and experimental approach to all aspects of discourse—the sentence, punctuation, and imagery—make her a true heir to writers such as Gertrude Stein. Like Stein, she takes risks with form, using repetition to infuse her poems with psychological truths. Her language is never static or flat; instead, it thwarts our expectations and requires that we question our assumptions about rhetoric and semantic structures. The acclaimed Irish poet Eavan Boland offers this comment on *The Hour of Pan/Ama*: "These poems achieve something which at first seems unlikely: they are both very finished and very experimental. They remain open and daring, while never failing to be crafted and persuasive. These are poems of powerful feeling and true accomplishment" (jacket notes).

CRITICAL RECEPTION

Nuala Archer has enjoyed a favorable critical reception. Victor Luftig, in an important article about Irish publishing ("A Migrant Mind in a Mobile Home:

Salmon Publishing in the Ireland of the 1990s'' in *Eire-Ireland: A Journal of Irish Studies*), says "Archer embodies the American sense of mobility and 'emancipation.' " He sees her as part of a tradition that includes James Joyce and Seamus Heaney as well as Eavan Boland and Medbh McGuckian. He writes:

> Whereas Europe offers Ireland analogous models of nations learning to shake loose traditional cultural authorities, the United States, as Archer makes clear, offers an example where such freedom already inheres, for better or worse. The American version of the 'migrant mind,' as exemplified by Archer, is capable of assimilating both the "poetic" language of linguistically self-conscious Ireland and the lurid language of American commerce. (119)

Luftig finds in Archer's work the dismantling of culturally proscribed taboos; he believes that her inclusiveness charts a new direction for Irish as well as American poetry.

BIBLIOGRAPHY

Works by Nuala Archer

Whale on the Line. Dublin: Gallery Press, 1981.
Two Women, Two Shores. Baltimore and Galway: New Poets Series and Salmon Press, 1989.
Pan/Ama. (chapbook) New York: Red Dust Press, 1992.
The Hour of Pan/ama. Galway: Salmon Publishing, 1992.
From a Mobile Home. Galway: Salmon Publishing, 1992.

Poems in Selected Anthologies

Unlacing: Ten Irish-American Women Poets. Ed. Patricia Monaghan. Fairbanks, AK: Fireweed Press, 1987.
The Legend of Being Irish: A Collection of Irish-American Poetry. Ed. David Lampe. Buffalo, NY: White Pine Press, 1989.
Resurgent: New Writings by Women. Ed. Lou Robinson and Camille Norton, Urbana: University of Illinois, 1992.

Studies of Nuala Archer

Kisner, Kathleen. "CSU's Multicultural Poet." *Cleveland Plain Dealer*, Sunday, May 31, 1992: 9H.
Luftig, Victor. "A Migrant Mind in a Mobile Home; Salmon Publishing in the Ireland of the 1990s." *Eire-Ireland: A Journal of Irish Studies* (Spring 1991): 108–19

JUNE ARNOLD (1926–1982)

Linda Dunne

BIOGRAPHY

June Arnold was a daughter of the aristocratic South. She was born June Davis on October 27, 1926, in Greenville, South Carolina, to Robert Cowan Davis and Cad Wortham Davis, both members of prominent southern families. After her father's death, when she was still a child, June, her mother, and her older sister, Fannie, moved back to her mother's native Houston. By all accounts, her life was a privileged one: she rode and showed horses at Pin Oaks Stable; she attended the best private schools, Kinkaid and Shipley; and when the time came, she "came out" as a debutante. In 1943, not yet eighteen, she went off to Vassar College, but hating the North, or perhaps just feeling homesick, she came back to Houston within a year and completed her undergraduate education at Rice University, graduating in 1948.

In conformity with the expectations of a young woman of her class, era, and culture, she married and had four children: Kate, Roberta, Fairfax, and Gus. But her marriage floundered. Unlike most of her peers, she returned to Rice University as a graduate student and received an M.A. in literature in 1958. After her divorce, she left Houston again, taking her children with her and moving to Greenwich Village. There she took writing courses at the New School and began her first novel, *Applesauce*, which was published by McGraw Hill in 1967 and was widely reviewed. She bought an abandoned factory at 54 Seventh Avenue and became one of the first New York loft dwellers. She had also become a lesbian and an active, even militant, feminist, participating, along with over seventy-five other members of the New York Women's Liberation Movement, in the illegal occupation of an abandoned building in Manhattan's lower east side in an attempt to create a woman's building. The building was occupied for the first thirteen days of 1971 before the women were ejected, and five arrested.

Following this failure to create a public space for women, Arnold moved in

1972 to rural Vermont with her partner, Parke Bowman. They bought an old farmhouse in Springfield with their own money and founded Daughters Inc., the first feminist press to specialize in novels. The authors on the Daughters, Inc. list included Rita Mae Brown, Bertha Harris, Elana Nachman, Monique Wittig, and Arnold herself. Daughters Inc. became one of the best known and important publishers of feminist and lesbian literature of the 1970s, and Arnold became an outspoken advocate of the separatist movement. During this period, she wrote for feminist periodicals and spoke at numerous conferences, including the Women in Print Conference in 1976, which she organized; the lesbian caucus of the Modern Language Association in 1976; the New York City Lesbian Conference in 1976; and the Southeastern Gay and Lesbian Conference in 1977. As a political separatist, she believed strongly in the importance of women establishing a completely independent communications network and took a strong public stand against feminists publishing with male-dominated presses. Ironically, Daughters Inc. was chosen to represent lesbian separatism in a major article by Lois Gould that appeared in the *New York Times Magazine* in 1977. During the 1970's, Daughters Inc. published eighteen novels and an anthology. Unlike the majority of feminist presses, Arnold and Bowman were able to pay their writers at a scale comparable to and sometimes even above that of commercial, male-dominated presses. In addition to supporting women writers, especially lesbians, through her own publishing activities, Arnold provided financial support to other lesbian feminist publications.

In 1977, tired of coping with New England winters, Arnold and Bowman brought Daughters Inc. back to New York, where they bought a brownstone at 22 Charles Street in the West Village. Arnold did not stay in New York long, however. Within a few years, she returned to her native Houston in order, she told friends, to write a novel about her mother. She died of cancer in Houston on March 11, 1982, and the novel, *Baby Houston*, was published posthumously five years later.

MAJOR WORKS AND THEMES

June Arnold has been categorized as a lesbian feminist, a southern writer, and an experimental writer. In her own non-fictional writings, she represented herself and her press as advocates of lesbian political fiction of high literary quality. In a published dialogue with fellow novelist Bertha Harris, she argued that "one of the lesbian writer's primary duties or tasks is to write in such a way that each woman reader learns to get in touch with her own source of truth" ("Lesbian Fiction" 42). For her this meant writing the truth, even when it might seem to be "just your own crazy individual perversions" (44) and even when it might seem to be inconsistent with a positive image of women. Through her own writing and the Daughters Inc. publications, Arnold actively fought the blatant censorship of the male publishing establishment, but she was also concerned about a new censorship among lesbians, manifested by a subtle demand that lesbians avoid their struggles and weaknesses, that they write only about "women being tender, sensitive, understanding, . . . working in groups" (45). In addition to envisioning a new honesty in fiction by women freed from male control, she believed that lesbian writers were creating a new kind of novel, one that was "developing away from plot-time via autobiography, confession, oral tradition into what might finally be a spiral . . . [a] spiral sliced to present a vision which reveals a whole and satisfies in some different way than the male resolution-of-conflict" ("Lesbians and Literature" 29).

Her own novels are consistent with her theories. Her first novel, *Applesauce*, was published in 1967, when Arnold was forty and was publicly known only as a southern divorcée. Published by McGraw Hill, it is an experimental novel that appears to be about a male protagonist, Gus Ferrarri, his three dead wives—Liza, Rebecca, and Lila, and his three children. But perhaps there is only one wife, or maybe all three wives are really extensions of Gus. It isn't at all clear. Although *Applesauce* appears to be a novel about heterosexual marriage and the relationships of parents and children, it can also be read, like the novels of earlier lesbian modernists such as Virginia Woolf, Gertrude Stein, and Djuna Barnes, as doing some gender bending and not being what it seems. As such, it introduces themes that were recurrent in Arnold's later works; the complexity of romantic, sexual, and family relationships; the problem of merging; the use of alcohol as a means of coping with the harshness of life; the social construction of gender difference; and the constructed nature of each individual's perceived reality.

These themes were brought into an explicit lesbian context in Arnold's next two novels, both of which were published by Daughters Inc. The authorship of Arnold's second novel, *The Cook and the Carpenter*, published in 1973, is attributed to the Carpenter, with a testimonial note from the Cook, thus establishing, simultaneously, both the fictional and the autobiographical nature of her project. Set in a women's commune located in an unnamed part of Texas, the novel's main action is based on the 1971 attempt to establish a woman's building in New York City. By fictionalizing the events leading up to and following this action, Arnold was able to describe and analyze the theories and strategies of lesbian-feminist separatist politics, as well as some of the conflicts within the movement and the attempts of women's groups to grapple with issues of power, violence, and personal jealousies. Another important narrative line explores the complexity of lesbian relationships and sexuality by following the development of a triangular relationship between the Carpenter, the Cook, and a character named Three. In addition to its political content, *The Cook and the Carpenter* is also notable for its stylistic innovations. For the majority of the book, all gendered pronouns are replaced by the single neuter pronoun "na" and "nan," "trusting the reader to know which character is female and which male," according to the publisher (who is, of course, also the unnamed author). This grammatical form of gender bending reaches a climax in the last section of the book when, having attempted the takeover, the commune begins to fall apart and the main characters, cleansed and transformed by their political rite of passage, are again able to claim their individual birth names and their gender identity.

Arnold's third novel, *Sister Gin*, was published two years later. While it is less experimental in style than the previous two works, *Sister Gin* is more complex in its characters and themes. The novel centers on the troubled long-term relationship of Su and Bettina, a relationship that at the novel's opening appears to be sustained primarily by Su's gin and Bettina's rum and Tang. This relationship is complicated by family ties, thwarted aspirations, the onset of menopause, and, most specifically, Su's affair with the seventy-seven-year-old southern belle and political activist Mamie Carter. Spiraling around this central story are a host of related stories: Su's earlier relationship with an abusive and alcoholic older woman; Bettina's fat sister, Adele; Su's mother Shirley, who could have been a lesbian if her feelings for women had not terrified her; Mamie Carter's vigilante band of old women, the Shirley Temple Gang, which abducts and punishes men who have committed acts of violence against women; the voicelessness of Bettina's mother's black servant, Miss May; and, of course, the relentless intrusion of Su's alter ego, Sister Gin. In *Sister Gin*, Arnold took the risk of ''outing'' qualities of her characters that lesbian feminists often attempted to keep in the closet: obsessions with food as substitutes for love, dependence on alcohol, the loss of sexual passion in long-term relationships and consequent sexual betrayals, menopausal mood swings, physical abuse in lesbian relationships, and general self-hatred. In *Sister Gin*, Arnold insisted on telling the truth of her own life, regardless of how acceptable this truth might be. For her, telling the truth was the ultimate political act, not inventing a lesbian utopia.

Toward the end of her life, Arnold returned to her hometown, Houston, Texas, to write her last and most complex novelistic memoir and one with almost no explicit lesbianism. In a move that might have been modeled on Gertrude Stein's *The Autobiography of Alice B. Toklas*, *Baby Houston* presents itself as the autobiography of Arnold's mother, ironically identified in the book only by her nickname ''Baby,'' as written by her daughter. Through this act of both daughter love and self-love, Arnold wrote her own story as well as her mother's in the voice of her mother. Her accomplishment was not only to give fictional birth to her mother, but also to perceive and re-create herself through the adoring eyes of her mother, and, finally, to describe her mother's death from cancer while she herself was battling the cancer that killed her before her book could be published. In her earlier novels, Arnold had often harshly and without pity exposed her own weaknesses and flaws. In her final novel, she escaped that trap by seeing both herself and her mother through the loving, demanding, and forgiving eyes of a mother. Arnold's depiction of the passion that can flow between a mother and a daughter is unsurpassed. *Baby Houston* is an astounding illustration of the feminist act of mothering oneself through unconditional self-love.

CRITICAL RECEPTION

The critical reception of June Arnold's novels has been mixed, and responses have tended to divide along political lines, with feminist publications being more positive than the mainstream press. Her first novel, *Applesauce*, was extensively reviewed, probably because it was issued by a major publisher. Because of its non-linear style, however, it confused most reviewers and was almost universally misinterpreted. One reviewer suggested that "Mrs. Arnold [*sic*] is more engaged in proposing riddles than providing answers," although he also called the book "a surrealist tour de force that evokes Dr. Seuss and Djuna Barnes" (Lewin 48). *The Cook and the Carpenter* and *Sister Gin*, on the other hand, being published by Daughters Inc. and having characters who are explicitly lesbian, received very little attention by the established publications and were reviewed largely in the feminist press. Responses to *The Cook and the Carpenter*, limited though they were, were generally favorable, *Sister Gin*, which received two rounds of reviews because it was reissued in 1989 by the Feminist Press, has inspired the most extreme reviews. Most readers praised Arnold for her "great insight and understanding of women, lesbians, menopause, aging and the aged" (Eaglen 546). Others, however, had a negative reaction to what one reviewer described as "a crusading element . . . every page shrieks we are old, we are sordid, we drink, but we are warm and wonderful human beings and just as capable of love as anyone else" (Fisher 23). *Baby Houston*, published posthumously in Texas five years after Arnold's death, was widely reviewed but with mixed results. While one reviewer praised it as "the novel of the year . . . wise, funny, heartbreaking and exhilarating" (Marcus 1987, 4), another was put off by the "pathological" relationship between the mother and daughter (Stone 10) and still another by the novel's "idiosyncratic . . . construction" (Blundell 94). It is worth noting that none of the reviews, outside the lesbian-feminist publications, named Arnold as a lesbian, and most even managed to avoid mentioning the lesbian content of her work.

BIBLIOGRAPHY

Works by June Arnold

Applesauce. New York: McGraw Hill, 1967. Reprinted New York: Daughters Publishing Company, 1977.
The Cook and the Carpenter. Plainfield, VT: Daughters Inc., 1973.
Sister Gin, Plainfield, VT: Daughters Inc., 1975. Reprinted New York: Feminist Press, 1989, with afterword by Jane Marcus.
"Feminist Presses and Feminist Politics," *Quest* 3: 1 (Summer 1976): 19–26.
"Lesbians and Literature" (Transcript from seminar presented at the MLA, San Francisco, 1975). *Sinister Wisdom* 1: 2 (Fall 1976): 28–30.
"Lesbian Fiction: A Dialogue" (with Bertha Harris). *Sinister Wisdom* 1: 2 (Fall 1976): 42–51.
"Feminist Presses and Feminist Politics (abridged)." *Sister Courage* 2: 5 (February 1977): 2, 7.
Baby Houston. Introd. Bevery Lowry, Austin, TX: Texas Monthly Press, 1987.

Studies of June Arnold

Bannon, B. A. Rev. of *Applesauce*. *Publishers Weekly* (January 23, 1967): 257.

Blundell, Janet Boyarin, Rev. of *Baby Houston*. *Library Journal* (May 15, 1987): 94.

Cannon, Taffy. Rev. of *Baby Houston*. *Los Angeles Times Book Review* (July 19, 1987): 4.

Clausen, Jan. "The Politics of Publishing and the Lesbian Community." *Sinister Wisdom* 1: 2 (Fall 1976): 95–115.

Desmoines, Harriet. "Retrieved from Silence: My Life and Times with Daughters Inc." *Sinister Wisdom* 5 (Winter 1978): 62–69.

Eaglen, Audrey B. Rev. of *Sister Gin*. *Library Journal* (February 1, 1976): 546.

Faderman, Lillian. *Odd Girls and Twilight Lovers*. New York: Columbia University Press, 1991.

Fisher, Emma. Rev. of *Sister Gin*. *Spectator* (March 3, 1979): 23.

Gould, Lois. "Creating a Woman's World." *New York Times Magazine*. (January 2, 1977): 10–11 and 35–37.

Harris, Bertha. Rev. of *The Cook and the Carpenter*. *Village Voice* (April 4, 1974): 33.

Johnson, George. Rev. of *Baby Houston*. *New York Times Book Review* (December 11, 1988): 42.

Levin, Martin. Rev. of *Applesauce*. *New York Times Book Review* (March 19, 1967): 48.

Marcus, Jane. Afterword. *Sister Gin*. By June Arnold, New York: Feminist Press, 1989, 217–36.

———. Rev. of *Baby Houston*. *Women's Review of Books* (October 1987): 4.

Monroe, Barbara. "Mother Wit: American Women's Literary Humor." Diss., University of Texas, 1991. 60–89.

Peters, Joan. Rev. of *The Cook and the Carpenter*. *Margins: A Review of Little Magazines and Small Press Books* (August 1975): 69–70.

"Polyperse." Rev. of *Applesauce*. *Time* (March 10, 1967): 100.

Rev. of *Applesauce*. *Prairie Schooner* (Spring 1967): 92.

Rev. of *Baby Houston*. *New Directions for Women* (November 1987): 22.

Rev. of *Baby Houston*. *Publishers Weekly* (March 13, 1987): 72.

Rev. of *Sister Gin*. *Belles Lettres* (Spring 1990): 22.

Rev. of *Sister Gin*. *Publishers Weekly* (August 18, 1989): 54.

Segrest, Mab. *My Mama's Dead Squirrel: Lesbian Essays on Southern Culture*. Ithaca, NY: Firebrand Books, 1985.

Stiles, Patricia. Rev. of *Applesauce*. *Library Journal* (March 1, 1967): 1029.

Stone, Eve Ottenberg. Rev. of *Baby Houston*. *New York Times Book Review* (July 26, 1987): 10.

Walters, Ray. Rev. of *Applesauce* reissue. *New York Times Book Review* (January 15, 1978): 27.

Webb, Marilyn. "Daughters Inc.: A Publishing House is Born." *MS* (June 1974): 35.

Zimmerman, Bonnie. "Exiting from Patriarchy." *The Voyage In: Fictions of Female Development*. Ed. Elizabeth Abel, Marianne Hirsh, and Elizabeth Langland, Hanover, NH: University Press of New England, 1983.

———. *The Safe Sea of Women: Lesbian Fiction 1969–1989*. Boston: Beacon, 1990.

JUDITH BARRINGTON (1944–   )
Ruth Gundle

BIOGRAPHY

Born in Brighton, England, in 1944, Judith Barrington has become primarily an "American" poet and writer, after several years as an uneasy "mid-Atlantic," introduced at readings, she says, as an American when in Britain, and as British when in the United States.

Barrington's parents spent most of their married life in Spain. When the Spanish civil war broke out, they caught one of the last boats out with their two young children. Barrington, the third and youngest, came into the world in the middle of an air raid toward the end of World War II.

Her family was middle class and conservative, as were the families of the other girls at the private girls' school in Brighton, which she attended from kindergarten to the upper sixth (some thirteen years), and memories of the school and some of her classmates appear in her writing. The tallest and youngest in her class, she was very shy. She would later write about the tangled relationships among the girls, and about caring "too much" when out of favor with her particular friends.

Barrington's older sister became a concert pianist, studying at the Royal College of Music while the poet was still very young. Since their mother was also musical, the three female members of the family would play trios together. Apart from this, Barrington was solitary, spending most of her teenage years riding her beloved horse on the Sussex Downs.

In 1963, while she was pondering whether to pursue the place she had been awarded at London University to study modern languages, her parents drowned in a tragic accident when the Greek cruise ship *Lakonia* caught fire off the Canary Islands. Determined to act grown-up, she pursued her independence vigorously. Although she did not come out publicly—or even to herself it seems—she had her first lesbian affair at this time, which was a source of additional trauma and guilt. Soon after her parents' death, she took a job in Spain working for a wealthy and powerful family who owned a castle and an international wine business. Part translator, part tour guide, part public relations officer, she moved from the life of a beach bum to the highest of the high life almost every day. Creating complex affairs with men she didn't care about, and secret ones with women she did, Barrington subsumed her shock and grief in a life of intense distraction.

In 1966 she returned to London. She married, divorced, and became a feminist. From 1971 to 1976, Barrington was deeply involved in the women's movement in London. She lived in a collective household of radical lesbians and worked for a year at the Women's Liberation Workshop. She attended conferences, participated in demonstrations and radical actions, and earned a precarious living as a furniture mover and driving instructor.

In 1976 she moved to Portland, Oregon, and began to teach women's studies part-time. Gradually she built a life centered on writing, with teaching and freelance journalism as sources of income. She began her current long-term relationship in 1979, and in 1984 founded the Flight of the Mind, an annual summer writing workshop for women, which has grown into a major event accommodating some seventy writers per week at a retreat center on the McKenzie River in Oregon's Cascade Mountains.

MAJOR WORKS AND THEMES

Barrington's major themes are loss, lesbian identity, speechlessness, and the power of speech. The central piece in *Trying to Be an Honest Woman* (1985) is a sequence of poems, "Four Days in Spain," which tells the story of a journey she made with her sister from Barcelona to Gibraltar to arrange for a permanent marker for her parents' graves. The poem is about the inability of the two sisters to talk about any of it: the deaths, the task at hand, and, most of all, their feelings. She articulates a state of inarticulateness—an approach that is characteristic of Barrington's work and can also be found in her writing about her early experiences as a lesbian.

In a widely anthologized poem simply entitled "Lesbian," Barrington begins to explore lesbian identity by addressing her fear of the word the first time she heard it spoken aloud. The poem ends with a characteristic emphasis on the power of speech. The title poem makes a connection between the problems and ultimate failure of a lesbian relationship and the pain the poet carries around from years of experienced and internalized homophobia.

History and Geography (1989) continues the poet's exploration of loss and grief with an unusual sequence of six villanelles for the poet's mother, which together form an elegy. Lesbian identity is explored in another long sequence, "The Dyke with No Name," which begins with a twelve-year-old fantasizing about an older woman who will pay attention to her, and whom she can rescue from danger, and progresses through teenage difficulties to a first lesbian relationship. Since this relationship takes place with no lesbian context, neither woman acknowledges it as such, and the "older woman" encourages the "dyke with no name" to get married. A very stilted, regularly syllabic poem, "Cryptic," describes from the inside the act of lying about love. In the final poem, Barrington leaps to the time when the "dyke with no name" will finally come out to herself and the world.

In 1991, Barrington edited a substantial anthology entitled *An Intimate Wilderness: Lesbian Writers on Sexuality*—an exploration of what lesbian literature has said about lesbian sexuality since the early 1970s.

CRITICAL RECEPTION

Trying to Be an Honest Woman was widely reviewed in the feminist and lesbian press. Not surprisingly, most reviewers traced a connection between the theme of honesty—the difficulty and importance of honest speech—and the work of Adrienne Rich, whose influence Barrington has frequently acknowledged, and whose words from *Women and Honor: Some Notes on Lying* form the epigraph. Writing in the *Women's Review of Books*, Adrian Oktenberg acknowledges the focus on honesty but notes that although Barrington's subject matter may be influenced by Rich, her style is not. Oktenberg likens her work to Marilyn Hacker's: "highly crafted and literate" (17). *Hurricane Alice* praises the work for "emphasizing the life-giving possibilities of love and language" ("Women's Ways of Being" 1). Valerie Miner, writing for *Out/Look*, focuses on the poems dealing with sexual marginality, saying it is "a lens through which to consider other marginalities—national, racial, linguistic, economic. From such poetry we learn about uniqueness and commonality" (94).

Calyx, *Belles Lettres*, and nearly every other feminist journal and newspaper praised *Trying to Be an Honest Woman*, an unusual occurrence for a first book of poetry from an unknown writer.

History and Geography also received extensive attention, this time from the mainstream literary press as well as the feminist press, with many reviewers now placing her in the shadow of Elizabeth Bishop. Meryl Altman, writing in the *Women's Review of Books*, says: "she engages wittily with cultural differences that are not necessarily power differences, and gives a prominent place to what Elizabeth Bishop, of whom her writing is sometimes, reminiscent, called 'questions of travel' " (16). Robyn Selman, in the *Nation*, also refers to Bishop: "Barrington's history, like Lowell's, is intensely personal; her geography, like Bishop's, extracts the familiar from the exotic and the exotic from the familiar" (288).

Both Altman and Selman discuss "The Dyke with No Name," which Altman says has "an economy of language . . . a healthy and resonating clarity" (16). Selman recalls that lesbian literature has, in recent years, produced many stories of "mature 'conversion' to the love of women," but that far less has been written about "women who discovered and explored their homosexuality in youth and adolescence" (288).

Julie Fay, writing in the *Kenyon Review*, takes a close look at the interplay between Barrington's forms and her subject matter. Of the villanelle sequence she says, "Form has served content well here: memories of her mother are as persistent as a villanelle's two refrains." Interpreting some of Barrington's symbols in "The Dyke with No Name," Fay comments on the imagery and use of word music: "In the same way a wedding album restrains its pages of photos, her allegiance to the heterosexual 'norm' binds her. Able at last to dismantle the fabrication, she jubilantly pronounces her lesbianism to herself and to those around her. Here, Barrington matches word texture to subject: assonance and anaphora achieve tension then release; consonants snag then loosen" (203).

Rachel Guido deVries, writing in *Belles Lettres*, praised her use of sounds ("her ear is delightful"); Evelyn C. White, in the *San Francisco Chronicle*, praised her courage ("These poems push against safe emotional boundaries."), and *Publishers Weekly* praised her control over her material (she "transform[s] ambivalence, volatile feelings and almost unspeakable observations into cogent, vigorous poetry").

HONORS AND AWARDS

In 1983, Barrington received the Jeannette Rankin Award from the National Women's Political Caucus for her feminist journalism. *History and Geography* was a finalist for the Oregon Book Award in 1989. In 1990 she received the Gerty Gerty Gerty in the Arts, Arts, Arts Award from the Barbara Deming Money for Women Fund. She has received numerous grants from private foundations and government-supported arts programs.

BIBLIOGRAPHY

Works by Judith Barrington

Trying to Be an Honest Woman. Portland, OR: Eighth Mountain Press, 1985.
History and Geography. Portland, OR: Eighth Mountain Press, 1989.
Ed. *An Intimate Wilderness: Lesbian Writers on Sexuality*. Portland, OR: Eighth Mountain Press, 1991.

Studies of Judith Barrington

Altman, Meryl. "Uneasy Understandings." *Women's Review of Books* 7, no. 1 (October 1990): 16.
deVries, Rachel Guido. "Loss and Power." *Belles Lettres* (November/December 1990): 38.
Fay, Julie. "Cathars, Kids and Catharsis." *Kenyon Review* 13, no. 1: 203.
Glazer, Jane. Review of *Trying to Be an Honest Woman*. *Calyx* (Spring 1986): 95.
Miner, Valerie. "Reading along the Dyke." *Out/Look* (Spring 1988): 94.
Moose, Ruth. "A Geography of Shared Lives." *Belles Lettres* (May/June 1986): 12.

Oktenberg, Adrian. "A Quartet of Voices." *Women's Review of Books* 3, no. 7 (April 1986): 17.

Selman, Robyn. "Balancing Acts." *Nation* (September 18, 1989): 288.

White, Evelyn C. "A Poet Charts Her Personal Landscape." *San Francisco Chronicle*, Book Review Section (October 15, 1989): 8.

"Women's Ways of Being." *Hurricane Alice* 4, no. 2: 1.

TERRY BAUM (1946–   )
Kendall

BIOGRAPHY

In 1990 Terry Baum sent friends and family a snapshot taken at a Gay Pride march above a "Happy Channukah" greeting. In it she wears striped tights, a T-shirt, and high-topped tennis shoes. She's bedecked with surgical rubber gloves, there's a dildo on her head, phallic vegetables hang from her belt. She holds a sign that reads, "Lesbians for Penetration." Baum's own persona is one of her bravest constructions: outrageous, politically unorthodox, confrontational, uproarious.

In a telephone conversation in December 1991, Baum said her middle-class Jewish upbringing in the suburbs of Los Angeles was "ordinary and stable." She attended Antioch College in Yellow Springs, Ohio, from 1964 to 1969, when Antioch was characterized by revolution, student movements for civil rights and peace, and feathers and bells. Baum planned to go into social work and began to discover political uses for theater. As a VISTA (Volunteers in Service to America) volunteer, she created theater with poor people as part of a project called "Folk Theatre of the Appalachias." She had her first directorial success with an Ionesco play at Antioch, then worked her way to New York City, where she directed for Circle Repertory Company and moved from theater into feminism.

In 1972, Baum migrated from New York to California, earned her M.A. in directing at the University of California at Santa Barbara, and founded two theaters before starting a feminist theater collective, Lilith, in 1975. With Lilith, Baum co-wrote four plays, *Lilitheater*, *Good Food*, *Moonlighting*, and *Sacrifices*. In 1976, Baum came out as a lesbian.

Dos Lesbos, co-written in 1980 with Carolyn Myers, was Baum's first specifically lesbian play. *Dos Lesbos* was followed by a string of performance pieces, all centered in lesbian experience and increasingly experimental in style. *Ego*

Trip; or I'm Getting My Shit Together and Dumping It All on You (1981) is the first piece Baum wrote and performed by herself, which led to additional shows including *Immediate Family* (1983), *The San Francisco Baumicle* (1985), *The Black Jewish American Lesbian Show* (created with Stephanie Johnson in 1986), and in 1987, *One Fool; or How I Learned to Stop Worrying and Love the Dutch*. Her one-act play, *Women in Line*, was produced in New York City in 1991. After two sojourns in Amsterdam and nearly a decade of touring her shows throughout North America and Europe, Baum has returned to San Francisco, where she now writes full-time and teaches playwriting for women.

MAJOR WORKS AND THEMES

Dos Lesbos (1980) is a domestic comedy about coming out. A lesbian couple in their living room contemplate coming out at work, coming out to parents, and coming out of their own internalized homophobia. They sing, dance, talk about man-hating, examine bisexuality, and romp their way through some clever one-liners to an affectionate and contented happy ending. *Dos Lesbos* has been a hit in lesbian communities for over a decade. It has been performed in Australia and New Zealand, translated and staged in Dutch and Swedish. It was published in 1985, and, at this writing, it continues to be popularly revived.

Baum's particular genius, however, has thus far been reserved for a series of performance pieces, each one more iconoclastic and socially incisive than the last. *Ego Trip* is a collage of autobiographical monologues and wild characters, including a five-thousand-year-old virgin and a secretary obsessed with stealing office supplies. *Baumicle* is stand-up comedy based on the daily newspaper, with a materialist-lesbian twist. *The Black Jewish American Lesbian Show* addresses racism and essentialism.

Immediate Family differs from the others in tone. A middle-aged working-class dyke visits the hospital room of her lover, who has long been in a coma. The tender and often hilarious one-sided conversation reveals the women's long-term intimacy, their lives outside "normal" society, the pressures on their union caused by social invisibility, and, of course, the legal barriers that deny the dyke status as "immediate family" of her hospitalized partner. The hospital room is a pool of light, the bedridden lover is the sound of a respirator, and the spiralling narrative follows the dyke's movement toward a decision to unplug the life-support system that sustains her partner in a vegetative state. *Immediate Family* was published along with *Dos Lesbos*. It has been translated and produced in French and Dutch and filmed for Dutch television.

Women in Line is an absurdist one-act play in which two women waiting in line find they're both filled with rage against men and subsequently fall in love. They decide to kill a man, and a third woman tries to prevent them. *Women in Line* was performed in a battered women's shelter in Oregon in 1985, and by Love Creek Theatre in New York City in 1991.

Baum's most recent piece, *One Fool*, is a ferociously comical exploration of sex and intimacy among lesbians in North America and Europe. The piece begins with an audience interaction in which Baum approaches numerous women and asks, "Are you The One?" Briefly and brilliantly, Baum plays out serial monogamy and the cycles of attraction, bliss, disenchantment, and separation that characterize so many lesbian relationships. She both blasts and celebrates lesbian courtship and coupling, and she takes hilarious liberties with sex—in one scene the "Fool" mimes making love to a coat rack; in another she masturbates with castanets.

CRITICAL RECEPTION

If "critical reception" means coverage in the gay and feminist press, Baum's work has drawn masses of it, generally in the shape of rave reviews, occasionally in-depth interviews and analyses. Even in mainstream newspapers, her reviews are primarily raves. Feminist critics have only recently discovered Baum, and while they are a decade behind Baum's progress as an artist, non-feminist academics have not recognized her at all.

Baum's reception in the press is proof of her grass-roots popularity. Literally hundreds of reviews praise her skill both as actor and writer. She is "shocking," "hilarious," "moving." Her "social commentary" is "perceptive," "caring," "outrageous." The only reservations are that her pieces are sometimes too long. In the *Village Voice*, Alisa Solomon writes that Baum "acts with an understated dignity and authenticity" and concludes that although *Immediate Family* is "about twice as long as it needs to be," it ends with "a twinge of triumph" (56). Bernard Weiner, for the *San Francisco Chronicle*, finds *Immediate Family* "remarkably honest" (E4). The *San Francisco Bay Guardian* named *One Fool* one of the Ten Best Shows in 1988 and called it "zany, raunchy, and wise" (December 28, 1988). Similar responses come from popular and alternative newspapers in Amsterdam, Kansas City, Boston, London, Seattle, Stockholm, and small towns like Fayetteville, Arkansas, and Fort Wayne, Indiana.

After fourteen years of creating feminist theater, Baum is finally noted in two serious critical essays appearing in *Modern Drama* in March 1989. Unfortunately, both assess *Dos Lesbos* as if it were Baum's only work. Jeanie Forte praises the play for emerging from "classic realism" and "pointing the way toward other discourses" (119). Forte admires Baum's "Brechtian sensibility" and finds *Dos Lesbos*, "in Barthesian terms, more a 'plural' text, wherein 'no single discourse is privileged' " (118). Jill Dolan calls it "lesbian farce," which "cannot seem to escape the constraints of realism" (150). Baum's later works, especially *One Fool*, will prove more rewarding to weavers of critical discourse.

Baum is a tireless theater worker, a hustler, and a veteran whose career in performance now spans more than two decades. From Australia to Germany, Baum's work appeals to bar-dykes, "chemical-free" lesbians, working-class women, women in collectives, cultural and materialist feminists, the rich, the impoverished, the middle class, the proper, and the perverse. Baum is still writing, and she consciously violates the boundaries of prescribed feminism. She distrusts elitist criticism that denigrates the popular and upholds the obscure. "If nobody understands it," she mused during a December 1991 telephone conversation, "nobody can be threatened by it. And if a piece of theater doesn't threaten anybody, I don't give a shit about it."

BIBLIOGRAPHY

Works by Terry Baum

Dos Lesbos (co-written with Carolyn Myers) and *Immediate Family*. *Places Please: The First Anthology of Lesbian Plays*. Ed. Kate McDermott. San Francisco: Aunt Lute Press, 1985. 1–40, 107–22.

One Fool or How I Learned to Stop Worrying and Love the Dutch. *Tough Acts to Follow*. Ed. Noreen C. Barnes and Nicolas Deutch. San Francisco: Alamo Square Press, 1992. 7–26.

Studies of Terry Baum

Adcock, Joe. "Italian Sausage Stars in a Poignant Scene." *Seattle Post-Intelligencer* (March 9, 1985).
———. "Terry Baum Looks at Death in the *Immediate Family*." *Seattle Post-Intelligencer* (May 5, 1985).
Alpert, Bill. "Drama Explores Anguish of Dying." *Seattle Times* (May 8, 1985): C3.
Barnes, Noreen C. "All the News That's Fit." *Bay Area Reporter* (March 28, 1991): 29.
———. "The Return of Terry the Fool." *Bay Area Reporter* (October 1990): 22.
Berson, Misha. Review of *Ego Trip*. *San Francisco Bay Guardian* (May 26, 1982): 57.
Collis, Rose. Review of *Immediate Family*. *London City Limits* (November 7, 1985): 41.
Dolan, Jill. "Breaking the Code: Musings on Lesbian Sexuality and the Performer." *Modern Drama* (March 1989): 146–58.
Dougherty, Robin. "Women Declare Women: Ladies of the Stage Come of Age." *Boston Phoenix* (April 1, 1988): B7.
Forte, Jeanie. "Realism, Narrative, and the Feminist Playwright—A Problem of Reception." *Modern Drama* (March 1989): 115–27.
Gelb, Hal. "Can a Tyrannical Lesbian Director Get Rich and Famous?" *Artbeat* (April, 1981): 14–16.
Guthmann, Edward. "Lesbian Writer's *Family*: A Labor of Love and Fear." San Francisco *Datebook* (June 30, 1985): 42.
Hurwitt, Robert. "Hilarious Tales of a Fool for Love." *San Francisco Examiner* (August 18, 1987): C2.
Justesen, Per. "Shocking Play About Lesbian Relationship." (Amsterdam) *Het Parool* (September 27, 1985): 19.
Landstreet, Lynna. "Liberating Laughter: Terry Baum is a Fool for Love." *Toronto Xtra!* (May 24, 1991): 28.
Simpson, Mona. "Perspectives on Lesbianism." *Daily Californian* (March 6, 1981): 13.

Solomon, Alisa. "Doubly Dying." *Village Voice* (January 16, 1986): 56.
Weiner, Bernard. Review of *Immediate Family*. *San Francisco Chronicle* (July 3, 1985): EH.
Zemel, Sue. "Terry Baum: Rage on Stage." *Bay Area Reporter* (September 22, 1983): 33.

ROBIN BECKER (1951–   )

Leslie Lawrence

BIOGRAPHY

The first of two daughters, Robin Becker was born on March 7, 1951, in Philadelphia, Pennsylvania. Her parents, both the children of Russian immigrants, spoke Yiddish as well as English in their home, giving Becker an early appreciation of the rich possibilities of language and also awakening her to the ways in which her family straddled the rim of mainstream American culture. Her maternal grandmother, the chief purveyor of Old World rituals and values, was a powerful presence throughout the poet's life. Becker recalls: "In my earliest memories my Bubbie is cooking kasha and bow ties, saying the prayers over the Hanukkah candles, threading a needle to fix a hem. On the High Holidays, we made an annual trip to the cemetery, where my Bubbie went from gravestone to gravestone, speaking with the dead" (personal communication with Leslie Lawrence, June 1992). While Becker's parents wanted her to know her heritage, they also wanted her to have the material comforts and educational opportunities they didn't have. Thus they sent her to Abington Friends, a small, private Quaker day school for girls; a place that introduced Becker to the pleasures and challenges of literature, sports, and the visual arts; the first place that showed Becker how fully she enjoyed female company.

At Boston University, Becker earned a B.A. in English in 1973 and an M.A. in creative writing in 1976. In 1977, she was hired to teach poetry and fiction writing at the Massachusetts Institute of Technology, where she still teaches.

Becker made her first trip to Taos, New Mexico, in 1979 as a fellow at the Helene Wurlitzer Foundation. She returned every summer for several years, establishing a deep relationship with the Southwest that is reflected in her work. In 1989, she lived in Taos for six months, completing a manuscript of poems. In recent years Becker has also spent time in Nepal, Italy, and in France, though her strongest and most consistent pull is still to New Mexico.

In 1985, Becker was invited to serve as poetry editor for the *Women's Review of Books,* a position she currently holds. Her book reviews have appeared in *Belle Lettres, Prairie Schooner, Sojourner,* and the *Women's Review of Books.* In 1991, she accepted a one-semester position as visiting poet at Kent State University. Becker is active in the Boston literary community as well as in several professional organizations. In 1992, she delivered a paper entitled "Making Common Cause: Bringing Poems by Lesbians into the Creative Writing Classroom" at the annual meeting of the Associated Writing Program.

MAJOR WORKS AND THEMES

In her paper on lesbians in the creative writing classroom, Becker discussed her own experiences as a young writer terrified of revealing her lesbianism. She recalled her tendency to write poems without pronouns and the pivotal moment when a substitute teacher, Maxine Kumin, questioned Becker's claim that "gender didn't matter." In her first book, *Personal Effects* (1979), a collection of poems by three women writers, Becker shows that she has accepted Kumin's challenge and honored her own intuitive knowledge that it is a poet's job to reveal, not to mask. Several poems expose the poet's sexuality. In "A Woman Leaving a Woman," a lover leaves the poet for a man whose "life makes sense." As she leaves, that woman thinks of her lesbian liaison as "a crime," one for which she was "the only witness." Here the reader sees the forces that tear . women apart: the lack of precedents and structure that would make lesbian coupling "sensible," and the homophobia (external as well as internal) that makes many lesbians and gay men view their love as criminal. In "Weekend," however, Becker shows that the opposing forces don't always win. While one woman has once again left another, in this case the separation is temporary and the connection is maintained. The poet writes about being "a misplaced city-dweller / breathing honeysuckle / and the smell of you / still on my fingers." Here Becker specifically evokes lesbian sex—a bold move in 1979!

Other poems in this volume introduce us to themes that will continue to permeate Becker's work. Some of those, though not directly connected to her lesbianism, are related to it. For example, in "Dreams of Smoke and Fire," addressed to a friend's mother (a woman who survived Warsaw and Dachau), the poet speaks of the daughter who now wears "an engineer's cap and blue jeans." Clearly, as a woman who doesn't dress as women traditionally do, this daughter will also face oppression and have to struggle to survive. In this same poem, we are also introduced to Becker's ongoing obsession with storytelling ("You tell me stories. / I crave them"), inspiring, true stories about survival, and fanciful, just-as-crucial stories about the future we imagine for ourselves. While we all enjoy stories, it appears that Becker's *craving* stems from her lesbianism: until very recently, the stories of lesbians have not been told, leaving the lesbian with no images on which to build a future.

In "Seizure," Becker writes about her sister's epilepsy and how it "lifted

[her] day after day / out of the afternoon, / unremembering.'' Certainly, a sei-zure is, in itself, a fascinating subject, but it becomes even more so when we see how the image of two worlds infects Becker's sensibility in later poems.

As its title suggests, *Backtalk*, published in 1982, highlights the poet's cheeky refusal to accept cultural norms. The volume contains some of Becker's most lyrical lesbian love poems, and while some of these again focus on the impe-diments to lesbian love, they deliciously evoke triumphant moments. ''We ʹs-turb the difficult compromises / with our steady wanting of each other, / but for a moment the afternoon light falls on your shoulder, our intimacy is loosed / into the air, and you move easily / down the path, parting the prairie grass'' (''Women in Love'').

Here we see how Becker uses images from nature to suggest the landscape of the body. This is sexy writing at its best, and it is, I believe, particularly lesbian to experience nature as sexual and sex as natural. (Lesbian poets Olga Broumas and Jane Miller offer other fine examples of this tendency.) Note Becker's ''Prairie'': ''We break off weeds / and put them in each other's mouths. / She slides her fingers / up the milkweed's stem / slits the pod / to watch the seeds float / in the fog beside me.'' We're not surprised when this gesture leads to lovemaking, but all too soon the realization of the ideal vanishes: ''Before we walk back, she's already walked back, / arranged herself into the familiar fictions.'' Here the reader is reminded of ''Seizure'' and the disjunction between two worlds, in this case, the world of secret lesbian love and the straight world that many of Becker's lovers normally inhabit.

''Echolaliac'' is most obviously about the speaker who ''tagged along'' with a lover while she painted, but it is also about one's irreconcilable desire for union and separateness at the same time. This is, of course, a universal problem, but it is doubly thorny in same-sex relationships where the love object can so closely mirror the lover. ''I am and am not another person in the room / where my words orbit theirs, the way / a refrain illuminates.''

Love, identity, the nature of reality—Becker tackles serious questions, but she can also be light and humorous, and this volume contains some of her funniest poems. For example, from ''After Making Love'': ''Afterwards I like to talk about it, / hear her describe the camels / parading one by one across the desert, / compare notes, find out how the experimental / parts worked.''

Giacometti's Dog is Becker's most recent, most ambitious, and best book. Published by University of Pittsburgh Press, it was released in 1990. This volume again contains many beautiful lesbian love poems, but these do not predominate. Becker's world has become larger—literally and figuratively. Many poems reflect her extensive travels and her desire to locate herself, culturally, psychologically, and spiritually; all reveal the poet's expanded subject matter. It is as if Becker's willingness to publicly claim her lesbian identity in earlier poems has opened up a space for her to explore all kinds of love. The volume's final poem rawly states: ''Now I see that love is really / the subject of our lives'' (''The Subject of Our Lives'').

In "Grief," about the suicide of Becker's sister, we see how tragedy has deepened the poet's sense of belonging to the human community. Here, all varieties of love are given equal import. "Already the grieving gather the candles / and clothing they need for the seasons of mourning, naming / themselves lover, mother, father, friend, brother, sister."

Several poems allude to love and acceptance the poet hadn't expected to receive. "This big man set a place / for me at his table, and I was met / at the door like any child, / though I, a woman, loved / his daughter and arrived / with my hair cut short" ("Letter from Your Father"). And again, from "Grief": "It is the kindness of the rabbi I remember now."

As its title indicates, *Giacometti's Dog* deals with the poet's engagement with the visual arts, and many poems explore the connection between art and love, a theme first introduced in a poem from *Backtalk* ("Studies from Life") where Becker twice says, "If love is seeing." In addition to the title poem, there are poems about Georgia O'Keeffe, Matisse, and Chagall. The latter speaks of love as "a two-headed journey, / terrible and wonderful" and asserts the power of love to unify the disparate aspects of self.

It is ironic but not surprising that as poets mature they often return to the subject of childhood, and *Giacometti's Dog* contains some of Becker's best poems on that subject. "Like Breath at Your Ear" describes a schoolgirl's first experience with masturbation and her discovery that she is under the sexual power of a girlfriend. "The voice blows syllables and you utter them now, with her, as though / there had always been two worlds, and you'd inhabited that / other one, calling and breathing across a vast and private space."

"Philadelphia, 1955" is about a child's discovery of a separate self—autonomous, responsible, capable of keen and luscious perceptions. "A child in a nightgown" steps outside into the "permissive dark" and discovers that "Everything that is her own is suddenly here / revealed." The poem concludes: "Oh wild and tentative solitude, so new, / so graceless. How can she carry it / from the spacious night back to the distressed / and loving people of her life?" In the context of the poem, this is not a rhetorical question, and so it is particularly satisfying to realize that Becker has found the answer to her childhood question: for who is the poet if not the messenger, carrying experience from one world to another.

CRITICAL RECEPTION

Becker has received much critical attention, especially for *Giacometti's Dog*. Lesbian, feminist, literary, and mainstream presses have all taken notice, and most have appeared equally at home and complimentary when commenting on both "lesbian" and "non-lesbian" poems. (Perhaps this sourcebook will shed new light on these difficult-to-define categories.) It seems that by the nineties, for Becker and her critics, "lesbian" is just one of many labels one can use for this poet. She has been praised for her lyricism, her vivid imagery, her ear for dialogue, her wit, her courage, her emotionality and lack of sentimentality, her ability to speak to all of us.

Josie Rawson (*Daily Hampshire Gazette,* August 29, 1990) sees a pattern in many of her poems: "First grounding us in *place* . . . then describing an event, then . . . moving into the territory of spirit and meaning." She sees in the poems "a quality of voice that allows for tragedy and the sublime" to exist at once.

Publishers Weekly reports that "she is at her best when using microscopic detail and apt particulars to magnify past and present moments and events, her poems quietly building to subtle, arresting epiphanies." *Remark* (Fall 1991) has said that Becker "is particularly fine on love between women, giving us a full-bodied love poetry that never drops into sleaze or mere personal reportage." And in the *Kenyon Review* (Spring 1991) Leslie Ullman asserts that Becker's travel poems "suggest a physical as well as a spiritual fearlessness" (190). She says her love poems are "alive with the presence of someone who is at home with the body. . . . They affirm not only the condition of love (be it lesbian, gay, or heterosexual), but the struggle of learning to love with its assaults against the self's composure" (192).

HONORS AND AWARDS

Robin Becker has won fellowships in poetry from the National Endowment for the Arts (1989) and the Massachusetts Artists Foundation (1985). She has received residency grants from the MacDowell Colony, the Michael Karolyi Memorial Foundation, the Ragdale Foundation, the Ucross Foundation, the Virginia Center for the Creative Arts, the Cummington Community of the Arts, and the Helene Wurlitzer Foundation of New Mexico. In 1992, she served as a jurist for the Cleveland State University Poetry Center's annual competition and judged the annual S.O.M.O.S. (Society of the Muse of the Southwest) contest jointly sponsored by the *Taos Review*.

BIBLIOGRAPHY

Works by Robin Becker

Personal Effects. Robin Becker, Helena Minton and Marilyn Zuckerman. Cambridge, MA: Alice James Press, 1979.
Backtalk. Cambridge, MA: Alice James Books, 1982.
Giacometti's Dog. Pittsburgh: University of Pittsburgh Press, 1990.

Studies of Robin Becker

Altman, Meryl. "Uneasy Understandings." *Women's Review of Books* (October 1990): 16–18.
Hope-McCarthy, Eleanor. "Robin Becker: *Giacometti's Dog.*" *New England Studies Association Newsletter* (Fall 1990): 456.

Mazur, Gail. *"Giacometti's Dog." Ploughshares* 16, no. 4 (Winter 1990–91): 281.
Morris, Leslie. "Robin Becker: An Interview." Northampton, MA: *Valley Advocate* (October 15, 1990): 7.
Publishers Weekly. May 4, 1990, 65–66.
Rawson, Josie. "Time and Art Heal in Becker's Poetry." *Daily Hampshire Gazette* (August 29, 1990): 28.
Remark. (Fall 1991): 19–23.
Schwartz, Patricia Roth. "Sappho's Heirs." *Bay Windows* (November 1, 1991): 19–20.
Ullman, Leslie. "Solitaries and Storytellers, Magicians and Pagans: Five Poets in The World." *Kenyon Review* (Spring 1991): 179–93.

BECKY BIRTHA (1948–   )
Rebecca Mark

BIOGRAPHY

Becky Birtha was born in 1948 to Jessie Moore Birtha and Herbert Marshall Birtha in Hampton, Virginia. While Becky celebrates her actual birthday on October 11, she has been giving birth to herself and to the many communities that she calls home throughout her writing career. Birtha knows what it means to belong to many people. She identifies with the African-American tradition and reminds us that her great-grandmother, Rebecca Birtha, was a slave. In addition, her family roots include Irish, Cherokee, and Catawba peoples, and from this multicultural heritage, Birtha finds a voice that bridges many cultures.

Living the first two years of her life in the college town of Hampton, Virginia, Birtha was born into an academic environment. Although her teachers encouraged her to become a writer, and exposed her to many writers whom she still cherishes, it was her mother, a children's librarian, who wrote articles about teaching African-American literature to Black children, who introduced her to African-American writers. Throughout her childhood, Becky Birtha heard the voices of her parents reading and telling stories to her and her sister, Rachel Roxanne Birtha Eitches. After Hampton, the Birtha family moved to Maryland and one year later to the Germantown section of Philadelphia. She went from the public Philadelphia School for Girls, where she took her first creative writing class, to college at Case Western Reserve.

On July 4, 1968, Independence Day, during a year when so many young Americans were protesting the war and declaring their independence from an older generation, Birtha left home. In 1969–1970, she dropped out of college and moved to Berkeley, California, where she experienced the height of the Berkeley protests, People's Park, and the closing of the university. After one year in California, Birtha moved back east to Buffalo where she lived for five years, returned to school at the State University of New York (SUNY) at Buffalo and Buffalo State, and graduated from SUNY Buffalo in a self-designed major in children's studies. After Buffalo, she moved back to Philadelphia and has lived there ever since, developing an extensive community of friends.

From the time Birtha left home, she has supported herself by working as a day-care, special education, and preschool teacher, a college instructor, and, in order to devote more time to her writing, as a legal librarian. While working at the law firm, she attended Vermont College and received her M.F.A. in creative writing by correspondence in 1984. She won a Pennsylvania Council on the Arts Individual Fellowship in Literature in 1985, a National Endowment for the Arts Creative Writing Fellowship in 1988, and a Pushcart Prize in 1988. Throughout her writing career, Birtha has been an active member of her Buffalo and Philadelphia communities, generously lending her voice at hundreds of readings, conferences, and workshops.

MAJOR WORKS AND THEMES

Becky Birtha has had three books published including *For Nights Like This One: Stories of Loving Women* (1983), *Lover's Choice* (1987), and most recently, *The Forbidden Poems* (1991). Over the past two decades, her work has appeared in nineteen anthologies and over fifty journals and periodicals including *Sinister Wisdom, Conditions*, the *Iowa Review, off our backs*, and *Sojourner*. In her stories and poems, Birtha gives voice to a lost generation of African-American foremothers (her own mother and grandmother wanted to be creative writers) and to the ordinary and extraordinary voices of lesbian communities from the seventies, eighties, and nineties. In 1976, when Birtha came out as a lesbian and began to see her audience as lesbian, she found new direction and energy for her writing.

Birtha's stories are about being alive and understanding love, and sometimes hate, between women. Not only do they cover the whole range of our emotional terrain, from youth to old age, from birth to death to birth, but Birtha's stories chronicle the political debates, relationship issues, self-healing journeys, incest recoveries, creative explorations, dreams, gardens, escapes, and friendships that have been the vibrant core of lesbian community. Like Sahara, the journeyer, in "In the Deep Heart's Core" from *Lover's Choice*, Birtha, the writer, creates home and mother love in all its tough and healing manifestations wherever she goes. Several of Becky Birtha's stories are about the love of childless women for children, a story Birtha experienced most of her life as she worked at day-care centers and schools, loving and helping to raise other people's children. With the publication of her first volume of poems, Birtha also celebrated the adoption of her daughter, Tasha Alfrieda Birtha.

While the plots of Birtha's stories address major issues in the lesbian community—should we be monogamous? in "A Monogamy Story," how do we deal with a lover's ex? in "Her Ex-Lover" and "A Four-sided Figure," and should we have children? in "Babies"—Birtha gives her readers interesting and idiosyncratic language with which to think about and to discuss these issues.

Through twists of plot and odd imagery, Birtha exposes and strips away the expected and the conventional. The most interesting plot twist that Birtha achieves is an exciting lack of closure. In "Babies," we want Lurie to follow her dream and have a child. She does not. In "Next Saturday," we expect Kacey and Jennifer to have hot sex. They do not. In "Ice Castle," we want Gail and Maury to get it together and stop wandering around in the snow. They do not. What does happen in each of these stories is much more interesting, much more honest, and sometimes more painful.

Birtha achieves these unconventional endings by opening up the lens of our perception and stretching out the amount of time she devotes to the inner workings of human change. She quite literally slows down our impulse to fall into romantic clichés, so easy to do with the themes Birtha addresses—coming out, having an affair, struggling with separation. Birtha creates characters whose interior world is more developed than their external actions, characters who are expert observers and who thus move far beyond superficial responses. By leading us into the wilderness of our emotions and reminding us that there is no terrain so terrible that we cannot listen, observe, and modify our conventional response, Birtha gives us the language to hear even the longest cries of pain, the grief, the death, and the return.

Although Birtha's stories are about life, she sees death as part of life. Like the old Black woman character in "In the Life," who lies down in the garden to meet her long-dead lover, Gracie, Birtha's stories show us how to embrace rather than resist death, and to see, as the narrator of "In the Life" sees, the inextricable connection between sexual passion and death. A wonderful result of this story is that it makes it impossible for us to strip old people of their sexuality.

Becky Birtha is a soft-spoken warrior, able to turn her wounds and our wounds into words and to let them heal under the often warming, though sometimes scorching, sun of community recognition. In *The Forbidden Poems*, Birtha lets the passions that she names in the poem "Storms" flow onto the page. She writes of living through the breakup of a long relationship, of all that this loss means; she writes of broken dreams, of being stood up, but most importantly, she writes of putting herself back together. Birtha reminds us that this is a lifelong process. In a recently-published piece, "No Longer Speakable," which appeared in *She Who Was Lost Is Remembered: Healing from Incest through Creativity*, Birtha writes about her own incest. In the poem "The Parents Pantoum," Birtha shares the pain of being told, "You remember wrong." In these words we hear the echo of a storm that has rumbled through the lesbian community during our latest healing crisis. Birtha teaches us in all her work to honor our memories, for without them, we have no voice.

CRITICAL RECEPTION

The critical reception of Birtha's works is slowly gaining momentum. The writer of a review for *Publishers Weekly* commented on Birtha's ability to "endow ordinary perceptions and occurrences with profound significance" (77). A positive critique of her work appeared in the *Times Literary Supplement* after the publication of *Lover's Choice*: "Becky Birtha's subject-matter is new and vital; she plays on the unexpected and approaches her material from an original viewpoint. This collection contains virtuoso performances. . . . Becky Birtha has a distinctive talent, and this book puts her in the forefront of writers contributing to the development of Afro-American women's literature" (Pullin 623).

BIBLIOGRAPHY

Works by Becky Birtha

For Nights Like This One: Stories of Loving Women. San Francisco: Frog in the Well, 1983.
Lover's Choice. Seattle: Seal Press, 1987.
Lover's Choice. London: Women's Press, 1988.
The Forbidden Poems. Seattle: Seal Press, 1991.

Studies of Becky Birtha

Bogus, SDiane. "All of Our Art for Our Sake." *Sinister Wisdom* 27 (Fall 1984): 92–106.
Brownworth, Victoria A. "The Mother's Tongue: Poet Becky Birtha Gives Voice to the Experience of Parenting." *Advocate* (April 23, 1991): 78.
Pullin, Faith. "Acts of Reclamation." *Times Literary Supplement* (June 3–9): 623.
Review of *The Forbidden Poems*. *Publishers Weekly* (February 1, 1991): 77.
Roberts, J. R., comp. *Black Lesbians: An Annotated Bibliography*. Tallahassee, FL: Naiad Press, 1981.
Selman, Robyn. "Loss Horizons." *Village Voice* (April 16, 1991): 70.

JULIE BLACKWOMON (1943–   )
Toni P. Brown

BIOGRAPHY

Julia Carter was born in Saluda, Virginia, on November 16, 1943, to Mary and Perlie Carter. When she was five years old, she and her family moved to Philadelphia, Pennsylvania, where she presently resides.

At the age of fourteen, Julia started writing. Her first piece was published in the Fitzsimons Junior High School newspaper. A high school English teacher, Miss Jacobs, recognized and encouraged the latent talent in this young black woman.

Carter was married in 1963 and moved to Springfield, Massachusetts. The marriage lasted three years. She returned to Philadelphia two days before her daughter, Robin, was born. In 1973, she acknowledged her love for women and "came out." Those first pieces were about lesbian identity, falling in love, and being attracted to women. The discovery of her lesbian self and her writing self was not just a coincidence, and in an affirmation of her newfound identity, she renamed herself Julie Blackwomon.

The favorable response to the 1977 publication of "Revolutionary Blues" validated Blackwomon's identity as a writer. Writing poetry became a natural form of expression; in time, however, her short fiction started to be accepted for publication just as frequently.

Julie Blackwomon has read her work to appreciative audiences in Philadelphia, Boston, New York, and Baltimore. Her poetry and stories have appeared in many feminist journals, magazines, and anthologies. A collection of her short fiction, *Voyages Out 2*, was published by Seal Press in 1990. She is currently working on a novel.

MAJOR WORKS AND THEMES

The first work published by the adult Julie Blackwomon was the poem "Revolutionary Blues." Black lesbians were just beginning to test their wings, noticing the scarcity of lesbians of color in the women's movement. The question that kept getting pushed to the back of the dark closets, Who can we trust?, was spelled out in Blackwomon's poem; "I *expect* to be shot in the back by someone who calls me sister."

Exploring the implications of the "otherness" of choosing the love of women from the standpoint of the African-American community, facing those hard places, those closed doors in our own houses, is what makes Julie Blackwomon's work so wonderful and so important. Blackwomon takes us back to childhood in "Kippy" (*Lesbian Fiction*; later rewritten as "So's Your Mama" in *Voyages Out 2*). With Blackwomon's first-person singular narrative, we become Kippy as she hangs out with the kids on "Miss Lottie's newly washed steps." Blackwomon's detailed depictions of the ways of being with one another, kids "bustin' " on one another until it gets just this side of uncomfortable, puts us right there and moves us smoothly and unavoidably into the heart of conflict. Before we know it, we have thrown our sweaters to the ground, placed our hands on our hips, and are ready to kick Jamie's "narrow butt." In Blackwomon's stories, we are the fighter *and* the crowd that goads her on.

In "Cat" (*Home Girls: A Black Feminist Anthology*, later rewritten as "Long Way Home" in *Voyages Out 2*), we go along with Cat through her "baby-dyke" crush and feel nervous as we lie dangerously close to Sheila on an old army blanket in "Fairmount Park." We feel the burning of the tops of our ears at the bulldagger and the blind-side smack of being caught in the act of making forbidden love. We forget we are the adults who bought the book that we can close at any time, shutting off the stomach-clinching terror. We don't close the book. We sit frozen as Cat sits while her father/our father bellows in our faces, "There will be no bulldaggers in my house." She has once again taken us by the hand, opened the door to the room we tiptoed past, and drawn us inside.

As an African-American lesbian, when I read Julie Blackwomon's work, I always respond, "Yeah, this speaks my language; there is no translation necessary." Like finding a sister-friend in the wilderness of lesbian literature, her work not only speaks to the lesbian experience but also brings us to the life of the African-American lesbian as she lives in a very real world.

In "Marcia Loves Jesus," we are brought to the salient point in the first line. " 'I've given up women for Jesus,' Marcia said in a soft voice that was equal parts boast and apology. 'Oh?' I said." This external/verbal and internal/thought dialogue speaks directly to the reader, giving us insight into the situation that the other characters do not have. It is as if the protagonist is leaning toward us, a hand shielding her words lest anyone else hear the detailed comments she is whispering.

Blackwomon's 1980s fiction reflected serious internal conflicts of being lesbian in the Black community. The 1990s brought her characters into the lesbian community with a more humorous tone. "Maggie, Sex, and the Baby Jesus Too" looks at the silly side of sexual and racial expectations. Blackwomon's wry sense of humor tickles us in "The Thing That Wouldn't Hide," brings us through unrequited love in "Marcia Loves Jesus," and reveals the conflict of a white woman who believes that her inner soul is black in "Ophelia" (*Voyages Out 2*). This humor faces us toward the truth about our lives just as unerringly as her more serious poems or fictional pieces have.

More recently, Blackwomon explores another ancient, sealed doorway: incest. In "Look Ma, No Hands," Blackwomon speaks directly to us as a trusted friend or sister. She sits across the kitchen table from us leaning in or speaking into our ear next to us in bed. She tells us of her process of writing the essay that could not be written for so long. She speaks in a voice insistent on telling the truth:

I am six years old and dreaming I am atop the counter of a smoke filled bar. The bar is made of heavy mahogany wood, and I am cradled in my own familiar bedcovers. But for some reason there is a brown beer bottle at the entrance to my vagina.
When I wake I find I am in my father's bed along with my seven-year-old brother. My father is on top of me. The sensation is not unpleasant. (231)

Blackwomon brings us through her evolution as she comes to realize the meaning and purpose of her writer's block and the missing puzzle pieces of her life. Through flashbacks she reveals the buried traumas of childhood that come to the surface disguised in her adult life.

Through Blackwomon's poetry and fiction, we look into the shining black joy of our love for women and our pride in our African-American heritage. We hold hands as we feel the pain of betrayal, the disappointment, the fear of abandonment. And as she tells us about her very personal pain, as she peels back the layers of scarred skin to the original wound, the scab that must be pulled off for healing to begin, we are right beside her. We hold her hand and encourage her forward as we continue to read every word. When she breaks free, that six-year-old/forty-nine-year-old woman/child riding that bicycle for the first time, we are there running beside her applauding wildly at her great accomplishment and at ours.

CRITICAL RECEPTION

Voyages Out 2: Short Lesbian Fiction is a collection of six short stories by Blackwomon and eight stories by Nona Caspers. This is the only collection of Blackwomon's work with the exception of her chapbook, *Revolutionary Blues and Other Fevers*, which is a collection of her poetry. All other examples of her work appear in various lesbian journals and anthologies.

Voyages Out 2 (Seal Press) was favorably reviewed by gay and lesbian book reviewers. The *Baltimore Gay Paper* commented on the realism of Blackwomon's style: "Blackwomon's stories have a gritty, urban feel" (28) the reviewer noted. Rosalind Warren, writing for the *Welcomat Book Review*, was the most detailed in her praise: "Philadelphia writer Julie Blackwomon has a wild imagination, a sound understanding of what makes people tick and the ability to articulate both in a witty, no-nonsense and readable style. Her first collection of stories is part of the Seal Press 'Voyages Out' series. . . . Every tale is a winner'' (17).

BIBLIOGRAPHY

Works by Julie Blackwomon

"Claudia.'' *The Cathartic* 2 (1975): 40
"Sisterhood.'' *The Cathartic* 2 (1975): 3.
"Revolutionary Blues.'' *Dyke* 5 (Fall 1977): 22.
"Ghost Story 2.'' *Sinister Wisdom* 2 (Fall 1979): 93.
"Kippy.'' *Lesbian Fiction: An Anthology*. Ed. Elly Bulkin. New York: Persephone Press, 1981. 77.
"Revolutionary Blues.'' *Lesbian Poetry: An Anthology*. Ed. Elly Bulkin and Joan Larkin. New York: Persephone Press, 1981. 132.
"Cat.'' *Home Girls: A Black Feminist Anthology*. Ed. Barbara Smith. Latham, NY: Kitchen Table Press, 1983. 159.
Revolutionary Blues and Other Fevers. Chapbook 1984, 1991.
"The Thing That Wouldn't Hide!'' *Lesbian Bedtime Stories II*. Ed. Terry Woodrow. Willits, CA: Tough Dove Books, 1990. 155.
Voyages Out 2: Short Lesbian Fiction. Seattle: Seal Press, 1990. 3–94.
"Look Ma, No Hands.'' *She Who Was Lost Is Remembered: Healing from Incest through Creativity*. Ed. Louise M. Wisechild. Seattle: Seal Press, 1991. 231.
"Maggie, Sex, and the Baby Jesus Too.'' *Riding Desire*. Ed. Tee Corinne. Austin, TX: Banned Books, 1991. 47.

Studies of Julie Blackwomon

Baltimore Gay Paper (September 7, 1990): 28.
Warren, Rosalind. *Welcomat Book Review*: Fall 1990, 17.

ALICE BLOCH (1947–   )
Em L. White

BIOGRAPHY

Alice Bloch was born the oldest of five children in her family in Youngstown, Ohio, in 1947. Her mother died when she was nine, and her father remarried. As the eldest daughter, she "became a sort of honorary parent" (*Lifetime Guarantee* vii).

Bloch attended the University of Michigan as an undergraduate. Later on, dissatisfied with "the petty quarrels and hypocrisy" (personal communication with the author) of graduate school in Romance studies at Cornell University, she left for Israel in 1969. She remained there for two years, studying at Hebrew University of Jerusalem and working as an editor.

Upon returning to the United States, Bloch lived in New York and was a co-founder of Gay Liberation House. She published *Lifetime Guarantee*, an account of her sister's death from leukemia, in 1981. *Law of Return*, an autobiographical novel about living in Israel, appeared in 1983. She has also published articles, commentaries, and poetry in several feminist and lesbian periodicals.

Alice Bloch currently lives in Seattle, Washington. She is employed as a technical writer and is working on another novel.

MAJOR WORKS AND THEMES

Bloch writes intensely personal accounts of her efforts to encompass her lesbian and Jewish identities. Both of her books may be considered in the context of coming-out stories. In *Lifetime Guarantee*, Bloch reveals her struggles to live her own life separate from the judgments and pressures of family while responding to crisis and grief. *The Law of Return* describes aspects of the difficulty faced by a devoutly religious Jewish lesbian. She expresses feelings of urgently developing lesbian identity in a woman who is surrounded by family members who consider her hard-won and happy self-knowledge as something as terrible as early death.

Bloch explores themes of pain and loss and growth. Spirituality is important to her, and there is a strong component of joyous religiosity and a sense that one has a responsibility to appreciate gifts received. The fragility of life is something very close to the consciousness of a Jewish woman who knows her history. Survival and mourning are themes she examines both within her own life and in those of her characters.

Lifetime Guarantee is a memorial to Bloch's sister, Barbara, who died of leukemia at the age of twenty. Bloch and her sister had planned to write the book together. *Lifetime Guarantee* is a survivor's account of a harrowing series of events. It combines memories of Bloch's feelings during Barbara's illness with some of her sister's letters and writings. Bloch demonstrates how one horrific event, while dominating one's life at a particular time, is never quite all that is going on. Jobs must be sought; a coming out once started must be continued; old lovers are lost; new ones are found; other family members become ill, die, get married; tension does not mitigate family rivalries, rejections, and power struggles.

Block relates how several family losses bring her to terms with memories of her mother's death and the mourning she was denied at that time. She seeks to find pattern and meaning and goals for living in the context of loss and strongly perceived mortality.

Lifetime Guarantee traces the author's efforts to identify the lines between the need to care for herself and for others whom she loves. She eventually makes a decision to follow her own life and moves away from her family shortly before her sister's death.

Her second book, *The Law of Return*, is a novelistic treatment of part of the author's observations and experiences during a two-year stay in Israel. Dissatisfied with a life in America where her spiritual values were unappreciated, the heroine journeys to a place where she feels welcomed, where she hopes to fit in. And to a great extent, she does. She becomes fluent in Hebrew, makes friends, and freely practices and studies her religion. She writes joyous, sensuously descriptive passages about the food, music, prayers, and people she encounters. These vivid descriptions of Israel in the 1970s are one of the great strengths of this book.

Eventually, the protagonist begins to question the imposition of rigid patriarchal values. She observes classist divisions within the society, exemplified by inequalities in housing and medical care, and she perceives the relationship between the classism and the determined relegation of women to subservient domestic roles. She is constantly pressured to marry. Her psychiatrist is determined to help her "work past" her lesbian feelings and to help her achieve a "real maturity" in life as a "happily married Israeli woman" (86). Her confusion deepens when her fiancé declares that he is gay. She eventually goes back to the United States to work for a gay rights organization in New York, where she enters her first lesbian relationship and confronts her family.

The protagonist and her lover do return to Israel to study, and she finds it changed for the worse: it is more violent, more hostile, and more in conflict than during her first visit. The protagonist seeks symbols of the enduring nature of the place, its noise, its crowds, and its uneasy but sustainable ethnic diversity which has been, for centuries, the spiritual center of several major religions.

Bloch uses carefully intricate strategies in writing intense descriptions of emotional events. She shifts frequently between her own thoughts and some of her sister's writings in *Lifetime Guarantee*, and she also moves smoothly from various points in the past to a present seven years after Barbara's death. *The Law of Return* also contains frequent shifts from first- to third-person narration and from past to present tense.

CRITICAL RECEPTION

In general, criticism of Bloch's work has been favorable. There is praise for her honesty and introspective directness. Readers delight in the immediacy of her descriptions, the "unusual richness and texture" of her words (Beck). "In sumptuous language, Bloch vividly evokes the Holy Land, its heat and dust, its dramatic beauty, the colors and feels and smells of its centuries, the noisy crowded exuberance of its cities, the transcendent strength and resilience of its people," according to Katherine Forrest. "Bloch is marvelous in her descriptions of streets and markets, town and villages, the sight and smell of a people. Beautiful is the portrait of Old Jerusalem etched in the sculptured prose of a poet," writes Bettina Aptheker.

One critic of *Lifetime Guarantee* offers a list of topics that she would, as a cancer patient, have liked to see given a more "thorough treatment" (Bertram). Most reviewers of *Lifetime Guarantee*, however, comment positively on Bloch's writing, including her "good strong woman-identified sensibility" in handling "important themes of survival, support, and affirmation of life" (*The Law of Return*). Some reviewers feel that reading the book has helped them to gain perspective on similar issues in their own lives.

Most of the critics who reviewed the books seemed to show acceptance of Bloch's lesbian themes, though one refers to her resolution of a quest for identity in *Law of Return* as "owning up" (*Publishers Weekly*). On the whole, however, the reception has been positive.

BIBLIOGRAPHY

Works by Alice Bloch

Lifetime Guarantee: A Journey Through Loss and Survival. Boston: Alyson Publications, 1981.
The Law of Return. Boston: Alyson Publications, 1983.

Studies of Alice Bloch

Aptheker, Bettina. "Jewish Feminists Claim Their Identity." *Demeter* (Monterey, California), February 1985.

Beck, Evelyn Torton. Rev. of *The Law of Return*. *The News* (Los Angeles), December 11, 1987.

Bertram, Diane. "A Journey Through Loss and Survival." *Womansight* 2: 5 (November 1981).

Bounds, Elizabeth M. "Survivor's Story." *Sojourner* (February 1982).

Craig, Sarah. Rev. of *The Law of Return*. *Windy City Times* (December 17, 1987).

Daly, Mary Ann. "Zion and Her Daughters." *Washington Blade* (March 9, 1984).

Forrest, Katherine V. Rev. of *The Law of Return*. *Advocate*. (February 1988).

Freitag, Bob. *"Lifetime Guarantee*, An Intense, Intimate Odyssey." *Out Magazine* (October 22, 1981).

Goldberg, Eve. Rev. of *The Law of Return*. *Lesbian News* (January 1984): 41.

Goodwin, Jackie. "Instant Citizenship; Delayed Lesbianism." *Body Politic* (September 1984): 40.

Gregory, Dianne. "Lesbian Jews' Dilemma." *Bay Area Reporter* (July 5, 1984): 24.

Hernandez, Judi. Rev. of *Lifetime Guarantee*. *Lesbian News* (December 1981).

Klein, Yvonne. Rev. of *The Law of Return*. *New Women's Times* (May/June 1984).

The Law of Return. Reviewed in *Lesbian Resource* Spring 1984; *Ms.* July 1984, 30; *Publishers Weekly* July 29, 1983, 69; *This Week in Mississippi* December 8, 1983, 14; *The Works* January 1984, n. pag.; *Lammas Little Review* November 1981; *Lavender Horizons* 1, no. 2, 10.

Lowenstein, Andrea. "Moving Through Loss and Survival." *Gay Community News* (November 7, 1981): 10.

Monteagudo, Jesse. Rev. of *Law of Return*. *Connection* (February 1984).

Newman, Felice. Rev. of *Lifetime Guarantee*. *Motheroot Journal* (Winter 1981).

———. "A Lesbian Understanding of Israel and Judaism." *off our backs* (June 1983): 19.

Starkman, Elaine. "Sisters." *Small Press Review* (May 1983): 1.

Sturgis, Susanna J. Rev. of *Lifetime Guarantee*. *off our backs* (December 1981): 22.

Taylor, Rebecca Sue. Rev. of *The Law of Return*. *Library Journal* (September 1, 1983): 1719.

SDIANE ADAMS BOGUS
(1946–   )
Rita B. Dandridge

BIOGRAPHY

SDiane Adams Bogus was born January 22, 1946, in Chicago, Illinois, the only girl of three children of Florence and Lawrence Bogus, hardworking factory employees. Bogus began writing poems as an adolescent and anticipated receiving a typewriter from her mother for her sixteenth birthday. When her mother died from cancer of the uterus, SDiane, grief-stricken at fourteen years of age, started journal keeping. She lived temporarily with an aunt across town and then with her paternal grandparents in Birmingham, Alabama, when her father was unable to raise her.

In Alabama, Bogus fell in love with the girl next door, a high-school classmate who reminded her of her mother and who, along with teachers interested in literature, helped to resurrect her writing talent. Bogus, however, graduated from A. H. Parker High School in 1964 without publishing a single poem because segregated Alabama did not allow black students to publish in the local newspapers, and Bogus had no mentors to guide her to publication. That September, she enrolled in predominantly black Stillman College in Tuscaloosa, Alabama, where she established *Stillman College Literary Magazine* and graduated as a *cum laude* English major in 1968. She was first called a "bulldagger" at Stillman even though she had been sexually intimate with girls since the age of eight, and in the face of heterosexual socialization, she had become aware of her lesbianism at sixteen. Her autobiographical short story, "A Measure by June," from *Sapphire's Sampler* (reprinted in *Azalea* and *GPU News*), graphically depicts the conflict she encountered with her sexual preference.

In 1968, Bogus was granted a fellowship to Syracuse University, where she dated men and women, pursued a master's degree in English through accelerated effort, and graduated in 1969. Inspired by her reading of Malcolm X's works and caught up in the black consciousness movement of the late 1960s, Bogus wrote numerous "black" poems and short stories, none of which found publication in the Syracuse University's magazine. She published her first poem, "Dippity-Did-Done or Can You Do," in Nikki Giovanni's anthology *Night Comes Softly* (1970), and the Syracuse poems later became *I'm Off to See the Goddam Wizard, Alright!* (1971).

Bogus assumed a teaching position in 1969 at predominantly black Miles College in Birmingham, Alabama. Young and heedless of taboo and convention, she was open about her lesbian relationship with a student and was not retained at the college. For the next twenty years, she taught in various public schools and held lectureships in English departments at Northwestern University, Miami University, City College of San Francisco, and San Francisco State University. She is currently an instructor at De Anza College in Cupertino, California, where she teaches writing, poetry, and gay and lesbian studies.

In May 1979, Bogus founded Woman in the Moon (WIM) Publications, a small poetry press and one of four major publishing companies owned by African-American women in the United States. The press was established in Compton, California, and has been in San Francisco since 1985. In 1988, Bogus received her Ph.D. in twentieth-century American literature from Miami University. She currently resides in Cupertino, where she and her devoted partner and lover, Trilby Masters Nelson-Gilbert, are preparing for WIM publication the *Lesbian and Gay Wedding Album*, a style directory and photodocumentary of lesgay marriages in America.

MAJOR WORKS AND THEMES

Bogus writes in several genres—poetry, short stories, plays, and essays—but she is known best as a performance poet, who has a one-woman show that brings to life characters from her seven volumes of poetry and prose. The themes of self-identity, woman-loving consciousness, spirituality, sexuality, and humanitarianism pervade her works. Bogus's first published volume, *I'm Off to See the Goddam Wizard, Alright!* (1971), came eleven years after she began writing unpublished "books" of poetry and traces her awareness of her black identity. It manifests her political activism during the black liberation movement of the 1960s and is an open assault on the wizard's (white America's) fantasies, myths, and fairy tales that have stifled blacks' individuality. The volume addresses the identity crisis of blacks who believe in destructive myths, and it celebrates Bogus's liberation from these fantasies and her recognition of herself as a proud black woman. In "Awareness," her love for her fellow African Americans enables her to write, "This awakening of mine / Has served to give me enumerable ecstasies with my people" (57).

Woman in the Moon (1977), the title of which became the name for Bogus's publishing company, explores women's identity and feminist consciousness. In four parts—"Woman in the Moon," "Of Birds and Bees," "Persona," and "Consciousness"—the volume moves from celebrating woman's growth, analyzing love, remembering relationships, to an awakening of women's surroundings. The fifty-eight poems consist of epigrams, dialect verses, monologues, ballads, and rhymes of pop history and Black feminist blend. Two important ones are "Franklin on U.S. History" and "Miss Brown."

Her Poems: An Anniversaric Chronology (1979) traces in sixteen poems the five-year relationship between Bogus and her lover at that time, Frances J. Hoxie, from its uncertain beginning, through a ritual union, to an acknowledgment of a shared noble vision. Replete with illustrations, only twenty-five signed and numbered volumes were printed, and these sold for $200 each.

Sapphire's Sampler (1982), her fourth and largest volume, consists of poetry, short stories, essays, and plays that explore women's issues and other universal subjects. From incest in the poem "Deep South Passion" to reincarnation in the essay "The Fixed and Common Notion," Bogus comments on human nature and people's capacity to love. Her intent was to offer various samples of her writing before she became known solely as a poet. Many of her poems here have been published in numerous periodicals and journals, and among the popular ones are "Lady Godiva," "Mayree," and "The Creator's Dalliance: Psalm 4."

Dyke Hands and Sutras Erotic and Lyric (1988) is also a mix of previously published poems and essays, and it divides into four parts: "Spirituality," "Race and Culture," "Love, Joy, Sex, and Loss," and "Selves and Selfhood." Instructive and uplifting, this collection concerns itself with issues related to self-definition. Racial, sexual, and personal topics offer strength and courage to women oppressed by a traditionally white, heterosexual society. "To My Mother's Vision" relates the author's struggles as a Black lesbian writer, and "After the Kiss" pays tribute to Winnie Mandela and Coretta Scott King, strong women who have struggled to bring change in a world that suppresses women's natural freedom.

The Chant of the Women of Magdalena and the Magdalena Poems (1990) is Bogus's most ambitious work to date and for which she was named one of the finalists for the Lambda Literary Award in June 1991. In two parts, preceded by a twenty-page preface, this volume continues the idea of self-definition celebrated in *Dyke Hands*. Part 1 relates the escape of thirty-two multicultural women from an English prison and their settlement in a mountain cave near Spain, where years later they defeat male explorers from England. Part 2 chronicles the backgrounds, natures, psyches, and virtues of these women. In this expanded repertoire of oppressed women taking control of their lives, Bogus implies that she represents every woman and that every woman represents her. Set in an English and American literary tradition, this volume draws from such writers as T. S. Eliot, Robert Frost, and Edna St. Vincent Millay; from such genres as the ballad, monologue, and haiku; and from such universal themes as regeneration, redefinition of self, and the celebration of nature.

For the Love of Men: Shikata Gai Nai (1990) steps beyond the circle of lesbian bonding to address gay men, often seated in Bogus's listening audience. The forty-two poems eschew the politically naive stance of some male-bashing lesbians in order to foster trust and encourage dialogue between lesbians and gays, a situation that is unavoidable as the Japanese subtitle suggests. The volume acknowledges issues common to same-sex partners, such as unfaithfulness in "Al Thinks of Tony," imprisonment in "Men behind Bars," greed in "Incontinence," and race denial in "Michael Jackson." Expanding Bogus's woman-centered consciousness to include human welfare and social reform, this work represents her broadest statement for humanitarianism and peace.

CRITICAL RECEPTION

Aside from several brief reviews on her first two volumes, Bogus has received most attention for her latest works. Mostly feminists and lesbians have reviewed her works, a phenomenon that certainly reflects the homophobia of academe and perhaps also the unavoidable restrictions placed upon the self-published black lesbian poet. These critics have generally commented on various aspects of her works, from her relevant themes, the riveting directness of her style, the poignant messages, to her varied subject matter.

Anne J. D'Arcy, editor of *Telewoman*, comments on Bogus's wide range of subjects on the back cover of *Sapphire's Sampler*: "This woman points a finger at everyone from the Pope to American traditions—how she manages to spit in your eye and capture your heart at the same time is beyond me. Witty! Audacious! Not exactly housebroken!" Similarly alerted to the diversity in Bogus's poetry, Becky Birtha points out the influences in *Sapphire Sampler*, ranging "from a child's reader in 'Elementary Erotica' ('Come, Lady. Come. / Come. Come. Come. / See What I Want.') (14) to, at the other extreme, a series of 'Psalms,' heavy with Biblical influence" (14, 20).

Terri L. Jewell in "'A Farewell to Harms: Women Reclaim the Sea," observes that in *The Chant of the Women of Magdalena and the Magdalena Poems*, "Bogus' imagination defies all traditional boundaries, and it is her daring that births her treatment of women and the sea. The subject of women as sailors and their relation to the sea and its forces has been ignored in literature" (29). In another review, Terri Jewell regards *Dyke Hands and Sutras Erotic and Lyric* as a cultural classic whose subject matter ranges from sexual eroticism to "Christian exuberance" and whose genres extend from autobiography to poetry of sexual fantasy (12). Karen Wolman, in "Every Which Way But Easy," sees a variety of struggles in Bogus's poetry: "the struggle to be a woman in a man's world, the struggle to be a black woman in a white world, the struggle to get and keep and honor the love of another woman" (73). Bogus's diverse subject matter heralds her as a significant writer who embraces the Black lesbian-feminist aesthetic while expanding the American literary tradition as she strives for truth and an independent poetic vision.

BIBLIOGRAPHY

Works by SDiane A. Bogus

I'm Off to See the Goddam Wizard, Alright! Inglewood, CA: WIM Publications, 1971.

Woman in the Moon. Stamford, CT: Soap Box Publishing, 1977. Reprint. Englewood, CA: WIM Publications, 1977.

Her Poems: An Anniversaric Chronology. Inglewood, CA: WIM Publications, 1979.

Sapphire's Sampler. Inglewood, CA: WIM Publications, 1982.

Dyke Hands and Sutras Erotic and Lyric. San Francisco, CA: WIM Publications, 1988.

The Chant of the Women of Magdalena and the Magdalena Poems. San Francisco, CA: WIM Publications, 1990.

SDiane Bogus Creativity. Video Cassette. Dir. Tee Corinne. WIM Publications, Jan. 23, 1990. 2 hrs.

For the Love of Men: Shikata Gai Nai. San Francisco, CA: WIM Publications, 1991.

SDiane Reading the Chant of the Women of Magdalena and Selected Magdalena Poems. Audio Cassette. WIM Publications, 1992. 90 min.

Studies of SDiane A. Bogus

Birtha, Becky. "Celebrating Themselves: Four Self-Published Black Lesbian Authors." *off our backs* 15 (August/September 1985): 19–21.

Jewell, Terri. "*Dyke Hands and Sutras Erotic and Lyric*: Poems and Lyrics by SDiane Bogus." *Womenwise* 12, no. 4 (Winter 1990): 12.

———. "A Farewell to Harms: Women Reclaim the Sea." *Lambda Book Report* 2, no. 10 (May/June 1991): 29.

"We're Moonstruck over SDiane Bogus." *Womyn's Words* (July 1990): 1.

Wolman, Karen Dale. "Every Which Way But Easy: Poet SDiane Bogus Comes Out on Top." *Advocate: The National Gay Newsmagazine* 14 (August 1990): 73.

SANDY BOUCHER (1936–   )
Carolyn Kyler

BIOGRAPHY

Sandy Boucher (Early) was born July 15, 1936, in Columbus, Ohio, where she grew up in a working-class family. She began writing when she was eleven. After receiving a B.A. in English literature from Ohio State University in 1958, she moved to New York City to accept a guest editor position at *Mademoiselle*. She married Jerry Boucher in 1961; they divorced in 1971. Boucher moved to San Francisco in the early sixties and worked as a proofreader, copy editor, library assistant, pathology transcriptionist, and secretary. In the early 1970s, Boucher came out as a lesbian, began living communally with women with whom she published a newspaper, *Mother Lode*, and became deeply committed to political activism. Boucher was a founding member of the Berkeley Feminist Institute (1980–1983), an independent teaching institution based on feminist principles. In 1990, she earned an M.A. in the history and phenomenology of religion from the Graduate Theological Union in Berkeley. Boucher was a fellow at the MacDowell Colony (New Hampshire) in 1975, received a fellowship in literature from the National Endowment for the Arts in 1979, twice received Money for Women Fund/Barbara Deming Memorial Fellowships (1983, 1991), and was awarded a Druid Heights Foundation writer's grant in 1991.

Sandy Boucher has written four books and many short stories and essays. She lives in Oakland, California, with her lover, Crystal Juelson, where she teaches writing workshops and is a writing consultant for women. She has spoken on such topics as women and Buddhism, sex and spirituality, and peace and justice. Currently, Boucher is working on two novels, one about the "anatomy of abuse" in a family, and one about a woman's erotic/spiritual journey. As a member of the San Francisco community, the lesbian-feminist community, the Buddhist community, and the radical political community, she says: "I more and more appreciate the stability and the richness of being part of this (these) community

(-ies). I especially cherish my lesbian-feminist friends from the early seventies, as we share such a passionate past of commitment, activism and discovery'' (personal communication with the author, 1992).

MAJOR WORKS AND THEMES

Sandy Boucher is very comfortable with being identified as a lesbian writer and believes that she writes from a lesbian perspective. Much of her work, fiction and non-fiction, is in some way autobiographical as she explores such issues as beginning and ending relationships, coming out, community, and change.

Boucher's first book of short stories, *Assaults & Rituals* (1975), required, according to its introduction, a reclaiming of the past: having discarded writing when she discarded heterosexual life, Boucher finally began to write again, as a lesbian, reworking old stories and creating new ones. *Assaults & Rituals* explores the consequences of living in the past or of breaking free. Tia Nuria in ''The Fifth Great Day of God'' is a woman who lives without memory, history, or language; when she is forced to confront her history, she becomes old. In ''Big Rock in the Road,'' George O'Day's disappointment in his own life poisons his relationship with his son, and in the story/poem ''For My Brother and Me,'' a sister recalls her older brother's suicide years before.

The only explicitly lesbian stories in *Assaults & Rituals* are the last two, ''Mountain Radio'' and ''Retaining Walls,'' which are linked by common characters and are connected autobiographically to Boucher (as she verifies in her essay ''Three Stories''). In ''Mountain Radio,'' the thirty-seven-year-old narrator, Sandy, recalls her first sexual experience with a woman when she was twenty-three, an experience she fled because ''I *didn't want to be like her*, as I defined it, meaning I didn't want to be treated as she was by everyone who came in contact with her (including *me*)'' (31). No longer running from being a lesbian or from that memory, Sandy thinks about seeing Lenora again, and she finally does see her, in ''Retaining Walls.'' The character/writer Sandy shows the story she has written, ''Mountain Radio,'' to Lenora. This visit to the past is both an assault and a ritual. For June, Lenora's lover, it is an assault on her present life with Lenora; for Sandy and Lenora, it is both a ritual of healing and an assault on the ''retaining walls'' that keep the past safely contained.

The Notebooks of Leni Clare and Other Short Stories (1982) continues and expands on the theme and paradoxes of change: change is inevitable, destructive, rare, redemptive. The past cannot be recaptured, but neither can it be escaped. The memory of a bear attack in ''Nothing Safe in Crabtree Meadow'' carries the realization that no one can fully protect either him/herself or another. In ''The Cutting Room,'' after listening uncomfortably to a homophobic conversation, Kelly decides to overcome her fear and come out to her coworkers. Her transition from being a ''nice heterosexual woman'' (51) to being a lesbian and then being out means taking a risk. But for Kelly, the realization that nothing is ever safe is freeing. Coming out, cutting herself open, is dangerous surgery, but it will, she hopes, save her life.

Dealing with the past can mean dealing with a place (''Kansas in the Spring''), with parents (''The Day My Father Kicked Me Out''), or with memories of sexual abuse (''Charm School''). Often it means coping with the loss of a relationship. In ''Me and Ahnie Silver,'' Rose Giannini experiences the worry, anger, absence, cruelty, and blaming of a relationship that is over before the breakup. Her house, symbolizing stability and recalling her parents and her history, helps Rose remember that she is ''larger than the events in my life, more enduring than any particular pain'' (37). Leni Clare, in ''The Notebooks of Leni Clare,'' is paralyzed by her lover's departure. She confronts herself as ''a woman who had never in her life made an active choice'' (103) and feels a need to change—even as part of her wishes she could crawl back into the past. In Part 2 of the story, aptly titled ''Everything Changes,'' Leni and Gretchen break up, Leni takes a new job doing physical labor and moves into a communal household. The story ends with Leni assuring Gretchen that ''you're my best friend always. That just doesn't change'' (150)—yet even this point of stability feels insecure.

Boucher's third book, *Heartwomen: An Urban Feminist's Odyssey Home* (1982), is an engrossing combination of travel narrative, interview, and memory, as Boucher explores a mostly rural region of Kansas, Nebraska, and Missouri, talking with women and thinking about her own roots in Ohio. The strongest parts of the book are the stories Boucher draws out of the women she meets. ''Why I don't believe I've ever told my life to anyone before!'' (117). Boucher seems personally connected to the women she meets, especially as their stories inspire memories of her own childhood. In spite of this autobiographical element, Boucher does not identify herself as a lesbian until late in the book, remaining silent even when Marian Ellet, one of the women she interviews, makes a comment linking ''crime and homosexuality'' (160). While she mentions lesbian authors—Willa Cather, Gertrude Stein, Barbara Deming—Boucher does not refer to her own sexuality until she speaks with Barbara Grier, co-founder of Naiad Press and a very out lesbian, in Kansas City. ''I have heard much about this woman since becoming a lesbian myself in the early seventies'' (212). Originally, Boucher planned to mention her lesbianism in the introduction, but she agreed with her editor to discuss it only in a later chapter since it was not the subject of the book and since her memories of the Midwest are primarily of a pre-lesbian life. Consequently, Barbara Grier becomes the primary lesbian voice in the book. '' 'They may not like us,' Grier says of heterosexuals, 'but they'd have to get used to us if they knew who we were' '' (228).

Like many of Boucher's stories, *Heartwomen* is about understanding and coming to terms with one's history. ''This is my place still,'' Boucher concludes. ''It is neither possible nor necessary to accept exile anymore'' (280). Still, Boucher reports that her parents, who she thought would like *Heartwomen*, did not—in part because in it she identifies herself as a lesbian.

Boucher's method in *Heartwomen* is to travel, interview women, and give space to many voices while also identifying her personal stake in the discussion. This multivocal method is even more explicit in "The Power of Consciousness: A Collage" (1979, 1986), an assembly of voices speaking of rape, in which coauthors Boucher and Susan Griffin comment only by selection and arrangement. Boucher uses the technique of *Heartwomen* with a different community in *Turning the Wheel* (1988), a documentary of women attempting to create an "Americanized, feminized, democratized" form of Buddhism (1). In her introduction, Boucher notes her initial hope that she could discuss lesbians practicing Buddhism and that she was thwarted when many of the lesbians she interviewed refused to be quoted on that subject. "As I worked on this book I was surprised at the level of homophobia present in our culture, in our Buddhist centers, and in ourselves" (xi). While mentions of lesbians and homosexuality are scattered through the book, it is not a central issue.

With Boucher's interest in spirituality has come a greater emphasis on eroticism. A recent story, "Humming" (1986), is uncannily similar to "The Woman Who Walked in the Night" (1975). In each story a middle-aged woman married to a man named Ralph embarks on a lesbian affair with a younger woman. But "Humming"—originally written for a collection of erotic stories—includes both Buddhist spiritual practice and highly charged sex scenes, additions reflecting Boucher's interest in sex as a sacred act.

CRITICAL RECEPTION

Sandy Boucher's work has not yet received much critical attention. *The Notebooks of Leni Clare* is mentioned in Bonnie Zimmerman's study of lesbian fiction, *The Safe Sea of Women*, as part of a tradition of lesbians writing about community, and by Valerie Miner in her essay "An Imaginary Collectivity of Writers and Readers" as an example of working-class fiction. Reviews of Boucher's most recent book, *Turning the Wheel*, tend to focus—not surprisingly—primarily on its Buddhism, and secondarily on its feminism. One of the best sources on Boucher's work is Boucher herself, who in her essay "Three Stories" describes her progression from writing about lesbians as abstractions, to writing about herself *for* herself, to becoming committed to "an examination of what is in our lives" (102).

BIBLIOGRAPHY

Works by Sandy Boucher

Assaults & Rituals. Oakland, CA: Mama's Press, 1975.
"The Woman Who Walked in the Night." *The Lesbian Reader*. Berkeley, CA: Amazon Press, 1975. 23–35.
Heartwomen: An Urban Feminist's Odyssey Home. San Francisco: Harper, 1982.

The Notebooks of Leni Clare and Other Short Stories. Trumansburg, NY: Crossing Press, 1982.
"The Power of Consciousness: A Collage." With Susan Griffin. *Rape: The Politics of Consciousness*. By Susan Griffin. 1979. rev. ed. San Francisco: Harper, 1986. 93–137.
Turning the Wheel: American Women Creating the New Buddhism. San Francisco: Harper, 1988.
"Humming." *Lesbian Love Stories*. Ed. Irene Zahava. Freedom, CA: Crossing Press, 1989. 27–41.
"In Love with the Dharma." *Ms*. (May-June 1991): 80–81.

Studies of Sandy Boucher

Boucher, Sandy. "There Stories." *The Lesbian Path*. Ed. Margaret Cruikshank. 1980. rev. ed. San Francisco: Grey Fox Press, 1985. 100–102.
Butler, Katy. Rev. of *Turning the Wheel*. *New York Times Book Review* (Oct. 30, 1988): 27.
Miner, Valerie. "An Imaginative Collectivity of Writers and Readers." *Lesbian Texts and Contexts: Radical Revisions*. Ed. Karla Jay and Joanne Glasgow. New York: New York University Press, 1990. 13–27.
Scott, Victoria. "The Feminine Side of American Buddhism." Rev. of *Turning the Wheel*. *San Francisco Examiner-Chronicle* (Sept. 4, 1988): 9.
Zimmerman, Bonnie. *The Safe Sea of Women: Lesbian Fiction 1969–1989*. Boston: Beacon, 1990.

BLANCHE McCRARY BOYD
(1945–   )
Madeline R. Moore

BIOGRAPHY

Blanche McCrary Boyd was born in Charleston, South Carolina, in 1945. She was educated at Duke University and Pomona College and received her M.A. from Stanford University in 1970 where she was a Wallace Stegner Fellow. She has taught feminist studies at Goddard College and is now professor of English literature at Connecticut College.

The Revolution of Little Girls is Blanche Boyd's third novel and her fourth book. *The Redneck Way of Knowledge*, a collection of essays published by Alfred A. Knopf in 1982, combined autobiography and journalism. Her previous novels are *Mourning the Death of Magic* (Macmillan, 1977) and *Nerves* (Daughters, Inc., 1973). Boyd's stories, essays, and articles have appeared in the *Village Voice*, *Esquire*, *Vanity Fair*, *Vogue*, *Premiere*, *American Film*, *New Age*, and numerous other publications. She has been a staff writer at the *Village Voice* and a contributor to National Public Radio's "All Things Considered."

Boyd received a Fiction Fellowship from the National Endowment for the Arts in 1988 to support her work on *The Revolution of Little Girls*. An excerpt entitled "The Black Hand Girl" appeared in *Best American Short Stories 1989*. She won a fiction fellowship from the South Carolina Arts Commission several years ago, was a nominee for the Southern Book Award in 1991, and has recently won the Ferro Grumley Foundation's award for the best work of fiction written in 1991. She has given numerous readings and has lectured widely on the relationship of fiction and non-fiction, including a series in Thailand and Malaysia for the U.S. Information Agency's Arts America Program. She makes her home in Stonington, Connecticut.

MAJOR WORKS AND THEMES

Blanche McCrary Boyd's sense of irony and defiance permeates both her novels and essays. In the best tradition of southern writers, Boyd situates her narratives on the boisterous porches of her family's past, and there she writes her way through her own history. Her writings frequently focus on the trials of a southern girl turned non-conformist. Blanche Boyd's artistic integrity can be seen in the way she elicits questions from the reader, not about political correctness, but rather about how intelligently the characters are depicted and how provocative the narrative's pattern is. Boyd anticipates a maturity in contemporary lesbian writers to acknowledge their sexual decisions and then to write the stories they know best. Despite the fact that she denied creating a form flattering enough for her subjects until she wove together the essays previously published by the *Village Voice* into a single patterned narrative named *The Redneck Way of Knowledge*, one can see the beginnings of the weave in her first novel, *Nerves*.

In *Nerves* (1973), we experience a flawed but passionate coming-of-age tale inhabited by the strong and troubled generations of women who try to make sense of their relationships and their isolation. Especially poignant is the fourteen-year-old Diane Hamilton's fear of defeat, and her tough and serious determination to grow up unscathed by a culture that equates femaleness with victimization. The tension this struggle creates between Diane and her mother, Lena, is the central theme of the novel. Her friendship with her neighbor Brookie is also important, and it is a precursor of Ellen's adventures with Hutch in *The Revolution of Little Girls*. Boyd thinks *Nerves* was an apprenticeship novel, yet it was an apprenticeship that was successful in many ways.

By the time we pick up *Mourning the Death of Magic* (1977), we're familiar with the complicated Southern family that lives in Charleston, South Carolina. There, the protagonist, Galley Rhett, muses that her "whole family, herself included, made her think of a monster living in a cave" (139). *Mourning the Death of Magic* is about Galley's memories of her dead mother, her confrontations with her Uncle Arlis, her relationship with her lonely father, her emerging awareness of racial oppression, her brief affair with a woman, her experimentation with drugs in college, and her attempts to kill herself. Mostly, though, it's a love story dominated by Galley's childhood obsession with her adopted brother, Shannon, and her later attraction to and love for her sister, Mallory. Galley yearns for Shannon, who leaves her when he moves to Palo Alto, California, where, in the novel's opening, he's answering Johanna Osborne's ad in the personals. She needs someone to read her Kierkegaard in exchange for Greek lessons. As it turns out, Johanna is ninety-two years old and really wants someone to help her die. Johanna Osborne's ad is the metaphor that unlocks the rest of the novel. Each character needs someone to help her/him mourn the death of what was magical but which no longer works.

Mourning the Death of Magic is a third-person narrative set in the early 1960s. The main characters' points of view make up alternating sections. Its greatness is read in the non-judgmental way Boyd presents us with the paradox that we don't just lose our illusions to find a fixed reality. Rather, we relinquish past illusions in order to create new ones.

The Redneck Way of Knowledge (1982) is a collection of essays, which together form a single coherent narrative. Boyd describes these essays as being like "trick pool shots," and she feels her form came out just right with this work. Rita Mae Brown said the work read like a person who had hit bottom and came up laughing. In the essays, Boyd takes us to the Spoleto Arts Festival, to Pope John Paul II's mass in Yankee Stadium, to the Charleston stock car races and amateur boxing nights, and to New York City where her Aunt Jenny rocks with the Rockettes. Many of the essays are superb social criticism—including "Ambush," which highlights what happened when the Communist Workers party confronted the Ku Klux Klan in Greensboro in November 1979.

Boyd's emerging lesbianism is never written as one definitive act, after which she is changed and so changes the world around her. Instead it is framed in narratives like "Be Here Then" starring Blanche, Shreve, and Dixie, who spread rumors about an avalanche of alligators about to descend on all the picnickers at the Charleston Jazz Picnic.

The Revolution of Little Girls (1991) won the Ferro Grumley Foundation's award for the best work of fiction written in 1991. It was also nominated for the Lambda Award, for Quality Paperback Books' New Voices Award, and for the first Southern Book Award for Fiction. Boyd's third novel is the tragicomic story of a southern lesbian suffering from a nervous breakdown who goes home to help her mother heal from her facelift. In the process, Ellen Larraine Burns comes to terms with her own suffering and her own past. As a child, Ellen is an outspoken rebel. "After the Tarzan serial at the movies every Saturday afternoon," the novel begins, "my friend Hutch and I would climb the mimosa tree in his backyard and take off our shirts and eat bananas. Neither of us wanted to play Jane." This understated voice represents the craft of a writer whose language has achieved an almost perfect pitch. And Ellen, who is immensely likable, never will want to play Jane. But along the way she learns that society, not Hutch, insists that she play Jane to Hutch's Tarzan, and in fact, her happiness with Hutch is destroyed when her mother, Irene, tells on the nine-year-old boy, after learning he's exposed himself to her daughter. Time passes both happily and unhappily for Ellen.

The next time I talked with Hutch, seven more years had passed, and I was tripping on mescaline at my mother's Christmas party. I was divorced and had recently proclaimed myself a lesbian revolutionary in a twenty-four page letter to my mother, who was not happy with this news. (15)

But the reader who expects Ellen's coming out to be the focus of the novel will be disappointed. The core of the novel is formed in Ellen's interactions with her mother, her teachers, her brother, her sister, their dead father, her teenage boyfriends, and not least of all the family's surrealistic plantation. Ellen tells us about her most important female lover after the fact; we learn she's left Ellen for her ex-husband and that her decision is irreversible.

For Ellen, lesbianism is not so much an identity as an activity. It's an activity every bit as important as her genderless childhood love for Hutch, as her hilariously argumentative interactions with her mother, as her grief over her dying sister, Marie, and as her consciousness of the contradictions inherent in growing up southern with a sense of racial ethics. But it's no more important. As such, *The Revolution of Little Girls* may be more revolutionary than those novels whose authors focus only on their protagonists' sexuality. Blanche Boyd has exploded the idea that gay and lesbian writers always write from the margins. She's moved the margins to the center. Her story is universal in the best sense of that word. It raises questions about the integration of the self, about the necessity of balancing irony with pity, and about the problems of finding spiritual answers in a secular world.

CRITICAL RECEPTION

Blanche Boyd has enjoyed an overwhelmingly enthusiastic reception from American critics, who applaud her novels for their eccentric characters, their probing philosophical issues, and their exacting sense of style. Even her earlier work was well reviewed. Martha Saxton says of *Mourning the Death of Magic* that it "is a significant experiment in fiction and, in spite of its title, a magically affecting collage of emotions" (210). And Alice Denham assesses *The Redneck Way of Knowledge* by asserting that "Boyd's articles on violence and politics are superb" (759).

The Revolution of Little Girls has elicited a wider range of critical voices including Ellen Cohen's statement—"Boyd's writing, while honest and original, is also disturbing and may leave many readers feeling unsettled" (104). Other critics (and I would include myself among them) feel that Boyd's greatness emerges from that unsettling sense of tragedy, tempered by her ironic overtones. Carol Anshaw sees the difficulty in the "obsessional exploration of self," which she thinks describes Boyd's autobiographical novels. Anshaw says, "Being one's own main subject is a high wire act, and it's a long way down if you trip on your ego. . . . Boyd's secret to staying aloft is an adroit use of irony—defined by a friend of hers as 'the ability to look at yourself and still get the joke' " (27). In an interview that she conducted with Blanche Boyd (*Mirabella*, 1991), Wendy Gimbel maintains that "Boyd believes painful gender confusion to be a state experienced by all women as they come into their own" (68). Agreeing with that understanding, Boyd adds the following: "Women identify with Ellen in a way I think is surprising. I mean, here's a kid who decides early on there's three categories in the world: men, women and me" (68). Boyd's celebration of Ellen's audacious individuality, her redneck rebelliousness, and her respect for sexual fluidity has resulted in a wise and wicked novel: *The Revolution of Little Girls*.

BIBLIOGRAPHY

Works by Blanche Boyd

Books Published

Nerves. Plainfield, VT: Daughters, Inc., 1973.
Mourning the Death of Magic. Riverside, NJ: Macmillan, 1977.
The Redneck Way of Knowledge. New York: Alfred A. Knopf, 1982; Bergenfield, NJ: Penguin, 1983.
The Revolution of Little Girls. New York: Alfred A. Knopf, 1991; London: Jonathan Cape Ltd., 1992.

Work in Anthologies

"What Is This Thing Called?" *Village Voice Anthology: Twenty-five years of Writing from the Village Voice.* Ed. Geoffrey Stokes. New York: Morrow, 1982. 80–85.
"South Carolina." *The Signet Classic Book of American Short Stories.* Ed. Burton Raffel. New York: New American Library, 1985. 419–22.
"The Black Hand Girl." *Best American Short Stories 1989.* Ed. Margaret Atwood and Shannon Ravenel. Boston: Houghton Mifflin, 1989. 49–59.
"My Town." *The Uncommon Touch: Fiction and Poetry from the Stanford Writing Workshop.* Ed. John L' Heureux. Stanford, CA: Stanford Alumni Association, 1989. 45–54.

Studies of Blanche Boyd

Allison, Dorothy. "Tableau with a Twang: Southern Crossed." *Lambda Book Report* 2, no. 11 (July/August 1991): 27–28.
Anshaw, Carol. *Voice Literary Supplement.* (June 1991): 27.
Cohen, Ellen. Review of *The Revolution of Little Girls. Library Journal* 116, no. 8 (May 1, 1991): 104.
Denham, Alice. "Southern Belles Lettres." *Nation* 234, no. 24 (June 19, 1982): 759–60.
Dorris, Michael. "See Ellen Grow." *New York Times Book Review* (June 30, 1991): 19.
Gimbel, Wendy. "Southern Discomfort." *Mirabella* (May 1991): 68.
Hyde, Sue. "Growing Up in a Most Peculiar Way." *Gay Community News* (August 4–10, 1991): 8, 10.
Saxton, Martha. Review of *Mourning the Death of Magic. Saturday Review* 4 (September 17, 1977): 210.

MAUREEN BRADY (1943–   )
Glynis Carr

BIOGRAPHY

Born June 7, 1943, to a working-class family in Mt. Vernon, New York, Maureen Brady has also lived in Florida, where she graduated from the University of Florida in 1965. Brady worked full-time as a physical therapist until 1974, then returned to New York to write. Supporting herself by working part-time as a physical therapist, she earned an M.A. at New York University in 1977 and began to eke out a writer's living, conducting writing workshops and teaching in colleges such as Hunter and Skidmore. In the "boom years" of the lesbian feminist movement between 1978 and 1982, she co-founded Spinsters Ink, one of the most important of the alternative feminist presses, and enjoyed close ties to the emerging community of lesbian writers. Her career was stalled in the mid-1980s, however, by her need to examine the impact of incest on her life. In the autobiographical essay "Insider/Outsider," Brady explains that during this time she began to perceive the community as "more and more closed as a unit, similar to the incestuous or alcoholic family, where blurring of separate boundaries is a requirement for protecting the system, not its individual people" (56); "being an insider [then became] restrictive" (55), and the focus of her work shifted. She no longer writes "the archetypal lesbian hero" but explores instead the "shadow feelings" not tolerated by the movement (56). Brady has had difficulty publishing this work, which she characterizes as a matter of "breaking ranks and trespassing boundaries" (56). Still, since 1990, she has managed to support herself exclusively by writing and teaching. She now lives in West Hurley, New York, an area adjacent to the artists' colony at Woodstock (of rock-and-roll fame).

MAJOR WORKS AND THEMES

Maureen Brady's primary artistic interest is fiction. Her novels and short stories are not formally innovative (the necessary flaw, perhaps, of an entire generation of writers who either had little interest in modernist aesthetic experimentation or subordinated it in order first to represent "what had never been"). Brady's fiction is carefully constructed in the realist mode. She relies on complex characterization and skillful use of symbolism, imagery, and allusion. Among her major themes is the conflict between women's desires for autonomy and for fusion in intimacy. Many of her characters have just left a relationship or are in the process of leaving, poised at the moment when its "give and take" necessitates either abandonment of the self or the other: her characters consistently choose the self. Brady is also much concerned with the pressure exerted by memory in the construction of lesbian identity. Many of her characters struggle to overcome the crippling legacy of alcoholic parents or childhood sexual abuse. Brady also writes love stories, both "coming out" stories and erotica. Ultimately, she is concerned with the transection of radical politics and personal growth, the way changing the self and changing the world complement, and complicate, each other.

Brady's first novel, *Give Me Your Good Ear*, is the first-person narrative of Francie Kelly, a woman breaking free from a stifling heterosexual marriage, experiencing her first inklings of desire for other women, and, most importantly, evaluating and reconstituting, on terms more fully her own, her troubled relationship with her mother. Francie struggles to "lift the fog that descended after [her father's] death" when she was eight years old. Obsessed with the past, Francie yet resists examining it, insisting that "it never works to try to put your relationships in reverse and travel back to 'a time when . . . ' " (13). The writing alternates between Francie's memories (in a child's voice) and her description of painful present events. Readers discover that Francie witnessed her mother stab and kill her father during the last of their chronic alcoholic fights; yet for many years, the two never discuss what really happened or what it means. Francie embodies the proverb that "you're only as sick as your secrets"; as she constructs an honest account of her life and clarifies her feminist philosophy, she eventually learns that even sorrow can have "a sweet taste" (134).

Brady is at her best describing the conditions, limits, and possibilities of mother-daughter bonds. *Give Me Your Good Ear* is dominated by Francie's self-image as the last player in a frantic game of crack the whip. Francie urgently needs to break the chain linking her grandmother, mother, and herself, yet in doing so, she preserves something of value and creates new rules of relationship: "the daughter who breaks the chain becomes the mother" (91). Also Brady's wry humor gently prods the emerging feminist culture, as when Francie compares women's construction of "truth" in consciousness-raising groups to the Catholic ritual of confession, finding that in both situations the "venial sins" are omitted.

Brady's second novel, *Folly*, is a complex book with a wide scope. Its central concern is to describe the creation of an activist women's community and to interrogate certain problems of coalition politics: what defines a community, what are the bases of alliance, how power will be distributed, and who speaks for whom. The narrative perspective is necessarily shared by several major characters but focalized primarily through Folly and Lenore, two white women battling racism, poverty, and homophobia. Crisscrossing their stories are three complex mother-daughter stories, two coming-out stories, two coming-of-age stories, and, of course, the overarching plot that concerns the women's efforts to unionize the factory. What unifies the novel is Folly and Lenore's realization that their vision of themselves, and of the world, has been profoundly conditioned by their white identity. Images of blindness and visual perspective describe the workings of racism. Brady's characters learn not only to see each other in new, liberating ways, but to act on that vision.

Compared to analogous but black-authored novels such as Alice Walker's *Meridian* or Sherley Ann Williams's *Dessa Rose, Folly* is hopeful, even euphoric: its interracial friendships are personally and politically transformative and strong enough to form the basis of long-term alliance. Thus Brady's plot reflects the white feminist imperative to forge female solidarity across lines of difference (an imperative not necessarily endorsed by black feminists). *Folly* is both bold (in its unflinching focus on white women's racism as a liability to radical politics) and timid (in its representation of black subjectivity), but by any standard, it is a major achievement. It significantly challenges and revises the literary tradition to which it belongs.

Brady's short stories, collected in *The Question She Put to Herself*, were first published in feminist journals such as *Conditions, Sinister Wisdom*, and *Feminary* and have often been anthologized. Rightly so: they are lesbian classics. The title piece, for example, is a marvelous, witty coming-out story, and "Chiggers" is a stomach-clenching tale of child molestation and its consequences. "Early Autumn Exchange" is a brilliant, compact mother-daughter story in which Brady combs out a tangle of similarity and difference between two women. Its center is the daughter's need that her mother recognize her autonomy, a need strangely undermined by her own inability to see her mother on the same terms. "Strike It Rich" concerns a girl's first awareness of class, while "On the Way to the ERA" is a political fable questioning the various merits of revolution and reform. "Corsage" pictures an adolescent girl whose home life is punctuated by verbal jabs and cuts from her mother; "Wilderness Journal" explores the same dynamic reproduced by two adult women lovers. "The Field is Full of Daisies" is the shuddery, horrific story of an auto accident, but in "Seneca Morning," a woman renews herself as she protests the deployment of nuclear weapons. "Care in the Holding" is simple erotica, and finally, "Novena" sketches the relationship between an unusual aunt and her niece.

In addition to fiction, Brady has also written essays, book reviews, and two dramas. Her prize-winning first play, "I Know A Hundred Ways to Die," was published in *Sinister Wisdom* in 1980 and produced in 1982. It concerns the question of hope and the restorative power of yearning as a young physical therapist works with her patient, Min, a rebellious seventy-eight-year-old lesbian who is ill and unsure of what to live for. As in *Folly*, Brady writes here with remarkable perception about old women: the dialogue between Min and Henrietta, her lover of at least two decades, is subtle, authentic, and moving. Brady's other play, "The True Story of the Elephant in the Living Room," has been produced twice, but is yet unpublished. Structured as a long soliloquy, it unfolds the consciousness of Marty, a forty-year-old "adult child" of an alcoholic father. The other characters are Marty as a seven- and eleven-year-old and "Daddy." Spectators witness Marty's internal drama as she reaches beyond her stifling childhood, shedding in the process a coat of negativity.

As part of her own recovery from incest, Brady wrote *Daybreak*, a Hazeldon meditation book typical of the genre. Readers concerned with the conservative, isolationist tendency of the recovery movement will be interested in Brady's discussion of the relationships between child abuse, creativity, power, and politics in "Insider/Outsider." Brady is now under contract with Hazeldon/Harper to produce a workbook, *Beyond Survival*, that uses writing as a tool for self-healing.

Also in progress is a new novel, *Rocking Bone Hollow*, an excerpt from which has been published in Tee Corinne's *Riding Desire*. Although it is impossible to discern the design of the whole from the anthologized episode, many elements typical of Brady's other work are present here: a lesbian in the process of leaving her lover, an internal struggle to clarify and meet one's own needs, and a quest for sustaining sexual values.

CRITICAL RECEPTION

Although Brady's work has been well received among feminists, she suffers like other lesbian authors from severe critical neglect. Brady has received a number of grants, residencies, and awards for her work (such as first prize from the Lesbian Community Theatre in 1980 for "I Know a Hundred Ways to Die"), and her fiction has been extensively and favorably reviewed in the alternative press. Reviewers, however, like Jacqueline St. Joan in her afterword to *Give Me Your Good Ear*, have focused almost exclusively on the sociopolitical contexts and themes of Brady's work, ignoring its formal qualities. Bonnie Zimmerman's *Safe Sea of Women* is currently the only treatment of Brady to emerge from the mainstream academic press. In this full-length study, Zimmerman reads contemporary lesbian fiction as the collective voice of the lesbian community. Although her method does not permit substantial readings of any one novel, she does discuss *Folly* and *The Question She Put to Herself* as they have shaped the tradition's major themes.

BIBLIOGRAPHY

Works by Maureen Brady

Give Me Your Good Ear. Argyle, NY: Spinsters Ink, 1979.
"I Know a Hundred Ways to Die." *Sinister Wisdom* 12 (1980): 67–78.
Folly. Trumansburg, NY: Crossing Press, 1982.

The Question She Put to Herself: Stories by Maureen Brady. Freedom, CA: Crossing Press, 1987.

"Insider/Outsider Coming of Age." *Lesbian Texts and Contexts: Radical Revisions*. Ed. Karla Jay and Joanne Glasgow. New York: New York University Press, 1990. 49–58.

Daybreak: Meditations for Women Survivors of Sexual Abuse. New York: Hazeldon/Harper, 1991.

Excerpt from *Rocking Bone Hollow*. *Riding Desire: an Anthology of Erotic Writing*. Ed. Tee Corinne. Austin, TX: Banned Books, 1991. 61–72.

Beyond Survival. New York: Hazeldon/Harper, 1992.

"The True Story of the Elephant in the Living Room." Unpublished play.

Studies of Maureen Brady

St. Joan, Jacqueline. Afterword. *Give Me Your Good Ear*. By Maureen Brady. Argyle, NY: Spinsters Ink, 1979. 135–41.

Weschsler, N. "*Folly*'s Author Talks About Race, Sex, and Class." *Gay Community News* 10.39 (April 23, 1983): 8.

Zimmerman, Bonnie. *The Safe Sea of Women: Lesbian Fiction, 1969–1989*. Boston: Beacon Press, 1990.

BETH BRANT (1941–   )
Dorothy Allison

BIOGRAPHY

A Mohawk of the Bay of Quinte, from Tyendinaga Mohawk Territory, Ontario, Canada, Beth Brant did not begin to write until 1981. Many of the details of her family and early life are reflected in stories in *Mohawk Trail*, her first collection of short fiction. Her grandparents had moved to Detroit from Canada hoping for better opportunities for their children. In Detroit, all of the children married white, and Beth speaks about being teased as a ''half-breed'' but there is no sense of alienation in her writing or identity. She has always been a woman of the turtle clan.

Beth dropped out of high school, married at seventeen, and had three daughters—Kim, Jenny, and Jill. She did not begin her career as a lesbian writer until the age of forty when she had an encounter with a bald eagle who instructed her to begin. She sent her first stories, ''Mohawk Trail'' and ''Native Origin,'' to *Sinister Wisdom*, the lesbian feminist journal that was then being edited by Michelle Cliff and Adrienne Rich. With their encouragement, she went on to edit *A Gathering of Spirit: A Collection of North American Indian Women*, first published in 1984 as a special issue of *Sinister Wisdom* and reprinted in 1988 by Firebrand Books, Ithaca, New York, and the Women's Press, Toronto, Canada. In 1985, she published her first book of stories, *Mohawk Trail*, simultaneously with Firebrand Books in Ithaca and the Women's Press in Toronto. She made the same arrangement for her second collection, *Food and Spirits*, which was published in 1991.

Now the grandmother of three boys, Beth lives in Melvindale, Michigan, with her lover, Denise Dorsz. She is working on a collection of essays to be called *Testimony from the Faithful*, about the legacies her father left, which for her includes a love of the natural world.

MAJOR WORKS AND THEMES

Beth tells about beginning to write only after an encounter with Eagle as she and her lover were driving through Seneca land.

He swooped in front of our car. . . . I got out and faced him as he sat in a tree, his wings folded so gracefully, his magnificent head gleaming in the October afternoon sun. We looked into each other's eyes. Perhaps we were ten feet away from one another and I was marked by him. I remember that I felt in another place, maybe even another time. He stared at me for minutes, perhaps hours, maybe a thousand years. I knew I had received a message to write. ("To Be or Not To Be Was Never the Question" 17)

The spiritual motivation is vital to understanding the work of Beth Brant. She writes as a member of her community, as an Indian, a lesbian, a mother, a working-class woman—a woman who feels no divided sense of self but an intimate link both with all her communities and with the tradition of tribal women behind her. When she tells us that Eagle brought her the gift of writing, she is being completely honest and forthright, as honest and forthright as her stories. She is clear too that the gift Eagle brought is also a responsibility, that the stories she tells are not personal but tribal while her insistence on being seen as both Indian and lesbian is an equal responsibility. "Homophobia is the eldest son of racism," she noted in "To Be or Not To Be Was Never The Question," her autobiographical essay in Betsy Warland's *Inversions*, "and one does not exist without the other" (18). In the same essay she also tells us, "I write because to not write is a breach of faith" (18).

Beth Brant's two books *Mohawk Trail* (1990) and *Food and Spirits* (1991) showcase short stories that are intensely personal and reflect her strong sense of tribal identity. Much of her work also reflects her experience as a half-breed woman raised in a working-class community in Detroit, and she has a particular talent for letting her characters present their daily lives in language both powerfully lyrical and startlingly blunt. Waitresses who keep their own council, old men with gentle hands, tiny girls chewing frybread after losing their mothers, women who have lost their children but not their hope, women on the verge of losing hope and holding on moment by moment to the decision not to drink— Beth Brant's gift is to make us not only see these people but feel them, their grief and determination, their confusion and hard-won moments of joy.

CRITICAL RECEPTION

A Gathering of Spirit attracted high praise in both its editions. It was a pivotal collection for both showcasing the work of Indian women and calling attention to how little opportunity they have had for publishing their work. Beth's story collections have not attracted the same degree of critical attention. The one scholarly examination—Cora Hoover's master's thesis at Yale University—focuses on *A Gathering of Spirit*. There have been only a few reviews of each collection in the feminist and lesbian press and little attention from mainstream reviews. Brant has pointed out the inadequacy of critical response to her work in her essay in Betsy Warland's anthology, *Inversions*. Since Brant is the author of some of the finest short stories currently available from the feminist and alternative presses, this neglect is hard to explain and may in fact reflect both the overwhelming racism in review journals and the apparent inability to deal with someone who gives equal emphasis to her identities as both a lesbian and an Indian. Most of her reviews have been done by other writers and poets noted for the quality of their own work. Gloria Anzaldúa praised her work in *Conditions* 10, and Joy Harjo did the same in *Sojourner* in January 1987. But while reviews and interviews have been sparse, Beth Brant's talent and insight have been widely recognized. She is extremely popular as a lecturer and speaker at lesbian, feminist, university, and Indian events. At scholarly conferences and community gatherings, Beth Brant is known for speaking both effectively and inspirationally, and her stories and books continue to be popular in both the United States and Canada.

HONORS AND AWARDS

In 1984, Beth Brant received her first recognition for excellence from the Michigan Council for the Arts, which awarded her another grant in 1986. In 1989, the Ontario Arts Council awarded her a grant, and in 1991, she received a literary fellowship from the National Endowment for the Arts. In 1992, she was a judge for the Astraea Foundation's National Lesbian Writer Award series.

BIBLIOGRAPHY

Works by Beth Brant

"A Long Story." *Sinister Wisdom*: Special Edition—A Gathering of Spirit 22/23 (1983): 90–96. Reissued as *A Gathering of Spirit: A Collection of North American Indian Women*. Ithaca, NY: Firebrand Books, 1988.
"Introduction." *Sinister Wisdom*: Special Edition—A Gathering of Spirit 22/23 (1983): 5–9. Reissued as *A Gathering of Spirit: A Collection of North American Indian Women*. Ithaca, NY: Firebrand Books, 1988.
Mohawk Trail. Toronto; Women's Press, 1985; Ithaca, NY: Firebrand Books, 1990.
"Her Name Is Helen." *An Intimate Wilderness: Lesbian Writers on Sexuality*. Ed. Judith Barrington. Portland, OR; Eighth Mountain Press, 1991. 74–77.
"To Be or Not To Be Was Never The Question." *Inversions*. Ed. Betsy Warland. Toronto: Press Gang, 1991. 17–23.

Studies of Beth Brant

Allison, Dorothy. Review of *A Gathering of Spirit*. *New York Native* (January 1984).
Anzaldúa, Gloria. Review of *A Gathering of Spirit*. *Conditions* 10 (1984): 145–53.

Charmley, Kerrie. Interview. "Beth Brant: Telling the Truth for Each Other." *Kinesis* (September 1989).

Daligga, Catherine. Review of *A Gathering of Spirit*. *Gay Community News* (December 1982): 56.

Harjo, Joy. Review of *Mohawk Trail*. *Sojourner* (January 1987).

Hoover, Cora. "The Making of *A Gathering of Spirit*." Master's thesis, Yale University, April 1991.

OLGA BROUMAS (1949–   )
Kate Carter

BIOGRAPHY

Olga Broumas was born in Syros, Greece, in 1949. While in Greece, at the age of seventeen, she published her first collection of poetry. A year later she came to the United States on a Fulbright Scholarship to study architecture at the University of Pennsylvania. She graduated from the University of Pennsylvania in 1969 and chose to pursue graduate study at the University of Oregon. It was there that she had her introduction to a formal writing program. She received her M.F.A. in creative writing from the University of Oregon and stayed on to teach in and to eventually coordinate the emerging Women's Studies Program. It was during this time that her book, *Beginning With O*, was chosen to receive the Yale Younger Poets Award. Broumas then received a grant from the Oregon Arts Commission to begin work on what was to become her second volume of poetry.

From here, Broumas began a long and committed career of teaching writing. She taught in the writing programs of the University of Idaho and Goddard College before receiving a Guggenheim Travel Award. She spent a year abroad in Europe and her native Greece, to which she returned for the first time since coming to the United States in 1969. During this time, she completed work on the collaborative volume *Black Holes, Black Stockings* with poet Jane Miller.

On returning, Broumas accepted a residency with the Women Writers Center, then located in Cazenovia, New York. During her time at Goddard, she had been exploring the integration of movement and body awareness with her teaching methodology. The less traditional structure provided by the Women Writers Center allowed Broumas to teach through an experiential process in which writers were encouraged to integrate bodily and intellectual presence into their creative work. After Broumas's year in residence, the Women Writers Center restructured and moved to Provincetown, Massachusetts, in 1982, becoming FREEHAND.

For the next five years at FREEHAND, Broumas expanded and refined her body-centered approach to teaching writing. After FREEHAND disbanded in 1987, Broumas continued her teaching in the creative writing program at Boston University. She currently holds a professorship at Brandeis University in Waltham, Massachusetts. Broumas has received many grants, awards, and fellowships over the course of her career. She is widely respected as an artist and as a teacher and continues to be fed by the pleasures of both.

MAJOR WORKS AND THEMES

Any discussion of Broumas's work must begin with stating the obvious: Olga Broumas was born and lived in Greece for eighteen years, and Greek is her native language. English is, therefore, a chosen language. Yet she has established and maintained the distinction of being one of America's foremost contemporary poets with her writing in English. Many people, when discussing Broumas's poetry, note her birthplace and move on. This is possible only because Broumas has such an incredible grasp of the English language and American idiom that she can use both with a facility that is apparent and natural. But beyond this, there needs to be a preliminary understanding of the differences between Broumas's native language and her chosen language.

The Greek language is limited to a comparatively small pool of speakers in the world. It is also a very old language. These two factors combine to produce a language that is very charged with layers of meaning, nuance, and subtlety. English is a much younger language with a vast pool of speakers and is not charged, and may never be charged, to a comparable degree. Broumas is writing out of the tradition of her native language and within boundaries of her chosen language. This establishes her use of language as the foundational theme in her work, adding an appropriate layer to the general discussion of how poetry itself charges the language from which it speaks.

Broumas's first full collection in English, *Beginning With O*, was chosen by the poet Stanley Kunitz to be the recipient of the Yale Younger Poets Award in 1977. In his foreword to that book, Kunitz remarks:

One is impressed by the poet's capacity to transmute complex information into the urgent stuff of poetry. It is not the kind of information that one has been led to expect in verse. . . . "How new!" one is quick to exclaim. But another thought supervenes, "How ancient is that lore." (xii)

The challenge from Broumas in this book is presented in her emphasis on the use of a cultural idiom, which can be understood in terms of the similarities to her native language. The women's community of the time was thrust into the process of creating a language that would embrace and incorporate the disparate traditions of its members. Its pool of speakers was small and self-selected and its language transformed rapidly, becoming more and more highly charged with nuance and meaning. *Beginning With O* opens with Broumas in a circular embrace of her native culture and her women's culture. The first poems, in a section entitled "The Twelve Aspects of God," present a pantheon of Greek goddesses who in turn take the reader by the hand to appeal, cajole, seduce, scream that yes, in fact, we as women are the goddess, the ancient goddess. And we're not always pretty. And there's no need to be. The female reader is challenged to take responsibility for her inherent power. What follows in the book is an account of a poet speaking in a language both very new and very familiar. It is from here that Broumas charts the territory that is to be her poetic home.

Soie Sauvage is the title of Broumas's second volume. This is a quiet book, one guided by solitude and introspection. Its tone is not that of a patient mother speaking to a child, but of a child's body of knowledge, of a child speaking from herself. The language is direct and exacting. The poet leaves little room here for misunderstanding. What is being spoken arises directly out of a need to voice understanding without compelling or forcing the understanding of her reader. The poems in *Soie Sauvage* bring an emotional depth to the previous body of Broumas's work. And it is in this volume that it becomes clear that the sensuality of the physical body found in *Beginning With O* has a concomitant emotional body whose sensations are as deeply desired and as deeply felt.

Pastoral Jazz can be seen as a continuation of *Soie Sauvage* in that the poems share a directness of language. But the poems in *Pastoral Jazz* speak in a language that has been fully transposed and embodied by felt emotion. The reader is challenged to make this jump with the poet with the understanding that there is no hand-holding. The success of this leap depends on the reader's desire to move with Broumas to a key in which the song can be sung simultaneously in language native to both. The poems here trust the resilience of the chosen language to buoy the poet through raw emotional landscapes of recognition and passage. It is a book in which Broumas confronts the wellspring of her passions in a language that cannot contain the charge of that in which those passions were first embraced. The language here metamorphoses into a vessel appropriate for such epiphanies.

Pastoral Jazz also holds a recognition of the vitality Broumas finds in the work of the Greek poet Odysseas Elytis, whose work she would later translate. In the poem "Mosaic" (whose form is based on a poem by Elytis), the duality of language and culture is suspended, and we are challenged to embrace the reverence and humanity that mark the channels of this volume.

Black Holes, Black Stockings, fuses Broumas's surety of emotion with Miller's ability to draw us into the language to the point of its implosion. What we find on the other side are Broumas and Miller together at their best. These poems remind us that relationship, in whatever manifest, requires the fullness of our being. When this presence is brought to the volume by the reader, the preliminary impediments to engaging with the book fall away. We no longer care about the mechanics of how they wrote the book, or why, or even who they were to each other to be doing such a thing. Instead, we find ourselves welcome to share the process of two women creating, two women creating together, two women honoring the force that allows them to be, two women, creating.

Prior to publishing *Perpetua*, her most recent volume, Broumas had completed her two translations of works by Odysseas Elytis. The process of translation is one to which Broumas has been intimately connected in the creation of her own work. She brought to her translations of Elytis's *What I Love* and *The Little Mariner* her ability to synthesize the deep contexts of her native language with the fabric of our spoken lives. The impact of these translations on Broumas's work cannot be understated. In their richness, the poems in *Perpetua* celebrate this miracle of integration, the fullness of being.

Perpetua presents a marked shift in Broumas's work. It would be easy to view this shift strictly as a stylistic change. It would be easy to explain it as a sort of poetic maturation. But what is consistently seen in *Perpetua* is that the poet is writing from a place of integration. There has been a transformation in the poet and in her work. The intensity of this transformation is evident as we realize that Broumas's writing emerges from a conscious effort to find the balance of comfort in relationship. When she speaks of her relationship to her body and to the bodies of others, we feel that comfort. When she speaks of her relationship to her father, to his death, we feel that comfort. And when she speaks of her relationship to herself, we feel that comfort. She has found more than peace between the divergent thrusts of her linguistic traditions and her cultural traditions. She has created a work whose integrity reflects the poet's journey into and through the process of accepting the entirety of the self.

There has been much mention made of Broumas's eroticism and her direct confrontation of the sensual body. This commentary, although valid, serves to direct and limit the reader's attention instead of encouraging a view broad enough to encompass all that Broumas's work has to offer. There is a subtlety, a complexity, to her work and her expression of eros, layered throughout, that is much more a means than an end. Broumas is indisputably a lesbian poet. Lesbians have been defined by society strictly on the basis of sexuality and are relegated to a place within (or without) society by virtue of that definition. It will be up to lesbian readers to provide a criticism that goes beyond the cultural definition of what is lesbian. It will be up to lesbian readers to address the nature of what is lesbian and to celebrate the tradition of the lesbian poet.

CRITICAL RECEPTION

There has been little scholarly criticism of Broumas's work as a whole. Although the reviews of *Beginning With O* were generally positive in terms of her craft, the lesbian content of her work was often the aspect singled out for censure. In discussing *Beginning With O*, Thomas Stumpf in the *Chicago Review* notes, "These poems insist on celebrating 'a woman/who loves a woman' . . . perhaps in time Broumas will come to care about something else" (472). The mainstream acceptance of feminist literary criticism as a valid critical modality has done much to prohibit such overt homophobia and heterosexism as cited above. But the fact that creative works by lesbian writers are typically viewed as genre writing indicates an unwillingness on the part of academic and literary critics to measure this work against traditional literary standards, thereby identifying it as substandard. Broumas's enduring and highly awarded literary career has established her a place in the forefront of contemporary American poetry. One wouldn't know it based on the extent of the criticism of her work. Until we afford the lesbian writer equal representation in critical thought and analysis, we hinder the evolution of the literary tradition in our country and become progenitors of its stagnation.

BIBLIOGRAPHY

Works by Olga Broumas

Poetry

Caritas. Eugene, OR: Self-published, 1976.
Beginning With O. New Haven: Yale University Press, 1977.
Soie Sauvage. Port Townsend, WA: Copper Canyon Press, 1979.
Pastoral Jazz. Port Townsend, WA: Copper Canyon Press, 1983.
Black Holes, Black Stockings (with Jane Miller). Middletown, CT: Wesleyan University Press, 1985.
Perpetua. Port Townsend, WA: Copper Canyon Press, 1989.

Translations

Elytis, Odysseas. *What I Love: Selected Poems of Odysseas Elytis*. Port Townsend, WA: Copper Canyon Press, 1986.
Elytis, Odysseas. *The Little Mariner*. Port Townsend, WA: Copper Canyon Press, 1988.

Studies of Olga Broumas

Reviews

Kunitz, Stanley. Foreword. *Beginning With O*. By Olga Broumas. New Haven, CT: Yale University Press, 1977. iv-xii.
McNaron, Toni. "The Importance of *Beginning With O*: A Reflection on Olga Broumas." *Sinister Wisdom* 1 (Winter 1979): 77–85.
Stumpf, Thomas A. "Three Prizewinners." *Chicago Review* 30 (1978): 472.

RITA MAE BROWN (1944–   )
Sharon D. Boyle

BIOGRAPHY

Novelist, poet, essayist, and social activist, Rita Mae Brown was born on November 28, 1944, in Hanover, Pennsylvania, a town approximately nine miles from the Maryland state border. Her biological parents unmarried, Brown was adopted while still an infant by Ralph and Julia Ellen Brown. Brown spent the first eleven years of her life in Hanover and then, in 1955, the family moved south to Fort Lauderdale, Florida. Brown attended Fort Lauderdale High School and excelled both academically and athletically.

After graduating from Fort Lauderdale High, Brown was awarded a scholarship to attend the University of Florida in Gainesville, where she was expelled because of her involvement in civil rights activism.

From Florida, Brown hitchhiked her way to New York City, where she supported herself for a time as a waitress. Awarded a scholarship to attend New York University (NYU), she studied English and classics and earned the bachelor of arts degree in 1968.

While at NYU, Brown helped to found the Student Homophile League. She gradually became disillusioned with the sexist attitudes of male members of the group, however, and focused her attention on the women's liberation movement. With activist Jane Arnold, Brown was instrumental in opening a women's center in the city; she was also one of the early members of NOW (National Organization for Women) and became the national administrative coordinator and editor of NOW's New York newsletter. She found herself increasingly at odds with NOW's policy of not addressing lesbian issues within the organization. NOW did not want to alienate members of moderate political conviction or politicians who might be convinced to support the group's causes.

Brown resigned her post at NOW in 1970 and settled in Washington, D.C.

She lectured in sociology for a year at Federal City College, and from 1971 to 1973, she worked as a research fellow at the Institute for Policy Studies, where she would later take the Ph.D. in political science. Her political essays were collected and published in 1976 by Diana Press as *A Plain Brown Rapper*. During her tenure at the Institute for Policy Studies, New York University Press published a collection of Brown's poetry entitled *The Hand That Cradles the Rock*.

Brown was urged to try her hand at the type of creative writing she had always wanted to produce; the result was *Rubyfruit Jungle*, first published in 1973 by Daughters, Inc. It is the story of Molly Bolt, a fiercely independent tomboy who, like Brown, is born illegitimate, grows up poor in rural Pennsylvania and is relocated to Florida. She eventually travels to New York and aspires to a career in filmmaking. After its 1977 reissue by Bantam, *Rubyfruit Jungle* climbed to the top of the best-seller list, and more than a million paperback copies were sold.

Brown's next work was not as successful as its predecessor. *In Her Day*, published in 1976, was a critical and commercial failure. Brown rebounded with *Six of One*, a novel chronicling the lives of Runnymeade, Pennsylvania's inhabitants.

In 1982 Harper published *Southern Discomfort*, Brown's fourth novel. Set in Montgomery, Alabama, the story examines the limiting effects of culturally imposed racial, economic, and gender constraints.

Brown's 1983 novel, *Sudden Death*, dealt more directly with lesbian relationships than either *Six of One* or *Southern Discomfort*. The novel examines the tenuous foundations on which relationships can be built, and the devastating effects outside pressures can have on those relationships.

In 1986 Brown gave her reading audience *High Hearts*, a novel that again takes to task cultural definitions of "masculine" and "feminine." The research on the Civil War that Brown compiled and incorporated into *High Hearts* lends the story an authenticity unequalled in her previous novels.

In 1988 Brown published two other works: *Starting from Scratch: A Different Kind of Writer's Manual* and *Bingo*, a novel that takes the reader back to Runnymeade, the small town straddling the Mason-Dixon line. Brown utilizes Runnymeade's geographical location not only to examine divisions between males and females but also to examine the extent to which these divisions are based on perceptions reinforced by culture, and vice versa.

Brown's 1990 work, *Wish You Were Here*, is a novel marking her debut as a mystery writer. She places a female protagonist in the private detective arena, a field typically dominated by men. Protagonist Mary Minor Haristeen gets help from her Welsh Corgi, Tucker, and her cat, Mrs. Murphy, who lend their expertise in helping her solve a multiple-murder mystery.

Rita Mae Brown currently lives and writes in Charlottesville, Virginia. She has been a member of the Emmy jury, has served on several panels for the National Endowment for the Arts, and makes regular rounds of the lecture circuit.

MAJOR WORKS AND THEMES

Rita Mae Brown has long refused to be categorized as a "lesbian" writer. In a 1978 interview in *Publishers Weekly*, she told Patricia Holt that she was "a writer, a woman, and Southern. And that's that." In spite of her refusal to be labeled, no one who has read Brown's works could deny their unifying theme: the struggle on the part of an individual to live as freely and fully as possible in the face of social/cultural restraints and expectations. Brown does not limit this struggle to lesbian characters but creates a diverse cast of individuals on which to place the burden of venturing toward self-fulfillment.

In *Rubyfruit Jungle*, the most autobiographical of Brown's works, the protagonist is lesbian, and the barriers she encounters are familiar to many lesbians. It is the first-person narrative of the coming-of-age of Molly Bolt: smart-aleck, tomboy, survivor. Discovering at seven years of age that she is adopted, Molly begins her journey to find out "who she is" and how she fits into the world around her. The first obstacle Molly encounters on this journey is her mother's view of what femininity means and what it means to be female. Carrie Bolt imprisons Molly in the house in order to teach her the fine arts of womanhood: canning, cleaning, and cooking.

In arguing with her mother about having to learn "woman's work," Molly learns that she is the biological daughter of a woman who, according to Carrie, would "lay with a dog if it shook its ass right." In a fit of rage, Carrie beats Molly, who escapes to the wheatfield behind the house. In fleeing from her mother, Molly also flees from what Carrie represents: a typical female life of cooking, cleaning house, and nursing children and a husband. In rejecting what her culture expects of her, Molly takes the important first steps in her journey toward self-discovery.

One of the taboos Molly breaks in her journey is acknowledging sex and her own potential for sexuality. The catalyst for her imprisonment in the kitchen was the formation of a partnership with Brockhurst Detwiler, a classmate. Discovering that Brockhurst is uncircumcised, Molly convinces him to show himself to other members of the class for a nickel. Carrie's discovery of Molly's enterprise convinces her that it is time Molly was molded into a proper woman: one who is safety stashed in a kitchen, far away from the world and all of its temptations, especially sex. Molly's escape from Carrie is the first indication the reader has that she is not willing to fit a mold designed by others.

Molly further undermines cultural expectations for women when she falls in love in the sixth grade with her best friend, Leota B. Bisland. The two go into the woods each day after school to practice kissing. When Molly's cousin Leroy discovers the girls, Molly invites him to join them. Leota makes Molly privy to her greater knowledge of sex after she invites Molly to spend the night at her house, where the friendship develops a sexual component.

Molly also learns of loss as a result of her relationship with Leota. While the two girls write to each other for a while after Molly's family moves to Florida, eventually the letters end and they do not see each other for ten years.

Later, as a student at Fort Lauderdale High School, Molly continues to explore her sexuality within the context of her relationship with Carolyn Simpson, the beautiful head cheerleader. With the disclosure of the sexual nature of their relationship to Molly's best friend Connie Pen comes Molly's first experiences with prejudice and homophobia. She realizes that she is expected to behave in certain culturally sanctioned ways: grow up, get married, and bear children. She learns that as a woman, she is to define herself within the boundaries of a monogamous, heterosexual relationship; if she chooses not to obey those regulations, she must be prepared to pay the consequences.

Molly does indeed pay the price for non-compliance with cultural regulations. While she is a college freshman, her academic scholarship and sorority membership are revoked because of her sexual relationship with her roommate, Faye Raider.

Upon her release from the university hospital's psychiatric ward, Molly discovers that Faye's parents have taken their daughter home; the two never see each other again. Carrie further contributes to Molly's isolation when she refuses to let her daughter explain her side of the story. In ousting Molly from the house, Carrie provides the impetus for Molly's journey to New York City.

Once in the city, Molly meets other members of the gay community: Calvin, who shows Molly how to survive on the streets, and Holly, who attempts to convince Molly to allow herself to be "kept." In addition to prejudice based on sexual orientation, Molly is exposed to racial, gender, and class conflicts. As she faces each incident of ignorance and prejudice, she learns that the individual is sacrificed for the good of the group. Through Molly's experiences and her refusal to function as one of the herd, she offers readers an opportunity to break through limiting dictates and stereotypes that imprison each of us.

Like *Rubyfruit Jungle,* Brown's second novel, *In Her Day*, takes a critical look at boundaries and expectations placed on an individual's race, class, and gender. *In Her Day*, however, pits two protagonists and their personal and political ideologies against each other within the context of the nascent women's movement of the early 1970s.

Carole Hanratty is a forty-one-year-old professor of art history at New York University. During a night out with friends Adele and LaVerne, she meets Ilse James, waitress, activist, and undergraduate student at Vassar, Carole's own alma mater.

The two women are immediately drawn to each other and become lovers. Oddly enough, it is not pressure outside the relationship that eventually tears Ilse and Carole apart. Rather, it is Ilse's inability to compromise in her dogmatic approach to women's liberation that causes tension between the two women. She attempts to indoctrinate Carole into her particular type of firebrand feminism, something for which Carole feels no affinity. Ilse begins to question the depth of her feelings for Carole, noting to herself that Carole seems philosophically opposite her in terms of how she views the world.

In turn, Carole has difficulty finding something for herself in the sociopolitical rhetoric espoused by the women with whom Ilse associates. She does not understand how all problems can be categorized as a result of "male supremacy or capitalism or racism." As a product of the Depression-era slums of Virginia, Carole is further alienated from the more affluent group of activists because of their "downwardly mobile" approach to appearance and hygiene; she cannot comprehend why people would choose to live in poverty if they have other options.

The tensions build in the relationship and reach a climax when Ilse refuses to believe that Carole grew up poor. To Ilse, Carole's education and her material possessions preclude a childhood spent in destitution. It is here that boundaries in the form of stereotypes are most visible in the book. For Ilse, appearances indicate what lies beneath. Carole points out to Ilse that she and the group live by stereotyping people, by refusing to acknowledge that each person is an individual and possesses the ability to change and to transcend social and economic restrictions. She further asserts that through stereotyping, Ilse's political movement is no better than the system it purports to correct. She introduces the idea of a group mentality versus the individual's right to think and behave as she sees fit. Ilse responds by saying that individuality has been responsible for keeping women separate from each other. She does not believe in "doing one's own thing," and insists that if they remain individuals, women stand no chance for equality; they must join each other and think, act, and move as a cohesive group. These conflicting ideologies between Ilse and Carole are what finally lead to the demise of their relationship; neither woman is ready to compromise what she believes in to save the union.

Although Carole and Ilse are lovers, their relationship seems to take a back seat to the social and political upheavals taking place around them. Unlike *Rubyfruit Jungle*, in which the protagonist experiences blatant discrimination based on her sexual orientation, *In Her Day* assumes that readers will already be familiar with the problems lesbians face in coming out to family, friends, and colleagues and examines a lesbian relationship from a political and social rather than an emotional angle.

Six of One, Brown's third novel, primarily examines relationships in a social rather than a sexual context. The love relationship between Celeste and Ramelle is secondary. While readers may be able to appreciate seeing a lesbian relationship flourish without its partners having to face discrimination, hardship, or even gossip, the lack of conflict detracts from the realism of the novel. While the actions and dialogue of the characters are humorous and often thought-provoking, the absence of a clear lesbian theme might render *Six of One* a disappointment to some readers.

The emotional content of *Sudden Death*, Brown's fifth novel, is more than sufficient to make up for what the other novels may lack. In *Sudden Death*,

Brown again explores the theme of maintaining one's individuality within the framework of a lesbian relationship; the setting is the highly competitive world of the women's professional tennis circuit.

The protagonists in this story are Carmen Semana, a world-class tennis player, and Harriet Rawls, a professor of religion at a small private college. Harriet has left her job in order to travel with Carmen, whose dream is to win the Grand Slam. Between Carmen and her dream is Susan Reilly, Carmen's first lover and a woman determined either to win the Slam herself or to make it impossible for anyone else to win it. Susan is greedy, manipulative, and competitive to the point of viciousness. She vows that no matter what it takes, she will stop Carmen from winning the Grand Slam.

Susan's "it" takes the form of her fabricating a story about Carmen and Harriet's impending marriage, and passing the "information" on to Martin Kuzirian, a sportswriter whose scruples are as few as Susan's. Susan advises Kuzirian to confront Harriet and not Carmen about the wedding, because "Harriet couldn't tell a lie if her life depended on it."

The subtheme of remaining true to oneself in any situation is one that appears in all of Brown's novels, including those using lesbian characters or themes. In *Rubyfruit Jungle*, for example, Molly refuses to lie about the nature of her relationship with Faye; Celeste and Ramelle and Carole and Ilse are not ashamed of their sexuality, and Carole's argument with her supervisor embodies her refusal to be crushed by cultural standards of what is normal and acceptable. And while not as forthright perhaps as Molly, Ramelle in *Six of One* does not deny her love for Celeste, including the physical nature of that love, to Curtis, Celeste's brother, who loves Ramelle and proposes marriage. Ramelle could easily accept Curtis's proposal, and the social sanction it offers, but chooses instead to maintain her identity as Celeste's partner.

Harriet too, rather than denying her lesbianism, affirms Kuzirian's accusations about her sexuality, and Nickel Smith, the protagonist of *Bingo*, tells the reader that she and Mr. Pierre, the hairdresser, are "the only two openly gay people in Runnymeade."

Brown's leading characters are not willing to sacrifice their individuality in order to fit neatly into socially constructed boxes that dictate behavior and beliefs. It is more important to them to remain true to themselves and seek happiness, rather than to fulfill cultural expectations and risk living miserably.

Harriet embodies this philosophy more so than Carmen who, after reading Kuzirian's column about the "wedding," publicly denies she is a lesbian. She is pressured by everyone around her, except Harriet, to lie about her sexual orientation. As the pressure mounts, the relationship between the two women begins to deteriorate. They argue over whether Harriet should have admitted her own lesbianism and whether Carmen should, as one newspaper column suggested, "find a boyfriend fast."

Before the French Open, the first of four tournaments of the Grand Slam, Lavinia Archer, the circuit organizer, announces that she has found Carmen not a boyfriend, but a husband. If Carmen knows what's good for her, Lavinia asserts, she'll marry this man as soon as possible; Carmen agrees. In order to deal with all of the pressure on her, or perhaps to ignore it, Carmen has an affair with a young woman who is as afraid of being called a lesbian as Carmen is. Like Carmen, she would rather lie to and about herself in order to maintain cultural acceptance than tell the truth and be able to look in a mirror. In that respect, Carmen's new liaison is the opposite of her relationship with Harriet. Carmen has sold out, Harriet maintains, for "the good opinion of people [she] wouldn't like if she met them."

But Carmen will not listen. The two women experience one final conflict over Carmen's affair, and Harriet, with little opposition from Carmen, walks out.

Carmen goes on to win Wimbledon and, by default, the U.S. Open. At the Australian Open, however, the last tournament she must win for the Grand Slam, Susan Reilly defeats Carmen in a spectacular match of sudden death overtime.

It is in *Sudden Death* that Brown best illustrates one of the most difficult questions facing gay men and lesbians: come out, or live firmly entrenched in the closet; do what is expected, or stand up and challenge those expectations? *Sudden Death* gives the reader two characters who obviously answer the question in different ways. Harriet is willing to risk social amenities for truth and self-respect; Carmen is not willing to risk anything for something she is not sure she truly wants. All she knows is that if she lies about her sexual orientation and marries a man, people will stop persecuting her.

None of Brown's other novels come close to matching the depth of emotion presented in *Sudden Death*; no other novel portrays so realistically the degree of fear, frustration, and deceit with which gay people must live. Its realism is painful, and no one enjoys reading about pain, especially one's own.

Brown's next publication, *Bingo*, seems to lack the depth and intensity of its predecessor. *Bingo* takes the reader back to Runnymeade, the small town split by the Mason-Dixon line, and home to Julia and Louise Hunsenmeir, the two fiery sisters introduced in *Six of One*. Although the novel does not deal specifically with lesbian issues, Julia's adopted daughter, Nicole (Nickel), is a self-proclaimed lesbian who seems not to be interested in women at all. *Bingo*, like *Six of One*, deals more with familial and social issues than sexual ones.

But in spite of the apparent lack of a lesbian consciousness in *Bingo*, the protagonist is lesbian, and it is her struggles that are central to the book's essence.

Nickel finds herself having an affair with her best friend's husband, a man she has known almost all of her life. Discovering she is pregnant, Nickel develops a new set of problems: guilt, impending motherhood, and a marriage proposal from Mr. Pierre. Needless to say, the overly pious Louise is quite taken aback by the news that her lesbian niece is pregnant and preparing to marry "the bearded lady," a nickname used for Pierre by Louise and Julia.

Bingo focuses on how Nickel resolves the conflicts she experiences within herself and with those around her. Since her lesbianism is not presented problematically and is very nearly ignored, it is a minor issue thematically.

In fact, the potential for a lesbian consciousness is negated in the last fourth of the book. In spite of the platonic nature of her marriage to Pierre, Nickel has nonetheless entered into a traditionally heterosexual institution in order to be "taken care of" by Pierre. For a woman who disavows conventionality, Nickel acts in a surprisingly conventional manner: she has an affair with a man, plans to keep and raise the child from that union, marries another man because he has the financial means to support her, and negates the possibility of a lesbian relationship with a young reporter. When teased by Pierre about the young woman, Nickel responds, "I've banished romantic love from my mind." And while she insists she would rather have "the love of good friends" over a passionate, romantic relationship, she seems to reject that philosophy long enough to have an affair with a married man.

Bingo also examines the pathos and humor of familial and social relationships and, like its predecessors, offers a theme of the individual working against cultural expectations.

In Brown's other novels too, characters question culturally based expectations and constraints. In *Southern Discomfort*, for example, Hortensia Banastre learns a painful lesson in class differentiation as she engages in a love affair with a young, Black boxer. Hortensia knows that because she is a woman, she is not supposed to possess a libido, much less gratify her desires in the arms of any man but her husband. She is also aware that because of her race and socioeconomic class, her contact with middle-class Blacks is to be superficial at best. Hortensia defies these limitations and risks her socially brilliant but loveless marriage, and her position with Mobile's elite, to be with the man she loves.

But in spite of her daring, Hortensia displays just how deeply ingrained social pressures are. She tells Hercules, her lover, that they must keep their relationship a secret, and admits to him that she is not yet able to leave her marriage. In spite of its loveless state, her marriage to Carwyn Banastre still affords her power and prestige in the community.

Even after Hercules' untimely death, after which Hortensia discovers she is carrying his child, she cannot openly break the codes of the culture in which she lives and admit to her relationship with Hercules; she leaves town to have her child and then passes the infant off as the child of a servant. It is only years later, when her son Paris, in a fit of insanity, tries to kill the child, that Hortensia is able to break free from the fear of social repercussions; she shoots Paris to save her daughter's life. In the symbolic act of killing Paris to save Catherine, Hortensia chooses to accept the responsibility for her actions. In freeing herself from what Paris represented, she can now begin a new life with Catherine as her daughter. By admitting her blood relationship to the child, Hortensia breaks free from the cultural definition of what is expected and acceptable, and realizes that she can no longer feign allegiance to a social structure in which she no longer believes.

High Hearts, too, explores a situation in which a woman transcends gender and cultural boundaries to be with the man she loves. Geneva Chatfield decides to cut her hair and dress as a boy in order to join her husband Nash's regiment at the outbreak of the Civil War. Nash is initially overjoyed to have his bride with him, but when Geneva outshoots and outrides him, he feels his manhood challenged. He also becomes the object of ridicule by the other men in the company who believe that Geneva, as Jimmy, is being corrupted by Nash when "he" sleeps in Nash's tent.

High Hearts provides an excellent illustration of how women and men are created not so much by their own desires and potential, but by what is dictated to them by cultural tradition. Because Geneva brilliantly performs feats usually reserved for men, Nash wonders what is left for him to do. He sees people in terms of gender and therefore in terms of what they are supposed to be, not what they can be. Nash, unlike Geneva and many of Brown's other characters, is unable to transcend outmoded sociosexual and cultural codes, and remains bound by what should be.

CRITICAL RECEPTION

Despite the impressive amount of writing Brown has produced, critical attention paid to her work remains scarce. Book reviews of Brown's early work appear mostly in publications not considered mainstream, and may be difficult to obtain, and articles offering critical analysis or interpretation of her works number approximately six.

The most immediate critical attention Brown's novels receive is the book review, which offers a brief synopsis of the plot and analyzes strengths and weaknesses in structure, characterization, or theme. One need only glance at the covers and inside pages of Brown's works and read adjectives such as "incredible," "hilarious," and "joyous" to see that reception of her books is generally favorable.

In a review of *Rubyfruit Jungle* for example, Marilyn Webb calls the book "an inspiring, bravado adventure story of a female Huck Finn" (37). She commends Brown's use of humor in making important sociopolitical statements, and finds *Rubyfruit Jungle* "an exciting, liberating book to read" (38).

In the *Washington Post*, reviewer Carole Horn agrees with Webb's initial appraisal of the novel and calls it "a funny, vivid, sometimes vulgar, often moving account of growing up lesbian" (D6). Horn also notes the class and gender struggles in the story and mentions that Brown makes it clear "that the woman who rejects the usual societal roles remains an outsider wherever she goes" (D6).

In their assessments of the book's weaknesses, however, the reviewers differ. While Webb ultimately feels the novel is "much too polemical" (38) and questions what she sees as "one put-down of women after another" (37), Horn believes the book's only weakness lies in Brown's portrayal of Molly. She is "too good, unfortunately and too doctrinaire to be believed" (D6). Molly never compromises her personal or political ideologies which, according to Horn, makes her "a superlesbian . . . less human less someone with whom we can honestly emphatize [*sic*]" (D6). On a positive ending note, Horn does laud the fact that a book like *Rubyfruit Jungle* is no longer condemned to remain within the confines of "the plain brown wrapper" (D6).

In spite of the generally favorable reception from the reviewers, it was not until ten years after its initial publication that *Rubyfruit Jungle* received critical attention. In 1983, Martha Chew published her article "Rita Mae Brown: Feminist Theorist and Southern Novelist" in the *Southern Quarterly*. Chew draws parallels between Brown's own political and personal life and the lives of the characters in her novels (which by this time numbered five). Chew points out that in the early novels, Brown works more within a lesbian and political context and asserts that as Brown becomes less politically active, so do her characters. As a result, "the novels [are] increasingly directed toward a mainstream audience" (61).

Chew further asserts that the reason for "the disappearance from the novels of the lesbian feminist political vision" is the change in Brown's lifestyle from "political activist and street-level organizer to that of Hollywood scriptwriter, celebrity novelist, and member of Charlottesville's polo-playing set" (63). One need only take a careful look at the progression, or perhaps more accurately the regression, of lesbianism in Brown's work to see that Chew's assertions are correct. After the publication of the critically acclaimed *Southern Discomfort*, in which the only lesbian episode is negated at the story's end by the revelation that one of the women is actually a man, Brown's subsequent novels pay little or no attention to lesbianism. When lesbianism does play a part in the story, it is often negated by the novel's close, as is Nickel's lesbianism in *Bingo*, or, as in *Sudden Death*, with the neurotic nature of most of the lesbian characters.

Chew concludes by stating that although the female characters in the rest of Brown's novels are not as rebellious as the prototypical Molly Bolt, "their rejection of the limitations that society attempts to place on them through class, race, and gender divisions is the essence of their being" (79).

Leslie Fishbein's study of *Rubyfruit Jungle* is not as magnanimous in its appraisal as is Chew's. Although Fishbein does allow that *Rubyfruit Jungle* "marked a significant new direction in lesbian literature" (155) by breaking the stereotype of the lesbian as depressed and neurotic, she points out what she perceives to be serious flaws in calling the novel "the celebration of lesbian feminism that many of its reviewers claimed it to be" (156).

To illustrate her point, Fishbein uses Webb's comparison of Molly to Huck Finn. Fishbein asserts that the only way the two are similar is in their efforts to break societal restraints placed upon them. Molly is unlike Huck "because she neither grows nor changes. She never learns anything new about the world; she is always uninhibited personally and sexually. She develops no new insights as a result of her experiences" (156).

Fishbein also agrees with Carole Horn, who questions the validity of *Rubyfruit Jungle*'s being called a feminist work. "The book is no feminist tract because there is no genuine affection for women; Molly never truly loves the women with whom she sleeps. Women make good lovers, but they are not portrayed as friends'' (157). Fishbein, like Horn, notes that Molly's primary relationships are with men.

Fishbein goes on to say that the book ''is as compulsive about homosexuality as heterosexuals have been about heterosexuality'' (158). *Rubyfruit Jungle* ''is completely narcissistic and selfish'' (158), Fishbein concludes, noting that the book ''becomes the perfect document of the ME generation: it takes the new selfishness and makes it both gay and good'' (159).

James Mandrell takes a different approach in his discussion of *Rubyfruit Jungle* and uses it as the center for an analysis of ''the relationship between gender and genre'' (149), specifically, the picaresque. Mandrell defines the picaresque as a genre in which there is a ''clear identification of the protagonist as an outsider, if not 'rogue' or 'delinquent,' '' someone who ''at least in economic terms [attempts] to enter the social mainstream'' (151). Mandrell explains that in creating Molly as ''a Southern lesbian from a poor, working-class family,'' Brown has condemned Molly ''to her marginality and thus ensured the novel a place as a picaresque'' (152). Mandrell then explores the importance of origin in the picaresque and draws parallels to Molly's origins.

In spite of its being limited, the scholarship available on Brown's work is diverse and interesting. As Brown continues to grow and change as a writer, critical attention paid to her work will increase as critics and scholars come to appreciate her contribution to writing and to the reading public.

BIBLIOGRAPHY

Works by Rita Mae Brown

The Hand That Cradles the Rock. New York: New York University Press, 1971.
A Plain Brown Wrapper. New York: Diana Press, 1976.
Rubyfruit Jungle. Plainfield, VT: Daughters, 1973. New York: Bantam, 1977.
In Her Day. Plainfield, VT: Daughters, 1976. New York: Bantam, 1988.
Six of One. New York: Harper and Row, 1978. New York: Bantam, 1979.
Southern Discomfort. New York: Harper and Row, 1982. New York: Bantam, 1983.
Sudden Death. New York: Bantam, 1983.
High Hearts. New York: Bantam, 1986.
Starting from Scratch: A Different Kind of Writer's Manual. New York: Bantam, 1988.
Bingo. New York: Bantam, 1988.
Wish You Were Here. New York: Bantam, 1990.

Studies of Rita Mae Brown

Chew, Martha. ''Rita Mae Brown: Feminist Theorist and Southern Novelist.'' *Southern Quarterly* 22 (1983): 61–80.

Fishbein, Leslie. *"Rubyfruit Jungle*: Lesbianism, Feminism, and Narcissism." *International Journal of Women's Studies* 7 (1984): 155–59.

Garrett, George. "American Publishing Now." *Sewanee Review* 96 (1988): 516–26.

Holt, Patricia. *"Publishers Weekly* Interviews Rita Mae Brown." *Publishers Weekly* (October 2, 1978): 16–17.

Horn, Carole. "Out of the Closet and the Plain Brown Wrapper." Rev. of *Rubyfruit Jungle,* by Rita Mae Brown. *Washington Post* (February 14, 1974): D6.

Irwin, Edward E. "Freedoms as Value in Three Popular Southern Novels." *Proteus* 6 (1989): 37–41.

Levine, Daniel B. "Uses of Classical Mythology in Rita Mae Brown's *Southern Discomfort." Classical and Modern Literature: A Quarterly* 10 (1989): 63–70.

Mandrell, James. "Questions of Genre and Gender: Contemporary American Versions of the Feminine Picaresque." *Novel* 20 (1987): 149–70.

Webb, Marilyn. "Daughters, Inc.: A Publishing House Is Born." Rev. of *Rubyfruit Jungle. Ms.* (June 1974): 35–38.

PAT CALIFIA (1954–)
Bryn Austin

BIOGRAPHY

"I would rather be a tribal storyteller than a self-conscious member of the literati or a leather missionary churning out tracts for a bunch of people who will never think of themselves as heathens." These words, penned by Pat Califia in the introduction to *Macho Sluts*, her 1988 collection of erotic short fiction, ably describe the path she has carved for herself as a writer. Once affectionately described by a reviewer as "the cuckoo in the lesbian nest," Califia has consistently proven herself to be a maverick in her own communities, whether among feminist theorists, lesbians, or sadomasochists, and even as a working-class Mormon girl growing up in the 1950s.

Born in Corpus Christi, Texas, in 1954, Califia is the oldest of six children. Her family was forced to move nearly every year of Califia's childhood as her father, a coal miner, looked for work throughout the western states. From the time she learned to read, she had the unorthodox plan of being a writer, often slipping away to her room to scrawl poems, science fiction adventure stories, and religious plays, in which her younger siblings begrudgingly performed. In her teens, Califia wrote several unpublished novelettes, now locked away in dresser drawers, and authored an occasional youth column for the *Salt Lake Tribune*, a daily newspaper.

In 1971, she left home to attend college at the University of Utah in Salt Lake City. In her first year there, she came out as a lesbian at the age of seventeen. But the impossible situation of falling in love with a woman who lived in her dormitory—in the heart of the desert—drove her to a nervous breakdown, and she dropped out of school. Once out of school and living on her own, she began her commitment to political work, becoming deeply involved in women's rights, housing rights, the anti-war movement, and the self-health movement. Though she immersed herself in the alternative community that Salt Lake had to offer, she found the conservative Mormon environment oppressive and finally, in 1973, found the courage to move to San Francisco. In the introduction to her 1980 self-health guide *Sapphistry: The Book of Lesbian Sexuality*, she writes of her move out of Utah, "I knew that living in Salt Lake was making me hate myself, but I didn't know how bad it was until I escaped. I kept feeling waves of tension melt away" (vii).

During her first two years in San Francisco, she worked on *Sister*, the publication of the Daughters of Bilitis, the first national lesbian group in the country. By the mid 1970s, she was well on her way to building what was to become an extensive career in public speaking on lesbian issues. Her involvement in sex education began in 1975 with a volunteer job at the San Francisco Sex Information switchboard. In 1978, she co-founded Samois, a lesbian feminist S/M support group, and the next year, she helped publish the group's first collection, *What Color Is Your Handkerchief: A Lesbian S/M Sexuality Reader*. Some of her early research on lesbian sexuality was published in the *Journal of Homosexuality* in 1979. That same year her essay "A Secret Side of Lesbian Sexuality," an article about the S/M community, was published in the *Advocate*, ushering in her long association with the national gay and lesbian newsmagazine, where she served in a variety of editorial positions and continues to be a regular contributor. Two years later Califia became the magazine's advice columnist, known as the "Adviser," and in the mid 1980s, she began writing a similar advice column, the "Sexpert," in the gay men's porn magazine *Advocate MEN*. In the early 1990s, she worked as the editor of the erotic publication.

Califia resumed her academic studies after several years in the Bay Area, earning a bachelor's degree in psychology from San Francisco State University in 1981. After living in New York for several years in the mid 1980s, and later in Los Angeles, she returned to San Francisco State University in 1992 to earn a master's degree in counseling. Throughout her prolific writing career, Califia has published five books, close to a hundred articles and essays in American and European publications, and dozens of erotic short stories in straight, gay male, lesbian, and S/M magazines. In addition, her poetry has appeared in numerous journals and anthologies.

MAJOR WORKS AND THEMES

Woven throughout the body of Califia's work is a tension between utopian and dystopian, hopefulness for positive change and warnings of what harm may consume us. The foreboding tone of many of her essays, seemingly written by an unwavering cynic, is countered by an unmistakable compassion for and faith in the communities that surface in her advice columns. In "Feminism and Sadomasochism," one of her early analytic pieces published in a 1981 issue of the feminist journal *Heresies*, Califia testifies that she is "motivated by her concern for the people who are frightened or ashamed of their erotic response to sadomasochistic fantasies" (30).

This tension is clear in the juxtaposition of the erotic short story "The Calyx of Isis" and the futuristic novel *Doc and Fluff: The Distopian Tale of a Girl and Her Biker*, published in 1990. "The Calyx of Isis," a lengthy story that is included in *Macho Sluts* but could easily stand alone as a novella, tells the tale of a lesbian couple's ultimate test of faith and S/M fantasy rolled into one. Before the quest begins, Califia crafts the sexual adventurer's dream scenario—an idyllic lesbian bathhouse in San Francisco complete with a benevolent millionaire proprietress. The setting, sadly unlikely to be reproduced in real life, is the result of mixing the modest dream of a sexual optimist with a little science fiction.

In *Doc and Fluff*, a science fiction template is refracted through the lens of a grave pessimist. In the not-too-distant future, the United States has been torn apart by warring juntas and largely overrun by fascists and Christian fundamentalists. Even Harpy Farm, a lesbian separatist planned community, is rife with infighting and discrimination. Ironically, within *Doc and Fluff* the dystopian tenor is not sustained to the end of the novel, and though the country's political plight is not improved, the two heroines neatly straighten out their troubled lives and get themselves on a path to fulfill their dreams. What is on one level a facile conclusion to an otherwise sophisticated novel is also an understandable playing out of the competing poles of optimism and pessimism that run throughout her writings as a whole.

As a writer, Califia invariably has taken the road less traveled, forging into territory where few lesbian writers have gone before. Though some in disagreement with her message have tried to cast her as the lunatic fringe, Califia's analysis is as sharp as her compassion is disarming, making it difficult for her detractors to dismiss her. More often than not, she directs her arguments and social critiques to the heart of the issue. Since the time of her earliest published works, Califia has played a pivotal role in the lesbian community's sexuality debates and the emergence of the voice of the S/M community.

Califia's work on sexual health and diversity are widely considered pioneering. Equally provocative is her sophisticated treatment of violence, particularly in *Doc and Fluff*. Most often fiction by women avoids or obscures the ways that violence affects people, both as victims and as perpetrators. In S/M writings specifically, a necessary strategy has been developed to ideologically distance sadomasochism from non-consensual abuse in order to defend and legitimate. Califia's use of violence as an element in her more recent work does not undermine this strategy, but rather it evolves from it historically and pushes the discussion to a higher level.

In *Doc and Fluff*, Califia juxtaposes rape and mutilation with intensely brutal but consensual S/M, a misogynistic assault on a woman with a pagan priestess's ritualistic torture of an abusive man. The priestess, Raven, justifies her actions, saying,

As women it is our task to preserve the balance . . . men rule us because they are willing to be violent. They are too stupid to realize that our capacity to be violent exceeds theirs.

Women have to stop being afraid of that potential, and learn instead to exercise it with wisdom and justice. (207)

Califia does not give readers a clean package of perpetrating villains and pacifistic heroines. Readers are forced to decipher for themselves the ways in which the opposing scenarios look similar and the ways in which they look different. And throughout, Califia paints this violent imagery with the kind of luxurious detail that others use to write of mawkish sunsets and fields of heather. The clever skill of her pen and the scrupulous care she devotes to her subject demand recognition and belie any charges that her employment of violence is simply for shock value.

CRITICAL RECEPTION

Califia's works have been widely reviewed nationally and internationally, chiefly in gay and lesbian, feminist, and S/M publications. Often her early works, particularly *Sapphistry*, garnered not only emphatic reviews but lengthy political diatribes, either accusing Califia of alienating and offending the lesbian community with her positive message on sadomasochism and sexual diversity or praising her for her non-judgmental and realistic approach to human sexuality. A decade later, after publishing *Doc and Fluff*, she was accused by others of alienating the S/M community with her graphic depictions of violence. But for the most part, her later works, such as *Macho Sluts*, *Doc and Fluff*, and *The Advocate Adviser*, a compilation of her columns, received more uniform praise, and all three were nominated for Lambda Literary Awards, honors given in the annual book contest for lesbian and gay writers.

Arguably the nadir of the reviews has not been negativity but rather the disappointing mediocrity of the criticism. Rare is the review that discusses the themes of her work or the challenging issues she raises. *Doc and Fluff*, her most ambitious work, suffered a similar fate. A complicated creation juggling charged subtexts such as racism and militarism, loyalty and spirituality, the novel received many favorable reviews, but none discussed its themes in much depth, and most delivered perfunctory admonitions against Califia's use of violence.

BIBLIOGRAPHY

Works by Pat Califia

Sapphistry: The Book of Lesbian Sexuality. Tallahasse, FL: Naiad Press, 1980.
Macho Sluts. Boston: Alyson Publications, 1988.
Doc and Fluff: The Distopian Tale of a Girl and Her Biker. Boston: Alyson Publications, 1990.
The Advocate Adviser. Boston: Alyson Publications, 1991.

Edited by Pat Califia

The Power Exchange: A Newsleather for Women on the Sexual Fringe. (Four issues published from 1984 to 1986.)
The Lesbian S/M Safety Manual. Denver: Lace Publications, 1988.

Works in Anthologies and Periodicals

"Lesbian Sexuality." *Journal of Homosexuality* (Spring 1979): 255–66.
"A Secret Side of Lesbian Sexuality." *Advocate* (Dec. 27, 1979): 19–23.
"Feminism and Sadomasochism." *Heresies* 12 (1981): 30–34.
"Jessie" and "A Personal View of the History of the Lesbian S/M Community and Movement in San Francisco." *Coming to Power: Writings and Graphics on Lesbian S/M*. Ed. Samois Collective 2nd ed. Boston: Alyson Publications, 1982. 156–82, 245–83.
"The Calyx of Isis." *Erotica: Women's Writings from Sappho to Margaret Atwood*. Ed. Margaret Reynolds. London: Pandora Press, 1990. 186–88.
"The Limits of the S/M Relationship, or Mr. Benson Doesn't Live Here Anymore." *Leatherfolk: Radical Sex, People, Politics, and Practice*. Ed. Mark Thompson. Boston: Alyson Publications, 1991. 211–32.
"Poems." *High Risk: An Anthology of Forbidden Writings*. Ed. Amy Scholder and Ira Silverberg. New York: Plume, 1991. 55–67.

Translated Works

Sapphistrie. Trans. Alexandra Bartoczko. Berlin: sub rosa Frauenverlag, 1981.
Macho Sloeries. Trans. Marijke Hajunga. Amsterdam: Stichting SMet, 1991.

JANE CHAMBERS (1937–1983)
Nancy Dean

BIOGRAPHY

Jane Chambers was born in March 1937 in Columbia, South Carolina, the daughter of a bookkeeper and a father whose struggles with alcoholism and mental illness finally led to her parents' divorce after ten years. After the marriage broke up, her father and her uncle left the house, ending their sexual abuse of her (conversation with Beth Allen, March 20, 1992).*Chambers grew up in central Florida, in the care of her grandmother, while her mother worked outside the home. The child entertained herself by cutting out heads from *Life* magazine, drawing bodies for them, and composing dialogues for those famous people who sat as little cutouts in the wicker chairs on her porch.

Soon she began hounding the local radio station, asking for parts. She wrote radio scripts: "Girl Scout Time" and "Hi Time." At eight, she was child host of "Let's Listen," a radio show for children. Later, with the arrival of TV, she wrote, produced, and moderated her own Sunday afternoon show called "Youth Pops a Question" (Glines 6).

After high school and a year at Rollins College, she moved to Los Angeles in 1956, determined to go to Pasadena Playhouse to study theater writing. She learned that women would be accepted only if there were seats remaining after the men were admitted. She inquired about directing and learned that women could study only acting at Pasadena Playhouse, not play writing or directing. Chambers stayed to study acting for two years and appeared in two films. When she returned to New York, she studied acting with Erwin Piscator and was cast in *Single Man at a Party*, which opened April 21, 1959 (Anderson 4). She earned her living working for a literary agent, acting in summer stock, auditioning,

---

*I want to thank Beth Allen for her remarkable generosity and care in providing materials and information for the preparation of this chapter.

working with the Poet's Theatre, and taking opportunities to direct. She wrote the book for a muscial called *Keep it Clean* and tried to place four of her one-act plays. In 1963, Chambers moved to Poland Springs, Maine, and became staff-writer for WMTW-TV, presenting women's news, a teenage feature, and "Merry Witch," a regular children's show, which she wrote and produced. Riding one of the sponsor's Motor Brooms, her "Vroom Broom," Chambers played the witch (Glines 11).

In 1966, a Job Corps Center opened near the TV station, offered her a job at twice the pay, and transferred her to New Jersey where she met Beth Allen, who became her lover and manager. She received her B.A. at Goddard College through the Adult Education Program in 1971 and formed the Corpswoman Theatre, playing to mainly Black audiences, a perspective that informed *Christ in a Treehouse*, which won the award for Best Religious Drama on Connecticut Educational TV in 1971, and *Here Comes the Iceman*, the first African-American sitcom optioned for prime time TV, although the series was never produced.

In 1972, she co-founded, with Margot Lewitin, the Women's Interart Theatre and was accepted at the Eugene O'Neill Playwriting Conference, where *Tales of the Revolution and Other American Fables* was presented. In that year, she wrote "Search for Tomorrow" for TV, which earned her the National Writers Guild Award for 1972–73. *Jamboree* was presented at Town Hall, and *Random Violence*, *Mine*, and *The Wife* were presented at the Women's Interart Theatre. At thirty-five, Chambers was making her living doing the kind of writing she wanted to do.

In 1974, after careful consideration, Chambers wrote *A Late Snow*, her first play produced that centered on lesbian life. (We know now that *The Eye of the Gull* was written three years earlier, but it was unknown before 1991.) Chambers knew that she risked her reputation in agreeing to have *A Late Snow* produced. Still, the play was well received, was optioned for an off-Broadway production, but then dropped for lack of financial backing, the producer remarking, "I can't get backers interested in a play about lesbians" (Glines 18).

In 1976, Chambers went to Los Angeles where the Mark Taper Forum planned to produce *The Common Garden Variety* (presented at Interart Theatre in 1974), a play that shows the conditions that keep women uneducated and impoverished. In those lean years Chambers struggled financially: she did editing work, received two grants, and although she refused to treat child abuse or violence against women, she wrote ten pornographic paperbacks, some written on typesetting machines to formula and published under pseudonyms.

In 1978, Chambers's father died of cancer, and in the next year, her uncle committed suicide with a gunshot to the head. Chambers traveled to his trailer in Georgia and "literally cleaned his brains off the walls" (Glines 19).

In Her Own Words describes how The Glines, a production company, called Chambers early in 1980 to ask her if she had "a gay play they could do." She sent *Last Summer at Bluefish Cove* to them; in ten days the play opened at the Shandol and was sold out. As many as fifty people waited in line for cancellations for what the *New York Post* called the "hit of [the] summer" (Stasio, 27). In 1981, The Glines staged *My Blue Heaven*, and *Kudzu* was optioned for Broadway and presented by Playwrights Horizons in November and December of 1981 as a pre-Broadway Workshop. During a rehearsal of *Kudzu* in November, Chambers experienced an uncontrollable spasm of her left arm. A brain tumor was soon diagnosed. She returned from the hospital paralyzed on the left side and saw herself dying as her father and uncle had, and she dreaded meeting those "tormentors of her childhood" after death (Glines 23).

Her last play, *Quintessential Image*, was presented at Town Hall as part of the celebration of the sixth anniversary of The Glines production company, October 1982.

The remarkable loving support the lesbian community gave Jane Chambers during her illness has become legend. Her letter "To my dear friends at Foot of the Mountain" gives witness:

Doctors said I was the fastest recovering brain surgery patient ever, I . . . woke up in the o.r. and went directly to intensive care where I held a production meeting for *Quintessential Image*. . . . When I first was admitted to the hospital, the head nurse on the floor . . . said, "The last time I saw you, you were onstage in *Bluefish Cove*. That play changed my life." I told her how afraid I was and she [said], "Don't worry, you'll never be alone here." And I wasn't. Every test I was sent to, there was a lesbian technician, nurse or resident waiting for me, to stroke my head, hold my hand and allay the fear. The lesbian community in NY was incredibly supportive. . . . They signed up for shifts and someone was always with me. . . . Never had to wake up fearful or feeling alone. This enormous love wrapped me in such a blanket of love that I never was truly fearful or depressed. I felt sure that this committed family of lesbians was simply not going to let me die, that they had removed all the terror and anger from me and all that was left for me to do was heal. . . . We can do that for each other; we can heal by loving, we certainly proved that. (unpublished letter)

MAJOR WORKS AND THEMES

Of Jane Chambers's twelve works written for the stage, six have a major lesbian presence (in order of writing): *Eye of the Gull, A Late Snow, Last Summer at Bluefish Cove, My Blue Heaven, Kudzu,* and *Quintessential Image,* but it would be quite accurate to say that all of Chambers's stage works as well as her novels are feminist. In her works centered on the lesbian experience, she focuses on relationships themselves rather than on the heterosexual world's view of the relationships. She was one of the first playwrights to depict the love of woman for woman as non-pathological, as just one version of loving. Her lesbians are funny, angry, manipulative, bored, loyal, strong, anxious—varied humans, not primarily in stereotypical butch-femme roles.

In *Eye of the Gull,* written in 1971 (a work unknown before 1991 when Vita Dennis asked Beth Allen about "other" works by Chambers and Dennis, under Allen's supervision, revised the play), Pat and Maggie run a rooming house at the shore, Gull House, and try to make a comfortable home for Pat's sister, Sara, who is mentally and emotionally disabled.

In *A Late Snow*, all of Ellie's ex-lovers visit her vacation house in a snow storm: Peggy, the perfect person she loved in college; Quincey, the graduate student who loves her and has lived with her a year, and Pat, the opportunist she lived with for five years. Ellie comes home with Margot, an attractive writer whose insight and experience are exciting to her. Before the next morning Ellie has realized that she must leave Quincey, and Ellie and Margot commit themselves to a new relationship.

In *Last Summer at Bluefish Cove*, Chambers depicts Lil, a cancer patient, falling in love with Eva, who has just left her husband. A group of loving friends supports Lil, who finally reveals to Eva that she may be dying. Although Lil tries to make Eva leave, to protect her, Eva refuses and challenges Lil to live out their love fully. The day of Lil's funeral, the women pack up her things, and we see Lil's influence on Eva and the other women, giving them her legacy of independence, strength, and zest for living.

My Blue Heaven (originally two one-act plays) concerns the same characters framed by an emcee at beginning and end. Molly writes a regular column about her idyllic life with Joe and their animals in the woods. A Christian book publisher comes by with a fabulous book offer but is horrified to learn that Joe in life is Josie, Molly's woman lover. In the second episode Josie and Molly get married when an old friend, now in the priesthood, comes by to see them. There is trickiness, humor, a homeyness in these two acts as they explore a loving and secure bond.

Kudzu, perhaps Chambers's best play, sets forth many of her strengths: her wit and humor, her gift for the language of the South, her wry perspective on human events, her staunch recognition of heroism in the gentle and bigotry in the powerful. In this play Martha and Katy take care of Ginger, Martha's Momma, and P.T., Martha's cousin. They await J. J. Chapman, an important journalist who is coming to speak to P.T. Martha and Katy are not sisters, as we first suppose, but lovers. As Ginger puts it, Martha has this "affliction" that she developed when she first met Katy. The play ridicules the bigot, racist P.T. (whom Beth Allen says was modeled on Chambers's uncle). The play alludes to men's exploitation of women and portrays the deep devotion and kindness between Martha and Katy. Ginger is a refreshing, funny "truthteller"; Katy is witty and strong but touched by Martha's gentle devotion and loyalty. This play was revised by Marsha Sheiness under Allen's supervision before its Theatre Rhinoceros production in 1988.

Quintessential Image, which Chambers first wanted to call "Quintessential Dyke," shows a slick, smiling TV hostess interviewing a world-famous woman photographer who insists that her love of Belinda was responsible for all her famous pictures. The TV talk show host tries to divert that line of conversation but fails repeatedly as she gets more anxious and tries to conceal her own relationship with her lover, Rachel. The play is a funny but tough-minded criticism of a homophobic society that wastes talented women by depriving them of training, financial support, and recognition.

In *Burning*, Chambers presents a powerful and unusual lesbian theme. Cynthia and her husband are able to use an old Massachusetts farmhouse during the summer, and unaware that Angela has fallen in love with Cynthia, they bring Angela with them to help with the children. In the farmhouse they find a hidden room still filled with the high emotions experienced there two hundred years before. Cynthia and Angela unconsciously take on those personae and experience the passionate attachment of Martha and Abigail from the days of witch trials in early Massachusetts.

Chasin Jason, published posthumously in 1987, is an earthy and comic monologue by the foster mother of a man who is considered to be the Son of God. There is a lesbian relationship in the early part of the novel.

CRITICAL RECEPTION

Of the many awards Chambers won, some of the most important are the Eugene O'Neill Fellowship (for *Tales of the Revolution and Other American Fables*, 1972), the Writers Guild Award (for "Search for Tomorrow" on CBS, 1973), a grant from the Creative Artists Public Service Program (1977), the Dramalogue Critics Circle Award (for *Last Summer at Bluefish Cove*, 1980), the Alliance for Gay Artists Award (for *A Late Snow*, 1982), the Fund for Human Dignity Award (1982), the Los Angeles Drama Critics' Circle Award (for *Last Summer at Bluefish Cove*, 1983), the Betty Award (for *Quintessential Image* in 1985 and *Kudzu* in 1987), and the Dramalogue Critics Circle Award (for *Kudzu*, 1988).

The Women in Theatre Program (formerly the American Theatre Association, Women's Division) created the Jane Chambers Playwriting Award to encourage the writing of new plays that address women's experience and have a majority of principal roles for women.

Jane Chambers's significant contribution to the development of lesbian culture was primarily her writing about lesbians as "normal," that is, non-pathological. Lesbians in her work are not sick, suicidal, or malevolent. They are ordinary, fascinating, and funny, struggling with their relationships and financial worries, as other people do. Perhaps this universality accounts for the ease with which her works have joined the mainstream and are now taught in colleges through textbooks and anthologies that include her in the accepted canon. Her works continue to be published posthumously.

The rapidity of Chambers's acceptance into anthologies to be used as textbooks in colleges attests to a sound critical evaluation of her work as does the performance of her plays all over the United States and in Israel, Europe, and South Africa.

BIBLIOGRAPHY

Works by Jane Chambers

Drama

Tales of the Revolution and Other American Fables. Eugene O'Neill Memorial Theatre, Waterford, CT. August 1972. (Three acts.)

Random Violence. Women's Interart Theatre, New York. March 1973. (Two acts.)

One Short Day at the Jamboree. Town Hall, New York. January 1974. (One act.)

Mine. Women's Interart Theatre, New York. May 1974. (One act.)

The Wife. Women's Interart Theatre, New York City. May 1974. (One act.)

A Late Snow. Playwrights Horizons, New York. May-June 1974. (Two acts.) New York: JH Press, 1989.

The Common Garden Variety. Mark Taper Laboratory, Los Angeles. February 1976. (Two acts.)

Last Summer at Bluefish Cove. Shandol Theatre, New York. February 1980. (Two acts.) New York: JH Press, 1982.

My Blue Heaven. Shandol Theatre, New York. June 1981. (Two acts.) New York: JH Press, 1982.

Kudzu. Playwrights Horizons, New York. November 1981. (Two acts.) Revised by Marsha Sheiness.

Quintessential Image. Town Hall, New York. October 1982. (One act.)

The Eye of the Gull. Footsteps Theatre, Chicago. 1991. (Two acts.) Revised by Vita Dennis.

Television

Curfew!: A Feminist Parable. WNYC-TV. January 1971.

Christ in a Treehouse. Connecticut Educational Television, August 1971.

Here Comes the Iceman, 1972.

Search for Tomorrow, CBS, 1972–73.

Novels

Burning. New York: Jove Press, 1978; New York: JH Press, 1983.

Chasin' Jason. New York: JH Press, 1987.

Poetry

Warrior at Rest. Ed. and introd. Beth Allen and Jere Jacob. New York: JH Press, 1984.

Posthumous Publications

A Late Snow. Gay Plays: The First Collection. Ed. William M. Hoffman. New York: Avon Books, 1979; *Contemporary Realistic Plays.* Ed. John R. Wolcott. Dubuque, IA: Kendall/Hunt Publishers, 1988.

Two more texts were contracted for publication in 1992:

A Late Snow, in *Staging Diversity: Plays and Practice in the American Theatre,* ed. Michael L. Quinn and John R. Wolcott. Kendall/Hunt Publishers.

The Eye of the Gull (revised by Vita Dennis under Beth Allen's supervision and produced at The Footsteps Theatre in 1991) is included in a gay and lesbian anthology published by Heineman/Methuen, 1993.

Monologue from *A Late Snow. Moving Parts: Monologues from Contemporary Plays,* edited by Nina Shengold and Eric Lane. New York: Penguin Books, 1992.

Studies of Jane Chambers

Anderson, Julia Gay. "Fiction Is a Lie about the Truth: Lesbian Characters in the Plays of Jane Chambers." Master's thesis, Kansas State University, 1986.

Coss, Claire. "On Jane Chambers: An Interview with Beth Allen and Jere Jacob." *Heresies* 17 (1984): 83–84.

Dace, Tish. "For Whom the Bell Tolled." *New York Native* October 24–November 6, 1983: 47.

———. *"Last Summer at Bluefish Cove." Other Stages* 2.20 (1980): 12–25.

Feingold, Michael. "The Good Little Girl Grows Up." *Village Voice* August 15, 1989: 93.

Glines, John. *In Her Own Words.* Program produced at Zebra Crossing Theatre, Chicago, 1989; Courtyard Theatre, New York, 1989.

Helbing, Terry. "Jane Chambers: A Reminiscence." *New York Native* April 11, 1983: 14.

Landau, Penny M. "Jane Chambers: In Memoriam." *Women and Performance* 1.2 (1984): 55–57.

"Plain Jane." *New York Native* August 24, 1981: 7.

Regelson, Rosalyn. "Jane Chambers' Lesbian Convention." *Soho Weekly News* June 11, 1980: 58.

Sisley, Emily. "Playwright Jane Chambers: The Long Road to *Last Summer at Bluefish Cove." Advocate* November 13, 1980: 31–32.

Stasio, Marilyn. "A Warm 'Summer' at the Glines." *New York Post* July 3, 1980: 27.

CHRYSTOS (1946–   )
Barbara Dale May

BIOGRAPHY

Born in San Francisco in 1946 to a mother of North European lineage and a father of Menominee ancestry, Chrystos is a self-identified "Urban Indian" whose traumatic childhood and troubled adult years are woven throughout her poetry. In direct, painful language she recalls her mother's severe depressions, her father's shame at his ethnic identity, and in a number of poems she suggests that sexual abuse by an uncle led her early on to a life patterned by self-destructive behavior. In her first book, *Not Vanishing*, she recognizes the efforts of her first lesbian lover who over a period of many years rescued her from a life of drugs, prostitution, suicide attempts and the revolving door of mental institutions. Likewise she acknowledges the support of Kate Millett who, in the late 1970s, when Chrystos was emerging from another period in a "looney bin," encouraged the poet to write for publication.

Chrystos's poems appear in a number of anthologies, among them the landmark volumes *This Bridge Called My Back: Writings by Radical Women of Color* (1981) and *Living the Spirit: A Gay American Indian Anthology* (1988). Poems appearing in these and earlier anthologies are collected, together with new material, in her two book-length works, *Not Vanishing* (1988) and *Dream On* (1991). In both books she describes herself as a self-educated writer and artist, and she underscores the importance of primary relationships, however problematic, to her life and work, dedicating her first book to her lover at the time, B. J. Collins, and her second book, published three years later, to her new lover, Ilene Samowitz.

A recovering alcoholic, she dates her life of sobriety back to October 1988, six months after publication of *Not Vanishing*.

Since 1980, she has lived on Bainbridge Island in the state of Washington.

MAJOR WORKS AND THEMES

Chrystos's poetry is fiercely political and fueled by a strong personal identification with the victims of violence. *Not Vanishing* includes poems about serial killers ("The Man without Fingerprints," "No More Metaphors"); abusers of children ("For Eli," "Bitter Teeth: about My Uncle, Jean LeMaitré"); and murderers of indigenous peoples ("I Dreamt Again of that Beach," "Vision-Bundle"). In these poems and others dealing with society's treatment of the eccentric (e.g., "Dr.'s Favorite Color," "Crazy grandpa whispers"), the poet consistently identifies with the beaten, the raped, the institutionalized, the murdered.

If Chrystos's subjects are violent, so is her style. It is unflinchingly angry, with anger manifested as both style and theme. In "I Walk in the History of my People," she writes: "Our sacred beliefs have been made into pencils /names of cities   gas stations / My knee is wounded so badly that I limp constantly / Anger is my crutch   I hold myself upright with it / My knee is wounded / see / How I Am Still Walking" (*Not Vanishing* 7). The same anger and sense of betrayal is echoed in "Savage Eloquence," anthologized in a number of books and reappearing in *Not Vanishing*, whose subject is the tribal struggle for Big Mountain. "We know you fences death laws death hunger death / This is our skin / you take from us," she writes, "these were our lives / our patterns our dawns" (*Not Vanishing* 41).

In much the same way that these poems and others, such as "Today was Bad Like TB," and "I am Not Your Princess," reflect the testimonial nature of this personal/political poetry, so do they reveal a seriously problematic aspect of Chrystos's work. "White girl don't / tell me about El Salvador or Nicaragua / especially if you go there for an educational / vacation / Tell me about First Street in Seattle / the bench where the drunk Indians hang out" (*Not Vanishing* 74), she writes, and then continues, "Stop crying / stop whining / Don't aim 5,000 miles away to a land whose words / you barely speak   if at all / Right here now   genocide / I'll tell you all about it" (*Not Vanishing* 75). This poem, by itself, is not particularly problematic, but it becomes so when the reader confronts its odd companion piece, "I Dreamt of that Beach again," in which the poet bemoans the violence in El Salvador, drawing upon a kind of, albeit questionable, ethnic privilege to justify a posture that might be considered self-righteous by some readers, and offensive by others, especially feminists of mixed race with a more global perspective. The problem is one that will be seen, as well, in the writer's second book, *Dream On*, where the questions of identity and politics are all the more troubling.

Although Chrystos is probably better known for her angry political poems and her identification with society's victims, it is her erotic poems in *Not Vanishing* that are the most original and lyrical. "O Honeysuckle woman / won't you lay with me / our tongues flowering / open-throated / golden pollen / We could drink one another / sticky sweet & deep'' (*Not Vanishing* 6) is a fine example of the lusty, joyous celebration in her finest lines. "Sailing," "Close your Eyes," "Woman," "Your Tongue Sparkles," and "Let me Touch" are all tender, rowdy, sensual lesbian poems. With frequent allusions to all the senses, but especially to those of taste, smell, and touch, these poems can quite fairly be described as delicious reading. In others, the lyrical drive is precisely the sensation of flight and freedom of movement, the dance that is joyous lesbian sex. In "Double Phoenix," the lover "whirls moves tightly her mouth shivers / birds appear in my hands / my toes skim stars / I'm wings in the night sky crying out in her breasts / my hips wet flowers" (*Not Vanishing* 43).

Chrystos returns in *Dream On* with her troubled political agenda with epithets to alienate. Not to recognize the existence of these hurtful components of this writer's work would be to ignore a key element in her writing, which, oddly, is at once offensive and intriguing. Some of the more invidious finds are "pinched white lady" (66), "chic white faggot headwaiter" (80), "whites, whites, everywhere; they're a plague" (118), and "those legion white lesbians" (130). Perhaps the most confusing, or rather, confused of these poems in either volume is one from *Not Vanishing* entitled "Yesterday he called her a pig" in which a white man insults his boss, a Black woman, because he "was egged on by some politically correct / white lesbians" (22). Regardless of the reader's posture, feminist, lesbian, ethnic, or all three, the poem is puzzling.

A clue to the seemingly free-floating rage in Chrystos's poetry is her relationship to her parents, which is fairly well laid bare to the reader in *Not Vanishing* and which resurfaces somewhat fleshed out in *Dream On*. She completely identifies with the paternal side of her heritage, the Menominee father, idealizing a language unknown to her and which she says, from shame, he never spoke to her. At the same time, she rejects her white heritage from her Lithuanian/Alsace Lorraine mother, describing her mother's language as "rubble mama broken bricks / glass shards rats dog shit" (*Not Vanishing* 25). Although Chrystos's idealization of the unspoken "fathertongue" provides the base for her political identity, it is the countervalent rejection of the "mothertongue," that is, half her heritage, half her identity, indeed, the mirror of her gender, that explains some of the internalized oppression so vivid in both *Not Vanishing* and *Dream On*. In a rambling prose poem somewhat reminiscent of personal journal entries, the poet analyzes her tortured relationship with her mother: "She is desperate for my pretense that she was a good mother I am desperate for her acknowledgment that my childhood was a painful chaos of beatings & her emotional absence I understand from a feminist viewpoint (poverty, my father's indifference, her own terror), why she behaved as she did—but I can't forgive her as long as she denies my reality" (*Dream On* 138). Clearly, in denying the existence of the maternal side of her ethnic identity, which is North European, that is, white, the writer is, at the same time, imposing a kind of personal punishment on the mother and demanding an unremitting penance from the culture that the mother represents.

Although Chrystos's "terrible stories" of a life of drugs, alcoholism, prostitution, sexual confusion, and abuse are woven throughout both books, it is her sexy and sometimes funny poetry that speaks to lesbians of all colors. Notable among a number of these works in *Dream On* are "Bright in your Dark Mouth," "Clear Sphinx," "Getting Down," and "Waking Up." A wonderful, celebratory poem that sings like a lesbian international anthem is "Lesbian Air" where "We are the sea of Lesbians the breathing wind of Lesbians we are the falling cherry petals of Lesbians we are the Lesbian moon rising full of our fallen warriors' songs we are the Lesbian sky" (143).

CRITICAL RECEPTION

Chrystos's name, since her inclusion in *This Bridge Called My Back*, is frequently associated with a number of other, more well known writers of color, such as Gloria Anzaldúa, Paula Gunn Allen, and Jewelle Gomez, some of whom have written supportive comments released with the publication of both *Not Vanishing* and *Dream On*. Nevertheless, her work has, for the most part, been unnoticed by national reviews and critical journals.

BIBLIOGRAPHY

Works by Chrystos

Dream On. Vancouver: Press Gang, 1991.
Not Vanishing. Vancouver: Press Gang, 1988.

CHERYL CLARKE (1947–　)
Elizabeth Randolph

BIOGRAPHY

In 1947, Cheryl Clarke was born in Washington, D.C., to Edna and James Clarke, the middle child of five children. She wrote her first poem at age thirteen in Catholic school, where she acquired her love of literature, her respect for the power and intelligence of women, and a "definite perspective on the world" (unless otherwise indicated, all quotations are from personal communication with the author). In spite of her skepticism about religion, Clarke was impressed by the competency of the nuns, who opened her up to appreciating women as role models, as friends, as capable people.

It was at home, however, that she learned to respect her own capabilities. Her parents had great faith in black women, preferring to see their daughters self-sufficient rather than stuck with a "triflin' " man. Her mother, whom Clarke describes as "very intelligent and well-read," pushed Clarke to do things, to "get out there in front of people." In fact, she credits her childhood music recitals with her ability to relate to the audiences that attend her poetry readings.

An emphasis on self-sufficiency and self-determination in the home combined with her education at historically black Howard University in the height of the 1960s created a deep need to uncover her own non-traditional role models. In 1963, she discovered James Baldwin, then, later, other male poets of the Black Arts Movement. Fascinated by her newfound heroes, she entered a graduate program in English at Rutgers University in 1969, where she found little support for black-identified women.

Clarke continued to teach herself historic and contemporary black literature, discovering such black women writers as Zora Neale Hurston, Ntozake Shange, Toni Morrison, Audre Lorde, and Gwendolyn Brooks, who were to become her primary literary role models. She began to write essays, criticism, and fiction as a way to "enter dialogue" with those writers.

She parallels her struggle to be an "out" lesbian writer with the struggle to be conscious and black-identified. In 1974, one year after coming out as a lesbian, she withdrew from graduate school and began to concentrate on her poetry. "It wasn't until I started reading to lesbians," she says, "that I got a sense of the impact poetry has on an audience." Finally, she found the support she needed, primarily among other black lesbian writers who encouraged her to publish her work.

Since then, Cheryl Clarke has published three books of poetry: *Narratives: Poems in the Tradition of Black Women* (Kitchen Table, Women of Color Press), *Living as a Lesbian,* and *Humid Pitch* (both Firebrand Books). In addition, her poems, essays, and book reviews have been published in numerous feminist, lesbian, gay, and African-American publications, including *Home Girls: A Black Feminist Anthology* (Kitchen Table, Women of Color Press), *This Bridge Called My Back: Writings by Radical Women of Color* (Persephone Press), *Blues Stones And Salt Hay: An Anthology Of New Jersey Poets* (Rutgers University Press), *Inversions* (Press Gang Publishers), *Piece Of My Heart* (Sistervision Press), *Conditions, Feminist Studies, Black Scholar, Belles Lettres, Gay Community News, Outweek, Advocate, Sojourner,* and *Bridges: A Journal for Jewish Lesbians and Their Friends.*

Since 1985, Clarke has been an editor of *Conditions,* a feminist magazine of writing by women with an emphasis on writing by lesbians. She also serves on the board of the Center for Lesbian and Gay Studies (CLAGS) of the City University of New York and on the education committee of the New Jersey Women and AIDS Network.

Clarke is an administrator at Rutgers University in New Brunswick, New Jersey, with specific responsibility in the area of lesbian and gay student life. She coordinates the Lionel Cuffie Lesbian and Gay Culture Series, a program that features exponents of lesbian and gay culture.

Cheryl Clarke has read her poetry all over the United States and Canada. She lives in Jersey City, New Jersey, and is presently at work on a book of lyric poetry entitled "experimental love."

MAJOR WORKS AND THEMES

For Cheryl Clarke, "Saying the Least Said, Telling the Least Told . . . ," the title of her essay on African-American lesbian writers, is as close as she comes to having a motto. Most of her work focuses on the lives of black lesbians whose images are generally lacking or distorted. She explains, "There is so much mythology and reality in the black lesbian experience that is the stuff of narrative poetry." The difference: Clarke discredits racist and heterosexist mythology, presenting realistic stories that confront the silencing and invisibility of black lesbians and the lesbian erotic. In doing so, she serves as a medium for censored voices and suppressed desire.

Clarke's first collection of poems, *Narratives: Poems in the Tradition of Black*

Women, was self-published in 1982, and then in a second edition by Kitchen Table: Women of Color Press in 1983. "Since I can remember," she writes in her foreword, "I've always wanted to be able to tell a good story. Fortunately, I had access to the good tales—the lives of black women." *Narratives* is full of such tales. From brazen to blue, triumphant to tragic, these stories of sexuality, aging, internalized racism, incest, and loving against the odds speak to the sometimes larger-than-life reality of the black lesbian experience.

In *Narratives*, as in much of Clarke's work, the women are bold. Her poem "Of Althea and Flaxie" chronicles the enduring love affair between two women who might have been mistaken as eccentric spinsters, had they hidden behind heterosexual pretense. Althea, a welder who likes to dress up in a suit and tie, and Flaxie, a true Southern lady with all of the accompanying frills, are icons of butch-femme identity. When her mother dies, Flaxie insists that Althea accompany her in the funeral procession, "and did not care how many aunts and uncles knew she slept with a woman" (*Narrative* 15).

Sexual imagery is plentiful in lesbian poetry, but Clarke infuses her images with irony and humor. Her wit is informed by her exposure to one of the hallmarks of black oral tradition—a relentless examination of everything, including the self, with the greatest scrutiny. In "The johnny cake," she reveals the interplay of irrepressible desire and youthful ignorance. When a woman drives a college friend home for his mother's funeral, she is drawn to his sensuous aunt. While the mourners grieve in the parlor, she tastes forbidden fruit in the kitchen. The narrator explains, "Death frees people for new experiences . . . / As no one in my family I cared about had died then / I knew nothing of grief" (50).

Clarke frequently challenges any attempt to squelch the lesbian erotic. To this end, she operates under the manifesto put forth in her essay "The Everyday Life of Black Lesbian Sexuality": "As long as my freedom to be sexual with women is endangered and under attack, as long as lesbian sexuality is the most invisible sexuality, politically, my poetry must be a medium for the sexual politics of lesbianism" (41).

In *Living as a Lesbian*, Clarke promotes the thesis in Audre Lorde's speech "Uses of the Erotic"—that the suppression of women's erotic serves to cut us off from creative, self-affirming power and information. In "Sexual Preference," the narrator challenges a lover, as she challenges a host of others who would sit in judgment. "I'm a queer lesbian. / Please don't go down on me yet. / I do not prefer cunnilingus / (There is room for me in the movement.)" Similarly, in "Nothing" the narrator shows the extent to which she'd go to keep a woman who satisfies her, despite what anyone else might think. "Tie her to the bed post / and spank her / lie to my mother / let her watch me fuck my other lover." She dares us to judge.

Clarke also examines racial politics, death, and violence in such cautionary tales as "Living as a Lesbian Underground." "Don't be taken in your sleep now," she writes. "Call your assassin's name now. / Leave signs of struggle. /

Leave signs of triumph. / And run . . . ,'' In "Miami: 1980," Clarke counts out the victims on the page in front of us: "Today 16 are dead in Miami / and skies are not yet darkened by Mount St. Helens ending 100 years of silence with molten rock / burning ash over Western skies / balancing the account.''

Clarke often reinforces her gritty realism with the strains of vocal music— blues, jazz, gospel, and rhythm and blues. With touches of Bessie Smith, B. B. King, Jimmy Rushin, and Billie Holiday, Clarke not only preserves stories of the black oral tradition, but preserves the language. The words of Bessie Smith, for example, provide an essential image—one of persistence—in *Living as a Lesbian*'s "I come to the city for protection": "The city fumes with expectations / and the smells of women / wanting women. / I been in love / six times in the last six months / and I ain't done trying yet.''

The music plays on in *Humid Pitch*. The major work in this volume, "Epic of Song," is a jazz/gospel/blues fantasy that explores erotic love between women, jealousy, and the loneliness inherent in being an entertainer on the road. The story focuses on Morning Star Blue, abducted from her well-revered seat in the church choir to serve in the fold of Mean Candy Sweat and the Road Temple Eagle Rockers. With her flawless voice and emerald eyes, Star charms the flamboyantly butch Candy and the jealous pianist Evalena. Soon, they are involved in an erotic triangle fashioned of passion, drama, and creative fulfillment. Candy's "famous, crowd-pleasing song" mirrors themes frequently seen in Clarke's work—independence and strength: "I'm a mean woman / and I don't need a man. / I make my bed soft, / take my lovin hard / drink my whiskey straight / and like my coffee sweet.''

Clarke's women are indeed triumphant in their struggles against racism and homophobia. In *Humid Pitch*, "The Day Sam Cooke Died" represents emergence into and acceptance of lesbianism. Its sixteen-year-old heroine, bored with her boasting boyfriend and overprotective parents, longs to live like her neighbor, who dresses "like a man." Her clandestine love for her former babysitter is the force that finally moves her to pack her bags and leave the day Sam Cooke dies. Similarly, in "Kitchen Mechanics Sequence," a poor young woman gets a brief reprieve from her hard life and runs away with a woman.

Clarke knows there is power in acknowledging who we are and that we are not alone. In "Frances Michael," she gives voice to these common, often unspoken flashes of recognition. She describes a teacher we might all have known, a woman as comfortable in science class as on the basketball court, "a black nun in a white order" whom students secretly refer to as "Mike," "Dyke," and "Ace of Spades." We see this flash of recognition again in "High School." Here, Clarke ponders the fine qualities of Sister Elsie Marie, "vigilant and voluptuous in her habit" and, like other authority figures we might have known at that age, most assuredly the objects of budding desire.

Clarke indeed says the least said and tells the least told. She tells of our triumphs. Whether her heroines escape from compulsory heterosexuality or slavery, they break the chains of captivity. And by allowing us a peek into their triumphant lives, by showing us their strength and independence, Clarke imparts hope to us all.

CRITICAL RECEPTION

Cheryl Clarke has been heralded by critics and reviewers who applaud her poetry for its honesty, humor, and lyrical song. June Jordan endorsed *Narratives*, concluding that the poems "present authentic stories of real live, hitherto unnoticed: sassy/hilarious/grim lives of black women honestly perceived with a clearly hardworking respect and without affectation" (jacket notes), and Jewelle L. Gomez, writing for *Womanews*, agrees, saying that *Narratives* "is a vibrant portrait of our lives and attendant mythology. . . . We recognize the lives and language even if the specifics have not been our own" (11).

Living as a Lesbian has been warmly received. Dorothy Allison, reviewing the collection for the *Village Voice*, writes that Clarke "has burst into lyrical song, jazz melodies played in counterpoint to uncompromising political judgements. . . . These poems reach for the hardest reality of queer city life" (21). Sydne Mahone writes in *Womanews* that "*Living as a Lesbian* is an affirmation of power. Cheryl Clarke creates a poetic testimony of her struggle, survival and triumph as a lesbian" (12).

Humid Pitch received similar reviews. Writing in *Belle Lettres*, Jane Campbell says, "Cheryl Clarke's poems reverberate with uncompromising toughness, piercing joy, and sensual delight. . . . Informing *Humid Pitch* are women's capabilities to survive, love, and nurture; one leaves the book with new reverence for our strength, complexity, and diversity."

Of the many critics who have commented on Clarke's work, perhaps Audre Lorde says it best: "Long a recorder of the difficult, juicy moment, the questions of difference, Cheryl Clarke gives us acute highlights along the journey traveled with resolve, pain and joy. The best of her language has a singing tautness that is direct and unavoidable" (jacket notes).

BIBLIOGRAPHY

Works by Cheryl Clarke

Narratives: Poems in the Tradition of Black Women. New York: Kitchen Table: Women of Color Press, 1982.
Living as a Lesbian. Poetry by Cheryl Clarke. Ithaca, NY: Firebrand Books, 1986.
Humid Pitch: Narrative Poetry by Cheryl Clarke. Ithaca, NY: Firebrand Books, 1989.

Studies of Cheryl Clarke

Allison, Dorothy. "Rhyme, Women, and Song" (Review of *Humid Pitch: Narrative Poetry by Cheryl Clarke*). *Village Voice Literary Supplement* (February 10, 1987): 52.

Campbell, Jane. *"Humid Pitch: Narrative Poetry by Cheryl Clarke."* Belles Lettres (Fall 1990): 53.

Gomez, Jewelle. "Cheryl Clarke's *Narrative Poetry*" (Review of *Narratives: Poems in the Tradition of Black Women*). *Womanews* (April 1983): 11.

Mahone, Sydne. "Truth To Be Told" (Review of *Living as a Lesbian: Poetry by Cheryl Clarke*). *Womanews* (May 1986): 15.

JAN CLAUSEN (1950–   )
Patricia Roth Schwartz

BIOGRAPHY

Although Jan Clausen is often considered a writer of urban sensibilities, her roots lie deep in the Pacific Northwest. Born in 1950 in North Bend, Oregon, the oldest of three daughters, to Phyllis and Victor Clausen, she lived on the West Coast until 1973, when she moved to New York. Her father was an employee in the timber industry, first in Oregon, then in the Seattle area; her mother was a concerned environmentalist. Clausen spent a lot of her childhood alone, reading or walking in the woods. Following her family's Unitarian/Universalist affiliation, Clausen joined the Liberal Religious Youth group in her adolescence in a "post-beat," "pre-hippie" era. Her earliest literary influences were Jack Kerouac, Norman Mailer, Bob Dylan, and Nikos Kazantzakis.

A Reed College dropout (leaving the spring of the Cambodia invasion), Clausen first began to share her poetry with members of her communal household in 1970, the same time in which she began to relate intimately to women, although she continued as well to relate to men until establishing a lesbian identity a few years later. Her first national poetry publications happened in 1973 in *off our backs* and *hanging loose*. In Park Slope, Brooklyn, where she settled, Clausen attended the New York Women's School, including a women's literature class taught by Elly Bulkin, and joined the peer writing group Seven Women Poets, initiated by Joan Larkin with Irena Klepfisz as another member.

In 1975, Clausen formed a partnership with Elly Bulkin, both intimate and working. The two were together for twelve years, serving as co-mothers to Elly's biological daughter, who was five at the time Jan met them. In 1975, Clausen wrote, then self-published, her first book of poems, *After Touch*. The following year, Clausen and Bulkin, along with Klepfisz and Rima Shore, started *Conditions* magazine, one of the first lesbian literary journals, which focused as well on multicultural writing.

Supporting herself often with clerical work, Clausen increased her political commitments to include work with the Committee for Abortion Rights and Against Sterilization Abuse. Although working on poems that were to form her second book, *Waking at the Bottom of the Dark*, Clausen also began to write short stories, work that documents the life she and her friends were leading: lesbians, political activists, city dwellers, mothers, and co-mothers. Further political involvement included anti-nuclear activism.

In 1980, Crossing Press published *Mother, Sister, Daughter, Lover*, a collection of the short stories Clausen had been writing. Her next writing project was her first novel, *Sinking, Stealing*, which deals with issues of lesbian co-mothering. Political work expanded to include the Women's Pentagon action.

While writing the essay ''A Movement of Poets,'' Clausen put *Sinking, Stealing* under contract with Persephone Press, only to find her publishers denouncing the manuscript as anti-Semitic because one of the characters, a Jewish man, is seen as a ''villain.'' Clausen terminated the publishing agreement; although the recipient of a National Endowment for the Arts grant in fiction in 1981, she shelved the completion of the manuscript until 1984 when the Women's Press in Great Britain published it, followed by Crossing Press in the United States in 1985.

In 1986, Clausen began her second novel, *The Prosperine Papers*, the story of a lesbian academic who loses her job and her lover, yet gains the truth about her grandmother's life and loves through an examination of her grandmother's personal papers. The following year Clausen traveled to Nicaragua as a member of the Brooklyn-Niagara Sister City project. As her relationship with Bulkin was dissolving, Clausen retained close ties to their daughter, a high school senior. A collection of Clausen's essays, *Books and Life*, started coming together in 1988. *The Prosperine Papers* was published in the fall of 1988 by Crossing Press, and *Books and Life* in 1989 by Ohio State University Press. During these years, Clausen traveled again to Nicaragua, as well as to Mexico, as the recipient of a poetry award from the New Haven Sister City Project. In 1989, *Out/Look* magazine published Clausen's highly controversial article ''My Interesting Condition,'' in which she describes her current relationship with a man, a political activist who has been a colleague. Clausen affirmed in her writing a continued commitment to liberation struggles, gay and lesbian rights included.

At the present, Clausen lives in Park Slope in Brooklyn, teaches writing at the Eugene Lang College of the New School for Social Research and in the Goddard College M.F.A. Program, continues her activism, and works on a novel, *The Observable Moment When Things Turn Into Their Opposites*.

MAJOR WORKS AND THEMES

City streets, scraps of urban parks, ghettos of women office workers, food co-ops, endless political meetings attended bone-weary after work, women trying to claim some power in a hostile world, women lovers snatching joy in each other's bodies before the alarm clock, before the child's cry, lesbian mothers sharing the raising of their children with women partners, pulling together, breaking up, starting over. . . . this is the territory of Jan Clausen, poet and fiction writer.

All of Clausen's works of poetry, as spare, intense, lyrical, and penetrating as they are, trudge such mundane ground, detailing, from the first thrashing of coming out—the ecstasy and the terror—in *After Touch*, through to the homely images of the everyday lives of lesbians living together, working, loving, struggling, mothering, explored in both *Duration* and *Waking at the Bottom of the Dark*. Clausen's poems speak of soul-deep exhaustion; of anger, personal and political, that will not be quenched; of hope stubborn as a weed blooming in a sidewalk crack. These works, which spiral out from the author's own life, usually narrated in first person, arrive with all of the immediacy of scenes we instantly recognize, having lived, as lesbians in the seventies, so many of them ourselves. Love in Clausen's poems courses through the system, often enough, as a drug. Lovers betray and disappoint; the society we live in barely allows our continued existence; the hoped-for salvation of lesbian community and leftist politics often turns on us as unfaithfully as any lover. Clausen, the poet, the woman, the fighter, however, continually finds rebirth, no matter how hard.

Despite their urban grittiness, Clausen's writings remain close to her childhood source of solace, that of nature: in the midst of peeling paint in fourth floor walk-ups, the poet still cans tomatoes, observes the solstice, and feels the heat of the coming summer infuse both the weather and her lesbian body.

The short stories that followed her poetry publications, do not leave the poems' neighborhood; they merely flesh out the author's always well-chosen images with razor-sharp characterization and gentle plot lines, as ordinary and as searing as our own days. In *Mother, Sister, Daughter, Lover*, the intricacies, passions, and occasional absurdities of our lesbian-feminist politically active urban communities are explored in depth. With far more attention to craft and form than the average lesbian story exhibits, Clausen brings this world to life in an enduring fashion. Not only has she chronicled the hearts of women like Alice and Leah, struggling to build a home with their daughter, but she has captured a pocket of a generation, a slice of a subculture as well. No other author has taken these snapshots, as valuable as they are rare. Characterized by a light touch, a frequent, surprising, instructive humor, these pieces—as well as the fiction in *Duration*, in which food co-ops, political groups, and neighborhood organizing all expand upon the concept of created family—remain refreshingly free of rhetoric, of any agenda other than the truth.

Clausen's novel-length works carry on. *Sinking, Stealing* deals with an issue far more common in our lives than, unfortunately, in our fictions. Josie, the novel's protagonist, finds herself with no legal rights in the matter of custody of the daughter she had co-mothered with her lesbian lover who has died suddenly in a car accident. Since Ericka, the child, finds the thought of living with her father unbearable, Josie takes the bold plunge of going underground with the girl. The odyssey the two find themselves on (detailed in part from the girl's perspective) involves a lesbian's eye view of America, something rarely, if ever, offered in print. The scenes in a dyke commune, bordering on parody, are especially deft. Josie ends as she began, with not much except her hard-won sense of self in a world that would offer her as little legitimacy as possible. Yet this novel, like Clausen's work as a whole, never sinks into self-pity or despair.

The Prosperine Papers, Clausen's second novel, employs the stylistic device of having part of the story told in the form of the writings of one of the characters. Dale, the protagonist, after losing her faculty job, her long-term lover, and her beloved grandmother, scrambles to maintain and to heal by making an exhausting survey of her grandmother's papers, which had been the old woman's request. She finds letters and journals that document the life of a young woman in heady times. Grandmother has had a beloved friend, Prosperine Munkers, an avid labor unionist during the IWW-led labor revolt on Minnesota's Iron Range before World War I. Prosperine, the papers thoroughly reveal, wanted a life and a full partnership with Dana's grandmother, who retreated in fear from such a forbidden love and settled instead for marriage and respectability. Dana's odyssey has traversed the past, as Josie's has the country itself. Yet each woman has traveled the furthest within her own soul. Dana, like Josie, ends up with nothing much— except the ground under her feet.

Clausen remains unique in lesbian fiction—with the exception of Barbara Wilson—as a writer whose main characters are white, from Protestant heritage, with a West Coast or midwestern lineage, a more or less middle-class background. Her exploration of lesbian life of the past, as well, has rarely been offered by our presses. The fact that Clausen's poetic personae and fictional protagonists often find themselves political activists in a wide range of causes stands as another hallmark of Clausen's contribution to lesbian-feminist writing. These portrayals stand as definitive in the documentation, by lesbian artists, of an era that may not have thoroughly changed the world yet certainly changed many of us.

No collection of lesbian-feminist writing would be complete without Clausen's work, which, as a body, holds together with remarkable coherence. Rooted so deeply in the seventies and eighties, these poems and stories remain fresh. Readers may smile a wry smile at where we've been; few will doubt the impact of Jan Clausen's ability to impart where we still are.

CRITICAL RECEPTION

Jan Clausen's work has received widespread attention from feminist, gay, and alternative publications in both the United States and Great Britain (where her books are published by the Women's Press). In Great Britain, mainstream papers as well have reviewed her work; this has not been the case in the United States (as is true for virtually all lesbian-feminist writers), although *Kirkus*, *Bookweek*,

Publishers Weekly, and *Library Journal* always review—and favorably—her releases.

The overt lesbian content of Clausen's work has always been both noted and applauded by her reviewers, mainstream included. Although far less popular than the authors of pulp and genre lesbian fiction, and even unknown to lesbian readers, Clausen has been admired by critics who appreciate the high literary quality of her work. The sometimes politically controversial issues her work has generated (particularly *Sinking, Stealing*) have engendered strong emotions in a few critics, resulting in some rather biased reviews. In general, though, Clausen finds favor with lesbian reviewers who appreciate both good writing and honest representation of segments of our subculture untouched by most writers published by feminist presses.

Clausen's two volumes of poetry, *After Touch* and *Waking at the Bottom of the Dark*, as well as her volume *Duration*, which contains poetry and fiction, received wide critical attention (unusual for feminist poetry) in periodicals as diverse as *Lesbian Contradiction* and the *Village Voice*. Judith McDaniel, reviewing *After Touch* in *Plexus*, calls Clausen "visionary in the larger sense" by the poet's giving, through "her immigrant eyes," details of "her own very particular experience" (4). Anne Blackford, in *Motheroot Journal*, praises Clausen's *Waking*: "I know I need the directness of these poems. They ask what we are allowing ourselves to lose, why our women's energy is still important in our own love and anger"(5). Writing about *Duration*, Lindsay Cobb, in *Rites* (Canada), says, "Jan Clausen is an invaluable writer for her depiction of the lesbian activist community, for no other has focused so accurately on the nuances of this life and the struggles that attend it"(14).

Clausen is better known for her fiction than her poetry, fine as that is; each of her book-length fictional works has been widely reviewed. *Mother, Sister, Daughter, Lover* was well received as Clausen's first fictional work after her poetry. She was especially praised for writing about the everyday lives of urban lesbian feminists, politically active mothers and co-mothers. The only negative criticism wanted the characters rendered as even more politically active and committed than Clausen's closely autobiographical fictional portrayals, which offer more complex characterization (Perenyi 11).

Reviews of the short story collection appeared in *Sinister Wisdom*, *Christopher Street*, the *San Francisco Bay Guardian*, *American Book Review*, *Motheroot*, and *Womannews*, among others. The *Village Voice Literary Supplement* says of the book's stomping grounds: "Grace Paley staked out this territory. Jan Clausen is filing a claim" (White 10).

Sinking, Stealing, Clausen's first novel, was favorably reviewed in the United States in the mainstream *Kirkus*, *Publishers Weekly*, *Booklist*, the *San Francisco Chronicle*, and *Library Journal*. Doris Grumbach says, in the *Small Press Review*, "Jan Clausen is a most accomplished storyteller. . . . with skill and insight, she tells the story of Josie" (27). The lesbian-feminist and gay press—*Equal Times*, *New York Native*, *Gay Community News*, and the *Women's Review of*

Books—on the whole applauds the novel; some dissension occurred around the Jewish identity of one character who is presented in a less than favorable light by Clausen. Louise Rice, in *Gay Community News*, particularly praises Clausen's attention in the novel to issues of lesbian parenting and co-parenting (7). In the *Women's Review of Books*, Adrian T. Oktenberg also appreciates Clausen's writing about "Mothers Outside the Law" (10). In general, critics enjoyed this book for its literary artistry and for its theme. Only the *New York Native*, rarely sympathetic to anything lesbian, claims the novel is "missing most of its guts" (Benal 6).

Clausen's second novel, *The Prosperine Papers*, also received wide coverage in the alternative press, with some mainstream coverage (more in Great Britain and Canada than in the United States but with a few more mixed reviews than her previous work. Reviewers seemed to struggle a bit, both with a main character who is older than Clausen's previous protagonists, slipping a bit on life's downside, and with the book's unusual format—the narrative set part in the present and part as an excursion into the past through the inclusion of the protagonist's grandmother's papers, which reveal a long-hidden lesbian love. On the whole, the book was applauded, and remains, except for Paula Martinac's *Out of Time*, unique in lesbian fiction as a presentation of a piece of our "herstory."

Publishers Weekly calls *The Prosperine Papers* a "marvelously poignant, witty tale" (109). Julie Nelson, in the *Washington Blade*, who dislikes the novel's "mundane yet unimportant details," nevertheless calls the work as a whole "enticing" (23). In *Gay Community News*, Pam Mitchell describes Clausen as a "gifted writer," and enjoys both her offering of "present day lesbiana" (7) and her "delicious prose" (11). Katherine Forrest lauds the novel for giving the "silences of our lives" the "lonely sanctity of memory" (5). The novel's "narrative excess" and "conflicting tone" were a problem for Julie Abraham in the *Women's Review of Books*, yet overall she appreciates the book for "taking our lives seriously" (19).

Although Clausen is the least known for her non-fiction, her two non-fiction volumes, *A Movement of Poets: Thoughts on Poetry and Feminism*, a long essay, and *Books and Life*, a collection of book reviews and essays, have been appreciated by critics as well.

In general, Jan Clausen is considered, in lesbian-feminist literary circles, an important and ground-breaking author. Her work has received more mainstream attention than many, and more attention in Great Britain and Canada (through her simultaneous publication with the Women's Press) than most American lesbian authors. Because her books have been judged as having literary merit, their lesbian content has been accepted by the mainstream without difficulty. Clausen's political activism has gained her a fair amount of visibility as well in the leftist and movement press, which has usually ignored lesbian authors.

Always on the cutting edge (one of the very first lesbian-feminist poets to publish; one of the only fiction writers to deal with the themes she has), Clausen's work has at times ruffled feathers—yet frequently it is important and noteworthy books that do so, books that stick in the mind, that serve as chronicles of who we are and where we've been.

BIBLIOGRAPHY

Works by Jan Clausen

After Touch. Brooklyn: Out and Out Books, 1975.

Mother, Sister, Daughter, Lover. Freedom, CA: Crossing Press, 1980; London: Women's Press, 1981.

A Movement of Poets: Thoughts on Poetry and Feminism. Brooklyn: Long Haul Press, 1982.

Duration. Boston: Hanging Loose Press, 1983.

Sinking, Stealing. Freedom, CA: Crossing Press, 1985; London: Women's Press, 1985.

The Prosperine Papers. Freedom, CA: Crossing Press, 1988; London: Women's Press, 1989.

Books and Life. Columbus: Ohio State University Press, 1989.

Waking at the Bottom of the Dark. Brooklyn: Long Haul Press, 1989.

Studies of Jan Clausen

Abraham, Julie. "Steam of Self-Consciousness." Rev. of *The Prosperine Papers*. *Women's Review of Books* 6: 7 (April 1989): 19.

Benal, Jolanta. "Holes You Could Drive a Bus Through." Rev. of *Sinking, Stealing*. *New York Native* (October 21–27, 1985): 6.

Blackford, Anne. "Waking at the Bottom of the Dark." Rev. of *Waking at the Bottom of the Dark*. *Motheroot Journal* (Spring 1990): 5.

Cobb, Lindsay. "Musing on Burnout: A Long-Term Radical's Report." Rev. of *Duration*. *Rites* (1983): 14.

Forrest, Katherine V. "Historical Papers Give Insight." Rev. of *The Prosperine Papers*. *Lambda Book Report* (December 1988–January 1989): 5.

Grumbach, Doris. Rev. of *Sinking, Stealing*. *Small Press Review* (November–December 1985): 27–28.

McDaniel, Judith. "Touch Poems." Rev. of *After Touch*. *Plexus* 4 (September 1980) 4.

Mitchell, Pam. "Casting Our Reflection on the Mirror of History." Rev. of *The Prosperine Papers*. *Gay Community News* (March 12, 1989): 7, 11.

Nelson, Julie. "*Prosperine Papers*: An Enticing Novel Is Buried beneath Realms of Cliches." Rev. of *The Prosperine Papers*. *Washington Blade* (July 1989): 23.

Perenyi, Constance. "Clausen Stereotypes Political Women." Rev. of *Mother, Daughter, Sister, Lover*. *Big Mama Rag* 8: 9 (October 1980): 11–12.

Oktenberg, Adrian T. "Mothers Outside the Law." Rev. of *Mother, Sister, Daughter, Lover*. *Women's Review of Books* 2: 11 (August 1985): 10–11.

Rev. of *The Prosperine Papers*. *Publishers Weekly*. (October 7, 1988): 109.

Rice, Louise. "Fact, Fiction, No Apologies from Lesbian Moms." Rev. of *Sinking, Stealing*. *Gay Community News* (July 13, 1975): 2, 7.

White, Carol. "*Sinking, Stealing* by Jan Clausen." *Village Voice Literary Supplement* 39 (October 1985): 10.

MICHELLE CLIFF (1946–   )
Mary S. Pollock

BIOGRAPHY

Michelle Cliff has always lived on the boundaries: the clash between the dominant and oppressed cultures in her native Jamaica, the diaspora that has resulted from this clash, and the dangerous marginality of lesbian existence inform her art. She writes in the Preface to *The Land of Look Behind* that "Jamaica is a place halfway between Africa and England, to put it simply, although historically one culture . . . has been esteemed and the other denigrated" (12–13). And she has struggled, she says, to understand the "Afro-Saxon" white supremacy she internalized as a child, and to find "what has been lost to me from the darker side, and what may be hidden, to be dredged from memory and dream" (12). In her autobiographical fiction, the refabrication of Cliff's racial history meshes with her effort to claim an identity with other women oppressed by the white patriarchal system: her mother, her aunt, her grandmother, her childhood friends, and the slave women who were her ancestors.

Born in Kingston on November 2, 1946, Cliff emigrated to New York with her parents three years later. Her only sister was born the following year, and for seven years, the family settled into an uneasy existence on the borders of the city's Jamaican community. In the Jamaican idiom, the light-skinned Cliffs were "red people," so family and friends urged them to "pass," to assimilate into the mainstream. Eventually, the family returned to Jamaica, where Michelle was enrolled in a private girls' school. She later returned to New York, earning the A.B. degree in 1969 from Wagner College in Grymes Hill.

After working from 1969 to 1971 as a reporter, and then as a production supervisor with the publishing house of W. W. Norton in New York, Cliff continued her education at the Warburg Institute in London, where in 1974 she received the M. Phil. degree in Renaissance studies. She is proficient in Latin (essential in her scholarly work), and through her travels, she has become fluent in French, Italian, and Spanish. After returning to New York in 1974, Cliff rejoined Norton, where she spent five years, first as a copy editor and later as a manuscript and production editor specializing in history, women's studies, and politics. Cliff's publishing experience made her uniquely qualified to co-edit and publish (with Adrienne Rich) the journal of lesbian culture, *Sinister Wisdom*, from 1981 to 1983.

Cliff's wide-ranging career also includes teaching. After she returned from London to New York, she accepted a part-time position at the New York School for Social Research during the 1974–1976 academic years. In 1980–1981, she took positions at Hampshire College and the University of Massachusetts at Amherst. In 1983–84, she taught in the adult degree program of Norwich University's Vermont Campus. Moving from the East to the West Coast in 1985, Cliff began teaching at Vista College in Berkeley and developed an experimental creative writing program for young Black writers with the Martin Luther King, Jr. Public Library in Oakland.

In "Sister/Outsider: Some Thoughts on Simone Weil," Cliff remembers that as a girl she lived a lonely existence, stalking the streets of New York, pretending she was a writer. But she faced particular difficulties. In the Preface to *The Land of Look Behind*, she explains that her first published piece of non-academic writing, "Notes on Speechlessness" (*Sinister Wisdom* 75, 11–17), was literally a set of notes about the problems of self-expression in an alien culture. Since then, she has developed this theme in essays, poetry, short stories, and two novels. Her work has continually gained in depth, power, coherence, and complexity since the mid-seventies, and it has been supported by grants from the National Endowment for the Arts and the Artists Foundation of Massachusetts.

Cliff leads a busy, but private, life, teaching, lecturing, and writing at her home in Santa Cruz, California.

MAJOR WORKS AND THEMES

Cliff's major works include *Claiming an Identity They Taught Me to Despise* (1980), a collection of loosely autobiographical essays in note form; *The Land of Look Behind* (1985), poems and essays; *Abeng* (1984), an autobiographical novel; its sequel *No Telephone to Heaven* (1987); and the short story collection *Bodies of Water* (1990).

The quotations and autobiographical notes in *Claiming an Identity They Taught Me to Despise* group themselves into ten sections that reflect Cliff's personal experience, her family history, and the histories intersecting within her of women and other colonized people. The most important filaments in the book are attempts to connect with her mother, her grandmother, and other women in her life. The fragmentary form suggests the difficulty of writing about these compromised and undermined relationships, and the simultaneous difficulty of structuring an identity from a past shattered by imperialism, racism, and misogyny.

These notes—compressed, terse, highly imagistic—are essentially poetic. But this quality of *Claiming an Identity They Taught Me to Despise* becomes more apparent within the context of Cliff's next work, *The Land of Look Behind*, a collection of essays, poems, and prose poems that includes a lengthy excerpt from the first book. One powerful autobiographical essay in this collection, "If I Could Write This in Fire, I Would Write This in Fire," explicitly revisits the themes of the previous book, to analyze in more definite terms the author's own agonizing complicity with the racism, misogyny, and homophobia of her upbringing. Strangely less personal than her prose, Cliff's poems explore these influences in history and everyday life. For example, "The Laughing Mulatto (Formerly a Statue) Speaks" is narrated by a mulatto woman, ironically carved in white marble, who remembers and mourns another woman who has died and two women who "chose to live as ghosts," denying their Blackness and their lesbian identity. These women, says the speaker, are lost to their sisters, and so nothing can protect them.

The intersection of race, gender, and history is a major theme of Cliff's first sustained work, *Abeng*. In this novel, Cliff intertwines the life of her autobiographical heroine Clare Savage with the history of the Jamaican people; in telling their parallel stories, Cliff builds on her previous formal experiments, weaving together historical narrative, proverbs, fiction, poetry, and quotation, and moving back and forth between the culture and language of the Jamaican people, Coromantee, and the culture and language of the English, the oppressors. Like her previous works, *Abeng* explores, through Clare's conflicts with her mother, her grandmother, and her first lover, Zoe, the destructive effects of economic and class tensions on relationships among women. But in this work Cliff also begins to balance the losses with the recovery of a matriarchal heritage, represented by the warrior Nanny, a powerful woman who led slaves in revolt against their white masters, caught live bullets, and wore a necklace of white men's teeth.

No Telephone to Heaven continues the chronicle of Clare's growth into an adulthood that is scarred by exile, prejudice, and relationships with men who are themselves victims of racism and imperialism. Like its predecessor, this novel takes shape as a dialogue among many genres, and its texture is broken by the clash between the island patois and the "buckra," or standard English of the privileged classes. In a commentary on her two novels, Cliff refers to Clare as a "crossroads character," whose life reflects a multiplicity of influences:

She is a light-skinned female who has been removed from her homeland in a variety of ways and whose life is a movement back, ragged, interrupted, uncertain, to that homeland. She is fragmented, damaged, incomplete. The novels *Abeng* and *No Telephone to Heaven* describe her fragmentation as well as her movement toward homeland and wholeness. ("Clare Savage as a Crossroads Character," 265)

The plot of Cliff's second novel, even more than the first, underscores Clare Savage's "crossroads" experience as it follows her wanderings from Jamaica to North America and back, to England, to the Continent, to the Aegean, and finally to Jamaica again, where she is murdered along with a band of guerillas, the descendants of those slaves led by Nanny who are trying to reclaim the identity and basic human rights destroyed by their colonial past and the imperialist present. As in *Abeng*, the central influences in the novel are Clare's real and symbolic female ancestors—her mother, her grandmother, and the Coromantee woman warrior of legend and history.

Finally, reclaiming identity from the wreck of history is also a major theme linking the stories in *Bodies of Water*. The main character in the title novella, for instance, begins to piece together her own identity as she recollects her brother's painful "cure" for homosexuality and copes with his battle against AIDS. *Bodies of Water* consists of three sections. "Columba," the first story in the collection, is set in Jamaica. Both this and the following story explore a theme Cliff broaches in *No Telephone to Heaven*—the psychology of boys whose lives are warped by economic and social oppression. These two stories make up Part One. Part Two consists of historical fictions based on the suppressed lives of actual women, and Part Three of stories about contemporary North America, reflecting Cliff's geographic stability in recent years. In the entire collection, Cliff continues to experiment with prose style, layering history, memoir, narrative, and poetry to suggest the multiplicity of voices that make up her culture and her life.

CRITICAL RECEPTION

Although Michelle Cliff's work has been duly noted in such major periodicals as the *New York Times Book Review*, the *Times Literary Supplement*, and the *Washington Post*, as well as in more specialized publications ranging from *Ms.* to the *Manchester Guardian*, for academic literary critics, her writing remains a country only recently discovered and still mostly unexplored.

Reviewers have praised Cliff's work for its descriptive style, innovative form, and relentless analysis of twentieth-century colonialism. For example, in a review of *Bodies of Water* for the *New York Times*, Elizabeth Nunez-Harrell writes of the "spare and taut language that sharply underscores the harsh reality of the worlds she re-creates" (22). Others, such as Francis Levy in a *New York Times* notice of *Abeng*, comment on Cliff's formal innovations. Reviewers of her later works have continued to note the non-traditional plot structures evolving in her fiction. Most often, reviewers mention Cliff's postcolonial themes. In a *Times Literary Supplement* review of four novels by West Indian women, Isabel Fonseca stresses the relationship between Cliff's style and content and notes that the "rich, inscrutable patois" of characters in all these works conveys the realities of an island culture that is distinct and rich, but alienated and marginalized (364). She also links Cliff's work to a frequent concern in postcolonial literature about the psychic alienation resulting from assimilation into the dominant culture.

Although not enough attention has yet been paid to Cliff by academic feminist critics, recently her work has been invoked in several general studies of contemporary women's literature. For instance, Bonnie Zimmerman's *The Safe Sea of Women: Lesbian Fiction 1969–1989* (1990) places *Abeng* within the evolving conventions of lesbian literature, especially as the novel concerns issues of selfhood and community. In "Resisting Amnesia" (*Blood, Bread, and Poetry*, 1986), Adrienne Rich assesses the importance of Cliff's work differently; writing about the need for art to fill gaps in women's history, especially Black women's history, she defines Cliff, and other contemporary Black women writers, "as historians who are making sure that the Black woman can no longer be severed from her context in history, who are making sure that she *has* a written history which will not be subsumed under the experience either of white women or of white or Black men" (149).

Lesbian identity is an important theme in Cliff's work. However, her statements about her own work, her choice of teaching appointments, and the preponderance of concern with racism and colonialism in her scholarly and creative work suggest that the *most* pressing and vital creative tensions in her writing come from her identity as a woman of color.

BIBLIOGRAPHY

Works by Michelle Cliff

Books

Claiming an Identity They Taught Me to Despise. Watertown, MA: Persephone Press, 1980.
Abeng. Trumansburg, NY: Crossing Press, 1984.
The Land of Look Behind: Prose and Poetry. Ithaca, NY: Firebrand Books, 1985.
No Telephone to Heaven. New York: Random House, 1987.
Bodies of Water. New York: Dutton, 1990.

Other Works

"Notes on Speechlessness." *Sinister Wisdom* 5 (Winter 1978): 5–9.
Editor. *The Winner Names the Age: A Collection of Writing by Lillian Smith*. New York: Norton, 1978.
"Sister/Outsider: Some Thoughts on Simone Weil." *Between Women*. Ed. Carol Ascher, Louise DeSalvo, and Sara Ruddick. Boston: Beacon Press, 1984. 311–25.
"Clare Savage as a Crossroads Character." *Caribbean Women Writers: Essays from the First International Conference*. Ed. Selwyn R. Cudjoe. Wellesley, MA: Calaloux, 1990. 263–68.

Studies of Michelle Cliff

"Cliff, Michelle." *Contemporary Authors*. vol. 16. 72–73.
Fonseca, Isabel. "Dreams of Leaving." Rev. of four novels by Caribbean women,

including *No Telephone to Heaven. Times Literary Supplement* (Apr. 1, 1988):
364.

Hodges, Beth. "An Interview with Michelle Cliff." *Gay Community News* (February 7,
1981): 8–9.

Levy, Francis. Rev. of *Abeng. New York Times Book Review* (Mar. 25, 1984): 20.

Nunez-Harrell, Elizabeth. "Abandoned for Their Own Good." Rev. of *Bodies of Water.
New York Times Book Review* (Sept. 23, 1990): 22.

Rich, Adrienne. "Resisting Amnesia." *Blood, Bread, and Poetry: Selected Prose 1979–
1985.* New York: Norton, 1986. 136–55.

Zimmerman, Bonnie. *The Safe Sea of Women: Lesbian Fiction 1969–1989.* Boston:
Beacon Press, 1990.

CLARE COSS (1935–   )

Rosemary Keefe Curb

BIOGRAPHY

Clare Coss, playwright, poet, psychotherapist, was born October 13, 1935, in New Brunswick, New Jersey. Clare's mother, Alistine Phillips Coss, was from New Orleans, spoke French as her first language, and returned home each year with Clare for the summer months. Clare's father, Harold Thornton Coss, descended from Thornton Coss (the last signer of the Declaration of Independence), and was the son of a small-town doctor in Illinois. Harold was a research scientist for Johns-Manville, where his many patents included the design for insulation on the *Nautilus*, the first nuclear submarine. Alistine, who had been a teacher in New Orleans, was a concerned public citizen, a dedicated hostess and homemaker whose charismatic style fascinated people and whose use of language inspired many of Coss's early writings. When Coss was sixteen her father died from cancer contracted through his work with asbestos, and her mother left New Jersey with Clare and her brother Hal—four years older and now a naturalist living in the Southwest—to join her parental family in New Orleans.

Clare Coss attended Friends Academy, a boarding school in Locust Valley, Long Island. She later received a B.A. degree in theater from Louisiana State University and an M.A. in theater in education from New York University. As a student she acted, directed, and wrote her first plays. In 1975 Coss was a "returning woman" in the School of Social Welfare of the State University of New York (SUNY), Stony Brook. This study helped prepare her for her second career as a psychotherapist. At Stony Brook she matriculated in the M.S.W. program as an out lesbian to fill the college's affirmative action quota that encompassed homosexuals.

Clare Coss and her living partner, Blanche Weisen Cook, met in 1967 while working against the Vietnam War as members of the Women's International League for Peace and Freedom. They left their husbands for each other and mark their first anniversary as the Full Moon in June 1969. Coss and Cook, a professor of history, journalist, and biographer of Eleanor Roosevelt, live in New York City and on eastern Long Island. They remain political activists against sexism, heterosexism, racism, and homophobia.

MAJOR WORKS AND THEMES

In the 1960s Coss began writing plays and also wrote and produced plays developed through sociodrama and improvisation with Maryat Lee at East Harlem's Soul and Latin Theatre. Later she founded a similar grass-roots theater in Calgary, Alberta.

In 1969, the American Place Theatre produced Coss's one-act metaphoric anti-imperialist/mother-daughter play, *Madame USA*. In 1971 and 1972 Coss served as drama critic for the *Drummer* in Philadelphia, writing a biweekly review column of New York theater openings and interviews with theater personalities.

In the summer of 1971, Coss was awarded a grant by the University of Massachusetts as playwright-in-residence at the Berkshire Theatre Festival, where Maxine Klein directed *The Star Spangled Banner*. Coss's two-act play set in 1848, depicting a confrontation between President Polk and Mexico's Santa Ana, was called a "Brechtian Marx Brothers' Manifest Destiny." (The U.S. invasion of Mexico paralleled the 1960s invasion of Vietnam.)

Coss's dramatic monologue *Titty Titty Bang Bang*, a triumph over patriarchal prescriptions from family and society, was produced by the Women's Theatre Troupe of Vancouver in 1974. In the spring of 1974, Coss collaborated with composer Thiago de Mello on the lyrics for *The Well of Living Waters*, Old Testament Story Theatre, produced at the Cathedral of St. John the Divine.

In 1975, Coss began work with Sondra Segal and Roberta Sklar at the Womanrite Theatre, which led to the establishment of the Women's Experimental Theatre, in residence at New York's Interart Theatre. Their trilogy of plays, *The Daughters Cycle*, performed by an exceptional acting ensemble, was acknowledged to be on the cutting edge of feminist theater in the 1970s. Through improvisation with the company, individual writing, and research workshops attended by hundreds of women, Coss, Segal, and Sklar developed, shaped, and wrote three plays: *Daughters*, *Sister/Sister*, and *Electra Speaks*. Margot Lewitin, Interart producer, housed this five-year project in the Interart Theatre Annex, providing support, encouragement, and artistic freedom.

Daughters, first produced in 1977, opens with the matrilineage of the five cast members; develops with family narratives; dramatizes memory scenes, litanies, and ritual oaths between mothers and daughters; and closes with audience participation in the matrilineage ritual. *Sister/Sister*, first produced in 1978, continues non-linear, free-flowing, overlapping styles for showing and telling family secrets and expands the concept of sisterhood. *Electra Speaks*, a feminist retelling of *The Oresteia* produced in 1980, fractures the patriarchal myth that guaranteed perpetual male domination over women. Electra searches and thrashes her way through to consciousness and empowerment. In Karen Malpede's book *Women in Theatre: Compassion and Hope*, Coss, Segal, and Sklar reflect that humor in the work is "a deliberate choice to ameliorate the pain of seeing the experience of women in the patriarchy. We have the intention to disturb, stimulate, challenge, call upon ourselves and other women to change" (239).

During *The Daughters Cycle* project, Coss kept a journal out of which she produced dramatic monologues: "Daughter of Alistine Melpomene Thalia: A Play Within a Play"; "Recollections of a 79-Year Old Sister," in which she imagines her mother calling her sister "a dirty rat—never took my advice about anything"; and Alistine Glodine," an autobiography of her mother. In the latter Alistine grapples with her daughter's lesbianism: "She told me a few years ago that she's a hermaphrodite—one of those women who lives with women. Whatever you call it. I told her I have all I can do just getting through the day" (34).

In 1982, several of Coss's works were given studio productions. "Alistine Glodine" was staged at L.A. Theatre Works. "Behind Closed Doors: The Private Hours of Don and Donna" was presented at the Twentieth Century International Writers Conference at Hofstra University and at the Women's Project, American Place Theatre. "The Dial Tone" was produced at Soho Rep. and "Growing Up Gothic" at the Interart Theatre. In 1983, Margot Lewitin directed a full production of *Growing Up Gothic* at Theatre for the New City, co-produced by the Interart. The play is propelled by the urgency of a girl to grow up fast enough to get out of her family alive.

Clare Coss's ability to listen and capture the voices of women led to another phase of her literary career, which she calls "recruitment of women" who have been forgotten, lost, or overlooked. Coss wants to bring to the stage models of women who tough it through all kinds of adversity and in some way realize and claim their dignity and humanity. Coss found Blanche Cook's mother a master storyteller. Her hilarious and poignant tales of singles weekends in the Catskills for older people led Coss to write the one-woman play *Sara: Lost and Found*, staged at the American Jewish Theatre in 1984–1985 and performed by Lynn Cohen. Sara is catapulted into a disastrous second marriage but lands on her feet with insight and independence.

While at Stony Brook, Coss wrote a paper on Lillian Wald, founder of the Henry Street Settlement, Visiting Nurse Service, and Neighborhood Playhouse. Amazed by how little was known or published about this great activist, she contacted Woodie King, Jr., producer of the New Federal Theatre, with whom she had worked at Mobilization for Youth in the 1960s. He commissioned her to write a one-woman play on Wald. *Lillian Wald: At Home on Henry Street* was produced in fall 1986 at the New Federal Theatre, performed by Tony Award winner Patricia Elliott, and is in the Theatre on Film and Video Collection at Lincoln Center Library for the Performing Arts.

In 1989, the American Place Theatre produced Coss's most openly lesbian major work, "The Blessing," directed by Roberta Sklar. Based on Coss's mother, the protagonist, Claudine Porter, is no longer able to take care of herself and enters a nursing home. While Claudine plots her escape from the home, her daughter Restive and her lover Nan try to make it work. The family agony of "putting someone away" tears through the characters. The daughter's lesbianism is incidental to the struggle between mother and daughter.

To antogonize Restive, Claudine pretends to deny the centrality of her lesbian relationship with Nan. Claudine taunts, "You or Nan should find a rich old geezer and marry him—then all four of us could live together and when he kicks off you'd inherit his dough and be set for life" (43). Claudine recoils from the word *lesbian* as "too explicit" despite her gleefully graphic heterosexual descriptions. She lets up on Restive by bestowing a literal and metaphoric recognition: "Oh yeah. My little lesbian" (77).

Coss has been working on two new full-length plays with lesbian themes. She is also conducting research for a one-woman play on Mary White Ovington, a white woman who devoted her life to anti-racism work and was a close colleague of W.E.B. Du Bois at the National Association for the Advancement of Colored People (NAACP). She also helped to produce Black playwright Angelina Weld Grimké's play *Rachel*, produced at Wald's Neighborhood Playhouse, a first in theater history in terms of integration.

In considering motivations for her work, Coss notes that she is concerned with the conflict of oppression and freedom, on political and personal levels. She also wants to create images of women onstage that we can all identify with. She longs for an end to that train of one-note sex objects, victims, crazy women, alcoholics, and shrews. She would like to see women who inspire us with their courage and illuminate the hidden positive and negative forces within our souls. She believes that having a lesbian and feminist consciousness has allowed her to be more open, to question more provocatively, to have a freer mind.

CRITICAL RECEPTION

Predictably, the most insightful reviews and commentaries on Coss's work have appeared in feminist journals and newspapers. In *Ms.*, Honor Moore describes *Daughters* as "a play constructed like a poem from archetypal moments between mothers and daughters condensed to short scenes, physical images, and repeated questions and phrases. The effect is stark revelation of the root of the mother-daughter relationship—its painful force, its gentleness, its centrality" (29). Laurie Stone's *Ms.* review notes that *Sister/Sister* "dramatizes a state of consciousness [about mercurial relationships between sisters and] proceeds as a series of scenes, poems, dances, monologues, and free-for-alls" (40).

Stages in Feminism: The Daughters Cycle of the Women's Experimental Theatre, edited by Esther Beth Sullivan and Charlotte Canning, is forthcoming and will be published with the complete revised text of the trilogy; it will feature comments from Coss, Segal, and Sklar and critical responses from theater scholars. The book will document the pivotal position of *The Daughters Cycle* in American Feminist Theatre history.

Most reviewers of *Lillian Wald* regard it as a fitting tribute to an overlooked but important woman. In *New Directions for Women* Alice Kessler-Harris praises the "luminescent, sometimes poetic language" (8) of the play. In the *New York Times* review of *Lillian Wald*, Walter Goodman notes that Coss "despite her admiration for her subject [avoids] a reverent tone." However, he seems to have missed the subtlety of Coss's characterization when he adds, "She is far too polite to suggest that Miss Wald, who seems never to have had a love affair with a man, may have felt sexual passion for one or more of the women in her 'family' on Henry Street whom she speaks of very warmly" (14).

BIBLIOGRAPHY

Works by Clare Coss

"Madame USA" (play). *Works* (Summer/Fall 1971): 56–84.

"Titty Titty Bang Bang" (dramatic monologue). *Aphra* (Fall 1971): 9–16.

From "Daughter of Alistine Melpomene Thalia: A Play within a Play" (poem). *Chrysalis* 5 (1977): 59–69.

*"Separation and Survival: Mothers, Daughters, Sisters" (essay). *The Future of Difference*. Ed. Hester Eisenstein and Alice Jardine. Boston: G. K. Hall, 1980. 193–235.

*"The Women Speak" (Act I of *Electra Speaks*). *Union Theological Seminary Quarterly* (Fall 1980): 223–53.

"Alistine Glodine" (dramatic monologue). *Sinister Wisdom* 18 (Fall 1981): 29–35.

"Recollections of a 79-Year Old Sister: An Excerpt" (dramatic monologue). *Feminary* 11: 3 (Summer 1981): 30–32.

*"Daughters" (play). *Massachusetts Review* 24: 1 (Spring 1983): 141–76.

*Notes on the Women's Experimental Theatre" (essay). *Women and Theatre: Compassion and Hope*. Ed. Karen Malpede. New York: Drama Book Publishers, 1983. 235–44.

*"The Daughters Cycle: The Women's Experimental Theatre" (Excerpts from *The Daughters Cycle*). *Heresies* 17 (1984): 54–58.

"Courageous Battle Challenges Cancer" (Sonny Wainwright essay). *New Directions for Women* (March/April 1985): 5–6.

"Lillian Wald: At Home on Henry Street" (play). *Heresies* 20 (1986): 31–37.

"A Street Corner in a Mountain Village, Guatemala" (poem). *Affilia* (Winter 1986): 59–61.

"Peace as a Way of Life" (essay on Erna Castro of Costa Rica). *New Directions for Women* 16: 6 (Nov./Dec. 1987): 14–15.

"Sara: Lost and Found" (play). *Ikon* 7 (Spring 1987): 131–41.

"Veteran Activist Leads Long Courageous Life" (essay on Annette Rubenstein). *New Directions for Women* 16: 2 (March/April 1987): 4.

Lillian Wald: Progressive Activist. (Introduction, play "Lillian Wald: At Home on Henry Street" and edited selection of speeches and correspondence.) New York: Feminist Press, 1989. 1–97.

*Indicates work written with Sondra Segal and Roberta Sklar.

"Single Lesbians Speak Out" (essay with edited interviews). *Lesbians at Midlife*. Ed. Barbara Sang, Joyce Warshaw, and Adrienne J. Smith. San Francisco: Spinsters/ Aunt Lute, 1990. 132–40.

Studies of Clare Coss

Curb, Rosemary. "Re/cognition, Re/presentation, Re/creation in Woman Conscious Drama: The Seer, the Seen, the Scene, the Obscene" (includes analysis of "Daughters"). *Theatre Journal* 37: 3 (October 1985): 302–16.

Goodman, Walter. "Stage: Patricia Elliott in 'Lillian Wald' " (review of Lillian Wald play). *New York Times* (Oct. 14, 1986): 14.

Kalisa. "Re-Membering: *Electra Speaks*" (review of *Electra Speaks*). *Womanews* 1: 3 (Feb. 1980): 3.

Kessler-Harris, Alice. "Playwright Captures Lillian Wald's Spirit" (review of Lillian Wald play). *New Directions for Women* 16: 2 (March/April 1987): 8.

Moore, Honor. "Can You Talk About Your Mother Without Crying?" (review of "Daughters"). *Ms.* (Nov. 1977): 29.

Pasternak, Judith. "Therapist/Writer Loves Both Roles" (essay on Clare Coss). *New Directions for Women* (May/June 1989): 9.

Stone, Laurie. " 'Sister/Sister'—Working It Out Onstage" (review of "Sister/Sister"). *Ms.* (Nov. 1978): 40.

Sullivan, Esther Beth, and Charlotte Canning, eds. *Stages in Feminism: The Daughters Cycle of the Women's Experimental Theatre*. New York: Feminist Press, 1994 in progress.

MARTHA COURTOT (1941–   )
Adrienne Lauby

BIOGRAPHY

The daughter of a beauty operator and a taxicab driver, Martha Courtot was born in a decaying neighborhood of Cincinnati, Ohio, on August 18, 1941, just a few months before the United States entered World War II. She attended Catholic grade and high schools. When she was ten years old, her father died suddenly, an event that marked her life with fear. Her mother supported Martha, her two sisters, and one brother through her work as a beautician.

As a working-class fat child, Courtot found herself in exile from the life of those around her. She objected to the institutionalized racism of the city that tried to make her complicit in the oppression of African Americans. When she graduated from high school, she realized she was destined for factory work. Instead, she saved one hundred dollars from her job as a file clerk and took a bus to New York City. There, she thought, her intelligence and interest in literature would gain her entry into a class-free world of writers. Unable at that time to reconcile her sexuality with Catholicism, she chose to have a sexual life and to ignore her spirituality.

Courtot "knew enough to call herself a lesbian" (unless otherwise indicated, quotations are from personal communication with the author) by the time she was twelve and related to another girl through high school, although they never declared themselves lesbian. However, working odd jobs in a large city, lonely and filled with the underground rage of her childhood, she fell in love with a man who seemed able to control all that she felt overwhelmed by. Together they had three daughters, Thea Lawton, Heather Lawton, and Cynthia McCabe. They married after Heather was born.

Courtot began college for the first time at age thirty, when she was pregnant with Cynthia, and earned an associate of arts degree from Edward Williams College in New Jersey. There, an English professor, Paul Keator, recognized her abilities. For years she'd poured words into cheap notebooks; now, finally, "I learned I was an intellectual and a gifted writer, a strong woman who could make choices about my life."

The new wave of feminism exacerbated existing tension in her marriage and the two eventually divorced. It was with great effort that Courtot continued in school while supporting her household.

Still searching for a classless society, Courtot became active in the lesbian-feminist revolution of the 1970s. She journeyed across the country several times and helped begin and/or was involved with several women's retreat/land collectives. These included A Woman's Place in New York and Nourishing Space in Arizona. Her life was filled with grass-roots activism, mothering, women's spirituality, lesbian relationships, and poetry. She had been reading and publishing her poetry since the mid–1960s and was almost immediately able to make a name for herself in the burgeoning lesbian poetry scene. Her record of those times is a personal history of feminist publishing, including poems printed in the landmark *Amazon Poetry Anthology*, and in highly regarded journals such as *Quest, off our backs, Woman Spirit, Heresies*, and *Sinister Wisdom*. During this period two collections of her poetry, *Tribe* and *Journey*, were published and widely circulated through the women's movement. Many of her poems entered the spoken lesbian tradition and were used in rituals and on various other occasions.

A scholarship awarded in part as a result of winning a poetry contest sent her to Seton Hall University in New Jersey, where she was able to earn a B.A. in sociology. Almost ten years later, Courtot received a master's in English with a creative writing focus from Sonoma State University in California. "My degrees cost my children and myself enormously," she says. "We paid for each one in sacrifice and pain."

In the 1980s, as middle-class women began to reclaim their privileges and many projects ended with economic hard times, Courtot was still raising two daughters. "I began to realize I had not been able to escape my class destiny, but had only opted out of the job market in order not to face it." She worked with frail elders to support her family until illness and funding cuts cost her her job after twelve years.

Early in this period Courtot read Mary Gordon's book, *In the Company of Women*, which, she said, "mirrored back to me a part of my inner self I'd never had mirrored in my adult life, a specifically Catholic spiritual essence." She realized her "Catholic self" was as deep and old as her "lesbian self," and found the two "completely intertwined." Finding hope in the radical thought of liberation theology and Catholic activists, Courtot returned to Catholic rituals. She has been active in her local Catholic community ever since, continuing to work on issues of justice for women in the church while reclaiming her Catholic birthright to fully participate in the liturgical life of the church.

With her children growing older, Courtot expected some easier years. Instead a sudden illness ushered her into a psychological cave, a "rich and difficult" journey into menopause and isolation lasting three years. Her writing changed. "My poetry had begun short and thin, then it grew long and wide. Now my ideas wanted longer forms." She currently writes more prose, publishing essays regularly in a local women's newspaper and working on the manuscripts of two novels. One of them is a detective novel in the Catholic genre; the other is based on her childhood. She has completed several new poetry manuscripts but, as yet, has been unable to find a publisher for them.

Courtot continues to suffer from CFIDS (Chronic Fatigue Immune Disorder Syndrome) and asthma. She is proud to be the grandmother of Sonia Brigid Lawton, a "lively new biracial female spirit of my long matriarchal tradition."

MAJOR WORKS AND THEMES

Lesbian consciousness in Martha Courtot's work is a way of seeing and speaking. Courtot speaks as a lesbian writing about the world, rather than offering an explanation of her lesbian self to others. Her assumed speaker is a lesbian whether the word is present in the poem or not. In the myths Courtot creates, lesbians are warriors, erotic beings, "a love which dares to speak its name."

Tribe, published in 1977, offers eleven poems that integrate hard daily truths as they link emotions with the natural world. Like most of Courtot's work, they describe a world of imagination and spirit. She envisions cultural myths to provide a context for living. Echoing the French writer Monique Wittig, she says, "If there is no history, I can invent it." "What is a woman? What woman?" she asks, and answers, "Hush. Stone knows."

In *Tribe*, Courtot's poems are somewhat "longer and fatter" than other work of this period. Several, including the title poem, are printed in prose. The fourth poem of this collection, an untitled homage to her mother, is unusually factual. "i could always tell when she was home / by the cigarette cough walking down the drive / that cough was a caress to me." The image is of a single mother who managed to love her children against the odds. The mother's self-destructive smoking is seen as an effect of living in a woman-hating society. Courtot repeats this blend of love and pain again and again. She returns to the mother-daughter theme in her middle work, much of which was dedicated to making life different for her daughters.

Language itself appears as a subject in much of Courtot's work. She involves herself in questions of speaking, to speak or to choose not to speak, perhaps not to have the choice. She writes of enforced silence, sometimes of speaking to an audience who refuses or cannot hear.

Many of Martha Courtot's poems and essays remain dispersed in the newspapers and magazines of the U.S. women's movement. The fact that even the most consistent and respected of these publications are rarely collected by libraries or indexed by standard reference sources makes a thorough research of her and other lesbian writers' works difficult. Courtot has published over eighty separate poems in over forty different venues. She has a partially indexed publishing record that may be helpful to future researchers, but many of her collected manuscripts remain unpublished. "I knew nothing about publishing, how to make goals for a writing career, how to establish a reputation, get my work reviewed, none of that," Courtot said. "I believe there was a time when I might have made a leap to more prominence but I only realized it later. And, those years were occupied by nurturing and sustaining my daughters rather than my literary reputation. This is a problem shared by most working-class writers, especially if they are mothers. We don't end up being the ones who are called on to lead workshops and do the editing. It's extremely difficult for us to fulfill our promise."

From the beginning, her poetry has expressed a deeply personal world where the lesbian collective consciousness sings and howls. Often Courtot's poet persona is a woman in nature. In *Journey*, a collection of eleven deceptively simple poems, her body "mimics the sand" (#5) and is "a bell / which rings and rings / and clangs against the Great Silence" (#7). She sees a bit of wood readied for carving and is reminded of a woman whose "future shapes / [are] crouching" (#8). She describes herself as looking like a mountain "whose birds have gone" (#10), and, in another poem, she writes, "I am the rain" (#11).

In her close observation of nature's moods Courtot resists romantic glorification while describing an inner world that is intricately linked with elements of nature. For instance, she speaks of a complicated relationship of separation and unity with another woman, saying, "I have been / both earthquake and desert" (#11). The mountains are like women sleeping after lovemaking, but they hold "terrible losses [in their] deepest clefts" (#6). The "underbelly of a gull [is] extravagance of ecstasy / for nine life times" (#3) but "when the wind blows / it is a dark sound" (#9). Courtot writes about bonds between women and about sexuality, and celebrates life.

Night River, her unpublished 1982 collection of forty-two poems, contains many portraits of women and poems specifically about her daughters. It includes "Lesbian Bears," which focuses on lesbians in the animal and vegetable world. After speaking of lesbian bears, plums, and pumpkins, Courtot declares, "ah, everything is lesbian / which loves itself."

In "This Is a Song for Our Dead," Courtot celebrates women who have died fighting for themselves and each other in the face of hatred by other women. Recognizing that these other women are "mirror enemies," Courtot offers forgiveness and a promise to live because "dying is not enough."

The experience of exile is another recurring theme. "Night-Noises" describes the fear of women alone at night in a house where nothing belongs to them, and in "Each Morning" the speaker constantly returns to the sea where she drifts beyond any hope of rescue. Powerful childhood factors, which Courtot speaks of in numerous essays, helped create her sense of exile. These factors were the racism toward black people that in Cincinnati was similar to apartheid, her experiences with a nun who for two years emotionally tortured her because she refused to deform her own experience to match middle-class expectations, the pervasive classism that limited her sense of what she might become, her experience as a fat child in a society that has little tolerance for difference, and her lesbian nature.

Being fat gave her an understanding of how a person could be treated badly just because of the way he or she looked. She suffered intense pain because to be fat in this culture is to be erased, made invisible by the projections and fears of the culture. In the poem "I Refuse To Be Invisible," Courtot refutes the oppression and projections that have been laid upon her: "the fat woman will learn to grow into her body / will learn to take up the space she is meant for / she will swell with pride when she walks into a room / will you be able to see her?"

The Woman Moving Through the Dark, published in 1983, contains forty-two poems and includes the nine-poem section "Fortieth Autumn." "The Witch in the Well" and Sections Four and Six of the "Holding Fast" sequence, among others, make this volume more directly confrontational than Courtot's other work.

In *The Woman Moving Through the Dark*, Courtot tells us blatantly, with no apology, "I refuse to be invisible." This book takes a step deeper into her own sense of the world, of what is just and unjust, not only for herself but for other exiles. Courtot insists, "who can see how beautiful i am?" and "i am necessary and beautiful / when you take up your camera to take a picture / of the world / do not leave me out."

The classism that was so pervasive in her childhood helped define for her a battleground for her own identity. Her mother's roots were working-class and hillbilly, as she describes in the long poem "Holding Fast," in which Courtot describes the exile experience of a working-class woman in a feminist community where the earth is quaking, and the room is full of women, joined by danger. "When you move away from me / nimble footed and thin / i realize you have your escape route planned / it is private and predictable / it does not include me." She celebrates her own simple roots and asks the reader to imagine amid the chaos of contemporary life women reaching out to help each other; "imagine us all together / surviving long enough / to know each other / for the first time."

Frequently Courtot's sense of injustice and oppression is linked with images of hope, as in the poem "The Woods Are Full of Bodies." Here the poet cannot help but notice the violence, the death and pain, which is graphically present on a walk through the winter woods, but her final image is of buried bodies that rise up and find peace in coming years.

One of the strongest poems in this book, "The Voice of the Owl," attempts to express the inexpressible rage toward the violence against women and children in this culture. Courtot uses the image of an owl that has been nailed to a post, which she glimpses while walking through the woods. She is impelled to include many different women in her lament: "i can feel the bodies of other women moving through me / women i have not known / tender and soft muscled and hard / thin, bird-like women sumptuous and strong fat women / Black women and white women / Asian women Jewish women / Chicana women / Native American women / martyred in public places."

The Woman Moving Through the Dark closes with a deeply personal statement of inner independence. "I have been the plundered earth too long / You can take the tractors of your mind / out of my body now / I am changing metaphors in the middle of my life. This one is killing me." *The Woman Moving Through the Dark* closes with Courtot's rejection of herself as metaphor: "I am a woman opening to herself / A woman with choices / I choose myself." In this book she prepared the ground for the powerful intimate poetry that will follow, a poetry in which the breaking of silences becomes paramount.

"This Is Something I Have To Tell You," a collection of forty-five poems with a twenty-nine-page essay on lesbian poetry, was Courtot's master's thesis which, at present, remains unpublished.

Courtot is a prolific writer of poems, many of which yield layers of meaning with critical reading. It is tragic that most are out of print or unpublished at this time. In a personal communication Courtot said, "My endings tend to be strong. I don't like fade away ends to anything, love or a poem." Hopefully, this will prove prophetic in terms of her writing career.

CRITICAL RECEPTION

Courtot has long been a favorite of lesbians who read and listen to poetry. Before her illness she regularly appeared at popular poetry readings. "I could take an audience and reach down inside each one until they felt the things I wanted them to feel," she said. As is true for many lesbian poets, major critical studies remain to be done on her work. Without the skill and time to push herself forward in the literary arena, she struggles to keep her work in print and is largely unable to promote herself in academic and literary markets. Even book reviews of her work are too few and too short.

The reviews she has garnered came in the context of the lesbian literary culture of the 1970s. At this time, Courtot was struggling to raise her daughters as a lesbian mother. She had to make difficult choices, such as uprooting herself and her children from the East Coast in order to assure custody of her youngest daughter. The reviews she did get exemplify the enthusiastic reception her work has met with in the lesbian-feminist community and the importance of her writing in shaping that community. "I want to say, Martha Courtot, I love your writing," Janis Kelly writes (88). Sharon Barba says this poetry "shares with Native American song a sense of the word's real power—to change, heal, to ward off evil" (113).

Kelly finds Courtot's technique and content so compelling, she uses most of her review to quote the poems directly. "Not many people can string together such a luxury of vowels," she says (88). Terry Wolverton praises her "strong sense of woman-identification [which] is ever present, from the love poems to those which express isolation," what Joan Nestle calls, "a dyke dance of rebellion and courage" (104). Wolverton also finds her vision "both pictorial and sensitive" (88).

Martha Courtot's work is intricate and very female in its strength and vision. Courtot has a substantial underground following of women across the United States, who look for her work in publications and treasure the poems they have. She deserves wider publication and stronger critical attention.

BIBLIOGRAPHY

Works by Martha Courtot

Collections

Journey. Ashland, OR: Pearlchild; 1977 (out of print).
Tribe. Pearlchild; 1977 (out of print).
Night River. 1982 (unpublished).
The Woman Moving Through the Dark. Ashland, OR: Pearlchild, 1983 (out of print).
"This Is Something I Have To Tell You." Master's thesis, Sonoma State University, Rohnert Park, CA, 1986.
Tribe (The poem "Tribe" in a small book). Don Olsen: Oxhead Press (Rt. 3, Box 136, Bowerville, MN 56438), 1991.
The Drowned Girl Now Rises. 1991 (unpublished).

In Anthology

"i am a woman in ice." *Amazon Poetry*. Ed. Elly Bulkin and Joan Larkin. Brooklyn: Out and Out Books, 1975. 33.
"i am a woman in ice." *Lesbian Poetry*. Ed. Elly Bulkin and Joan Larkin. Watertown, MA: Persephone, 1981. 98.
"Tribe" (excerpts). *Image-Breaking, Image-Building*. Ed. Linda Clark. New York: Pilgrim Press, 1981.
"A Spoiled Identity." *Shadow on a Tightrope: Writings by Women on Fat Oppression*. Ed. Lisa Schoenfielder and Barb Wieser. San Francisco: Spinsters, 1983. 199–203.
"Lesbian Bears," "Each Morning," and "Childhood Secret." *New Lesbian Writing*. Ed. Margaret Cruikshank. San Francisco: Grey Fox, 1984. 1–4.
"Tribe." *The Political Palate*. Ed. Bloodroot Collective. Bridgeport, CT: Sanguinaria, 1985.
"Before I Had a Name for God." *A Faith of One's Own: Explorations by Catholic Lesbians*. Ed. Barbara Zanotti. Freedom, CA: Crossing Press, 1986. 31–37.
"Childhood Saints One: Maria Goretti." *A Faith of One's Own: Explorations by Catholic Lesbians*. Ed. Barbara Zanotti. Freedom, CA: Crossing Press, 1986. 127–30.
"Desire." *The Poetry of Sex*. Ed. Tee Corinne. Austin, TX: Banned Books, 1992. 34–37.

Studies of Martha Courtot

Barba, Sharon. Rev. of *Tribe* and *Journey*. *Thirteenth Moon* 4.1 (1978): 113.

Kelly, Janis. Rev. of *Journey* and *Tribe*. *Sinister Wisdom* 4.3 (1978): 86–91.

Nestle, Joan. Rev. of *Lesbian Poetry: An Anthology*. *Sinister Wisdom* 18 (Fall 1981): 97–107.

Wolverton, Terry. Rev. of *Journey* and *Tribe*. *Chrysalis* 3 (1977): 88

DORIS DAVENPORT (1949–   )
Helena Louise Montgomery

BIOGRAPHY

doris davenport was born on January 29, 1949, in Gainesville, Georgia. Her "momma," [Miss] Ethel Mae Gibson/Davenport, moved her children to her hometown, Cornelia, Georgia. "That's just thirty miles down the road," davenport quickly informs folks who admit knowing where Gainesville rests but have no geographical sense of Cornelia, which is set at the foothills of the Appalachians. (Unless otherwise indicated, all quotations are from personal communication with the author during May 1992.) "[Cornelia/Gainesville] it's all the same area." And it is "this area," where the red Georgia clay sticks to everything inside and out, that davenport writes about.

Cornelia's folks didn't separate their yards or themselves from one another with chain-linked or wooden fences during the 1950s and 1960s; barriers remain non-existent even today. Miz Cooke, davenport's third and fifth grade teacher, brought that open-mindedness into her classrooms and encouraged her students to excel.

davenport attended her freshman year at Paine College in Augusta, Georgia, in place of twelfth grade at Cornelia Regional. "[It was] all Black Methodist. I loved it . . . that's where I got my value systems from; my love of learning and reading. The English department was all women . . . [those women] had the most lucid minds—I thought all women were like that."

davenport graduated cum laude in 1969. She received her M.A. in English from the State University of New York at Buffalo in 1971, but she postponed work on her Ph.D. when her sister Tanya, at the age of fifteen, developed a brain tumor that took her life. Realizing she could not help support her family without completing her education, davenport eventually went back to school, to the University of Southern California, where she received her Ph.D. in literature in 1985.

davenport's successes, both educational and personal, lend credence to her having grown up in the midst of a community lacking visible boundaries, with Miz Cooke, who encouraged her to live and learn while being the oldest of seven children—helping her "momma" to raise six siblings—five sisters and a brother. The fire that propels davenport to live and to celebrate life was also the catalyst to self-publish her three books of poetry: *it's like this* (1980); *eat thunder & drink rain* (1982), and *Voodoo Chile Slight Return* (1991).

"*Voodoo Chile* was rejected by [at least] six alternative, feminist, and black presses," davenport admits without a bitter tone, and quickly adds, "I wanted my work out and [self-publishing] was the most expedient way to do it . . . and I did." *eat thunder & drink rain*, originally published in 1982, received a second printing in 1983 by Iowa City Women's Press. It was also translated into Italian in 1988.

In addition to her writing, davenport's teaching experience is also extensive. Her most recent appointment was as an assistant professor of English at the University of North Carolina in Charlotte.

Her areas of academic expertise include African-American literature/multiethnic literatures; contemporary critical theory (ethnic-feminist); pedagogy in/of education; women's studies, and creative writing (poetry). These areas of expertise and the existing umbilicus connecting her to Cornelia, Georgia, and to her family, immediate or otherwise, can be viewed as the impetus for and the foundation supporting the diverse content of her poetry.

MAJOR WORKS AND THEMES

In 1991, davenport received a grant from the Kentucky Foundation for Women that enabled her to live and write in Italy for a month. A personal gift afforded davenport the opportunity to take 1992 off from teaching in order to complete a major work in progress—*The Cornelia Book*. "I want to recreate the uniqueness of [Cornelia], this small isolated community at the foothills of the Appalachia . . . rich with literature and oral culture." davenport moved back to Cornelia in April 1992, a move that reunites her with her community's rhythms, their heartbeats, and "the intonations of [their] voices."

The Cornelia Book won't be the first time this down-home southern community has been given voice. In *Voodoo Chile slight return: poems*, Miz Anna speaks about sex, religion, and death. davenport brings forth Miz Anna's colorful exposé of a neighbor quieting her husband's "white lightning" whooping and hollering for a moment's peace of mind in "Miz Anna—On Death":

i done seen / all kindsa things / uh.huh. / all kinds of 'em. / Take death, now. / Some folk up & die, / some folk though, / you can't kill. / like Lean's husband. . . . said she gave / Wolf—just to keep / him quiet a minute— / some rat poison, & some red devil lye, / in his meat loaf, / for supper. / next morning—he had his usual breakfast, kissed Lean on the cheek, / and said he sho / did like that meatloaf davenport interweaves the hard truth of social realities among these Cornelia voices. This community did not escape history's ugliness. Regardless of where Black communities existed—north or south—indignities of institutionalized slavery were relentless. In "just *one* question—for the world's only real 'minority,' '' davenport bluntly queries the white male political social structure:

i now wonder / what it feels like / to spread blood all over the lanes / of the world, for centuries / to rape / murder, lynch / & legislate people / out of their / rights, their land, their lives . . . just one question— / just how *does* / it feel to be a

white

male?

davenport's poetry challenges the heterosexual status quo and the mirror imagery of its existence in the lesbian community when she responds to the feminist small press publishers in her poem "about my poetry manuscript rejected for the sixth time by 'alternative' feminist-black-lesbians smallpress-publishers" when *Voodoo Chile* was rejected by them:

poems almost / perfect / years ago / still traveling / from place to place / boomerang style. while Legba / voices & Oya voices & Oshun voices / newer, stronger, raw-Chango / softer tones, / ancient rhythms Obatala polyphonous chants / in my heads. / i wait impatient for their Ogun-emergence / in visions i see / between sounds, / hear in silence / continue, as always, / to sing . . . Yemaye / my Spirits / my Ancestors / my Mama / so i can't be stopped. / nothing / can stop / these words. (43)

This last poem's expressed confidence, "nothing can stop these words," is a declaration that davenport will not be silenced by publishers who refuse voice to those whose views and realities do not fit into the scheme of things.

While *Voodoo Chile* in many instances challenges readers, davenport's second published work, *eat thunder & drink rain*, requires an open heart (a disengagement from the cerebral)—a desire to "be free to hear & feel & care & share & hurt & say [you] hurt and wanna feel better." A healing process also requires living in truth, removing illusion. davenport's poem "sweet nighter" suggests substituting the mundane with a kaleidoscopical imagination, including one very important condition—truth. In another poem, "just for the record," davenport takes a very old untruth that women (and men) have believed for years, an untruth intended to keep women in their place, preventing access to power and self-confidence:

one of his ribs he / gave to eve and / that's why he got / one less. that's the / best joke i ever / heard. (whoever wrote / the bible was not only sexist but full of shit) / the fact is / we got more ribs because we are / more complete. / because we are complete. (32)

Another collection of poems, *it's like this*, employs the spiritual, the political, and the personal, with the personal interwoven within each segment. davenport draws her audience closer, eliminating distance with vivid imagery, provoking thoughts and feelings that are difficult to disregard, unless one is in total denial of truth. Her poem "Sojourner, you shouldn't have done that" is a perfect example of her imagistic creativity:

Sojourner. . . . / you told them what was what . . . i got one question. / why did you bare your chest? you set an awesome precedent. / now, everytime they see us coming, / they get ready for a show. / they get ready for a comedy. / or a tragedy, to some. but entertainment / to most. and if we don't bare our chests, / they come right up and rip off the dress / pull out our hair / pull off a tit, sometimes, in the enthusiasm . . . / we knew you were a womon, too—but / all black wimmin inherited your theatrics. so now / what are we supposed to do??????? (4)

In one breath, davenport can transport her readers from a very painful time in history, make them feel the consequences of a particular event, and then take them right into the most private room in their homes—the bathroom. davenport's poem "the toilet tissue theory of life" demonstrates how simple life could be if we would only let the natural order of things exist:

each day is / another leaf. / a year, / a whole roll. except for exceptional instances, / just good for wiping. (6)

Honesty is a constant in davenport's three books of poetry. Her bittersweet words are difficult for some to hear simply because "she tells the truth. Harsh and a bit incisive sometimes but her message is always clear: Loving and Living always and only" (*it's like this* 46).

davenport refuses the three-monkey syndrome—silence, blindness, and deafness—whether expressing love, frustration, the spiritual, a recollection, or anger at past or present social ills existing within the lesbian or heterosexual communities; sugar coating the truth is not her style.

Although davenport's style of poetry assumes a more personal vein than other poets, there is much more than the world of Cornelia, Georgia, breathing life into her published works. Her poetic stories are very similar to many of her readers' personal stories, which allows one to relate to davenport's autobiographical work while experiencing her life through her writing.

davenport has also authored a number of articles, listed in the bibliography. These works are also important, particularly if one is interested in the experiences of an "out" outspoken black lesbian writer/professor.

CRITICAL RECEPTION

Self-published manuscripts receive little or no attention from critics, whether these critics are from the mainstream arena or the feminist, lesbian "clique." Regrettably, davenport's three self-published works have not received any formal critical attention to date.

BIBLIOGRAPHY

Works by doris davenport

Books

it's like this. Los Angeles, CA: Self-published, 1980.

eat thunder & drink rain. Los Angeles, CA: Self-published, 1982 (2nd printing 1983, Iowa City Women's Press).

Mangia Il touna & Bebi La Pioggia [Italian translation of *eat thunder . . .*]. Introd. and trans. by Franco Meli. Milano: Cooperativia Libraria I. U. L. M. Scrl, Arcipelago Edizioni, 1988.

Voodoo Chile: Slight Return. Charlotte, NC: Soque Street Press [PO Box 135, Cornelia, GA 30531], April 1991.

Articles

"A Signifying Short Story." *Azalea* 3, no. 3 (Fall 1980): 25.

"Claiming Another Identity: Wimmin's Spirituality." *Day Tonight/Night Today* 3 (June/ July 1981): 15–18.

"Black Lesbians in Academia: Visible Invisibility." *Lesbian Studies: Present and Future.* Ed. Maraget Cruikshank. Old Westbury, NY: Feminist Press, 1982. 9–11.

"The Pathology of Racism: A Conversation with Third World Wimmin." *This Bridge Called My Back: Writings by Radical Women of Color*, Ed. Cherrìe Moraga and Gloria Anzaldúa. 1981; reprint New York: Kitchen Table Press, 1984. 85–90.

"Pedagogy &/of Ethnic Literature: The Agony and the Ecstasy." *MELUS* 16, no. 2 (1989–1990): 51–62.

"Music in Poetry: if you can't feel it/you can't fake it." *Mid-American Review* 10, no. 2 (June 1990): 57–64.

NANCY DEAN (1930–   )
Ginnie Goddard

BIOGRAPHY

Nancy Dean was born into a male-centered home in Westchester County, New York. Ambitious and successful, her father held the position of head of urology at Memorial Hospital (later Sloan Kettering) for twenty years and claimed a personal bibliography of 103 published articles. At home he was domineering and dogmatic, holding narrow ideas of personal conduct. Her mother deferred to him in all matters in which he expressed an opinion.

As would be expected for the child of a prominent physician, Dean received an expensive East Coast education at the Greenwich Academy, Rye Country Day School, and the Masters School in Dobbs Ferry before entering Vassar College in 1948. "The great thing about Vassar was that it taught me that I had a brain" (unless otherwise indicated, all quotes are based on personal conversations with the author). Distanced from her narrow and judgmental family, Dean began to open up both intellectually and socially. It was at Vassar that Dean met her first lover, Ann Reinberg, and began a relationship that lasted from her sophomore year until after they graduated. "Ann had a brilliant critical mind and showed me that I had been thinking in boxes, making lists to memorize."

With Ann's guidance and the freedom to audit any class she wanted, Dean began the first steps of her intellectual journey. Along the way, she developed a passionate interest in art history, Greek sculpture, and Russian and Greek drama, studies that helped her come to terms with her sexual preference. After years of hearing her father describe homosexuality as unnatural and aberrant, she discovered a culture that accepted and even revered it. Learning that the Greeks, whom she so admired, would have approved her choices helped her to accept her own orientation.

In 1952, Dean graduated with honors and received a tuition grant to continue her studies at Harvard, where she earned her master's degree in 1953. By then she had separated from Ann, who wanted a future as a married woman. After their split, Dean moved to Virginia, where she taught in public and private schools and began a new ten-year relationship. In 1956, Dean and her lover accepted an invitation to teach in Turkey. Encouraged by the dean there, a Barnard graduate, Dean began saving to finance further graduate studies. She returned to the United States and enrolled in a doctoral program in English literature at New York University. There, Dean specialized in Chaucer and Medieval Studies. Her dissertation topic was "Chaucer's Use of Ovid in His Early Poems."

By 1963, Dean had earned her Ph.D., and she embarked on two new committed relationships—one with Beva Eastman, her partner for the past twenty-nine years, and the other with Hunter College, where she taught for twenty-seven years, becoming a full professor and finally president of the faculty.

Hunter was the perfect place for me to work. They gave me so many interesting things to do. I taught Composition, Introduction to Literature, Chaucer, Medieval Literature, Short Story Writing Workshops, Women's Studies, and courses I made up, like "Walker & Welty," and something called "Women Centered Literature," which permitted me to teach lesbian texts among others. But I stayed at Hunter mostly because of the students, their energy, their commitment, and their variety. Most of the people I taught were inner-city students who knew that the way out was through education. They were motivated to work hard and they loved to learn.

Dean was actively involved with the women's movement during the sixties and seventies. In 1977, she learned that less than one percent of all foundation money went to women. In response, she and a group of lesbian friends formed Astraea, a foundation with a strong lesbian orientation, dedicated to funding organizations that supported women's development. She resigned ten years later, and with Beva Eastman, she formed Open Meadows, a foundation with an all-lesbian board, which provides financial support for tax-exempt women's organizations that foster ethnic and cultural diversity.

In the fall of 1991, Nancy Dean retired from Hunter College to devote herself to play writing.

MAJOR WORKS AND THEMES

Nancy Dean's professional field was education, but her need to express a more personal side of herself has surfaced in her writings, particularly in play writing. Although she studied short story writing under Albert Guerard at Harvard, it was not until 1969, when she took her first sabbatical from Hunter, that she took up the form again. The result was two published stories, "The Gathering" and "Requited Love." Her next sabbatical produced a first novel, *Anna's Country*, published by Naiad Press in 1981 under the pseudonym Elizabeth Lang.

In this novel and in "The Gathering," Dean describes lesbian life from the point of view of an outsider. In "The Gathering" the narrator discovers her voyeuristic admiration for the lesbians she observes. In *Anna's Country*, a straight woman discovers her own repressed homosexuality. Dean continued with the discovery of a lesbian identity in her first play *Larks and Owls* (1984), a comedy about a daughter who, upon returning home from college, tries to conceal her lesbian relationship from her mother, whom she later discovers has been trying to conceal her own lesbian affair.

In play writing, Dean feels she has found her medium. She studied the form with Marsha Sheiness and shifted her dramatic focus to the core relationships between lesbians. Rather than continue to contrast lesbian life with heterosexual life, she creates characters who struggle to define themselves, develop their own identities, and fulfill their own talents while operating within the context of a central relationship. *Returning Home* (1985), for example, is a one-act play in which two women examine their relationship in light of an affair that one of them had with a student. This play is closely linked with *Which Marriage* (1990), which also explores a long-standing relationship in light of one partner's affairs with a number of women. The idea that two people can be in the same relationship and see it completely differently—one operating out of denial, the other out of deceit—is an ongoing theme in Nancy Dean's work. *Burning Bridges* (1991), Nancy's most emotionally developed play, addresses the question of whether one particular partner will stifle one's development more than another and what factors influence whom one chooses in a relationship. Another important theme in Dean's work is that of chosen family and the lesbian's commitment to it. *Blood and Water* (1988) was inspired by the support Jane Chambers received from the lesbian community during her critical illness. In it, a woman is torn between responsibilities to her chosen lesbian family and to the biological family that all but abandoned her. During this personal struggle, she recognizes that her father's cruelty has enabled her to truly value her chosen family. *Ophelia's Laughter* (1988) takes place four years after Hamlet's death. Although lesbian themes in this play are not in the forefront, it does relate to women's struggles to discover their individual talents and interests and to develop them fully, an important component in Dean's work as a whole.

Dean has written several other plays that feature homosexual characters but that do not have strong lesbian themes. *Hetty Peppers Stew* (1987), based on O'Henry's story "The Fourth Ingredient," shows the convoluted way in which four homosexual people pursue their romantic interests. And *Gloria's Visit* (1990) takes a light-hearted look at misplaced generosity in a lesbian relationship.

CRITICAL RECEPTION

Anna's Country was reviewed extensively in the gay press and was very well received: "a worthwhile, enjoyable novel," says Marjorie Morgan in *Gay News*. "It gives us back the truth about our lives," writes Suzanne Pharr in *Motheroot*

Journal. "Here is a major novel of lesbian life. Anna's journey from suburban housewife to loving lesbian woman is one of the true and important stories of our times," according to Sidney Abbott in *New Directions for Women. Larks and Owls* (1984) was a semifinalist in the national competition of lesbian plays sponsored by Theatre Rhinoceros of San Francisco. *Blood and Water* had its national premiere in Dallas, Texas, but it was not well received. "A bit too earnest and self-conscious a comedy," writes Jerome Weeks in the *Dallas Morning News.*

BIBLIOGRAPHY

Works by Nancy Dean

Theater

Larks and Owls (1984), staged reading by the Meridian Theatre, New York, 1986.
Returning Home (1985), staged reading at Eccentric Circles Theatre, New York.
Hetty Peppers Stew (1987), staged reading at the Women's Coffee House, at the Gay and Lesbian Center sponsored by the Women's Collective.
Blood and Water (1988), produced by Theatre Gemini, Dallas, Texas.
Ophelia's Laughter (1988), staged reading at the John Houseman Studio Theatre, New York.
Wrath and Avocados (1989), staged reading for Actors Alliance, New York, at Hunter College.
Gloria's Visit (1990), staged reading for Actors Alliance, New York, at Musical Theatre Works.
Which Marriage (1990), staged reading for Actors Alliance, New York, at Musical Theatre Works.
Burning Bridges (1991), produced by the Women's Playwrights Collective at the Gay and Lesbian Community Center, New York.

Novels/Short Stories

"The Gathering." *Room of One's Own.* The Growing Room Collective, 1976. 2–9.
Anna's Country. Tallahassee, FL: Naiad Press, 1981. Published under the pseudonym Elizabeth Lang.
"Requited Love," *Ikon* (Winter 1985): 74–81.

Studies of Nancy Dean

Abbott, Sidney. Rev. of *Anna's Country*, by Elizabeth Lang (pseudonym of Nancy Dean). *New Directions for Women* (March/April 1982).
Morgan, Marjorie. Rev. of *Anna's Country*, by Elizabeth Lang (pseudonym of Nancy Dean). *Gay News* (December 25, 1981).
Pharr, Suzanne. Rev. of *Anna's Country*, by Elizabeth Lang (pseudonym of Nancy Dean). *Motheroot Journal* (Winter 1981).
Weeks, Jerome. Rev. of *Blood and Water*, by Nancy Dean. *Dallas Morning News* (August 31, 1988).

JACQUELINE DE ANGELIS
(1950–   )
Terry Wolverton

BIOGRAPHY

Jacqueline de Angelis was born on March 21, 1950, in Youngstown, Ohio, to a mixed Italian and Polish working-class family that maintained close ties to its varied ethnic roots. Her immediate family included an older sister and a younger brother, but she was also surrounded by a vast network of extended family. She attended Chaney High School, where she was active in journalism and became the first female in that school's history to cover athletic events. Despite the interest in journalism, de Angelis aspired to become a painter and never imagined that she would be a writer.

She attended Youngstown State University for one year, where she majored first in psychology and then in horticulture (with an emphasis on "woody plants"). It was at the university that she first came into contact with a group of poets and painters who managed a coffeehouse. De Angelis began writing poetry during that year, publishing her work in the local poetry magazine under various pseudonyms, too intimidated to let her friends know that the poems were hers.

In 1969, she moved to Fullerton, California, to join her parents, who had moved there a year earlier. She remembers the relocation as traumatic; she knew no one except her family, but the loneliness inspired her to begin keeping a journal and to write more poetry. She studied English at Fullerton Junior College and California State University at Fullerton before transferring to the University of California at Irvine, where she studied comparative literature and graduated with a B.A. in cultural anthropology. While at Irvine, she met a number of writers, among them Charles Wright, Robert Peters, James McMichael, Ron Sukenik, and Lynn Sukenik, whom de Angelis credits with introducing her to the work of Katherine Mansfield and making her fall in love with the form of the short story. There she was also heavily influenced by her contact with visual artists and art historians, including Moira Roth, Barbara Rose, and Dickran Tashjian. She supported herself through college by working at Disneyland, an experience that provided the background for her book, *The Main Gate*.

In 1972, she married Glen Wright and moved to Los Angeles. During this time she taught poetry in the public schools in a program for mentally gifted minors and at a private school for adolescents with learning disabilities. In 1975, her marriage to Wright ended, and de Angelis came out as a lesbian.

It was in that same year that she discovered the Woman's Building, a multidisciplinary feminist arts organization in Los Angeles and became involved in its writing programs. In 1976 she met Aleida Rodríguez, with whom she formed a literary and romantic partnership that would last until 1988. In 1978, the two co-founded *rara avis* magazine, a literary journal with the mission of publishing excellent writing from diverse perspectives (feminist, gay and lesbian, multicultural). In 1981, this effort expanded into Books of a Feather Press, which published Eloise Klein Healy's *A Packet Beating Like a Heart*, an anthology of Latina writers, *Maintiendo El Espiritu* (published in cooperation with the Woman's Building), and the anthology *Southern California Women Writers and Artists*. Both the magazine and the press were discontinued in 1984.

That year also saw the publication, by Paradise Press, of de Angelis's short story, *The Main Gate*, in a letterpress edition. In 1984 de Angelis won a residency at Dorland Mountain Colony, a writers' and artists' retreat, and a Vesta Award in writing from the Woman's Building.

Since the mid-seventies de Angelis has supported herself through work in publishing, including work for an advertising and public relations agency; editing books for NASA, which required her to have a security clearance; editing gothic romances and western novels; and working in her current position as communications creative director for Kaiser Permanente. She also teaches creative writing at a private Catholic girls' high school. She is currently working to compile a collection of her short stories and writing a novella about life in the near future.

MAJOR WORKS AND THEMES

Although Jacqueline de Angelis has produced an extensive body of work in both short fiction and poetry, much of this work remains unpublished. The concerns of her work are primarily literary, which has served to exclude her from those lesbian and feminist publications with more political agendas, and, no doubt, the lesbian and gay content of much of her work has been a barrier to inclusion in some mainstream literary journals. She is a writer whose level of exposure is inconsistent with her considerable abilities.

De Angelis identifies herself as a writer of short stories and is adamant in her belief that her work in this form is not a prelude to the production of a longer work of fiction, but that the short story is a distinct form, the potential of which has yet to be fully realized. She insists that it is "the mode of the future." (Unless otherwise noted, all quotations are from personal communication with the author.)

All of her work, whether fiction or poetry, is deeply rooted in a sense of place. "Interior Improvisations," a cycle of poems written between 1979 and 1985, deals with her father's death and, as she describes it, "the death of the old paradigm." It begins in the Cleveland Airport and proceeds both forward in time and inward to the landscape of private thoughts and personal symbology, symbols which hinge primarily on the workings of matter—the way plants grow, the functioning of machines, the behavior of animals, the construction of the universe—and which de Angelis details with the eye of a scientist, both informed and curious.

Her fiction is no less rich in material description, but in her stories, the profusion of detail is more likely to reveal a deadpan humor and finely wrought sense of irony. *The Main Gate*, a short story published as a limited edition letterpress book, explores an unrequited love affair between two young women who are both employed at Disneyland. As we come to expect with de Angelis's work, the setting is critical to the story, which provides a backstage view of life at "the happiest place on earth," where the magic flight of Tinkerbell routinely ends in her "crashing into a large wet mattress in Frontierland's break area." Also typical is that the characters never seem quite conscious of their circumstances, or of their true feelings. Rarely does de Angelis focus the reader's gaze directly on the central plot of her stories; instead she seems to be attending to a myriad of absurd details—the Muzak that plays "Mona Lisa" or the forty-six-year-old ex-tightrope walker who plays Tinkerbell—while the main event takes place slightly off camera.

The same strategy of emotional dislocation is utilized in "Filling in the Blank," a story about the dissolution of a marriage between a gay man and a lesbian as both hover on the edge of becoming conscious of their true preferences (de Angelis has written a second story on this theme, called "Harmony"), and in "Baby," in which a lesbian relationship is threatened when one member of the couple declares her desire to have a baby. In each case, the stories are buoyed by the use of a dark humor, which "makes the painful parts palatable" and allows the deeper issues to emerge without overwhelming the reader.

A strong working-class sensibility pervades de Angelis's fiction, both in its fascination with the workings of matter and in its irreverence for status and institutions. The characters in her stories always work, she says, "because I do." Indeed, the struggle of the writer who must work to support herself becomes the subject of "Lunch," a series of stories written by de Angelis on her lunch hour at work.

Her newest fiction is influenced by science fiction, future fiction, and cyberpunk, and includes a long short story, "Our Lives Are Nothing But a Complex of Electromagnetic Interactions" and a novella-in-progress.

CRITICAL RECEPTION

The paucity of critical attention given to the writing of Jacqueline de Angelis reveals the state of neglect in which lesbians and West Coast writers languish. While her story "Baby" received praise from a *Publishers Weekly* review of the anthology in which it appeared, de Angelis has yet to receive the serious attention befitting her work.

BIBLIOGRAPHY

Works by Jacqueline de Angelis

Book

The Main Gate. Los Angeles: Paradise Press, 1984, letterpress edition.

Work in Anthologies

"Filling in the Blank," short story. *Southern California Women Writers & Artists*. Ed. Jacqueline de Angelis and Aleida Rodriguez. Los Angeles: Books of a Feather Press, 1984. 151–58.

"No Matter What I See from This View No Matter How Long I Look and Look Again the Situation is the Same" and "Lunch #3." *In a Different Light*. Ed. Carolyn Weathers and Genny Wren. Los Angeles: Clothespin Fever Press, 1989. 94–96.

"Baby," short story. *Indivisible: New Short Fiction by Gay and Lesbian West Coast Writers*. Ed. Terry Wolverton and Robert Drake. New York: Penguin, 1991. 211–16.

Work in Periodicals

"Los Angeles." *Gramercy Review* 2, no. 4 (1977): 19.

"Jack and Mary." *Pigiron* 5 (1978): 82.

"Request," "The Training of Magpies," and "Saucers." *rara avis* 1 (1978): 58–60.

"Suellen in New York," poem. *Momentum*. (Spring 1978): 170–72.

"Cleveland Airport," "Alone," and "St. Joan #3," poems. *rara avis* 3 (1978): 24–26.

"Interior Improvisations," poems. *Bachy* 15 (1979): 64–66.

"Talgo to Cordova," short story. *Boxcar* 5 (Winter 1980): 80–81.

"No Matter What I See from This View No Matter How Long I Look and Look Again the Situation Is the Same," short story. *rara avis* 5 (Summer/Fall 1981): 67–70.

TERRI DE LA PEÑA (1947–   )
Camille D. Loya

BIOGRAPHY

Terri de la Peña, novelist, short story writer, and book reviewer, was born on February 20, 1947, in Santa Monica, California. Her father's family settled in Santa Monica in the early 1800s; her mother is from Chihuahua, Mexico. As the middle daughter of five children, de la Peña grew up hearing Spanish spoken in the home, but her parents expected their children to speak English. The bilingual sensibility in her work stems from this early experience.

De la Peña identifies herself as a Chicana lesbian feminist, a reader as well as a writer. Growing up, she sensed that she was different. Her feelings about these many differences are clearly acknowledged in the "coming out" story "Good-Bye Ricky Ricardo; Hello Lesbianism." This short autobiographical story explores what made this young woman retreat into a world of fiction writing, creating not one, but several lives for her characters, and finding refuge from what seemed like the only constant in her life—feeling different. She felt different because she did not physically blossom as a teenager but maintained the lankiness that other girls were outgrowing; she was not interested in boys, whereas her school friends had suddenly discovered them; her teeth weren't straight; she had acne; and in short, she just did not feel good about herself. De la Peña chose to shelter herself from the pain of feeling different through her affinity for the written word.

Others, including her family, saw a young woman isolating herself from the world, escaping into her room to be with her stories. Of course, what these friends and family failed to see were the people with whom she shared her life— various characters that de la Peña herself brought to life. These early characters helped de la Peña create an inner life while her natural shyness kept her from developing much of a social life.

When these initial characters first appeared, de la Peña did not know that she was embarking on a career that would lead to recognition as a "writer." She certainly was unaware that she would, in due course, become a *lesbian* storyteller.

From adolescence to young adulthood, de la Peña submitted her short fiction to mainstream publications such as *Mademoiselle* and *Redbook*. Those early attempts at becoming a published writer were unsuccessful. Those rejections kept de la Peña in the literary closet; yet she maintained her love for writing.

In 1970, while de la Peña was a secretary in the Chemistry Department at the University of California at Los Angeles (UCLA), two fictional Chicano brothers first made their appearance in her imagination. After work every evening, de la Peña carved out their world. It took ten years and six drafts before she realized that she had something in common with the gay brother. De la Peña "came out" to herself as a lesbian, finally having a name for the feelings she had suppressed all of her life, yet she was still unwilling to "come out" as a writer.

By the early 1980s, de la Peña realized that she could write and publish stories about Chicanas(os). Several books were already available, but one market had not been tapped, and it happened to be the type of writing de la Peña wanted to do most—fiction about Chicanas, especially Chicana lesbians. It was at this time that she gave up her novel about the Chicano brothers and began writing short stories. In 1986, one of her short stories, "A Saturday in August," earned one of the Chicano Literary Prizes from the University of California at Irvine. The floodgates opened, and a significant amount of quality work poured forth. In 1988, de la Peña was awarded a scholarship to attend the fifth annual Flight of the Mind Summer Writing Workshop for Women. She recalls, "It was a significant act of self recognition; acknowledging myself as a writer and allowing myself the luxury of a full week devoted to my craft" (*Lesbian News* 4–5).

In just a few short years, de la Peña's name and work have become fixtures in feminist/lesbian anthologies—*Finding the Lesbians*, *Lesbian Bedtime Stories*, *Word of Mouth*, *Cats (and Their Dykes)*, *Chicana Lesbians*, *Riding Desire*, and *Blood Whispers*, to name a few.

In addition to being widely published, de la Peña frequently participates in workshops and conferences that focus on the particular issues of Chicanas, lesbians, and on fiction writing. De la Peña has participated in numerous readings of her work in the western United States.

Among her numerous affiliations are membership on the editorial board of New York University Press's Lesbian Life and Literature series, membership on the editorial board of the feminist journal *Hurricane Alice*, membership in PEN Center West, membership on the Board of Directors of the June L. Mazer Collection (a Los Angeles lesbian archive), membership in the UCLA Latino Faculty and Staff Association, and membership in the UCLA Lesbian and Gay Faculty/Staff Network.

Finally, de la Peña has created a life that embraces all of her differences and turns them into the ingredients that make up a unique and successful individual.

MAJOR WORKS AND THEMES

Through her writing, Terri de la Peña explores both the internal and external conflicts felt by Chicanas. She does this from the perspective of a Chicana lesbian. Searching for identity, crossing borders, and maintaining one's integrity are the major threads running throughout the body of de la Peña's work.

In "A Saturday in August" (1988), de la Peña's first published short story, Alicia Orozco meets Marti Villanueva at a march for the Equal Rights Amendment. Initially, Alicia is intimidated by what she considers to be Marti's outrageous behavior, especially her easy identification as a lesbian. However, Alicia and Marti feel compelled to reach out to one another because they need that connection. They yearn for *una familia*. Through Alicia and Marti, de la Peña illustrates for the reader the dilemma of being insider/outsider within one's own group—however that is defined.

"Tortilleras" (1989) builds on the themes of isolation and connection by showing the lengths that Chicana lesbians go to in order to protect themselves from isolation while at the same time taking personal risks. Veronica Melendez and Michi Yamada go to see a film by graduate student Renè Talamantes primarily to cheer up Veronica. The title of the story refers to the film by Renè, a character described as a "fine mestiza dyke." The film consists of black and white close-ups of two Latinas clad in transparent robes, performing what seems to be a mating dance of sorts. This story is refreshing in that it consists entirely of the interactions and thoughts of lesbians of color.

In many of de la Peña's short stories, and in her novel, there is simultaneous celebration and loss, love and alienation, recognition and disconnection. In "La Maya" (1989), Adriana Carranza is enjoying her vacation on Mexico's Isla Mujeres, thinking about visiting the Mayan pyramids; "she did not want to view them with an Anglo lover. And so she had come alone" (1). Realizing that she and Liz existed on different wavelengths and were increasingly growing apart, Adriana finds herself having erotic dreams about Latinas and wonders if being in Mexico has made her more open to such fantasies.

In "Sequences" (1990), Monica Tovar meets Jozie Krozinski through a personal ad in *The Wishing Well*. After their initial meeting, Jozie invites Monica on a weekend trip to the mountains. Monica is attracted to Jozie, but is scared of being in a relationship, and is especially dubious because Jozie is not Chicana.

"Labyrs" (1990) is a humorous story about what happens when lesbians are faced with ignorance about lesbian culture. In this story, the narrator is questioned about the meaning of the labyrs that she is wearing around her neck. She says, "This is a battle-ax—the legendary weapon used by Amazons. For me, it's a symbol of empowerment" (32). The narrator feels frustrated at the ignorance of heterosexuals when it comes to lesbian cultural symbols while she is expected to be aware of heterosexual symbols. The narrator draws a comparison with the ignorance of the Anglo culture: "I recall how none of my white co-workers ever question the tiny Mexican flags which adorn my office calendar. My cultural

symbols—clues to my identity—are ignored. No wonder I often feel invisible''
(32).

Picking up on the notion of cultural identity, ''Bouquets'' (1990) is about two
Chicana lesbians negotiating the fine line between being true to themselves as
Chicana and lesbian and still protecting themselves against societal prohibitions.
Whatever the societal constraints, de la Peña envisions a homecoming of sorts
for Chicana lesbians when they can find each other and not have to translate
their lives to be understood.

Similarly, ''Mariposa'' (1990) shows the reader two Latina lesbians discovering that there is the possibility of a deep love if they can trust each other
enough to be vulnerable.

In ''Beyond El Camino Real'' (1991), the reader meets Monica Tovar and
Jozie Krozinski again—this time at the end of their relationship. The story
contains Monica's reflections on the reasons why the relationship was doomed.
Monica's feelings of ambivalence are made clear to her when she and Jozie
make their way cross-country to Jozie's native New England and Monica feels

stirrings of alienation from her homeland. Away from the ethnic diversity of California,
far from the brown people of the Southwest, she had faced the daily reality of being a
woman of color in a country dominated by whites. She had not liked the confrontation.
(86)

It is with feelings of sadness that Monica realizes that she cannot be fulfilled in
relationship with Jozie. She realizes that Jozie is threatened by Monica's need
to socialize with other Chicanas.

''Once a Friend'' (1989) and ''Tres Mujeres'' (1990) are explorations into
family life and the sometimes complex relationships that can exist among sisters,
mothers and daughters, and aunts and nieces. While the importance of family
and home may be an ethnic stereotype, de la Peña depicts the sometimes volatile
aspects of family life in a way that is genuine and familiar.

Conflict plays an important part in much of de la Peña's work. Often the
conflict is between the Chicana lesbian as an individual striving to maintain her
integrity in a lesbian world that is racist and a Chicana world that is blind to
her lesbian self-identity. The result is a woman who is rendered invisible by the
people most important to her sense of herself as a whole person. Many of de la
Peña's characters are immobilized by self-doubt, fear, and low self-esteem. De
la Peña shows that the cost of living as a Chicana who also identifies as a lesbian
is sometimes high.

The spring of 1992 brought the publication of de la Peña's first novel, *Margins*.
This novel makes a significant contribution to the body of literature about lesbian
lives. Of particular distinction is that de la Peña writes as a Chicana who also
identifies as a lesbian—not the other way around. This perspective is altogether
uncommon up to this point in lesbian literature.

Margins focuses primarily on the relationships and struggles of Veronica

Melendez. The novel opens some eight months after a car accident kills Veronica's lover, Joanna Nuñez—with Veronica at the wheel. In this work, de la Peña masterfully creates authentic characters—characters with complex emotions who touch the reader across many levels. In addition, what makes this novel especially important to the Latina reader is that the bilingual dialogue is significant. This is important because for many Latina readers, the Spanish language is a substantial element in defining identity.

Certainly, finding one's identity and then holding on to that sense of self is a major theme running through *Margins*. Veronica finds herself almost paralyzed from guilt and grief over her lover's death. This is made all the more painful by the fact that the lesbian relationship between the two women was kept a secret. Eventually Veronica learns to love again, but only when she truthfully acknowledges herself as a lesbian person.

An unequivocal lesbian consciousness pervades de la Peña's work. It is, however, a consciousness that is informed by an extremely profound ethnic awareness. De la Peña's characters have a certain integrity that comes from this coming together of identities. De la Peña's short stories and especially her novel are memorable because they give the reader genuine insight into the lives of Chicana lesbians. Her characters are reflections of reality, bringing Chicana lesbians to life as lover, friend, sister, and daughter.

CRITICAL RECEPTION

There has been little critical attention paid to de la Peña's works. It is expected that this will change with the publication of the novel, *Margins*. Mary Ann Daly's review of *Margins* in the *Lambda Book Review* notes the cultural marginality of de la Peña's characters and her use of Spanish in the dialogue as a way of providing a "cultural index to the characters" (15).

BIBLIOGRAPHY

Works by Terri de la Peña

"Good-bye Ricky Ricardo, Hello Lesbianism." *The Coming Out Stories*. Ed. Julia Penelope and Susan Wolfe. 2nd ed. Freedom, CA: Crossing Press, 1989. 223–33.

"La Maya." *Intricate Passions: A Collection of Erotic Short Fiction*. Ed. Tee Corinne. Austin, TX: Banned Books, 1989. 1–10.

"Once a Friend." *The One You Call Sister*. Ed. Paula Martinac. San Francisco: Cleis Press, 1989. 49–62.

"Return to the Chicano Studies Research Center: A Chicana Renaissance." *La Gente de Aztlan* (May 1989): 22.

"A Saturday in August." *Finding Courage*. Ed. Irene Zahava. Freedom, CA: Crossing Press, 1989. 141–50.

"Tortilleras." *Lesbian Bedtime Stories.* Ed. Terry Woodrow. Little River, CA: Tough Dove Books, 1989. 83–92.

"Bouquets." *Matrix Women's Magazine* (July 1990): 23.

"Labyrs." *Word of Mouth: Short Stories by Women.* Ed. Irene Zahava. Freedom, CA: Crossing Press, 1990. 31–32.

"Mariposa." *Lesbian Bedtime Stories.* Ed. Terry Woodrow. Little River, CA: Tough Dove Books, 1990. 7–17.

"Palabras." *Sinister Wisdom* (Spring 1990): 38–39.

"Sequences." *Finding the Lesbians: Personal Accounts from around the World.* Ed. Julia Penelope and Sarah Valentine. Freedom, CA: Crossing Press, 1990. 162–71.

"Tres Mujeres." *Frontiers: A Journal of Women's Studies* 14, no. 1 (1990): 60–64.

"Beyond El Camino Real." *Chicana Lesbians: The Girls Our Mothers Warned Us About.* Ed. Carla Trujillo. Berkeley, CA: Third Woman Press, 1991. 85–94.

"Blue." *Riding Desire.* Ed. Tee Corinne. Austin, TX: Banned Books, 1991. 149–53.

"Catnap." *Cats (and Their Dykes).* Ed. Irene Reti and Shoney Sien. Santa Cruz, CA: HerBooks, 1991. 105–8.

"Desert Quartet." *Lesbian Love Stories.* Ed. Irene Zahava. Freedom, CA: Crossing Press, 1991. 154–61.

"Frankie." *Blood Whispers.* Ed. Terry Wolverton. Los Angeles: Silverton Books and the Gay and Lesbian Community Services Center, 1991. 27–28.

"Mujeres Morenas." *Lesbian Love Stories.* Ed. Irene Zahava. Freedom, CA: Crossing Press, 1991. 85–93.

Margins. Seattle: Seal Press, 1992.

Studies of Terri de la Peña

Daly, Mary Ann. "A Study in Character: Terri de la Peña's Latina Lesbians Light Up the Page." *Lambda Book Report* (July/August 1992): 15.

ALEXIS DeVEAUX (1948–   )
Jewelle L. Gomez

BIOGRAPHY

Alexis DeVeaux was born on September 24, 1948, in New York City, where she was raised by her mother, Mae DeVeaux (Gould), along with her eight siblings. Her father, Richard Hill, was incarcerated during much of her childhood and died in 1975. Her mother was supported by state aid and was assisted in the management of her family by DeVeaux's paternal grandmother, Ruby Moore Hill. Both women, along with Alexis's maternal grandfather, James DeVeaux, Sr., formed a strong extended family, all of whom lived within blocks of each other in Harlem. When Alexis was fifteen, her mother announced she was "moving her family out of the ghetto" (unless otherwise indicated, quotations are from personal communication) and relocated to the South Bronx.

DeVeaux did much community-based work early in her career—assistant instructor in English for the WIN program of the New York Urban League in 1969, and creative writing instructor for the Frederick Douglass Creative Arts Center in Manhattan in 1971. In 1972, she was a community worker for the Bronx Office of Probations, and in 1975, she served as a cultural coordinator for the Black Expo for the Black Coalition of Greater New Haven (Connecticut). Alexis graduated from Empire State College, part of the State University system of New York, in 1976 and received her M.A. in American studies from the State University of New York (SUNY) at Buffalo in 1989.

DeVeaux has taught creative writing and contemporary black women writers at several schools: SUNY Buffalo, 1991–92; Wabash College (Indiana), 1986–87; Vermont College, 1984–85; and Sarah Lawrence College (New York), 1979–80.

In addition to academic pursuits, DeVeaux established several community arts projects such as the Coeur de l'Unicorne Gallery, in which she exhibited her paintings. With Gwendolyn Hardwick, she formed the Flamboyant Ladies Theatre Company (1977–84), which created performances exploring the lives of black women and sponsored regular Sunday salons in Brooklyn where women shared their art. DeVeaux also created the Gap Tooth Girlfriends Writing Workshop (1980–84), which produced two volumes of original poetry and fiction. On her own she has written seven plays that have been produced nationally; two of them, *The Tapestry* and *Circles*, were broadcast on national public television in 1979.

When asked about the beginnings of her writing career, DeVeaux responds, "I was the one always documenting what was going on when my mother was out. I was the one always telling on my brothers and sisters." She goes on to say that this initial impulse to observe and relate was further fed by the influence of her Uncle Frank:

He used to come by our house and entertain us with stories for hours. He would act out the stories, putting on different things from around the house to make costumes, making us laugh. And he'd be talking about getting over on white people. A definite trickster figure. From him I realized that the stories were important because they showed you how to resist and survive. You could be smart even if you had nothing material.

DeVeaux's poetry and fiction have been translated into Japanese, Dutch, and Spanish, and have garnered a number of awards including first prize for fiction from the Institute for Afro-American Affairs, New York University, 1972; Art Books for Children Award from Brooklyn Museum in 1974 and 1975; Unity in Media Award for political reporting from Lincoln University in 1982 and 1983; the Fannie Lou Hamer Award for excellence in the arts from Medgar Evers College in 1984; and the Humanitarian Award in 1984 from MADRE, an organization addressing the concerns of women in war-torn Latin American countries.

She was also the recipient of a Creative Artists in Public Service grant from the New York State Council on the Arts in 1981 and a National Endowment for the Arts Fellowship in Fiction in 1981.

Alexis DeVeaux was an editor at large for *Essence* magazine from 1978 to 1990 and continues to write for it regularly. She is currently an assistant professor in women's studies and American studies at SUNY Buffalo, where she will receive her Ph.D. in American studies in 1992.

MAJOR WORKS AND THEMES

The range of Alexis DeVeaux's writing spans journalism, poetry, theater, and fiction for adults and young people. In all of her work the essence of jazz and the root of Africa can always be felt. The concept of sisterhood is also an important element in much of her work. In the play *The Tapestry* (first performed in 1975 and broadcast on public television in 1976) she begins to introduce these themes. Using the spelling and rhythmic verses of poetry, the play captures a pivotal moment in the life of Jet, a young black woman. She is balancing the strenuous demands of law school, the idealism that has led her to her studies, and the realities of black life and poverty. As she struggles to prepare for final exams, she's confronted by the surrealistic images of her past—her family, the church choir—which are both comforting and menacing.

Jet's internal conflicts are also manifested in her relationship with Axis, a jazz musician, who says "i like a woman who knows how to be a woman for a man." Jet rebels against this "narrow damn view," and Axis shifts his attentions to Jet's neighbor and friend, Lavender. In the end Jet understands that she has to let go of all of these people she's dependent on because they have, in fact, become dependents. Jet's determination not to be infantilized by Axis is a tug-of-war that parallels the vision of baptism that progresses throughout the play. And like the cold water signifying her rebirth, the shock of Lavender's betrayal of their sisterhood pushes Jet into complete independence.

Her play *A Season to Unravel*, performed at the Negro Ensemble Company (New York City) in 1979, also examines the psychological struggle of a young black woman but begins to weave the full range of complexities of that struggle. The main character, Erzula, is faced with the physical embodiment of the many facets of her personality as she attempts to determine which is the real persona. Here the question of desire becomes more problematic—touching on desire for other women as well as the unresolved pain resulting from incestuous desire.

A later theatrical presentation, *No*, explores even more fully the elements that her earlier work introduces. Produced at the New Federal Theatre in 1981, *No* is an assemblage of poems, scenes, and stories that bring her woman-centered vision more clearly into focus. The play as produced has not been published, but some of the work appears in the unnumbered portfolio of poems *Blue Heat*.

Of varying lengths, the pieces look toward the time and place where loyalty and desire are successfully completed rather than thwarted. One of the most dramatic and sensuous sections is entitled "Erotic Folktale #7." Delivered in the shape of an African griot tale, it tells of a woman named Usawa who was "between a time in the land of FA (which was somewhere on the skirts of Brooklyn) who was dizzy for a sculptress named Blackberrie." The feelings are mutual, but Blackberrie has committed herself to celibacy until the piece of wood she wants to work with has finally "breathed." Usawa accepts the restrictions, going on with her life until the miracle of breath fills the wood. Blackberrie carves the first stroke and calls to say "I'm coming over." Here one woman's ambition and vocation is supported by another rather than betrayed. The language DeVeaux uses is a comfortable blend of lyricism and vernacular, a hallmark of her most successful work.

When asked what issues or ideas sit down with her at the typewriter, DeVeaux responded, "I always think about resistance, community, being empowered, love or the absence of love, the future and its possibilities." These ideas fill much of *No* including an often-reprinted section, "The Riddles of Egypt Brownstone,'' which tells of a young girl, Egypt Brownstone, who is born to a young mother in East Harlem. It is a childhood of stoop ball and women holding court from their tenement windows. Egypt enjoys the mythology of riddles and the energy of playing in the city street but does not enjoy the secret fondling of Prince, the store owner her mother dates. He promises extra groceries with each abusive encounter, leaving Egypt caught between disgust and fear of depriving the family of food. It's a dilemma resolved only when Egypt begins her menstrual cycle and her mother begins to note Prince's unusual interest in her daughter and the change in the smell of her daughter's body. Her mother announces that Egypt is ''not to go to Prince's store no more she had stopped shopping there.''

With explicit words, names, and references DeVeaux continually forges the link between African peoples on the African continent and in the United States. Her two most popular books are both quintessentially of Africa and of the United States—*An Enchanted Hair Tale* and *Don't Explain*. *Don't Explain* is an epic poem of the life of legendary jazz singer Billie Holiday.

DeVeaux maintains the varied rhythms of jazz and blues to retell Billie's rise to stardom and the terrible toll racism and sexism take on her and others in show business. DeVeaux places Billie Holiday and the other African-American innovators of jazz and blues within an African historical context; they are part of a long line of geniuses culminating in many African things such as jazz or style or hair.

In her book for young adults, *An Enchanted Hair Tale*, DeVeaux tells the story of a boy named Sudan. Sudan is at the mercy of his childhood friends' derision but is saved by a friend of his mother's, Miss Pearl, who is with a traveling circus called the Flying Dreads. Weaving mythical images (and the exuberant illustrations of Cheryl Hanna), DeVeaux continues to emphasize the woman-centered vision of her interpretation of African-American culture. An added element of her work is often her own illustrations. They are part of several of her books and show a deep connection to both African heritage and the stark western, urban landscape. Her drawings, which adorn *Na-ni* and *Spirit in the Streets*, have both a haute couture sophistication and folk craft that help carry the complexity of her imagination.

DeVeaux brings these complex rhythms to her readings of her work and can be said to have continued the tradition of African-American storytelling carried forward by Nikki Giovanni and Audre Lorde in the 1960s and to have helped launch the idea of the contemporary performance poet. Each of DeVeaux's essays exhibits this same, expansive political and literary vision and applies it to the many aspects of black life. She places herself within the parameters of her magazine articles, giving them added resonance. Each takes on the rhthym of jazz—from her 1984 celebration of gay liberation in the *Village Voice* to her interview with Nelson and Winnie Mandela written on the occasion of his release from more than a generation of imprisonment in South Africa. In all of her work, both fiction and non-fiction, DeVeaux is able to pull together the strands of ethnicity—both historic and contemporary—and weave them through the patterns of class and gender as experienced in this country to create a fuller picture of African-American life.

In her introduction to *Gap Tooth Girlfriends—The Third Act*, the anthology that was a product of her workshop, she wrote: "Continuity. The will to survive. Belief in the unseen. Sheer and delicate. Belief in self. In another Black woman. A risky idea" (13). Her writing—plays, poems, fiction, journalism—has all been an artful reaffirmation of her commitment to that risky idea.

CRITICAL RECEPTION

The clear African-American cultural context and the lyrical style of the work of Alexis DeVeaux makes it immediately appealing to black audiences and the press of the black community. But the consistently woman-identified themes present a problem for most reviewers. The performance of *No* at the Henry Street Settlement in 1981 set off a flurry of letters and competitive reviews in Harlem's *Amsterdam News*, most of which addressed the nature of lesbianism in the African-American community rather than the dramatic quality of the writing. Yusef A. Salaam's review neglected any literary criticism in favor of assessing her political positions (from "sharp" to "naive"). In citing police statistics about the death rate of black men at the hands of whites, Salaam attempted to dismiss DeVeaux's anger at the fate of black women at the hands of black male violence. He ends his review with a flat denial of lesbian existence in African culture.

That piece is answered subsequently by Rhea Mandulo for the same paper in which she urges people to see the work. She minimizes its lesbianism and feminism and finds the play's worth in its ability to deal "poetically, dramatically and soul-searchingly with a very personal point of view" (27).

John S. Patterson, writing for a general interest paper in Greenwich Village, called *No* a "succession of stunning images—an elegant demonstration of flamboyant, gorgeous, black American physicality." He found her love poems "so firmly focused on the adoration of an individual . . . that the surrounding world exists only through the eyes of the subject." While he thought it "lack[ed] inner structure," he said that was "compensated for . . . with a flash . . . aggressivity [*sic*] and boldness" (17).

Interestingly enough, the fullest, mainstream appreciation of DeVeaux's work has come from Mel Gussow of the *New York Times*. Reviewing the production of *No*, he identifies the "black roots and black rage at the heart" and sees its evolutionary relationship to Shange's *For Colored Girls Who've Considered Suicide when the Rainbow is Enuf*. He calls her language "lush to the point of being rhapsodic, a forest of colors, foods and smells" (14).

There still remains no critical work done on DeVeaux's epic prose poem on the life of Billie Holiday, *Don't Explain*. It is, as Cheryl Clarke said of *Blue Heat*, a portfolio collection of some poems from *No* and elsewhere, "Eloquent, insightful, poignant'' (156) and ''a woman centered and woman identified poetics'' (158).

BIBLIOGRAPHY

Works by Alexis DeVeaux

Books

Na-ni. New York: Harper and Row, 1973.
Spirits in the Street. New York: Doubleday, 1973.
Don't Explain: A Song of Billie Holiday. New York: Harper and Row, 1980.
Blue Heat, Poems. Brooklyn, NY: Diva Publishing, 1985.
An Enchanted Hair Tale. New York: Harper and Row, 1987; paperback reissue, 1991.

Plays

The Tapestry and *Circles*. *Nine Plays by Black Women Playwrights*. Ed. Margaret Wilkerson. New York: New American Library, 1986. 56–84.

Productions

Circles. Frederick Douglass Creative Arts Center, New York, 1973.
The Tapestry. Genesis Arts Co., San Diego, CA, 1991, and KCET-TV, Los Angeles, 1976.
A Season to Unravel. Negro Ensemble Company, New York, 1979.
No. New Federal Theatre, New York, 1981.

Essays

''Renegade Spirit: Standing up for Gay Liberation in the Reagan Era.'' *Village Voice* (June 1984): 8.
''Going South: Black Women and the Legacies of the Civil Rights Movement.'' *Essence* (May 1985).
''New Body, New Life: Dealing with Black Women's Health Issues.'' *Essence* (June 1988).
''Alice Walker: Rebel with a Cause.'' *Essence* (September 1989).
''Forty Fine: A Writer Reflects on Turning Forty.'' *Essence* (January 1990): 57.
''Walking Into Freedom with Nelson and Winnie Mandela.'' *Essence* (June 1990): 13–15.

Short Stories

''The Riddles of Egypt Brownstone'' and ''Remember Him A Outlaw.'' *Midnight Birds*. Ed. Mary Helen Washington. New York: Doubleday, 1980. 78–81 and 90–91.
''Adventures of the Dread Sisters.'' *Memory of Kin, Stories about Family by Black Writers*. Ed. Mary Helen Washington. New York: Doubleday, 1991. 32–37.

Studies of Alexis DeVeaux

Clarke, Cheryl. Rev of *Blue Heat: A Portfolio of Poems and Drawings*. *Conditions* 13 (1986): 154–58.

Davis, Curt. Rev. of *No. Other Stages* (May 7, 1981): 5.

Gomez, Jewelle. "Commanding Performances: Alexis DeVeaux and the Flamboyant Ladies Company." *New York Native* (March 26, 1984): 12.

Gussow, Mel. Rev. of *No. New York Times* (June 6, 1981): 14.

Lewis Williams, Julinda. Rev. of *A Season to Unravel. Black American* 18 no. 6.10.

Mandulo, Rhea. Rev. of *No. Amsterdam News* (June 20, 1981): 27.

Patterson, John S. Rev. of *No. Villager* (June 4, 1981): 17.

Salaam, Yusef A. Rev. of *No. Amsterdam News* (May 16, 1981): 36.

Tate, Claudia. *Blackwomen Writers at Work*. New York: Continuum, 1983. 49–59.

RACHEL GUIDO deVRIES
(1947–)
Susan Sherman

BIOGRAPHY

Rachel Guido deVries was born on September 9, 1947, in Paterson, New Jersey. The daughter of Southern Italian-American parents, she has a younger brother and sister. During her formative years, her father drove a truck, and her mother, a housewife, worked for some time as a meat-packer at an A&P supermarket. DeVries vividly recalls "sitting around the table with my mother and her five sisters, listening to them talk about families, marriage and their lives as women." (Unless otherwise noted, all quotations are from personal communication with the author.) She attended high school at Manchester Regional High and comments wryly that she enrolled at the St. Joseph's Hospital School of Nursing in Paterson, New Jersey, because "I had a very articulate cousin who was a nurse. None of my family had gone to college, and I thought if I became a nurse I could be articulate too!"

DeVries received her R.N. in 1968, and in 1974, deVries and her husband, Marten, went to Kenya to do child development research. Although she had been writing since she was little, it was in Kenya that deVries "met a novelist who read my work and encouraged me to pursue writing full-time." From 1975 to 1976 she studied creative writing and women's studies at the Women's Writers' Center in Cazenovia, New York (a non-degree-granting program), during which time she came out as a lesbian and got divorced. She received a B.S. in general studies with honors from the University of Rochester (New York) in 1976 and attended Syracuse University (New York) from 1976 to 1978 in the master's program in creative writing. Her thesis was a book of poems titled *An Arc of Light*.

From 1978 to 1982, Rachel Guido deVries was resident faculty member and co-director of the Women's Writers' Center. She was director of the Feminist Women's Writing Workshops at Wells College from September 1990 to September 1991 and was on the resident faculty of the workshops in July 1989 and 1990. Since 1989, deVries has been an adjunct instructor of creative writing and English at the Onondaga Community College in Syracuse, New York, and an instructor of creative writing at the Humanistic Studies Center, University College of Syracuse University.

One of her major undertakings has been the Community Writers' Project in Syracuse, New York—a multicultural program of readings, forums, and cultural presentations that publishes a newsletter and attempts to bring together members of the immediate community with writers and scholars of national importance. She served as co-director of the project from 1984 to 1987, when she became director.

Since 1984, deVries has also worked as a poet-in-residence in the Alternate Literary Programs in the Schools (six-day residencies at elementary and high schools throughout upstate New York) and has conducted workshops for convicted felons as a poet-in-residence at the Central New York Psychiatric Center in Marcy, New York. DeVries currently lives in Cazenovia, New York.

Rachel Guido deVries's awards include a 1987 fiction fellowship from the New York Foundation for the Arts, a 1987 fellowship to the Millay Colony for the Arts, and a 1989 New York State Council on the Arts Writer-in-Residence Award for a four-month residence at the Oswego Art Guild.

MAJOR WORKS AND THEMES

As a novelist and poet, Rachel Guido deVries deals most often with her Southern Italian heritage and her lesbian identity: "[M]y experience as a Southern Italian-American includes writing about blood families and families I create." Nowhere is that concern more evident than in her published work of fiction, *Tender Warriors* (Firebrand, 1986).

DeVries dedicates her novel to her "mother and father, who taught me how to love, how to fight, how to survive" (7), and it is an altogether appropriate dedication because *Tender Warriors* is a book about the endurance of an Italian-American family weighted down by pressures both external and internal that would seemingly make their holding together impossible.

Tender Warriors opens with a declaration by the focal character, Sonny deMarco, that "he was damned if he was going to let anybody—not even his father—stop him from getting by" (11), setting the theme of survival that will come full circle by the novel's end as well as introducing the writing style of the book, which powerfully weaves present narrative action and memory, the story line, and the characters' relationship to events, past and present, into a seamless whole. Sonny's father has thrown him out (or Sonny has left home) after a bitter fight, and Sonny is working as a short order cook. Quickly, we learn through Sonny's memories that he has a sister, Lorraine, who is a drug addict (we later discover she is a recovering addict who lives in a trailer with her children and her husband, who is black). We also learn about Sonny's sister, Rose, and father, Dominic, who has a history of physically abusing the family.

The second chapter introduces us directly to Rose, who is a lesbian in a supportive relationship, as well as a nurse and a photographer. It also introduces us to Josephine, their mother, who supplies much of the background motivation for the actions and events that ensue—even though she is, ironically, a character whose influence is in her absence; she has been dead for two years.

Sonny, who suffers from a serious brain disease, cannot accept his mother's death. His odyssey takes place in his mind and in his conversations with his friends, particularly Moses O'Toole, as Sonny moves back and forth from fantasy to reality to fantasy—reality fading more and more from his consciousness as the story line progresses. DeVries's writing moves powerfully and persuasively through his fluctuations until it builds to an almost unbearable crescendo. Ironically, it is Rose, the lesbian, who has most contact with the external world, who is most able to connect the pieces of the family through the inevitable and violent confrontation at the novel's end.

DeVries is currently working on a new novel, *The Lost Era of Frank Sinatra* (working title)—the image of Frank Sinatra functioning metaphorically in a book exploring Italian-American culture immediately after World War II to the present. Two of the main characters, Jude and Liz, are lesbians exploring their relationship to their culture inside the larger society.

The focus of much of Rachel Guido deVries's poetry is on lesbian relationships, often containing strong but delicate erotic elements and, of course, her Southern Italian-American heritage. Although her poems have been extensively published in magazines and anthologies, her three most recent collections remain unpublished. *Cave Songs* (1985), which was a finalist for an Ohio State University award in poetry in 1989, is about "losing the familiar, entering the cave and learning the music of solitude." *The Notmother Poems* (1990) explores the choice not to have children, particularly in the light of being a lesbian, and all the poems in her most recent manuscript, *How to Sing to a Dago and Other Canzonetti* (working title, 1992), are about the Italian-American experience and the way she, as a lesbian, fits within that tradition.

CRITICAL RECEPTION

Tender Warriors, deVries's widely read and reviewed novel from Firebrand Press, is her only novel published to date. The feminist press gave the book almost universal critical acclaim, with comments like that in the *Feminist Publishers News* (vol. 2, no. 2) being typical: "After reading what seems is an endless stream of tepid novels revolving around hot sex, one picks up another novel to review with a moan and a sigh. Much to one's surprise and delight *Tender Warriors*, a novel by Rachel Guido deVries, breaks the pattern" (10). *Lesbian Connection* (Spring 1987) observes that the novel is "notable as a story with lesbian characters in which the main theme is not lesbianism. About a working class Catholic family striving to heal itself'' (32). Lee Lynch, in the *Women's Review of Books* (July–August 1987), writes that ''DeVries has written a moving, careful novel which feels its way through suffering to a shattered family's salvation: Sonny. He contains—is—the volatile, easily bruised spirit of love. Yet it is so blocked in him that it threatens, literally, to burst in his brain and kill him. Rosa, the lesbian, who is ironically the savior of the family, mobilizes Lorraine and crusty, macho Dominic to thwart death and release the love that can bond them all'' (18).

Some of the more traditional venues recognized the novel's lesbian content as well as its literary value. Tom Dial, a staff writer for the *Syracuse Herald*, mentions that Rose is a lesbian as well as commenting that ''DeVries writes with a strong, rhythmic flow, but it is far removed from the stream-of-consciousness style that so befuddles the average reader. This is a clear, concise novel that explores the inner feelings with outer portrayals'' (13). The *Windy City Times* (July 31, 1986) has a laudatory review calling *Tender Warriors* ''a subtle, honest novel of working class people . . . .There are a number of surprises and moments of dramatic tension that make the book compelling reading'' (21). The review explicitly talks about lesbianism: ''Lesbianism is not the focus of the book, but an element in the family dynamic, yet interestingly, the only graphic love scene in the book occurs between Rosie and her lover.''

BIBLIOGRAPHY

Works by Rachel Guido deVries

Books

An Arc of Light (out of print). Cazenovia, NY: Wild Goose Press, 1978.
Tender Warriors. Ithaca, New York: Firebrand Books, 1986.

Anthologies

Ariadne's Thread. Ed. Lyn Lifshin. New York: Harper and Row, 1982.
''Poems.'' *The Limits of Miracles*. Collected by Marion Deutsche Cohen. South Hadley, MA: Bergin and Garvey, 1984. 14.
''The Tangerine Plymouth and the Gilded Cage.'' *My Father's Daughter: Stories by Women*. Ed. Irene Zahava. Freedom, CA: Crossing Press, 1990. 227–34.
''Mama's Life: A Long Distance Monologue.'' *My Mother's Daughter: Stories by Women*. Ed. Irene Zahava. Freedom, CA: Crossing Press, 1991, 225–28.

Studies of Rachel Guido deVries

Dial, Tom. Review of *Tender Warriors*. *Syracuse Herald* (June 29, 1986): 13.
Katz, Judith. ''*Tender Warriors*: Sense of Place.'' Review. *Equal Time* (June 25, 1986).
Lynch, Lee. Review of *Tender Warriors*. *Women's Review of Books* (July–August 1987): 18.

Math, Mara. "Dyke & 'Queer' Son Confront Italian Patriarch." Review of *Tender Warriors*. *Gay Community News* (November 2–8, 1986).

Romano, Rose. Review of *Tender Warriors*. *Common Lives/Lesbian Lives* 22 (Spring 1987): 107.

"*Tender Warriors* by Rachel Guido deVries." Review. *Feminist Publishers News* (San Francisco) 2, no. 2: 10.

"*Tender Warriors* by Rachel Guido deVries." Review. *Lesbian Connection* (Spring 1987): 32.

"*Tender Warriors* by Rachel Guido deVries." Review. *Windy City Times* (July 31, 1986): 21.

SARAH ANNE DREHER (1937–   )
Deborah T. Meem

BIOGRAPHY

Sarah Dreher was born Sarah Anne Alleman on March 26, 1937, in Hanover, Pennsylvania. An only child, she describes feeling "caught in the middle" between her rich well-connected father, Winnemore Alleman ("the kind of person who deadened everything around him, made lively people feel squashed" [Schwartz 16]), and her ambitious social-climbing mother, Marian Dreher (a self-described flapper from a poor coal-mining family who tried to push her daughter into an "upwardly mobile, social-butterfly life" [Schwartz 16]). After private prep school, Dreher attended Wellesley College. There she was nearly expelled "when my college roommate started the rumor that a friend and I were lovers" (unless otherwise noted, all quotations are from personal communication with the author), although, as she says, "I wasn't even out to myself then and I was as homophobic as the rest of them" (Roth 2). Dreher graduated from Wellesley in 1958 with a major in psychology. After earning an M.A. (1961) and a Ph.D. (1963) in clinical psychology from Purdue University, she worked first in a state mental hospital, then at Purdue's University Mental Health Service. During that period Dreher's "adult" writing began with "a coming out novel I plan to finish some day." She was fired from Purdue "for being an existentialist in a Freudian setting" (Barnes 29) and took a job counseling students at the University of Massachusetts. This move coincided roughly with the rise of the women's movement, and Dreher at last came out as a lesbian. She later left the University of Massachusetts to open a private practice.

In 1974, Dreher agreed to participate in a revue entitled *Girl of Our Dreams* for International Women's Week. That event led to her first connection with the theater since high school; since then, she has collaborated on two feminist musicals and written solo one musical and eight "serious" plays. In addition to plays, Dreher also writes mystery novels. As it became clear around 1980 that she was beginning to have more plays performed, and her writing was about to be published, she took her mother's maiden name, "because I sure didn't want my father's family to get the credit." Dreher has published four novels featuring lesbian travel agent-cum-detective Stoner McTavish.

Sarah Dreher now lives in Amherst, Massachusetts, with her partner and two dogs, combining her clinical psychology practice with writing. She has recently finished a play and is planning a fifth Stoner McTavish mystery, "to take place in Walt Disney World." Also percolating is a "serious book . . . about life before the women's/gay liberation movements. About being a lesbian in the horrid fifties."

MAJOR WORKS AND THEMES

Ruby Christmas (1980) was Dreher's first serious, non-musical play. Dreher admits, "Most of my work is autobiographical, more or less" (*Lesbian Stages* iii), and a number of characters and themes in *Ruby Christmas* bear this out. It is a family play, based loosely on Dreher's own family. Harriet, the mother, is obsessed by her memories of poverty—"the dirt and the hunger, and the coal dust you can never really wash off your skin" (II.ii.189). These memories have led her into a long-term unhappy marriage with Frank, the selectively deaf scion of a "good" family who, like Dreher's own father, "raised passive-aggressiveness to [an] art form." Frank never appears onstage in *Ruby Christmas*, but his portrait dominates the room where all action takes place, and the VCR (on which he watches tapes of old football games) is audible offstage throughout the play. Thus when Bronwyn, the lesbian daughter, comes home for Christmas bringing her lover Kelley, the confrontation between daughter and mother takes place in Frank's "domain." Harriet and Bronwyn ultimately fail to recapture the closeness they had enjoyed during Bronwyn's childhood.

8 × 10 Glossy is another "coming home" play. In this play, lesbian photographer and activist Carter visits her mother and sister in their small town on the first anniversary of her father's death. Sister Julie, unhappily married with small children, must deal with her growing emotional and physical attraction to local divorcée Dana. Meanwhile, their mother, Ketty, is rebuilding her life and strengthening her bonds with daughters and friends. But *8 × 10 Glossy* is ultimately Carter's story; she strips away layers of pretense and self-protection and allows herself to feel pain. She is able to come down from the ladder she uses to insulate herself from unpleasant truths and face squarely the buried memory of her father's abuse of her as a child. Like *Ruby Christmas*, it is a play in which the offstage/absent father exerts powerful influence on the action. But unlike *Ruby Christmas*, in *8 × 10 Glossy*, the women are able to forge bonds of love among themselves and break free from the father.

Base Camp (1983) is yet another early Dreher play about overcoming the fear of closeness. It explores group dynamics among five women stranded in a mountain tourist cabin after a freak October snowstorm. It explores the kinds of damage that can be done by an egotistical and divisive "harmony-breaker." And it explores the agony of opening an old inner wound kept closed—but never healed—by willful woodenness. Claire Stoddard engages in an emotional power game with Meredith Bryant, owner of Rockchuck Lodge and Claire's former lover. Her devastating critique of Meredith's ability to love nearly blocks the budding relationship between Meredith and Natalie Wenniger. *Base Camp*, like *8 × 10 Glossy*, describes the "unblocking" of love.

Backward, Turn Backward (1984) revisits the themes of lesbian daughter coming home, rapprochement between long-separated sisters, newly surfacing memories of child abuse, and the passive-aggressive father. In *Backward, Turn Backward*, sisters Rae and Lynda seek and find common ground on which to build a relationship with a future. Rae is a lesbian farmer, come home for the first time in years in response to Lynda's telegram stating "Come at once Father dying." Lynda is happily married with children, stuck for a decade caring for the invalid father, Monroe, never acknowledging her childhood sexual abuse by him. Their story takes place in the kitchen of their father's home, while Monroe himself lies comatose upstairs. But when Rae is left alone in the house with the "dying" old man, he appears in the kitchen and talks at her. Dreher notes that "Monroe's language, attitudes, etc. are exactly my father's—in fact, much of the dialogue in the play (his, anyway) is copied directly from my father." In *Backward, Turn Backward* it is never clear whether Monroe "is intended to be real or a specter, a haunting figment of the two sisters' imaginations" (Schwartz 16). Whether real or imaginary, Monroe's "presence" galvanizes Rae and Lynda into mutual understanding, and ultimately into constructive action.

The paranormal, expressed both as psychic activity and as blending of past and present, informs much of Sarah Dreher's other work. Her play *Hollandia '45* (1983) conflates past and present action as the main character, Kit Fortescue, lives and converses simultaneously with her World War II nursing companions in New Guinea (particularly her lover Mary Cleveland) and with her perniciously interfering present-day niece, Marian Johnson. Another play, *Alumnae News: The Doris Day Years* (1987), also switches back and forth a number of times between Wellesley College in the mid-1950s and Stacey Holcomb's rural home in 1966. *Alumnae News* fictionalizes Dreher's Wellesley experiences, particularly the unfounded accusation of lesbian behavior during her first year there. The play begins with Karen Martin's surprise arrival at Stacey's house ten years after graduation. The two women gradually open up to each other, finally acknowledging their long-buried passion only after the arrival of Terry Beck, Karen's old roommate and the villain of the piece (the one who maliciously reported Stacey's "lesbian behavior" to the Dean). This play's optimistic tone results from Dreher's seeing the 1950s and 1960s through the more liberated lens of the 1980s.

Dreher's time-blending technique appears yet once more, in her most recent play, *Open Season* (1991). *Open Season* focuses on the lives of Kate Cameron and Corey Simms, a middle-aged lesbian couple, former activists, who have retreated to Vermont to mourn the death of the women's movement. The diagnosis of breast cancer for Corey coincides with the opening of the hunting season; the ravages of patriarchal medicine and patriarchal weaponry appear to be closing in on Kate and Corey's idyllic space. The threatened present highlights their weakness, which seems the more pronounced in light of their apparent inability to take positive action. Interspersed among the Vermont scenes are flashbacks to "the Women's Movement Years," where Kate and Corey fall in love, where women call each other "Sisters," where life seems as focused as "liberating a boys-only bar," where "today Indiana, tomorrow the world" seems possible, even inevitable. These memories of the past blend into the present as Kate and Corey sort through old activist mementos stored in the barn. Their past eagerness to act against injustice contrasts bleakly with their helplessness to act against cancer. Corey's fear of losing control of her life—and possibly her death—causes Kate to withdraw emotionally in fear of losing Corey. They rediscover the purpose in their lives through their young friend Madrigal, whom they have patronized ("Madrigal, what you don't know about long-term love would fill volumes") and dismissed ("Generation gap"). Yet Madrigal, it turns out, does "Things . . . against the Patriarchy." Her present-day vitality and purpose rekindle the fires of activism and hope in Kate and Corey, and *Open Season* ends looking forward, not back.

In 1978, Sarah Dreher wrote a "comic gothic horror romance" (Barnes 29) entitled *This Brooding Sky*. This wacky lesbian farce toys with common literary genres and character types. It also shows Sarah Dreher at work in a comic mode, which she employs to great advantage in the four Stoner McTavish novels. While the Stoner books are mysteries and contain both suspenseful action and serious themes, the prevailing tone is lighthearted. *Stoner McTavish* (1985) introduces the cast of characters: Stoner herself, the lesbian travel agent named after Lucy B. Stone, who has a habit of getting involved in sticky situations; her Aunt Hermione, a benign witch and psychic; Marylou Kesselbaum, Stoner's partner at the travel agency; and Gwen Oxnard, who begins the series married to Bryan Oxnard. *Stoner McTavish* is set primarily in the Grand Tetons, where Stoner rescues Gwen from the evil husband (in the process pushing Bryan over a cliff to his death). By the time we revisit Stoner in *Something Shady* (1986), she and Gwen are lovers. This second novel picks up the gothic mood of *This Brooding Sky* (although with less slapstick and more psychological tension). Its plot turns upon Stoner's admission into Shady Acres, a mysterious mental institution in an old Victorian mansion in Castleton, Maine. There, with help from Gwen, Marylou, Hermione, and several new friends both within and without the asylum, she unearths the secret behind a series of unexplained disappearances and a murder.

The third Stoner McTavish book, *Gray Magic* (1987), represents a departure from its predecessors in that it takes up fundamental questions of good and evil in the world. *Gray Magic* is set in Arizona, where Stoner and Gwen have traveled, apparently on vacation. But Stoner soon meets an ancient Hopi woman named

Siyamtiwa, who renames her ''Green-Eyes'' and assures her that she was called there to be a combatant for good in the upcoming battle against the forces of evil, represented by Coyote. Good, defined as Harmony, or *hozro*, is upheld by a network of women: Stoner, Siyamtiwa, Gwen, the proprietor of the tourist lodge, a Navajo nurse, Hermione, even a female eagle and crow. Evil, or breaking of harmony, is here a male principle; Stoner is called to fight against it partly because as a lesbian never involved with men, she is immune to the Ya Ya sickness Coyote uses to suck power from women. *Gray Magic* differs from Dreher's earlier novels, indeed from nearly all mystery novels, in endorsing a supernatural solution to the battle. Stoner does not kill the villain at the end, as she killed Bryan Oxnard; the sacred Ya Ya *kachinas* rise up and destroy him, and the evil principle is neutralized until the next cycle.

Sarah Dreher's most recent mystery, *A Captive in Time* (1990), also takes risks not ordinarily found in detective novels. Stoner takes an accidental ''detour in time'' and finds herself in Tabor, Colorado Territory, 1871. Again, as in *Gray Magic*, she has been summoned to take part in an elemental battle between good and evil. But this time the battle is described as foreordained by the ''Witch's Book.'' The Witch/Old Woman is now Blue Mary (Aunt Hermione in an earlier life); Stoner is the Fool, Blue Mary's ally in the struggle against Rev. Henry Parnell, the Sanctified Man, embodiment of male evil. Like Siyamtiwa and Coyote, Witch and Sanctified Man represent two sides of a balanced essence. When the balance tips too far either way, good and evil wage war until harmony is restored.

In short, Sarah Dreher's plays and novels consistently see the world from a lesbian perspective. Dreher uses this perspective to take up fundamental issues: love relationships, family dynamics, female solidarity, fear and prejudice, paranormal phenomena. Never arguing for lesbianism as a lifestyle, Dreher's writing assumes the centrality of female experience.

CRITICAL RECEPTION

At present the response to Dreher's work has primarily been in the form of reviews. It is expected that critical studies will be forthcoming.

HONORS AND AWARDS

Playwriting fellow, The Artists Foundation, Massachusetts Council on the Arts, 1980.

Winner, Massachusetts Playwriting Festival, The Artists Foundation, 1984 (*Backward, Turn Backward*).

Winner, First Annual Lesbian Playwriting Contest, Theatre Rhinoceros, San Francisco, CA, 1985 (*8 × 10 Glossy*).

L.A. Weekly Theater award, "for outstanding achievement in playwriting," Los Angeles, CA, 1986 (*8 × 10 Glossy*).

Alliance for Gay and Lesbian Artists in the Entertainment Industry media award, Los Angeles, CA, 1987 (*8 × 10 Glossy*).

Jane Chambers Memorial International Gay Playwriting Contest, New York, NY, 1987 (*Alumnae News: The Doris Day Years*).

Lesbian Stages chosen for inclusion in the New American Writing/ United States Information Agency Book Program, a worldwide exhibit of books by small independent U.S. presses, 1990.

BIBLIOGRAPHY

Works by Sarah Dreher

Plays

8 × 10 Glossy and *Ruby Christmas*. *Places, Please! The First Anthology of Lesbian Plays*. Ed. Kate McDermott. San Francisco, CA: Spinsters/Aunt Lute, 1985. 41–91, 137–91.
Lesbian Stages (contains *Alumnae News: The Doris Day Years, Base Camp, Backward, Turn Backward, This Brooding Sky, Hollandia '45*). Norwich, VT: New Victoria, 1988.
Open Season (unpublished), 1991.

Novels

Stoner McTavish. Norwich, VT: New Victoria, 1985.
Something Shady. Norwich, VT: New Victoria, 1986.
Gray Magic. Norwich, VT: New Victoria, 1987.
A Captive in Time. Norwich, VT: New Victoria, 1990.

Other

"Waiting for Stonewall" (article). *Sexual Practice, Textual Theory: Lesbian Cultural Criticism*. Ed. Susan J. Wolfe and Julia Penelope. London: Basil Blackwell (forthcoming).

Studies of Sarah Dreher

Barnes, Noreen C. "Seeing the World Through Lesbian Eyes." *Bay Area Reporter* (Nov. 22, 1990): 29, 38.
Meem, Deborah T. "Chee and McTavish: The Relationship of the Detective to the Supernatural." *University of Cincinnati Forum* 17, no. 2 (Winter/Spring 1991): 5–7.
Roth, Patricia. "Nancy Drew for Lesbian Grownups." *Bay Windows* 6, no. 25 (June 1988): 2, 14–15.
Schwartz, Patricia Roth. "Phantoms and Lesbian Frolics." *Bay Windows* 8 (Dec. 27, 1990): 16, 26.

ELANA DYKEWOMON (1949–   )
Anna Livia

BIOGRAPHY

Elana Dykewomon, self-identified as "a Jew, a poet, a survivor of psychiatric assault, a separatist for 17 years, hip-deep in lesbian community" [Contributor's note, *For Lesbians Only* 584], started life as "Elana Nachman." She was born in New York City on October 11, 1949, to middle-class Jewish parents. Her father is a lawyer; her mother was a researcher for *Time* magazine but lost her job for smuggling arms to Israel. The family moved to Puerto Rico when Elana was eight; when she was twelve, she was institutionalized for adolescent suicide attempts, after which she attended a "progressive" boarding school in Massachusetts.

Dykewomon studied literature at Reed College in Portland, Oregon, and received a B.F.A. in creative writing from the California Institute of Art. It was at Cummington Community College of the Arts that, at the age of twenty-one, she finished her first novel, *Riverfinger Women*.

In 1979, she learned to print and has earned her living printing and typesetting ever since. A veteran speaker and creative writing teacher at feminist and lesbian conferences, music festivals, and women's studies conventions throughout the United States, she is also a seasoned political activist speaking out against psychiatric assault and fat oppression while promoting lesbian separatism and a strong Jewish identity.

In 1981, she set up Diaspora Distribution with Dolphin Waletzky "to distribute the work of lesbians to lesbians." In 1987 Elana Dykewomon became editor of *Sinister Wisdom*, a journal "for the Lesbian Imagination in the Arts and Politics," founded in 1976.

MAJOR WORKS AND THEMES

Elana Dykewomon conceived of *Riverfinger Women* as a pornographic novel, one step over from the Beebo Brinker series but with a happy ending. It was rejected by two mainstream presses before being accepted by Daughters, Inc., established in 1972 to publish books by women. From the perspective of the 1990s, it is difficult to see anything pornographic in the novel, but in the early 1970s, any explicitly lesbian text was considered pornographic. Though the novel deals with sexual violence, sadism, humiliation, and prostitution with sometimes searing directness, these practices typify heterosexual relationships, a sordid background against which the lesbian heroine stands out as a brilliant, troubled seeker with a warm and comprehending heart. One of the author's explicit aims was to show the ordinary heroism of lesbian relations.

Written as an open text in which continual reference is made to the act of creation, and laced with documents of the 1970s (an army recruiting ad, letters from the women's page of a local newspaper), *Riverfinger Women* shows reality itself to be problematic and easily appropriated. Style, setting, and characterization predominate over plot. The plot is simple: Inez Riverfinger comes to consciousness as a lesbian, falls in love with her schoolfriend, has a late adolescent affair against a background of pain and degradation (as personified by her straight friend, Peggy Warren), loses her lover to a man, ends up in California, and masterminds an enormous (and enormously successful) drug-smuggling plot. *Riverfinger Women* features heroism and a happy ending.

While *Riverfinger Women* was published under the name "Elana Nachman," by 1976, when *They Will Know Me by My Teeth* came out, Elana had changed her surname to "Dykewoman." This was at once an expression of her strong commitment to the lesbian community and a way to keep her "honest," since anyone reading the book would know the author was a lesbian: a public burning of the closet. The work bears the legend, "This book was printed, financed, typed, corrected and bound entirely by lesbians." It was published by Megaera Press, the name coming from the Greek for one of the Furies.

The stories and poems in this collection are written from very much within the lesbian community, addressing such issues as surgical breast reduction, masturbation, and class, as well as inventing creation myths, harvest myths, and mythic lesbian communities. The stories are set in bars, halfway houses, in public places, and on lesbian land. Though the genres vary from social realism to myth and legend, all tell a story of the search for community, for the challenge of comprehension. Even the solipsism of masturbation is transformed into a feeling of oneness with the female world. The collection ends on a triumphant, empowering note: "And what is most wonderful about my desire / Is that I desire what I myself have to give" ("The Journal She Kept" 117).

Elana Dykewomon's third book was published in 1981, and it was in this poetry collection that she adopted the spelling "Dykewomon," changing the "a" of "Dykewoman" to an "o" to avoid etymological implications of connectedness with men. This collection bears the legend "for lesbians only" and was designed and handprinted by the author in a limited edition of 550. Many of the poems are love poems, poems about the aching contentment of sex, but also, surprisingly, about the pleasures of solitude. If *Riverfinger Women* is characterized by a yearning for, and eager fumbling toward, lesbian community, and

They Will Know Me by My Teeth by an examination of the meaning of community and the stresses and strains individual experience places upon it, then *Fragments from Lesbos* sees the lesbian hero contemplating the view. It is a very visual, very sensuous collection; many poems describe the thoughts of a traveler, a cross-country driver as she considers the meteorological, the geographical, the material, often in terms of a woman's body, a woman's spirit.

Some of Elana Dykewomon's most influential writing has taken the form of articles and poems that were copied and recopied by hand and machine before being published in anthologies and journals. "The real fat womon poems," which were published in *Sinister Wisdom* (No. 33, 1987), and "Traveling Fat," which was published in *Shadow on a Tightrope: Writing by Women on Fat Oppression*, deal movingly and incisively with fat oppression and liberation, making the radical connection between social sanction of dieting and diet surgery in twentieth-century America and Chinese foot binding. "The Fourth Daughter's 400 Questions" (published in *Nice Jewish Girls: A Lesbian Anthology*), which addresses questions of Jewish identity and culture, has been widely used in lesbian seders and study groups all over the States.

Throughout her work, poetry or prose, novel or essay, the same themes recur: the lesbian as active, dynamic hero on center stage, a counter to the supposed heterosexual universal; the need for honesty, however difficult or painful it might be, and a belief that breaking silence will strike a common chord in other women; a call for lesbians to take themselves seriously, value themselves, taking responsibility for creating community. Against this backdrop walks the figure of the outsider: the Jew, the fat woman, the lesbian, the woman moving between communities, but with a new strength in solitude.

CRITICAL RECEPTION

Riverfinger Women was favorably received by feminist critics, who greeted it as one of the first feminist-influenced lesbian novels. They have commented particularly on its poetic language and circular structure. Bonnie Zimmerman in *The Safe Sea of Women* describes the novel as "the writing of a text . . . as both means and metaphor for the creation of the lesbian self" (74). In discussions of the later works, more attention has been paid to the fact that the books were for sale to women, or to lesbians, than to the content. Having once passed the hurdle of the front cover and the author's chosen name, however, reviewers have responded positively. Terri Poppe, reviewing *They Will Know Me by My Teeth* in *off our backs*, is concerned that women may be prevented from reading the collection and is disturbed at the request that the book be reviewed by a lesbian (18). Marcia Womangold, on the other hand, praises the book as "an exploration of alternative writing styles for women, a breakaway from the masculine mode" (18).

BIBLIOGRAPHY

Works by Elana Dykewomon

Books

Riverfinger Women. As Elana Nachman. Plainfield, VT: Daughters, 1974; Tallahassee, FL: Naiad Press, 1992. German translation by Irmtraut Ruber and Karin Wilms: *Frauen aus dem Flüss*. Berlin: Amazonen Frauenverlag, 1977.

They Will Know Me by My Teeth. Northampton, MA: Megaera Press, 1976.

Fragments from Lesbos. Langlois, OR: Diaspora Distribution, 1981.

Articles

"Traveling Fat." *Shadow on a Tightrope: Writings by Women on Fat Oppression*. Ed. Lisa Schoenfielder and Barb Wieser. San Francisco: Aunt Lute Books, 1983. 144–54.

"Journal Entry." *For Lesbians Only: A Separatist Anthology*. Ed. Sarah Hogland and Julia Penelope. London: Onlywomen Press, 1988. 547–84.

"On Passing." Editor's Note. *Sinister Wisdom* 35 (Summer/Fall 1988): 3–6.

"Surviving Psychiatric Assault and Creating Emotional Well-Being in our Communities." Editor's Note. *Sinister Wisdom* 36 (Winter 1988–89): 3–7.

"The Fourth Daughter's 400 Questions." *Nice Jewish Girls: A Lesbian Anthology*. Ed. Evelyn Torton Beck. Watertown, MA: Persephone Press, 1989; Boston: Beacon Press, 1989. 148–60.

Studies of Elana Dykewomon

Poppe, Terri. Review of *They Will Know Me by My Teeth*. *off our backs* (January 1978); 18.

Womangold, Marcia. Review of *They Will Know Me by My Teeth*. *Sojourner* (October 1976); 18.

Zimmerman, Bonnie. *The Safe Sea of Women: Lesbian Fiction 1969–1989*. Boston: Beacon Press, 1990.

KATHERINE V. FORREST
(1939–   )
Mary C. Ware

BIOGRAPHY

Katherine V. Forrest was born in 1939 in Canada. Although both parents died while she was in high school, Forrest resolved to continue her education by completing public school and later enrolling in some college courses. After emigrating to the United States in 1957, Forrest became a U.S. citizen. According to her own accounts, Forrest's most valuable education was gained through a variety of life and travel experiences and through being a voracious reader.

Forrest worked in the business world in several capacities, including management, before becoming a full-time writer in 1979. She was able to make the shift to full-time writing because of the encouragement and support of her partner, Sheila, to whom most of her books are dedicated. This full-time commitment to her writing career has proven successful, as she spent many hours in the early years honing her craft and becoming the writer she is today.

Forrest began her career with eight rewrites of her first novel (still unpublished), and then produced *Curious Wine* (1983), a love story; *Daughters of a Coral Dawn* (1984), a science fiction novel; and *Amateur City* (1984), her first Kate Delafield mystery.

Forrest launched her publishing career with Naiad Press, a small women's publishing house specializing in books for the lesbian reader, and has retained that association, despite the fact that she has had considerable success, as measured by numbers of copies sold, translations into languages other than English, and movie rights (for *Murder at the Nightwood Bar*, which has been optioned by film director Tim Hunter). When asked about her fidelity to Naiad Press (since many authors who start publishing with small presses move to mainstream publishers after establishing a following), Forrest is candid in her response:

The reason authors go to mainstream publishers is money. But I think there are several absolutely overwhelming advantages to being published by a gay press. First, the truth and validity of what you write is valued, appreciated, and recognized at a gay press. Second, you're working with people who are totally sympathetic to what you're trying to do, and there's a commitment to the importance of what you're doing. . . . Third, a gay press can keep the books in print better than a mainstream press. (McDonald 44)

Forrest lived in Los Angeles from 1979 to 1992; at the present time, she lives in Salem, Oregon, where she is a supervising fiction editor for Naiad Press. She has written a total of eight books, including the aforementioned, plus three other Kate Delafield mysteries (*Murder at the Nightwood Bar*, 1987; *The Beverly Malibu*, 1989; and *Murder by Tradition*, 1991); *An Emergence of Green* (1986), a work of contemporary fiction; and a short story collection, *Dreams and Swords* (1987). Her works have been widely reviewed, including in the *New York Times Book Review*, and *The Beverly Malibu* was the recipient of the Lambda Literary Award in the mystery category.

Currently, Forrest spends much of her time editing and assisting new writers who are being added to Naiad's collection of authors. She laments the time this takes away from her own writing, but feels that the gay and lesbian community deserves new writers, and she recognizes her contribution to their development.

Another activity Forrest enjoys is her membership in the Third Street Writing Group. Established over a decade ago, the Group reads and critiques each other's writing. Forrest recommends such groups to other writers, for she finds that the variety of life experiences and skills held by group members enriches all who participate as they share their works in progress with their peers.

As for her self-identity, Forrest identifies herself as a lesbian writer—one who is a lesbian, who writes for and about lesbians. This is her foremost identity and one of her strongest contributions to lesbian fiction.

MAJOR WORKS AND THEMES

Curious Wine, which has sold over 100,000 copies, is Forrest's best-selling work, both in the United States and in other countries. Forrest wrote this book, she says, because "there were few books that, to me, conveyed the passion and the beauty of our relationship" (McDonald 45). The plot of *Curious Wine* centers around Diana Holland, a personnel representative for a Los Angeles trust company, who is on the rebound after a failed five-year relationship with a man. Holland meets Lane Christianson, a San Francisco lawyer, during a weekend trip to Lake Tahoe. The women discover love for one another. Their attempts to fight the unfamiliar feelings are unsuccessful and eventually they let love take its course. The emotions and dialogue evoked are familiar to any woman who has fallen in love with a woman for the first time. Love scenes are plentiful, realistic, and sensual. The book is truly a lesbian love story.

The four Kate Delafield detective novels are probably the best known of Forrest's works, with readers hungrily awaiting each sequel. *Amateur City* was the first of the Kate Delafield series and established Delafield as a detective for the Los Angeles Police Department. In this novel, Kate is unattached and mourning the death of her lover, Anne. The plot details her investigation of the death of a corporate executive and the beginnings of Kate's romantic interest in Ellen O'Neill.

The next novel in the series, *Murder at the Nightwood Bar*, introduces Kate to the world of gay bars, as she investigates the murder of Dory Quillin, a lesbian who frequents the Nightwood, a Los Angeles lesbian bar. She meets a love interest, Andrea Ross, solves the crime, as usual, and wrestles with her closeted existence, which she compares to the lives of those in the "community" that she sees as she frequents the bar during the investigation. As Forrest says, "I wanted to bring Kate out more—it's the story of a woman's journey to community. I think that Kate Delafield personifies the lives of many lesbians in this country, living in isolation, and I wanted to connect her to a community of women" (Levin 6).

The Beverly Malibu required extensive research, which is evident as the reader follows the murder investigation of a former Hollywood director, Owen Sinclair, who has been poisoned. (The book takes its title from the name of the apartment building near Beverly Hills, occupied by a strange assortment of tenants, where the murder took place.) The plot unwinds with many historical references to the McCarthy era, the blacklist years in Hollywood, and the activities of the House Un-American Activities Committee. As the plot unfolds, Kate finds a new romantic interest, Aimee Grant, niece of the mysterious Paula Grant, who discovered Owen Sinclair's body.

Murder by Tradition has Kate investigating the violent murder of a gay man by a straight muscular "he-man." Aimee Grant, who appeared in the previous Kate Delafield mystery, reappears as Kate's lover. Kate debunks the murderer's self-defense plea, while fighting homophobia on many fronts. She also wrestles with issues of how much of her work and its problems to share with Aimee as well as the theme (developed through all the Kate Delafield books) of the costs and benefits of staying "in the closet" in her professional life at the Los Angeles Police Department.

Themes evident throughout the Kate Delafield series include the ability of a strong intelligent lesbian woman to solve crimes and to act as capably as any man. The series also deals with Kate's integrity; in fact, when faced with moral decisions, she agonizes realistically for pages. The love of a woman—both affection and sexuality—are realistically portrayed in this series (and in all Forrest's novels); finally, Forrest addresses Kate's progress, albeit slow, from a completely closeted existence to one with increasing bonds to the gay and lesbian community. Forrest seeks to portray lesbian women as positive images—something lacking in much of the mainstream press. This portrayal of strong lesbian women is, in fact, one of Forrest's major goals.

Forrest's other works do not fit into the mystery or romance categories; however, all are worthy of mention. *An Emergence of Green* deals with a number of issues not addressed in other works. Carolyn Blake, a wife trapped in an unhappy marriage, meets Val Hunter, a painter, swimmer, and mother of an adolescent boy. The two women fall in love, leading to major changes in their lifestyles and the end of Blake's marriage. Most of Forrest's other major characters who are lesbian are already lesbian at the start of the novel and know who they are. In this novel, the agonies of individuals who are not sure who they are, in terms of affectional preference, are probed, as well as the complexities of love triangles, adolescent youth as part of a lesbian family, and a cultural climate inhospitable to lesbian and gay couples. It is a realistic and gripping portrayal.

Finally, some of Forrest's early work was science fiction. *Daughters of a Coral Dawn* created a lesbian utopia, and one selection from *Dreams and Swords* (a short story collection) also featured a science fiction plot with a strong lesbian character, Captain Drake, whom many readers and reviewers would like to see reappear in future works. Her science fiction also reflects Forrest's most consistent themes—the strength and self-sufficiency of women and the beauty of their love.

Through conversations with Forrest, it was possible to identify several other themes that she feels are important throughout her work. These include issues of abuse of power in the business world, as evidenced in *Amateur City*; the abuse of power that incest represents (in *Murder at the Nightwood Bar*, as Dory Quillin was an incest survivor); and the general abuse of power of "straight" individuals over gay individuals, evident in many of Forrest's works. The issue of body image is another important lesbian (and woman's) issue with which Forrest deals. Forrest's character Andrea Ross has no breasts, and Val Hunter is portrayed as an "enormous woman." The ways these incidents of body image affect Forrest's characters is evident in her writing.

CRITICAL RECEPTION

Katherine Forrest has received attention from both mainstream and gay reviewers for her work, almost since its first appearance. Most early reviews (1983–1987) were basically short and positive, appearing in mainstream publications such as *Library Journal*, *Booklist*, *Science Fiction Chronicle*, and *Publishers Weekly*, and gay publications such as the *Advocate*, the *Lesbian News*, and the *Wishing Well*. Her more recent works have received more mainstream attention (i.e., *New York Times Book Review*) and perhaps, with more lengthy reviews, have come some more critical comments. The *New York Times Book Review*, for example, says of *The Beverly Malibu* that Forrest's prose "lacked grace," but the review includes positive comments such as, "The author tells an interesting story . . . her detective plies her trade with admirable efficiency and more hard-to-come-by integrity" (Stasio 41).

Although she was not the direct target of specific criticism, Forrest, as supervising editor for Naiad, has also received some indirect criticism from reviewers who attack Naiad Press for emphasizing genre novels and books that "sell," rather than publishing literary works (Snowden 38). Forrest's response to those critics is useful in situating her works and their purpose. She stresses the point that, before writing any work, she considers her audience. She cites numerous audiences within the lesbian/gay community and indicates that she deliberately writes some of her work (e.g., mysteries) to appeal to the audience that seeks mystery stories. She is not, she makes clear, trying to write *the* classic work of lesbian fiction when she writes a Kate Delafield mystery, although she certainly would not object if some of her works became "classics." Forrest feels it is important for lesbian women to read and that it is motivating for individuals to read works that validate them and their lives, while they are reading the types of works (e.g., mysteries, science fiction, contemporary fiction) they like and choose to read.

There was not much evidence of overt homophobia affecting recent mainstream reviews of Forrest's work, but marked changes must be noted over the past seven years in how reviewers worded their comments. For example, in a 1984 Library Journal review of *Daughters of a Coral Dawn*, Forrest's work was labeled "unabashedly lesbian," and libraries were told to "use caution" in purchasing, ostensibly for fear of offending patrons (826). By 1991, *Library Journal* was saying "Lesbian LAPD detective Kate Delafield's fourth appearance should quash any doubts concerning Forrest's abilities as a mystery writer, mainstream or otherwise" (141). It seems sad, however, that doubts would need to be quashed, or that her quality of writing as a mystery writer would need qualifiers such as "mainstream" or "otherwise." Covert homophobia in reviewer's words is lessening over time, but it is not gone, or writers would not have to protest too much about the quality of Forrest's work, "mainstream or otherwise."

BIBLIOGRAPHY

Works by Katherine V. Forrest

Curious Wine. Tallahassee, FL: Naiad Press, 1983.
Amateur City. Tallahassee, FL: Naiad Press, 1984.
Daughters of a Coral Dawn. Tallahassee, FL: Naiad Press, 1984.
An Emergence of Green. Tallahassee, FL: Naiad Press, 1986.
Dreams and Swords. Tallahassee, FL: Naiad Press, 1987.
Murder at the Nightwood Bar. Tallahassee, FL: Naiad Press, 1987.
The Beverly Malibu. Tallahassee, FL: Naiad Press, 1989.
Murder by Tradition. Tallahassee, FL: Naiad Press, 1991.

Studies of Katherine V. Forrest

Hopbell, Ph. "Katherine Forrest—In Process." *Lambda Rising Book Report* 1, no. 9 (1989): 1, 9.
Levin, Jenifer. "Aboard the Scorpio IV and Other Places with Katherine V. Forrest." *Visibilities* 2, no. 4 (1988): 4–7.

Lynch, Lee. "Katherine Forrest: A Giant Talent in the World of Gay/Lesbian Literature." *Dallas Voice* (March 18, 1988): 14.

McDonald, Sharon. "Katherine Forrest: A Passionate Gutsy Storyteller." *Advocate* (Oct. 2, 1984): 44–45.

Nash, Tammye. "Katherine Forrest: A Hero among Literate Lesbians." *Dallas Voice* (March 18, 1988): 14.

Parks, J. Review of *Daughters of a Coral Dawn*. *Body Politic* 1:6 (September 1984): 38.

Review of *Daughters of a Coral Dawn*. *Library Journal* (April 15, 1984): 826.

Review of *Murder by Tradition*. *Library Journal* (July 1991): 141.

Snowdon, Shane. "Of Girls and Gorillas: Naiad Press." *San Francisco Bay Times* (Sept. 26, 1991): 38–39.

Stasio, Marilyn. "Mysteries." Rev. of *The Beverly Malibu*. *New York Times Book Review* (Dec. 10, 1989): 41.

Zaki, Hoda M. "Utopia and Ideology in *Daughters of a Coral Dawn* and Contemporary Feminist Utopias." *Women's Studies* 14, no. 2 (1987): 119–33.

SUZANNE GARDINIER (1961–)
Susan Krause

BIOGRAPHY

Suzanne Gardinier was born on January 25, 1961, in New Bedford, Massachusetts. Her mother was a secretary at the time, and her father a newspaper reporter. She grew up in Scituate, a town on the coast south of Boston, where she attended public schools and sang in the Congregational church choir and in various regional competitions.

At sixteen, she began college at Drew University; at seventeen, she fell in love with a woman. After two years, she transferred to the University of Massachusetts at Amherst (B.A. 1981), where she worked as a student organizer on women's and anti-racism issues.

Between 1981 and 1984, Gardinier lived in San Francisco and Cambridge, Massachusetts, working as a retail clerk in bookstores and liquor stores and as a temporary secretary. In 1983, she quit drinking. After being accepted into the graduate writing program at Columbia University (M.F.A. 1986) in 1984, Gardinier moved to Manhattan. During her graduate work, Gardinier also began to teach.

She has taught writing at the State University of New York (SUNY) at Old Westbury, Rutgers University at Newark, and several other colleges; between 1986 and 1988, she worked for the Teachers College Writing Project, training teachers in the New York City public schools. Between 1988 and 1990 she served as assistant editor at *Grand Street* magazine. She now consults in public school districts on the teaching of writing and has lived with Georgia Heard in Sag Harbor, New York, since 1988.

MAJOR WORKS AND THEMES

In a time when many people are recharting the landscape of history to include and to reflect all points of view, and to challenge a history written to protect the interests of a few, Suzanne Gardinier's is a much needed voice. Her poetry explores the terrain of the long-silenced and recontextualizes achievements that have been presented as the definitive version of events. In *Usahn: Ten Poems & A Story* (Grand Street Books 1990) and the soon to be published *The New World*, heroism is reconsidered: "Listen to the manifold voices / of those you crushed struggle into speech / to give myself to help make what will come" *(The New World* 1:1). The New World, then, is both history and possibility.

There is much ground to (re)cover before the new New World can be sustained. "Stranded like anyone, the isolation / made solitude, I try to understand" *(Usahn* 12) ends the first poem, "Voyages," from the poet's first book. Gardinier's sense of the world and the work that needs to be done is rooted in these lines. Stranded metaphorically and literally as a woman and as a lesbian, the poet recognizes that we are all stranded, and if we hope to make real progress we must try to understand each other's as well as our own isolation; conversely, we must also grasp all of the ways that our lives are intertwined.

Much of *Usahn* is a precursor to *The New World*. One thread continued, but now tightly woven with others, is the personal and historical voyages that traverse the territory of the sea voyages of Columbus, Verrazano, Hudson, and Block; the voyages (migrations) of native peoples fleeing persecution and the forced migrations of African peoples; the voyages of refugees; the daily voyages to work and school; the voyages of the tongue along a lover's body. Throughout this epic poem, Gardinier refuses to see these varied explorations as isolated events having little to do with each other or with the condition of the world today.

In discussing *Usahn*, Richard Howard asserts, "Despairing but not in despair; brave and even-tempered, Suzanne Gardinier's writing is an adventure" (jacket notes). Gardinier's virtuosity of language and form carries over to the operatic, epic poem *The New World*. In the Poem "To Peace," the language captures the anger and the love the poet has for the city. Juxtaposition is at the heart of much of Gardinier's work, as is her clear-eyed vision. The attention she pays to detail, whether on the street or in a diner, adds to the chronicle of lives and landscapes converging. Nothing is too mundane. The lives of people are what makes history.

History repeats itself, we often hear, yet we insist on viewing events as if they have sprung full-blown from the cosmos like Athena from Zeus' head. Suzanne Gardinier refuses to indulge this fantasy.

CRITICAL RECEPTION

Gardinier's only published book, *Usahn: Ten Poems & A Story*, was printed in an edition of five hundred copies and has not been widely distributed. In the only review (*Ms.*, 1991), Adrienne Rich called the book "small in size but ambitious in reach" (71), and praised the poet's "powerful rhythmic sense, her control of the various strands of language she's working with" (72). Her poems have appeared in mainstream anthologies like *Under 35: The New Generation of American Poets* (Doubleday, 1989) and *The Best American Poetry* (Scribner's and Macmillan/Collier, 1989 and 1990), but at this early point in Gardinier's career, most of the critical response to her work is yet to come.

HONORS AND AWARDS

Gardinier was nominated for two Coordinating Council of Literary Magazines/ General Electric Awards for Younger Writers in 1987 and 1989; her work has also been nominated for a Pushcart Prize (1991), and for a PEN/Revson Fellowship (1991). Suzanne Gardinier won the 1992 Associated Writing Programs Poetry Award.

BIBLIOGRAPHY

Works by Suzanne Gardinier

Books

Usahn: Ten Poems & A Story. New York: Grand Street Books, 1990.
The New World. Pittsburgh: University of Pittsburgh, 1993.

Essays

"At Home (Marianne Moore)." *Parnassus* 16, no. 2 (1991): 61–77.
"Bootleg, Jackleg Medicine: Curing As Only Generations Can (Thylias Moss & Marilyn Nelson Waniek)." *Parnassus* 17, no. 1 (1992): 65.
"Two Cities: On *The Iliad*." *Kenyon Review* (Spring 1992): 5–12.
"A World That Will Hold All The People (Muriel Rukeyser)." *Kenyon Review* 14, no. 3 (Summer 1992): 88

Studies of Suzanne Gardinier

Rich, Adrienne. "Poetry for Daily Use." *Ms.* (September/October 1991): 70–75.

SALLY MILLER GEARHART
(1931–   )
Cynthia Secor

BIOGRAPHY

Sally Miller Gearhart was born April 15, 1931, in Pearisburg, a small, rural Virginia town. She was raised by her mother, an executive secretary, and her grandmother, a schoolteacher who ran a rooming house. Gearhart's father, divorced from her mother, was a dentist and a charming, philandering alcoholic. He took little interest in her upbringing. That was left to these strong German-Scots women (with their bit of Cherokee blood) and Gearhart's African-American nurse. Men living in the rooming house gave Gearhart access to the male world, telling her stories and teaching her to shoot. Shooting a bird, her first kill, left her with a lifelong distaste for blood sports and the macho emotions and behaviors associated with the culture of hunting.

Sweet Briar College provided Gearhart with a fine liberal arts education, widening her horizons in acceptable and not so acceptable ways. Not surprisingly, she discovered the romantic and carnal love of women. As important, however, Sweet Briar, the Episcopal girls' camp in West Virginia where she counseled, and the Methodist church watered the deep roots of her lifelong passion for philosophy and religion.

Gearhart went through her M.A. and Ph.D. in four years. Bowling Green State University and the University of Illinois gave her a fine background in theater and, not incidentally, a good feeling for traditional values and the unbending conservatism of the heartland. In the midwest and in Texas, where she taught for the next fourteen years, there was no lesbian life but the closet life. She lived as a lesbian during those years, enduring silence, blackmail, and enough dyke drama for a lifetime. She led two lives—that of the enormously popular and successful professor of speech, debate, and theater and that other life, the one shared only with a few trusted friends and colleagues.

These were the closet years, marked by heavy drinking, wild driving, butch-femme roles (Gearhart did both), and social friendships with gay men who provided the necessary male escort for church and college functions. It was a time of sexuality, celibacy, and domestic violence. The respected professor who published in church journals and was desirous of becoming a Lutheran minister was also a woman of passion, given to women, alcohol, and thwarted dreams.

The world turned in the summer of 1968 when Gearhart went to California to study group encounter techniques at the Western Behavioral Sciences Institute in La Jolla. Aristotle met Carl Rogers. Gearhart spent the next year with a new lover, studying philosophy at the University of Kansas. Reading Robin Morgan's "Goodbye to All That" and spending a summer doing consciousness raising with new and old friends—the conversion to feminism was complete. That fall she moved to San Francisco.

The rest, as they say, is history. Gearhart emerged as one of the Bay Area's leading lesbian feminist activists. A fine teacher and public speaker, she became associated with most of the major lesbian and gay political issues of the next two decades. She is perhaps best known for her participation statewide in the campaign to defeat Proposition Six, the infamous Briggs initiative to bar lesbians and gays from teaching. She debated John Briggs on television and stumped the state with Harvey Milk. The lesbian and gay community asked her to chair the city's victory rally the night Proposition Six was defeated and to lead the candlelight march the night Mayor George Moscone and city supervisor Harvey Milk were assassinated.

Thanks to open-minded colleagues and administrators at San Francisco State University, Gearhart's work as a lesbian teacher, theorist, writer, and spokesperson was properly acknowledged as professional achievement, and she was given tenure and promoted to full professor.

During the eighties, Gearhart for a time entered a new closet, choosing at first to remain silent about her involvement in the S/M community. As a member of the Outcasts, she found a new cause—as a sexual radical. She has published little on this experience. But she has been less reticent about her activities with animal rights, futurism, and cultural feminism. Ever active, she sings with a lesbian "barbershop quartet," is just shy of a brown belt in aikido, and has time for a house on the land, her cat companions, and her pit bull Brindle.

Gearhart's interest in metaphysics has deepened. Her reading of the Seth books by Jane Roberts has given her a new understanding of her own earlier works including *The Wanderground*. A child of the rural depression South, a closeted professional of the McCarthy years, and activist during the heyday of lesbian and gay pride—it may ultimately prove of even greater significance that Gearhart has been a citizen of California these twenty-odd years in which a state blessed with economic largesse, easily accessible public education, wondrous stands of redwoods, and endless miles of open beaches has given way to a state beleaguered with pollution, overcrowding, ethnic/racial violence, AIDS, and the slow relentless, irreversible destruction of the natural environment. Gearhart is, after all, a fine writer of speculative fiction.

MAJOR WORKS AND THEMES

Gearhart's reputation as a fiction writer rests on *The Wanderground*. Violence is the central issue in her fiction. In *The Wanderground*, the violence is physical. It results from male behavior. To explore the phenomenon of male violence and possible alternatives, she creates the Wanderground and the City. The woman-centered female culture in the hill country and the nascent culture of the male gentles are in stark contrast to the violent, misogynistic male culture of the distant City below.

The concerns, values, practices, and rituals—the spirituality and soft technology that the hill women evolve in isolation—contrast sharply with the violent, domination-driven, objectifying practices that characterize the hard culture Gearhart creates for the men. The scene in which self-selected hill women meet with the gentles (men in the process of evolving their own new spirituality and technology) makes it perfectly clear that Gearhart believes in a modified gender essentialism that recognizes biological differences in perception and behavior, while allowing for spiritual, political, and possibly social alliances.

At the simplest level, the settlements in the hill country represent the separatist communities created by lesbian women in the seventies. At a more complex level, they represent a radical imagining of a culture stressing communication, relatedness, empathy, and oneness with nature.

The emotional texture of the novel depends on the loving, sensual, psychic energies evoked by the images of the feminine and the natural, and the abrupt collision of these soft stirrings with the fear, defensive rage, and panic engendered by the kill-for-fun-and-thrills images characteristic of the City segments of the narrative.

If the hill country dramatizes seventies ecofeminism and women's spirituality, the City dramatizes compulsive heterosexuality and prefigures the sexual radicals' insights of the eighties into the aesthetic and ethical basis of S/M scripting and postfeminist butch-femme role-playing. Choice, vulnerability, trust, and intensity are values that inform the text. Depending on the reader's practices, these values may be associated most compellingly with images characteristic of either the hill country or the City. The novel would seem to argue that gender is constructed and that the psyche can be evolved.

Four of the chapters in *The Wanderground* were first published as short stories. "Kreuva and the Pony," which appeared in *Ms.* magazine in 1976, is typical. This evocative, sensual narrative—depicting as it does sensations, perceptions, and a worldview askew the dominant culture—sets the style for her short fiction. Together, as in *The Wanderground*, such tales constitute a believable and moving universe. Taken singularly they are amusing—at their best thought-provoking—and they are always on subjects of interest to feminists concerned with the world we live in and the creatures, human and otherwise, who populate or might be imagined to populate this world.

Here Gearhart expresses her attentiveness to and sympathy for the potentially oppressed, be they loner children, trees, animals, or elderly women confined to nursing homes. The best of the current stories, "The Chipko" (1987), depicts a group of women bent on saving a stand of virgin oaks from loggers bent on earning their livelihoods. These militant but non-violent women generate energy in a manner suggestive of an exercise in collective martial arts.

In these texts, as in *The Wanderground*, Gearhart teaches us to see the other in stranger-than-life figures and to acknowledge the other in familiar figures. Gearhart believes that to see and to acknowledge the other is to participate in the fullness of creation and to desire its preservation.

As a respected activist and popular professor at San Francisco State University, Gearhart has frequently been called on to give speeches, to write, to do guest lectures, and to take part in workshops, panels, and debates on religion, the church, spirituality, feminism, lesbian feminism, S/M, lesbian and gay rights, First Amendment issues, technology, communication, and education. She gained national visibility as a result of her appearance in two popular documentary films, *Word Is Out* (1977) and *The Times of Harvey Milk* (1984). The former is available in book form.

Gearhart began writing on religion in the early sixties while teaching at a Lutheran college in Texas. By the seventies, however, she was writing critiques of traditional religious theory and practice from a radical lesbian feminist perspective. The best known of these texts is *Loving Women/Loving Men*, authored and edited with William Johnson (1974). *A Feminist Tarot* (1975), which she authored with Susan Rennie, established her as a spokeswoman for cultural feminism and women's spirituality.

"Womanpower: Energy Re-Sourcement" (1975) circulated widely in mimeographed form before it was printed in 1976 and reprinted in 1982. This essay is key to an informed reading of *The Wanderground*. Here Gearhart argues for the moral responsibility of women to each other and to the earth. This responsibility informs the actions of the hill women in *The Wanderground* and the Weavers and Stillers in "The Chipko." Similarly, "The Future—If There Is One—Is Female" (1982) and "An End to Technology: A Modest Proposal" (1983) expand discursively the moral and technological arguments represented in *The Wanderground*.

Gearhart spent forty years in the classroom teaching rhetoric, theater, debate, and speech communication before retiring in 1992. "Womanization of Rhetoric" (1979) argues that persons who study and teach public discourse have been advocates of violence. She believes that the contemporary shift of emphasis from rhetoric as persuasive to communication as interactive and relational signals a shift to a female model of personal interaction. This shift is presented as an antidote to violence and, as such, an alternative to our self-destruction as a species. This essay provides the clearest statement of her position on the use and abuse of language.

Zude/Jez, Gearhart's most recent fictional work, focuses on intellectual violence. In this text, still in progress, she addresses two related but separate issues:

the violence implicit when separatism is not a willing choice and the violence done when language is used to coerce agreement. Like *The Wanderground*, the new text is speculative fiction. The narrative, employing several cultures, deals with the perceived conflict between individual rights—namely choice and privacy—and the need to assure the survival of the community. Here, for the first time, Gearhart integrates into her fiction her professional life as a teacher of speech communication and her political activity as a major spokesperson for the lesbian and gay movement.

CRITICAL RECEPTION

Published criticism of Gearhart's fictional work centers on *The Wanderground*, her only published novel. Significantly, this speculative fiction classic, which portrays so concretely the work, dreams, and theory of lesbian cultural feminists of the seventies, is still in print some thirteen years after its initial publication by a small alternative press. It continues to sell briskly (15,000 copies over the last eight years). In the early years, it was reviewed in mainstream and women's publications such as the *San Francisco Chronicle* and *Sister Lode*. It has been translated into German, Swedish, and Danish. A favorite with individual readers, it is also frequently assigned in women's studies courses.

This novel immediately won for Gearhart a devoted lesbian and feminist following. The culture of the hill women was felt by many to embody our best hope for a world in which nature can triumph over the violence characteristic of human communities. *The Wanderground* continues to have wide appeal for feminists concerned with violence, ecofeminism, women's spirituality, and metaphysics.

Significantly, the novel is frequently cited by authors seeking to characterize the beliefs and activities of lesbian separatists in the seventies—a time marked by separatist analysis of the dominant patriarchal culture and by the creation of lesbian living collectives in both urban and rural areas (Zimmerman, 1984, 1990; Faderman, 1991).

Here the hill country is read as an imaginative representation of Lesbian Nation. While understandable, the literalness of these readings is reductive of a philosophically and experientially complex text. The hill women's culture is not meant primarily to signal idealistic or youthful experiments in collective living. Gearhart writes explicitly of women who have fled the city in the face of genocidal violence; the hunts and purges depicted represent the burning years, the Salem witch hunts, Nazi Germany, and the sporadic but frequently very damaging harassment of the closet years.

The hill women are not lesbians, as that identity has been constructed and reconstructed throughout patriarchal time. Gearhart's radical imagination creates for us autonomous women living in community with each other and in harmony with nature, evolving the intuitive power that such relatedness might be imagined to engender.

Cherrìe Moraga and Barbara Smith (1982) address the specificity of the text differently, pointing out that the experience which engenders the text is not that of a third world woman and that the author in speaking out of her own reality is not inclusive of such experience.

Sarah Hoagland (1988), in her study of lesbian ethics, examines concepts from both the non-fiction and *The Wanderground*, specifically Gearhart's insistence that women have control of the frequency of pregnancy and that the hill women learn to shield when remembering the harsh events that have earlier befallen other hill women. Hoagland's interest is in boundaries, both physical and psychic. She challenges Gearhart's depiction of vulnerability when she has Seja bare her own throat in a display of vulnerability so that Margaret, recently raped and humiliated by men from the City, can let go her fear and rage. Hoagland sees the risk entailed as unnecessary and perhaps counterproductive as well. Provocatively, Hoagland embeds in her discussion of this episode a critique and condemnation of S/M practices that result in the reduction of tension rather than the breaking of dysfunctional patterns.

Lucy Freiburt (1983) and June Howard (1983) read *The Wanderground* in the context of utopian and science fiction. They place Gearhart in the line of Mary Shelley, Charlotte Perkins Gilman, Marion Zimmer Bradley, Marge Piercy, Ursula Le Guin, Joanna Russ, Dorothy Bryant, and Mary Staton. Gearhart, however, reports herself widely read in the works of both male and female science and fantasy fiction writers. Freiburt is concerned with the system of values emerging from the organicism that underlies the society of sisters living in harmony with the mother earth. Here the oneness of creation is privileged. In this vein, it would prove fruitful to place this text in the context of Carol Gilligan's *In a Differenct Voice* or Mary Field Belenky's *Women's Ways of Knowing*. Howard somewhat perversely uses *The Wanderground* as the occasion for an attack on cultural feminism and gender essentialism. In contrast to Freiburt, Howard privileges race and class, and summarily dismisses gender as an essential determiner of oppression.

In her discussion of contemporary lesbian activism, Lillian Faderman points out that cultural feminists of the seventies, given their utopian social visions, often went on to become involved in movements on behalf of peace and the environment (281). This observation seems particularly appropriate to a writer such as Gearhart, whose passion for animal rights clearly outweighs her interest in goddess worship.

Cheris Kramerae and Jana Kramer (1987) and Mario Klarer (1991) appropriately foreground language in their discussions of Gearhart's work. Klarer's discussion of Gearhart's utopian female poetics provocatively grounds in classical rhetoric her use of memory, telepathy, and what he terms "regressive mediumlike orality" (323). He rightly relates her poetics to the ecofeminism of the text, but in a curious way his emphasis on fertility myths, comparisons of *The Wanderground* with *The Waste Land*, and insistence on calling the hill women Wandergrounders subtly subvert the feminist intention of the text.

It is hard to assess the impact of homophobia per se on the reception of Gearhart's fiction and non-fiction. Opposition did, however, significantly delay publication of two of the works cited—"The Lesbian and God-the-Father" and "The Future—If There Is One—Is Female." Her explicit challenge to patriarchal assumptions rankled publishers.

More important in the long run is the fact that little of broad significance has been written about Gearhart's contributions as an educator, political activist, and writer. Her published and unpublished work needs to be collected and given sustained critical attention. Until this is done, it will continue to be difficult to place individual works in the broader philosophic and metaphysical contexts they deserve.

BIBLIOGRAPHY

Works by Sally Miller Gearhart

Fiction

The Wanderground: Stories of the Hill Women. Boston: Persephone Press, 1979.
"The Chipko." *Love, Struggle, and Change*. Ed. Irene Zahava. Freedom, CA: Crossing Press, 1988. 169–83. Rpt. in *Finding Courage: Writings by Women*. Ed. Irene Zahava. Freedom, CA: Crossing Press, 1989. 99–110. Rpt. in *Ms*. (Sept./Oct. 1991): 64–70.
"Roxy Raccoon." *Through Other Eyes: Animal Stories by Women*. Ed. Irene Zahava. Freedom, CA: Crossing Press, 1988. 81–89.
"Flossie's Flashes." *Lesbian Love Stories*. Ed. Irene Zahava. Freedom, CA: Crossing Press, 1989. 89–91.
"Roja and Leopold." *And a Deer's Ear, Eagle's Song and Bear's Grace: Animals and Women*. Ed. T. Corrigan and S. Hoppe. San Francisco: Cleis Press, 1990. 136–47.
"The Dying Breed." *The Fourth Women Sleuth Anthology: Contemporary Mystery Stories by Women*. Ed. Irene Zahava. Freedom, CA: Crossing Press, 1991. 56–65.
Zude/Jez. Work in Progress. 1992.

Non-Fiction

"The Miracle of Lesbianism." *Loving Women/Loving Men: Gay Liberation and the Church*. Ed. Sally Gearhart and William R. Johnson. San Francisco: Glide Publications, 1974. 118–52.
With Susan Rennie. *A Feminist Tarot: Guide to Intrapersonal Communication*. Monticello, NY: Persephone Press, 1975.
"Womanpower: Energy Re-Sourcement." *Woman-Spirit* 2, no. 7 (Spring 1976): 19–23. Rpt. in *The Politics of Women's Spirituality*. Ed. Charlene Spretnak. Garden City, NY: Doubleday, 1982. 184–206.
"Womanization of Rhetoric." *Women's Studies International Quarterly* 2 (Summer 1979): 195–201.
"The Future—If There Is One—Is Female." *Weaving the Web of Life: Nonviolence and*

Women. Ed. Pam McAllister. New York: New Society Publishers, 1982. 266–84.

"If the Motarboard Fits . . . Radical Feminism in Academia." *Learning Our Way: Essays in Feminist Education*. Ed. Charlotte Bunch and Sandra Pollack. Trumansburg, NY: Crossing Press, 1983. 2–18.

"An End to Technology: A Modest Proposal." *Machina Ex Dea: Women and Technology*. Ed. Joan Rothchild. New York: Pergamon Press, 1984. 171–82.

Studies of Sally Miller Gearhart

Faderman, Lillian. *Odd Girls and Twilight Lovers: A History of Lesbian Life in Twentieth-Century America*. New York: Penguin Books, 1991.

Freibert, Lucy M. "World Views in Utopian Novels by Women," *Women and Utopia: Critical Interpretations*. Ed. Marleen Barr and Nicholas D. Smith. Lanham, MD: University Press of America, 1983. 67–84.

Hoagland, Sarah Lucia. *Lesbian Ethics: Toward New Value*. Palo Alto, CA: Institute of Lesbian Studies, 1988.

Howard, June. "Widening the Dialogue on Feminist Science Fiction." *Feminist Re-Visions: What Has Been and Might Be*. Ed. Vivian Patraka and Louise A. Tilly. Ann Arbor, MI: Women's Studies Program, University of Michigan, (1983). 64–96.

Klarer, Mario. "Re-Membering Men Dis-Membered in Sally Miller Gearhart's Ecofeminist Utopia *The Wanderground*." *Extrapolation* 32, no. 4 (1991): 319–30.

Kramerae, Cheris, and Jana Kramer. "Feminist's Novel Approaches to Conflict." *Women and Language* 11, no. 1 (Winter 1987): 36–39.

Moraga, Cherrìe, and Barbara Smith, "Lesbian Literature: A Third World Feminist Perspective." *Lesbian Studies: Present and Future*. Ed. Margaret Cruikshank. Old Westbury, NY: Feminist Press, 1982. 55–65.

Zimmerman, Bonnie. "The Politics of Transliteration: Lesbian Personal Narratives." *Signs: Journal of Women in Culture and Society* 9, no. 4 (Summer 1984): 663–82. Rpt. in *The Lesbian Issue: Essays from "Signs."* Ed. Estelle B. Freedman et al. Chicago and London: University of Chicago Press, 1985. 251–70.

———. *The Safe Sea of Women: Lesbian Fiction 1969–1989*. Boston: Beacon Press, 1990.

JEWELLE L. GOMEZ (1948–   )
Linda L. Nelson

BIOGRAPHY

Jewelle Gomez was born on September 11, 1948, in Boston, Massachusetts, where she lived with her maternal great-grandmother, who had recently retired from her job in a textile factory, until she was twenty-two. Her childhood and adolescence in Boston were characterized by a depth of family support and encouragement, as well as by the emerging civil rights and anti-war movements.

"I had a very family-oriented childhood, although it was not what you would consider the traditional nuclear family," Gomez said in a recent interview (unless otherwise noted, all quotations are from personal communication with the author). Her parents separated when she was two years old, and she was sent to live in Washington, D.C., for six years with her paternal grandparents before returning to Boston. In addition to her great-grandmother, she spent much time with her maternal grandmother, who had returned to Boston in order to be near her mother and her granddaughter after living and working for years in New York. Gomez often spent weekend time with her father, a bartender who lived nearby, and her stepmother, a cook, and recalls their return from work late at night when she would be visiting: "He'd be reading the newpaper, and he would comment on everything in [it]. And so I had this sense of the news being directly related to me in this way. That had a strong impact on me. . . . he would some- times just be making jokes about what was in the paper, and his jokes were just very, very funny. And he did this while we watched TV too; we watched TV together a lot. I feel like there was this thing about sharing my youth with adults which was very special."

A good student whose abilities exceeded the reach of her family's finances— her great-grandmother, after retiring, went on public assistance—Gomez found herself shuttled between the college and business tracks in one of Boston's all- girl public high schools in the middle–1960s, finally having to attend summer school when an incoming administration realized that the civil rights movement would create the new economic base necessary for her to attend college. Accordingly, she received a full scholarship to Northeastern University, at which she was awarded the National Negro Scholarship Service Tuition Award from 1968 to 1971, and from which she graduated in 1971.

She found Northeastern, the largest private school in the country, overwhelming, recalling the ratio of black students to white as approximating 600 to 30,000. As a result, Gomez participated in student strikes and takeovers of administration buildings to protest the glaring racial inequality of the school's policies.

While there she was also employed through Northeastern's co-op program. She had always known she wanted to be a journalist, and in 1968, after the assassination of Martin Luther King, Jr., she got a chance to work on one of the first black television shows, "Say, Brother," at Boston's public television station, WGBH. "It definitely changed my life," Gomez remembers. "I learned a lot more about black culture. And politics. And the work place. About the power of work."

The show was cancelled, however, around the time of her graduation, and Gomez got a job in New York City working on the pilot shows of "The Electric Company" for Children's Television Workshop. Soon after moving to New York, she enrolled at the Columbia School of Journalism, where she was a Ford Foundation Fellow, and from which she earned a master's degree in journalism in 1973.

She worked for the next seven years, however, at various non-journalism-related jobs, which included teaching high-school students film and play writing and stage-managing various theater groups. It was during this period, inspired by the Black Arts Movement and by seeing Ntozake Shange's *For Colored Girls . . .* , that she began to write poetry. She gave her first public reading at the Cornelia Street Cafe in New York City, "and when I was finished I was a poet, I knew I was a poet, I knew that that was exactly what I needed to do, that all of the time I had been thinking in my head I'm going to be a journalist, I'm going to be a writer, it was all vague, I didn't know exactly what I meant. But once I read in front of people I knew exactly what it meant: it meant that I could put words together that would affect people. That people would be touched, moved, excited. And that that's what it meant to be a writer and I knew that I was one."

Having decided that in order to consider herself a poet she would need to publish a book, she began to save the money necessary to self-publish her first volume, *The Lipstick Papers* (1980). Gomez's journalism training, however, has served her in good stead: she has published more than a hundred and fifty reviews, articles, and essays over the last ten years in addition to two books of poetry (*The Lipstick Papers* and *Flamingoes and Bears*, 1987), and a novel (*The Gilda Stories*, 1991). All of her work is inspired not only by her personal understandings of race and class issues but by her lesbianism. Surrounded by women growing up, Gomez presumes a female context. Within this female world, sexuality and eroticism have never been invisible: "I always knew I was a lesbian. . . . I understood that [sexuality] was a natural part of life . . . and I tended to be more practical about it than traumatized. . . . It seemed natural to me that I was always attracted to females: it never seemed odd, it just seemed the way it was."

In addition to her published work, Gomez has become a prolific public speaker, delivering papers and lectures primarily on lesbian and gay issues. "I think of my public speaking as my political activity," she says. "And I do it as an artist: the art of creating a speech that actually moves people. Oratory is a very important part of the black tradition. And of the Native American tradition: the whole idea of . . . the Native American song that is a history and that is a lesson. . . . The sense of who I am as a writer very much grows out of my political grounding in the 1960s and the 1970s, the anti-war movement. And I will never be divorced from that. I bring that to everything I do."

Jewelle Gomez is now the director of the Literature Program at the New York State Council of the Arts, where she actively supports small presses and individual writers whose voices might otherwise be marginalized by the narrow constraints of mainstream publishing. She has also worked on the editorial collective of the lesbian literary journal *Conditions* (1982–83) and is presently a consulting editor for the feminist review of books *Belles Lettres*. She has taught women's studies, literature, and writing courses at Hunter College (1989–91) and the New York Feminist Art Institute (1985–88); edited the poetry sections of *Essence* (1978–81) and *Out/Look* (1989–90) magazines; and conducted research and interviews for a film documenting the lesbian and gay movement for PBS, *Before Stonewall* (1982–83). In addition, she is on the board of directors of the Open Meadows Foundation and serves on the board of advisors for the Hunter College Women's Studies Department, the Cornell University Human Sexuality Archives, and the National Center for Lesbian Rights. She was awarded the Beard's Fund Award for fiction in 1986 and a Barbara Deming Award in 1990.

MAJOR WORKS AND THEMES

Jewelle Gomez's poetry, fiction, and essays effectively blend political activism with her own evolving aesthetic of language and narrative. A veteran of the anti-war and black arts movements of the 1970s, Gomez draws her primary audience from the lesbian community, while her broad themes draw from many genres of U.S. literature.

While Gomez is well known for her critical and political work, much of which, delivered orally at political community events, remains unpublished, the same feminist themes drive her literature: the quest for female independence and the voices of it; the sense of belonging to a denigrated and seemingly monstrous community of outsiders; a search for a new kind of family and community; and a mandate to use one's power responsibly.

The poems of *The Lipstick Papers* (1980) were written thoughout the 1970s. These early poems resound with the very voices Gomez found missing in her extensive reading of American literature: from Assata Shakur having her baby in jail on Rikers Island in New York City to a poem addressed to the belatedly recognized Puerto Rican poet Julia de Borgos. These poems are the work of a woman fighting to hear the particulars of her own voice—black, female, lesbian—in the late-twentieth-century United States. Moving from the poems of *The Lipstick Papers* to those of *Flamingoes and Bears* (1987), Gomez creates continuums of place and history that she joins with the complexities of richly imaged and more sexually explicit characters: from one of Gomez's own lovers, the humorously characterized "Chakabuku Mama"; to Jenny, singing in a bar off Boston's Combat Zone and dying at the hands of her "irate lover man"; to the brown sisters in creased pants doing the two-step on VJ Day in their Harlem apartment; to "Our Feminist Who Art in Heaven," from whom the poet asks forgiveness for having "politically-incorrect sex." The seemingly odd, allegorical marriages of flamingoes and bears who sleep entwined despite the reproach of parents and peers presage the vampire-human couplings of *The Gilda Stories* (1991).

These characters, much like the women with whom Gomez grew up, are quintessential survivors, a theme that Gomez explores in *The Gilda Stories*. For more often than not in Western literature, the survivor is viewed by those different from her as a monster. Gomez employs the gothic language and characteristics of vampire mythology to explore what is essentially just such a community of ultimate outsiders—non-humans who require human blood for survival. Gilda, whom Gomez first introduces as The Girl, is an escaped slave whose first chance to use her power responsibly for herself comes when a bounty hunter attempts to rape her. As the novel progresses, The Girl is taken into a brothel whose mistress, Gilda, initiates her as a vampire, passing on to her her name. As a black lesbian vampire, Gilda will live for hundreds of years, bringing the costs of survival into sharp focus. Gomez transports her character across the United States in a picaresque adventure plot on a quest for family in a narrative so full of concern for the meaningful details of the land through which she travels that it is more reminiscent of Mark Twain than of contemporary lesbian writers. Yet Gilda's sexuality is never at issue: Gomez's vampire community is unquestioningly, joyfully, polymorphously perverse. What is of question is what gives one life meaning when that life comprises several hundred years. Gilda's answer: a chosen family made up of that diverse group of humans whom she has come to love as she traverses U.S. history. As with her character Gilda, whose responsibility it is to leave a dream in exchange for the blood she must take, Gomez's works inspire hope that we can create change.

CRITICAL RECEPTION

Gomez's poetry has been well received by the feminist and lesbian presses, prompting commentary such as "empowering," "irreverent," and "sensual," and her anthologized short fiction and novel, *The Gilda Stories*, have secured her place within the lesbian literary world. Much of this criticism tends to focus primarily on the intrinsically feminist themes around which all of her work revolves. As noted feminist critic Susan Sherman wrote of *The Gilda Stories* in *New Directions for Women*, "On the surface a vampire story spanning two centuries . . . [it] is a novel intensely concerned with the ethical implications of human interaction" (10). Allison Green elaborated on this in *Bay Windows*: "Above all, it is a profoundly moral book; it places us on earth to do good works, to encourage people's dreams, and to see beyond our daily worries to the world we are creating. It gives us hope, and it gives us a responsibility" (28). In one of the few insightful comments upon the language of the book, Kamili Anderson wrote in *Conditions*, "She has cajoled the language to serve her own immense expressive needs, in effect 'de-*man*-cipating' language to speak in the name of woman unbound" (120). Lesbian critics have been highly appreciative of Gomez's willingness to write erotic material, particularly in her poetry and anthologized short fiction. "Gomez's words follow women journeying boldly or cautiously to the ends of intimacy, towards their truest, most vulnerable or indestructible selves" (Anderson 122). The few stylistic comments that appear in these reviews reflect on the originality of and lack of pretension in Gomez's voice and on her use of imagery, but they do not locate her in any literary context.

By virtue of their self-publication, Gomez's first two books received limited notice outside the feminist lesbian community. *The Gilda Stories*, however, is published by Firebrand Books, and thus has been more widely publicized and distributed. Yet even it has received virtually no attention from the black or "alternative" straight presses, including publications for which Gomez has been a critic, such as the *Nation* and the *Village Voice*. Her exclusion, as a successful black woman writer and public administrator, from comment in the black press seems to echo the ongoing discomfort of the black literary establishment with explicitly lesbian themes. The alternative and mainstream white presses seem merely not to know what to do with *Gilda*'s independent, black, lesbian vampire. The trade papers, such as *Booklist* and *Publishers Weekly*, have noted the appearance of *The Gilda Stories*, but have effectively dismissed it stylistically. The organic form and the absence of a singular narrative climax to the novel have proven unbearable to these reviewers. "[I]f plot and action are your meat, go elsewhere," wrote Scott Winnent in *Locus*. And *Publishers Weekly* accused the novel of using issues of race and sexual preference as "mere fodder for an ultimately uninteresting romance novel" (277).

Since the feminist and lesbian presses have yet to review Gomez's work within the broader contexts of black literature or of American literature as a whole, the effect of being homophobically excluded from the body of mainstream cultural criticism is to cut her work off from its literary roots. Such segregation, of course, merely mirrors the ongoing segregation of American culture. As a result,

Gomez's themes, which are of import to all of American literature, continue to be dismissed as "political" rather than incorporated into the literary heritage of which they are a part.

BIBLIOGRAPHY

Works by Jewelle L. Gomez

Books

The Lipstick Papers. New York: Grace Publications, 1980.
Flamingoes and Bears. New York: Grace Publications, 1987.
The Gilda Stories. Ithaca; NY: Firebrand Books, 1991.

Essays

"A Cultural Legacy Denied: Black Lesbians in Fiction by Women." *Home Girls*. Ed. Barbara Smith. New York: Kitchen Table Women of Color Press, 1983. 110–23.
"Surpassing the Isms: Racism and Anti-Semitism in Our Neighborhoods." *Between Ourselves* (Washington, D.C.) April 1985. 8.
"Showing Our Faces: A Century of Black Women Photographed." *Ten-Eight* (London) (Fall 1987): 13–19.
"Recasting the Mythology: A Critical Analysis of Vampire Fiction." *Hot Wire* (November 1987): 42–44.
"Imagine a Lesbian . . . a Black Lesbian. . . . " *Trivia: A Journal of Ideas* 12 (Spring 1988): 45–60.
"The Spirit of Mildred Pierce: Outsider Status as a Source of Power." *Lambda Book Report* (September 1989): 6.
"Lorraine Hansberry: Uncommon Warrior." *Reading Black, Reading Feminist*. Ed. Henry Louis Gates, Jr. New York: New American Library, 1990. 307–17.
"Art Out Front." *Our Right to Love*. Ed. Ginny Vida. New York: E. P. Dutton, 1990. 1–4.

Studies of Jewelle L. Gomez

Anderson, Kamili. Rev. of *Flamingoes and Bears*. *Conditions* 14 (1987): 120–22.
Brownworth, Victoria A. "No Either/Or: Jewelle Gomez Won't Settle." *Outweek* 22 (May 1991): 54–55.
Cook-Daniels, Loree. Rev. of *The Gilda Stories*. *Lambda Sci-Fi* (November 1991).
Findlen, Barbara. "Bold Types: Jewelle Gomez." *Ms.* 2.1 (1991): 87.
Green, Allison. "The Good Life." Rev. of *The Gilda Stories*. *Bay Windows* 7 (Nov. 1991): 28.
Hamer, Diane. "Love Bites." Rev. of *The Gilda Stories*. *Gay Community News* 26 (May 1991): 7, 11.
Hines, Kim. "Strumpets, Vampires, and Intrigue." Rev. of *The Gilda Stories*. *Equal Time* 19 (July 1991).
Johnson, Angela. "Blood, Hunger and Immortality." Rev. of *The Gilda Stories*. *off our backs* 21, no. 8 (August–September 1991): 14.

Kolbe, Miranda. Rev. of *Flamingoes and Bears*. *Gay Community News*.

Kuda, Marie. Rev. of *The Gilda Stories*. *Booklist* 1 (June 1991).

Rev. of *The Gilda Stories*. *Publishers Weekly* 10 (May 1991): 277.

Schwartz, Patricia Roth. "Living On: Novelist Gomez Turns to 'Genre' to Keep Hope Alive." *Bay Windows* 7 (Nov. 1991).

Sherman, Susan. "Making Family History Come Alive." Rev. of *The Gilda Stories*. *New Directions for Women* (Nov.-Dec. 1991): 10.

Smith, Kennedy. "Gilda's Bite Is Irresistible." Rev. of *The Gilda Stories*. *Washington Blade* 8 (Nov. 1991): 43.

Troxell, Jane. "Minnie Bruce Pratt and Jewelle Gomez." *Washington Blade* 8 (Nov. 1991): 42–43.

———. Rev. of "Don't Explain." *Women on Women*. *Lambda Book Report* 2, no. 5 (June/July 1990): 16–17.

Winnett, Scott. Rev. of *The Gilda Stories*. *Locus* (July 1991).

Woodson, Jacqueline. "Blood Connections." Rev. of *The Gilda Stories*. *Outweek* 22 (May 1991): 53–54.

MELINDA GOODMAN (1957–   )
Donna Allegra

BIOGRAPHY

Melinda Goodman grew up in New York City's Manhattan and in Englewood, New Jersey, the second daughter in a Jewish family of four children. Her first poetic work, composed around age eight, was song lyrics for the civil rights movement and against the Ku Klux Klan, coauthored with her elder sister, Robin. By age eleven she was taking her writing seriously, inspired by Louise Fitzhugh's *Harriet the Spy*.

Around age thirteen, Goodman was introduced to the work of Nikki Giovanni and *The Last Poets* by her sister and an older female lover. The poetry spoken over the airwaves made a strong impression on her, particularly as it combined with political consciousness. Giovanni's use of rhythms influenced her writing style.

In junior high school, she wrote for her English class a poem, "So You're On The Subway," which enjoyed a tremendous reception. That memory stayed with her, although she was not to take up her writing again until age eighteen.

A lover brought her into contact with the exciting political activity going on at City College (New York) and in the liberation movements, but there were no gay politics to speak of. The women's movement at that time struck her as too filled with racism, and the women were much older than she. In the early 1970s, no gay youth organizations were available to provide support on issues of sexual identity, homophobia, sexual abuse, and drug dependency. These elements of lesbian adolescence later became major themes explored in her first book of poems, *Middle Sister*.

In high school, Goodman's energies went into developing her persona. She knew herself to be a lesbian, but few of the classmates to whom she was attracted had any such self-awareness.

Goodman entered Hampshire College in 1975 with the expectation of pursuing documentary film. A poetry workshop with Andrew Salkey nurtured her blossoming talent.

In 1976, Goodman saw Ntozake Shange's *For Colored Girls Who've Considered Suicide/When the Rainbow Is Enuf*, then on off-Broadway. Its impact on her was such that she combined her poetry with Frieda Jones's to produce a play, *Tiny Pyramids*, which was performed at Hampshire College in 1977. Her writing sphere broadened to the theatrical.

In college, Goodman was involved with men, even though she knew she was a lesbian. She came across some feminist poetry that convinced her that being a lesbian could integrate with the politics of anti-racism and revolution so important to her. In particular, Judy Grahn's *The Common Woman* voiced a white woman's perspective she could relate to. Pat Parker's poetry was also crucial because Parker wrote about interracial relationships with insights that Goodman needed.

At Hampshire College, Goodman was introduced to Audre Lorde, who became an important mentor. Lorde's powerful reading style had a profound effect on Goodman, who knew she wanted to go to New York City to study with Lorde. In 1980, Goodman returned to New York City and connected with Audre Lorde in workshops at Hunter College (1981–1985). Lorde encouraged her to pursue an M.F.A. at Columbia University, where she took workshops with Carolyn Forche and Molly Peacock. She also studied with Cherrìe Moraga and Joan Larkin. But it was Lorde who taught Goodman that one could influence political consciousness and change society with words. This was important to Goodman during the late 1970s and early 1980s, when radical activism appeared to be the most effective way to alter society.

From 1987 to 1990 Goodman served as an editor for *Conditions*. She left to continue her graduate work at New York University. Since 1987, Goodman has worked as an adjunct professor of English at Hunter College, and since 1989, at Bronx Community College as a teacher of literacy. She has also taught theater at the University of Massachusetts at Amherst, worked as an exercise therapist, made video documentaries, and been a scientific photographer.

MAJOR WORKS AND THEMES

During college and the ensuing years, Goodman tried to capture the flavor of her lived experience. Her poems take those energies and address the loneliness and fears of a young person. The vignettes in her collection, *Middle Sister*, are like snapshots of moments taken from a film. There is a slow zoom lens quality where the stream of details racks up a tension released in a final image.

There are four sections in *Middle Sister*. "Raccoon Coat," "Cobwebs," and "Don't Think I Don't Know Where They Get It From" from Part 1, *Platforms*, distill moments from childhood, growing up with adults who are not like the parents shown on TV.

"Platforms," also in the first section, captures the affect of teenagers who both giggle and assume a cool attitude toward painful feelings and events. "Just How Crazy Brenda Is" and "Platforms" bespeak the poignancy of being a teenage lesbian and feeling lonely among friends. "Platforms" leaves the reader aching over the alienation of having an affair with another girl but being unable to name it lesbian.

Emotion hides in Goodman's detailed observations. Her final lines are usually abrupt, but they leave the reader feeling complete or appropriately surprised. "Countdown" and "Jailbait," for example, convey an adolescent's sexual awareness where she is knowing, but not entirely understanding. In part 2, *Women Were Our Mothers*, "Night Stalking," "Lemon Juice," and "Getting Out and Seeing People," particularly capture textures from the landscape of love affairs.

Part 3, *Spin Cycle*, stems from adult life in New York City. A major aspect of Goodman's poetic technique is to stack precise descriptions that add up to a revelation larger than the sum of the parts. "Fast Break after Breakfast" and "Shell Shocked in Chincoteague" exemplify this technique.

The poems in parts 2 and 3 convey themes of not getting a lover—of connecting for a moment only to unravel too soon. Part 4, *Turtles On a Rock*, continues observations of her life and the backdrop of world politics. She recounts living pain and social commentary. "Body Work" relentlessly catalogues the horrors of contemporary life. "Women Have Always," the final poem, scales a transcendent note of hope.

When Goodman is performing, her absurdist edge holds the forefront on stage. Jokes hidden on the written page take on substance when Goodman delivers the poem. She often has a double punch line. "New Comers," a poem in her most recent manuscript, completes a narrative to laughter's satisfaction over a classic lesbian scenario, but the final line floors the reader with the unexpected spin that she delivers.

CRITICAL RECEPTION

Performing poets are not generally reviewed, and Goodman is no exception, but audiences are eager to hear her read and are enthusiastic about her appearances.

In review in *Conditions* 15, Donna Masini gives an analytical ovation to *Middle Sister*. She summarizes themes in Goodman's work:

The ways we fail one another—the mother that fails her daughter who is very high, very scared and needing her, the woman who fails her lovers and the lovers who fail her, the governments that fail their people, failures of understanding, communication, the acts of imagination we cannot or will not make. (151)

Masini sums up key aspects of Goodman's work, the importance of the ordinary in our poems; of the need to use the things of our lives" that are at the base of

Goodman's writing (152). Finally, Masini's study points out that "in her best poems the visions and meditations are locked down with a series of highly specific and striking details . . . the surprising emotional discoveries are made through her choice of and attention to specifics" (149).

From 1985 to 1987 Goodman was the recipient of the Esther Longstreet Poetry Fellowship. In 1987 she received the Columbia University Fellowship Citation. In 1991 she was chosen to receive an Astraea Foundation Lesbian Poetry Award.

BIBLIOGRAPHY

Works by Melinda Goodman

"Anagram." *Boxspring*. Amherst, MA: Hampshire College, 1978. 2.
"Untitled." *Boxspring*. Amherst, MA: Hampshire College, 1978. 3.
"Yeah, I'm a Bitch" and "Countdown." *Freshtones: An Anthology of Women's Writings*. Ed. Pat Lee. New York: One & One Communications, 1978. 17, 98.
"Hackensack House Warming." *Common Lives/Lesbian Lives* 14 (Winter 1984): 48.
"Wedding Reception." *Conditions* (November/December 1985): 17.
"Bullets." *Heresies* 21 (1987): 26.
"Body Work" and "I Am Married to Myself." *Early Ripening: An Anthology of American Women Poets*. Ed. Marge Piercy. London: Pandora Press, 1988. 68–71.
"Just How Crazy Brenda Is" and "Wedding Reception." *Gay and Lesbian Poetry in Our Time*. Ed. Joan Larkin and Carl Morse. New York: St. Martin's Press, 1988. 132–38.
Middle Sister. New York: MSG Press, 1988 (self-published).
"February Ice Years." *Conditions* (1990): 68–69.
"Open Poem." *Outweek* 17 (November 7, 1990): 59.
"Lullabye for a Butch." *The Persistent Desire: A Femme-Butch Reader*. Ed. Joan Nestle. Boston: Alyson Publications, 1992. 234–37.

Studies of Melinda Goodman

Masini, Donna. "Checking the Closets." *Conditions* 15 (1988): 148–52.

JANICE GOULD (1949–   )
Marie-Elise Wheatwind

BIOGRAPHY

Janice Gould was born on April 1, 1949, in San Diego, California. Her father, Geoffrey Gould, is a first-generation American whose working-class parents immigrated to the United States from Great Britain when he was four years old. Having received a degree in physics from the University of California at Berkeley, Geoffrey Gould was working for Scripps Institute on the development of sonar at the time that Janice, the second of three daughters, was born. Vivian Beatty Gould, Janice's mother, was of Native American ancestry. Both of Vivian's parents were of the koyangk'auwi, or Maidu tribe, of northern California. Vivian, the youngest of fourteen children, was five or six years old (there are no official records of her birth) when her mother died. She was adopted shortly thereafter by Beatrice, Clara, and Henrietta Lane, three sisters who took Vivian to live with them in Berkeley, California, where she received a parochial education, eventually going off to Julliard School of Music and Columbia University. By the time Janice was born, Vivian had enjoyed a brief career as a professional singer but was content to be at home, supported by her husband, raising their family.

The year Janice Gould turned nine, her family moved to the San Francisco Bay Area, so that her father could return to school at the University of California, Berkeley. They moved into Beatrice Lane's house in the Berkeley Hills and continued to live there after ''Mama Bea'' died when Janice was thirteen years old. Gould attended public schools in Berkeley, graduating from Berkeley High School in 1967. Following high school, Gould moved to Salem, Oregon, where she attended Willamette University. She studied music there for one semester before dropping out. During the next several years, Gould moved back and forth between California, Colorado, and Oregon, attending junior college and business college, and working as a ranch hand, a cannery worker, a waitress, a book-keeper's assistant, and at various other odd jobs.

"Those were difficult years for me," Gould recalls. "Although I had known I was a lesbian since I was a little girl, my mother had a hard time accepting this about me. When I was a teenager and young woman, she did her best to pressure me to conform, and often humiliated me for not trying to be more feminine, and date men. But I refused to compromise myself.

"In spite of the free speech movement and civil rights activities of the sixties, even in Berkeley, there was still a lot of homophobia and intolerance. Homosexuals were still being committed to mental institutions for 'deviant behavior' by their families. I was unsure of myself, of how to survive, and how to feel accepted in the society I lived in" (unless otherwise noted, all quotations are from personal communication with the author).

Trained as a musician by her mother (she plays oboe, piano, guitar, mandolin, mandocello, and accordion), Gould performed folk music in coffeehouses and wrote poetry during these years. Her first poem was published in a textbook of student poetry while she was a student of Edith Jenkins at Merritt College in 1972.

By the time Janice Gould was in her early thirties, she had committed herself to a life of writing. Determined to complete her education, she enrolled as a full-time student at Laney College in Oakland. After achieving a grade point average of 4.0, she was admitted as an affirmative action student at the University of California (UC), Berkeley in 1981. While at Berkeley, Gould was awarded a President's Fellowship to conduct fieldwork in an Athapaskan language near Fairbanks, Alaska. She received a B.A. in linguistics in 1983, graduating with high honors and distinction in scholarship.

A year later, Gould entered the M.A. program in English at UC Berkeley. Her master's thesis focused on the writing of American Indian women writers. She was instrumental in designing a course entitled "Literature of Twentieth Century North American Women of Color."

In 1987, Gould moved to Albuquerque, New Mexico, and began her doctoral studies in American Indian literature at the University of New Mexico. She was awarded a poetry fellowship from the National Endowment for the Arts for 1989, which enabled her to complete a manuscript of her poems. Firebrand Press published her first book of poetry, *Beneath My Heart*, in 1990. In 1992, Gould was awarded an $11,000 Astraea National Lesbian Action Foundation grant for emerging lesbian writers.

MAJOR WORKS AND THEMES

The question of identity, both as an American Indian and as a lesbian, informs much of the writing that Janice Gould has published over the last two decades. Because of the personal and often autobiographical content of her work, Gould submitted her early writing only to lesbian and feminist journals and anthologies for consideration. She found a receptive and empathetic audience for her poetry in magazines such as *Calyx*, *Fireweed*, *Ikon*, and *Sinister Wisdom*.

Janice Gould's early poems explore the angst of unrequited or unacceptable lesbian love, as in "An Oregon Story" (in *A Gathering of Spirit*, edited by Beth Brant), "Tanana Valley" (in *Calyx*, Volume 8), "The Black Bear" (in *Ikon* #7), and "The Woman I Love Most" (in *The Berkeley Poetry Review*, Issue 20). The strength of Gould's poetic voice, however, is in her refusal to lament or bemoan her plight as a lonely lesbian in a patriarchal world. Her poems reveal distinctly individual women, holding their own in this world, either by singing "in a way that Patsy Cline would have understood" or by keenly observing the natural world and attempting to internalize the spiritual and emotional power of that beauty and solitude. This is especially apparent in "The Woman I Love Most." In this poem Gould describes what she wants to do to her prospective lover, using imagery and metaphors that are evocative and sensual. She then confesses in equally striking imagery to what extent she will express her anger and frustration if this imaginary lover does not love her in return. The poem gives a succinct and complex portrait of a woman who possesses feelings of both exquisite tenderness and ferocious intensity.

Much of Gould's early published work also includes the unique perspective of a woman who is Native American. The landscape of her homeland, the voices and experiences of her ancestors, and a sense of being caught between two cultures (but feeling that she belongs to neither) are themes that can be found in many of her poems in *Beneath My Heart*, including "Coyotismo," "Dispossessed," "The Beaver Woman," "No Nation," and "We Exist."

"History Lesson" (first published in *Ikon* #7) synthesizes the issue of Native American identity with the realities of cultural exclusion and genocide—realities that are familiar concerns for gay rights activists today. Divided into over a dozen stanzas with several different dates as subheadings (beginning with 1832 and ending, ironically, with 1984), "History Lesson" serves as a fragmented record of Gould's tribal history—a history that was trivialized or completely ignored in her history books in public schools. Written as a direct contradiction to an educational system that teaches children how to "fit in" to the larger society, "History Lesson" offers a convincing testimony of a people who have first been removed from their land, and then silenced in the classroom.

"I wrote 'History Lesson' while I was studying linguistics," Gould recalls. "It was an attempt to tap into the collective tribal memory of the Maidu people, and to speak for some of them. I feel that many of my poems come out of this 'collective memory' experience. A poem I wrote about my great-grandmother, for example, ["Prayer Path"] was one that I envisioned because I felt that I was actually seeing with her eyes."

Beneath My Heart is dedicated to the memory of her mother. Many of the poems express grief at the loss of her mother. "In some ways," Gould explains, "the loss of my mother was connected to the older grief I feel at having lost the ancestral members of my tribe. Except, of course, the love and grief I feel for my mother is more profound and intimate. But the sense of loss I feel, even now, is not just the loss of my mother and her people, but for a whole way of being. It is in this vacuum, this void, that I must try to reconstruct a sense of who I am, where my place is in the world. I hope my poems convey that.''

CRITICAL RECEPTION

All of the critical responses to Janice Gould's first book, *Beneath My Heart*, have been enthusiastic and favorable. At the time of this writing, the responses have been limited to book reviews. Patricia Roth Schwartz's review, ''Beautiful and Useful: A Woman's Work of Poetry,'' appeared in the *Lambda Book Report* (October/November 1990) shortly after *Beneath My Heart* was published. In her full-page review, Schwartz cites many examples from the book, illustrating how Gould's work interweaves ''past, present, and dream-time with searing anger and unimaginable loss, yet [is] suffused with stubborn persistent hope'' (25). Although Schwartz mentions that Gould's ''love for women ultimately sustains'' her, the reviewer does not focus so much on Gould's lesbian identity as she does on the mother as a source of life ''both earthly and spiritual.'' Schwartz concludes that the poems in *Beneath My Heart* are ''thoroughly Native American.''

Margaret Randall's review, ''Another Miracle Worker,'' published in *Sojourner* (January 1991), is a generous look at Gould's work. The review spans five columns across two pages in *Sojourner*'s ''Books'' section. Randall identifies Gould as a ''miracle worker'' because she contributes to the ''poetic chorus that is changing the language of American poetry: demanding more of it, committing it to renovated configurations of deeply confronted experience'' (36).

In what seems at first like a contradictory statement, Randall insists that Gould's work ''is not a usual first book—uneven but promising'' (36). She then explains that ''*Beneath My Heart* is the work of a mature poet, ranging broadly in content but always zeroing in with fierce steadiness.'' Randall focuses on the various aspects of Gould's search for identity: culturally, emotionally, and sexually, as well as imaginatively, through the ''spirit of fauna and flora'' and creatures (literal as well as figurative) of the ''natural world'' (36). Randall's review is both thoughtful and thorough, offering numerous selections of Gould's poetry to substantiate her judgment that Gould is ''among our most important and enduring'' poets.

In a comprehensive review of thirty-four books sent to her by *Ms.* magazine, Adrienne Rich, in an article entitled ''Books: Poetry for Daily Use'' (September/October 1991), writes that she is ''drawn to Janice Gould's clear, plainspoken poems . . . where tribal memories and relations meet lesbian desire, humiliation, pleasure, painful childhood flashbacks, moments of pure fulfillment'' (71). Rich's review concludes that Gould's ''every work is taken up, turned to the light, and placed with deliberate choosing, as in 'The Room,' '' which she quotes in its entirety (71). While this review of Gould's work is not as lengthy as the two aforementioned reviews, it is nevertheless noteworthy, given the historical context of the women's and feminist writing and publishing community, which Rich offers as the foundation of her article. Because Adrienne Rich is a lesbian-feminist poet whose work is respected in both academic and literary circles, her praise of *Beneath My Heart* has helped introduce Gould's poetry to a wider audience.

BIBLIOGRAPHY

Works by Janice Gould

"Dispossessed." *Sinister Wisdom* 22/23 (1983): 58.

"Going Home" and "Tanana Valley." *Calyx: A Journal of Art and Literature by Women* 8, no. 2 (Spring 1984): 75, 83.

"An Oregon Story," "The Caves," and "Dispossessed." *A Gathering of Spirit: Writing and Art by North American Indian Women*. Ed. Beth Brant. Montpelier, VT: Sinister Wisdom Books, 1984. 68, 182, 184.

"Mama at the Hospital." *My Story's On*. Berkeley, CA: Common Differences Press, 1985. 183.

"Small Subversions." *Sinister Wisdom* 28 (Winter 1985): 84.

"The Spirit Bundles," "Journey," and "The Beaver Woman." *Ikon*, 2nd ser., 4 (1985): 104–5.

"The Woman I Love Most," "Caves on a Mountain." *Berkeley Poetry Review* 20 (Fall 1986): 14–16.

"History Lesson," "The Black Bear," and "Lost for Years," *Ikon*, 2nd ser., 7 (1987): 53–55.

"Our Lives Go On." *Living the Spirit*. Ed. Will Roscoe. New York: St. Martin's, 1988. 207.

"They Look for the Deepest Green," "We Exist," "Caves on a Mountain," and "The Children Who Never Departed." *Naming the Waves*. Ed. Christian McEwen. London: Virago, 1988. 55–59.

"Stories Don't Have Endings" (under the pseudonym Misha Gallagher). *Spider Woman's Granddaughters*. Ed. Paula Gunn Allen. Boston: Beacon, 1989. 221.

Beneath My Heart. Ithaca, NY: Firebrand Books, 1990.

"Foster Family." *Evergreen Chronicles* 5 (Spring 1990): 8.

"We Exist." *Making Face, Making Soul/Haciendo Caras*. Ed. Gloria Anzaldúa. San Francisco: Aunt Lute Foundation, 1990. 8.

"Mornings Are Like This." *OutLook* 14 (Fall 1991): 63.

"My Crush on the Yakima Woman," "A Married Woman," and "Foster Family." *An Intimate Wilderness*. Ed. Judith Barrington. Portland, OR: Eighth Mountain, 1991. 101–5.

"Companion" and "Homeland." *Berkeley Poetry Review* 25 (1991–1992): 47–48.

"Companion." *The Poetry of Sex*. Ed. Tee Corinne. Austin, TX: Banned Books, 1992. 92.

"Nightfall" and "What Happened to My Anger." *Frontiers: A Journal of Women Studies* 12 (1992): 151–52.

Studies of Janice Gould

Randall, Margaret. "Another Miracle Worker." *Sojourner* (January 1991): 36–37.
Rich, Adrienne. "Poetry for Daily Use." *Ms.* (September/October 1991): 70–75.
Schwartz, Patricia Roth. "Beautiful and Useful: A Woman's Work of Poetry." *Lambda Book Report* (October/November 1990): 25.

CAMARIN GRAE (1941–   )
Kate Burns

BIOGRAPHY

"Sometimes I want to write more than I want to live or be or go on vacations or make love or relate to other people or eat or breathe. Sometimes I feel driven. Sometimes I don't think it's healthy to enjoy writing so much" (unless otherwise indicated, all quotations are from personal communication with the author). These words of Camarin Grae help to explain the achievements of a writer who, in the short span of eight years, published seven novels, started and managed a lesbian feminist press, and simultaneously maintained a professional career. Since 1983 when she published *The Winged Dancer*, Grae has provided readers with popular lesbian mystery, adventure, and science fiction novels.

Born on October 23, 1941, Grae has lived most of her life in Chicago, Illinois. After completing her education in the Chicago public schools in 1959, she moved five times in six years to pursue undergraduate studies and to relocate with a new husband. At the age of twenty-three, while her infant daughter napped, Grae began to write novels but waited ten years before she attempted to publish. During those years, she balanced her family life with her studies and her writing. In 1968 she received a B.A. degree in psychology from Roosevelt University in Chicago. Grae then went on to complete an M.A. in clinical psychology at the University of Illinois in Chicago in 1971 and continued there to conclude her doctoral studies in the same field (1974).

While in graduate school, Grae came out as a lesbian at the age of thirty. She ended her ten-year marriage and, in the process, lost custody of her then eight-year-old daughter because the judge handling the case in 1973 said she "lived on the fringes of radicalism, associated with 'known homosexuals,' " was perhaps one herself, and "did not hold God or religion in high esteem." In spite of the custody battle trauma, Grae and her daughter preserved a close relationship that they continue to cherish.

Grae acquired a position as a staff psychologist at the counseling center of a university in Chicago shortly after completing her doctorate. Her professional life compelled her to take a *nom de plume* for writing her novels. Although she chose not to reveal her lesbian identity in her career, she was active as a feminist on campus, chairing the Rape/Assault Intervention Committee, leading groups for women on assertiveness and self-determination training, helping found the Women's Center, and bringing in feminist speakers. Off campus she participated in numerous lesbian-related activities and organizations such as the lesbian chorus, women's music festivals, and gay pride parades. For the past six years, she has directed the Psychological Services Department at the same university and participates in the Association for Women in Psychology, the professional organization of her discipline.

Grae's psychotherapeutic orientation is in the area of insight-oriented cognitive psychotherapy, which directly influenced her writing of *Paz* and *Soul Snatcher*. Her novels highlight other self-declared influences: feminism, secular humanism, rationality, domination/submission fantasies, dreams of community, cynicism, and pollyannishness. ''I see myself as a middle-of-the-road lesbian, not radical, but firmly feminist. I don't find men repulsive because they are males, but sexism by anyone does repel me. . . . I write novels because it allows me to experience feelings beyond what I get in real life. In real life, I get a taste. In my novels, I create a multi-course meal.''

After writing *The Winged Dancer*, a murder mystery concerned with sexual domination and submission in lesbian relationships, Grae, with the help of her then lover, started her own publishing company based in Chicago called Blazon Books in 1983. The press successfully published *The Winged Dancer*, *Paz*, and *Soul Snatcher*. A year's leave of absence from her job enabled Grae to study printing press operation and graphic design in San Francisco. By the time she wrote *The Secret in the Bird* (1988), which also addresses sexual power issues, she tired of the tedious demands of self-publishing and closed the press. Lesbian feminist publisher Naiad Press then negotiated to publish all of her novels.

Two of her novels have received critical acclaim. *The Secret in the Bird* was nominated for the Lesbian Fiction Award in the first annual Lambda Literary Awards in 1989. *Slick*, a grass-roots detective novel, was nominated in the category of Lesbian Mystery in 1991.

MAJOR WORKS AND THEMES

Psychological themes predominate in the novels of Camarin Grae, effectively combining her professional interests as a psychotherapist with her talent for mystery, science fiction, and adventure writing. Her characters struggle in their search for lesbian identities that embrace both personal desires and political values. At the center of their internal conflicts are power issues in relation to sexual desire, self-esteem, family dynamics, and utopian communities.

Her first novel, *The Winged Dancer* (1983), introduces themes that re-emerge in several of her subsequent books. First-person narrator Kat Rogan confronts two sides of herself that previously remained dormant while she lived comfortably in Chicago's lesbian feminist community. Her involvement in two murder cases causes her to be incarcerated unjustly in the fictional country of Miragua in South America. In a women's prison she discovers feelings that shock her as she manipulates the oppressive power structure in order to survive: she finds pleasure in dominating others. When she is sold to a prison farm and is forced to act submissively, a counter pleasure in being dominated equally surprises her. Both desires, the novel suggests, stem from the patriarchal family model she knew as a child in which her father dominated her mother. The conclusion resolves the conflict between Kat's sadomasochistic, or S/M, obsessions and her egalitarian feminist values. Her sexual attraction to power inequality vanishes after she fully experiences both dominant and submissive roles. Grae implies that by acting out S/M fantasies, Kat exorcises her S/M desire. Kat then begins again on equal ground in a new relationship that promises lasting commitment and a deeper intimacy than any relationship she experienced before.

Similar power issues are mirrored in the political history of Miragua's indigenous tribes. Grae describes a dominant tribe, a submissive tribe, and an egalitarian tribe. The Winged Dancer, a statue once created by the egalitarian tribe, symbolizes individual and community empowerment through freedom and equality for the present-day inhabitants of Miragua.

Like Kat, Drew McAllister in *Paz* (1984) is also puzzled to find herself aroused by unequal power dynamics when she plays a game of sexual cat and mouse with Rit Avery, a charismatic lawyer in Chicago's women's community. However, Drew's primary concern is with the ethical and personal considerations of her new ability to implant beliefs into other people's minds. She discovers her mind "zapping" ability after healing from a brain injury and, at the same time, falls in love with her best friend. Thus, Grae presents both a coming-out novel and an analysis of Drew's development from the shy person she was before to a woman with new confidence due to her impressive powers.

Oppressive institutions are contrasted with Grae's women-centered conceptions of community. When the CIA forces Drew to use her powers to their advantage, Drew decides she would be safer and more effective in a separate community of lesbians. She creates that community, Dega J, on a secret South American island where she becomes the awe-inspiring leader, Paz (Spanish for "peace"). Problems that typically threaten utopian communities do not exist on Dega J because Paz telepathically instructs all members to follow principles of self-fulfillment and respect for others.

In *Soul Snatcher* (1985), Grae employs the symbol of the *doppelganger*, the double, to examine the role that self-image plays in childhood and adult development. The protagonist Sharla Jergen's *doppelganger* is her estranged twin sister, Meredith Landor. Although the women's physical resemblance is enough to confuse friends and family, their personalities are opposites. Sharla is as troubled and lonely as Meredith is self-assured and admired. Grae attributes the difference to the disparate environments in which they were raised. In an attempt to acquire the confident and attractive demeanor of her sister, Sharla secretly impersonates Meredith, who has left her Chicago home to work in San Francisco for the summer. The narrative becomes a coming-out story as Sharla reads Meredith's personal journal in order to research the life she plans to imitate. Retracing Meredith's maturation, she discovers her own creative talent, feminist orientation, and love for women that provides her a sense of belonging in the lesbian community. In short, by adopting a positive identity she develops into a vibrant and fulfilled woman.

However, one flaw corrupts her progress: she fails to grasp that it is her new self-image that has increased her happiness, not her adoption of Meredith's life history. Here Grae gives the *doppelganger* theme a sinister twist. Convinced that Meredith stole all of the good personality traits in the womb, Sharla resorts to violence and empty magic rituals to switch souls with her sister. An ambiguous ending leaves the reader to conclude whether or not Sharla learns from her mistakes.

The Secret in the Bird (1988) returns to power dynamics in lesbian sexuality. The protagonist, Rena Spiros, has a mysterious compulsion to kill and dissect birds. This baffles her as much as her obsession for domineering lovers. Shunning traditional therapy, she is drawn to Lou Bonnig, who promises to heal Rena by guiding her through a personal detective adventure devised to unearth the childhood traumas responsible for her troubles. Once again, Grae implies that actual expression of domination fantasies releases a dependency on this kind of sexual desire as Rena learns to enjoy an egalitarian relationship after her adventure with Lou culminates in an S/M spanking scene. Although the sexual tension of power inequality is depicted in the novel, it is presented as a type of desire that can and should be overcome in favor of an idealistic lesbian sexuality free of any power imbalance.

The Secret in the Bird also presents another version of the lesbian utopia in the women-run farm community of De Nova, established by Lou. Conflict, and even animosity, within the collective create an interesting and perhaps more realistic depiction of women working together to achieve the sometimes difficult task of living according to feminist values.

Grae continues to explore the concept of lesbian land in *Edgewise* (1989). This time, the utopia is Circle Edge, a spiritual community in the Rocky Mountains that honors the benevolent female forces of the goddess figure Kwo-am. Potential convert Jude Alta sets out to determine whether the Kwo-amity religion is a dangerous cult or a legitimate avenue for woman-inspired revolution. A schism eventually divides the membership, motivating Jude to found a new community based on humanist and feminist values rather than on religious prophesies. Jude's ''community-corporation,'' a town called New Page, allows for more diversity among members. It balances protective self-sufficiency with efforts to encourage feminist reform outside the town boundaries as well. The novel concludes with only a brief description of New Page, leaving little to convince readers that there exist solely "fulfillment and completeness" (360) and "no rape, violence, racism, or sexism" (359).

Written one year later, *Slick* (1990) brings together several key characters from Grae's previous novels at a San Francisco gathering of alternative utopian communities. Organizers of and participants in this Other Ways conference include Amagyne from *Edgewise*, Meredith from *Soul Snatcher*, Lou from *The Secret in the Bird*, and Marinda from *Winged Dancer*. Marinda brings with her the statue of the Winged Dancer to be exhibited during the proceedings as an inspiring representation of the ideals of equality and cooperation that all of the communities share. *Slick* tells the story of the abduction of the statue and the women's efforts to recover it. It is mainly a light mystery/adventure novel although Grae discusses approaches to utopian living, and sexual power relations are touched upon in the relationship between Randy and Marce, two principal characters. Grae's lesbians deliberate whether to work with or against patriarchal, capitalist, and exploitative institutions in order to solve the crime.

In Grae's latest science fiction novel, *Stranded* (1991), conflict arising from difference is minimized on the utopian planet of Allo. There exists only one sex and one race. When three Allo citizens, Jenna, Billy, and Cass, descend upon earth to stop the Allo mutant Zephkar from taking over, they must confront sexism, racism, and homophobia for the first time. In this good-versus-evil story, religion is once more lampooned. Zephkar, the embodiment of evil, brainwashes thousands to join his growing fundamentalist cult based on Christian foundations but advocating indulgence in sin rather than restraint.

As she did in *Paz*, Grae speculates on the implications of telepathic powers. The characters from Allo exist inside human hosts with access to thoughts, sensations, and emotions. For Grae, the ethics of using this advantageous ability is a major point of discussion. Feminist/humanist values are again presented as the best hope to improve a society so enmeshed in power struggles.

CRITICAL RECEPTION

Grae's novels have been reviewed in a few mainstream city newspapers. She has received more attention from gay and lesbian newspapers. Although reactions to her work vary widely, most are favorable. In general, her writing is described as being both psychologically complex and entertaining. Joyce Bright locates her in "the on-going dialogue that is world literature," comparing her to Gogol, Dostoevsky, and Mishima (6). Several other reviewers emphasize the science fiction and mystery adventure plots, describing her books as "curl-up-by-the-fireplace" (Chauncey) and "lightweight" (Glazier) reading.

Clearly, the most discussed aspect of Grae's fiction is the portrayal of power dynamics in lesbian relationships. Because they focus directly on such relationships, *The Winged Dancer* and *The Secret in the Bird* have been reviewed more than her other novels. Whether critics agree or disagree with Grae's interpretations of dominance/submission and S/M sexuality in her novels, they invariably praise her for dealing with power as an issue. In her review of *The Secret in the Bird*, Elizabeth K. states, "[T]hese novels perform a service of examining theoretical concepts in an all-women environment without the distractions and complications of heterosexual muck" (1988). Although one critic finds *The Winged Dancer* to be "neither an apology nor an exploitation of lesbianism" (*"The Winged Dancer*," 1983), several other critics find her analysis of S/M simplistic in her implication that S/M is a cure for internal needs stemming from socialization in a patriarchal environment (see Elizabeth K. and Jessie Lasnover). However, Jeanyne Bezoier Slettom, of the *St. Paul Pioneer Press/Dispatch*, applauds the books for breaking from the domestic love novel tradition. In *The Safe Sea of Women: Lesbian Fiction 1969–1989*, Bonnie Zimmerman states, "Grae pushes the lesbian myth of sex and romance to its extreme limit, and then over the edge into its exact opposite" (111). She places Grae's works in the tradition of the lesbian "bridging novel" since unequal relationships develop into equal ones as characters overcome differences between them (112).

It is usually in the context of Grae's utopian models that inequalities are bridged. Several critics comment on her choice of fantasy settings, which they believe imply the impossibility of feminist utopias in present societies (Glazier, Gwylan, Elizabeth K., Zimmerman 112). Edna Barker suggests that Grae's utopias simply reverse the power structure now in existence rather than offer a new idea of community. Zimmerman characterizes Dega J in *Paz* as a "benevolent dictatorship" based on a "cult of leadership" because all members of Dega J must consent to a mind zap by Drew, who is reborn as the mythical Paz (155). In general, Grae herself has one or more of the characters in each novel undermine the utopian ideals and thus call into question their feasibility.

Little has been written about Camarin Grae's work outside of what is found in book reviews. The volume of her work alone is a significant contribution to lesbian popular fiction. That she writes well-plotted novels which confront difficult issues within lesbian communities only confirms her place in lesbian literary history.

BIBLIOGRAPHY

Works by Camarin Grae

The Winged Dancer. Chicago: Blazon, 1983. Tallahassee, FL: Naiad, 1986.
Paz. Chicago: Blazon, 1984. Tallahassee, FL: Naiad, 1986.
Soul Snatcher. Chicago: Blazon, 1985. Tallahassee, FL: Naiad, 1986.
The Secret in the Bird. Tallahassee, FL: Naiad, 1988.
Edgewise. Tallahassee, FL: Naiad, 1989.
Slick. Tallahassee, FL: Naiad, 1990.
Stranded. Tallahassee, FL: Naiad, 1991.

Studies of Camarin Grae

Alfonso, C. F. "Camarin Grae Manages to Get Another Word in: *Edgewise.*" *Washington Blade* (Sept. 15, 1989): 30.

Baim, Tracy. "Chicago Writer Zaps Mystery Lovers with 'Paz.' " *GayLife: Chicago's Gay and Lesbian Newsweekly* (Dec. 6, 1984).

Barker, Edna. "Morality Play in Mystery Drag." Rev. of *The Winged Dancer. Body Politic* (Toronto, ON, Can.) June 1984.

Bright, Joyce. "Bits and Pieces." Rev. of *Soul Snatcher. Mom . . . Guess What! Newspaper* (Sacramento, CA) Nov. 1985. 6.

Brownworth, Victoria. "Lesbians from Out of this World: Camarin Grae's Hermaphroditic Aliens." Rev. of *Stranded. Lambda Book Report* (Jan.-Feb. 1992): 33.

Chauncey, Sarah. Rev. of *The Winged Dancer* and *Paz. Lambda Book Report* (May 1987): 8.

Glazier, NutMeg. "Critic's Corner." Rev. of *The Winged Dancer. Changing Herizons* (Binghamton, NY) Feb. 1984.

Gwylan, Sally. "*The Winged Dancer*: A Review." *Sisterlode* (Albuquerque, NM) Mar.-April 1984.

K., Elizabeth. Rev. of *The Secret in the Bird. ATLANTA: Newsletter of the Atlanta Lesbian Feminist Alliance* (Sept. 1988).

Lasnover, Jessie. Rev. of *The Secret in the Bird. Lesbian News* (Los Angeles, CA) (July 1988): 36.

MacPike, Loralee. Rev. of *The Winged Dancer. Lesbian News* (Los Angeles, CA) (Feb. 1984): 40.

Ogletree, Julie. "Polar Simplicities Mar Lesbian Mystery." Rev. of *Soul Snatcher. Gay Community News* (Boston, MA) (Jan. 1986): B2.

Slettom, Jeanyne Bezoier. " 'Kat-mouse' Mystery Has Feminist Slant." Rev. of *The Winged Dancer. St. Paul Pioneer Press/Dispatch* (Feb. 11, 1984).

Sturgis, Susanna J. "Women's Worlds." Rev. of *Soul Snatcher. Women's Review of Books* (June 1986): 13.

Williamson, Karen. "A Feminist, Lesbian Nancy Drew." Rev. of *The Winged Dancer. Xenia Daily Gazette* (Xenia, OH) Jan. 26, 1984.

"*The Winged Dancer*: Mystery with Unusual Depth." *Common Ground* (Buffalo, NY) (Dec. 1983): 8.

Zimmerman, Bonnie. *The Safe Sea of Women: Lesbian Fiction 1969–1989.* Boston: Beacon, 1990.

JUDY GRAHN (1940–)
Diane Lunde

BIOGRAPHY

Judith Rae Grahn is a working-class writer and a self-defined lesbian feminist. She was born in Chicago, Illinois, on July 28, 1940, and raised in a small town in New Mexico. Her parents were Elmer August, a cook, and Vera Doris, a photographer's assistant. Grahn began writing articles at the age of six and poetry at the age of ten or eleven, although she stopped writing when she left home at seventeen. By the time she was sixteen, she identified herself as lesbian, and at eighteen, she followed her first female lover to the college town in West Texas where Vonnie was studying. In *Another Mother Tongue* (1984), she describes her initiation into lesbian culture at that time.

In 1961, Grahn was dismissed from the air force for the "crime" of being a lesbian. During the following years, she worked odd jobs at night to earn money for school. After she earned certification as a medical technician in 1962, she worked days and attended school at night. From 1963 to 1965 she attended Howard University, where she studied sociology until she became seriously ill with brain fever and fell into a coma. A year later she began writing again, openly as a lesbian. During the late sixties and early seventies, she became a poet, publisher, editor, critic, essayist, and cultural historian. While researching *Another Mother Tongue*, she gave talks at various colleges, and in 1984, she earned a B.A. in women's studies from San Francisco State University. That year she also co-founded the Gay and Lesbian Studies Program at the New College of California, where she continued to teach.

For the past thirty years, Grahn has been politically active in the gay movement. She picketed the White House for gay rights in 1963 with the Mattachine Society, a group of fifteen men and women. In 1969, she joined with a small group of women to form the Gay Women's Liberation Group, which founded the movement of lesbian feminism and articulated the ethics and political perspective that Grahn continues to develop in her writing. Members of the group opened a women's bookstore in Oakland, A Woman's Place, where Grahn gave readings. Finding that her writing was too radical for the small press publications, Grahn and artist Wendy Cadden founded the first all-women's press in 1969, the Women's Press Collective, which began with a mimeograph machine in Grahn's basement in San Francisco. Besides lesbian-feminist literature, they published works on rape, classism, racism, multiculturalism, and women's spirituality. Grahn has estimated that the collective printed 60,000 volumes by about 200 women during the eight years before it merged with Diana Press (Yalom 97).

By 1975, Grahn's poetry was widely read in the United States and abroad, and much of her poetry was being performed as theater. In 1978, her early chapbooks were collected in a single volume, *The Work of a Common Woman* (1978), which has become a classic of lesbian literature. Poems from the collection have been translated into Dutch, German, Italian, French, and Spanish. "So much depends on making sure your work is relevant, making sure that it is useful to other people," Grahn has said (Yalom 97).

She reads and lectures at colleges and universities all over the country, forty to sixty readings and workshops yearly, and she has taught courses on Gertrude Stein at Stanford University and at the New College of California. Among her works is an anthology of Stein's writings with essays by Grahn, *Really Reading Gertrude Stein* (1989). She also teaches women's writing and mythology workshops at her own school, LavenderRose Women's Mystery School. Among her current projects is completion of the Queen Chronicles. *The Queen of Wands* (1982) and *The Queen of Swords* (1987) will be followed by *The Queen of Cups* and *The Queen of Diamonds*, with musical tapes. Grahn has several tapes and recordings to her credit, and her current poetry includes the use of electronic media and acoustic sound.

MAJOR WORKS AND THEMES

Grahn's writing is marked by accessibility and integrity and is packed with information about the facts of women's lives, their oppression, the violence perpetrated against them. Her earliest work initiates themes upon which she has continued to elaborate in poetry, fiction, non-fiction, and drama: lesbian identity, women's power and their buried spiritual tradition, and her feminist vision of personal and social transformation. Grahn's strategy is to discover and to include the facts of women's lives and history, a project inseparable from her transformation of language. In the prose and prose poems of *The Work of a Common Woman* (1978), for example, she retrieves the word *common* from the negative connotations accrued in Euro-American culture. Grahn uses *common* to mean the ordinary experience and energy that bind women together. Thus in the liturgical poem "Vera, from my childhood," Grahn swears an oath to her mother that women are "as common as the best of bread" and they "will rise," in spirit and in strength.

Grahn's poems speak to a woman-centered spirituality of this world, rather than transcendence. In the *She Who* poems (written 1972, published 1978), she explores a ritual language that marks and reclaims the ordinary events of women's lives. The poems include a birth poem, a funeral poem, a plainsong from an older woman addressing a younger woman, and a poem celebrating menstruation; there is also a poem of insults, which defuses the insulting names that men have called women ("a cunt a bitch a slut a slit"), and a boasting rune that has become canonical in lesbian literature. As Alicia Ostriker notes in *Stealing the Language*, She Who "is less a name than a grammatical configuration pointing toward a potentially unlimited array of possible states and acts, which the sequence begins to exemplify" (202). She Who is both goddess and everywoman, a multivalent figure that Grahn later explores under the name of Helen.

Grahn writes from the political and philosophical perspective she helped shape, the conviction that the personal is political. As Adrienne Rich says in her introduction to *The Work of a Common Woman* (1978), "'A Woman Is Talking to Death'' is "a political poem to the extent that it is a love poem, and a love poem insofar as it is political—that is, concerned with powerlessness and power" (12). Linking events of the narrator's life with historical facts of institutional violence and oppression (racism, classism, sexism), the narrator discovers the complex matrix of her personal and political location; through that self-awareness she learns how to transform her pain and powerlessness into strength and love. In a form that is anti-literary in the sense that there are no conventional literary allusions and little poetic language, Grahn explores relationships between the facts of women's experience and the patriarchal fictions about their lives. "This poem is as factual as I could possibly make it" (112), she says in her introduction to the piece. In the process of exploring the facts, Grahn also redefines the word "love," rejecting conventional definitions of private romantic love and sentimentality. Instead, her definition focuses on the need to actively change how we all relate to one another socially, politically, economically, emotionally, erotically—in order to reclaim our own power. The transformation at the end of this poem is Grahn's vision of women's empowerment and communal bonding.

The poems in *The Queen of Wands* (1982) were inspired by an "ancient Babylonian" text, "A Tablet of Lamentation," which records the story of a queen whose country has been invaded and who has been carried into captivity. Grahn connects this story with other myths of a female god of beauty, fire, love, light, thought, and weaving, and especially with the story of Helen of Troy. These figures are juxtaposed or conflated with the Queen of Wands and also with ordinary working women; the poem looks forward to the middle-class Helen in *The Queen of Swords*.

Between *Wands* and *Swords*, Grahn's ambitious book *Another Mother Tongue* (1984) was published. It combines autobiography, history, legend, poetry, and etymology in order to discover women's history, gay history, and the language of gay culture. Characteristically, she began her research by exploring epithets flung at gay men and lesbians in contempt, and as she researched their meaning she uncovered the knowledge buried in these words. The book offers a wealth of information about pansy, faggot, Amazon, lavender (associated with spiritual power and transformation), the "lower class word" bulldike, which she brilliantly connects with the Celtic warrior queen Boadicea. Grahn discovers the tribal origins of many gay customs as well as the leadership roles that gay men and women have performed. Throughout the book she weaves her research discoveries with her own experience as a lesbian in contemporary gay culture.

In her introduction to *The Queen of Swords* (1987), Grahn claims that "the goddess Helen" signifies many ancient goddesses and is also an image of everywoman: "In *Wands* I placed her as a worker (as all workers) in industrial capitalism and as a romantic figure in Euro-American folklore." In the verse play "The Queen of Swords" Grahn creates a contemporary version of the Sumerian goddess Inanna, who descended to the underworld and confronted Ereshkigal, a figure of death and transformation. Grahn's modern-day Helen is a middle-class housewife, bored with her life, who takes off one night and ends up at an underground lesbian bar, the Crow Bar, owned by Ereshkigal, the consumate dike. Neti, the gatekeeper in the original myth, becomes Nothing, the bartender; the seven Sumerian judges become a chorus of seven Crow dykes, trickster characters whose incessant punning and wordplay rupture conventional language and meaning.

Helen must pass through seven gates, and gate by gate she is reminded of her ancient history. Ereshkigal, the Crow dykes, and Penthesilea the lesbian Amazon (Ereshkigal in disguise) force her to remember the part she played in the Trojan War, to remember the Amazons and Queen Boadicea and other women warriors. These acts of re-membering the old Greek and Sumerian myths from a gynocentric perspective, naming and claiming women's history, including lesbian history, and of restructuring the language, allow Grahn to create a ritual drama that reclaims women's power.

The second part of *The Queen of Swords* consists of two poems that resonate with the subject of the verse play. "Descent to the Roses of the Family" explores white male dominance and violence, "the battery, the arrogance and the alcohol." The poem begins with a family gathered around the eighty-five-year-old father who suddenly makes a racist statement, and "I saw each of us falling / into the gall of old habits," the verbal and physical abuse, the frustration and self-hatred that come together in the white mind and invest the word *nigger* with everything forbidden. Through the lens of this epithet Grahn examines the interconnection of oppressions.

With *Mundane's World* (1988) Grahn turns her attention to the novel form. The plot of the book is both a mystery story and the story of five "mostly brown young girls" coming of age in the city of Mundane. A community of interconnected names, places, people, plants, animals, the living and the dead, Mundane is Grahn's vision of a world before patriarchy, and perhaps after it, a world where women dancing passionately together can make the rain come down. The culmination of the story is a ritual ceremony for the five girls who have reached the age of menstruation, a magical celebration of women's culture, women's vision, and women's psychic energy. Because Grahn believes that along with their psychic power women need to reclaim science for their own use, it is significant that the structure of *Mundane's World* reflects current holistic field theories in physics, mathematics, and the natural sciences.

In each of her books, Grahn has continued to develop what she calls a metapoetics of woman-centered theology and political philosophy, a perspective firmly grounded in the lesbian-feminist community. In her book *The Highest Apple* (1985), where she discusses a specifically lesbian poetic tradition, Grahn describes lesbian writing as "mythic realism," in which women characters are "portrayed realistically on one level, yet with deep connections to a communally held myth at the same time" (87). It is this communal bonding that Grahn creates through her writing.

CRITICAL RECEPTION

Although Grahn has received critical attention from men, her work has predominantly attracted the attention of women readers and critics because, as Rich notes in her introduction to *The Work of a Common Woman* (1978), Grahn is concerned with *"the primary presence of women to ourselves and each other"* (10). Rich focuses on the power of language to transform our lives, on the capacity of poetry to criticize conventional language by creating new relationships between words. She notes that "the apparently innocent and casual in Grahn's work is often the most subversive" (20). Rich speaks of the Common Woman poems as a study on the theme of power and powerlessness, and she argues that Grahn redefines the word *common* here, just as she redefines *lover* in "A Woman Is Talking to Death." Both Rich and Alicia Ostriker (*Stealing the Language*, 1986) speak of Grahn as a visionary poet. Ostriker links her with writers like Mary Daly who affirm that "the quest for an integrated female self is inseparable from linguistic revolution" (202). Ostriker acknowledges that "one of the most powerful statements about the linked social and personal dimensions of women's love is Judy Grahn's underground classic 'A Woman Is Talking to Death' "(177).

Mary Carruthers ("The Re-Vision of the Muse," 1983) places Grahn's work in the new movement of lesbian poetry that focuses on social, psychic, and linguistic concerns. Carruthers places Grahn in the tradition of Walt Whitman, Allen Ginsberg, e. e. cummings, and Gertrude Stein, noting that Grahn uses similar techniques of repetition and incantation, creating "dance-like, ritualistic patterns" in her poetry. The ritual, sacred quality of Grahn's poetry is also the focus of Ruthann Dobson's review of *Swords* ("New Testaments," 1988), in which she describes Grahn's writing as "scriptural," meaning "both sacred and irreverent." Dobson claims that feminist scripture speaks to our relationship to our selves but also to what we consider otherness, in a language that articulates integrity and transformation. In discussing Grahn's verse play, she draws attention to Grahn's "wonderful language" that collapses the false dichotomies that separate the daily and the mythic.

In her article "Judy Grahn's Gynopoetics" (1988), Sue-Ellen Case also notes the ritualistic quality of much lesbian feminist poetry and the characteristic concern with "neomythology": reclaiming and transforming the old Mediterranean myths, retelling them from a gynocentric perspective. Case notes that the dramatic structure of "The Queen of Swords" is based on interrelationships rather than on the linearity of Aristotelian drama, and she argues that the Aristotelian necessity of violence and fear is also absent from Grahn's play. Case suggests that it is more useful to compare Grahn's poetics with Sanskrit drama, where the spectator is moved "to a feeling of collective unity, in the present and in all time zones" (66).

Ursula Le Guin ("Up to Earth," 1989) connects *Mundane's World* with *The Work of a Common Woman*, in that both works are about common, ordinary life and people. Le Guin focuses on Grahn's "highly individual, slightly eccentric, wonderfully varied, witty, funny, surprising and effective prose" (8), noting the influence of Stein in both style and structure. Le Guin also places *Mundane's World* in a context of other women novelists who have created prehistoric or ahistoric environments as an effort to understand the history and ordinary life of women.

HONORS AND AWARDS

Grahn has received an American Poetry Review Award for Poem of the Year ("A Woman Is Talking to Death") in 1979, a National Endowment for the Arts Individual Grant for Poetry in 1980, and an American Book Award, Before Columbus Foundation, for a multicultural book of merit (*The Queen of Wands*), in 1982. She has also received an American Library Association "Gay Book of the Year" award (*Another Mother Tongue*) in 1985, a "Woman of Words" San Francisco Women's Foundation award for recognition of writers, with Alice Walker, Tillie Olsen, Janice Mirikitani, Alice Adams, and Josephine Miles (in memoriam) in San Francisco in 1985, a Lambda Literary Award for non-fiction (*Really Reading Gertrude Stein*) in 1989, and she was an Honored Gay Writer by the Out/Look Foundation, with Allen Ginsberg, Samuel Steward, and others, in 1990.

BIBLIOGRAPHY

Works by Judy Grahn

The Common Woman Poems. Oakland, CA: Women's Press Collective. 1969; Oakland: Diana Press, 1977.

Edward the Dyke and Other Poems. Oakland, CA: Women's Press Collective, 1971; Trumansburg, NY: Crossing Press, 1978.

She Who. Oakland, CA: Diana Press, 1978.

A Woman Is Talking to Death. Oakland, CA: Diana Press, 1978; Trumansburg, NY: Crossing Press, 1978.

The Work of a Common Woman. Oakland, CA: Diana Press, 1978; New York: St. Martin's Press, 1980; Trumansburg, NY: Crossing Press, 1984; London: Onlywomen Press, 1985.

True to Life Adventure Stories, vol. 1 (editor). Oakland, CA: Diana Press, 1978; Trumansburg, NY: Crossing Press, 1983.

True to Life Adventure Stories, vol. 2 (editor). Trumansburg, NY: Crossing Press/Diana Press, 1980.

The Queen of Wands. Trumansburg, NY: Crossing Press, 1982.

Another Mother Tongue: Gay Words, Gay Worlds. Boston: Beacon Press, 1984.

The Highest Apple: Sappho and the Lesbian Poetic Tradition. San Francisco: Spinster's Ink, 1985.

The Queen of Swords. Boston: Beacon Press, 1987.

Mundane's World. Freedom, CA: Crossing Press, 1988.

Really Reading Gertrude Stein: A Selected Anthology with Essays by Judy Grahn. Freedom, CA: Crossing Press, 1989.

Studies of Judy Grahn

Avi-ram, Amitai F. "The Politics of the Refrain in Judy Grahn's 'A Woman Is Talking to Death.' " *Women and Language* 10 (Spring 1987): 38–43.

Carruthers, Mary J. "The Re-Vision of the Muse: Adrienne Rich, Audre Lorde, Judy Grahn, Olga Broumas." *Hudson Review* 36 (Summer 1983): 293–322.

Case, Sue-Ellen. "Judy Grahn's Gynopoetics: The Queen of Swords." *Studies in the Literary Imagination* 21 (Fall 1988): 47–67.

Dobson, Ruthann. "New Testaments." Review of *The Queen of Swords*. *Women's Review of Books* 1 (April 1988): 8.

Evans, Nancy H., and Jean W. Ross. "Grahn, Judith L. [*sic*] Grahn" (including an interview). *Contemporary Authors*, edited by Hal May and Susan M. Trotsky. vol. 122. Detroit: Gale Research, 1988.

Frankel, Judy. "Judy Grahn." *Feminist Poetics: A Consideration of the Female Construction of Language*. San Francisco: San Francisco State University, 1984.

Le Guin, Ursula K. "Up to Earth" review of *Mundane's World*. *Women's Review of Books* 6 (February 1989): 8.

Montfiore, Jan. " 'What Words Say': Three Women Poets Reading H.D." *Agenda* 25 (Autumn-Winter 1987–1988): 172–90.

Ostriker, Alicia. *Stealing the Language: The Emergence of Women's Poetry in America*. Boston: Beacon Press, 1986.

Rich, Adrienne. "Power and Danger: *The Work of a Common Woman* by Judy Grahn" (introduction to *The Work of a Common Woman*). Freedom, CA: Crossing Press, 1978; reprinted in Adrienne Rich. *On Lies, Secrets and Silence*. New York: W. W. Norton, 1979. 247–58.

Stimpson, Catherine R. "Going to Be Flourishing" review of *Really Reading Gertrude Stein*. *Women's Review of Books* 7 (May 1990): 6–7.

SUSAN GRIFFIN (1943–   )
Barbara Adams

BIOGRAPHY

Susan Griffin was born on January 26, 1943, in Los Angeles, California, the second daughter of Walden and Sarah (Colvin) Griffin. Her father was a fireman who did carpentry and janitorial work part-time. His immediate family had moved from Grand Manan Island off the coast of New Brunswick when he was very young, becoming U.S. citizens. Griffin's mother, a homemaker, was born in San Francisco and has lived most of her life in California. The Griffins divorced when Susan was six, and at that time her father and maternal grandmother moved the sisters, deciding that their mother's alcoholism left her incapable of taking care of them. Susan was sent to live with her maternal grandparents in Los Angeles, while her sister, Joanna (born 1936), to whom she was very close, was sent to a great-aunt in Davis, California. In the years that followed, Griffin lived alternately with her mother, grandmother, and father, until her father's death when she was sixteen. She then moved to the home of her best friend, where she had been living and working as a mother's helper.

Griffin has written of her parents and the disruption of these years in her 1992 work, *A Chorus of Stones*. Her childhood years with her mother were marked by neglect and sporadic abandonment. Griffin was aware even then that this behavior stemmed from her mother's alcoholism, and she eventually came to some reconciliation in poems of the early 1970s such as "Grenadine" and "Mother and Child." The latter poem, however, caused a nearly two-year break in their relationship. Griffin speaks of her mother as a "very bright woman" who, having been discouraged from studying for a career by her husband and father and having no job skills, remarried soon after her divorce. Since the late 1970s, when her mother stopped drinking, Griffin says that their relationship has been close and caring, a guarded peace (unless otherwise noted, all quotations are from personal communication with the author).

When Griffin moved away from home at sixteen, her friend's parents became her legal guardians, and it was in this family that she developed an early political consciousness and a strong awareness of Jewish culture. Her own background had been nominally Christian: her mother's parents were Masonic, her father's practiced "a very sweet kind of Christianity," and she had attended a Presbyterian church for some time, until a new minister displayed his anti-Semitism. In later years, Griffin's connection to Judaism, and in particular to the Holocaust, which is a prominent theme in her work, was strengthened by her four major relationships with Jewish partners and by her study and research.

Griffin showed an early aptitude in both writing and painting, and at fourteen, she decided to write seriously. Attending Reseda High School, she worked within a creative writing program and won a writing contest. Then, as the recipient of several scholarships, she attended the University of California at Berkeley from 1960 to 1963, majoring in both English and (honors) history. As a student, Griffin became part of the leftist organization Slate, precursor to the free speech movement. She came to feel that her creative writing "steadily deteriorated" at Berkeley. Seeking to avoid the influence academic writing was having on her ("literary theory was tying me up in knots"), she switched to San Francisco State University from 1963 to 1965. During that time Griffin lived in North Beach, immersed in a circle of friends who were artists and performers. She began writing plays and studied improvisation and mime with the R. G. Davis Mime troupe and subsequently with the collective committee of the San Francisco Mime Troupe. In 1965, Griffin completed her B.A. (*cum laude*) in English literature with a creative writing emphasis at San Francisco State.

From 1965 to 1968, Griffin was an editorial assistant at *Ramparts* magazine, and a writer/editor at the *Sunday Ramparts* newspaper, a situation she describes as "enormously sexist." In 1966, Griffin married John Levy; their daughter, Rebecca (the "Becky" of Griffin's early poems; now named Chloe), was born in 1968. Finding herself too secluded and protected in marriage, Griffin divorced her husband in 1970 and became primary caretaker of their daughter. She wrote of the difficulties of single parenthood in her early work and in the poems of "The Tiredness Cycle" (1972–74). During their daughter's teenage years, in particular, Griffin and her ex-husband, a linguist and English language teacher, along with his relatives, remained friendly and provided a unified family for her. Chloe, who recently graduated from Mills College, is a writer of fiction and screenplays; she and Griffin remain close.

In the introduction to her 1982 anthology, *Made from This Earth*, Griffin gives an account of her own coming-of-age in a conservative Republican family in California during the postwar years. She traces her evolving political consciousness, from the end of McCarthyism, through the civil rights, anti-war, and radical left movements. In particular, she describes the personal and experiential awareness that gradually transformed into her own feminism and her action in the emerging women's movement. Her commitment to basic women's issues, early in the feminist movement of the 1970s, is reflected in her interviews on abortion, her essays on motherhood, and her work on the politics of rape. A contributing editor of *Chrysalis*, Griffin was strongly supportive of the emerging women's presses.

Griffin speaks not only of the social silence but of her self-imposed silence on lesbianism. Her older sister, Joanna (now a writer living in New Mexico), had come out when Susan was a girl, which had been somewhat disquieting, as she describes in *A Chorus of Stones*. Griffin had had a relationship with a woman before her marriage, but she felt unable to handle the social ostracism at that time. Griffin began to identify as a lesbian a few years after her marriage ended, living, from 1972 to 1974, with a woman who was not herself out. Her sustained lesbian relationships have been with writer Kim Chernin (1978–1983), to whom she dedicated *Pornography and Silence* as well as three love poems in *Unremembered Country*, and since 1990, with Nan Fink, writer and co-founder of *Tikkun*.

Griffin had already published several essays and her first small volume of poetry by the time she received her M.A. in English/creative writing from San Francisco State in 1972. She taught English there (1974–75) and at the University of California at Berkeley (also women's studies, 1973–75). She has continued to live in the San Francisco Bay Area and has supported herself by her writing, lecturing, and teaching—in workshops, private tutorials, Poetry in the Schools, visiting artist positions, and a 1991 instructorship at Mills College. In the past two decades, Griffin has published six collections of poetry, six books of non-fiction or mixed genres, and three plays.

In 1983, Griffin became debilitated with an unidentified illness, which was not clearly diagnosed until 1987 as chronic fatigue immune dysfunction syndrome. In her 1992 essay, "The Internal Athlete," she writes movingly of her experience of this illness and her slow, nine-year near-recovery. Her two most recent books, *Unremembered Country* and *A Chorus of Stones*, were written during this difficult period.

MAJOR WORKS AND THEMES

Both the volume and range of her work have established Susan Griffin firmly as a major voice of the twentieth-century feminist movement. She has written as a poet, philosopher, essayist, playwright, cultural historian, and political theorist. Since the late 1960s, her work has appeared in a wide range of literary and feminist journals as well as national magazines, including *Ms.* and *Ramparts*. In the period from 1971 to 1982, she published eleven volumes; among these, two prose works in particular were integral to the feminist discourse of the 1970s. Her essay on rape, "the all-American crime," appearing in *Ramparts* in 1971 and expanded in *RAPE: The Power of Consciousness* (1979), was a groundbreaking statement influential in both the anti-rape and women's shelter movements. Breaking the "conspiracy of silence" around rape, Griffin identified it as an act of domination and "mass terrorism," "a symbolic expression of the white male hierarchy'' (23–24). Griffin's 1977 work, *Pornography and Silence: Culture's Revenge against Nature*, remains one of the central texts of the anti-pornography movement. In it, Griffin argues that pornography is the denial of both materiality and spirituality, a male-defined culture's rage against the inevitability of human limitation, vulnerability, and death.

Griffin's complex understanding of nature, of woman's connection to it and to the body as a way of knowing, is the foundation of all her writings. As with the mind/body or culture/nature dualism, she also rejects the separation of the political or ideological from the poetic or psychological. In her 1982 essay, ''The Way of All Ideology,'' Griffin argues for the cultivation of diversity and for the informing role of imagination, emotion, and experience in the undivided self and culture. This effort toward integrity, which Griffin consistently maintains throughout her work, is not without ambivalence or struggle.

Ultimately, Susan Griffin's poetry is intrinsically political, rooted in the senses, the imagination, and the intellect. Poetry is for her central to feminist expression and to the feminist movement itself. She reflects on poetry as ''a way of knowledge'' in a group of nine essays, written from 1973 to 1982, which have been brought together in her excellent 1982 anthology, *Made from This Earth*. These essays also discuss women writers influential to her work and understanding (such as Tillie Olsen, Adrienne Rich, and Sylvia Plath); the evolution of her feminist, lesbian, and aesthetic consciousness; and the value of women's presses and women's community.

Griffin's first book of poems, *Dear Sky,* was published in 1971 by Alta's Shameless Hussy Press, soon followed by three other collections of poetry and prose poems, all published in 1973 by small feminist presses: *Let Them Be Said, Letter,* and *The Sink.* Some of this work is reprinted in her larger 1976 collection, *Like the Iris of an Eye,* which is divided into four parts. All the work reflects Griffin's sense of her experience as a woman: the complexities of the body, family, women's friendships, motherhood, and patriarchal society. Written over nearly a decade, the poems range from the directness and cool anger of ''I Like to Think of Harriet Tubman'' to the imagistic intricacies of ''Breviary,'' which threads together war, violence against women, Christianity, and the educating force of society.

Stylistically, Griffin's poetry has been characterized by a naturalness of voice; a clarity of images, often domestic and familiar; and short lines that create a sense of both hesitancy and immediacy. The poems also frequently employ the devices of repetition, interruption, and the interleaving of voices—fragmenting devices that paradoxically build a new form, the voice of inner consciousness.

This notion of contrapuntal and interwoven voices provides the infrastructure for two other poetically based works: Griffin's first major play, *Voices* (1975), and her long prose collage, *Woman and Nature* (1978). Griffin began writing plays as an undergraduate. Among her plays, *Voices* is the piece that has been most widely presented. It has been produced for radio, television, and stage throughout the United States, as well as in England, Germany, Sweden, Yugoslavia, and Switzerland. Originally written for public radio, *Voices* blends the speeches of five different women: a single-parent graduate student, a successful actress, a depressed survivor of an abusive childhood, an idealistic bohemian, and a mother of grown children. As the women question the shape and meaning of their lives, they seem, as Griffin intended, to be different facets of a single female psyche; her stage directions indicate that the action of the play occurs "in the mind."

The dialogic device is mostly complexly realized in Griffin's book-length, annotated prose poem, *Woman and Nature: The Roaring inside Her*, where the voices and values of Western patriarchal culture are ultimately infiltrated by the voices of women and nature, which absorb and transform them. In the first section, "Matter," the objective and impersonal male voice dominates, declaring (and confusing) facts and truths observed about the material universe; the infrequent female voice speaks only of its muteness and suffering. In the three sections that follow—"Separation," "Passage," and "Her Vision (The Separate Rejoined)"—as male culture appears to triumph in its control and pervasiveness, nature rebels, and the harmonious, multivocal female principle is gradually reasserted through the body, earth, and matter itself. No conceptual explanation, however, can give a sense of the richly imagistic, textured, and fluid language that embodies Griffin's ideas in this work; the poem is ultimately an experience, not an idea.

Woman and Nature creates its own form—an amalgam of dense research (from theological treatises to lumbering manuals to medical texts) and visionary lyricism. This need to invent a new instrument has been described, by Rachel Blau DuPlessis, as accompanying the "subversive critique of culture" inherent in both modernism and feminist writing: "an encyclopedic impulse" by which women "transform values, rewrite culture, subvert structures" (150–51). Griffin's most recent book, *A Chorus of Stones: The Private Life of War* (1992), similarly creates its own form—a personal narrative embellished by scientific accounts of cellular processes and historical passages on the development of weapons. The work is an associative narrative tapestry, into which Griffin has woven her own family history, the life histories of other artists, and the stories of the victims of war she has interviewed—survivors of atomic bombs and radiation poisoning, downwind veterans, men in combat. Griffin considers this work a continuation of her thinking on the relationship of "the body and social justice."

Both personal and public themes inhabit Griffin's latest collection of poetry, *Unremembered Country* (1987), but in comparison to *Like the Iris of an Eye* a decade earlier, its political concerns are more global. In many of the poems, written between 1978 and 1987, the immediate subject seems to be foreground for a universal condition or crisis, evoking a deep sense of *mythos*. For example, one of the four sections in this collection, "Our Mother," is a series of strikingly simple poems, visually specific, about a mother being perceived by her children, yet each poem resonates with the sense of the mother as earth, Gaea—life itself.

In the long, multisectioned "Prayer for Continuation" (1985) and "On the Edge," Griffin describes our tenuous place in a world marred by concentration camps, pollution, and nuclear warfare. In the midst of social madness, the writer's role as witness to the suffering can still be of use. A deep weariness—of absence, grief, and death, of human atrocities—pervades the final poems of this collection. "Hunger," a poem responding to a famine in West Africa, exemplifies the sense of holistic connectedness Griffin seeks.

CRITICAL RECEPTION

Recognition of Susan Griffin's work has come in a variety of forms. In addition to extensive publication in numerous journals, since the mid-1970s, her longer and collected work has been presented by major publishers: Harper & Row, Women's Press (London), and Doubleday. Griffin's essay on rape has appeared in eleven anthologies, and her poetry has been represented in more than twenty-four anthologies since 1971, including every major U.S. collection of women's poetry. Griffin has given numerous readings and lectures throughout the United States, as well as in England, Holland, Belgium, West Germany, and Japan. Her writing has also been acknowledged by a variety of awards and honors: she received the Ina Coolbrith Prize in Poetry (1963), an Emmy Award (for a KQED production of *Voices*, 1975), a National Endowment for the Arts grant (1976), the Malvina Reynolds Cultural Achievement Award (1982), and a Schumacher Fellowship (1983). Griffin received an honorary doctorate in humane letters from the Starr King School for the Ministry (1985), the Kentucky Foundation for Women Grant (1987), a Silver Medal for Literary Excellence in Poetry from the California Commonwealth Club (for *Unremembered Country*), and a Women's Foundation Award for Women in the Arts (1988). Most recently (1990), Griffin has received a MacArthur Foundation Grant for Peace and International Cooperation, the Barbara Deming Memorial Fund Award, and a MacDowell Colony Fellowship.

Among Griffin's wide-ranging work, her writing on rape and pornography has received the most extensive critical attention, from popular media debates to philosophical analyses. Likewise, *Woman and Nature* has been frequently discussed by cultural theorists, usually as a representation (and often a critique) of the radical feminist and essentialist positions. In *Gender and Knowledge*, Susan Hekman acknowledges Griffin's "attempt to accomplish the reformation of language in a feminist direction" as well as the significance of her ideas for the ecofeminist movement (46, 113); however, she believes that the privileging of "feminine irrationality" within a male/culture woman/nature dualism has led Griffin, among others, to posit "an a-historical 'feminine nature' that does not allow for historical, social, and cultural definitions of the feminine" (41).

Griffin's literary writing has received favorable attention in periodicals but little sustained critical analysis. Her play *Voices* has generally been positively reviewed wherever it has been performed. A representative review, in 1978, praises its "carefully built-up detail of character with an elegant, precise, poetic style" while observing that it "relies on individual monologue performance skills, rather than organic stage interaction" (Wandor 37). Griffin's other literary work has been well received by the feminist press and in general by women reviewers, and *Woman and Nature* in particular has been respected for its radical and creative form. Adrienne Rich and Valerie Miner praised *Woman and Nature* as both scholarly and visionary, and Gloria Garfunkel in the *Harvard Educational Review* described it as "brilliant in both form and content" (117). Reviews of Griffin's poetry have tended to be brief, descriptive, and appreciative rather than analytical. In the 1970s, a feministic perspective in and of itself often distressed male critics; one reviewer in *Choice* (May 1977: 372) dismissed the pain, grief, loss, and anger of the political poems in *Like the Iris of an Eye* as "whining." Apart from the predisposition of a generation of male critics to see any political awareness in poetry as "rhetoric," even some sympathetic critics have difficulty with the concept of the female principle in Griffin's writing. In *Impertinent Voices*, Liz Yorke simultaneously acknowledges Griffin's goal "to transform the *relation* between the hierarchies of oppositional dualities" (41), her re-generation or re-visioning, and yet sees her thought as somehow still snared in "old essentialist stereotypes" that "deny diversity and difference among women" (40). This line of criticism seems, unfortunately, to misread or ignore the pervasive themes of inclusiveness in Griffin's poetry.

BIBLIOGRAPHY

Works by Susan Griffin

Writings

Dear Sky. Berkeley, CA: Shameless Hussy Press, 1971.
Le Viol. Montreal: L'Etincelle, 1972.
Let Them Be Said. Oakland, CA: Mama's Press, 1973.
Letter. Berkeley, CA: Effie's Books, at Twowindows Press, 1973.
The Sink. San Lorenzo, CA: Shameless Hussy Press, 1973.
Voices: A Play. New York: Feminist Press, 1975; rev. ed. New York: Samuel French, 1979.
Like the Iris of an Eye. New York: Harper & Row, 1976.
Woman and Nature: The Roaring inside Her. New York: Harper & Row, 1978; London, 1985; Germany, 1988.
RAPE: The Politics of Consciousness. San Francisco: Harper & Row, 1986. (Originally published as *RAPE: The Power of Consciousness*. Harper & Row, 1979).
"Thoughts on Writing: A Diary." *The Writer On Her Work*. Ed. Janet Sternberg. New York: W. W. Norton, 1980. 1: 107–20.
Pornography and Silence: Culture's Revenge against Nature. New York: Harper & Row, 1981; London, 1981.
Introduction. *Movement: A Novel in Stories*, by Valerie Miner. Trumansburg, NY: Crossing Press, 1982. vi–x.

"The Way of All Ideology." *Signs: Journal of Women's Culture and Society* 8: 3 (1982): 641–60. (Also in *Feminist Theory: A Critique of Ideology*. Ed. Nannerl O. Keohane. Chicago: The University of Chicago Press, 1982, and *Made from This Earth*.)

Made from This Earth: An Anthology of Writings. New York: Harper & Row, 1982. (Originally published in London: Women's Press, 1982)

Unremembered Country. Port Townsend, WA: Copper Canyon Press, 1987.

"Ideologies of Madness." Nov. 1983 Schumacher Lecture. *Exposing Nuclear Phallacies*. Ed. Diana E. H. Russell. New York: Pergamon Press, 1989. 75–83.

A Chorus of Stones: The Private Life of War. New York: Doubleday, 1992.

"The Internal Athlete." *Ms.* (May/June 1992): 37–38.

Thicket. Playscript, 1992 (available from author).

Audio Recordings

Susan Griffin Reading from Her Work. Berkeley: University of California Extension Media Center, 1974.

Pornography and Silence. Los Angeles: Pacifica Tape Library, 1981.

"A Woman Thinks about War." *Take Hands Singing and Speaking for Survival*. Washington, DC: Watershed Foundation, 1984.

Studies of Susan Griffin

DuPlessis, Rachel Blau, and Members of Workshop 9. "For the Etruscans: Sexual Difference and Artistic Production—The Debate over a Female Aesthetic." *The Future of Difference*. Ed. Hester Eisenstein and Alice Jardine. New Brunswick, NJ: Rutgers University Press, 1980. 128–56.

Freedman, Diane P. "Living on the Borderland: The Poetic Prose of Gloria Anzaldúa and Susan Griffin." *Women and Language* 12:1 (Spring 1989): 1–4.

Garfunkel, Gloria. Rev. of *Woman and Nature*. *Harvard Educational Review* 50:1 (Feb. 1980): 116–17.

Hekman, Susan J. *Gender and Knowledge: Elements of a Postmodern Feminism*. Boston: Northeastern University Press, 1990.

Phelan, Shane. *Identity Politics: Lesbian Feminism and the Limits of Community*. Philadelphia: Temple University Press, 1989.

Stevens, Jackie. "Being and Otherness: A Conversation with Feminist Theorist and Poet Susan Griffin." East Bay (Berkeley) *Express* 14 Apr. 1989: 11–21.

"Susan Griffin." From a public dialogue between Griffin and Nannerl Keohane, Oct. 1980. *Women Writers of the West Coast: Speaking of Their Lives and Careers*. Ed. Marilyn Yalom. Santa Barbara, CA: Capra Press, 1983. 41–55.

Wandor, Michelene. Rev. of *Voices*. *Plays and Players* (March 1978): 37.

Yorke, Liz. *Impertinent Voices: Subversive Strategies in Contemporary Women's Poetry*. London: Routledge, 1991.

ROSA (CUTHBERT) GUY
(1925?–   )
Beva Eastman

BIOGRAPHY

The reported facts about the birth and early years of Rosa Guy are sketchy and conflicting. It is known that she was born on the first of September in Trinidad as the third child of Henry and Audrey Cuthbert. However, both 1925 and 1927 appear in the bibliographical material as her year of birth. Soon after her birth, her parents emigrated to the United States, where she and her sister, Ameze, joined them around 1932. Her mother became ill with cancer in 1933, and the sisters were sent to live with cousins in the Bronx. When her mother died sometime in 1934, the sisters returned to Harlem to live with their father.

Her father remarried, but the Depression caused him to lose his business, and he died around 1937. The two sisters became wards of the state and lived for the next few years in foster homes and institutions. Ameze was two years older and tried to care for her younger sister. However, when Ameze became ill in 1939, Rosa left school to take care of her, and she also began working in a brassiere factory in the garment district.

In 1941, Rosa Cuthbert married Warner Guy one week before the outbreak of World War II. Through a friend at work, she was introduced to the American Negro Theatre, where she began to study. Her husband was sent overseas during World War II, and her first and only child, Warner, was born in 1942. Shortly after her husband's return in 1945, the family moved to Connecticut. In 1950, Rosa Guy divorced her husband and moved back to New York City. At that time, she joined the Committee for the Negro in the Arts and met John Killens. This relationship was most important, as she and Killens founded the Harlem Writers Guild the following year.

The Harlem Writers Guild was most influential in Guy's life. It provided some of the training missed when she stopped her formal education, and John Killens encouraged her to continue with her writing throughout this period. She also attended New York University in New York City and studied under Viola Brothers Shaw. In 1960, Rosa Guy met Maya Angelou at a meeting of the Harlem Writers Guild. Together with Abbey Lincoln, they founded the Cultural Association for Women of African Heritage (CAWAH) to support black civil rights groups. Rosa Guy, Maya Angelou, and Paule Marshall, as members of CAWAH, organized a protest at the United Nations in the winter of 1961 on the day the death of Patrice Lumumba was announced. The protest, originally planned to be a small, quiet sit-in within the Chambers of the Security Council of the United Nations, quickly turned into a massive demonstration.

With the civil rights movement escalating in the 1960s, the societal violence became personal when Rosa Guy's former husband was killed in 1962. Shortly after his death, she left for Haiti, where she began work on her first novel, *Bird at My Window*, which was published in 1966. After Martin Luther King's assassination in 1968, Rosa Guy traveled throughout the South for the first time to learn directly how the civil rights movement had affected the lives and visions of young people. In 1970, *Children of Longing* was published, which is a series of essays written by young adults and accompanied by Guy's interviews and personal commentary. This book marked a turning point for Rosa Guy, for it brought together her concerns as activist and writer. After this book, she began to write serious novels for young adults.

In the early 1970s, guy traveled extensively in the Caribbean and lived in both Haiti and Trinidad. During the next ten years, Guy's famous trilogy *The Friends*, *Ruby*, and *Edith Jackson* were published in 1973, 1976, and 1978 respectively. This trilogy with young adult female characters as central is "the work upon which her reputation is based" (Norris 34). The young women, sensitively portrayed, face very realistic challenges of inner-city life as they grow to adulthood.

By the end of the 1970s, Guy had begun another trilogy, which has one young male adult as the central character who solves crimes and grows to adulthood. In 1980, Guy traveled to Senegal, where she found Birago Diop's African tale of *Mother Crocodile*, which she translated and published in 1981. Her sister, Ameze, to whom Guy was very close, died in 1981, and again Guy left the United States. This time she went to Geneva, Switzerland, which eventually became where she did much of her writing.

Guy returned to the United States in 1983 for the publication of two of her novels: *A Measure of Time*, a splendid tribute to Harlem seen through the extraordinary character Dorinne Davis, and *New Guys around the Block*, the second book in the second trilogy. New York City became her permanent home, but she still returns periodically to Geneva to write. In 1985, *My Love, My Love; or the Peasant Girl*, a fable set on a Caribbean island, was published. This novel became the basis for the successful 1990 musical *Once on This Island*. Guy now lives mainly on the upper West Side of New York City and enjoys her family of one son and five grandchildren.

MAJOR WORKS AND THEMES

Rosa Guy has expanded the traditional, male *bildungsroman* as developed in the nineteenth century by German writers by focusing on inner-city young women who struggle to "shape a life against overwhelming odds" (Norris 31). Guy's most powerful settings are in Harlem, where she strongly shows both the glory of past Harlem and the present decline and disintegration of the Harlem community. She portrays the multiculturalism of life in Harlem, for many of her novels present a variety of West Indian, African-American, and Hispanic characters making decisions within their own traditions. The effect of internalized racism is a strong theme throughout all of her books as her diverse characters interact and react.

Although Rosa Guy depicts strongly the loss of talent and promise through the destructiveness of inner-city poverty, she also depicts just as clearly characters who must make their own choices, for "nothing is worse than being one of the faceless" (*Edith Jackson* 56). Guy presents honestly the serious problems that face young women growing up. Violence, both external and internal to the home, is real in many of her books. Incest and rape are portrayed, as well as the isolation of many young women facing this experience. Her characterizations are thorough, and she often portrays the life of young women who are motivated by "the feelings of being wanted and wanting to be wanted" (*Music of Summer* 106).

Ruby is Guy's only novel that portrays an explicit lesbian relationship. This book presents the story of the two sisters, Ruby and Phylissa Cathy, who live with their tyrannical, violent father. Ruby has an isolated existence until she falls in love with Daphne Dupre. When the father learns of the affair, he brutally beats Ruby. The affair continues secretly and ends as the school year ends. Daphne is going off to college. Ruby, who defines herself totally in relation to others, is devastated by Daphne's leaving and attempts suicide. She is rescued by her father, and her attempt at suicide breaks through his possessiveness. The novel ends ambiguously with her father inviting a young man to visit Ruby.

Each of Guy's books has at least one strong woman character, and several present warm and supportive friendships between women. Guy remarked, when interviewed: "I believe in the strength of black women" (Fraser). In her most recent book, *The Music of Summer*, Guy acknowledges directly an acceptance of woman's sensuality and response between women when she writes, "She stilled the urge to fall on her knees, to kiss the tiny feet in their dainty mules, to bury her face in the fullness of [Madame Armand's] breasts, mingle with her softness" (143). However, none of Guy's other novels discuss lesbianism.

CRITICAL RECEPTION

Each novel of Rosa Guy has been well reviewed. The response to *Ruby* mainly focused, as can be expected, on the lesbian relationship, especially since it was the first novel for young adults to present a lesbian affair. The review in *Publishers Weekly* stated: "This is a very sensitive novel in which adolescent homosexuality is viewed as nothing so frightening, but perhaps just a way-step towards maturity" (80). Zena Sutherland's review considered that "the affair between Daphne and Ruby [was] treated with dignity" (42).

The review of *Ruby* in the *Horn Book Magazine* is also positive:

Ruby, deeply sensitive and lonely, finds love in a secret homosexual relationship with Daphne, a beautiful, arrogant Black classmate. Their experience fills a desperate need at a crucial time in the lives of both girls, affording them an early insight into the depths and complexities of human relations and emotions. (652)

Because the affair between Ruby and Daphne ends, most reviewers treated the issue of the lesbianism as a "stage" toward maturity and thus praised Guy for writing such a sensitive book about relationships between young women. However, Regina Williams, in the *Interracial Books for Children Bulletin*, wrote that "sexism is reflected . . . in the aggressive/passive relationship between Ruby and Daphne," and that "*Ruby* reinforces sexist stereotypes about heterosexual males, heterosexual females, and lesbians by implying that *real* lesbians are 'masculine' types like Daphne, while 'feminine' types like Ruby are destined to 'go straight' " (15).

Ruby was selected by the American Library Association as one of the Ten Best Books for Young Adults in 1976. However, although both *The Friends* and *Edith Jackson* were adopted for use in the school curriculum in England, *Ruby* was excluded because of the controversial lesbian theme (Lawrence 104). With such limited information, Guy's attitude toward homosexuality is not clear. Judith Mitchell perhaps summarized Guy's attitude by stating that Guy "believes the need to love and be loved is paramount. To assuage that hunger, young people may fall in love within or outside of their own gender. What determines the success or failure of the relationship may have more to do with personality than with being male or female" (32).

HONORS AND AWARDS

New York Times Outstanding Book 1973 for *The Friends*

New York Times Outstanding Book 1979 for *The Disappearance*

Coretta Scott King Award 1982 for *Mother Crocodile: An Uncle Amadou Tale from Senegal*

Parent's Choice Award 1983 for *New Guys around the Block*

BIBLIOGRAPHY

Works by Rosa Guy

Novels

Bird at My Window. Philadelphia: Lippincott, 1966.
The Friends. 1973.
Ruby. New York: Viking, 1976.
Edith Jackson. New York: Viking, 1978.
The Disappearance. New York: Delacorte, 1979.
Mirror of Her Own. New York: Delacorte, 1981.
Mother Crocodile: An Uncle Amadou Tale from Senegal. New York: Delacorte, 1981.
A Measure of Time. New York: Holt, 1983.
New Guys around the Block. New York: Delacorte, 1983.
My Love, My Love; or The Peasant Girl. New York: Holt, Rinehart, 1985.
Paris, PeeWee and Big Dog. New York: Delacorte, 1985.
And I Heard a Bird Sing. New York: Delacorte, 1986.
The Ups and Downs of Carl Davis III. New York: Delacorte, 1989.
The Music of Summer. New York: Delacorte, 1992.

Anthologies, Essays

Children of Longing. New York: Holt, Rinehart, 1970.
"Black Perspective: On Harlem's State of Mind." *New York Times Magazine* (April 16, 1972): 17.
"The Human Spirit." *Caribbean Women Writers: Essays from the First International Conference*. Ed. Selwyn R. Cudjoe. Wellesley: Calaloux, 1990. 128–33.

Short Story

"Wade." *Ten Times Black*. Ed. Julian Mayfield. New York: Bantam, 1972. 42.

Play

Venetian Blinds. Produced in New York, Topical Theatre, 1954.

Studies of Rosa Guy

Contemporary Authors. vol. 17. Detroit: Gale, 1976.
Contemporary Literary Criticism. vol. 26. Detroit: Gale, 1983.
Fraser, C. Gerald. "Novelist Savors Link to Broadway." *New York Times* (Nov. 17, 1990); 13(1).
Lawrence, Leota S. "Rosa Guy." *Afro-American Fiction Writers After 1955*. Dictionary of Literary Biography, vol. 33. Detroit: Gale, 1984.
Norris, Jerrie. *Presenting Rosa Guy*. Boston: Twayne, 1988.
Something about the Author. vol. 62. Detroit: Gale, 1990.
Stevenson, Peggy Lee. "Conflicts of Culture, Class, and Gender in Selected Caribbean-American and Caribbean Women's Literature." *DAI* 50 (1990): 3222A. Howard University.

Reviews of Ruby

Donelson, Kenneth, and Alleen Pace Nilsen. "The New Realism of Life and Other Sad Songs." *Literature for Today's Young Adults.* 2nd ed. Glenview, IL: Scott Foresman, 1985.

Mitchell, Judith N. "Loving Girls." Rev. of *Ruby*, by Rosa Guy. *Alan Review* 10 (1982): 32–34.

Rev. of *Ruby*, by Rosa Guy. *Horn Book Magazine* 52 (1976): 652.

Rev. of *Ruby*, by Rosa Guy. *Publishers Weekly* (April 19, 1976): 80–81.

Sutherland, Zena. Rev. of *Ruby*, by Rosa Guy. *Bulletin of the Center for Children's Books* (Nov. 30, 1976): 42.

Williams, Regina. Rev. of *Ruby*, by Rosa Guy. *Interracial Books for Children Bulletin* 8 (1977): 14–15.

MARILYN HACKER (1942–   )
Suzanne Gardinier

BIOGRAPHY

Marilyn Hacker was born on November 27, 1942, in the Bronx, New York City, daughter of Albert Abraham and Hilda (Rosengarten) Hacker. Her father was an industrial chemist, her mother a teacher at a Bronx elementary school; both were the first in their families to attend college. She grew up in a three-room apartment full of books, including Modern Library editions of *War and Peace* and Machiavelli's *The Prince* stamped with the imprint of Macy's. "I was sort of an infant feminist," she says (unless otherwise noted, quotations are from personal communications with the author). In fifth grade she wrote a humorous verse-essay about women's double burden of housework and wage work and cultural misogyny.

She attended the Bronx High School of Science, where she remembers poetry—Robert Frost, e. e. cummings, T. S. Eliot, Edna St. Vincent Millay—not as part of the curriculum, but as part of the counterculture: "It was somehow associated with being a rebel; it went along with black turtleneck sweaters and clandestine smoking. I remember somebody passing around *Howl* under the desks, when we were supposed to be reading *Silas Marner*." By the time she began attending the Washington Square College of New York University at the age of fifteen, she was writing sonnets; she majored in Romance languages, and her reading passions turned to European literature, particularly Russian novelists. For a year, she studied painting full-time at the Art Students League.

At the age of eighteen, she married science fiction writer Samuel R. (Chip) Delany. In 1967, she moved to San Francisco; from 1967 to 1970, Hacker served as editor of *City*, a mimeographed magazine that first published the "Common Woman" poems of Judy Grahn; in 1970–71 she was co-editor with her husband of the science fiction anthology series *Quark*. In 1970, Hacker moved to London; it was there that American and British magazines first began to publish her work.

Delany joined her there in 1972. Between 1971 and 1976, Hacker was an antiquarian bookseller in London and first visited Paris on book-buying expeditions; in 1974, the year of her final separation from Delany, their daughter was born, Iva Alyxander.

In March of 1976, after the publication of *Presentation Piece*, Hacker returned to New York, having accepted the Jennie McKean Moore Chair at George Washington University for the following September. "I remember hanging out with gay guys," she says of her time in San Francisco, "and wondering what it would be like if this existed for women." In New York at that time she found that parallel society of women's bookstores, bars, coffee shops, meetings, and periodicals. She began identifying herself as a lesbian in 1976.

Between 1977 and 1982, Hacker was part of the editorial collective of the *Little Magazine*; between 1982 and 1986, she edited the feminist literary magazine *13th Moon*. Since 1990, she has served as editor of the *Kenyon Review*; she has also taught at many universities and given workshops through the Writers Community of the Writers Voice and the Poetry Society of America. She lives in New York with her life partner, Karyn London, and with her daughter, Iva, and she divides her time between New York, Paris, and Gambier, Ohio.

MAJOR WORKS AND THEMES

The six words that end the lines of a sestina can be a charm that spells out a poet's life. In the sheer abundance of the sestinas that flash from Marilyn Hacker's six books is her Houdini panache, her trademark escape after escape from the net of the form into sense and music and revelation. In "words-structure-wire-beams-wall-room" (*Presentation Piece* 67) is the formal house she has built and lived her poet's life in; in "brain-eye-glass-air-like-French" (*Taking Notice* 102) is her cerebral elegance, her *esprit*, her unembarrassed delight in the life of the mind. In "leaves-wine-oil-frosting-butter-coffee" (*Taking Notice* 96, with an epigraph from Gertrude Stein's *Tender Buttons*: "A table means does it not my dear it means a whole steadiness") is the sensual balance to the intellect's pleasures, the sustenance this poet finds in kitchens; in "father-hand-black-classes-slavery-man" (*Assumptions* 33) is her acute vision of the human place where the personal and the political meet. Between her first book's "pleased-read-poetry-death-seasons-subjects" (*Presentation Piece* 108) and her fourth book's "daughter-friend-bread-mother-lover-myself" (*Assumptions* 11) are the themes she has danced through the sestina's demanding, obsessive steps for these first fifty years of her life and the first fifteen years of her career as a publishing poet: keeping words as companions through the upheavals of love, death, and the changing of the seasons, and keeping companions—her daughter, her mothers, her lovers and friends—as nourishment for the work of making words.

"About the skull of the beloved" begins Hacker's first book's first poem (*Presentation Piece* 3); the last poem of her most recent volume, mourning her mother-in-law's stroke, ends with this stanza:

A hemisphere
away from understanding where you are,
mourning your lost words, I am at a loss
for words to name what my loss of you is,
what it will be, or even what it was.

(*Going Back to the River* 95)

Throughout her work, Hacker grounds herself in the mind, in the realm above the neck—while meditating ceaselessly on food and kisses and providing us with lesbian love poetry of a sexual explicitness that has never before existed. She has never been part of the anti-literary or anti-intellectual tradition in lesbian poetry, but she broadens the parameters of the literary to include daily meals and Motown, both fellatio (in her earlier work) and cunnilingus (in the later), not only troubadours and Renaissance sonneteers and W. H. Auden and James Wright (all of whom she insists on holding near), but an extensive network of women friends whose names appear in her poems as frequently as rhymes. The voice she has trained to traverse this wide terrain reflects the varying moods of the renegade: sometimes partisan, sometimes courtly, angry, funny, lovesick, gallant. This voice shares something with Billie Holiday's, late in life, singing some jaunty Rogers and Hart tune like "You Took Advantage of Me," in a voice full of booze and agony; Hacker's standards are the fixed, traditional forms, and her agony is the loss knelling through the lines previously quoted and throughout her work. In *Separations*, the loss is of a young man who was her lover; in later books, it is of other lovers, of friends, of mothers lost first to illness, then to death. In discussing *Presentation Piece*, Richard Howard called the poems both "witty" and "desperate" (jacket copy, *Presentation Piece*); in "Nightsong," the poet describes her plan to "stay at home and teach my wound to spell" (*Presentation Piece* 77). Her method is to begin with the patterned steps of the sestina, the sonnet, the pantoum, the villanelle; in *Separations*, in syllabic tercets, she repeats a godfather's advice for weathering adversity: " 'Whatever / happens, keep on dancing' " (29).

One aspect of the lesbian literary tradition, particularly among poets, is what might be called "the awakening": a previously heterosexual woman becomes aware of herself as a lesbian and is changed to her foundations, awakened, born again. Hacker's first two books were written before this awakening; her third describes her version of it, and the following three continue to explore its ramifications.

In *Presentation Piece*, dense with formal accomplishment, Hacker tacitly describes the woman poet's dilemma in "She Bitches about Boys": "To live on charm, one must be courteous. / To live on others' love, one must be lovable" (16). The forms are here still more pyrotechnics than subversion, and the audience is mostly male. Under the display is a tension between the pleasure of official approval and the constraint of the silences it demands.

Separations is a book of the dead, an agonized circling around ghosts and absences. One lost love is called "little brother" and "the mad boy," faces we find and lose and find again in Hacker's work years later. Both these books appeared not only before Hacker's self-definition as a lesbian but before her contact with the wave of the feminist movement of the mid-1970s, including its poetry. In *A Movement of Poets* (Brooklyn: Long Haul Press, 1982), Jan Clausen writes: "That woman can be the center of the poetic universe, can be *assumed* as author, subject, and audience of the poem—that is the staggering achievement of the past ten years or so of the feminist poetry movement"(10).

"Revolutions feed on comedy," asserts one line in *Taking Notice* (11), part of a sequence of sonnets addressed to "a man half listening to a woman speak" ("Sequence" 9); it is a note seldom sounded in *Separations* and one essential to Hacker's poetic persona thereafter. Both comedy and revolution speak in this book, both hemmed in on all sides by difficulty. In "Little Green-Eyed Suite," we find this complicated contribution to the lesbian literary canon:

> "Is it any improvement," said Chip
> (in the Hungarian restaurant),
> "to go from a man who's gay
> to one who wishes he were?"
> I wish I were a Lesbian.
> (I pepper the lentil soup.)
> "Honey," says Bill,
> "if you could take a *pill*
> to be a Lesbian, you'd
> walk on down the street and home
> in on Ms. Wrong before you got to the post office!"   (23)

The post office looms large in *Taking Notice*, as does the international telephone bill, and the solitude that these imply; but for all its limning of absences, Hacker's work is as crowded with characters as is a Russian novel and as centered on narrative unfolding. There are many poems of company here, some of the most beautiful born of the company of the poet's child—from "Huge Baby Blues" (written from the tightrope of a partial alphabet, "with the letters that can be used in an eight-segment wiring diagram," 44) to the supple, musical "Iva's Pantoum":

> Our friend gives you a sharp knife,
> shows how the useful blades open.
> Was any witch's youngest daughter
> golden and bold as you? You run and
>
> show how the useful blades open.
> You are the baby on the mountain. I am
> golden and bold as you. You run and
> we pace each other for a long time.   (51)

In "Peterborough," the poem's conflicted speaker says, "I want to love a woman / with my radical skin, reactionary im- / agination" (88); by "Home, and I've" the tone is calmed, and the gender of the loving "you" of "Sequence" has changed:

                         . . . both
        solitude and company
        have a new
        savor: yours.   Sweet woman, I'll woman-
        fully word a nomen-

        clature for what we're doing
        when we come
        to; come to each other . . .   (95)

The lesbian awakening here is no world-changing revision of the voice of the first two books, and no ecstatic cataclysm; the title sequence of twenty-five sonnets begins with an epigraph from Adrienne Rich's "Twenty-One Love Poems," The two women lovers navigate quarrels and absences and winters that sting like those the heterosexual lovers in Hacker's first two books endure; but, like Rich's, the love poems of "Taking Notice" exist in the context of the difficult world, where for two women who love each other the wind blows with a different intensity. "Mined with self-destruction" (113), "the unhealed woman" (115) and her lover, "a farm woman, a raw boy" (166), walk this new rocky land together, huddled against winter and apart in summer's ease, anxious and impatient and disconsolate, sustained by moments of delight. They do all this within the elegant confines of sonnets, with rhyme schemes broken from tradition into rebel patterns of the poet's own making, seating Wittgenstein and Gertrude Stein beside each other (115), linking "woman" with "risked in" (110).

If *Taking Notice* marks a turning in Hacker's work, where she plows the energy of new risks into new language, *Assumptions* offers the fruits of that labor, an abundant reaping. Although bearing its own griefs, the book is her happiest, full of the strong painter's light of southern France falling on a world of women, on the redeemed pleasures of gossip, shopping, kitchens:

                         . . . What grace is
        implicit in our customary roles
        —confidante, chatelaine, cook, hostess, mother—
        when, our own women, we have latitude
        to choose them and enact them for each other.

                                        (*Assumptions* 31)

By this point, the forms in which Hacker works have as much in common with patriarchal tradition as with the *fripes*, the used-clothing markets this poet loves so well, where the savvy may discover and claim textures and patterns that have served others' uses and adapt them to their own.

"The Assumption / of Mary," she writes in "Two Young Women," "moves certain unbelievers" (13); under the holiday rubric, this moved unbeliever creates a gallery of mothers: some kind, some wicked, some lost to death, some to historical silences, some, with joy, found. In the section called "Inheritances," she paints her own mother, "harridan, pincurled in a washed-out housedress" (16), and describes one *fripes* gift from her:

> Naked or clad, for me, she wore
> her gender, perpetual chador,
> her individual complex
> history curtained off by sex.
> Child, I determined that I would
> not be subsumed in womanhood. (20–21)

The book also focuses on *dis*inheritances; it is characteristic of Hacker that these are rendered with intimate, domestic power, from the countess who would disinherit her daughter ("Did I say, she was beautiful, / that youth, in her scintillant pallor, paled / to decorative nursery pastel?" 82) to her own daughter's heritage:

> "No tar-brush left," her father's mother said.
> "She's Jewish and she's white," from her cranked bed
> mine smugly snapped.
>   She's Black. She is a Jew. (19)

Among the book's most comprehensive redemptions of disinheritance are two ballads: "Graffiti from the Gare Saint-Manqué" and "Ballad of Ladies Lost and Found." Both are concerned with the place where individual experience meets history; the voice of the first is brash and sure in its alliances—

> We hope chairpersons never ask: why are
> unblushing deviants abroad on grants?
> My project budget listed: Entertain
> another Jewish lesbian in France. (56)

—and in its insider dissents:

> Then the advocates of Feminitude
> —with dashes as their only punctuation—
> explain that Reason is to be eschewed:
> In the Female Subconscious lies salvation.
> Suspiciously like Girlish Ignorance,
> it seems a rather watery solution. (57–58)

"Ballad of Ladies Lost and Found" is a more somber search for genuine loyalties and lost ancestors, for "the gym teacher, the math department head," "Big Sweet who ran with Zora in the jook" (89), "the bulldaggers with marcelled processes" (90), "Bessie, whose voice was hemp and steel and satin" (91). "Where's Emily?" the poem asks. "It's very still upstairs" (91). This poem ends the book, with a quote from Margaret Fuller—"The life, the life, will it never be sweet?"—and a note of resignation, from the poet now "midlife at midnight when the moon is full" (92).

Into this quiet, chastened meditation bursts *Love, Death, and the Changing of the Seasons*, a book whose title (listing the sonnet's customary topics) and epigraphs (from William Shakespeare and Ezra Pound) provide a traditional counterpoint to the most explicit rendering of a lesbian love affair ever to appear in literature in English. *Love, Death* is a lesbian classic, ranging over cultural archetypes from bars to butch ("Although the butch coach gave them out . . . I bet you don't wear shoulder pads in bed" 8) to gender-bending ("You, little one, are just the kind of boy / I would have eyeballed at the bar, and cruised" 17) to passing ("Do people look at me and know I'm gay?" 101) to thirty-odd dykes gathered for a poetry reading (51). Beside these are familiar archetypes of Hacker's own making, like the late meal with wine, the vistas of France, and long-distance travel and communication.

The book tracks the arc of a courtship and a separation between a younger woman and the previously circumspect narrator, who blesses and curses "what's waking up no wiser than it was" (3): "Well, damn, it's a relief to be a slut / after such lengths of 'Man delights not me, / nor woman neither,' that I honestly / wondered if I'd outgrown it" (11). The voice here has a new expansiveness, born of rediscovered sexual passion; it works almost exclusively within sonnets, the traditional form that most nearly repeats the rhythms of sexual tension and release. More than ever, the tone is intimate, gossipy, private-made-public, which heightens both the page-turning drama of the book and Hacker's redemption of the trivialized aspects of women's lives; she calls it "the left-brain righteousness that makes me / make of our doubled dailiness an art" (71).

A crucial part of this "doubled dailiness" is lovemaking; the book renders it, as often in fantasy as in reality, with a directness that is unprecedented. The long history of silence about lesbian sexuality hovers over *Taking Notice*'s reference to "our surfaces' silken / sparking" (110); that silence is ecstatically broken throughout this book: "I'd like to put my face between your legs," begins one sonnet, "lick you, my fingers in you, till you moan" (179); "First, I want to make you come in my hand," imagines another, "while I watch you and kiss you" (21). This language and these images are the core of the book's power and of its contribution not only to the lesbian canon but to all literature. "Fill the lacunae in" the poet asks of her lover on the book's first page; between there and the rapid denouement, 172 sonnets later, she shoulders and meets that challenge herself.

Love, Death ends with the agony of love's dissolution; *Going Back to the*

River, Hacker's most recent volume, charts the subsequent subdued resignation. While humor is not absent here, the poems are most often rooted in grief: "Then," "Separate Lives," and "Country & Western" in that of the old lost love ("She will never know I cried for her / in a motel outside Memphis" 32), and "Going Back to the River" in that of the altered terrain of the new:

> Life's not forever, love is precarious.
> Wherever I live, let me come home to you
> as you are, I as I am, where you
> meet me and walk with me to the river.   (88)

"Elevens," addressed to James Wright, begins with an epigraph from Robert Grave's "To Juan at the Winter Solstice": "There is one story and one story only." Literally, the story is of the ancient hero's marriage to the goddess, and of his death at her command; more broadly, it is the story of fate's circuit, and of its tragedy. For all Hacker's wit and wisecracks and bravado, this is her work's most evident theme; where Adrienne Rich paces the landscape of history, and Audre Lorde paints the ancient goddesses and her own embattled love and rage, Marilyn Hacker offers the comforts—the food, the markets, the patterned music—and the losses of a figure just as firmly rooted in the lesbian world: a woman whose heart has been broken, singing her way through.

CRITICAL RECEPTION

Marilyn Hacker's work has won more mainstream acclaim than that of any other lesbian poet except Adrienne Rich. Her first book, *Presentation Piece*, won both the Lamont Prize and the National Book Award, and Christopher Ricks, in the *New York Times Book Review*, placed her "squarely, and very elegantly, in the indirect T. S. Eliot line" (2). "I don't see how anyone who knows versification can help but admire and relish her abilities," wrote Hayden Carruth on *Separations*. "Add to this her thematic adultness and intelligence, her compelling poems of lust, anger and grief, her sense of experience truly lived, and you have a formidable poet to contend with" (13). For others, she has felt too much: "Hacker, in short, takes her losses too seriously, nursing her grievances and dwelling on them with the single-mindedness of a Malvolio," according to Robert Holland (292). The explicit lesbian sex in *Love, Death, and the Changing of the Seasons* brought admiring warnings from the *Wall Street Journal*: "Marilyn Hacker, winner of the National Book Award for Poetry, poses a hard question for many readers with her immensely accomplished new verse novel," wrote Raymond Sokolov. "The language is brisk and modern; it communicates explicitly. But this is also a very explicit lesbian romance . . . The bold description of physical sex stops just at the edge of the pornographic, but the description is lavishly rendered and it often rhymes" (34). But these are varied, considered responses to a poet who is taken seriously in mainstream literary circles; *Publishers Weekly* echoes many other journals in praising Hacker's "intelligence, wit and elegance" and her "brilliant use of form" (March 2, 1990: 77). With the mainstream cavils have come praises: "She is our latter-day Byron," wrote J. D. McClatchy in the *New York Times Book Review* (16). "No one sings quite like this," wrote Carol Muske two years later. "A capella, she's a whole choir" (13).

Among feminist reviewers, response to Hacker's work has been astute and admiring. "Hacker's voice manages to be intimate and intellectual at the same time," wrote Kathleen Aguero. "It is as if the constraints of her forms, in making her work so carefully with language, assure an honest and unsentimental vision as well" (13). Marilyn French, in a review of *Love, Death*, roots Hacker's "deeply satisfying" sonnets in the soil of Sir Philip Sidney, Petrarch, John Berryman, and Shakespeare, and adds: "Hacker's is very much a *woman's* sonnet sequence: it embraces all elements of life equally. Nothing is too insignificant to be included" (447, 445). The poem's characters are "acquainted with what is disgusting, foolish, childish, erotic, maternal, joyous, serene, painful—with everything real" (446). In *Assumptions*, wrote Carol Oles, "Hacker continues to explore the forms, powers and attributes a woman can assume . . . [her] work is political, looking toward a new order of things. . . . More than ever, her poems make us forget to admire their technical brilliance. They deepen and expand our conception of what it is to be a woman" (506)

Gay and lesbian responses have been similarly appreciative. Michael Klein found the poems of *Going Back to the River* "formal in the best way . . . effortlessly memorable," and commented on the book's "restless, intuitive power" (20). Dorothy Allison found in *Love, Death* "technically effective, emotionally evocative portrayals of lesbian sexuality in explicit, almost rauchy terms" and noted that Hacker "has opened her own life to art and fashioned poems that are both rueful and revealing" (21). Adrian Oktenberg called *Love, Death* "the only book of poetry I know that qualifies as a 'page-turner' " (5): "Hacker's book is made with that casual mastery of craft which has become the author's hallmark. It can only have come from a perfect balance of 'heart, body and brain' that is rarely achieved. It should be read for years, and cherished" (6).

In direct contradiction to the spirit of her work, Hacker is a poet who is frequently ghettoized; in establishment contexts she often becomes The Feminist Poet, or The Lesbian, and in feminist and/or lesbian contexts The Worldly Success or The Formalist. None of these quarantined neighborhoods is large enough to contain her; her work merits more critical studies concerned with the totality of her contribution, in all its "reactionary anarchist" complexity (*Taking Notice* 103).

HONORS AND AWARDS

Marilyn Hacker was one of the four winners of the 1973 Discovery Award given by the New York 92nd Street YM/YWHA Poetry Center; her first book,

Presentation Piece, was the 1973 Lamont Poetry Selection of the Academy of American Poets and the winner of the National Book Award in 1975. She has received many grants in support of her work, among them a Creative Artists Public Service Grant in 1980, a Guggenheim Fellowship in 1980–81, grants from the National Endowment for the Arts in 1973 and 1984, and an Ingram-Merrill Fellowship in 1984–85. In 1984 she was awarded an editors fellowship by the Coordinating Council of Literary Magazines for her work on *13th Moon*. She received the Robert Wynner Award of the Poetry Society of America in 1987 and 1989, and the Lambda Literary Award in 1991.

BIBLIOGRAPHY

Works by Marilyn Hacker

Presentation Piece. New York: Viking Press, 1975.
Separations. New York: Alfred A. Knopf, 1976.
Taking Notice. New York: Alfred A. Knopf, 1980.
Assumptions. New York: Alfred A. Knopf, 1985.
Love, Death, and the Changing of the Seasons. New York: Arbor House, 1986.
Going Back to the River. New York: Random House, 1990.
The Hang-Glider's Daughter: Selected Poems. London: Onlywomen Press, 1990.

Selected Essays

"Mortal Moralities (Josephine Jacobsen)." *Nation* (November 28, 1987): 644.
"The Trees Win Every Time: Reading Julia Randall." *Grand Street* (Autumn 1988): 155–66.
"Begin to Teach (Adrienne Rich)." *Nation* (October 23, 1989): 464.
"Unauthorized Voices (U.A. Fanthorpe and Elma Mitchell)." *Grand Street* (Summer 1989): 147–64.
"An Invitation to My Demented Uncle." *Ploughshares* (Winter 1989–90): 1–5.
"Provoking Engagement (June Jordan)." *Nation* (January 29, 1990): 135–39.

Studies of Marilyn Hacker

Aguero, Kathleen. "Ties That Bind." *Women's Review of Books* (September 1985): 13.
Alexander, Elizabeth. *Village Voice Literary Supplement* (April 1990): 6–7.
Allison, Dorothy. "Rhyme, Women, and Song." *Village Voice Literary Supplement* (February 1987): 21.
Barrington, Judith. "Feminist Formalist." *Women's Review of Books* (July 1990): 28.
Carruth, Hayden. Review of *Separations*. *New York Times Book Review* (August 8, 1976): 13.
Disch, Thomas M. "A la recherche de Marilyn Hacker." *Little Magazine* (Summer 1975): 5–9.
French, Marilyn. "Laura, Stella and Ray." *Nation* (November 1, 1986): 442–47.
Gates, Beatrix. "Of Time and the River." *Nation* (January 21, 1991): 64–67.
Holland, Robert. "Six or Seven Fools." *Poetry* (February 1977): 292–93.

Klein, Michael. "Going with the Flow." *Lambda Book Report* (April/May 1990): 20–21.

Larkin, Joan. "Women's Poetry: Once More with Form." *Ms.* (March 1981): 78–80.

McClatchy, J. D. "Figures in a Landscape." *Poetry* (July 1981): 231–41.

———. "Three Senses of Self." *New York Times Book Review* (May 26, 1985): 16.

Molesworth, Charles. "Fondled Memories." *New York Times Book Review* (October 12, 1980): 14.

Moore, Honor. "Word Puzzles against Chaos." *Ms.* (April 1975): 48–49, 113–14.

Muske, Carol. "Reading Their Signals." *New York Times Book Review* (June 21, 1987): 13.

Oktenberg, Adrian. "Write Your Heart Out." *Women's Review of Books* (March 1987): 5–6.

Oles, Carol. "Mother Wit." *Nation* (April 27, 1985): 509.

Ricks, Christopher. Review of *Presentation Piece*. *New York Times Book Review* (January 12, 1975): 2.

Sokolov, Raymond. "Speaking Volumes." *Wall Street Journal* (November 11, 1986): 34.

ELOISE KLEIN HEALY (1943–   )

Loralee MacPike

BIOGRAPHY

Born in El Paso, Texas, and raised in Remson, Iowa, and North Hollywood, California, Eloise Klein Healy is the left-handed poet of the urban goddess/woman. Her family moved to Iowa to farm, and Healy considers herself a "farm girl" at heart. While her mother ran the local cafe, Healy was free to roam anywhere in town after school. She was a reader ("the sole user of the public library," she says) and much more in contact with adults than with other children. When her father took a job as a special effects man in Hollywood in 1953, she began an urban life in which she viewed the city through the eyes of a child connected to the sensory material of nature.

Healy completed high school at Providence High in Burbank, California, and graduated from Immaculate Heart College in Los Angeles in 1965 with a degree in English. In 1968, she also received her M.A. and teaching credential from Immaculate Heart. She taught at Immaculate Heart High School for five years, then at the college for seven more. She has also taught at the Wright Institute and the California School of Professional Psychology, as well as being one of the core faculty at the Los Angeles Woman's Building. Between 1972 and 1980, she was married to Matthew Healy, a therapist. Since 1980 she has taught poetry, composition, and women's studies at California State University, Northridge, where she was also director of the Women's Studies Program from 1988 to 1991. She currently also teaches a master class in poetry at the University of California at Los Angeles. Healy is thus very much a part of the academic poetry world of urban Los Angeles.

MAJOR WORKS AND THEMES

Healy's first published volume, *Building Some Changes* (1976), shows its strong imagist roots. It is a collection of early poems put together for a book-prize competition; there is no cohesive theme, and the poems are image- and metaphor-driven, heavy on closure, as if rushing to an ending. Most are addressed to or are about specific people and incidents. The single long poem, "Furnishing," begins the linking of moments that becomes one of Healy's major ideas in her subsequent work. The volume did win the prize, and under a National Endowment for the Arts grant, 8,000 copies were printed and distributed free around the country.

It is only with *A Packet Beating Like a Heart*, her second volume of poetry, that Healy begins to develop a specifically lesbian poetic identity. Beginning with this book, Healy has inextricably interwoven lesbian identity and a sense of place, both natural and urban. The opening poem wishes explicitly for a return to the "simple . . . predictability" of a tomboy childhood as a retreat from "the awesome landscapes of a female future," which is likened to walking "out in the corn / where I might get lost and never found." Although she "live[s] in the city of Los Angeles," she understands that we are all, urban and rural, "from the country still," and city/country blur into a common sunlight under which the poems' narrators test out their love for women. These narrators become tail-wagging old dogs, become cars wanting to park in front of their loves/houses or needing the "junk fuel" of passion or driving at breakneck speed toward love or careening off the center divider as metal carflesh rips. "How do I love you?" she asks in "Entries: LA Log"; "Let me count the lanes." The volume captures the inchoate rapture and fear of an awakening lesbian self as poems like "Edging" rush breathless, reckless of syntax and recursive in a way Healy has of circling round and round her topic until the poem poises briefly at the center and then explodes. But the volume is not sexually unconflicted, for Healy includes poems about heterosexuality as well: a Catholic schoolgirl's first experiments with a boy, a woman saying goodbye to her last male lover, a woman trying to woo her woman lover from that woman's male lover.

And even lesbian love can be tinged with violence, as in "This Is Not Making Love," where the narrator protests against the request to "surrender . . . give in," or with rejection as when she mourns a lover's departure in "Finally." Women's road is rocky, as in "Driven to Meet You in Rainy Weather," but Healy perceives that the storms are necessary to teach her how to work with women to build life. *A Packet* combines Healy's rootedness in landscape with a woman's awakening to other women: "I went willingly / to the ends of my map for you" ("I Spent the Day with You"). "Each poem" becomes "me inching out across the ice" to save the woman-loving woman in herself from the frozen lake ("The Words 'Begin Again' "). Overall, *A Packet Beating Like a Heart* is a departure (significantly, in a car) in which

> I am becoming someone else
> step by step at a time
> like an explosion
> sequencing larger

frame frame frame frame frame
("Going Away")

In her third book, *Ordinary Wisdom*, Healy practices techniques of seeing
that turn out to be part of the process by which the concerns in *Packet* get
transformed into the more integrative art of *Artemis in Echo Park*. She says, in
"In the Passageway," "to me, transition is everything," and the concepts of
both change and transit take form as she immerses herself in the emotional
resonances of Chinese ideographs as a way of transmitting feeling through image.
Healy's concern with women is muted in this volume, with the moon and trees
"work[ing] together dividing things / since they were girls" ("Dividing the
Fields") and the equation of humanness with the simplicity of loving ("To Speak
for Human Feelings"). Ironically, Healy visited China only in 1982, after *Ordinary Wisdom* had been published.

It is with *Artemis in Echo Park* that Healy's lesbian sensibility comes to full
flower. She begins with the evocation of Artemis, the ancient goddess of fertility
and life. Within an urban Los Angeles landscape apparently abandoned by the
goddess, she carefully unearths subterranean womanpower and celebrates that
nature's force "will return, / repossessing and collecting its dues" ("Payment"). Real bears have gone north, but the homeless woman begging with her
baby in "The Real Bears Have Gone North" is surrogate wildlife with whom
Healy later identifies herself as she contemplates coming out to her father in
"The Introductions." The girl "wearing a black tank top / and no bra" buying
food in the supermarket leaves the goggle-eyed males with the smell of horses,
which reappear in "The Concepts of Integrity and Closure in Poetry As I Believe
They Relate to Sappho," as "the waves [run] away like mares," blending human
and animal and natural. Healy's world is a transitional one in which margins
merge. Wisteria, in the poem of that name, is "simply a wild girl" who needs
"a good haircut"; the Arrowhead bottled water in "Public Water" becomes a
mystic river; and even poem titles convey crossover liminality: "This Is Not
Really a House at All," "The City Beneath the City," "Cactus Girls," "Wild
Mothers." "This Place Named for Califia" is an island just beyond our view,
"real enough to be necessary" and populated by women "necessary enough to
be real."

These poems also move beyond the slightly distanced, wry eroticism of *A
Packet Beating Like a Heart* into something elemental, slightly frightening,
resonant. In "Another Poet Writes about Love," she compares a male colleague's
desire for completion in tenderness to her own desire to mulch under the vegetation so she can immerse herself in "good black earth" as landscape and
womanlove join in the ultimate fertility. Later, in "Cactus," she opposes the
male desire to her own attraction to spiny cactus: "Love is how close you can
get and even bleed / and even want to pick it up again."

There is another undercurrent in *Artemis in Echo Park* that was not present
in Healy's earlier work. That is a wider political consciousness, which is a

natural outgrowth of her concern over the connections between our physical and our inner landscapes. In "Toltecs" she analyzes how mainstream culture shapes boys into gang members. In "Like a Wick, I Thought" the bag lady's song becomes incantation, her cigarette a wand, as "the gods appear at the fringes / just where the grip is about to give way" ("Going Down to Sunless Seas"). Her period of lesbian "discovery" over for now, Healy turns in this volume to a subtler analysis of the relationships among sexuality, nature, body, civilization, and life forms of all sorts.

Interestingly, in this volume Healy also begins working in more structured forms, specifically the sestina ("This Art, Your Life"), a form Marilyn Hacker uses frequently and which Healy handles with consummate skill.

Healy's poetic trajectory, then, has been a movement through image and sign into the wild joy of lesbian self-identification and on through to an attempt to make sense(s) of our bodies and our emotions in a world beneath which the goddess is ever stirring. For Healy, it is through "poetry, / the hungry wisdom" ("A Packet Beating Like a Heart") that we ultimately piece together our identities.

CRITICAL RECEPTION

Artemis in Echo Park was mentioned in *Ms.* magazine, September/October 1991, as featuring "Deceptively cool, light-fingered poems on women, metropolis, and desire, around Los Angeles" (75). It has also been reviewed in the lesbian and gay press.

HONORS AND AWARDS

In 1985 Healy was awarded a Vesta Award by the Woman's Building, Los Angeles, for poetic achievement. She has been artist in residence at the MacDowell Colony (1985) and the Dorland Mountain Colony (1980), and in 1989 she received a California Arts Council grant.

BIBLIOGRAPHY

Works by Eloise Klein Healy

Building Some Changes. Venice, CA: Beyond Baroque Foundation, 1976.
A Packet Beating Like a Heart. Los Angeles: Books of a Feather Press, 1980.
Ordinary Wisdom. Los Angeles: Paradise Press, 1981.
Artemis in Echo Park. Ithaca, NY: Firebrand Books, 1991.

TERRI L. JEWELL (1954–   )
S. Mari Madyun

BIOGRAPHY

Terri L. Jewell was born in 1954, in Louisville, Kentucky, to Miller LaRue Jewell, Jr., and his wife, Mildred. She was the only daughter born to the Jewells, and she had one half-brother, Marcus. Jewell's education included two years at the University of Louisville, where she majored in biology. She earned her B.S. in health education at Montclair State College in New Jersey in 1979.

While attending Montclair State, Jewell became very political in the women's movement in New York through her participation in marches and readings that dealt primarily with feminist issues. Jewell made many discoveries working in the women's movement. Her main discovery was that her love for women extended beyond the political arena. Jewell had come to the realization that she was a lesbian. Identifying herself as such created changes in her political consciousness.

As a black lesbian, Jewell understood that her life would involve additional complexities that the white lesbian would not have to endure. Jewell wanted to address the issues that were indigenous to her lifestyle through writing about the ills of homophobia, sexism, and racism in society. Ironically, Jewell discovered the lack of support and understanding in the mainstream lesbian movement for black women. Thus, she uses the tool of writing effectively to challenge all ideologies.

Jewell's work has appeared in over three hundred periodicials in North America and abroad. She won the National Women's Music Festival and Writers Conference Board of Directors Award in 1990, the American Society for Aging poetry competition in 1988, the Michigan "New Voices" State Poetry competition in 1986, and the Kentucky Poetry Society competition in 1983. Other honors include being invited as a guest poetry editor for *Sojourner* in 1989 and for the Kentucky Authors' Banquet in Louisville in 1988. Currently, Terri L. Jewell resides in Lansing, Michigan, and is working on her new project, *Gumbo Ya-Ya: Voices of Black Women*, a book of quotations.

MAJOR WORKS AND THEMES

The subject of interracial dating is still an issue most would rather not discuss, even today. Consequently, it is thought to be non-existent in the lesbian community. In Jewell's piece "An Alliance of Differences" (February 1985), we are radically challenged with the notion of black and white love.

The work begins with a summary of the attitudes that people have about black and white relationships, which Terri Jewell and her lover, Amy, had to endure. The question asked is not about the moral dilemma of homosexuality, but rather, it centers on how a white woman could be intimately involved with a black woman. "Admittedly or not, blacks and whites are still curious creatures when coupled in public," Jewell writes (25). The curiosity concept that is described here is sometimes the premise for the intermingling of these two races. However, this same concept can create hostilities between the races because of the lack of knowledge about their cultures.

Throughout the work, Jewell passionately analyzes the stark contrasts in their backgrounds and beliefs. The thrust of her recollections about her experience with Amy is not a typical "coming-out" story, but a "coming together" of differences separated by age, class, and race. Thus, "contemplating the age differences between us, I shuddered at visions of my friends labeling me a 'crib-robber' " (25). Jewell was thirty years old, ten years Amy's senior, when they met. However, the age differences and the nuances that are typically ascribed to those ages were the least of their concerns.

The differences in their economic classes created some strife in their relationship. Jewell grew up in a lower middle-class all-black area in the 1950s, and Amy's environment was typically white middle-class in the 1960s. Inevitably, each woman had to incorporate within their love relationship the other's contrasted viewpoint of the world.

However, the poignant idea represented is Jewell's inability to function in this world as an individual. Unfortunately, mainstream society dictates to us how we should think and live our lives. Jewell describes how "her parents and the black community had taught her all there was to know about the white man's soul in order for her to survive" (25). The idea of "survival of the fittest" is perpetuated in our society as being the sole source of our existence. Stereotypically, the "white person" is viewed as the fittest in our society and that by which all others are measured. By extending this idea into our homophobic society, the "hetero" is represented as the ideal sexual being, and all others deviate from the norm. Jewell acknowledges that she is directly affected by both hierarchies. But because Amy is white, she is challenged only in regard to her sexuality.

The unsettling issue of Amy's ability to be accepted into mainstream society is a difficult one to accept. However, Jewell resists any insecurities about the matter. Despite the differences that these women must deal with in order to continue loving, they set aside their societal baggage realistically. They grow, they love, they shrink, they hate, they make the best of what their situation has to offer. They discover their humanistic qualities within themselves and about each other. Thus, they forge this "alliance of differences."

Again, Jewell connects us to her past in "A Short Account of My Behavior" (July 1990). The issues discussed are universal concerns that are applicable to anyone. Specifically, though, the "coming-out" to her mother is expounded throughout the article. Jewell provides accounts about how her mother critically views each stage of her life. The interaction between Jewell and her mother is clearly seen as hostile and uncaring. Her mother seems personally assaulted by Jewell's homosexuality. She asks, "Are you trying to kill me?" (52), as if being a lesbian is a crime. However, the underlying issue is the idea of expectations. Jewell's mother is disappointed with the road that her daughter has chosen to take.

According to her mother, this road would lead to inevitable destruction. Thus, "they [society] will KILL you just for being alive" (52). Because Jewell's mother grew up during a time when blacks were not given the full opportunity to participate in the society, she made sure Jewell would be able to have everything in life she did not receive. However, Jewell does not behave in a manner that is acceptable for society's standards. By combating the system, one limits one's opportunities in the norm of society. Thus, Jewell's mother feels disappointed about her decision. The idea that one can create one's own destiny is the first step toward self-determination. This idea has been nullified in the black community since the onset of slavery in this country.

"You're not some little white girl who can get away with this" (52), says Jewell's mother. The idea here is that because one is black, one must follow societal rules on all levels—including sexuality. The mother is not denouncing the issue of homosexuality per se, but she is emphasizing the notion that blacks are not on a par with whites. White women have the freedom to define who they are. On the other hand, blacks are seen as a group, not as individuals. Therefore, they lack the ability to step outside of this group and be their own persons. Unfortunately, this type of ignorance has perpetuated self-hatred within the minds of blacks, thus internalizing the "group mentality" concept as the way of life.

Because our society has created double standards for the livelihoods of blacks and whites, a black gay woman is doubly ostracized. The dilemma is projected even further when Jewell's mother accuses her of "going around hugging and kissing the ENEMY" (52). Jewell's mother struggles to understand why her daughter cannot recognize these truths. One is moved by the painstaking way in which Jewell's mother "chastises" her for being gay, as if she is doing so out of spite.

CRITICAL RECEPTION

Unfortunately, there are at present no concrete reviews of the works of Terri L. Jewell.

BIBLIOGRAPHY

Works by Terri L. Jewell

"An Alliance of Differences." *I Know You Know—Lesbian Views and News* (February 1985): 25.
"A Short Account of My Behavior." *Outlines: Voice of the Gay and Lesbian Community* (July 1990): 52.

Works-in-Progress by Terri L. Jewell

We Sistahs Touched by Fire: Creative Writings by Black Lesbians (poetry and fiction from 42 women).
DreadWoman/LockSister (personal essays and photography from black women).
Gumbo Ya-Ya: Voices of Black Women (quotations book).

MELANIE KAYE/KANTROWITZ
(1945–   )
Nuala Archer

BIOGRAPHY

Articulation and activism have been interwoven in Melanie Kaye/Kantrowitz's life since her earliest days. In 1950, when she was a five-year-old kid living in Brooklyn—in Flatbush, a swirling Jewish ghetto/community of first- and second-generation immigrants, including Holocaust survivors—she stood up in front of her classmates and defied the kindergarten teacher who described bomb drills as "only a game." From her mother, she had learned how "our government had dropped bombs on children and their eyes had melted and people were burned and killed" (unless otherwise indicated, quotations are from personal communication with the author). Summoned to school, Violet Wolfgang Kaye defended her daughter, proud of her role as class conscience and rebel. In telling of her childhood, Kaye/Kantrowitz recounts with delight and recognition her mother's political and intellectual backbone. "This was my Jewish upbringing," she states. "Jewish was the air I breathe . . . everything I took for granted."

With only a few photographs of her grandparents who came to the United States from Poland and Russia—and very little of their language—Kaye/Kantrowitz remembers fragments of her identity by seeing with fresh eyes that names shed by one generation, like ragged coats, can be pieced together and worn by the next generation—her generation—as coats of many colors.

In one phrase, "assumed comicality," Melanie Kaye/Kantrowitz reveals cracks of pain and betrayal in her mother's courage when she insisted that the name *Kantrowitz* be shortened to *Kaye* in 1942. In another understated sentence she compresses the historically anti-Semitic contradiction of enforced identification and enforced invisibility: "My father says everyone called him Mr. K. anyway, at the vacuum cleaner store, where he did sales and repair, for business, because Kantrowitz was too long, too hard to say."

Fleshing out the implications of her own abbreviated name and piecing it back together is central to Melanie Kaye/Kantrowitz's biography. Exposing the connection between these very personal abbreviations and the historical horrors of anti-Semitic mutilation and extermination is what enables her to painstakingly create an imagination fierce enough to begin inventing another tongue.

At sixteen Melanie Kaye/Kantrowitz marched in her first demonstration against nuclear testing. At seventeen she moved away from home and began her studies. The pressures, sudden changes, and her daily, isolated battle with bulimia, a disease she didn't have a name for then, brought her to the brink of suicide. That same year, 1963, she began working in the Harlem Education Project, her first experience in a non-Jewish environment, where she spent her time with a proud community transforming a garbage-filled lot into a park. Over the years she began to recognize how her upbringing had brought her to 133rd Street and Lenox and prepared her for this commitment. In a phone conversation she added, "The civil rights movement saved my life." At eighteen she became financially self-supporting and continued moving between her studies at City College and her work in Harlem. Then in 1966 she moved to Berkeley, married at twenty-three, and divorced at twenty-six years of age.

In 1972, living in Portland, Oregon, she came out as a lesbian. For the next seven years she threw herself into the anti-war and women's liberation movements in Portland. While teaching at Portland State University she actively participated in the first women's caucus in comparative literature, which resulted in the first Women's Studies Program in Portland. Having been fired from an assistant professorship with the University Scholars Program at Portland State University (PSU) because the director of the program said he "wanted someone to have that job with whom he felt comfortable having lunch," Melanie Kaye/Kantrowitz taught as a half-time instructor with the Women's Studies Program at PSU. Her courses included such titles as Feminist Theory and Practice, Woman as Creative Artist, and Violence against Women and the Movement to Stop It.

In 1975 she earned a Ph.D. from the University of California in comparative literature with a thesis entitled "The Sword Philippan: Woman as Hero in Stuart Tragedy" (the plays of Shakespeare, John Webster, Thomas Middleton, and John Ford). In 1978 she worked at a Rape Relief Hotline in downtown Portland, and by the time she left Oregon in 1979, she had begun to get in touch with her Jewish identity through avid reading rather than *schmoozing* at Jewish women's gatherings, a rejection she says that "closely paralleled my pre-feminist contempt for women's consciousness-raising groups" and is a "tribute to the mind's ability to resist information which threatens."

Over the next few years a circuitous trajectory brought Melanie Kaye/Kantrowitz to northern New Mexico, where she helped organize a women's coffeehouse and a demonstration against militarism at Los Alamos Science Museum. Her own writings and readings were by this time informed with "strong Jewish content," and by 1980 her first book of poetry, *We Speak in Code,* was published by Motheroot Publications. The more Melanie Kaye/Kantrowitz became conscious of her own Jewishness outside of a Jewish ambiance, the more painfully aware she became of the anti-Semitism and willful ignorance in the women's movement. She learned much from the political analysis being written within the Black, Chicana, and Native American communities, but none of these studies completely "fit" her or her culture.

Nice Jewish Girls: A Lesbian Anthology, edited by Evelyn Torton Beck, was published by Persephone Press in 1982 and contained a poem by Kaye/Kantrowitz entitled "Notes of an Immigrant Daughter: Atlanta." Between 1983 and 1987 Kaye/Kantrowitz was editor and publisher of *Sinister Wisdom. The Tribe of Dino: A Jewish Women's Anthology* originally appeared in numbers 29/30 of *Sinister Wisdom* in 1986 and was co-edited by Kaye/Kantrowitz and Irena Klepfisz. It subsequently was revised, expanded, and republished by Beacon Press. During these years as an editor, Kaye/Kantrowitz continued to teach at Vermont College, Norwich University. No sooner was she tenured there in 1990, the same year *My Jewish Face & Other Stories* was published as an Aunt Lute Foundation Book, than she took an unpaid two-year leave of absence and moved to New York City. In 1992 she left her academic position altogether and is presently piecing together her work as the executive director of Jews for Racial and Economic Justice in New York City and her work as a writer. She has found the space and quiet of Taos, New Mexico, a conducive place to finish her two most recent books, the first a book of essays entitled *The Issue is Power: Essays on Women, Jews, Violence and Resistance,* published in the fall of 1992; the second, a novel with a working title of *Eyes.*

MAJOR WORKS AND THEMES

Becoming conscious of the complex connections between her radical Jewishness—not so much a religious heritage as one of passionate political analysis and activism—and her identity as a lesbian, informs all of Melanie Kaye/Kantrowitz's writings. Many of her poems, stories, and essays confront and resist the violence of everyday life in the United States—in families and relationships, between women and women, women and men, mothers and daughters, wives and husbands.

The way she writes about these issues is as much a significant theme as the content itself. There is both an urgency and a clarity of voice in all her writings. Formalism and academic notions of appropriate structure are exploded. There is also a consciously chosen loudness, a rawness and pushiness of tone that defies a particular brand of American politeness and prettiness that would minimize the oppressions of privilege and the racism and anti-Semitism inherent in assimilation.

Melanie Kaye/Kantrowitz writes with the voice of an outlaw who has done the necessary heartwork to speak with conviction and wit about the connections between an individual's survival and the larger revolution. Personal recovery and political action are inextricably connected in her work.

The healing process is portrayed throughout Kaye/Kantrowitz's writings as a complex network of synergies that includes and connects the personal, social, political, and spiritual ambivalences that can become strategies of bold action in fighting for justice. Class shifts and the sometimes inevitable "fuzzy boundaries" between the self, the family, and the community are explored in relation to the foundational question of power and empowerment where visibility—as a radical Jewish lesbian feminist peace activist—is key.

Melanie Kaye/Kantrowitz divides her first book of poetry, *We Speak in Code* (1980), into five sections. The first untitled section includes three introductory poems. "Survival Is an Act of Resistance," "Colors," and "On Being a Lesbian Feminist Artist." The second section is entitled Jewish Food: the third, Living with Chaos: the fourth, Naming: the fifth, We Speak in Code. An integral part of this book is visual art by Paula King, Michele Goodman, and Lee Pickett.

In these poems there is a sense of much hope in hearing other women's voices, their welter of experiences, the interconnectedness, as a "circulatory system" of all women. Pushing through boundaries imposed by male "boredom, shock, and disgust," Kaye/Kantrowitz finds herself as an out-lesbian poet on ground where no one has stood before, helping to create a "climate of female outrageousness." In these poems, her body remembers such people as her grandmother Helen, from whom she didn't learn enough Yiddish to know what was locked in her "birdbones." "Jewish Food: A Process" is a moving poem that speaks to the self-violence of bulimia, a misinterpretation of hunger as a need for cupcakes instead of a hunger for shame's end, a hunger for a woman to use herself against "those who keep us bloated." This poem ends in a desire for choice, a hunger "for power to feed ourselves." Several of the poems are written in an incantatory voice for example, "Ritual: For the Portland Women's Night Watch." The final poem in *We Speak in Code* is a performance piece entitled "Ritual: We Fight Back." This poem names and honors those women from all over the United States who have resorted to violence against those men who have repeatedly beaten, raped, and threatened to kill them. Each biographical note is written in the first person and is followed by the refrain: "I AM A WOMAN. I FIGHT BACK."

In *The Tribe of Dina: A Jewish Women's Anthology*, the diversity of the secular Jewish feminist and lesbian voices from around the world dispels any early notion of what it is to be Jewish. Here these women claim the necessary power to define themselves and to express their experiences in writings that belong in the Jewish literary canon. The connections between feminism, peace activism, freedom for the Palestinians, and a just Israeli society are explicitly drawn. The best interests of Jewish life, both in America and abroad, are enlarged by examining anti-Semitic stereotypes that often have been internalized. These women's writings fight against the intimidation and invisibility that demand good victims. A deepened awareness of denials makes room for pride. Insisting on speaking out about their Jewishness and their lesbianism reveals both the incredible risk involved and the courage.

In her most recent book and first collection of fiction, *My Jewish Face &*

Other Stories, Melanie Kaye/Kantrowitz continues to expand on the themes of lesbian relationships, Jewish identity and family, political activism, and resistance against violence. All the stories, written from the point of view of female protagonists, have an autobiographical feel, so that the very genre of the short story seems to be shifting.

Like Monique Wittig, Kaye/Kantrowitz describes the everyday violence that women confront and labels it war. In her story "The Day We Didn't Declare War and the Day We Did," she begins, "We just weren't ready to kill and anything else seemed too dangerous. . . . If we weren't ready, who was?" "Vacation Pictures" and "The Woman in Purple" are stories that focus on individual women, their growth and relationships as they open themselves to risking change. The dialogue between these women—as between the women in "Towers," "The Printer," and "Burn"—is raw, demanding, honest, and painful. Impatience, wry humor, and a street-smart sensibility combine to make these stories important political fiction. Kindness, dignity, and trustworthiness form the foundations of Melanie Kaye/Kantrowitz's portrayal of women's lives both delicate and besieged.

CRITICAL RECEPTION

Melanie Kaye/Kantrowitz's reputation as a fine editor and writer is widespread in the United States, particularly in the feminist and lesbian literary communities. Although there has not yet been a comprehensive study of her writings, her essays are often quoted and referenced in other essays. Gloria Anzaldúa and Irena Klepfisz are only two of many contemporary writers who have publicly acknowledged their gratitude to Melanie Kaye/Kantrowitz's energetic exploration of themes of identity and coalition.

Both her non-fiction and fiction have been favorably reviewed in the *Religious Studies Review*, *Publishers Weekly*, *Daughters of Sarah*, *Judaica Book News*, *Lilith*, The *Washington Blade*, *Sojourner*, and the *Lambda Book Report*.

WORKS BY MELANIE KAYE/KANTROWITZ

We Speak in Code: Poems & Other Writings. Pittsburgh: Motheroot Publications, 1980.
"Brooklyn 1956: The Walls Are Full of Noise" and "Trojan" *Lesbian Poetry*. Ed. Elly Bulkin and Joan Larkin. Watertown, MA: Persephone, 1981. 149.
"Notes of an Immigrant Daughter: Atlanta." *Nice Jewish Girls: A Lesbian Anthology*. Ed. Evelyn Torton Beck. Watertown, MA: Persephone, 1982. 109–13.
"Jewish Food, Jewish Children." *The Tribe of Dina: A Jewish Women's Anthology*. *Sinister Wisdom* 29/30 (1986): 131–36.
"To Be a Radical Jew in the Late 20th Century." *The Tribe of Dina: A Jewish Women's Anthology*. *Sinister Wisdom* 29/30 (1986): 264–87.
"Mathematical Model." *Sinister Wisdom* 31 (Winter 1987): 47.
"War Stories, 197–:" *Sinister Wisdom* 33 (Fall 1987): 20–31.
"Elements." *Common Lives/Lesbian Lives* 25 (Winter 1988): 29–32.

"Kaddish" and "Nagasaki Day: Los Alamos." *Naming the Waves: Contemporary Lesbian Poetry*. Ed. Christian McEwen. Freedom, CA: Crossing Press. 1989. 87–93.

The Tribe of Dina: A Jewish Women's Anthology, co-edited with Irena Klepfisz. 1st ed. Montepelier, VT: Sinister Wisdom Books, 1986; 2nd expanded ed., Boston: Beacon Press, 1989.

"The Issue is Power: Some Notes on Jewish Women and Therapy." *Jewish Women in Therapy*. Ed. Rachel Siegel and Ellen Cole. New York: Harrington Park Press, 1990. 7–18.

My Jewish Face & Other Stories. San Francisco: Aunte Lute Books, 1990.

Action and Awareness: Handbook on Anti-Semitism. Ed. Linda Eber, Melanie Kaye/Kantrowitz, and Irena Klepfisz. New York: New Jewish Agenda, 1991.

"eyes." *An Intimate Wilderness: Lesbian Writers on Sexuality*. Ed. Judith Barrington. Portland, OR: Eight Mountain Press, 1991. 131–32.

The Issue Is Power: Essays on Women, Jews, Violence and Resistance. San Francisco: Aunt Lute Books, 1992.

WILLYCE KIM (1946–   )
Kitty Tsui

BIOGRAPHY

Willyce Kim was born on February 18, 1946, in Honolulu, Hawaii, a second-generation Korean American. In 1968, she graduated from San Francisco College for Women, Lone Mountain, with a B.A. in English literature.

When she was in the sixth grade, Kim kissed her first girl in the coat room after gym class. ''The church taught that homosexuals were living in a state of mortal sin. . . . There were a lot of butchy-looking women in Hawaii that are coaches of basketball teams, even boy's teams. Everyone loves them. I still don't know if these women were gay or not. They were all devout Catholics'' (Cade 33).

In the early 1970s, Kim joined the Women's Press Collective that published the works of such lesbian pioneers as Judy Grahn, Pat Parker, Sharon Isabel, and Kim herself. A supervisor at the graduate library of the University of California at Berkeley since 1983, Kim considers writing her serious work.

MAJOR WORKS AND THEMES

Kim is a poet whose writing began in the heady days at the birth of the women's liberation movement. Along with Judy Grahn and Pat Parker, she gave readings at women's bookstores, bars, and coffeehouses. She was the first Asian lesbian to be published in this country, and her second chapbook, *Eating Artichokes*, remains a lesbian classic. Among Asian lesbian writers in America today, only a handful remain in print, mostly in anthologies, a sad commentary on the reality of our contemporary literary landscape. As one of only two Asian lesbians with books currently in print, her voice is an important one.

Her two novels, *Dancer Dawkins and the California Kid* and *Dead Heat*, are both action-packed adventures peopled with a cast of Technicolor characters.

The good guys have names like Ta Jan the Korean, a.k.a. Penelope Francis Lee, Jessica Nahale Riggins, and Janes Philips Joyce. The bad guys are named Fatin Satin Aspen, a.k.a. Morris Minnow, Sweet Lou, Vinny "the Skull" LaRoca, Diamond Jimmy, and Fat Al. There are canine characters, Killer Shep, a talking (well, kind of), aging German shepherd who has arthritis, and Gypsy, an adorable Hungarian vizsla. The heroes of our Western adventure, Dancer Dawkins (so named by her parents) and the California Kid (originally known as Willie Guthrie), meet when the fast-moving Kid sideswipes Dancer's car and takes off a door. Fighting off an asthma attack, Dancer slugs the Kid. After this inauspicious beginning, they find a common love, food, and team up to rescue Dancer's girlfriend from the clutches of a cult. In the process they foil a fiendish plot to defoliate the Napa Valley wine country.

Kim writes about love, sex, fun, friendship, and food. She can make the reader's mouth water with descriptions of buckwheat pancakes, spaghetti squash stuffed with mushrooms, onions and green peppers, and smothered with tomato sauce laced with cheddar, sushi and even some deadly sashimi, and vanilla bean ice cream.

In the sequel, *Dead Heat*, our heroes are reunited when a broken-hearted Dancer visits her friends in San Francisco to seek solace in food and gambling. The Kid falls in lust with a bisexual gangster's moll, Cody Roberts, a woman jockey; leaves Omaha with her trusty dog and heads West for her first stakes race; and the heat is on! This time our heroes team up to foil a mobster's plot to throw a crucial race.

Kim makes good use of an innovative form, short vignettes, that move to a climax at roller-coaster pace. She writes in a spare episodic style and combines wit and deadpan humor with a thick plot, vibrant characters, and great visuals.

Her characters are women who are brazen, bold, and strong. Women who swear, smoke Camels, and carry a knife. Women who use their eyes to steer a path through a crowd or stop a mad dog in its tracks. Women who fight and fuck. Women who battle addictions and phobias and triumph to emerge into sunlight. Women who love themselves and each other. Her characters are everyday women—you and I—outrageous, believable, fallible.

The prevalent themes in her work are the value of friendship, the power of love, and the importance of the (lesbian) family. In Kim's writing, all three themes combine as her one signature theme, to live openly and joyously as a lesbian is the ultimate act of affirmation.

CRITICAL RECEPTION

Kim's work has garnered positive reviews from both gay and lesbian publications like the *Feminist Bookstore News* and mainstream trade publications like *Publishers Weekly*. Her characters have been described as fabulous, funny, and believable. But it is her unique style of writing that prompts the most attention.

The *Publishers Weekly*, for example, reports that Kim's "characteristic technique of breaking down the plot into brief scenes successfully conveys the sense that aimless events are converging into a mosaic of meaning, independent of the efforts of her anti-heroines—and perhaps far beyond their ken" (September 2, 1988, 98). Another reviewer writes, "I expected this experimental format to be disconcerting, but found myself so undistracted I barely noticed the divisions of the chapter headings" (Lynch 1988). And, according to *Feminist Bookstore News*, "*Dead Heat* . . . steals my heart . . . [Kim's] ability to capture a complexity of actions and emotions (never mind situation) and distill them into snapshots with a few, very carefully selected words would be enough, but she scatters them across pages, like a photo album, until suddenly the tension drives them into a fast-paced mental movie with a sound track of dry humor and a technicolor of dyke bravado" (Lynch, 1988).

BIBLIOGRAPHY

Works by Willyce Kim

Curtains of Light. Albany, CA: self-published, 1970.
Eating Artichokes. Oakland, CA: Women's Press Collective, 1972.
Under the Rolling Sky. Oakland, CA: Maud Gonne Press, 1976.
Dancer Dawkins and the California Kid. Boston, MA: Alyson Publications, 1985.
Dead Heat. Boston, MA: Alyson Publications, 1988.

Works in Anthologies

Lesbians Speak Out. Oakland, CA: Women's Press Collective, 1974.
Lesbian Poetry. Ed. Elly Bulkin and Joan Larkin. Watertown, MA: Persephone Press, 1981.
Intricate Passions. Ed. Tee Corrine. Austin, TX: Banned Books, 1989.
Women on Women: An Anthology of American Lesbian Fiction. Ed. Joan Nestle and Naomi Holoch. New York: Plume, 1990.
Bushfire. Ed. Karen Barber. Boston, MA: Alyson Publications, 1991.
Poetry of Sex. Ed. Tee Corinne. Austin, TX: Banned Books, 1992.

Journal Contributions

Women's Press 2, no. 2 (1972).
Everywoman 33 (May 1972).
Furies 2, no. 2 (March/April 1973).
Plexus 5, no. 1 (February 1978).
Sinister Wisdom 17 (Summer 1981): 52.
Conditions Ten 3 (1984): 67.
Ikon, 2nd ser., no. 3 (Spring/Summer 1984).
Phoenix Rising 18 (October/November 1987).

Studies of Willyce Kim

Cade, Cathy. "Shy Woman, Bold Poet." *A Lesbian Photo Album*. Oakland, CA: Waterwoman Books, 1987. 21.

Feminist Bookstore News 11, no. 3 (September 1988): 74.

Field, Jack. *Tulsa Week Magazine* (1986): 8.

"From the Small Presses." *Feminist Bookstore News* 7, no. 5 (January/February 1985): 32.

Katz, Judith. "Dancer Dawkins/Moll Cutpurse: Two Novels Explore Gender." *Equal Time* (July 24, 1985): 9.

Lynch, Lee. "Laughing Lesbians." *Women's Review of Books* 3, no. 5 (February 1986): 5.

Lynch, Lee. "Lesbian Love Tales." *San Francisco Sentinel* (November 1988).

Malloy, Alice. "Kudos for Kim." *Mama Bears News & Notes* 2 (April/May 1985): 1.

Monteaguda, Jesse. *Front Page* (September 24, 1985): 5.

Publishers Weekly (September 2, 1988): 98.

Washington Blade (October 4, 1985): 21.

IRENA KLEPFISZ (1941–   )
Michelle Kwintner

BIOGRAPHY

Irena Klepfisz was born in Warsaw, Poland, in 1941. Her father was killed in the Warsaw Ghetto uprising. Together with her mother, her only surviving relative, she moved to the United States in 1949. She was educated in the New York City public schools and the Workmen's Circle Yiddish schools. After attending City College of New York, she studied English literature at the University of Chicago, where she received a Ph.D. in 1970.

Klepfisz has taught English, creative writing, women's studies, and Yiddish. She is a political activist and has lectured, written, and led workshops on feminism, office work and class, homophobia, Jewish identity, Yiddish culture, anti-Semitism, and politics of the Middle East. She was the founder and editor of *Conditions*, a feminist and lesbian magazine.

Klepfisz is committed to making known to American Jews the works of female Jewish authors. Her translations of Kadia Molodowsky and Fradel Schtok represent a part of this contribution. Her new play, *Bread and Candy: Songs of the Holocaust*, was performed in New York City in 1990. Klepfisz is currently executive director of New Jewish Agenda, a progressive political organization.

MAJOR WORKS AND THEMES

Lesbian and Jewish Identity

The weaving, unweaving, and reweaving of several distinct—though by no means separable—threads of self is the stuff of Irena Klepfisz's poems and essays. Her primary identities are Jewish and lesbian. These two threads, as she asserts in one piece, constantly inform her thinking:

I write as much out of a Jewish consciousness as I do out of a lesbian/feminist consciousness. They are both always there . . . . They are embedded in my writing, totally
embedded and enmeshed to the point that they are not necessarily distinguishable as
discrete elements. (*Dreams of an Insomniac* 68–69)

Although Klepfisz describes these elements as inseparable, it is clear that a
certain tension, painful and at times fragmenting, exists between the two. The
homophobia she has encountered in the Jewish community and the anti-Semitism
she recognizes in the lesbian/feminist movement have made necessary certain
choices: a negotiation between self and community. She describes, for example,
the sorrow, anger, and sense of loss she suffered when, after coming out as a
lesbian, she found no place in the secular Yiddish world, the world of secular
Jewish labor organizers, that had taught her the politics of the oppressed. She
realized that "this legacy did not include gay people among the oppressed"
(*Dreams* 72).

Nevertheless, Klepfisz has bridged the gap between these two elements of her
identity. And in a talk given at an American Jewish symposium, she described
the parallelisms between the oppression of Jews and of gays.

Like Jews, gays live in every culture and class, reside in every country on this planet.
Like Jews, gays have at various times been identified as the pariahs of society. . . . And
though it is not popular to point this out, gays, like Jews and Gypsies, were victims of
Hitler's extermination camps. Like Jews, gays understand the perils of passing, its de-
structive nature, its capacity to undermine the core of an identity, to rob us of spirit.
(*Dreams* 75)

She therefore sees the need for coalition. And she mourns the loss of energy
that exclusion of particular groups causes. Furthermore, she discourages the
Jewish community from seeing itself as benevolently making space for gays and
lesbians. Gays and lesbians contribute to the Jewish community an energy that
is not to be trivialized, an energy that is vital. Klepfisz has been able to reaffirm
her pride in being a lesbian and a Jew without needing to submerge parts of
herself because of social intolerance.

Survival

Klepfisz's Jewish identity begins with her escape, during childhood, from the
Nazi genocide of the Jews during World War II. Her survival of *der khurbn*
(Yiddish for "the destruction") and the recognition that she could easily have
died with the rest of her family inform her relationship to existence. Her poem
"*Bashert*" begins with a dedication "to those who died" and "to those who
survived" no matter how. It continues with a long sequence about her childhood
reminiscences of surviving in Poland, her learning of the suicide of another child
survivor, and about "being equidistant from two continents." "*Bashert*" (Yiddish for "fate") is about grappling with the inevitable.

Concomitant with this inability to take existence for granted is a strong sense of loss: loss of family, loss of culture, death of the Yiddish language. But Klepfisz shuns—and in fact scorns—the commercial glamorization and romanticization of the Holocaust. For her, it is concrete and ordinary experience that is steeped in this past. The loss and emptiness is palpable day in and day out. In an early poem, "The Widow and Daughter," she writes that the presence of her dead father in the three-room apartment shared by her and her mother stared out of a picture "till the apartment seemed to burst with his eyes." At night, when the mother and daughter sat down to dinner in their kitchen, his absence was so palpable that "they could taste his ashes" (*A Few Words in the Mother Tongue* 38).

Her strong connection to Jewish history and to the past drives Klepfisz's perception of the future. This past fuels her commitment to the preservation—and the renewal—of the Yiddish world, of secular Jewish culture that was destroyed during World War II. Having grown up in America, in a world of survivors, in a world of *yidishkayt* that had been uprooted, Klepfisz had taken for granted the solidity and permanence of the *yidishe svive* (the Yiddish environment):

So for all the talk *vegn khurbn*, for all my awareness of an absent father, aunts, and grandmothers, when I sat down at Brukha and Monye's *dritn seyder*, third seder . . . and looked around me and saw our whole community; or when I looked at a newsstand and saw the big, bold letters of *Der forverts*—it was hard for me to conceive that an entire world had been destroyed. (*Dreams* 147)

With the recognition that this world of *yidishkayt* was indeed very fragile, that her sense of self was tied to its existence, Klepfisz decided to contribute to the renewal of Yiddish culture. Through her teaching of Yiddish, through her writings, through her translation of Yiddish women authors, Klepfisz has attempted to revive this rich heritage and, in particular, to create a context for Jewish feminist life through a connection to the past.

Bilingualism

Klepfisz's experimentation with bilingual English/Yiddish poetry, inspired by Gloria Anzaldúa's mixture of Spanish and English, is an example both of her effort to create a living Yiddish art that can reach a wide American audience and of her attempt to shape a voice that integrates the different strands of her identity. Since language and experience cannot be separated, for Klepfisz to write of Jewish life without Yiddish would be conceptually and aesthetically impoverishing. As she writes in her poem "Fradel Schtok," the words "*heym*" and "home" have the same meaning but the "shift in vowel was the ocean / in which I drowned" (*A Few Words in the Mother Tongue* 228).

Voice

In Klepfisz's essays, we find a similar attempt to fashion a voice that suits her identity. Her introduction of Yiddish vocabulary in some of her more recent prose is part of this effort. But also her essays formally reflect a particular way of thinking. Never linear or static, this style represents the dynamic process of working out, negotiating, and renegotiating. In the preface to *Dreams of an Insomniac*, her collection of essays, she writes:

I see value in retaining the knots we experience in articulating concepts and theories. . . . By retaining the difficult process by which we reach conclusions . . . we endow ideas with a three-dimensional reality which makes them accessible and operative in the world. (xiii)

But it is also sensitivity to material exigencies that has affected Klepfisz's prose style. She is aware that economic conditions sometimes make a non-linear style necessary for women and, in particular, for working women. As she says in her essay "The Distance between Us: Feminism, Consciousness and the Girls at the Office," for some women, the choice is between experimentation with prose or else silence. And there is this material awareness, this attention or sensitivity to class and to women's lives throughout Klepfisz's work. She has written several poems about women and office work. Among these is "A poem for Judy / beginning a new job," in which the speaker is pained by the loss of creative talent and sheer time that Judy's office job requires. For Klepfisz, style is separable neither from content nor from material constraints.

CRITICAL RECEPTION

Until the publication of *A Few Words in the Mother Tongue* and its companion volume, *Dreams of an Insomniac*, in 1990, Klepfisz received little critical attention. With the appearance of these new books, Klepfisz is beginning to become more widely known as a poet and essayist.

Klepfisz has been praised for her poetic experimentation. Marge Piercy writes that in "Work Sonnets," a sequence that alternates between poetry and prose, "Klepfisz has incorporated many devices normally of importance in fiction into a tight sequence of poems: the importance of viewpoint and the changes of perspective on the same events" (12). And Meryl Altman has said, in describing Klepfisz's poetic technique and creative goals, that "Klepfisz's forms are various, inventive; her objective is not to heal . . . but to reveal, to make the senseless suffering not 'meaningful'—not symbolic—but palpable on the page" (16).

Adrienne Rich, in the introduction to *A Few Words in the Mother Tongue*, discusses Klepfisz in the context of immigrant American literature and of contemporary women writers torn between two cultural traditions. She praises Klepfisz's experimentation with bilingualism and fashioning of a voice to express her difference. Klepfisz does not "drop Yiddish phrases in a cosy evocation of an idealized past.'' Rather, her bilingual poems ''painfully explore the world of a writer located not only between landscapes, but between languages'' (21–22).

Klepfisz's essays have received recent attention in book reviews. Ellen Stone lauds Klepfisz's ability to distill and articulate issues that stem from her involvement with lesbian/feminist politics and the Jewish community (''Darkness Is the Incubator'' 1991). Evelyn Torton Beck, in her introduction to *Dreams of an Insomniac*, asserts that ''the power of Irena Klepfisz's work lies in the force of its moral and artistic integrity'' (xvii).

BIBLIOGRAPHY

Works by Irena Klepfisz

Keeper of Accounts. Watertown, MA: Persephone Press, 1982.

Different Enclosures: The Poetry and Prose of Irena Klepfisz. London: Onlywomen Press, 1985.

The Tribe of Dina: A Jewish Women's Anthology. Edited with Melanie Kaye/Kantrowitz. Boston: Beacon Press, 1989.

Dreams of an Insomniac: Jewish Feminist Essays, Speeches, and Diatribes. Portland OR: Eighth Mountain Press, 1990.

A Few Words in the Mother Tongue: Poems Selected and New. Portland, OR: Eighth Mountain Press, 1990.

A Jewish Women's Call for Peace: A Handbook for Jewish Women on the Israeli/ Palestinian Conflict. Edited with Rita Fabel and and Donna Nevel. Ithaca, NY: Firebrand, 1990.

Bread and Candy: Songs of the Holocaust. Bridges 2:2 (Fall 1991): 13–43.

Studies of Irena Klepfisz

Altman, Meryl. Review of *A Few Words in the Mother Tongue. Women's Review of Books* 8:1 (October 1991): 16–17.

Piercy, Marge. Review of *Keeper of Accounts. American Book Review* 5 (September 1983): 12.

Stone, Ellen. ''Darkness Is the Incubator.'' *Bridges* 2:1 (Spring 1991): 122–28.

LOLA LAI JONG (1949–)
Judy Chen

BIOGRAPHY

Lola Lai Jong is a Chinese-American lesbian born of immigrant parents in Chicago, Illinois, where she has lived all her life. Her mother was Cantonese, raised in Shanghai. Her Toisanese father was originally from Chicago, but was also raised in Shanghai. He and his parents, who were both born in Nanaimo, British Columbia, went to live in China in 1927. Fearing communist reprisal, he returned to the United States in 1948; Lai Jong's mother and older sister joined him in 1949 ("Three Chinese Women" 193). Lai Jong is the younger of two daughters. Her mother converted to Christianity after nine years in the United States, and raised her children in the Chinese fundamentalist church. Her family lived in a boarding house, in a room behind a friend's restaurant, and then in an apartment behind her mother's restaurant. They moved into a two-flat apartment building purchased by Lai Jong's parents when she was twelve years old.

The author's chosen last name, Lai Jong, means "beautiful dignity" in the Cantonese dialect. She has overcome assimilation in two ways: she first came out as a lesbian sixteen years ago (after seeing Phyllis Schlafly on television), and later came out as a "Pacifica Asian Lesbian" (or PAL) four years later. She names herself a woman of color separatist who is a "recovering assimilated" person (unless otherwise indicated, all quotes are from personal communication with the author).

Lai Jong describes her class background as "confused," though it is typical of many Chinese Americans. "In China, my mother was a dentist; in America, she cooked chop suey." Her mother had had servants in Shanghai, but was forced to learn how to "cook rice" to feed her family in the United States and eventually cooked for the customers in her restaurant. Though her parents were middle-class/upper middle-class in China, neither of them finished high school. Lai Jong's mother had apprenticed and earned her dentistry license in China but could not practice in the United States because of exclusionary licensing regulations. As a child, Lai Jong was "always aware my mother was angry because she couldn't be a dentist here." According to Lai Jong, "People looked down on [my mother] because she cooked chop suey," even though her mother was the first Chinese woman in Chicago to open her own restaurant. Lai Jong's father had been a lab technician in Shanghai, yet he sold vegetables from a truck in Chicago. He attended electronics school and became an auto mechanic at age thirty-five. In addition to the changes resulting from immigration to the United States, the havoc wrought by the Sino-Japanese War and their Toisan heritage (which is often linked to working-class economic and social status in both China and the United States) adds to the mix of her family's class background.

A self-taught carpenter, Lai Jong has also worked as a battered women's advocate, a crisis-line staff member, a helper in her mother's restaurant, and a secretary. She has written two secretarial manuals. She is raising a teenaged son, the product of a six-year marriage that she entered at the age of twenty. Lai Jong attended the Illinois State Teacher's College for one year on full scholarship, "flunk[ing] out" the second semester. After working for six years and ending her marriage, she attended Truman City College for two years while continuing to work full-time. Lai Jong has participated in four creative writing classes, with instructors who have included Kitty Tsui and Canyon Sam.

A community activist since the 1970s, Lai Jong has led organizing efforts in the Asian and Pacific Islander lesbian and the women of color communities in the upper Midwest for the last twelve years. A staff member of the Womyn of Colors program at the Michigan Womyn's Music Festival since 1987, she strives to build community among Asian and Pacific Islander lesbians. She is best known to the Chicago women's community as a founder and performer with two lesbian of color performers groups (Cravolinajong, 1985–1988; InterLOC Productions, 1988–present), and as a frequent speaker and reader.

Lai Jong helped found the Chicago Asian Lesbians in Motion, the current PAL's Networking-Chicago, the Asian Pacific Lesbian Network, the Asian American Literary and Arts Society (Chicago), and a Chicago lesbians of color writers group.

Though she decided to become a writer at age nine, Lai Jong didn't begin this career until her early thirties, when she started identifying as both Asian and lesbian. In her search for "a reflection of what it means to be a Chinese Lesbian in the isolation of the Midwest . . . [she] started 'writing [her]self into visibility' " (autobiographical statement, 1987). Her mother, who died in 1992, is her primary role model and a frequently appearing character in Lai Jong's work. Despite the pressures of time, a low income, single mothering, and a certain amount of isolation as a Chinese lesbian writer and organizer, she affirms, "I will always write."

MAJOR WORKS AND THEMES

Lai Jong's goal in creative writing is twofold. First, she strives to "interface [her] studies of Chinese folktales, myths and customs with adventures of Lesbians

in Old China and of Chinese Lesbians in Amerika'' (ibid). Second, she hopes
that sharing her stories will help break isolation among other Asian and Pacific
Islander lesbians and, indeed, for herself. The author tells how an elementary
school principal suggested that Lai Jong's sister's tongue be surgically shortened,
in order to remove the girl's accent. Breaking silence, as a working-class, second-
generation Asian-American lesbian, moves Lai Jong to write her primarily autobiographical poems and stories.

The process of writing remains "excruciating." She must "shut off the voice
that says, 'How dare you,' '' and ignore middle-class American lesbian feminist
speech that "uses fancy or big words that I don't understand."

Distinctive themes and strategies developed in her work include the author's
attempts to reflect her Chinese lesbian identity, an exploration of Cantonese
language rhythms and voice in English, and a revisionism of Chinese cultural
values and mythology to include woman-positive, lesbian-identified, clearly Chinese ethics and tales. In the second half of *Sudden Clarity* (1988), a self-published
collection of poems and stories, Lai Jong also begins to balance non-linear,
multiple story lines. This is a means of bringing the "old" into the "new" to
create self. These themes and techniques characterize many first- and second-
generation Chinese-American woman authors; however, most of them exclude
lesbian characters from their writings.

Lai Jong's early work seems an attempt to create a mirror into which she can
gaze and say, "That's who I am." These first articles, poems, and stories
acknowledge her experience of and resistance to multiple oppressions. "Three
Chinese Women" (1981; published 1988) defines lesbian separatism in a context
of a legacy of resistance by her female relations. Lai Jong asserts that her
separatism ("a focus, rather than an exclusion") and identity cannot be torn
from the "life-loving ways of my foremothers" (188), even when, as in the
practice of footbinding, "women [are] forced to become token torturers of their
daughters" by patriarchy (189). This is a personal yet scholarly account of
marriage, divorce, unraveling of footbandages, and other acts of oppression of
and subterfuge by her maternal grandmother, mother, and the author herself.

In "Re-Membering" (1981), she recalls secretly destroying a white doll given
by a patronizing teacher, in an act of silent rebellion against assimilation. She
is "the spirit who survives" ("Chrysanthemum" 1987), who is then ready to
construct a new self to go along with her political and sexual liberation. Much
of *Sudden Clarity* explores the sexual, ethical, and ethnic aspects of this new
self.

As a pioneer Asian-American lesbian writer in the Midwest, Lai Jong lives
outside the vibrant West and East Coast Asian and Pacific Islander lesbian
communities that came of age during the last decade. She has used her work,
therefore, to make a community of women for herself on paper: "Out of my
isolation, I create Asian lesbians in my writing," she explains. *Sudden Clarity*
was published "because I felt so alone, ... [and] if even one Asian lesbian out
there read it, ... she would know she wasn't the only one who felt that way."

This focus has changed as the local and national visibility of Asian and Pacific Islander lesbian communities and writers has grown. The result is the presence in her later pieces of more than just one Asian lesbian character.

"Motherbonding" is the midpoint of *Sudden Clarity*, and this poem marks the shift from a search for affirmation in the previous chapter to an assumption of a Chinese lesbian context. With this poem Lai Jong begins a discussion of her family background, solely in terms of the feminine. Stories retold by Lai Jong, found as well in "Eighty-Six" (33) and "Breaking Patterns" (35), describe the resistance to patriarchy and later, racism, passed on mother to daughter. Some of these stories trace back to her great-grandmother. From protecting a daughter from footbinding to secretly caring for oneself as a woman, the author names these as acts of love and finds lesbian identity a natural place in her family's legacy.

In the second half of the book, Lai Jong also begins to use Cantonese in full sentences, rather than just words. In "20 April 86" (37) ("I dreamt in Chinese . . . "), she speaks partly without translation into English. The author's first language was Cantonese, and she is currently relearning the language by listening to family conversations and watching Chinese movies on videotape, identifying speaking styles and patterns. For example, in the short story "Beautiful Dignity" (1990), the narrator uses the term "doubly happy" (3), referring to the the phrase "double happiness," whose written image suggests marriage. "Don't Correct My Grammar" (1990) and "Jung Gwok Yun" (1990) reclaim not only Cantonese words, but also the use of its grammatical structure when speaking English.

The richness resulting from her use of two language resources does not come without cost. Besides the pain of being forced to speak English as a schoolchild, and the work of relearning her first language, some of the author's expression escapes her. "I think in Chinese, translate to English. Often there is no translation of feeling. . . . Because America stole Chinese from me at an early age, I often register a blank," she says.

Lai Jong incorporates Chinese mythology in much of her writing. Rather than relying on the popular or translated version of a story, which may have male, Eurocentric, and heterosexist assumptions and center on the aristocracy, she researches several versions from different eras of the same tale. In this way, she acquires "a rhythm, a focus, a thought" and is able to recreate what Lai Jong believes to be the original woman- and lesbian-positive story. For example, in "Loving Revenge" (1990), the narrator's gradual reaching out, in recovery from sexual abuse, to a lover is compared to the slow but inevitable joining of the Weaving Maiden and Cowherder folktale constellations.

In "Beautiful Dignity," Lai Jong writes a new myth. Two young women discover their love for each other as "seung gee," or lesbians ("two stems growing from the same branch"), and find a place for themselves in their family and culture. The mother of the narrator not only accepts her daughter's sexuality, but encourages her to pursue Sui Gwong. With the two mothers' aid, Sui Gwong escapes an upcoming marriage and the lovers hit the road for freedom. Though they come from upper-class families, they flee to become workers in the silk factory sisterhood societies of Guangdong province. These were women worker societies with a public reputation as havens for marriage resisters and lesbians, as recorded by Han Suyin in the 1950s (*My House Has Two Doors*, Triad Grafton, 1980, 120–21). Lai Jong mixes traditional secrets, such as how wrapping a bride's groin with knotted cloths can be used to prevent marital consummation, with the newer secrets and hopes of lesbian sexuality and a mother's support for it.

CRITICAL RECEPTION

What little critical reception Lai Jong's work has received has focused on her life as an activist and performer as well as her career as a writer. Most commentators have been journalists with lesbian and gay newspapers of the Midwest. Neither her writing nor her performance work has received critical attention (other than the occasional paragraph) from lesbian, women's, or Asian-American literary publications. While the existing commentaries are positive, seldom do they go beyond praising her personal courage for breaking stereotypes, to actually analyzing themes and techniques or judging the quality of her writings.

There are several reasons for this situation. First, Lai Jong has published only a small body of work (though she has given thirty-two public performances and talks since 1982), and her self-published chapbook has no promotional agent or publishing house. Second, individual and institutional racism in the women's community, and undoubtedly sexism and homophobia in the Asian-American community, limit access to her writing. For example, one women's bookstore buyer initially rejected *Sudden Clarity* because "it opens the wrong way" (personal experience of contributor, September 1989) (that is, the pages run right to left, as Chinese books do). Third, her style and strategies may be unfamiliar or difficult to understand for the white or non-immigrant reader.

And finally, there is a paucity of written forums within lesbian of color communities, especially Asian and Pacific Islander lesbian communities, that foster dialogue and provide critical opportunities among writers. These forums, which white lesbian authors have, include journals, newspapers, anthologies, and bookstore readings. The increased presence during the last decade of lesbians of color editors and authors within the mainstream of lesbian literature has been necessary and valuable. This is different, however, from having internal dialogue among Asian and Pacific Islander lesbians who write, or among lesbian authors across communities of color. The most recent flourishing can be dated to the publication of *Making Face, Making Soul/Haciendo Caras* (Aunt Lute Foundation Books, 1990) and to *Piece of My Heart* (Sistervision, 1991), as well as the longer history of special journal issues and other support from lesbian institutions, but we still need to create more of these forums.

Lai Jong occupies a distinct place in many worlds of autobiographical writing. For the white lesbian or non-immigrant lesbian reader, her work may seem simplistic, overly symbolic, or emotional. In contrast, the Chinese reader open to lesbian culture may see Lai Jong's work as truth-telling, reflecting myth through the modern day, and openly expressing anger, pain, bitterness, or love. European-based writers are pressured to avoid such approaches, and Lai Jong's style of direct communication, like that of Chrystos, is a much-needed voice in lesbian literature.

Among women of color writers, including those lesbian and lesbian-positive, Lai Jong joins a growing community of women who focus on family relationships among women and who are passing on the legacies of their ancestresses.

Among lesbian separatist writers, Lai Jong's focus is indeed rare. Like some other Jewish separatist and lesbian of color separatist writers, she does not limit her discussion to the individual self, other lesbians of the same generation, or the present/future: memory and female family form the base of the separatism that Lai Jong is creating.

Among Asian-American women writers, especially those who are Chinese, she shares the goal and practice of an autobiographical retelling, revisioning, and reclaiming of Asian and Asian-American life from the male, colonial, and upper-class versions. These women aim no more rage, however subtly shown, on imperialism in their homeland or racism in North America than they do on misogyny by their Asian fathers, brothers, and sons. Most male Asian-American writers avoid this issue, to their own loss. Though Lai Jong (and others, including Suniti Namjoshi) uses mythological and matrilineal themes more than most other Asian and Pacific Islander lesbian writers such as Chea Villanueva, Kitty Tsui, and C. Allyson Lee, she is among the least "nice" in the spectrum of modern Asian-American women writers. Perhaps Lai Jong is one of the bridges between the generation of more reflective writers (including Amy Tan and Cathy Song) and the emerging in-your-face cutting edge (for example, Jessica Hagedorn). (Thanks to Julia Watson in her review of *This Bridge Called My Back* for pointing out this distinction [*The Forbidden Stitch*, ed. Shirley Geok-Lim et al., 1989, 254].) Like Gloria Anzaldúa and Kit Yuen Quan, Lai Jong explores language living on the "borderlands" of working-class, immigrant culture, lesbian worlds.

The larger importance of Lai Jong's work lies in the questions it raises: What is the role of writing in creating community, where there is little or none? How can traditional Chinese literature and common culture be transformed to affirm a lesbian identity that is unmistakably Chinese? (And do we believe there is only one authentic Chinese myth or voice, anyway?) How can writing create a flexible reality, spanning time and distance, that brings together many selves—daughter of immigrants, mixed-class Chinese American, lesbian reaching past white assimilation, child who almost lost her native tongue? Lai Jong brings a vibrant, separatist, story-filled voice to the new movements of Asian and Pacific Islander North American lesbian, and women, writers.

BIBLIOGRAPHY

Works by Lola Lai Jong

"When the Lesbians Came." *Common Lives/Lesbian Lives* (Winter 1983): 81–83.
"Chrysanthemum." *Naming the Daytime Moon.* Ed. Julia Parsons et al. Chicago: Feminist Writers Guild, 1987. 124–25.
"Three Chinese Women." *For Lesbians Only: A Separatist Anthology.* Ed. Sarah Hoagland and Julia Penelope. London: Onlywomen Press, 1988. 187–96.
Sudden Clarity. N.p.: Jong Publications, 1988.
"Chrysanthemum." *Asian Lesbians of the East Coast News* (April 1989): n. pag.
"I Dreamt in Chinese." *Outlines* 3.9 (Feb. 1990): 39.
"Faith." *Literary Express* (Summer 1991): 3.
"Beautiful Dignity" (audiotape). Forthcoming, 1994.

JACQUELINE LAPIDUS (1941–   )

June V. Rook

BIOGRAPHY

Jacqueline Lapidus was born in New York City on September 6, 1941. Both of her parents were lawyers, and she grew up in an environment where education and achievement were high priorities. Referring to herself as a "lifelong word-smith," Lapidus says she cannot remember a time when she was not involved in writing; she was on the editorial staffs of both her high school and college literary magazines. Jacqueline Lapidus graduated from Swarthmore College in 1962 with high honors in history, was elected to Phi Beta Kappa, and received a prize for poetry.

In the spring of 1964, longing for adventure, Lapidus left for a six-month trip to Europe, intending to return in the fall to use a scholarship to the Columbia University School of Journalism. This journey turned into twenty-one years of living abroad, first in Greece, then in Paris. While living in Greece, on the island of Crete, Lapidus taught English and wrote most of the poems that make up her first volume, *Ready to Survive* (1975). During this period, Lapidus married Aris Fakinos, a Greek novelist and journalist. When a group of army colonels staged a coup d'état in 1967, Lapidus's husband was in danger of imprisonment for his opposition to the regime, and they fled to Paris along with other artists, writers, and intellectuals. Settling in Paris, Lapidus worked on helping to produce exile publications for the Greek resistance movement, translated two of Fakinos's novels from Modern Greek into English, and earned a living as a teacher, translator, literary agent's assistant and magazine editor, including a stint at the French *Reader's Digest*.

After she and her husband parted in 1973, Lapidus became active in the newly emerging women's movement. She worked at organizing English-speaking fem-inist groups and was instrumental in the development and promotion of feminist networks and campaigns, including the French preparatory committee for the

International Tribunal on Crimes against Women, which was held in Brussels in March of 1976. Lapidus also helped to found a women writers' workshop, for which she organized the submission of poems to American feminist publications. Much of the poetry in Lapidus's second volume, *Starting Over* (1977), comes out of this period.

Also during this time, Lapidus had become friendly with a number of Brazilian expatriates, including several feminist organizers. While studying the culture and language, she fell in love with her Portuguese teacher, a Brazilian woman. During their seven-year relationship, she made four extended trips to Brazil, as well as trips to Portugal and Greece, including a disappointing but poetically fruitful voyage to Lesbos. These travels inspired many of the poems in *Ultimate Conspiracy*, Lapidus's third volume, published in 1987.

In 1985, Jacqueline Lapidus returned to live in the States and settled on Cape Cod, where she was drawn to the landscape and the active women's and gay communities.

In the last few years, Jacqueline Lapidus's life has taken another interesting turn. Through the influence of a lesbian Episcopal priest, Lapidus began to read extensively in theology. In the spring of 1992, Lapidus earned a master's degree in theology from Harvard Divinity School and is interested in exploring the various relationships between feminist, liberation, Jewish, and Christian theologies. In an essay written for application to divinity school, Jacqueline Lapidus stated that she views her involvement in both writing and feminist activism "as a vocation, not consciously chosen but, rather, work to which I was called."

MAJOR WORKS AND THEMES

One of the major influences on Jacqueline Lapidus's poetry has been the experience of living abroad for more than twenty years. The climate, history, and physical landscape of Greece had a powerful effect on Lapidus, who was used to a fast-paced, urban environment. In an article by Patricia A. Roth in *Bay Windows*, Lapidus describes the effect Greece had on her: "I discovered something transcendental out there. . . . The vastness was what moved me. The minimalist landscape, the very dark sea, the mythical resonances, as well as the simple life." These elements are reflected in many of the poems in her first volume, *Ready to Survive*.

A growing involvement in politics, notably, working with the opposition to the forces that staged the 1967 coup d'état, also informs many of the poems in *Ready to Survive*. In "Letter to a Son in Exile," she adopts her mother-in-law's voice to describe the ill effects of the regime on the area around Athens. In "A Map of Greece," the narrator laments the fact that "Someone else will cross the green borders, / travel the red-veined roads . . . / while we stare at Greece through a barred window."

In "Rereading Earlier Poems," the poet nostalgically contrasts the closeness to nature and the warmth of the people in Greece with the claustrophobic dinginess of city life in Paris. A long poem called "Titus' Skull," about the return from Venice to Crete of a relic purported to be the skull of Titus, bishop of Crete at the time of Paul, reveals, with ironic wit, the centuries-long hypocrisies and power struggles of the political and religious forces surrounding the island.

A second major influence on Lapidus's work has been her involvement in the feminist movement and her emotional and sexual identification with women. Many of the poems in her second volume, *Starting Over*, are about the painful struggles and awarenesses that came out of this period. Some poems in *Starting Over* deal with the inevitable anger, disappointments, and losses that accompany radical change and growth. In "Letter to a Lost Sister," the poet addresses a former fiery radical feminist who dropped out and disappeared and was rumored to have "become a hausfrau / in California, cooking meals / and changing diapers. . . . / and the rest of us are hacking / through the jungle without maps."

Other poems in *Starting Over* concern troubling subjects; "My Aunt in a Mental Hospital" describes the aunt as "a bundle of old clothes / without a name her family / keeps her, frightening as a secret." Many of Lapidus's poems reveal a strong sense of humor, such as "Nursery Rhymes My Mother Never Taught Me" and "Avertissement," which cleverly plays on words in two languages.

Throughout Lapidus's poetry, there is an emphasis on the physical and a profusion of images of the body and its parts. Perhaps one result of the separation from the poet's home territory is a heightened awareness of her physical presence as the one familiar constant. It is, in a sense, the one territory where we all always live, and it is through the body—both psyche and soma—that Lapidus reaches out to make connections, to validate and concretize experience, and ultimately to seek the spiritual through emotional and sexual relationship. This is very much a part of the work in *Ultimate Conspiracy*, Lapidus's third volume of poems, especially the last two sections, "Voyage to Lesbos" and "City without Walls."

In *Ultimate Conspiracy*, Jacqueline Lapidus's poetry reaches full fruition both in vision and in voice. Many of the poems are longer, and the voice seems to increase in strength and sureness. The lesbian-feminist sensibility becomes more naturally incorporated as an integral element in the poet's vision, allowing for a gynocentric interpretation of the Greek myths of Orpheus and Eurydice in "Eurydice." There is also a poem about Odysseus's return as seen through the eyes of Penelope, who has had "peace these twenty years" and who found "laughter in the gay company of women." The poem ends with Penelope's resolve not to grovel to her husband.

The opening poem in *Ultimate Conspiracy*, "Matrilineage," is a genealogy that names and documents the lives of the poet's female relatives. It is written in a quasi-biblical style:

I am Jacqueline
daughter of Judith

daughter of Helen
daughter of Erszébet
... I am writing for ...
... all the women whose names were never written
and all the women now alive who claim the power of naming.

This poem is an example of the importance of validation and substantiation of women's experience that is very much a part of Lapidus's poetry, and "the power of naming" is one means by which this is accomplished.

In "Voyage to Lesbos," a series of poems about a lesbian couple's trip to the Greek island of Lesbos, the speaker searches in vain for traces of love between women there. Each poem bears the name of an island or town on the journey: "Athens," "Piraeus," "Mytilene," "Eressos," and so forth, and in the poem "Athens," the names of Sappho's lovers are listed, not only to document and validate, but perhaps to counteract the "whitewash" about Sappho's "affectional preference." The lovers take "revenge" by locking their door "at the YWCA / and fuse, faces flushed, / palms damp, tongues tasting the names of Sappho's lovers."

In Section 4, "City without Walls," a seven-part sequence of poems called "Paraibana" relates the journey of two women lovers to Cabo Branco in the northeast of Brazil, and their subsequent involvement with a neighbor and *her* lover. The romantic specter of Maria Bonita, legendary armed leader of a peasant revolt, hangs over the adventure (along with a full moon), inspiring some daring actions and illicit passions to erupt among the four women. When morning comes, jealousies and regrets intrude, ending the euphoria of a freedom to love beyond the conventions to which even most lesbians adhere. Yet there was, at least momentarily, in this freedom, a spiritual component that is triumphant in "Design for the City of Women," the closing poem in *Ultimate Conspiracy.* "Design for the City of Women" is a utopian vision of a society in which women can live in harmony with nature, by the sea, comfortable with their bodies, sharing energy and ritual in an unself-conscious eroticism. In this all-female society, everything revolves around the body, and the body and its secretions take on a mystical power. Here the spiritual and the physical become one. This is a revolutionary vision, at once erotic and spiritual. The text of "Design for the City of Women" also appears as the text of *Yantras of Womanlove*, an artistic rendering of photographs by Tee Corinne.

Jacqueline Lapidus has written a fourth volume called *Promisetown*, as yet unpublished although many of the poems have appeared in magazines and anthologies. The poems in *Promisetown* are masterfully crafted, many with a definite end rhyme. The title work is a sonnet sequence about a passionate and clandestine love affair. The long narrative lines flow expansively to form what Lapidus has called a "distended sonnet." They incorporate the naturalness of speech while the line endings break to maintain the rhyme, sometimes even in the middle of a word. These poems are very sensual, erotic, with richly textured language that conveys the savory essence of Provincetown, a haven for gays and artists, in all its aspects.

Promisetown again proves that Jacqueline Lapidus is a poet with a unique voice who has not stopped expanding the boundaries of consciousness.

CRITICAL RECEPTION

Jacqueline Lapidus's poetry has been favorably reviewed in various women's literary reviews and small-press publications.

Marge Piercy called Jacqueline Lapidus's poetry ''strong, intelligent and often quite witty, a poetry of a woman becoming always more conscious of herself, her mind, her life, her body, her politics'' (back cover, *Ready to Survive*). Piercy called *Starting Over* ''a coherent whole, full of fine individual poems that fit into each other in an architectural whole'' and stated that the poems ''range from anger to humor to lyrical, ecstatic love poetry'' (back cover).

In reviewing *Ultimate Conspiracy* for the *Women's Review of Books*, Marilyn Hacker says: ''Complex, savory, specific, these poems render the interpenetration of quotidian and extraordinary on three continents, and create their own world, generous, unpredictable, matrifocal, polyglot, resonant with secrets and silences as the author recounts its infinite variety.'' Hacker writes that Lapidus's ''Paraiba'' sequence reminds her of Elizabeth Bishop's poems set in Ouro Preto and says they are both ''poets of *saudade*, which means at once nostalgia, homesickness, sadness and not-entirely-unpleasurable longing.'' Hacker notes that *Ultimate Conspiracy* is a ''descendant of the bold North American lesbian writing of the 1970s, when Grahn, Griffin, Lorde and Rich, among others, first stated that naming a lesbian choice was a political act'' (24).

In a review of *Ultimate Conspiracy* for *Bay Windows*, a Massachusetts paper, Patricia A. Roth remarks ''the constantly compelling sense, expressed in imagery lush and sensual as the places it springs from, of narrative movement, bringing both poet and reader continuously to destinations not easily attained.'' Roth also states that ''the sequences 'Voyage to Lesbos' and 'City without Walls' are the work of the seasoned and serious practitioner of the art: the poet in whom mastery of craft has fused with specific, hard-won vision to create work that matters and will endure.''

BIBLIOGRAPHY

Works by Jacqueline Lapidus

Poetry

Ready to Survive. Brooklyn, NY: Hanging Loose Books, 1975.
Starting Over. Brooklyn, NY: Out & Out Books, 1977.
Yantras of Womanlove. Tallahassee, FL: Naiad Press, 1982. Long poem sequence in collection of photos by Tee Corinne.

Ultimate Conspiracy. Provincetown, MA: Lynx Publications, 1987.
Promisetown, 1988 (unpublished).

Prose

The Marked Men (translation), novel by Aris Fakinos. New York: Liveright, 1971.
Literary and film critiques, news reports, events listings, editorials in *POW*. Paris, France:
     English-speaking Feminist Group, 1975–76.
"Collective Work and Individual Creativity: The Experience of a Women Writers' Work-
     shop." *Penelope* 3 (1980), Paris, France: Feminist Studies Group, University of
     Paris—VII & Center for Historical Research, School for Advanced Studies in the
     Social Sciences, 1980. In French.
"Freehand: An Apprenticeship by the Sea." *Provincetown Arts* (Fall 1986).
"International Feminism in Action: The Case of the Three Marias." *Conditions* 14 (1987):
     137–57.
"To Love Is to God" Review of Carter Heyward's *Touching Our Strength* and *Speaking
     of Christ*. *Women's Review of Books* 7:9 (June 1990): 17.

Unpublished Manuscripts

The Restricted Zone (translation), novel by Aris Fakinos, 1972.
Discours & essais d'Emma Goldman. Translation of *Red Emma Speaks*, with Nathalie
     Stern, 1975. In French.

Studies of Jacqueline Lapidus

Hacker, Marilyn. "A Pocketful of Poets." *Women's Review of Books* (July 1988): 24.
Roth, Patricia A. "Looking for Lesbos." *Bay Windows* (February 11, 1988): 1, 17–18.

JOAN LARKIN (1939–   )
Cynthia Werthamer

BIOGRAPHY

Joan Larkin was born April 16, 1939, in Boston. She attended Swarthmore College and received her M.A. from the University of Arizona. She began writing in high school, and says, "I always knew I was going to be a writer." (Unless otherwise noted, quotations are from personal communication with the author.) She married a painter, Robert Ross, in 1961; they moved to Tucson, where she held a teaching assistantship at the University of Arizona. When the marriage dissolved in 1964, Larkin moved to New York City. Within two years of her father's death in December 1964, she was married again, to Jim Larkin, fifteen years her senior and gave birth to her daughter, Kate, in 1967. "In between the two marriages I had the briefest of lesbian affairs; it scared me to death," she admits.

In 1969, her second marriage over, Larkin secured a job teaching writing at Brooklyn College and sought out other women writers, because "I was always interested in women poets." By the early 1970s, she had established her lesbian identity, although she "had come out many times" before then. With Jan Clausen and Irena Klepfisz, she formed a lesbian writers' group, Seven Women Poets. During the heyday of lesbian feminist publishing, Larkin co-founded Out & Out Books, a women's independent publishing company, in 1975. In the same year, Out & Out Books published Larkin's first collection, *Housework*. (Out & Out Books became inactive in 1981.) With Elly Bulkin, Larkin co-edited *Amazon Poetry* (Out & Out Books, 1975) and *Lesbian Poetry* (Persephone Press, 1981) before her second book, *A Long Sound*, was published by Granite Press in 1986. The anthology *Gay and Lesbian Poetry in Our Time*, which Larkin co-edited with Carl Morse (St. Martin's Press, 1988), won the 1989 Lambda Literary Award for poetry. Since then her poems have appeared in *Outweek* and the

Brooklyn Review, and her poetry appeared in a collection of lesbian erotic poems edited by Tee Corinne (Banned Books, 1992). Her poems also have appeared in a number of anthologies.

In "Poetry and Recovery," an interview with Bulkin after the publication of *A Long Sound*, Larkin explains why ten years had elapsed between her first and second collections of poetry: her alcoholism and recovery from the disease. "I didn't know that recovery is a gradual process," she says. "In time I had more energy, and things started to come into focus" (84). Her recovery, which began in 1980, has been a major focus of her poetry of the past decade, along with examinations of women's lives and families.

Larkin's relationship with her daughter Kate, to whom *A Long Sound* is dedicated, is one Larkin also considers crucial to her poetic development. "I raised her completely by myself; that's one of the life accomplishments I'm proudest of," she says.

Larkin now lives in western Massachusetts. She continues to teach in the English Department of Brooklyn College.

MAJOR WORKS AND THEMES

In both her collections of poetry and her anthologized work, Joan Larkin has occupied herself with unflinching, direct observations of women's lives and the entanglements of family bonds, in reality and in memory. Her first book, *Housework*, is illustrated with prints of watercolor paintings, by Mimi Weisbord, of doll houses, some precariously balanced—an indication of the childhood life that is shattered by, and juxtaposed with, adult reality. The prologue poem of the collection, "Rhyme of My Inheritance," uses stark images and heavy rhythms to tear "the pages of my past" (7).

The poet speaks often in the voice of a woman on her own, especially in the first two sections ("Housework" and "Needs"), in poems such as "Breaking Bread Alone," "Your Absence," and "Self-Pity." The third section, "Stop," speaks of brushes with and against other women, of exploring their bodies and thoughts, and of the pain of intimacy, whether with women or men. The fourth of the volume's five sections, entitled "True Stories," deals with family and, paradoxically, includes seven poems based on fairy-tale imagery. But the fairy tales are frightening and flawed ("The seven-league boots had a leak" 61); the painting that fronts the section is entitled "Doll House with Icebergs." The final section, intense and defiant, is aptly titled "A Certain Notion of Strength." The poet takes a newly formulated feminism and hurls poems infused with that feminism as if they were snowballs containing ice chunks. (A good example is "'Vagina' Sonnet," a poetic snowball hitting its witty target.) The section's title is a line repeated throughout the book's closing poem, "Notations—The F Train," which juxtaposes a late-night subway scene with soothing stanzas of water, nature, and women's connections to nature, the place from which female energy flows and is nurtured.

The voices in *A Long Sound* are clamorous. They represent many voices besides the poet's own: the voices of recovering alcoholics. Larkin says that in order for her to heal, she had to listen to the voices of those in the "community"—the recovering as well as the gay community. In "Poetry and Recovery," she states that these voices are at the "center" of the book, and that the collection's emphases are "themes of recovery, of letting go and of the persistence of the life force" (86).

Larkin acknowledges that the poems in the second book are more personal, stronger and clearer than those in the earlier collection, working several of the same themes with more concrete craft. Where the poems of *Housework* seem, at times, to be intentionally distanced from the reader, those of *A Long Sound* are so direct as to be almost brutal: the voice of a woman wondering whether she has drunkenly allowed a man to have intercourse with her ("Rape"); of a woman telling the stark story of her alcoholic past ("A Qualification: Pat H."); of a woman trying to reach some sense of existence, and of the physical world, through sobriety ("In Western Massachusetts, Sixteen Months Sober"). The narratives are vibrant and unpitying; the section is titled "Talk to Me." The sense of connection between poet and personae is almost palpable, as Larkin explores what it means to love, to be loved, and to come to love oneself in a recovering community.

The section "I Couldn't Have Told You" contains a crown of verses entitled "The Blackout Sonnets," bleak statements cased in elegant craft about a teenage girl going out on a New Year's Eve date with a young man she allows to intoxicate and then seduce her. The poems describe the self-hatred, despair and resignation of the eighteen-year-old speaker with the power of natural speech. The themes of adolescence, of low self-esteem, of dealing with parents, and of becoming an individual are interwoven, in the intonation of someone making a first-time confession.

In the Bulkin interview, Larkin speaks of balancing the tightness of poetic form, such as the sonnet, with the danger of the content: "The harder it is for me to say something the more comfortable I am saying it in a form" (89). The image of a woman's torn body after an abortion, likened to torn paper, is one that also appears in these sonnets and in several other strongly formed poems ("The Choice," "Open Question").

Particularly in the last two sections of the book, the poet's lesbian voice is clear and integral. As in *Housework*, the collection's final poems speak hopefully of balance, of women's strengths, and of the power and possibility of healing. Larkin uses the shifting images of other women to contrast, and hence to heighten, the realities experienced by the poems' speakers ("Struck," "Hard Differences"). Yet the world created by two women loving is not, by definition, safe ("Because Again," "Sleeping on the Left Side"); it can, however, be one of salvation or at least hope ("Alba," "Translation"). "The Power of Naming" is a paean to women's ways of knowing and empowering. The last poem in this powerful collection connects the healing power of self-recognition and self-love with the healing power of recovery; like the entire book itself, it describes "How the Healing Takes Place."

In a version of the Bulkin interview published in *Sojourner*, Larkin connects her themes of lesbianism and recovery: "It's as stigmatizing to say, 'I'm an alcoholic' as it is to say, 'I'm lesbian' or 'I'm gay.' So it's understandable that there aren't many role models in lesbian writing. . . . (A)dd to that a whole other area to expose. . . . I hope that more lesbians will come into recovery; I see that happening" (21).

CRITICAL RECEPTION

In a review of *Housework* in *Ms.*, Adrienne Rich sounds themes that have resonated for most of the reviewers of Larkin's work: the strength of Larkin's poetic craft and the honesty and clarity of her poetic presentation. Calling the book "passionate without self-deception," Rich marvels at the rhythmic tensions and half-rhymes Larkin establishes in poems such as "Rhyme of My Inheritance": "[T]his stanza . . . came of an ear consummately aware of the possibilities of language" (47, 105). As for the poetic content, Rich applauds Larkin's use of "domestic" images embodying awareness of "a keenly female sense of the mined terrain of everyday life," including the "danger" of women "having found each other" (105). Carll Tucker, in the *Village Voice*, also lauds Larkin's voice that "neither pities herself nor seeks pity" and adds, "Her best poems cut like broken glass" (40).

Critical reception for *A Long Sound*, a more widely reviewed collection, is even stronger. A review in *Sojourner* (May 1987) describes the strength of the poems coming from Larkin's resistance against "the myth that the alcoholic/ insane poet is a glorious, romantic figure," a legacy passed down through the confessional school of poetry. The exactness and clarity of her imagery "lessens our isolation and guilt, while empowering us with a sense of faith. . . . Unlike her predecessors, she has chosen life" (36). As a complement to life-affirming poems of recovery, the lesbian love poems "catch those moments when someone becomes memorable and important" and strike "the responsive chord of shared experience" (37). On the other hand, Marilyn Hacker, in the *Women's Review of Books*, notes that in *A Long Sound*, "Women lovers can reinforce each other's pain as well as their power, cannot make for each other the first step that must start in the self." She adds, however, that one of the book's strengths is the "gained power" of "lesbian relationship and culture as given, as background, not polemical focus" (24).

BIBLIOGRAPHY

Works by Joan Larkin

Housework. New York: Out & Out Books, 1975.
A Sign I Was Not Alone. Recording. Readings by Joan Larkin, Audre Lorde, Honor Moore, Adrienne Rich. New York: Out & Out Books, 1980.
A Long Sound. Penobscot, ME: Granite Press, 1986.

Works Edited

Amazon Poetry. Ed. Elly Bulkin and Joan Larkin. New York: Out & Out Books, 1975.
Lesbian Poetry: An Anthology. Ed. Elly Bulkin and Joan Larkin. Boston: Persephone Press, 1981.
The Women Writers Calendar. Trumansburg, NY: Crossing Press, 1982.
Gay and Lesbian Poetry in Our Time: An Anthology. Ed. Joan Larkin and Carl Morse. New York: St. Martin's Press, 1988.

Studies of Joan Larkin

Bulkin, Elly. "Joan Larkin on Poetry and Recovery." *Sojourner* (Feb. 1987): 21–22.
———. "Poetry and Recovery: An Interview with Joan Larkin." *Ikon*, 2nd ser., 8 (1987–88): 84–90.
Goldstein, Nancy. "Sober Poetry." Rev. of *A Long Sound*. *Sojourner* (May 1987): 36–37
Hacker, Marilyn. "A Pocketful of Poets." Rev. of *A Long Sound*. *Women's Review of Books* (July 1988): 23–24.
Lux, Thomas. "A Sound Long Overdue." Rev. of *A Long Sound*. *New Letters Review of Books* (Univ. of Missouri–Kansas City) (Spring 1988): 5.
Rich, Adrienne. "There Is a Fly in This House." Rev. of *Housework*. *Ms.* (February 1977): 46–106.
Tucker, Carll. "Alternate Currents." Rev. of *Housework*. *Village Voice* (Mar. 8, 1976): 40.

ANDREA FREUD LOEWENSTEIN
(1949–   )
Joy Holland

BIOGRAPHY

Andrea Freud Loewenstein was born in Boston, Massachusetts, on November 7, 1949, the eldest of three children. Her father, Paul Loewenstein (d. 1990), was a metallurgist, and her mother, Sophie Freud, a social worker and, subsequently, a professor of social work. Andrea is one of the great-granddaughters of Sigmund Freud, the founder of psychoanalysis. Her parents and grandparents escaped from Europe before and during World War II, and her heritage as a secular Jew, and as an intellectual, has had a profound effect on both her fiction and her academic concerns.

Freud Loewenstein grew up in Cambridge and then in the suburb of Lincoln, Massachusetts, the town that provides the setting for many of the episodes in her second novel, *The Worry Girl*. She attended Lincoln Sudbury High School and Clark University in Worcester, Massachusetts, from which she graduated with honors in English in 1971. The civil rights movement was an important formative influence, and as a teenager, she spent two summers working in the South, one of them in a freedom school in Mississippi. In these years she first began to experience the sometimes conflicting dual magnetisms of literature and community service. After two years as a high school teacher in Baltimore and at Children in Crisis in Boston, she began social work school and then moved into literary studies, receiving an M.A. in English from the University of Wisconsin at Madison in 1975.

It was during her years in Madison that she began both to explore lesbian relationships and to take herself seriously as a writer of fiction and poetry. However, Freud Loewenstein's political and social concerns also drew her to teaching, and between 1975 and 1984, she built a distinguished career in adult education. Her experience as a teacher of creative writing, literature, and drama at Framingham Prison for women in Massachusetts, provided important material for her first novel, *This Place*. She next founded the Jefferson Park Writing Center, a community school in a low-income housing project in Cambridge, writing award-winning grant proposals that kept the center afloat for three years. Many members of the community became involved in the activities of the Writing Center, which aimed to replace isolation and helplessness with connectedness, awareness, and empowerment.

Throughout her career, Freud Loewenstein has written short stories, poems, essays, and reviews, contributing regularly to publications such as *Gay Community News*, *Sojourner*, the *Women's Review of Books*, the *Nation*, and *QW*.

After the publication of her first novel in 1984, she went to London, where she spent two years and met her partner, Joy Holland. During this period she began work at the University of Sussex on a doctoral degree, which she completed in 1991. A revision of her dissertation, on the connections between misogyny and anti-Semitism in the work of three British male writers of the 1930s and 1940s, is scheduled for publication by New York University Press in 1993. In England, Freud Loewenstein also wrote a young adult novel, *Hollywood Dreams*, which is not yet published.

On returning to America, she lived initially in Boston, where she founded another innovative writing project at the Bay Cove Mental Health Center. She then moved to Vermont, where she taught at Goddard College, became director of the off-campus M.F.A. program, and wrote the episodes and conceived the shape of her autobiographical novel, *The Worry Girl*, published in 1992. Missing the stimulus and the varied population of the city, she moved to New York in 1991, where she teaches part-time at Brooklyn College and continues to direct the Goddard program from her Brooklyn base.

MAJOR WORKS AND THEMES

In *This Place* (1984), Freud Loewenstein recreates the closed world of a women's prison from the point of view of two inmates and two therapists. The major formal device of the novel is its use of these four viewpoints, three of which are conveyed in the third person. For the fourth character, the vividly hallucinating Telecea, the author stresses the inwardness and isolation of madness by the use of the first person. The novel is remarkable for the vibrancy of these alternating voices, which constitute the developing relationships and unfolding events of the novel. Indeed, capturing the immediacy and individuality of a voice is one of Freud Loewenstein's major strengths as a fiction writer, and this, above all, makes her work compelling reading.

The four characters whose lives interweave through the course of the novel are Ruth Foster, a white therapist; Sonya Lehrman, a Jewish art therapist; Candy Peters, a white inmate, an ex hooker and addict; and Telecea Jones, a black life prisoner whose powerful delusions thrust the novel toward its violent climax. A number of minor characters—inmates, therapists, prison guards, Victor, the lover

Ruth is in the process of discarding, and several of her friends—complete the cast.

Two major concerns shape the unfolding of the narrative. First, the prison setting provides a forum in which the author can scrutinize the choices and limitations confronted by lesbians of different races and classes. In so intimately juxtaposing therapists and inmates, Freud Loewenstein explores and exposes both the shortcomings and complexities of the client-therapist relationship and the impact of bad faith and dilettantism on an inmate community.

Second, that same setting provides a hothouse atmosphere in which lesbianism flourishes. Through the relationship between Candy and her lover, Billy, Freud Loewenstein explores inequalities of love, the complexities of sexual relationships between black and white, and butch-femme dynamics. Also Ruth becomes increasingly dissatisfied with her heterosexual relationship, and a growing attraction between therapists Ruth and Sonya culminates in an interrupted and abortive night of love. The lesbian relationships in *This Place* are the only sexual relationships that count. In evoking both the pleasures and the pressures of lesbian relationships, Freud Loewenstein explores the power dynamics of sexual attraction and conveys a rich and complex vision of the varieties of love between women.

Amber Hollibaugh writes of *This Place* that "its gift is the risks that Loewenstein took when she created these women, never sinking their voices into political correctness, never making them appear less than they are worth. Loewenstein rose to match her characters' challenges. She risked the safety of a too clean, too white, too simple world for women, for one that is uniquely distinct and powerful" (230). *This Place* is a long novel, a tour de force of voice, an attempt to construct a polyphonic, multilayered, multivalent world.

In her relatively brief second novel, *The Worry Girl*, Freud Loewenstein reaches back into childhood and through fifteen interconnected episodes recreates some of the pleasures and agonies of growing up as a member of an assimilated Jewish family in an overwhelmingly Protestant, upper-middle-class suburban town. If the issue of Sonya's Jewishness in the earlier novel remains latent, locked in at the level of subtext, the narrator's Jewishness and its meanings become an overt focus in *The Worry Girl*.

The novel begins with the voices of the narrator's (Rachel's) grandparents and parents, refugees from the Holocaust who provide the background of values, warnings, and exhortations on the basis of which Rachel attempts to make sense of her world. The episodes focus variously on Rachel's Jewishness, on her being a child of survivors and being related to Freud, on her position in the class and gender systems and the social hierarchy of her school, her friendships and enmities, her questioning and growing understanding of issues of race, the difficulties of individuation and separation, and her nascent lesbian sexuality.

Rachel's position in the family is that of the *Sorgenkind* (the term from which the title derives), the difficult child who is often also the eldest. Intensely merged with her mother, the narrator experiences her father as a rival and an enemy.

Mother and daughter join forces to ensure that Rachel's progress through school will be as smooth as possible given her peculiar admixture of talents and failings: an extreme verbal and imaginative faculty, and an equally extreme incapacity in spatial skills.

Of particular importance to her well-being is her friendship with Sydney, a cool and charismatic character who helps to mediate between Rachel and the cruel world of children. But the mutual dependency of Rachel and her mother leads to painful dramas of separation and survival in some of the later episodes of the novel. In the final episode, Rachel's refreshingly serene and optimistic acceptance of her emerging lesbian sexuality develops as a completely logical outcome of her earlier emotional involvements.

Rachel's voice combines a child's clear-sightedness with an adult's ironic comprehension, conveying social and cultural insights through detailed observation. Formally, *The Worry Girl* crosses the boundaries of conventional forms in two ways. First, in fictionalizing an avowedly autobiographical base, it questions the conventional distinction between truth and fiction. Second, in constructing a unified fictional world out of discrete stories, it blurs the distinction between novel and short story collection.

Freud Loewenstein's non-fiction writing consists of an extensive file of book and theater reviews, journalism, literary essays, and her critical book, *Engulfing Women and Loathsome Jews: Metaphors of Projection in the Work of Wyndham Lewis, Charles Williams and Graham Greene.* In this work, she traces the relationship between misogyny and anti-Semitism through a detailed examination of literary texts. Drawing extensively and critically on object-relations theory, she reconstructs the psychological system through which each writer configures the world, showing how categories of Otherness coalesce and interweave. Examining the incredibly various and inventive ways in which good and evil qualities can become polarized and projected to form stereotypical figures of Jews and women, Freud Loewenstein lays bare the roots of violence and hatred. She provides a reasoned and convincing demonstration of the interconnections between oppressions based on ideologies of race and gender.

This book and *The Worry Girl* can be seen as two different manifestations of an ongoing meditation on the meaning of being a woman, a lesbian, and a Jew in a post-Holocaust world.

CRITICAL RECEPTION

This Place received numerous reviews, mostly in the feminist and lesbian press. On its publication in England, an article in the *Guardian* demonstrated a greater interest in the writer's relationship to Freud than in her work. Particularly insightful and sympathetic reviews were those of Renee Neu Watkins and Amber Hollibaugh. Watkins shows an astute appreciation of the formal qualities of the novel and of the effect of the interweaving voices. "*This Place* works as a collective Bildungsroman in which women separate themselves from male domination. . . . What is most unusual about Loewenstein's worldview is her sense of the way personalities are constructed and reconstructed through interaction.''

Hollibaugh stresses the immediacy and vibrancy of Freud Loewenstein's writing and her refusal to buy into easy stereotypes. She notes that ''Andrea Freud Loewenstein took a lot of chances in writing this book,'' but in her view, the author successfully faces the challenges she sets herself (230). While the informal, oral response in the lesbian community was also positive on the whole, *This Place* was criticized on two counts. According to some critics, the character of Sonya, who is Jewish, becomes the locus of evil, selfishness, and negativity in the novel. In retrospect the author says, ''I think they were right, but I would have appreciated a more direct and helpful criticism—an attempt to raise my consciousness instead of being dismissed'' (personal communication with the author, 1992). In other informal discussions of the novel, women considered that Freud Loewenstein should not attempt to write in the voices of Black or working-class women. She still feels, however, that white writers should avoid creating all-white monolithic fictional universes.

At the time of this writing, reviews of *The Worry Girl* are only beginning to appear. The reception of the work in *Lambda Book Report* and *Booklist* has been positive. Jyl Lyn Felman writes of it: ''As in *This Place*, Loewenstein continues to transgress not only the subject matter of our lives, but the very form as well'' (26).

BIBLIOGRAPHY

Works by Andrea Freud Loewenstein

Novels

This Place. Boston and London: Pandora Press, Routledge and Kegan Paul, 1984. Paperback, 1985.
The Worry Girl. Ithaca, NY: Firebrand Books, 1992.

Critical Book

Engulfing Women and Loathsome Jews: Metaphors of Projection in the Work of Wyndham Lewis, Charles Williams and Graham Greene. New York: New York University Press, 1993.

Short Stories and Poems

''Crab Queen.'' *Conditions* 10 (1984): 51–63. Anthologized in *The Stories We Hold Secret.* Greenfield, MA: Greenfield Press, 1986. 28–44.
''Hungry Like a Wolf.'' *Conditions* 11/12 (1985): 55–61.
''The Mother Right.'' *Stepping Out.* Ed. Anne Oosthuizen. London and New York: Pandora Press, 1986. 135–50.
Seven poems anthologized in *Beautiful Barbarians.* London: Onlywomen Press, 1987. 87–90.

"The Same Old Story." *Word of Mouth.* Ed. Irene Zahava. Freedom, CA: Crossing Press, 1990. 83–86.

Studies of Andrea Freud Loewenstein

Hollibaugh, Amber. *"This Place* by Andrea F. Loewenstein." *Conditions* 11/12 (1985): 223–30.

Jacobson, Kent. "A Way Out of No Way: Humanities at Jefferson Park." *Brandeis Review* (1986): 13–16.

Lambda Book Report (May/June 1992): 26.

Watkins, Renee Neu. "Dramas of Confinement." *Women's Review of Books* 2:4 (January 1985).

AUDRE LORDE (1934–1992)
Elaine Maria Upton

BIOGRAPHY

"Black women's words are statements that we were there," writes Audre Lorde (Foreword, *Wild Women in the Whirlwind* xii). The words and the lives exist in intricate interplay. If ever a writer's life and work come together as a model of congruency, then surely the life and work of Audre Lorde form such a model. Born in New York City on February 18, 1934, Lorde has lived and worked courageously to uncover and create her selves as black, woman, lesbian, and warrior for human dignity.

Her life began amid the hard times of the Depression in Harlem with her parents, Linda Belmar and Frederic Byron Lorde, immigrants from the island of Grenada, and two older sisters. She completed high school in New York, and before traveling to Mexico in 1953, she took up several abodes in New York City and lived in Stamford, Connecticut. She worked as a nurse's aide, as a factory worker, and as a domestic worker in private homes, and she began to take courses at Hunter College in 1951. In 1954 she spent a year as a student at the National University of New Mexico. She received a B.A. degree from Hunter College in 1959 and a master of library science degree from Columbia University in 1961. In 1962, she married Edwin A. Rollins. She gave birth to two children, Elizabeth and Jonathan. The couple was later divorced.

Audre Lorde's life, like so much of her poetry and prose speaking, became an exploration and an affirmation of women loving women. Over the years, Lorde formed many supportive relationships with women. She lived for nineteen years in partnership with Frances Louise Clayton. Clayton helped with raising Lorde's two children and with Lorde's early confrontation with breast cancer. Lorde died from cancer on November 11, 1992. At the time of her death, Lorde had been living in St. Croix, the Virgin Islands with her partner—the scholar, writer, and social activist Gloria I. Joseph.

Lorde lived in New York most of her life, and after receiving her degree from Columbia University, she went on to work as a librarian in several New York libraries and as a lecturer at branches of City College of New York. Beginning in the spring of 1968, she was poet-in-residence at Tougaloo College in Mississippi, and in 1978, she became a professor of English at John Jay College of Criminal Justice in New York. In 1981, she became a professor of English at Hunter College.

Her honors include a 1968 National Endowment for the Arts grant, a 1972 Creative Arts Public Service grant, and a 1974 nomination for the National Book Award for *From a Land Where Other People Live* (poems). In 1975, Lorde was presented with the Woman of the Year Award by Staten Island Community College and also won the Broadside Press Poet's Award. She was elected to the Hunter College Hall of Fame in 1980, and in 1981, she received the American Library Association's Gay Caucus Book of the Year Award for *The Cancer Journals*. Lorde was awarded the Manhatten Borough President's Award for Excellence in the Arts in 1988. Her collection of essays *A Burst of Light* won an American Book Award in 1989. In 1991, she won the Walt Whitman Citation of Merit and was named poet laureate of New York. Lorde has received honorary doctorates from Hunter, Oberlin, and Haverford Colleges.

Lorde's life and work were celebrated at a conference entitled "I Am Your Sister" held in Boston in October of 1990. A February 1991 article in *Sojourner* reports that more than one thousand women from twenty-three countries attended this event (Alexander and Bowen 14).

Yet any listing of dates, employment, and honors in Lorde's life is the merest outline of a life merging national and international social and political activism, the raising of two children, engaging in the struggles and joys of friendships and lesbian partnerships. Lorde's writing is richly filled with the substance of her active life as lesbian, mother, friend, witness to our time, spiritual warrior, and woman of deep social conscience and commitment. Her writing is an eloquent testimony to a life lived in art and to art practiced in life.

Before her death, Lorde held an African naming ceremony and took the name Gambda Adisa, which means Warrior: She Who Makes Her Meaning Known.

MAJOR WORKS AND THEMES

To write about any great artist, as indeed Audre Lorde is, is to encounter an overwhelming range of highly textured detail and vivid, warm pictures and sounds. From her early books of poetry, from *First Cities* (1968) to *The Black Unicorn* (1978) to *Our Dead Behind Us* (1986), Lorde shows over more than two decades a deepening commitment to poetry as what she calls "the disciplined attention to the true meaning of 'it feels right to me' " ("Poetry Is Not a Luxury," *Sister Outsider* 37). Indeed, for Lorde, "poetry is not a luxury," but a necessity for registering our very personal and at the same time urgently socially relevant feelings, dreams, struggles, survivals, and realizations, especially as women, black women and women of color, and as lesbians. Those marginalized in the U.S. American and Western social, economic, and political life are often the subjects of Lorde's poetry.

In the poetry one can find a movement from the introspection and metaphorical charge found in the earliest collection, *First Cities*, to a focus on love and interpersonal relationships, notably in "Martha," the early overtly lesbian poem in *Cables to Rage* (1970), published in London by Paul Breman. What will come to characterize Lorde's subsequent poetry—an intense engagement with modern urban traumas, with racism, wars, poverty, and political and social injustice throughout the world—is seen in Lorde's third and fourth books of poetry, *From a Land Where Other People Live* (1973) and *New York Head Shop and Museum* (1974), both published by the Broadside Press that promotes the work of black poets such as Haki Madhubuti (Don L. Lee), Gwendolyn Brooks, Margaret Esse Danner, and Etheridge Knight.

Major themes in Lorde's poetry coincide with themes in her speeches and published prose collections (which include speeches). *The Cancer Journals* (1980), *Sister Outsider: Essays and Speeches* (1984), and *A Burst of Light* (1988) are poetic prose works that, like her poetry of the 1970s and 1980s, reveal the richly varied theme of silence versus speaking out, the necessity of speaking/ writing—speaking/writing for survival, speaking/writing in order to assert the difference that one constitutes as woman, black, and lesbian. Lorde's poems give voice to what has often been taboo, hidden, or ignored. "Black Mother Woman" (*From a Land Where Other People Live*) is one poem that gives voice to uneasy and complex mother-daughter relationships. "Need: A Chorale of Black Women's Voices" displays the agonies of violence against black women. "Woman" (*The Black Unicorn*) expresses the dream of fulfillment from hunger that the speaker finds between another woman's breasts. *Zami: A New Spelling of My Name*, a biomythography (1982), openly charts the territories of women's lovemaking. "Political Relations" (*Our Dead Behind Us*) reveals the hidden (literally under the table) connections between personal (i.e., lesbian) desire and the public political domain acted out in this poem set in a hotel in Tashkent. *The Cancer Journals* makes a refrain of "the transformation of silence into language and action" and provokes us into knowing that "there are so many silences to be broken" (22–23).

Related to this theme of silence versus speaking out is the theme of marginalization, or what Lorde herself might call "outsiderness." A considerable amount of contemporary literary criticism and philosophy is devoted to a discourse on the "other" or "otherness," but for Lorde this attention to otherness or outsiderness is no mere trendiness or ivory tower posturing. With Lorde the concern, as usual in her writing, grows out of (her) lived life and her direct witness and encounter. In Lorde's writing the outsider is the black, the person of color, the black woman and the lesbian particularly, not only in the United States but throughout the African diaspora. *From a Land Where Other People*

Live and *The Black Unicorn* present a large array of poems about being different in the Western, economic, and social structures. We find love spoken in another tongue, the death of Malcolm X connected to the travesties against peoples who are different and threatening throughout the world—in Hanoi, Bedford Stuyvesant, or Angola. We learn of the amazons of Dahomey and the women of Abomey whose lives have been hidden beneath Western social structures. Essays and speeches in *Sister Outsider* confront the otherness of being a black woman, a black lesbian, and a lesbian mother of a son.

In Lorde's poetry and essays, what would be the Other or object in much Western writing becomes the subject, part of the self or selves that one is or chooses. The authorial voice of her poems and prose speaks with an immediacy and a direct engagement with the subject, whether the subject be a South African black woman or Carriacou women or the presumably Hispanic children of ''Jose and Regina'' who are dubious survivors of daily war or a female pupil of a severe Catholic nun or the one-breasted Eudora. The subject is one with the speaker and author's voice. Thus, the reader also is forced from the realm of passive observer to engagement with the plight and feeling of the subject. Lorde's poetry and prose never are a luxury. The reader must be responsive, responsible, provoked to feeling and action.

One of the prominent feelings to which the reader must respond in Lorde's writing is anger and often rage. Anger and rage are also marginalized or relegated to the outsider in Western societies. In Lorde's writing it is the territory especially of black women. ''Every black woman in America lives her life somewhere along a curve of ancient and unexpressed angers,'' writes Lorde (''Eye to Eye,'' *Sister Outsider* 145). Anger is what black women taste as they confront racism, sexism, and homophobia. The racism comes too often from white feminists, as well as from other people. Lorde counsels that black women must move beyond the various ways of internalizing others' hatred of black women, move beyond angry forms of attack on each other.

Another feeling, experience, and source of power that is marginalized in Western societies is what Lorde calls ''the erotic.'' In *Zami*, and in her groundbreaking speech ''Uses of the Erotic: The Erotic as Power'' (delivered at the Ninth Berkshire Conference on the History of Women in 1978, and later published in *Sister Outsider* and also separately as an Out & Out Pamphlet), Lorde celebrates the hidden and rejected ''erotic'' power within women. She cites Western villification, abuse, and devaluing of what is most vital and precious within us—that which is dark and female, the source of the erotic. Lorde locates the erotic in the ancient realm of Chaos, the place of creativity and ultimately of harmony, the place where women celebrate the joy of life and all feelings in language, giving and receiving, acts of friendship and lovemaking, and healing work. The rational (male) world has led us to distrust the (female) erotic, which women must now reclaim.

Another related major theme of Lorde's writing is the theme of survival. *The Cancer Journals*, *A Burst of Light*, *Zami*, and so much of the poetry become the instruments for survival. Essays and journals record Lorde's struggle and encounters with cancer—the medical diagnostic procedures, a mastectomy and the agonizing feelings of loss, and the searches in the United States, Germany, and Switzerland for therapies and healing. The immediate recognition of her mortality, the support of friends and lovers, the occurrences of nature, the pain, and the longing for life are all revealed. What comes across as uncommon in Lorde's experience is her integrity in confronting the many changes in her body and the love and support of other women in her life. Lesbian life is an intricate tapestry of relationships and expressions of caring.

Along with the reality of cancer survival is the global challenge of survival in an ecologically degenerating world, and in a world of racism, sexism, and homophobia, as well as survival of the poor and of those who are abused in many ways. Lorde's poetry images forth a vast wreckage and wrenching concrete detail of racist, sexist, homophobic, and otherwise inhuman events. "A Litany of Survival" (*The Black Unicorn*) is one of the most powerful expressions where the poet gives voice to the voiceless who "were never meant to survive." The poem presents a juxtaposition of both allusory and concrete detail of the lives of the poor, of those who live in fear, and of those who are pushed to the edges of existence. The parallelisms, repetition, and accumulation form a panoply of the desperate or wretched, who form a rising chorus of need and longing. The poem is a crescendo to the concluding inescapability of its own logic and the ironic logic of the lives of its subjects "never meant to survive."

One of the most important means of survival in Lorde's works, as noted earlier, is the act of speaking out. But when Lorde speaks she does more than assail oppressors. She creates. Creation is another theme and motif throughout her writing. Many poems and essays are about language or speaking out or about poetry itself. One uses language as an act of creation to remember ancestry, to witness keenly through tightly woven language, to name and rename ourselves as black, women, lesbian, and in all roles related to these roles or selves. Creation as remembering, bonding, witnessing, visioning, and naming constitutes a crucial, perhaps ultimately the most crucial, theme in Lorde's work. In *The Black Unicorn*, Lorde's poetic vision and power accumulate into the creation of a diasporic consciousness of African women. For example, in "Walking Our Boundaries," the reader enters a world of women who show the persistence of a precolonial intimacy with the land and with each other. The seasons, the weather, the fruit of the land, the women's laughter, their livelihood from the land, and uncertainties emerge in dynamic, sensitive, and subtle relationship. The mythical black unicorn is an impetus for creation of a live black magic where birth happens amid ancient African rites.

In *Zami: A New Spelling of My Name*, Lorde pronounces the act of creation through an uncommon genre, what she calls a biomythography, blending what might be called fiction and personal history and mythmaking. Art and the act of creation are foregrounded. The dreams, imaginations, loves, and visions of the narrator blend into the formation of a surreal and sometimes transcendent reality.

As in Lorde's other work, the narrator writes of that which has so often been taboo. Lovemaking with numerous women lovers—the pleasures, pain, and loss are set forth in colorful motion.

The story forms a quest through the narrator's journeys. The quest and the mythic aura are punctuated with questions. Who is the elusive and often silent, yet strong mother, Linda? Who are the Carriacou women who bond with each other and create an earthy, sensual warmth in the narrator's imagination? Who is the one-breasted Eudora, who will die, and whose memory rings through all other relationships with women lovers? Who is Afrekete, whose presence focuses the central sensual and spiritual quest of the narrator? The narration raises these questions and thus foregrounds the artifice of delineations of reality and fantasy or dream, of physical and spiritual home, of male and female roles, of art and life. Lorde, the artist, and Zami, the artist within the art, create a complex territory of women loving women, a territory seldom enough explored and open to creation and art itself.

The artistry of *Zami* lies in its undulating prose, richly sensual imagery, feminine cyclical structure, and a disarming forthrightness juxtaposed with the ethereality of dream. *Zami* intensifies Lorde's project of speaking the (often lesbian) unspoken and merging life and art.

CRITICAL RECEPTION

Mainstream academic journals and academic critics have, for the most part, yet to become aware of the power of Lorde's writing. A few of these mainstream journals, such as the *Hudson Review* and the *Denver Quarterly*, have published interviews or critiques of Lorde's work, and *Callaloo* and *Signs*, academic journals devoted to black literature and to women's literature, respectively, have published work about Lorde. In *Signs* (Summer 1981), there is an extensive conversation between the white lesbian poet Adrienne Rich and Audre Lorde. An article by Mary Carruthers in the *Hudson Review* and an essay by black feminist critic Barbara Christian both look at Lorde in the context of her contemporaries—other women writers. Carruthers looks at the way lesbian writers such as Adrienne Rich, Judy Grahn, and Olga Broumas invoke the poetic muse differently than heterosexual poets. In her book *Black Feminist Criticism: Perspectives on Black Women Writers* (1985), Christian sees Lorde's *Zami*, like narrative fictions of Gloria Naylor, Alice Walker, and Ntozake Shange, as a revelation of a formerly hidden lesbianism in black women's lives. Lorde's unearthing is the most consistently affirmative of lesbian life, and the unearthing that all these writers perform alludes to a history of silence about lesbianism and the black lesbian's perceived need for silence, as in the case of Harlem Renaissance women poets like Angelina Weld Grimké.

Most of the attention to Lorde's work so far comes in what are usually non-academic or non-mainstream publications. These reviews provide information that is useful, even vital, to many readers, especially to feminist women, lesbians, and black readers of the black publications. Well known alternative and feminist publications such as *Sojourner*, *Ms.*, *off our backs*, *Conditions*, *Sinister Wisdom*, and *Radical Teacher* have published highly appreciative interviews, reviews, and commentary on Lorde's work as a lesbian, black woman, and social activist. *Ebony*, *Crisis*, and *Essence* are some of the black publications that have reviewed Lorde's work, yet some black publications fail to appreciate the lesbian protrayals that are central to so much of Lorde's writing.

For example, although there are two essays on Lorde's poetry in *Black Women Writers: A Critical Evualation*, edited by black poet Mari Evans, the essays do not adequately treat the lesbianism in Lorde's poetry. In one of the essays entitled "In the Name of the Father: The Poetry of Audre Lorde," Jerome Brooks fails even to acknowledge the lesbian relationships portrayed in the poetry. He simplifies and dismisses Lorde's own complex relationship to her mother, cites Lorde's quest for her father, and proclaims, "The poetry, then, is a prolonged spiritual search for the father" (270). Similarly, writing in the historic black journal *Crisis*, Joe Johnson claims that in *Zami* Lorde seeks to take on a male sex role. Although Johnson does acknowledge that the erotic in *Zami* is liberated from "the oppressive male models of power," he seems to contradict himself by asserting that Lorde relegates eroticism "to love scenes" and "merely dishes out hot flashes for devotees and voyeurs" (47).

In a more lesbian and African–culturally sensitive critical analysis of Lorde's *Zami* and *The Black Unicorn*, the black lesbian critic Chinosole writes of Lorde's bringing to readers her "fullest and deepest wisdom" in her presentation of matrilineal diaspora (379). Chinosole's is a rich, multilayered essay eliciting the cultural complexities in *Zami*, its ground-breaking generic acts, its display of cultural oppositions, its sustenance from West African and West Indian legend and myth, and in all, its matrifocality, beginning with the narrator's relationship to her mother. Chinosole notes that in *Zami*, as in many of Lorde's poems, the world of myth sustains artistic creation and also points the way to the future of women loving, sharing, and sustaining each other.

Probably the most important reception of Lorde's writing and her life of social activism is that manifest by the numbers of readers and admirers whom she has inspired—women struggling against sexism, lesbians struggling against homophobia and striving to create their own lives, and blacks seeking to create a meaningful existence beyond the many injustices suffered across the globe. One such manifestation of Lorde's reception is in the outpouring of appreciation at the I Am Your Sister Celaconference in Boston, October 1990. Although it must be noted that a group of Latina women, *Hermanas Latinas*, felt excluded from the conference planning, these women nevertheless acknowledge Lorde's gifts to them (see the "Open Letter" in *Sojourner*, February 1991, 14).

Lorde is a spiritual warrior fighting against the silences and hatreds that invade the lives of the many "outsiders"—victims of racism, apartheid, poverty, cancer, and homophobia. She is a creator with compassion and the joy of life in spite of hardships. Her large capacity to conjure and vividly name the deepest fears and the hopes and life-sustaining dreams of many make her voice, indeed not a luxury, but necessary bread.

BIBLIOGRAPHY

Works by Audre Lorde

First Cities. New York: Poets Press, 1968.
Cables to Rage. London: Breman, 1970.
From a Land Where Other People Live. Detroit: Broadside Press, 1973.
New York Head Shop and Museum. Detroit: Broadside Press, 1974.
Between Our Selves. Point Reyes, CA: Eidolon Editions, 1976.
Coal. New York: Norton, 1976.
The Black Unicorn. New York: Norton, 1978.
Uses of the Erotic: The Erotic as Power. Out & Out Pamphlet. Freedom, CA: Crossing Press, 1978.
The Cancer Journals. Argyle, NY: Spinsters Ink, 1980.
Chosen Poems: Old and New. New York: Norton, 1982.
Zami: A New Spelling of My Name. Freedom, CA: Crossing Press, 1982.
Sister Outsider: Essays and Speeches. Freedom, CA: Crossing Press, 1984.
Apartheid USA and Our Common Cause in the Eighties. Authored jointly with Merle Woo. Freedom Organizing Pamphlet. Latham, NY: Kitchen Table Press, 1986.
I Am Your Sister: Black Women Organizing across Sexualities. Freedom Organizing Pamphlet. Latham, NY: Kitchen Table Press, 1986.
Our Dead Behind Us. New York: Norton, 1986.
A Burst of Light. Ithaca, NY: Firebrand Books, 1988.
Undersong: Chosen Poems Old and New. New York: Norton, 1992.

Studies of Audre Lorde

Alexander, Jacqui, and Angela Bowen. "Why Audre?" in "Reflections on *I Am Your Sister.*" *Sojourner* 16.6 (February 1991): 14.
Baldwin, James, and Audre Lorde. "Revolutionary Hope: A Conversation Between James Baldwin and Audre Lorde." *Essence* 15.8 (December 1984): 72–74.
Bethel, Lorraine. Review of *The Black Unicorn. Gay Community News* (February 10, 1979): 1, 5, 6.
Bovoso, Carole. Review of *Zami. Essence* 13.11 (March 1983): 20.
Brooks, Jerome. "In the Name of the Father: The Poetry of Audre Lorde." *Black Women Writers 1950–1980: A Critical Evaluation.* Ed. Mari Evans. New York: Doubleday, 1984. 269–76.
Bulkin, Elly. " 'Kissing Against the Light': A Look at Lesbian Poetry." *Radical Teacher* (December 10, 1978): 7–17.
Carruthers, Mary J. "The Re-vision of the Muse: Adrienne Rich, Audre Lorde, Judy Grahn, and Olga Broumas." *Hudson Review* 36 (Summer 1983): 293–322.

Chinosole. "Audre Lorde and Matrilineal Diaspora: moving history beyond nightmare into structures for the future." *Wild Women in the Whirlwind: Afra-American Culture and the Contemporary Literary Renaissance*. Ed. Joanne M. Braxton and Andreé Nicola McLaughlin. New Brunswick, NJ: Rutgers University Press, 1990. 379–99.

Christian, Barbara. "No More Buried Lives: The Theme of Lesbianism in Audre Lorde's *Zami*, Ntozake Shange's *Sassafras, Cypress, and Indigo*, and Alice Walker's *The Color Purple*." *Black Feminist Criticism: Perspectives on Black Women Writers*. Ed. Barbara Christian. New York: Pergamon Press, 1985. 187–204.

Clarke, Cheryl. Review of *The Cancer Journals*. *Conditions 8* 3.2 (Spring 1982): 148–54.

Johnson, Joe. Review of *Zami*. *Crisis* 92.9 (November 1985): 10, 12, 47–48.

Joseph, Gloria. Review of *Zami*. *Black Scholar* 14 (Sept.-Oct. 1983): 4–5.

Smith, Barbara. "The Truth That Never Hurts: Black Lesbians in Fiction in the 1980's." *Wild Women in the Whirlwind: Afra-American Culture and the Contemporary Literary Renaissance*. Ed. Joanne M. Braxton and Andreé Nicola McLaughlin. New Brunswick, NJ: Rutgers University Press, 1990. 213–45.

Tate, Claudia. *Black Women Writers at Work*. New York: Continuum, 1983. 100–116.

LEE LYNCH (1945–   )
Glynis Carr

BIOGRAPHY

Like most contemporary U.S. lesbian writers, Lee Lynch has not yet attracted a biographer. Readers, therefore, must rely on Lynch's own writing for glimpses into her life. Specifically, they must consult *The Amazon Trail*, a collection of syndicated newspaper columns written for the gay press during the 1980s. These lively essays—in which Lynch skillfully combines the genres of travelogue, news report, memoir, and editorial—paint a fascinating, if incomplete self-portrait of the artist. Lynch would seem to be a woman of many contradictions: a "penniless bourgeois"; an adventurer who yearns for security; a city person who feels most at home in the country; a shy woman whose circle of friends is endless; a feminist critical of "politics"; a "sober dyke" who equally celebrates gay bars and gay Alcoholics Anonymous simply because "we are there."

Born in 1945, Lee Lynch claims New York City—where much of her early fiction is set—as her hometown. "I came," she writes, "from the kind of family that has two sides: the side that wouldn't shop in a thrift store and doesn't have to; and the side that did, but didn't want to talk about it" (*Amazon Trail* 95). Lynch aspired to be a writer even as a youngster, but her provocative and well-researched essays on gay literature strongly suggest that she could also have been a teacher or scholar had she so desired. Her essay "Cruising the Libraries" is both hilarious reading and serious scholarship on lesbian literary history, encoding, reader response, and canon formation in this century. It outlines a full course of lesbian literature, as dense as any graduate seminar, but more passionate than most.

Lee Lynch went to school in Connecticut and came out in 1959 or 1960, proudly asserting an "old gay" rather than "movement gay" identity. Her memoirs of the 1960s and 1970s concern her struggle to find other lesbians, working-class bar culture, communal living, and feminist politics. Lynch began to publish short stories in the late 1960s, but the 1980s were her watershed years. She wrote prolifically, established a good working relationship with Naiad Press, and produced a book almost every year between 1983 and 1991 (*Toothpick House*, 1983; *Old Dyke Tales*, 1984; *The Swashbuckler*, 1985; *Home in Your Hands*, 1986; *Dusty's Queen of Hearts Diner*, 1987; *The Amazon Trail*, 1988; *Sue Slate, Private Eye*, 1989; and *That Old Studebaker*, 1991). In 1984, at the age of thirty-nine, she traveled west across the United States for the first time, eventually relocating in a rural area of Oregon with her lover, artist Tee Corinne, who she married. Lee Lynch now lives there in a trailer and describes herself as happily committed to her work, lover, and the gay community—her chosen and created "family."

MAJOR WORKS AND THEMES

The Amazon Trail, discussed above, amply demonstrates Lynch's talent for non-fictional prose. These enthusiastic essays are densely informative advertisements for the work of gay artists and activists. Some promote feminist and gay institutions such as bookstores, writers' conferences, and music festivals, while others are itineraries that describe Lynch's travels through "gay geography" and urge the ongoing creation of more "gay space" by inspiring others to live openly and visibly. *The Amazon Trail* is written with wit and verve, in a pithy, sententious style (as when she writes that women's studies is the cutting edge of academia and teachers are its "vulnerable blades"). To structure both individual essays and the volume as a whole, Lynch extensively uses metaphors of geography and place. *The Amazon Trail* generously encourages gay culture by praising the community's creativity and ability to sustain itself under pressure, but occasionally the essays are unsatisfactorily thin. The danger of celebration alone, divorced from thoughtful critique, is that it can become superficial.

For example, the essays exuberantly "celebrate difference" among lesbians, but gloss over the problems such as racism and class conflict created by difference, a tendency that betrays the centrality and serious treatment of these issues in her fiction. But her fiction, too, sometimes glosses over lesbians' problems and idealizes lesbian community in problematic ways. Using Barbara Smith's terminology, one could say that Lynch's characters possess verisimilitude, but are perhaps *too* authentic; that is, although they are realistically drawn and do reveal "problems, contradictions, [and] flaws," many of them are not finally "sufficiently complex" (696). Lynch creates archetypal heroes, idealized figures who often solve their problems by asserting countercultural and feminist clichés. For example, during one of the crises in her relationship with Annie in *Toothpick House*, Victoria declares, "We have to find out how to be together and change together without becoming indistinguishable from each other or inseparable. As you said, we have to learn how 'not to lose our ability to be alone' " (206). Some readers will value such passages as nourishing and inspirational—serving the same purpose for today's lesbians as the nineteenth-century black feminist "uplift novels" did for their audience—while others will censure them as strained, stilted, and overly didactic. Like many of her contemporaries, Lynch does not experiment much with language, nor fully use the literary resources developed in this century since modernism. Her books can be severely literal, sometimes to the point of awkwardness.

But these formal qualities and the ease of reading they permit are perhaps directly related to Lynch's overriding purpose: to represent working-class lesbians and lesbian community in such a way that we are nourished, consoled, and emboldened to resist heterosexist oppression. The strength of Lynch's work is its power to make visible so many "buried lives," and to do so in such a way that normalizes, even glorifies, lesbian experience. Thus her work provides a necessary psychological corrective to the dominant culture's mainly derogatory representations of homosexuality.

Another of Lynch's formal techniques recapitulates her major interest in the creation and sustenance of lesbian community: her books employ what Bonnie Zimmerman has described as an "intertwining narrative technique" (141). Lynch's works are "intertwined" in that her characters frequently appear in more than one book, as when Annie Heaphy, the protagonist of *Toothpick House*, reappears in *Home in Your Hands* or when Dusty and Elly figure in three works: *Toothpick House*, *Home in Your Hands*, and *Dusty's Queen of Hearts Diner*. Lynch also unifies and structures her collections of short stories by alternating pieces that might be described as "self-contained" with ones that are part of a series (for example, the "At a Bar" stories that serve as structural backbone for both *Old Dyke Tales* and *Home in Your Hands*. To read any of Lynch's works, therefore, is to enter a fictional world in which community is both thematically and structurally central.

Lee Lynch is a superb short story writer. Her first collection, *Old Dyke Tales*, underscores two social processes: the individual one of "coming out" and the collective, historical process of lesbians coming together to forge visible and viable communities. Many of these stories narrate incidents from the lives of painfully isolated women, women who have been tragically victimized by the heterosexual mainstream and have suffered much loss. Others are brave tales of lesbians reaching out to find and love each other, constructing a culture of survival and resistance. The second collection, *Home in Your Hands*, is much less concerned with the devastating effects of heterosexism than with working-class lesbians' achievement of economic and cultural self-determination, what might be called a "lesbian nationalism." As the title suggests, "home" is the central metaphor of this book. In a variety of ways, lesbians "come home" to themselves and build "homes" with each other, spaces that are either private sanctuaries or public sites of opposition to dominant culture.

One of Lynch's formal techniques is to create intergenerational dialogue among lesbians. In many of the *Old Dyke Tales*, an older or elderly first-person narrator tells her story to a much younger listener. The emphasis in such tales is on the sameness of lesbian experience despite generational difference. In this way,

Lynch rather brilliantly, if problematically, constructs *both* a history of lesbianism that underscores the changing material and cultural conditions of women's lives *and* an essentialist definition of lesbian identity and experience that transcends time and culture.

Just as Lynch erases generational difference between lesbians, she sometimes erases racial difference as well. For example, "The Abrupt Edge," in *Old Dyke Tales*, is a both a coming-out story and a story of interracial friendship. As in many such stories, the white protagonist learns something of importance from her black friend and employs that knowledge toward some achievement. Here, the white woman recognizes her own difference from heterosexual society by meditating on the racial difference of her friend, just as Dusty, in *Dusty's Queen of Hearts Diner*, overcomes internalized homophobia by learning the "simple lessons of [racial] pride and courage" taught by Rosa, her Hispanic friend. Lynch's texts thereby tend to collapse and subsume all specific differences (racial, sexual, and so on) into one simple Difference. They tend to claim that since everyone is Different, we are all really the Same, a move undoubtedly helpful in constructing a basis for a more inclusive, tolerant society, but also clearly problematic for those readers attempting to understand the specific intersection of race, class, and gender in women's lives. Not all Lynch's work elides difference, however; in the final story of *Old Dyke Tales*, the divisive force of racism disrupts the lesbian community from (literally) the book's margin. This story erases neither race nor the problem of racism; it thoughtfully probes the importance of race and the psychological mechanisms sustaining racism and linking it to other forms of oppression.

Old Dyke Tales and *Home in Your Hands* provide a rich reading experience. In these collections, Lynch brings together many lesbian voices in dialogue about issues of urgent concern: lesbians' need for creative work and economic self-sufficiency, for friendship and community, ways to confront the everyday pathologies of heterosexist society, the process of recovery from devastating addictions, the need to restructure "love" so that it works for lesbian couples, and other issues of relationship and sexuality. Lynch's erotic writing is among the best. Of particular interest to many will be her sympathetic represention of butch-femme relationships in all her work. Here, butches and femmes are neither the pathetic apes of heterosexuality nor quaint survivals of a less enlightened, "prefeminist" age, but admirable women whose way of life deserves respect. Other characters are concerned with the tension between their unruly sexual desires and monogamous commitment to a partner. Lynch's most profound achievements are that she realistically captures a wide spectrum of contemporary lesbian experience and even-handedly explores the moral and ethical problems it entails.

Toothpick House is Lynch's first published novel, a love story that brings together two women, Annie Heaphy and Victoria Locke, against the backdrop of the early women's liberation movement of the 1970s. *Toothpick House* could easily be read as political allegory, with Annie representing "old gay" culture (that is, butch-femme bar culture) and Victoria's friends Rosemary and Claudia representing "movement gay" culture (one self-consciously created by feminists in the early 1970s, in which lesbianism was sometimes a matter of political choice, not being "born queer"). In such a reading, Victoria would be the figure who mediates between the two, a "Yalie" strongly attracted to feminism yet horrified that Rosie and Claudia could logically and dispassionately "choose" to be lesbians. Victoria herself yearns for some kind of life different from that expected of her by her parents, both from wealthy families in decline, yet she can articulate her desire only after meeting and falling in love with Annie, a tough yet emotionally cowardly woman who feels trapped in "endless circles" and fears she will waste her life as a "bar dyke." Victoria is surprised by her own lesbianism; neither "old gay" nor "movement gay," her task in the novel is to develop a new identity. As the lovers forge a life together, they also forge a new kind of gay community that combines the best qualities of each faction. In the process, Annie and Victoria negotiate a sharp difference between them in class, each giving something of value to the other.

Lynch's second novel, *The Swashbuckler*, is a much more sophisticated book than the first. Like *Toothpick House*, it is a love story in which the lovers must undergo personal and political transformation before their relationship will work, but here Lynch takes greater artistic risks, experimenting with the use of both first- and third-person narrators and using techniques such as internal monologue to achieve a greater psychological depth of characterization.

The portrait of Frenchy, the protagonist, is powerfully, even magnificently drawn. At the novel's beginning, Frenchy is a rather pathetic woman who exerts enormous control to maintain her life in rigidly segregated components: at work and home (where she is closeted) and at the bar (where her "true" identity as a swashbuckling bulldagger may freely be expressed). As a result, Frenchy is divided within herself and detached from all others. "Closing in on thirty [years old] and . . . running out of steam" (59), Frenchy begins to change, mostly because the effort required to manage her life has become exhausting, but also because she cannot quell a disturbing attraction she feels for another butch, Mercedes. Mercedes has been in and out of jails and hospitals for many years, since being raped and consequently having a daughter whom she cannot adequately support. The obstacle these lovers face is that both are butches, neither will become femme for the other, and neither knows how to live outside the complex and rigid sexual "language" of butch-femme culture. Ultimately, *The Swashbuckler* is about liberation from sexual roles that no longer fit, about becoming "more than a butch." During a separation of many years, both lovers grow, gradually shedding their self-limiting and self-defeating ideas like old skins. Like *Toothpick House*, *The Swashbuckler* narrates how "old gay" identity was radically and permanently altered during the 1960s and 1970s. In this novel, Lynch sustains her interest in representing lesbian community as a vital, necessary support for personal transformation, even broadening its definition by including characters deftly drawn across several lines of racial and ethnic difference: Frenchy is Quebecoise, Mercedes is a Puerto Ricana, Edie is Jewish, and Esther is an African-American. This novel is less didactic than the first, and more humorous, too.

Dusty's Queen of Hearts Diner is Lynch's most mature novel. Like much of her previous work, this story concerns the efforts of working-class lesbians to rewrite the homophobic "narratives of damnation" scripted for them by the dominant culture. But here Lynch surpasses her earlier work by attending more closely to the historical and sociopolitical contexts of her story, experimenting with narrative form, and alluding to lesbian literary tradition. The result is a richer, more carefully constructed novel, one that reads much less like myth or fable than her previous works. Still, the characters are types. The novel centers on Dusty and Elly, a butch-femme couple who have recently moved from the city to Dusty's hometown to set down roots. Each has taken the magnificent risk of quitting her job to buy and refurbish an old diner. The main plot concerns the couple's resistance against a homophobic hate campaign, led by a priest and a local businessman, to ruin their business and run them out of town. Into this plot, Lynch expertly weaves the first-person narrative of Dusty's life story: her abandonment by her father, her mother's attempt to survive by remarrying a man who sexually abused Dusty, her hitch in the navy during the McCarthy era, her unintentionally played role in the navy's lesbian purges, her alcoholism and recovery. Lynch's juxtaposition of past and present episodes emphasizes the psychological consequences of oppression. Dusty, "born queer," must come to terms with the shame that has been heaped upon her. Increasingly, she rejects the meanings ascribed to her by the dominant culture and the limitations it would place on her life. Much supported by her friends and lover Elly, Dusty comes to expect more from life than vilification. She also learns that she has more— much more—to offer life. *Dusty's Queen of Hearts Diner* is a profoundly optimistic novel in that it maps a way out of the impasse that occurs when lesbians, in attempting to survive heterosexist oppression, internalize so much of the hatred that surrounds them that they become, ironically, their own harshest critics, severest detractors, and strictest police.

Sue Slate, Private Eye is an extremely clever, fast-paced detective story. The fact that its protagonists are cats places it in that playful and parodic lesbian genre including Virginia Woolf's *Flush* and May Sarton's *The Fur Person*. Sue Slate, a hard-boiled lesbicat from San Francisco, unravels a mystery involving three missing kittens, a murdered gay man, and a conspiracy between a fundamentalist church and a pharmaceutical company to experiment on gay people with AIDS.

Lynch's 1991 novel, *That Old Studebaker*, is a thoroughly contemporary novel in which the problem isn't how to find other lesbians, but how to find *likeable* ones. But none of the potentially interesting implications of her dilemma are explored with the depth or seriousness that characterizes Lynch's earlier work.

CRITICAL RECEPTION

Barbara Christian has written that, historically, black women's literature has been supported not by scholars but by " 'ordinary' black women" readers (64).

The same could be said of the working-class lesbian literature written by Lee Lynch. Lynch has always commanded an eager audience of "ordinary" lesbians, but has been virtually ignored in academe. She is popular with publishers of lesbian and feminist journals: many of her short stories, later collected or worked into the novels, first appeared in such places as the *Ladder*, *Sinister Wisdom*, *Common Lives/Lesbian Lives*, and *On Our Backs*. Also, her work has been widely and favorably reviewed in the alternative press. Bonnie Zimmerman is the one scholar who notices Lynch. In her *Safe Sea of Women*, Zimmerman discusses several but not all of Lynch's books, placing them in the context of contemporary lesbian literature as a whole and emphasizing their treatment of the tradition's major themes.

BIBLIOGRAPHY

Works by Lee Lynch

Toothpick House. Tallahassee, FL: Naiad Press, 1983.
Old Dyke Tales. Tallahassee, FL: Naiad Press, 1984.
The Swashbuckler. Tallahassee, FL: Naiad Press, 1985.
Home in Your Hands. Tallahassee, FL: Naiad Press, 1986.
Dusty's Queen of Hearts Diner. Tallahassee, FL: Naiad Press, 1987.
The Amazon Trail. Tallahassee, FL: Naiad Press, 1988. [An expanded version of the limited edition volume *The Amazon Trail* (Grants Pass, OR: Variant Press, 1986).]
Sue Slate, Private Eye. Tallahassee, FL: Naiad Press, 1989.
"Cruising the Libraries." *Lesbian Texts and Contexts: Radical Revisions*. Ed. Karla Jay and Joanne Glasgow. New York: New York University Press, 1990. 39–48.
That Old Studebaker. Tallahassee, FL: Naiad Press, 1991.

Studies of Lee Lynch

Christian, Barbara. "But What Do We Think We're Doing Anyway: The State of Black Feminist Criticism(s) or My Version of a Little Bit of History." *Changing Our Own Words: Essays on Criticism, Theory, and Writing by Black Women*. Ed. Cheryl A. Wall. New Brunswick, NJ: Rutgers University Press, 1989. 58–74.
Smith, Barbara. "The Truth That Never Hurts: Black Lesbians in Fiction in the 1980s." 1990. Rpt. *Feminisms: An Anthology of Literary Theory and Criticism*. Ed. Robyn R. Warhol and Diane Price Herndl. New Brunswick, NJ: Rutgers University Press, 1991. 690–712.
Zimmerman, Bonnie. *The Safe Sea of Women: Lesbian Fiction, 1969–1989*. Boston: Beacon Press, 1990.

PAULA MARTINAC (1954–)
Penny Perkins

BIOGRAPHY

Paula Martinac was born and raised in Pittsburgh, the youngest of three sisters, to a housemaker mother and a tool-and-die-maker father. Pittsburgh in the 1950s and 1960s, when Martinac was growing up there, was very working class, very Catholic, and very ethnic—descriptions which all fit Martinac's family. (Regarding the latter, Paula is a composite of three nationalities: Croatian, Irish, and Polish. The name "Martinac" is Croatian.)

In keeping with the family's roots, Martinac was sent to Catholic school for twelve years, an experience which, she says succinctly, "was horrible." Although the nuns didn't hit the girls, they did have "scary, bony hands," which often were occupied with beating the boys. (Unless otherwise noted, all quotations are from conversations with Martinac during April 1992.)

When she was eighteen, Martinac left her hometown to go to Fordham University in the Bronx (New York), but attended the Catholic university (where men outnumbered women ten to one) only one year before transferring to Chatham College in Pittsburgh, where she graduated in 1976 with a B.A. in history. She later stated in her paper " 'Holding the Women': Historical Fiction and the Need to Imagine," presented at the 1992 OUT/WRITE conference for lesbian and gay writers:

I don't really remember why I became a history major in college except that my favorite professor talked about history as a living study of how the past, present, and future are interdependent. We still studied a lot of facts and dates that made you want to die, but there were also broad philosophical concepts that challenged the intellect. I believed that, knowing history, I could become anything.

After working a year, Martinac moved to the south to enter the College of William and Mary in Williamsburg, Virginia, where she graduated in 1979 with a master's in history. Her study was a one-year program focusing on the New Social History, an outgrowth of sixties radicalism, where sources such as tax records, census reports, newspapers, and diaries were used to recreate the history of people who had never been considered important enough before to have a history—poor people, women, and people of color. This training was later to have a major influence on her work.

Martinac had been attracted to women consciously since she was around nineteen years old, but she didn't come out (i.e., fall in love) until she was twenty-four. At that time, she was in West Virginia working at her first job as a historian—as a museum curator for the West Virginia Department of Culture and History—where she researched, dated, catalogued, and conserved the museum's collection of period costumes.

Martinac's coming-out experience resulted in a three-year on-again, off-again relationship with the woman she fell in love with, but for the most part, Martinac found it difficult to be a lesbian in West Virginia. "The only group I went to was NOW, and the only gay bar was seedy and its clientele was mostly men." This stifling sexual atmosphere, coupled with a distressing sexual harassment ordeal at work, impelled Martinac to look for other employment. After receiving job offers only in other parts of the South, and increasingly desirous of a multifaceted women's community, Martinac moved to New York City in 1982 without a job prospect.

She soon landed a job at the Prentice-Hall publishing company in Fort Lee, New Jersey, where she also found an apartment. Immediately, Martinac began going into New York three or four nights a week—volunteering for *Womanews*, a radical feminist lesbian newspaper, now defunct, where she met like-minded writer/artist types—and quickly and happily found both women's and writers' communities. One of the tangible results of this overall life change was Martinac's first published story, "The Good Daughter," which appeared in *Forum: A Journal for Lesbians* (now defunct) in 1983 when she was twenty-nine.

Although "The Good Daughter" was Martinac's first published short story, she had been writing since she was seven years old. Her very first story, she recalls, was about a deer. Her second story, also written at the age of seven, was about a pretty nun. (Apparently not all the nuns in young Martinac's world were scary: "The story was very adoring—the plot was that I loved her.")

The short stories continued until Martinac was eleven, when she started writing mininovels of about eighty pages during her summer vacations. She completed one a summer until she was fourteen, and still has the four manuscripts. The next few years, from fifteen to seventeen, Martinac—in an enterprise reminiscent of Emily Dickinson's hand-bound manuscripts—created little poetry books. Still in her imitative phase, the first book of poetry was "very much like *Winesburg, Ohio*." The next two manuscripts presented themes typical for her age: love poems to boys and poems about dying. But then ("thank goodness"), before that trend could continue, it was time to go to college.

In college, busied with academic work, Martinac stopped writing creatively for several years. "I wrote a few stories in my junior year, but my parents had hammered into my head that writers didn't make any money, so I had sublimated my creative desires into journalism." It also seems that she was sublimating other desires as well. Perhaps the greatest contribution to Martinac's long, dry spell from writing—from the time she was eighteen to twenty-four—was the confusion about her sexual identity. "I only started writing stories again when I came out as a lesbian." She sees these events as being very strongly connected: "You can't write unless you have a sense of who you are, and you can't have a sense of who you are without being comfortable with your sexuality." Martinac began writing "a lot" of lesbian-themed stories after arriving in New York and finding herself more connected to a lesbian and feminist community.

Even given the long relationship between Martinac and her writing (from age seven on), she still never "really" thought of herself as a writer until 1987 when she was thirty-three years old—even though she has been producing work steadily, on and off, her entire life—when she was submitting several pieces of a collection of short stories to various journals and magazines.

Since 1987, however, Martinac has left ample evidence that she is indeed a "real" writer. She has published seven short stories in various journals and anthologies, including *Conditions*, *Sinister Wisdom*, and *The Portable Lower East Side*; she edited an anthology, *The One You Call Sister: New Women's Fiction*, published by Cleis Press; and she has published a collection of short stories, *Voyages Out 1: Lesbian Short Fiction*, with Carla Tomaso, and an award-winning ghost-story/historical novel, *Out of Time*, both from Seal Press. Martinac recently finished another novel, *Home Movies*, to be published by Seal Press in August 1993, which chronicles a young lesbian's coming-of-age and grappling with loss and change, both in her own relationships and with her uncle's battle with AIDS. Martinac is presently in the midst of writing another novel, *Beards*— "It's the story I've always wanted to write"—about the marriage of convenience between a lesbian and a gay man after World War II.

Martinac has worked in book publishing as a design and production manager for the last ten years, most recently at the Feminist Press. She currently works part-time, which allows her to devote mornings to her writing. Martinac is also active in lesbian and gay politics and currently serves as the board co-chair of the New York City Lesbian and Gay Community Services Center. At the center, she was instrumental in the establishment of the innovative reading series there, "In Our Own Write," which showcases both emerging and established lesbian and gay writers. She has been a member of the *Conditions* collective since 1989, and regularly reads her work at various forums throughout the metropolitan New York area and around the country.

MAJOR WORKS AND THEMES

In her novel, *Out of Time*, Paula Martinac writes about a woman who finds a scrapbook of photos of four lesbians from the 1920s and becomes obsessed with the dead—or not so dead—women's lives. The book is written in the first person from the point of view of Susan van Dine: lesbian, perennial graduate student, participant in a wheel-spinning relationship, and soon-to-be ghost-chasing antiques dealer. Not a historical novel per se, *Out of Time* is more "about the historical process, the process of uncovering lesbian lives" and about the continuity of women's lives over time. The book is written mainly in the present with charming sallies back into the past, and juxtaposes Susan's insistence on intuition (or ghostly hallucinations) in discovering the lives of the women in the scrapbook against her historian girlfriend's insistence on archival research. By the end of the book, both Susan and Catherine, as well as intuition and research, are proceeding hand in hand.

The motif in the book between knowledge of the head and of the heart was, interestingly enough, mirrored by Martinac's process of researching and writing the book. As she recounted in her presentation at the 1992 OUT/WRITE conference:

I went to the Lesbian Herstory Archives and read every book and clipping I could get my hands on about lesbians in the 1920s. There wasn't much. So I immersed myself in the twenties. I spent hours squinting over microfilm of newspapers and staring at photographs in the public library. . . . I read novels of the period. . . . I read books and articles written by feminist activists of the twenties. I studied standard histories about the women's movement directly before and after suffrage.

In this sense, Martinac the author behaves strikingly like Catherine, the narrator's girlfriend and by-the-book rational historian. But Martinac's next statements demonstrate the need in the writing process for something beyond bare facts:

And then [after completing the tasks described above], because I'd learned a lot about the period but relatively little about what life was like for *lesbians*, I imagined. My imagination led me to write the novel as a ghost story. It also had to be part mystery, because lesbians' lives *are* a mystery to be unraveled through intuitive thinking. Research only takes us so far.

Given the fact that Martinac suffered a six-year writer's block during the period she wrestled with her sexual identity—and given that the successful denouement of this private struggle included her rebirth as a writer—it should come as no surprise that Martinac's fiction contains a full house of lesbians whose sexuality is just a part of the overall composition of their lives, loves, and situations.

In *Voyages Out 1: Lesbian Short Fiction* (an innovative but short-lived series by Seal Press of Seattle that collected the short fiction of two emerging authors and presented them together), Martinac focuses on stories about lesbians and the worlds lesbians create, inhabit, and move in and out of. Martinac's eight stories revolve around the issues of love, sex, and family from a distinctly lesbian point of view.

As Loralee MacPike states in a review of *Voyages Out* in *Lesbian News*, this is fiction that is "permeated by, yet not focused solely on, lesbian coming-out, coupledom, and identity." Martinac creates characters, narrators, and heroines "whose lesbianism does not need to be justified, whose identity does not need to be sought, whose sexuality does not need to be proclaimed." Instead, the characters' sexual orientation becomes "the mode through which [the character] makes connection both with her history and with her inmost self."

The stories in *Voyages Out* include "Mineola, Mineola," a humorous tale with much pathos about a young woman's coming out and her confusion of great sex with long-distance love; "The Tenants," where an Italian-American landlady grieving her dead sister rents the sibling's apartment to two women, a lesbian couple that later break up; "Strangers in the Night," about a father visiting his lesbian daughter for the first time after his wife dies and the strain and acceptance that goes on between them; "Cysters," where the stresses in a lesbian's life seem to manifest in an ovarian cyst; "Like Mother, Like . . . ," a touching tale about a conservative straight daughter who just doesn't understand her progressive lesbian mother's life; "A Matter of Convenience," where the narrator just can't continue with an affair any longer because not being in love with the other woman makes her "too sad"; "Sex among the Bukovacs," a charming and amusing story about how sex is (or mostly is *not*) talked about in the Bukovac family, and the intersection of this silence with one daughter's coming out to them; and the final piece, "Shelter," where a homeless woman walks into the office of a feminist collective newspaper and throws into sharp relief the chasm that exists sometimes between well-meaning politics and the harsh realities of people's lives.

Roy Olson, in a review of *Voyages Out* appearing in *Booklist*, describes Martinac as a writer who "limn[s] the experiences of ordinary people [more often than not, *lesbian* people] in simple, unpretentious prose" and who writes of "the emotional politics between family members." It's true: Martinac's characters in this collection explore their relationships both with their lovers and with their families. And the family—in terms of its acceptance or non-acceptance of a mother's/daughter's/sibling's sexual orientation, as well as its meaning and dynamics in and of itself—is another of Martinac's conspicuous themes.

The genesis of *The One You Call Sister: New Women's Fiction*, which Martinac conceived of, proposed to a publisher, and edited, came from trying to make sense of her relationship to her own biological sisters in her fiction. Martinac had finished the story "Kay, Grown Up"—an autobiographical account of Martinac's older sister who used to create miniromance novelettes but, because she was the "pretty" one, went on to become a mother and housewife as the family had preordained—and was looking for other fiction to read about sisters and their relationships. After a serious search of published work, Martinac found "very little in the way of non-fiction and even less in terms of fiction" (Introduction, *The One You Call Sister* 8). She decided to develop the anthology she could not find herself, and proposed the idea to Cleis Press (whose anthologies she had always admired). Cleis liked the idea and accepted it without any stories in hand.

In her introduction to *The One You Call Sister*, Martinac chronicles her motivation for compiling the book:

[My two older sisters] have had a profound influence on me and what I have made of my life, and this is what led me to this anthology.

A few years ago, someone suggested to me that sisters, perhaps more than mothers, are the prototypes for our relationships with other women as friends and lovers, because they are our first female peers. The more I thought about it, the more it made sense for me as a lesbian and a feminist and the more I became interested in what other women had to say about their experiences with their sisters. (7)

The anthology, in addition to being the only one of its kind (i.e., contemporary fiction about biological sisters), contained a wide-ranging and emotionally moving series of stories, and consequently was extremely well received. To her credit, the anthology exhibits Martinac's talents as a reader and editor as well as a writer, and displays her commitment to feminist issues while insisting on an inclusive multicultural participation in the dialogue.

CRITICAL RECEPTION

As other writers have voiced, and readers of this anthology are likely to surmise, having a wider audience or a burgeoning gay and lesbian publishing industry does not ensure expanded critical attention for the lesbian writer, particularly from mainstream channels. Although Martinac's work has been well received and well reviewed in the gay and lesbian, feminist, and alternative press, her collection of short stories, novel, and anthology—like the vast majority of lesbian authors and works—has attracted, at best, only moderate non-gay mainstream attention.

And this is so even given Martinac's 1990 Lambda Literary Award for *Out of Time* for Best Lesbian Fiction—a prestigious honor in the lesbian and gay writing community. Moreover, *Out of Time* was also a finalist for the 1990 Gay and Lesbian Book Award of the American Library Association, and *Voyages Out* was a finalist for the 1989 Lambda Literary Award for Best Lesbian Debut.

What non-gay attention Martinac has garnered has come mostly from the feminist and alternative press in terms of reviews, but it should also be mentioned that both *Publishers Weekly* (the bible of the mainstream publishing world) and *Booklist* (another must-read for mainstream book buyers) carried reviews of both *Voyages Out* and *Out of Time*.

In general, the reviews of Martinac's work have been positive, although perhaps more so from the gay and lesbian press and/or women reviewers. One suspects, however, following a closer comparison of all the criticism generated regarding her books, that this reaction is more reflective of reviewers' individual appreciation of femaleness or lesbianism rather than any real dispute about the quality of Martinac's work. That is, mainstream reviewers and/or male reviewers, even while commending the quality or the sincerity of the writing, tend not to *celebrate* this work—and its quiet championing of lesbians and their lives (as well as their desires for each other) as normal and deserving of being the fulcrum of plot and narrative—as much as lesbian or gay, feminist, or women reviewers do.

And that intriguing observation has as much to say about the state of the world in general as it does about any one person's—or, more specifically, any one lesbian writer's—body of work.

BIBLIOGRAPHY

Works by Paula Martinac

"The Good Daughter." *Forum: A Journal for Lesbians* (1983): 14, 23–27.
"Like Mother, Like. . . . " *We Are Everywhere: Writings by and about Lesbian Parents*. Ed. Harriet Alpert. Freedom, CA: Crossing Press, 1988. 70–82.
"The Tenants." *Conditions* 15 (1988): 36–39.
"Kay, Grown Up." *The One You Call Sister: New Women's Fiction*. Ed. Martinac. Pittsburgh: Cleis Press, 1989. 19–25.
"Little Flower: A Love Story." *Binnewater Tides*. Rosedale, NY: Binnewater Tides, 1989. n. pag.
"Mineola, Mineola." *Sinister Wisdom* 38 (1989): 100–105.
The One You Call Sister: New Women's Fiction. Ed. Martinac. Pittsburgh: Cleis Press, 1989.
Voyages Out 1: Lesbian Short Fiction. Stories by Paula Martinac and Carla Tomaso. Seattle: Seal Press, 1989.
"Heroines." *Conditions* 17 (1990): 50–54.
Out of Time. Seattle: Seal Press, 1990.
"Pitching Woo." *Queer City: The Portable Lower East Side*. New York: Portable Lower East Side, 1991. 23–30.
Beards, novel in progress (Dec. 1992).
Home Movies. Seattle: Seal Press, 1993.

Studies of Paula Martinac

Galst, Liz. "Everyday Lesbians." *Women's Review of Books* 7:4 (January 1990): 11.
Minkowitz, Donna. "Ghost Writing." *Village Voice* Oct. 30, 1990.
Roth, Patricia. "Sisters and Other Courageous Women." *Gay Community News* January 14–20, 1990.
Smith, Kennedy. "Paula Martinac's Engrossing Ghost Story *Out of Time*." *Washington Blade* Oct. 19, 1990: 37.

VICKI P. McCONNELL (1949–)

Sharon Silvas

BIOGRAPHY

From the Kansas heartland that sprouts wheat and tornadoes comes Vicki P. McConnell, born in 1949. She insisted on reading at age four, especially stories about animals, soldiers, and athletes.

Childhood with one older sister was centered in Hays, Kansas, where McConnell's mother worked at the city library and Old Fort Hays blockhouse (favorite haunts that McConnell has used in her novels) and for nineteen years in the registrar's office of Fort Hays Kansas State University (FHKSU). Her father taught physical education and coached football at FHKSU. Vicki had bad luck riding bikes (a brain concussion) but a flair for the theatre (star of "Gay Bunny," second grade).

In high school, McConnell and her best friend formed an early literary contract—to create eleven original pieces of writing. She had bad luck with musical instruments (pushed down a flight of stairs atop a cello) but good luck with acting (Best Character Actress, Best Thespian). In her senior year (1967), McConnell completed her first novel, *The Goddess Dies* (unpublished), and *Teen Life* published her first poem.

At FHKSU, she searched for the Bohemian spark, belonging to the writers' group "The Passionate Few," winning a Best Actress award, adapting Flannery O'Connor's "Greenleaf" for the stage, serving as president of Alpha Psi Omega drama fraternity and making the Dean's List. In 1971, she received a bachelor's degree in theatre with a minor in English. After a year of teaching high school in Grainfield, Kansas, she moved to Oklahoma City.

In that incarnation, McConnell worked for a single-rig oil driller, and her lesbian life was centered in the bars. But the Goddess works Her mysteries, politicizing even bar dykes—McConnell became president of the Gay Community Alliance and edited its newspaper, the *Oklahoma Gaily*. She also appeared in a television news profile of Oklahoma lesbians and marched in her first gay pride parade, nationally televised from Dallas in 1973.

In 1974, McConnell moved to Denver, Colorado, "to follow love, of course" (unless otherwise noted, all quotations are from personal communication with the author). For the next fifteen years with the Rockies as a backdrop, she wrote in venues both gay and straight. She published poetry, short stories, and book/movie reviews in national gay publications including *Lesbian Tide*, *Furies*, *Big Mama Rag*, *Dinah*, *Motheroot*, *Leaping Lesbians*, and *Guide Magazine*. She belonged to Diana's Grove feminist collective and the Feminist Writers Guild, and she wrote and produced three original lesbian comedies. She edited the Denver-chapter NOW newsletter for a year, won seven regional and three international petroleum-industry newsletter editing awards, developed original seminar training materials on "Women in Petroleum," and wrote for *Colorado Woman News*.

At the age of twenty-nine, McConnell published *Berrigan* under the pseudonym Gingerlox. The book captures the innocent fervor of "whizzing from one political powwow to another, full of change-the-world energy" (161) and is a coming-out tale that imitated her own. Over the next two years, she wrote *Passengers*, an unpublished novel deemed by one reviewer as "too ponderous." In 1982, *Mrs. Porter's Letter* introduced investigative reporter Nyla Wade; the book is based on a short story that Sarah Aldridge suggested McConnell turn into a novel. McConnell then developed a series with this character in *The Burnton Widows* (1984) and *Double Daughter* (1988). Claim the words, change the people—McConnell used feminist spellings of *womon* and *womyn* in the latter novel. Her lesbian feminist sleuth was among the first in the now-loaded contemporary mystery genre. Nyla Wade followed on the heels of M. F. Beal's Kat Guerera (*Angel Dance*, 1977) and Eve Zaremba's Helen Keremos (*A Reason to Kill*, 1978) and appeared well before Katherine Forrest's Kate Delafield (*Amateur City*, 1984).

After ghosting the autobiography in 1986 of an oil entrepreneur ("a real life Alexis Carrington"), McConnell became assistant editor for two plastics-industry trade magazines. She has won four of the publisher's EEE (Edgell Editorial Excellence) Gold Writing Awards as well as the ABCD (Above and Beyond the Call of Duty) Award as project editor in 1988. In 1989, she moved to Los Angeles as senior field editor, and in 1992, to Seattle. McConnell is a member of Sisters in Crime, a regular contributor to the *Advocate* and *Square Peg* magazines, a copy editor of novels for several lesbian publishers, and a free-lance copy writer.

MAJOR WORKS AND THEMES

As a young reader, McConnell observed that "male characters did all the power adventuring." As a young dyke, her embrace of feminism gave her new understanding and definition of power—a connection to the female, lesbian self that allowed her to fully claim her voice as a writer and create women in her fiction whose power adventures exceed anything the Hardy Boys or Ernest Hemingway could envision. In her four novels, women save each other from the danger of ignorance and violence. They discover and claim their lesbianism as a positive reality, as a wondrous way of loving. They challenge patriarchal heterosexist authority—individually and at the highest order—the law of the straight world's land. They refuse to be silenced.

This expression of the resilient universal lesbian voice is at the core of McConnell's writing. If "a man is as good as his word," McConnell has gender bent this male tenet with novels that pivot upon the power of words—as *women* write them and prove the essence of their character in letters, love poetry, journals, and newspaper articles. Words that record the truth and affirm gay identity are characters in these novels, consistent symbols of power, perhaps even weapons.

In *Mrs. Porter's Letter*, a single-page flier, written by women, routs out a murderous pimp. The written history of a castle built and owned by lesbians in *The Burnton Widows* costs three gay people their lives. Reporter Nyla Wade ruthlessly turns the pen into a sword, smiting out harbingers of homophobia and misogyny. Evil even shows itself as a pen stabbed into an oak desktop by an enraged man striking out where women have shared their words of love. In *Double Daughter*, the words are simple and violent, written on bricks used to gay bash: OUTLAW LEZ TEACHERS and FAG BUSTERS. The implication in McConnell's attachment to the words we write and say and hear in a homophobic world is that every word counts; each demands that we listen and be careful; there is a price for taking on lies or for telling them. She believes our words are our legacy.

There is also a reach for lyrical prose in McConnell's work, a penchant for poetic imagery. Her first successes were as a poet, so it is no wonder poetry is the underpinning of her fiction. Her characters are often poets (Berrigan, Pat Stevens in *Double Daughter*, Joan Ruddye in *The Burnton Widows*). McConnell's own college poet's collective, "The Passionate Few," appears in two of her novels, but poets are not always the good guys. Witness Arthur Quaid in *Mrs. Porter's Letter*. Nyla says of him, "It seemed fitting that a man who called Gertrude Stein and Mary Daly rhetoric writers would also have to title his sonnets only a *Semblance of Love*" (80). Nor are her poets stodgy academes; professor Marty Evans's lover in *Double Daughter* pens the poetry book titled *White Boys in Love*.

McConnell's characters are partially revealed through poetry (even in Cybil Porter's lyrical letters) or guided by it, as Nyla is on her journey to Burnton, Oregon, and throughout *Double Daughter*.

In 1979, McConnell self-published *Sense You*, a chapbook of eighteen poems she dubbed "erotica politica." The images juxtapose classic and modern Amazons and their words "spelled out with my tongue, laid upon the bosom of a flower, naked on the half shell'' (2) and ''grown as nipples that dapple the underside of the moon'' (6). Poet Chocolate Waters said succinctly of the collection, ''Finally you wrote some wet poems'' (12).

There is an element of translation required in poetry that McConnell extends into the character of Nyla Wade. Her translation of the layered meanings in poems and other words written and spoken ultimately solves crimes in which she is involved. She must decode the peculiar language of Ritchie Dennis and Mitch Masters in *The Burnton Widows* and the clues in the automatic writing from psychic Gladdie Aimwell in *Double Daughter*. In this aspect of the character and the resolution of the mystery plots, McConnell proves that the weapon of words can bring justice.

While the poetry in McConnell's novels is uneven, it is used as a form of connection, often between lovers. Here appears the softer power of words, strength shown through sensuality, vulnerability, sentiment. No surprise, since feminist poets were McConnell's early mentors: Audre Lorde, Adrienne Rich, and Rita Mae Brown's ''The Self Affirms Herself.''

Both McConnell and her characters do just that—Brown's poem epitomizes McConnell's narrative perspective. This theme of self-affirmation begins awkwardly though directly in *Berrigan* but gains sophistication throughout the three mysteries. The interaction of women in the novels suggests our most important job is to discover and mirror the best in ourselves and in each other. The result of this action within the individual soul can create a community of strong supportive women capable of taking powerful action together. Power begets itself and can be shared—with selected gay men and straight friends (a philosophical line that is politically correct or incorrect depending upon the reader).

McConnell's fiction feeds the spirit. We share herstory and the process of an evolving present. We second-wave feminists can see the way we've changed—moving, integrating, turning the edge of anger into insight—as McConnell herself does in the growth of her style over the course of these novels. As Natalie Goldberg puts it in *Wild Mind*, ''style comes from the inside; it is personally imbued'' (13). There is an irrepressible hopefulness and humor imbued in McConnell's images that eventually loses its naivete and is replaced by irony and wisdom. This sea change involves us; we feel the struggle and the victory.

For even as Berrigan must suffer the greatest losses, she still refuses to be vanquished, still welcomes the opening of her own spirit and the pain of love. And even when Nyla Wade finds love and moves through the difficulties of intimacy, she refuses complacency. As she trades the fuel of raw anger for the greater fuel of spirit in a new way of ''knowing,'' she stays wary. She values her karmic friends as her true family, but knows time is not endless for us anymore. The world is still a scary and unsafe place for women. Nyla knows there is still much to be done.

McConnell's characters endure: her women love each other, moving their soft and strong shoulders, tugging hair tender and persistent, taking and urging and sometimes losing each other and invariably coming to the rescue with a two-by-four through the door.

Read in chronology, McConnell's books show an evolution of the author's craft, spirit, and self. Likewise her characters, who gain in complexity, build community, refine their subtleties, and keep on courageously risk taking, setting boundaries, and breaking barriers to empower themselves and define life as ever more possible. Read in whatever order, this work is the real stuff of power adventures.

CRITICAL RECEPTION

McConnell's work has been reviewed almost exclusively by the gay press, which in the main finds her books exactly as intended: woman inspiring and spirit affirming. Alden Waitt in *off our backs* wrote that Nyla Wade is "an intelligent, credible, and life-sized woman who discovers herself while she solves a mystery. Treat yourself to a memorable mystery with a modern, original heroine." Nancy Walker of *Gay Community News* mentioned McConnell's "deliciously intricate" plots and subplots, while Joyce Bright in *the Advocate* called Wade "the upbeat female voice of Dashiell Hammett." Vic Ramstetter proclaimed in *Dinah* that "Nyla Wade is Lesbiana's answer to Miss Marple." *Plexus* called *Mrs. Porter's Letter* "mystery at its best, women at their best, a wonderfully funny, fast-paced novel of suspense." And Jesse Monteagudo of the *Weekly News* said "Nyla Wade is worthy to stand beside Joseph Hansens's gay male investigator David Brandstetter."

Of *The Burnton Widows*, Pat Wilson wrote in the *Baltimore Gay Paper* that "never before has there been a detective like Nyla Wade, a journalist with bulldog tenacity and inquisitiveness, and a real lesbian." And Stephanie Gotlob in *Gay Community News* wrote "Mystery lovers rejoice, Nyla Wade is back! *The Burnton Widows* is multifaceted, multidimensional, with excitement, murder, and intrigue . . . leaves its readers anxiously awaiting the third book."

Lee Dangerouse reviewed *Double Daughter* in Ft. Lauderdale's *The Inform Her* as a book written

with a persistence that political conscience and mystery need not be mutually exclusive. Nyla Wade is not of the tough-and-clever P.I. ilk, nor the wordly-wise police detective type. She is softer, valuing love that requires some work, justice that is never easy, and friendship that may demand putting her own life on the line. Still, she forces the barriers of prejudice by asking the critical questions.

In *Bad Attitude*, critic Nina Freed said *Double Daughter* is "well written if a bit TOO politically correct. Although I admit there is something appealing about the word WOMON with its two O's wide and open . . . despite its lack of sex scenes, *Double Daughter* is able to convey a sensuousness that lingers long after the novel ends." And Jesse Monteagudo suggested the writing in this novel shows "how it's done—down to the inclusion of gay male characters and the obligatory (though not forced) phobic villain."

Kathleen Maio criticized McConnell's grasp of genre elements and "love scenes obsessing on vulval, vaginal, and breast imagery" but said readers "may appreciate a mystery that not only validates but celebrates lesbian history and lifestyle."

In its first printing, *Berrigan* played to mixed reviews, as seen in these comments: "slow in places and with the air of a first novel that makes the reader wince" (Peggy Durham, *Sister Advocate*) and "a well-written book about a woman's search for herself" (Melora Miller, *Empty Closet*). Joyce Bright called *Berrigan* "funny, sad, and instructive" in *Mom, Guess What!*, while Debra Dragovich of *New Women's Times* proclaimed it "probably the best from Naiad" (in 1979). And in *Dinah*, Paula Ellen Hinds wrote, "The book is a word sculpture of a woman giving birth to herself—the creation is painful, joyous, sensual, and real."

In *Motheroot Journal*, Andrea Chesman blasted Naiad for bad jacket copy and editing on *Berrigan*, while Jeanne Bowles in *Plexus* simply trashed the book. In the *Washington Blade*, Janice Eklund called the characters "one dimensional and the plot compensatively overdeveloped" but also added that "the pace is good, the construction tight if somewhat overblown, and overall the novel is genuinely amusing. Gingerlox could be a really fine writer some day. She is certainly worth watching." More balanced reviews appeared in *Big Mama Rag* by Sandia Belgrade and in *off our backs* by Chocolate Waters.

In the Afterword that appears in the 1990 edition of *Berrigan*, Denver attorney and comedienne Katie O'Brien reprised her reaction to McConnell's first novel twelve years after its original printing: "I felt like a river had been put through a quarter-inch pipe. Here is poetry and unpredictability. Here are our foremothers as well as our stereotypes, fleshed out with all their contradictions" (162).

All of McConnell's novels have appeared on best-seller lists, from *St. Elmos' OUT* to *Small Press Review, ClaireLight, Washington Blade, Sojourner,* and *Category Six. Double Daughter* was nominated for the American Library Association's Best Books for Young Adults list.

BIBLIOGRAPHY

Works by Vicki P. McConnell

Berrigan. Tallahassee, FL: Naiad Press, 1978.
Sense You. Denver, CO: Gena Rose Press, 1979.
Mrs. Porter's Letter. Tallahassee, FL: Naiad Press, 1982.
The Burnton Widows. Tallahassee, FL: Naiad Press, 1984.
Double Daughter. Tallahassee, FL: Naiad Press, 1988.
"Slicks." *Erotic Naiad.* Tallahassee, FL: Naiad Press, 1992.

Studies of Vicki P. McConnell

Dunbar, Jill, and Catherine Sapinsky. "Nancy Drew for Grownups." *Ms.* April 1985: 101–104.

Maio, Kathleen. "Murder in Print." *Wilson Library Bulletin* September 1984: 54–55.

Reddy, Maureen T. "Lesbian Detectives." *Sisters In Crime.* New York: Continuum, 1988. 121–146.

Rich, B. Ruby. "The Lady Dicks." *Village Voice Literary Supplement* June 1989: 24–25.

Zimmerman, Bonnie. *The Safe Sea of Women.* Boston: Beacon Press, 1990. 160–161.

JUDITH McDANIEL (1943–   )
Roberta Hobson

BIOGRAPHY

Judith McDaniel began her path to "becoming the person [she] always wanted to be" as a military daughter at Ft. Sam Houston in San Antonio, Texas, on November 9, 1943 (telephone interview, February 17, 1992; unless otherwise indicated, all quotes are from the interview). Her mother, whom Judith describes as "extraordinary," provided her with a comfortable, happy childhood. Attentive and loving, she was also her girl scout leader and confidante who remained in the home until Judith's first year of college, when she returned to teaching. She inspired Judith with a sense of adventure, teaching her to play "splits" with jackknives, not only a dangerous game, but atypical of mother-daughter lessons. As a teenager in Europe, Judith, inspired by her mother, had "tremendous opportunities and did some rather extraordinary wilderness things."

Judith's father provided a regimented military life. He was absent for most of her infancy, and meeting him in 1946 provided one of her earliest memories. Although she describes military life as "contained, predictable and safe" (*Sanctuary* 33), she moved twenty-one times before college. This mobility forged Judith's close relationship with her two younger sisters as they were growing up. When she moved, she recalls, "I always took my friends with me." Because many childhood friendships were ended abruptly, in later life friends became very important to her. "I go a long ways to hold onto them," she says.

McDaniel denies feeling isolated in the military life. Rather, her mobile childhood provided diverse experiences that benefited her. Yet she admits she remained sheltered from worldly conflicts. Experiences fairly atypical for girls occurred: she learned to spit and ride a horse western style at various air force bases. However, she "never had a childhood friend of a different race." Her high school years were spent in Germany, where she "never met a European person, never learned a word of the language, never stepped off the base and into a foreign culture" (Ibid).

In this sheltered environment, Judith McDaniel did not discover her adult identity. In the pre-college years McDaniel did not identify as a lesbian, but she feels that her childhood experiences contributed to that identity as an adult.

I learned to do things on my own . . . I was encouraged by my parents to travel alone when I was fifteen, sixteen, and seventeen. Sometimes that was really scary . . . they essentially let me test the waters and I think that I have had a sense of security about myself and about who I am, and the OK-ness that came from that.

At age seventeen (1960), McDaniel attended an International Girl Scout event that she describes as "a fabulous experience." For the first time, she was part of something larger than herself. Scouting, too, empowered her. There were thousands of young women, and she likens it to the Michigan Women's Music Festival: a kind of female utopian community, albeit temporary.

I remember a lot of mud. It rained for days. Women mud wrestled with one another. I met the Queen of Denmark, and Lady Baden-Powell, wife of the founder of the Boy Scouts. She was an incredible old woman, and at sixteen, I could even then appreciate her. The epiphany was the moment when we were five thousand, winding with flags on a march through the stadium and the sense of the line-up going on and on and on filing past the Queen of Denmark.

Her sense of solidarity and empowerment resonates in the retelling. The following year McDaniel "testified" to her experience in an article based on this event for the national magazine *Girl Scout Leader*. It was published in 1961, the year she began college.

After attending Exeter University in England as an undergraduate, McDaniel enrolled in Antioch College, where she received her B.A. degree (1966). At Northeastern University she earned her M.A. (1968), and her Ph.D. from Tufts University (1975). Her dissertation was entitled "Fettered Wings Half Loose: Female Development in the Victorian Novel: Charlotte Brontë, Elizabeth Gaskell, George Eliot."

Ironically, her decision to be a literary critic was not born from a love of other people's writing; rather it developed from McDaniel's inability to speak in her own voice.

When I was in fourth grade, I started writing stories, I loved writing . . . I don't know why I stopped . . . but I did. I tried to write again in high school . . . in college . . . in graduate school, I tried to write both poems, stories, and plays. It was just not successful— I wasn't able to do it. What happened was that I became a professor of literature so that I could discuss what other people wrote, instead of writing my own. It wasn't until I came out as a lesbian that I was able to start writing again.

Finding her own voice as a lesbian allowed McDaniel to become a writer. In 1975–76 she began publishing her first work in lesbian journals, *Sinister Wisdom* and *Conditions* among them. In 1978 McDaniel and Maureen Brady founded Spinsters Ink, an alternative lesbian-feminist publishing house based in Argyle, New York. Both had work they could not publish in the commercial world. During this time McDaniel taught at many universities, mostly in the northeastern United States. She experienced tenure denial as an assistant professor at Skidmore College (1975–82). Its effect was profound, but liberating: "I've been fired for a lot of years now . . . I have published about a book every other year since I was fired." McDaniel says that the academy controlled her creativity. "I couldn't have written most of my books in that environment . . . I certainly would never go back to academe as a full-time tenure-track person." Since 1982, McDaniel has also continued to teach. She teaches literature and creative and technical writing as adjunct faculty at several community and state colleges. She also instructs at Greatmeadow Correctional Facility (University Without Walls) and at another maximum security prison for men.

MAJOR WORKS AND THEMES

The denial of tenure at Skidmore College was a turning point in McDaniel's life. Not only was it a consequence of finding her voice as a lesbian writer, but it marked the beginning of a personal journey of recovery and self-discovery. Writing served as the means for analysis, expression, and reflection. Personal issues of loss, risk, control, and the desire to "fix things" are ubiquitous and recurrent themes in her search for self-knowledge.

For example, her mother's death (1978) was the subject of *Elegy; from a hill in Hebron* (1979–80), a booklet of six short poems of quiet and loving memory. Still waters soon erupted in grief and angry questions that became the grist for *November Woman* (1983). Conflicting emotions are metaphorically expressed in stark visualizations. In the poem "Speaking Bitterness; to my sister," McDaniel is tangled with resentment in a push-pull struggle with a needy younger sister, "you the one she wanted . . . the baby . . . we could afford" (15). As an adult, her sister, in trouble with heroin, pleaded to McDaniel to be protector and mother. *November Woman* seeks boundaries and examines the skirmishes between her and her sister. She also examines her relationship with her mother, a relationship that she cannot relinquish. "She was fifty-nine, and I was not ready to lose her. I was drinking; I was not able to mourn her death until several years later when I stopped drinking. I moved through it, without feeling it."

McDaniel's first novel, *Winter Passage* (1984), embodies her coming out and the consequences of exploring and voicing this in academic writing. The three female characters are Anna, a Ph.D teaching in a Vermont college who is fired because the chair of the literature department dislikes her lesbian-feminist poetry; Elizabeth, who turns away from a potential relationship with Anna because she is afraid to leave the protection of patriarchal society; and Clair, wife and mother, a people pleaser who always rationalizes avoiding her own creativity as a painter. McDaniel says, "All three of those characters were important parts of myself and my experiences." Although McDaniel was two years into the Alcoholics Anonymous (AA) Twelve-Step recovery process at the time *Winter Passage* was published, her own alcoholism remained a silence. She was just beginning to face the earth-shattering changes that recovery demanded.

McDaniel began writing poems for *Metamorphosis: Reflections on Recovery* in 1983, although the collection was not published until 1987. Her conscious struggle for sobriety began (unsuccessfully) in the summer of 1977 with her decision not to drink for thirty days. It took more than four years to make it to day two. The pain and emptiness of sobriety in the first year is recorded in poems like "The Doe" and "The Descent," which describe the physical addiction. *Metamorphosis* is McDaniel's personal journey through hell to a self-crafted peaceful place. It is also a critique and interpretation of the AA's Twelve-Step program, which remains her tool for sobriety. *Metamorphosis* is, in many ways, McDaniel's most important and difficult work; it enabled her to face herself, perhaps for the first time.

I knew I wanted to live honestly, and that the alcohol wasn't letting me do that. I lied to my lover about having an affair for a year, and basically that was devastating to me. I'm a person who was raised by my mother to value the truth and be an honest and open person, and I was not able to live up to that. Recovery did not make me a different person; my values remained the same—only now I could live up to them. That's what I mean by becoming the person I always wanted to be.

Reading *Metamorphosis*, one can easily identify with McDaniel's metaphors for loss—descriptions of amputation and feelings of powerlessness, her explanation of ego death, and women's profound alienation. McDaniel explores addictions, to which lesbians, first as women and then in relationships with other women, are particularly vulnerable. She believes statistics claiming that one in three lesbians is alcoholic or addicted. "Alcoholism is a stress-related disease. I had a genetic predisposition, my father is an alcoholic, my grandfather was, but I also know that I drank myself into my alcoholism . . . trying to first hide as a lesbian and then trying to be open as a lesbian and deal with the repercussions of that" (21). McDaniel is quick to point out that while she was growing up, theirs was a teetotalling family; she never saw her father drink until after her mother died.

In her last several years of drinking, "there were a lot of flashpoints." These included

tenure at Skidmore, attempting to develop myself as a creative writer, and take that risk, moving into the national lesbian community and working on a national level with my professional organization the Modern Language Association, and with Spinsters press.

McDaniel believes the alcohol blunted her senses and efforts:

In many ways the alcohol kept me from knowing how dangerous what I was doing was—
and it kept me from doing it as well as I might have done it—and it certainly kept Maureen
[her lover of eight years] and me from developing our relationship.

She had to desire sanity and then surrender to turn away from addiction. AA
demands profound changes and counsels one to turn it over to God. For McDaniel
that "huge leap of faith" was defined as nature. She resurrected childhood
strengths: "I have always found my spirit life in nature. I still do. I believe in
an inspirited universe, I'm not a monotheist, I'm not an atheist, I'm a polytheist."

McDaniel would like to "fix" AA's patriarchal language and ideology. She
reinterpreted it for herself, and uncovered its purpose for other women as well.
Its power "was reminiscent of the 1960's consciousness raising groups. Finding
out that you weren't alone" (*Metamorphosis* 23). She speaks of alcoholism as
a gift. It gave her "the understanding to connect to another's experience" (Ibid).
Her belief "that hope is somehow embedded in the most despairing of circumstances" (Ibid) is apparent in her determination to help heal her own.

Witnessing the despair of others and putting her own life at risk is the subject
of *Sanctuary: A Journey* (1987). It is a book of poetry and vignettes about
making connections, taking action, finding safe places and, ultimately, learning
the value of risk taking. Witnessing the Women's Peace Encampment at the
Seneca Army Depot protest in 1983, she remarks, "I learned most when I was
dragged kicking and screaming through some of the most painful experiences
of my life . . . certainly going to Nicaragua was one" (*Sanctuary* 28). *Sanctuary*
records McDaniel's journey to Nicaragua in August 1985, as a Witness for Peace
delegate, where she was captured by the Contra rebels and held captive in the
jungle for twenty-nine hours.

McDaniel worked to create "safe places" in the United States by "witnessing"
and telling the story of the sanctuary movement. It grew out of a "new underground railroad" harboring and transporting refugees from Nicaragua and Guatemala after the 1980 Salvadoran government imposed a state of siege on that
country and mass killings began. She acted as a "monitor," seeing and telling
of the torture and mutilation. She began to realize the importance of "witnessing
when the reality of the lived experience is denied by the culture at large" (128–
29). She analogized it to the experiences of women being denied or ignored in
her own patriarchal culture. The "war zones" of Nicaragua raised McDaniel's
consciousness to the "war zones" in her own country. *Sanctuary* also documents
the struggle of the Hopi and Navajo Indians of the Southwest to retain their
lands against government-backed business.

For McDaniel the discomfort of physical risks involved in witnessing is secondary to the benefits gained from heartfelt connections.

Witnessing forces me to see my life more clearly. Recently, I went to Guatemala and
did some work with families of refugees here, that I almost couldn't do because I was
terrified—not physically. It was seeing the aged mother of a young man who had had to

flee for his life and having her know that I had been with her son and have her touch my arm over and over again, and say Herardo's name and cry . . . that kind of thing— those are not comfortable places for me.

McDaniel wrestles with intimacy in her most recent writing. Her newest novel, *Just Say Yes*, parallels her current quests for self-knowledge. McDaniel is currently in a year-old relationship that she considers a marriage. For years prior, her life had been an interweaving of a variety of friendships. Only in this relationship with Jan has that pattern shifted toward deep intimacy with one person. This new intimacy is reflected in both the direction and content of her work. "I don't do my work without the support of my intimate relationship. It is the fabric of my life." In her prose, McDaniel now explores intimacy and sexuality.

Just Say Yes (1991) is a novel set in Provincetown, Cape Cod, Massachusetts— a summertime mecca for lesbians and gays. Between snippets of feminist theory and interjections of social issues, McDaniel's characters breeze through summer romances on the dunes. The mesh of political activism and steamy sex is sometimes awkward. For McDaniel this book was about "what limits you could take, and break . . . sexual content was the risk I took . . . I was curious to see what turned people on, what was exciting to me."

Lindsay, the main character, is a graduate student who works nights in Provincetown waiting tables. Her days are spent cruising the beach, and in her after-work hours, she indulges in sexual adventures that test her previous limits. By book's end, she is in a serious relationship.

In *Never Say Never*, a sequel to *Just Say Yes*, Judith McDaniel will continue to explore sexuality, but the focus will be elsewhere. "It will be a light-hearted funny romance. . . . The focus may be faith issues." Her major characters will find relationships in the beginning of the book, reflecting her own "married" reality. She will bring back Rachael and the Unitarian minister from *Just Say Yes*. This time the threesome's focus will be their sense of family.

In *Just Say Yes*, McDaniel advocates practicing new behaviors until they become familiar. She also addresses hiding behind masks to explore, practice, and grow into these new behaviors. Incrementally, McDaniel's writings have served both to mask and to give voice to her own personal growth. Expressing her innermost fears in art makes inner exploration bearable. Writing is safer than doing, she explains: "The explosions and flying shrapnel of our emotional lives are not usually fatal in art" (*Inversions* 128–29).

Her focus on social/cultural themes reemerges in *Home Tales* (1991), a play that examines the plight of the homeless. Currently, McDaniel is working on a novel set in Central America for which she will seek a commercial press. Additionally, she hopes to publish a novel for young adults about a teenage alcoholic. This story, *First Tries Don't Always Work*, is a composite of young alcoholics McDaniel has worked with. A chapter from it appears in the anthology

Out From Under: Sober Dykes and Our Friends (1986), edited by Jean Swallow and published by Spinsters Ink.

When we spoke in February 1992, McDaniel was no longer active in Witness for Peace, though she was still involved with the Fellowship of Recovering Alcoholics. She has been working with the Feminist Action Network, which she helped found several years ago. They are women of color and white women who work on local issues doing anti-racist and anti-homophobia training. She and Jan recently relocated from Albany, New York, to Tucson, Arizona.

CRITICAL RECEPTION

McDaniel's political writings appeal to didactic themes in critics' eyes. Sheila Collins in *New Directions for Women* is reverent in her review of *Sanctuary*. She gives high praise for McDaniel's self-discovery and process of "self-disclosure." McDaniel's book, she writes, is "a valuable guide to the wisdom that is essential to the spiritual salvation of North Americans" (17). In the *Women's Review of Books*, Margaret Randall is less emotive but similarly appreciative of McDaniel's personal quest. "McDaniel's sources are recovery from alcoholism, an insistence on breaking through the disinformation barrier . . . feminism, solidarity, internationalism, spirituality, a desperate quest for peace, the circle of witness and an ear to the earth" (5–6). Karen Anderson, in *National Woman's Studies Association Journal*, is also enthusiastic although somewhat critical. *Sanctuary* is "an illuminating discussion of the multiple meanings of sanctuary . . . and finds connections between sexuality and the politics of war and peace." Anderson says McDaniel lacks analysis; in noting the importance of lesbian feminists in the Women's Peace Encampment, McDaniel "does not analyze the reasons for this or its implications for the definition of a feminist pacifism . . . she noted the centrality of homophobia to community hostility to the demonstration but did not analyze the connections between sexual politics and militarism" (127).

Winter Passage, "an elegant novel," portrays the growth of friendship between characters with "subtlety and surprise . . . . McDaniel's poetic eye is especially acute in descriptions of light and land," says Valerie Miner in *Woman's Review of Books*. She finds McDaniel's literary control the "ultimate limitation of the book." She wished to see more spontaneous process in daily living. "Analysis outweighs action, [it] is occasionally like eaves-dropping in a therapy session." Miner finds *Winter Passage* "too tightly contained"; she wants a "longer roomier story in which the characters and readers could dance around" (12–13). Similar criticisms were voiced about *Just Say Yes*. Sue Rochman in the *Ithaca Times* praises the blending of the personal and the political: "There is tasty, well-written sex, not mere allusions to sexual fulfillment . . . a welcome change from the typical lesbian romance." Although Rochman praises McDaniel for placing murder in a romance novel and bringing the reality of gay and lesbian lives into the forefront, she says that the treatment of "political issues—racism, classism, hetero-sexism—is, at times, ingratiating.'' As a result of McDaniel's not wanting to leave any type of lesbian out, sometimes ''it seems a bit too forced'' (12). Donna Minkowitz in the *Village Voice* congratulates McDaniel for producing the best of ''trash'' reading, ''a prime specimen of voluptuous snack-fare that almost out-classes itself.'' At first Minkowitz found the anti-gay hate crime ''unsettling; it felt like my boss had called and asked me to work on my vacation.'' However, McDaniel is successful at ''absorbing such a weighty subject.'' Unlike Rochman, she finds that ''the murder thrills and hot sex are never lost in the redeeming social value.'' Critics and the reading public alike look forward to McDaniel's upcoming publications, which they expect to maintain McDaniel's thoughtfulness, adventuresomeness, and provocative weaving of the personal and the political.

BIBLIOGRAPHY

Works by Judith McDaniel

Elegy; from a hill in Hebron. Argyle, NY: Spinsters Ink, 1981.
November Woman. Glens Falls, NY: The Loft, 1983.
Winter Passage. San Francisco: Spinsters Ink, 1984.
The Stories We Hold Secret: Tales of Women's Spiritual Development. Ed. Carol Bruchac, Linda Hogan, McDaniel. Greenfield Center, NY: Greenfield Review Press, 1986.
Metamorphosis: Reflections on Recovery. Ithaca, NY: Firebrand Books, 1987.
Sanctuary: A Journey. Ithaca, NY: Firebrand Books, 1987.
Home Tales. Script for a performance piece produced by Paula Sepinuck, Swarthmore College, Painted Bride Theater, May and June 1991.
Inversions: Writings by Dykes, Queers & Lesbians. Ed. McDaniel. Vancouver, British Columbia: Press Gang, 1991.
Just Say Yes. Ithaca, NY: Firebrand Books, 1991.

Studies of Judith McDaniel

Anderson, Karen. ''*Sanctuary: A Journey.*'' *National Women's Studies Association Journal* 1 (August 1988): 127.
Collins, Sheila D. ''U.S. Reflected in Nicaraguan Eyes.'' *New Reflections for Women* 17 (May-June 1986): 17.
''First Tries Don't Always Work.'' *Out From Under: Sober Dykes and Our Friends.* Ed. Jean Swallow. New York: Spinsters Ink, 1986. 177–86.
Miner, Valerie. ''*Metamorphosis.*'' *Women's Review of Books* 3 (October 1985): 12–13.
Minkowitz, Donna. ''*Just Say Yes.*'' *Village Voice* (July/August 1991).
Randall, Margaret. ''Down Dangerous Roads.'' *Women's Review of Books* 5 (October 1987): 5–6.
Rochman, Sue. ''Hot Fun in the Summertime; Judith McDaniel's Lesbian Romance.'' *Ithaca Times* (Ithaca, NY) July 25–31, 1991: 12.

ISABEL MILLER, pseud. (1924–)

Elizabeth M. Wavle

BIOGRAPHY

Isabel Miller (Alma Routsong) was born on November 26, 1924, in Traverse City, Michigan. Her father, Carl John Routsong, was a police officer. Her mother, Esther Miller Routsong, was a nurse. Miller realized at an early age that she wanted to be a writer. From 1942 to 1944, she attended Western Michigan University. Her studies were interrupted in 1945, when she joined the WAVES, serving as a U.S. Navy Hospital Apprentice for two years. In 1947, she married Bruce Brodie, a veterinarian, and they had four daughters. Isabel Miller resumed her studies, and in 1949, she graduated with honors from Michigan State University with a degree in art, although she still had aspirations of becoming a writer. In 1953, Miller published her first novel, *A Gradual Joy*, with Houghton Mifflin, which won the Friends of American Writers award in 1954. This novel, as well as her second novel, *Round Shape*, was written under her maiden name, Alma Routsong. In 1962 she divorced Bruce Brodie.

In January 1963, she moved to New York City and began writing her historical novel, *A Place for Us*. It is with this work that she started writing under the name Isabel Miller. Isabel is an anagram for "lesbia," and Miller was her mother's maiden name. Unable to find a publisher, she published the book at her own expense as a Bleecker Street Press edition and then took to the streets of New York, selling 1,000 copies out of a shopping bag. She contacted the Daughters of Bilitis to arrange for a reading from the novel. Literary agent Charlotte Sheedy purchased one of these private editions and convinced McGraw-Hill to republish the novel as *Patience and Sarah*. In 1971, this novel was awarded the first Gay Book Award by the Task Force on Gay Liberation of the Social Responsibilities Round Table of the American Library Association because "it presented a positive image of homosexuals and their lifestyle" ("Isabel Miller Wins" 2).

From 1968 to 1971, Isabel Miller also worked as an editor at Columbia University. She became active in the gay liberation movement, participating as an officer in Daughters of Bilitis and riding the bus to Albany to march for gay rights on the capital. She was arrested during a Daughters of Bilitis police raid. From the mid–1970s until 1986, she worked as a proofreader for *Time* magazine. In 1986, she published *The Love of Good Women* with Naiad Press, which also published *Side by Side* in 1990.

Presently, Isabel Miller resides in upstate New York. She has finished *A Dooryard Full of Flowers*, a sequel to *Patience and Sarah*, which will be published by Naiad. She is at work on a new novel.

MAJOR WORKS AND THEMES

Alma Routsong's first two novels, *A Gradual Joy* and *Round Shape*, were released by the major publishing house Houghton Mifflin. Written during the author's pre-liberation life in the 1950s, these novels do not deal with lesbian themes and identity.

A Place for Us, which was republished as *Patience and Sarah*, is the first novel that Isabel Miller wrote using her pseudonym, and as such, it is the first of her novels to deal with love between women. She believed that lesbianism was so misunderstood that she made it her mission to change the world so that a lesbian lifestyle would be easier for others. Her message was that it's "just love." The novel was inspired by the lives of Mary Ann Willson, a painter, and Miss Brundidge, her companion, who are known to have lived, loved, and farmed in Greene County, New York, during the early part of the nineteenth century.

A Place for Us (a.k.a. *Patience and Sarah*) is about love. Set in New England during the early nineteenth century, the novel is about the relationship of its two main characters, Patience White and Sarah Dowling. The story is told in a first-person style, which alternates point of view between the two women. Upon meeting, Patience and Sarah fall in love. The word *lesbian* was not used until the latter part of the nineteenth century. Therefore, Patience and Sarah do not have a name for their love, although they know "that there'd been women like us before, because the Bible complained of them" (151).

Patience and Sarah do not have a model to follow. They must define their own relationship. Each woman defies conventional nineteenth-century norms. Patience aspires to be a painter. Sarah has grown up assuming the role of the family son on the farm, because she has only sisters and she is the largest of them. Neither woman plans to marry a man. Patience and Sarah know that they want to make a life together and that to do so, they must move west, to a new world that they will create.

In *Patience and Sarah*, Miller has portrayed a natural, loving relationship between two women, which is based upon sharing, respect for each other, truth, and hard work. In their new home, Patience declares that "work is endless and we could never lack for topic: I had my whole life and every thought and fear and wish to tell, and hers to hear, and every day would bring more'' (190). At a time when lesbianism was considered by many to be a sickness or deviance, Isabel Miller wrote a positive, uplifting book about two women loving each other. By placing the novel in the nineteenth century, she provided a sense of history that this "love" had always been. Sarah delivers Miller's timeless message when in closing she states simply, "you can't tell a gift how to come" (190).

Isabel Miller's next novel, *The Love of Good Women*, was published by Naiad Press in 1986. Dedicated "to all the women of all my consciousness-raising groups," this novel is about change and growth in the lives of the two central characters, Gertrude and Milly. Setting the novel during World War II and the postwar years, Miller again employs the technique of alternating point of view. Unlike Patience and Sarah, Gertrude and Milly are not involved in a lesbian relationship with each other. By telling the story in the third-person narrative style, and in alternating sections between Gertrude and Milly, the author is able to convey simultaneously each woman's emerging sense of self-identity and subsequent exertion of independence.

Gertrude is the devoted and dutiful wife of Earl Sunup. She is the mother of his four children. She exists to serve and to please her family. She thinks of little else. Milly is married to Earl's brother Barney, although she thinks that she may love women. Like many women during World War II, Gertrude and Milly go to work to fill positions left vacant by men fighting in the war.

Gertrude's independence comes when she refuses to turn her earnings over to Earl. She begins to call herself Trudi, rather than Gertrude. She learns to drive and she begins to despise Earl and "his" children. Milly's emerging lesbian identity is expressed when she falls in love with Lil, the live-in housekeeper she hires while Barney is away at war. Eventually, Trudi marries Barney, while Milly forms a permanent relationship with Lil.

In *The Love of Good Women*, the issue of lesbian identity affects both Milly and Gertrude. From the beginning of the novel, Milly is identified as a lesbian: "In those days, Milly was in danger of loving any woman who held out her hand and some who didn't" (1). When Milly finally has her first lesbian sexual experience, with a married psychologist named June, she is "overwhelmed with happiness" (124).

As with *Patience and Sarah*, Miller has conveyed the message that lesbianism is just about love. For Gertrude, there is a very slow awakening process as she accepts Milly's lesbianism and considers the possibility for herself. She thinks of a time when Milly paid her frequent visits and she sensed that Milly was attracted to her: "Sometimes Gertrude felt that if she turned her mouth toward Milly's, Milly wouldn't mind" (92). Gertrude admits to herself, seven years later, that she had been tempted, but the potential consequences had kept her from taking action.

As the novel concludes, Miller leaves the reader with the sense that each woman will continue to change and grow as she discovers more about her self-identity and the possibilities that life has to offer. If Trudi finally acts upon her own thoughts of lesbianism, she will eventually tell Milly because "sooner or later, you have to speak of the most beautiful thing in your life" (209).

In *Side by Side*, the story of Patricia Burley and Sharon Almo parallels that of Patience and Sarah. By placing the novel in the 1950s and 1960s, however, Miller offers a continuum of lesbian existence, while also providing a history of the emergence of the modern gay and lesbian liberation movement. Characteristic of her style, Miller again employs an alternating first-person narrative between the two women. As in *Patience and Sarah*, she portrays a natural loving relationship between Patricia and Sharon. The pair have known each other since infancy.

During adolescence, Patricia and Sharon's friendship and love for each other add a sexual dimension. The two are separated after Sharon innocently tells her mother about their sexual experience. She is sent to live with her grandmother in a small, isolated town. Patricia, on the other hand, is sent to see a therapist. Her father informs her that "this is a problem. It is a disease. It is a recognizable disease with a name. Look it up. It is also, incidentally, a crime" (25). She puts on a show of being cured and conforming, while seeking solitude in drawing, much like Patience did with her painting.

Eventually both Sharon and Patricia find themselves and each other in New York City. In this novel, Miller's characters develop a strong and positive lesbian self-identity as they seek out and find the lesbian community in New York. They are involved in a lesbian organization, APFU (A Place for Us), which bears the original name of Miller's first lesbian novel. At APFU they encounter all types of lesbians. They participate in a march following the Stonewall Riots, carrying signs which read "GAY IS GOOD" and "GAY IS PROUD."

When Sharon's grandmother dies, leaving Sharon her farm, they decide to move there. After some searching, they find the country lesbian community. This is the first of Miller's novels in which the lesbian community is visible. She conveys the importance of community through Sharon's narrative:

They are the family that's glad you two got together. They are the father that's proud you're a girl. And something more yet. They are there. . . . They bring our world up to size and round it out. (233)

Miller again invokes the sense that life is not stagnant. There will always be growth and change. For Patience and Sarah, and Patricia and Sharon, "next time we'll be born on the same day" (234).

In a keynote address in 1978 to the Annual Lesbian Writer's Conference, Isabel Miller stated the following:

Living as a lesbian in a predominantly heterosexual world diminishes our spirits and impoverishes our emotions. It makes us invisible. Lesbian art can be a powerful force in making us visible. If we had more literature about us, we could accept as important the things that happen to us and the things we feel. There probably isn't anything like art for educating emotions. (qtd. in J. Fisher 5)

In each of her lesbian-identified novels, Miller has portrayed lesbian identity as a natural expression of love. Through use of a variety of historic settings and transference of characters between the novels, Miller has provided a unique understanding of lesbian experience, identity, and history. Through her work she has contributed to changing the attitude of the world toward lesbians.

CRITICAL RECEPTION

Criticism about the work of Isabel Miller is found primarily in the form of book reviews. In addition to being widely reviewed in the lesbian press, *Patience and Sarah* was reviewed in the major mainstream and library reviewing sources. Regina Minudri wrote in *Library Journal*:

[If young adults] are curious about lesbianism, this is a far better introduction than the current sensational material because these women are not stereotypes nor are they author subjected to the debatable speculations on causative factors as in *The Well of Loneliness* nor guilt-driven as in *The Children's Hour*. (2495)

In another *Library Journal* review, Cynthia Harrison stated that the book "merits a wide readership" (215). Rhoda A. Weyr wrote in the *New York Times Book Review*:

This novel captures even the reader with neither experience of nor particular sympathy for lesbianism. Even those who cannot feel comfortable with the subject will recognize the stillness of passion and its first 'melting' intensity as true. . . . Patience and Sarah remain alive long after the book is closed. (40)

Bell Gale Chevigny stated in the *Village Voice* that *Patience and Sarah* "has been an underground classic in the Women's Movement and that many young gay women cherish and find support in it. . . . the book was doubtless intended to move and delight a more general audience as well—and I am sure that it will" (25). *Patience and Sarah* is considered by many to be a lesbian classic that has stood the test of time, largely because Miller did not portray lesbians that were unhappy, suicidal, or deviant, as many of the novel's predecessors had. The book has not gone out of print and has been translated into several languages. *Patience and Sarah* "has remained a landmark in the literature" (Roberts 34).

Neither *The Love of Good Women* nor *Side by Side* has been reviewed as extensively as *Patience and Sarah*. This is because beginning in the late 1970s there was a proliferation of gay and lesbian publishing. On a historical spectrum, these novels were not as "unusual," perhaps, as *Patience and Sarah* was when it was published during the beginnings of the gay liberation movement.

Nonetheless, Zachary Sklar called *The Love of Good Women* "warm-hearted and wise" (743). Tracy Scott stated:

[This] novel's greatest strength is its depiction of work on the Zyglo assembly line. The scenes are realistic, funny and riveting. The matter-of-fact treatment of lesbian relationships, including love scenes, is also a pleasure. (18)

In *Gay Community News*, Buffy Dunker wrote that "the women at the factory are full of talk, about men and work and sex and relationships. They like Trudi a lot: they protect and educate and encourage her to take charge of her life" (5).

Eleanor Parkhurst called *Side by Side* "a thoroughly enjoyable (and at times touching) thought-full book" (17). In reviewing *Side by Side* for the *Lambda Book Report*, Sarah O. Buxton wrote:

Most lesbians are familiar with Miller's *Patience and Sarah*. For many, it is the most important novel they have ever read; for some, it's the first lesbian novel they ever read; and, for others, it's the only lesbian novel they have read. Miller has now created competition for her first novel. Full of the style and grace that Miller showed in *Patience and Sarah*, *Side by Side* is a special book. (24)

Isabel Miller moved lesbian literature in a new direction through her writing. With *Patience and Sarah* she demonstrated a prototype of lesbian writing that featured a positive lesbian voice. In so doing, she opened up the world for those who would follow.

BIBLIOGRAPHY

Works by Alma Routsong

A Gradual Joy. Boston: Houghton Mifflin, 1953.
Round Shape. Boston: Houghton Mifflin, 1959.

Works by Isabel Miller (Alma Routsong)

A Place For Us. New York: Bleecker Street Press, 1969.
Patience and Sarah. (Originally published as *A Place for Us*.). New York: McGraw-Hill, 1972.
The Love of Good Women. Tallahassee, FL: Naiad, 1986.
Side by Side. Tallahassee, FL: Naiad, 1990.
A Dooryard Full of Flowers. Tallahassee, FL: Naiad, 1993.

Studies of Isabel Miller

Abraham, Julie. Rev. of *The Love of Good Women*. *Nation* 243 (1986): 741.
Buxton, Sarah O. "Isabel Miller Returns: Patience and Sarah in Post-Stonewall." Rev. of *Side by Side*. *Lambda Book Report* (Jan. 1991): 24.

Chevigny, Bell Gale. "Frontierswomen in Love." Rev. of *Patience and Sarah*. *Village Voice* 20 Apr. 1972: 25+.

Craig, Patricia. "Bomb-babies." Rev. of *The Love of Good Women*. *Times Literary Supplement* 26 Feb. 1988: 214.

Dunker, Buffy. Rev. of *The Love of Good Women*. *Gay Community News* 10 May 1987: 5.

Fisher, A. Rev. of *Patience and Sarah*. *Leaping Lesbian* 3.3 (1979): 54+.

Fisher, Alma. "A Review of *Patience and Sarah*." *Radical Teacher* 24 (1983): 26–27.

Fisher, Joy. "The Patience & Sorrow of Isabel Miller." *Lesbian Tide* (May 1978): 5.

Friedman, Carole. Rev. of *A Place For Us*. *Homophile Action League Newsletter* (Nov.-Dec. 1969): 7+.

"Isabel Miller Wins First Gay Book Award." *Focus* (Sept. 1971): 2.

Jain, L. Rev. of *Patience and Sarah*. *Body Politic* (July 1972): 14.

Kaganoff, Penny. Rev. of *Side by Side*. *Publishers Weekly* 4 Jan. 1991: 68.

MacDonald, S. Rev. of *Patience and Sarah*. *Lesbian Feminist* (June 1977): 9.

McMaster, Cynthia H. Rev. of *Patience and Sarah*. *Library Journal* 97 (1972): 215.

Minudri, Regina. Rev. of *Patience and Sarah*. *Library Journal* 97 (1972): 2494–95.

Mitchell, Judith. "Search and Find." Rev. of *Patience and Sarah*. *Voice of Youth Advocates* (Feb. 1983): 17–18.

Mountaingrove, Ruth. Rev. of *Side by Side*. *off our backs* (Feb. 1991): 14.

Nasadica, M. Rev. of *A Place For Us*. *Radical Therapist* (Aug. 1970): 19.

Noble, Muffie. Rev. of *Patience and Sarah*. *Lavender Woman* (July 1972): 9.

Parkhurst, Eleanor. "Side by Side Again." Rev. of *Side by Side*. *off our backs* (Aug.-Sept. 1971): 16–17.

Roberts, Michele. "Is Everybody Happy?" Rev. of *The Love of Good Women*. *New Statesman* 19 Feb. 1988: 34.

"Routsong, Alma." *Contemporary Authors: A Bio-Bibliographical Guide to Current Authors and Their Works* 49–52. Detroit: Gale Research Co., 1975.

Scott, Tracy. "Factory Work Transforms Housewife." Rev. of *The Love Of Good Women*. *New Directions for Women* (Sept. 1971): 18.

Rev. of *Side by Side*. *Booklist* 15 Jan. 1991: 1007.

Sklar, Zachary. Rev. of *The Love of Good Women*. *Nation* 243 (1986): 743.

Spurling, John. "The New Style." Rev. of *Patience and Sarah*. *New Statesman* 84 (1972): 264.

Trova, Judith. "What's It All About, Athena?" *Lesbian Voices* 1 (Feb. 1976): 42–47.

Weyr, Rhoda A. Rev. of *Patience and Sarah*. *New York Times Book Review* 23 (Apr. 1972): 40.

Zimmerman, Bonnie. "Beyond Coming Out: New Lesbian Novels." *Ms.* (June 1985): 65–67.

KATE MILLETT (1934–   )
Anne B. Keating

BIOGRAPHY

Kate Millett was born Katherine Murray Millett in St. Paul, Minnesota, on September 14, 1934. She was the second of three daughters born to James Albert Millett, a civil engineer of Norman-Irish extraction, and Helen Millett (née Feeley), also of Irish descent and a college graduate who sold insurance after Millett's father left the family. Millett was educated in Catholic schools in St. Paul. She graduated from the University of Minnesota in 1956 with a B.A. in English, *magna cum laude*. During the summer of 1952, she worked as an aide in a local insane asylum.

Millett was admitted to Oxford University in 1956. She earned her passage to England and Oxford working in a factory. It was during that time that she developed her first significant relationship with another woman. From 1956 to 1958, she studied Victorian literature at St. Hilda's College, Oxford, and earned her postgraduate degree with first class honors, the first American woman to do so.

In 1958, after returning to the United States, Millett taught English at Woman's College, now the University of North Carolina at Greensboro. She arrived in New York in the spring of 1959. In 1960, she taught kindergarten in East Harlem. In 1961, she left New York for Japan in order to develop a sense of herself as an artist. She worked in Japan from 1961 to 1963. In the spring of 1963, she had her first one-woman sculpture show at the Minami Gallery in Tokyo. While she was in Japan she met the Japanese sculptor Fumio Yoshimura, with whom she returned to the United States and later married in 1965.

When Millett returned to the United States, she struggled to find a job and worked as a file clerk. She describes this period as one in which she held an "Oxford degree, but couldn't type." This was an important consciousness-raising moment in Millett's life, one that she marks as the beginning of her political life as a feminist. In the fall of 1963, she started teaching freshman composition at Hunter College. Millett was to hold this job through the spring of 1964. The following fall, in 1964, she was admitted to do Ph.D. work at Columbia University. She split her time between working on her doctorate at Columbia and teaching English at Barnard and becoming involved in campus politics. Her involvement culminated in her being fired from Barnard for supporting and being a member of the Columbia student strike of 1968. Millett started working full-time on her dissertation on New Year's Day 1969, finishing "Sexual Politics" in eighteen months.

During this period she became involved in the civil rights movement. In 1964, during Mississippi Summer, she became a member of Congress of Racial Equality (CORE). In 1965, she was a founding member of the New York chapter of the National Organization of Women (NOW). She was the NOW chair of the Educational Committee from 1966 until 1970. In 1968, while she was on the Educational Committee, she wrote the pamphlet *Token Learning: A Study of Women's Higher Education in America*. In addition to her work at NOW, Millett was a founding member of Columbia Women's Liberation, a member of Downtown Radical Women, Redstockings, and Radical Lesbians.

The fiftieth anniversary year (1970) of the passing of the Nineteenth Amendment giving women the vote was a pivotal year for Kate Millett and for the American women's movement. Millett's dissertation "Sexual Politics" passed with honors, and Doubleday published it in July of that year. The book, a product of Millett's involvement in the liberation politics of the women's movement, was a best-seller. On a par with French feminist Simone de Beauvoir's *The Second Sex* (1952) and Betty Friedan's *The Feminine Mystique* (1963), *Sexual Politics* became one of the most influential theoretical works on feminism in the history of the contemporary feminist movement. Millett's theory of sexual politics remains a keystone concept in the foundation of the women's movement and in feminist literary criticism.

On the strengths of *Sexual Politics*, the media adopted Millett as the "leader of the women's movement," an action that in August 1971 was to culminate in an unauthorized *Time* cover story on Millett announcing her as the "Mao Tse Tung of Women's Liberation." The label "leader of the women's movement" was one Millett detested, as it went against the non-hierarchal tenets of women's liberation. In that same year, at a meeting at Columbia University where Millett was scheduled to speak on the subject of bisexuality, she was asked by a member of the audience whether she was a lesbian. Millett answered that she was. *Time* magazine, which had been largely responsible for creating "Kate Millett," the media figure, used this incident in a follow-up article on the women's movement in a December 1970 issue. The article argued that the Columbia revelation would discredit Millett, "cast further doubt on her theories, and reinforce the views of skeptics who routinely dismiss all liberationists as lesbians" and, by extension, cast doubt on the women's movement as a whole (Cohen 247).

Initially there was a show of support for Millett from fellow feminists who staged a "Kate is Great" press conference on December 18, 1970, to announce women's liberation's support of gay liberation. However, after this incident, changes within NOW and the women's movement, the advent of gay liberation, as well as Millett's own growing sense of dislocation between her private self and the "Kate Millett" created by the media, propelled her to start drafting the manuscript of a new book in the spring of 1971 that would become *Flying*.

During the summer of 1970, Millett began shooting *Three Lives*, a documentary film recording the lives of three women as they discussed being women in America. The film was completed by September of 1972. Her next significant achievement was the publication of *The Prostitution Papers* in 1973. It was the product of work done in the summer of 1970 and had first appeared in the anthology *Woman in Sexist Society*. In the spring of 1973, Millett was appointed visiting professor at Sacramento State College. Here she met "Sita," a college administrator with whom she fell in love and who subsequently became the subject of *Sita*. That same spring Knopf accepted *Flying* for publication. That summer Millett traveled to England to work on a campaign to save Michael Malik, a Trinidadian civil rights lawyer condemned to death. When she returned to the United States, her family, believing she had "gone over the edge" from working too hard, had her committed to a mental hospital. Though the commitment was overturned, she was again incarcerated by her family the following month. Though Millett cleared herself once more, she was declared manic-depressive by the admitting psychiatrist, a record Millett was to carry with her from that day forward.

In the winter of 1974, *Flying* was published. It was the first of a new genre of autobiographical books that Millett was to write during the next sixteen years. *Flying* was an account of the eighteen months following the publication of *Sexual Politics*. *Flying* broke free of the traditional literary genre of autobiography by focusing on both the private and public experiences of women. *Flying* was also unabashedly lesbian. The book received uniformly negative reviews.

In 1977, *Sita* was published. With *Sita*, Millett broke completely away from the public self of "Kate Millett" to focus on the private world of a dying love affair. *Sita* was the account of an obsession, and reviewers were once more derisory in their reviews of the book. In 1978, her sculpture show, called "The Basement," was held at the NoHo Gallery. In 1979, *The Basement* was published. *The Basement* was an unusual book, a cross between a feminist essay and an autobiography, subtitled *A Meditation on a Human Sacrifice*. In *The Basement*, Millett told the story of the murder and death of Sylvia Likens, a sixteen-year-old girl.

In 1979, Sita committed suicide, and Kate Millett wrote, designed, and privately published *Elegy for Sita* in a limited edition of 350 copies. In 1982, after a trip to Iran to observe and participate in the women's movement, an action for which she was seized by the Ayatollah Khomeini's police and expelled, she published *Going to Iran*.

In 1978, Millett began restoring the fields and buildings of an abandoned dairy farm outside of Poughkeepsie, New York. Millett had initially purchased seven acres in the winter of 1971 with the royalties from *Sexual Politics*. Royalties from *Sita* and *The Basement* were used to buy the remaining seventy-three acres in the late seventies. This was the beginning of an experiment in communal living called "the Farm." Millett conceived the Farm as a place where women artists and writers could come to work on their art. In the beginning, women came to help Millett with the building and farming. By 1986, after approaching self-sufficiency through sales of Christmas trees, the Farm accepted its first artists in residence. Since that time, the Farm has been fully self-sufficient, and the number of women who have worked there is well over a hundred. Today, Millett splits her time between her Lower East Side loft in New York City and the Farm.

MAJOR WORKS AND THEMES

Kate Millett's overtly lesbian work begins not with *Sexual Politics*, but with *Flying*. However, a brief mention of *Sexual Politics* is necessary to understand Millett's motivations in writing *Flying*, *Sita*, *Elegy for Sita*, *A.D.*, and *The Loony-Bin Trip*, the five intensely autobiographical and personal books that followed *Sexual Politics*. *Sexual Politics* and the media's response to it were directly responsible for making a public figure of Kate Millett. It was the tension with this public identity, and the alienation from the self that it caused, that inspired these autobiographical books.

Millett started focusing on central issues of language and subject matter in *The Prostitution Papers*. As a text, *The Prostitution Papers* examined the experiences and views on the outright buying and selling of female flesh and the subsequent disintegration of the self. Her introduction to the work gave shape to a whole new body of work on which she expanded in subsequent books:

It is my impression that emerging peoples have great difficulty with form. . . . I should like to see the new movement give women in the arts a confidence in the value of their own culture . . . and a respect for its experience, together with the freedom . . . to express this in new ways, in new forms.(60)

While *The Prostitution Papers* explored language and subject, it was *Flying* that marked Millett's first experiment with form. The story of the eighteen months after the publication of *Sexual Politics*, *Flying* was densely packed with the details of everyday living. Made up of complex, multilayered themes and plots, *Flying* was an attempt both to capture the variegated fabric of daily life as well as the unique sound of the American language. As one of the first mainstream American lesbian autobiographies, Millett focused on the Columbia University "coming out" incident as the entry point into a new life. Dante's *vita nuova* idea of the ideal community gave shape to what she later described in the preface to the 1990 edition. *Flying* was Millett's *vade mecum*, or handbook, about lesbian life and identity. Designed for a lesbian audience, the book chronicled the "invention" of a life that combined feminism and lesbianism, despite the ambiguities inherent in both at the time.

Sita was the autobiographical narrative of the dissolution of a love affair with a university administrator from Sacramento State. Like *Flying*, *Sita* was a complex, multilayered narrative. It was the record of an obsession, of Millett's "one-sided fidelity" to an exotic woman, ten years her senior, who had ceased to share the same passion for their affair (v).

Elegy for Sita was privately published in 1979. Completed three years after *Sita*, *Elegy* was a work commemorating Sita whose suicide came suddenly and without warning just two years after she and Millett had resolved to settle for "a lifetime liaison . . . perfected and serene"(vii). *Elegy for Sita* featured four prose essays accompanied by a series of Japanese brush drawings and poems.

A.D. is the story of Millett's relationship with her Aunt Dorothy, one of her father's sisters who helped Millett finance her passage to Oxford. Though not overtly lesbian, the passion Millett had for her unpredictable and sometimes terrifying aunt was an example of a young woman's erotic attachment to a revered older woman.

The Loony-Bin Trip is Millett's most recently published work and is once more in the autobiographical genre she has been honing since writing *Flying*. *The Loony-Bin Trip* focuses on the events leading up to her last incarceration in an insane asylum in Ireland. It is an exposé of the abuses in the mental health establishment and the first of Millett's books to focus on the Farm as a major part of her life. *The Loony-Bin Trip* is a reprise of *Flying*, bringing to full circle many of the themes of the public-private dialectic, as well as a strong defense of the inviolate nature of the mind.

CRITICAL RECEPTION

Critical approaches to Millett's work can be divided into the cultural politics of book reviewing and the closer reading of literary criticism. The disparity between the two is clear in the critical response to Kate Millett's work. Book reviews of Millett's work outweigh critical studies and have, up to the publication of *The Loony-Bin Trip*, been largely negative. The handful of critical studies that exist of Millett's work are, on the whole, positive treatments of her work.

Kate Millett's writing requires a careful and at times complex reading that can take into account innovations and inventions in literary style and a collapsing of the cultural and social barriers that traditionally have sharply divided private experiences from the public self. Additionally, readers and critics of Millett's work must account for an exhaustive search for and meticulous accounting of the emergence of an identity both freed from the normative social constraints of the feminine, heterosexual, catholic, and modest, while at times haunted and conflicted by the inability to break entirely free from these constraints.

Book reviewers, often expressing their personal distastes and biases, have, on the whole, dismissed Millett's work after *Sexual Politics* as self-involved, ponderous, at times paranoid, and always anti-literary. The few literary critics who have tackled her work have recognized her innovations in literary style and have admired how she has broken away from the traditional genre of self-reflexive, but personally detached, autobiography.

Negative reviews, scarce critical studies, and few biographical statements about Millett have resulted in the absence of a clear statement on her work as a whole. Biographical errors and gaps abound, and only a handful of books and articles have been written that contain significant material on her. The most substantial biographical work to date is Marcia Cohen's *The Sisterhood* (1988), a journalistic account of the lives of Betty Friedan, Gloria Steinem, Kate Millett, and Germaine Greer and their role in the formation of the contemporary women's movement. There have been a few scholarly articles written on Kate Millett's work. The most significant of these are Annette Kolodny's "The Lady's Not for Spurning: Kate Millett and the Critics" (1976) and Suzanne Juhasz's "Towards a Theory of Form in Feminist Autobiography: Kate Millett's *Flying* and *Sita*; Maxine Hong Kingston's *The Woman Warrior*" (1979).

Kolodny's work explores the synthesis between the public and private selves that Millett attempted in *Flying*. She points out that "change and transformation are what *Flying* is all about" (249) and criticizes the book reviewers who assumed that Millett's problem was self-absorption or a compulsion for public confession, by reminding readers that book reviewing is practiced with the "assumed knowledge of a literary history which . . . tacitly accepts a commonly agreed-upon 'traditional canon' " (256).

Juhasz, in her analysis of *Sita*, points out that in *Sita* Millett completely rejected the public figure of "Kate Millett" to concentrate on writing about the private world of women. It was because of this, Juhasz writes, that reviewers literally hated the book. "The underlying assumption . . . seems to be that 'Kate Millett' is interesting or worthy of attention only when she is that public person, the celebrity who does things in the public world" (227–28).

Millett's autobiographical work emerged from her need to document the American language and map the imagination. Mike Woolf, in "Henry Miller and Kate Millett: Strange Bedfellows, Sexuality and Introspection" (1985), explores a connection between Henry Miller's and Millett's work, drawing the conclusion that the link between Miller and Millett was "the sense that the drama of self-liberation is the essential material out of which creative expression is made" (279).

Among the briefer statements on Millett's work are Catherine Stimpson's description in "Literature as Radical Statement" (1980) and Bonnie Zimmerman's comments on *Sita* in *The Safe Sea of Women: Lesbian Fiction, 1969–1989* (1990). Zimmerman, a lesbian-feminist literary critic, compares Millett to Monique Wittig, the French lesbian-feminist writer, and writes that "the interplay of power in *Sita* and of violent longing in [Wittig's] *The Lesbian Body . . .* prefigure the development of a new erotic discourse in the 1980s" (111).

In 1974, in *Flying* Millett recorded a conversation she had with Doris Lessing in which she expressed her doubts over creating literature out of the private experiences of women.

"feeling so vulnerable, my god, a Lesbian. Sure an experience of human beings. But not described. Not permitted. It has no traditions. No language. No history of agreed values."

"But of course people wish to know," Lessing countered. "And you cannot be intimidated into silence. Or the silence is prolonged forever." (358)

As the politics of homophobia and the moral constraints on writing the private loosen up, Millett's work may be reclaimed by readers, especially lesbian readers, as a piece of women's history. It is the bold writing of one individual who has not been afraid to explore every detail of her life and psyche in order that a few of those explorations might open a window forever on the experience of being a woman and a lesbian.

BIBLIOGRAPHY

Works by Kate Millett

Token Learning: A Study of Women's Higher Education in America. New York: New York Chapter of the National Organization for Women, 1968.

Sexual Politics. Diss., Columbia University, 1970. New York: Doubleday, 1969; New York: Avon, 1971; New York: Ballantine Books, 1978; New York: Simon and Schuster, 1990.

"Prostitution: A Quartet for Female Voices." *Women in Sexist Society*. Ed. Vivian Gornick and Barbara K. Moran. New York: Basic Books, 1971. 60–125.

The Prostitution Papers. New York: Ballantine Books, 1973. "Sexual Politics: A Manifesto for Revolution (1968)." *Radical Feminism*. Ed. Anne Koedt et al. New York: Quadrangle Books, 1973. 365–67.

Flying. New York: Alfred A. Knopf, 1974; New York: Ballantine Books, 1974; New York: Simon and Schuster, 1990.

"The Shame Is Over." *Ms*. 3:7 (Jan. 1975): 26–29.

Sita. New York: Farrar, Strauss and Giroux, 1976; New York: Ballantine Books, 1978; New York: Simon and Schuster, 1992.

The Basement. New York: Simon and Schuster, 1979.

Elegy for Sita. New York: Targ Editions, 1979.

Going to Iran. New York: Coward, McCann and Geoghegan, 1981.

"All Spruced Up: A Place Where Women and Trees Grow and Flourish." *Ms*. 16:11 (May 1988): 30–31.

"From the Basement to the Madhouse." *Art Papers* 12:3 (May/June 1988): 23–28.

The Loony-Bin Trip. New York: Simon and Schuster, 1990.

A.D. New York: Simon and Schuster, forthcoming 1993.

Studies of Kate Millett

Arbuthnot, Lucie B. "Main Trends in Feminist Criticism in Film, Literature, and Art History: The Decade of the 1970's (Berger, Haskell, Millett, Rosen)." Diss., New York University, 1982.

Bender, Marilyn. "Some Call Her the 'Karl Marx' of New Feminism." *New York Times* 20 July 1970: 30.

Bryant, Rene Kuhn. "Drowning in Claustrophobia." Rev. of *Flying*, by Kate Millett. *National Review* 30 (Aug. 1974): 989.

Clemons, Walter. "Distress Signal." Rev. of *Flying*, by Kate Millett. *Newsweek* 15 July 1974: 84.

Cohen, Marcia. *The Sisterhood*. New York: Simon and Schuster, 1988.

Dawson, Kipp. *Kate Millett's Sexual Politics*. New York: Pathfinder Press, 1971.

Dermansky, Ann. "Millett Still a Gadfly." *New Directions for Women* Sept./Oct. 1990: 12–13.

Dinnage, Rosemary. " 'I Am One with the Mad.' " Rev. of *The Loony-Bin Trip. New York Times Book Review* 3 June 1990: 12.

Durbin, Karen. "The Dangerous Fun of Special Pleading." Rev. of *Sita. Village Voice* 30 (May 1977): 80.

Hardy, Barbara. "De Beauvoir, Lessing—Now Kate Millett." Rev. of *Sexual Politics. New York Times Book Review* 6 Sept. 1970: 8.

Haynes, Muriel. "Sexual Energy." Rev. of *Flying. New Republic* 6 July 1974: 28–29.

Jelinek, Estelle, ed. *Women's Autobiography: Essays in Criticism*. Bloomington: Indiana University Press, 1980.

Juhasz, Suzanne. "Towards a Theory of Feminist Autobiography: Kate Millett's *Flying* and *Sita*; Maxine Hong Kingston's *The Woman Warrior*." *Women's Autobiography: Essays in Criticism*. Ed. Estelle Jelinek. Bloomington: Indiana University Press, 1980. 221–37.

Klemesrud, Judy. "The Lesbian Issue and Women's Lib." *New York Times* 18 Dec. 1970: 47.

Kolodny, Annette. "The Lady's Not for Spurning: Kate Millett and the Critics." *Women's Autobiography: Essays in Criticism*. Ed. Estelle Jelinek. Bloomington: Indiana University, 1980. 238–59.

Langer, Elinor. "Confessing." Rev. of *Flying. Ms.* (Dec. 1974): 69–71, 108.

Lehman-Haupt, Christopher. "Candor as an Anesthetic." Rev. of *Flying. New York Times* 15 July 1974: 23.

———. "He and She—I & II." Rev. of *Sexual Politics. New York Times* 4–5 Aug. 1970: 31, 33.

Leonard, John. Rev. of *Sita. New York Times* 13 May 1977: Sec. 3, 25.

"The Liberation of Kate Millett." *Time* 31 Aug. 1970: 18–19.

Lowenstein, Andrea. "A Complex Tale of 'Madness,' Drugs and Hospitalization." Rev. of *The Loony-Bin Trip. Sojourner* 15 (Aug. 1990): 12.

Mailer, Norman. *Prisoner of Sex*. Boston: Little, Brown, 1971.

Malapede, Karen. "*The Loony-Bin Trip* by Kate Millett." *Women's Review of Books* 8:1 (Oct. 1990): 7–8.

Marotta, Toby. *The Politics of Homosexuality*. Boston: Houghton Mifflin, 1981.

May, Clifford D. Rev. of *Going to Iran. New York Times Book Review* 16 May 1982: 14.

Milton, Marianne. "Kate Millett's Disturbing Journey." Rev. of *The Loony-Bin Trip*. *Washington Blade* 14 Sept. 1990: 33.

Oates, Joyce Carol. "To Be Female Is to Die." Rev. of *The Basement*. *New York Times Book Review* 9 Sept. 1979: 14–25.

Rev. of *The Prostitution Papers*. *Library Journal* 98 (July 1973): 2066.

Robb, Christina. "Kate Millett: Free at Last." Rev. of *The Loony-Bin Trip*. *Boston Globe* 31 May 1990: 77, 82.

Sanborn, Sara. "Personal Doings." Rev. of *Sita*. *New York Times Book Review* 29 May 1977: 13, 20.

Smith, Barbara. "She's Come a Long Way—and Hates It." Rev. of *Flying*. *National Observer* 3 Aug. 1974: 17.

Stimpson, Catherine. "Literature as Radical Statement." *Columbia Literary History of the United States*. Ed. Emory Elliott. New York: Columbia University Press, 1980. 1073.

Thom, Mary. " 'A Farm of Our Own' (Kate Millett's Artists' Collective Farm)." *Ms.* 16 (March 1988): 74.

"Who's Come a Long Way, Baby?" *Time* 31 Aug. 1970: 16–21.

Wilson, Jane. "Sexual Apologetics." Rev. of *Flying*. *New York Times Book Review* 23 June 1974: 2–3.

Woolf, Mike. "Henry Miller and Kate Millett: Strange Bedfellows, Sexuality and Introspection." *Dutch Quarterly Review of Anglo-Saxon Letters* 15 (1985): 278–92.

Yalom, Marilyn. "Kate Millett's Mental Politics." Rev. of *The Loony-Bin Trip*. *Washington Post Book World* 13 May 1990: 7.

Zimmerman, Bonnie. *The Safe Sea of Women: Lesbian Fiction, 1969–1989*. Boston, Beacon Press, 1990.

VALERIE MINER (1947–   )
Lisa L. Higgins

BIOGRAPHY

Valerie Miner was born on August 28, 1947, in New York City, the daughter of working-class parents. Her Irish Catholic father, John Daniel, worked as a merchant marine for forty-four years before retirement. Her mother, Mary (McKenzie), an Edinburgh immigrant, worked as waitress and hostess at coffee shops until the age of seventy-seven. Miner grew up in New Jersey (Metro New York), the Pacific Northwest, and California. In 1969, she received her bachelor of arts degree in English literature and journalistic studies from the University of California at Berkeley. The following year, she earned a master's in journalism, also at Berkeley. Miner was an honor student as a graduate and as an undergraduate, and she won the Edna Kinard Award for Outstanding Woman in Journalism at Berkeley in 1968. In addition, Miner studied English literature at the University of Edinburgh (1968) and the University of London (1974–75).

After college, Miner spent seven years living abroad in Canada and Britain, working as a free-lance journalist and lecturer/instructor in English, Creative Writing, and Journalism departments. She was married briefly from 1970 to 1974. While living in Canada, Miner co-authored a book of essays, *Her Own Woman* (1975), and she co-authored the first of two anthologies of feminist short stories in London, *Tales I Tell My Mother* (1978).

Upon returning to the United States, Miner settled once again in California where she served as a lecturer in the University of California at Berkeley's undergraduate interdisciplinary program from 1977 to 1989. During these years, she authored five novels and a collection of short stories; co-authored the second volume of short stories, *More Tales I Tell My Mother* (1987); and co-edited a collection of essays. In addition, Miner published numerous short stories and essays in anthologies and journals, presented literary readings and guest lectured in the United States and abroad, presented papers at academic conferences, received numerous honors and awards (including the PEN Syndicated Fiction Award, 1986, and the Australia Council Literary Awards Grant, 1988), and reviewed over one hundred books, particularly fiction by women, lesbian, working-class, and international authors.

Currently, Miner lives in Tempe, Arizona, with her lover of eleven years and is an assistant professor of English and core faculty member of women's studies at Arizona State University. She has recently completed her sixth novel, *A Walking Fire*, about the lives of a working-class American family from the 1940s through the 1980s, focusing on American intervention in Southeast Asia and Central America. Miner describes the plot as *"King Lear* from Cordelia's point of view" with a revision of setting and gender (personal communication with Miner, January 20, 1992).

MAJOR WORKS AND THEMES

Valerie Miner's novels and short stories include some overtly autobiographical elements; reflect lesbian, class, feminist, and political themes; and combine literary and journalistic writing in compelling reportage. Unlike much popular lesbian fiction, Miner's works are experiments in form and style.

Miner's second novel, *Movement: A Novel in Stories* (1982), most exemplifies the elements mentioned above. The life of Susan, the main character, is similar to Miner's. They share geographical migrations, working-class parents (seaman and waitress), occupations, feminist and progressive political consciousness, and sexual identification. Miner's experimentation in form is explained in the foreword:

Susan's stories are interwoven with short-short stories about completely different women who are experiencing other kinds of movement. I write these stories to break through the isolation and the individualism of the *Bildungsroman*, the conventional novel of development. (xiii)

Thus, while the autobiographical elements of the novel are of interest, of more interest are the ways in which Miner conveys women's lives during the tumultuous sixties and seventies. She weaves narratives reflecting realistic issues that affected women cross-culturally.

Several stories in Miner's collection *Trespassing and Other Stories* (1989) show similar themes. The title story, "Trespassing," establishes the prevailing theme in the collection: a lesbian couple visit their weekend cabin only to find a hunter trespassing on their posted property. As the women wait for the man to retrieve the poached deer, they battle the invasion of bats and wasps (or do the bats and wasps battle the weekend intruders?). Josie and Kate must also deal with the suspiciousness of the local residents, who challenge weekenders, especially same-sex couples, with raised eyebrows and invitations to attend Sunday church services. Other stories in the collection, whose settings include Europe,

America, Africa, and Asia, examine the notion of trespassing within individuals, families, classes, and countries.

Miner's lesbian consciousness is evident in the two preceding works; *Movement* is as much about Susan's sexual choices as her political and professional ones, and *Trespassing* includes lesbian characters more often than not. However, Miner's two most overtly lesbian works are *Blood Sisters* (1981) and *All Good Women* (1987). In *Blood Sisters*, Californian Liz Devlin travels to London, where she meets her Aunt Polly and cousin, Beth. The cousins struggle to resolve political conflicts—women's roles within the Provisional Wing of the IRA (Irish Republican Army) and the separatist politics of the feminist movement—that threaten their newfound identification as sisters. In addition, the extended family, as well as Liz, work to accept her lesbian identification, placing the lesbian narrative within a larger social and cultural context.

While Miner's works do not focus exclusively on lesbian characters and lesbian communities, she does identify her work as lesbian or woman-identified:

I am particularly engaged by relationships among women which cross cultures, classes, and sexual choices. It's far more interesting to make connections between lesbians and heterosexual women than simply to write about a particular group all the time. One of my strategies is to incite readers' consciousness about choice. (*Rumours* 21)

Like *Blood Sisters*, *All Good Women* illustrates this strategy. In the latter, four working-class, single women meet at secretarial school and eventually share a house together in San Francisco. The novel is set before, during, and after World War II, and it shows the effects of the war on the women. Teddy, the lesbian character, comes out in the fledgling bar scene, falling in love first with a neighbor who enlists in the WAFs and then with her remaining housemate, Moira. Teddy's story is not the central focus of the novel, however. The dominant focus is the war and the way it forces these women to cope with such issues as Japanese internment camps, orphaned Jewish Holocaust survivors, military drafts and injuries, and women's employment in factories. The personal interactions and familial relationships of each young woman are also woven into the complex plot.

In Miner's two remaining novels, the sexual preference of the main characters is ambivalent. *Murder in the English Department* (1982), however, is a woman-identified novel. Nan Weaver is a divorced, celibate, assistant professor at Berkeley. Her colleague, Angus Murchie, an aging, sexist Milton scholar, is murdered early in the novel by a female graduate student terrorized by his sexual advances. Nan finds the body and witnesses the fleeing graduate student. During the remainder of the novel, Nan tries to cover for the student while negotiating class boundaries between herself and her working-class sister's family. Nan's primary relationships in the novel are with her sister, her niece (a university student), the female graduate student, her best friend/lawyer, and her gay colleague, Matt.

Similarly, *Winter's Edge* (1984) focuses on woman-identified women and working-class issues. Margaret and Chrissie are best friends on the verge of retirement, living in San Francisco's Tenderloin district. Once again, Miner merges the personal and the political as she shows the two elderly women in conjunction with a local political campaign. Chrissie and Margaret are old friends but in constant conflict over Chrissie's socialist political activism. Miner creates a diverse community, placing the women in a setting of working-class neighbors and middle-class employers, all choosing sides in the election except Margaret. While Chrissie's sexual preference is ambiguous or even ignored, Margaret's heterosexuality provides for a very erotic love scene with the Unitarian minister.

Valerie Miner's fiction is compelling because of her successful revisions of conventional forms and topics. Her stories convey her interest in individuals' struggles to define themselves in relation to their families and society but provide no clear-cut answers to questions raised about class, politics, or sexual preference.

CRITICAL RECEPTION

Valerie Miner's fiction has been widely reviewed in mainstream, alternative, and feminist publications. In addition, a few interviews with the author have been published. Reception of Miner's work is favorable overall, although she points out that some reviewers complain about open endings and other ambiguous elements (*Rumors* 21). Amazingly, scholarly criticism about her fiction is almost non-existent. Ellen Cronan Rose's article in the *Doris Lessing Newsletter* traces Lessing's influence on *Movement*. Maureen Reddy discusses *Murder in the English Department* in her book about women's detective fiction, *Sisters in Crime* (1988). In addition, *Blood Sister* and *Movement* both receive mentions in Bonnie Zimmerman's *The Safe Sea of Women* (1990). Other scholars are currently researching Miner's fiction, but there is still a need for more critical examination of this prolific author.

BIBLIOGRAPHY

Works by Valerie Miner

Fiction

Blood Sisters. London: Women's Press, 1981; New York: St. Martin's Press, 1982.
Movement: A Novel in Stories. Trumansburg, NY: Crossing Press, 1982; London: Methuen, 1985.
Murder in the English Department. London: Women's Press, 1982; New York: St. Martin's Press, 1983.
Winter's Edge. London: Methuen, 1984; Trumansburg, NY: Crossing Press, 1985.
All Good Women. London: Methuen, 1987; Trumansburg, NY: Crossing Press, 1987.
Trespassing and Other Stories. London: Methuen, 1989; Trumansburg, NY: Crossing Press, 1989.

Fiction, Co-Author

With Zoe Fairbairns, Sara Maitland, Michele Roberts, and Michelene Wandor. *Tales I Tell My Mother*. London: Journeyman, 1978; Boston: South End, 1980.

With Zoe Fairbairns, Sara Maitland, Michele Roberts, and Michelene Wandor. *More Tales I Tell My Mother*. London: Journeyman, 1987.

Non-Fiction

Rumors from the Cauldron: Selected Essays, Reviews, and Reportage. Ann Arbor: University of Michigan Press, 1991.

Non-Fiction, Co-Author

With Myrna Kostash, Melinda McCracken, Erna Paris, and Heather Robertson. *Her Own Woman*. New York: Macmillan, 1975.

Non-Fiction, Co-Editor

With Helen E. Longino. *Competition: A Feminist Taboo?* New York: CUNY Feminist Press, 1987.

Studies of Valerie Miner

Reddy, Maureen. *Sisters in Crime*. New York: Continuum, 1988.

Rose, Ellen Cronan. "Lessing's Influence on Valerie Miner." *Doris Lessing Newsletter* 6, no. 2 (1982): 15.

Zimmerman, Bonnie. *The Safe Sea of Women*. Boston: Beacon, 1990. 55, 139–40.

HONOR MOORE (1945–   )
Jocelyn Sheppard

BIOGRAPHY

Honor Moore was born October 28, 1945, in New York City, the eldest of nine children born to Paul and Jenny McKean Moore. Majoring in English literature at Radcliffe College, where she took a degree in 1967, Moore then studied for two years at the Yale School of Drama.

Moore is a prolific and widely published author who began writing in the late 1960s. Her poems, essays, and reviews have appeared in a wide range of newspapers (*New York Times, Boston Globe, Los Angeles Times*), magazines (*Ms., Harper's Weekly, Sojourner*), journals (*AWP Chronicle, Coda: Poets & Writers, Ploughshares*), and anthologies (*The New Woman's Survival Sourcebook*, 1975; *Women in American Theatre*, 1981; *Lesbian Poetry: An Anthology*, 1981; *Writing in a Nuclear Age*, 1984; *Gay and Lesbian Poetry in Our Time*, 1989; and *Poets for Life: 46 Poets Respond to AIDS*, 1989).

Moore's career has included substantial teaching and workshop experience. Since 1976, she has participated in many workshops on women's writing, including sessions in New York City, Pittsburgh, and Syracuse, New York, and at the University of Iowa, Wells College, and the University of Connecticut's Women's Center. Moore has also served as an adjunct professor at New York University from 1980 to 1982 and as a visiting scholar at James Madison University in 1980. Moore has been featured in a long list of public lectures and panels with titles such as "Women and Their Work," "The Gay/Lesbian Writer in Context," "The Scholar and the Feminist," and "The Writer as Witness." Her public readings have frequently been part of benefits for a variety of causes, among them AIDS awareness, nuclear disarmament, and animal rights.

Moore has promoted the works of writers and performers in many ways. She founded the Writers in Performance literary series at the Manhattan Theatre Club (1971); she co-founded the Harvard Dramatic Club Summer Players in Cambridge, Massachusetts (1966); and she was one of the original contributing editors for the women's journal *Chrysalis* (1977). Currently Moore serves on the Board of Directors at Poets and Writers, the Music Theatre Group, and the Jenny McKean Moore Fund for Writers. Her memberships include the Poetry Society of America, the Dramatists Guild, and the PEN American Center; she is also an associate at the Barnard Center for Research on Women. Moore's honors reflect the diversity of her career: in 1975 she received a Creative Artists Public Service (CAPS) grant in play writing from the New York State Council on the Arts, and in 1981 Moore was awarded a National Endowment for the Arts creative writing fellowship in poetry.

Moore published a play, *Mourning Pictures*, in 1977; a book of poems entitled *Memoir* appeared in 1988. Since 1980, she has been cataloguing the works of her grandmother, American artist Margarett Sargent (1892–1978). This interest has led to Moore's co-curating a retrospective of Sargent's works, a project that will orginate at the Wellesley College Art Museum in 1993 and then become a traveling exhibit.

MAJOR WORKS AND THEMES

Moore's writings cover a range of topics (community, separation, death, rape, nuclear holocaust) and emotions (friendship, love, vulnerability, jealousy, anger) and use vivid images, humor, and directness to describe the speaker's personal and political condition. Moore has stated, "My poetry is political because I write as a conscious woman in a patriarchal culture." She also characterizes her writing as "woman-loving" and "woman-identified," so that issues connected with lesbian identity are implicit in works as early as *Mourning Pictures* and are explicit in later poems and essays. Moore's works often combine traditional poetic forms (such as the sestina, the sonnet, and the villanelle) with contemporary language and rhythms to convey the emotional intensity of her particular experience. Yet while autobiography resonates in these works, Moore warns that readers should not assume that her poetry, drama, and essays represent transcripts of her life: she uses autobiography as a means to a greater artistic end.

In 1974 Moore's career got a big boost when poet and critic Richard Howard published "My Mother's Moustache" in the *American Review*, a poem that has since been reprinted several times and which underscores Moore's fascination with relationships between mothers and daughters. The poem describes the disastrous results of the speaker's attempt to imitate her mother's waxing of facial hair; finally deciding not to aspire to conventional notions of beauty, the speaker compromises by lightening, but not removing, her own facial hair. Also in 1974, *Mourning Pictures*, a play about a mother's six-month bout with cancer and its effect on her family, was produced on Broadway.

In 1978 Moore published poems about sexual abuse and about love between women, and it is after this point that her writing contains more explicit lesbian images and references. "First Time: 1950" describes sexual abuse by a babysitter when the speaker is five years old, while "Poem: For the Beginning" chronicles passion, separation, and jealousy in a lesbian relationship. The themes of anger and healing reappear in many later poems, including "Shenandoah," "Premonition," and "Poem for the End." The poem "First Night" describes how silences must be broken in order to express desire, pain, and love. Here and in other poems, Moore uses the word *tongue* to denote an important source of (lesbian) sexuality and community that invariably is linked with the power of language.

In the 1980s, Moore's poems have continued to deal with issues of personal identity and integrity in a rapidly changing society. "Spuyten Duyvil" is a long poem about the imagined impact of nuclear disaster, exploring the potential loss of the world in terms of broken human relationships and representing Moore at her most political. Other types of pain inspire Moore's poetry as well: "Memoir" details the speaker's bewilderment and sorrow upon hearing of a friend's death from AIDS, while "New Haven, 1969" describes the speaker's experience of acquaintance rape and resulting pregnancy. Moore can achieve self-knowledge through these poems, and a line in "Spuyten Duyvil" reveals that her words are directed outward as well: "I never wanted a child, / but I saved everything important / so those who came after could learn."

CRITICAL RECEPTION

Moore has commented that it is difficult for her to attribute resistance to her work to its lesbian content. On the other hand, she remembers sending *Memoir* to twenty-one publishers before finding one willing to publish her book. Its lesbian eroticism appears not to have hurt critical reaction to *Memoir*: not surprisingly, Marilyn Hacker notes this as a positive aspect of the book and goes on to compare Moore's technique with that of Marianne Moore. Reaction to *Mourning Pictures*, though, demonstrates the obstacle that sexism can present. Clive Barnes offers a lukewarm review in the *New York Times*, stating that he is "not convinced that this very personal memorial should have been opened to the public" (41). While Brendan Gill compares *Mourning Pictures* to T. S. Eliot's *Four Quartets*, he says of the playwright who writes about cancer and death: "he must not induce suffering in us unless it can be made fruitful" and faults Moore's play for not doing so (113). The fruitfulness of *Mourning Pictures*, however, is addressed by Susan Braudy, who calls the play "a deep sounding of one woman's development as a daughter, a woman, and a writer" (104). Moore believes that much of the play's emotional intensity toward women is inaccessible and therefore invisible to male reviewers.

BIBLIOGRAPHY

Works by Honor Moore

"Word Puzzles against Chaos—Poetry by Marilyn Hacker and June Jordan." *Ms.* 3 (April 1975): 48, 113–14.

"A Raucous New Persona Called 'I'—Three New Poetry Anthologies." *Ms.* 5 (December 1976): 110–12.

Mourning Pictures. The New Women's Theatre: Ten Plays by Contemporary American Women. Ed. and introd. Honor Moore. New York: Vintage, 1977. 189–253.

"Theater Will Never Be the Same." *Ms.* 6 (December 1977): 36–39, 74–75.

"My Grandmother Who Painted." *The Writer on Her Work.* Ed. Janet Sternburg. New York: Norton, 1980. 45–70.

" 'Imagining Events I Pray Will Never Occur': The Responsibility of the Poet in a Nuclear Age." *Coda: Poets & Writers Newsletter* 12 (June/July 1985): 14–17.

Memoir. Goshen, CT: Chicory Blue Press, 1988.

"The Lesbian Writer and the General Reader." *AWP Chronicle* 22 (March/April 1990): 7–8.

Studies of Honor Moore

Barnes, Clive. "Theater: Death and Life." Rev. of *Mourning Pictures. New York Times*, (11 November 1974, late ed.): 41.

Braudy, Susan. "Ladies and Gentlemen, My Mother Is Dying." *Ms.* 3 (November 1974): 100–104.

Gill, Brendan. "Mighty and Dreadful Death." Rev. of *Mourning Pictures. New Yorker* 50 (18 November 1974): 113.

Hacker, Marilyn. Rev. of *Memoir. Women's Review of Books* 6 (March 1989): 11.

"Honor Moore." *Contemporary Authors.* vols. 85–88. Ed. Frances Carol Locher. Detroit: Gale Research, 1980.

Selman, Robyn. Rev. of *Memoir. Village Voice Literary Supplement* 72 (March 1989): 3.

Stone, Laurie. "Act I for Women Playwrights." Rev. of *The New Women's Theatre. Ms.* 6 (August 1977): 37–38.

CHERRÌE MORAGA (1952–   )
Skye Ward

BIOGRAPHY

The daughter of a Chicana mother, Elvira Moraga, and an Anglo father, Joseph Lawrence, Cherrìe Moraga was born September 25, 1952, in Whittier, California. Influenced by a large matriarchal family that kept strong ties to her mother's homeland in Mexico, Moraga spent most of her adolescence in the working-class communities of San Gabriel. Her mother and aunts were avid storytellers; her paternal grandmother was a vaudeville actress who instilled in her a love for theater. Referring to her background, she commented, ''The strongest creative influences on me have been the rich cultural images of Chicano/Mexican people— our passion and intimacy. . . . The oppositions of race collide inside of me—my writing is always an attempt at reconciliation'' (unless otherwise noted, all quotations are from a personal conversation with Skye Ward, August 22, 1991).

Not academically trained as a writer, Moraga took creative writing classes during the time she came out as a lesbian in 1974. Her first poems were lesbian love poems. She comments on the impetus for her writing: ''Fundamentally, I started writing to save my life. Yes, my own life first'' (*Art in America*, Con Acento. March 7, 1990, unpublished). She acknowledges the correlation between coming out as a lesbian and improving her writing:

I knew writing is what I would do—it's my life work. When I came out, I started to write well, lifting up the lid of secrecy. What is most feared is always ultimately the most beautiful in its naming. . . . Everything I write is wrought out of gut struggle.

In the early 1980s Moraga moved to the East Coast, where she lived in Massachusetts, New Hampshire, and then New York. In 1981 she co-founded Kitchen Table: Women of Color Press. The publication of *This Bridge Called My Back: Writings by Radical Women of Color* (1981) catapulted Moraga and her work into a political arena—she became highly visible as a writer. The pressure she experienced from being a spokesperson for Chicana lesbians and a movement writer for women of color had a chilling effect on her work. She recalls, "After *Bridge* . . . I felt like my communities were standing over my shoulders whenever I tried to write. . . . When one has to represent a community, you can lose the integrity and freedom of your own individual perspective."

In 1982, Moraga was a fellow at the MacDowell Arts Colony in New Hampshire, and a year later, she won the New York State Community Artist Program Award. While in New York, Moraga was selected, in 1984, as playwright-in-residence for the Hispanic Playwrights Lab at the INTAR (International Arts Relation) theater; she worked under the mentorship of director Maria Irene Fornes. Moraga and Fornes were reunited in 1990 to collaborate on her award-winning play *Shadow of a Man*. This is how she summarizes her shift from writing poetry and autobiography to playwrighting:

My motivation to write has always been about reunion with my people, and an ever-expanding definition of who my people are. In 1984, I turned to theater in the hopes of finding a more direct form of communication between me and my people. I turned to theater when my own single voice as a poet could not contain the voices inside me that wanted to be heard—voices with their own tone, rhythm, their own special language blending English, Spanish, Mexican caló, American slang . . . it was a great revelation and relief to discover that I was not limited to my own personal biography as a writer, but that a much larger community of people could inhabit me and speak through me: *La Raza*. (*Art in America*, Con Acento, unpublished)

Much of Cherríe Moraga's early writing was done in isolation; she was not "an active part of la causa" (*Loving in the War Years* 113). Her politicalization in the Chicano and feminist movements was a catalyst for developing an internal critique and dialogue with Chicano culture, which provided a framework for Chicana feminist writers that remains unparalleled.

From 1986 to 1991, Moraga was employed as a lecturer of writing and theater in Chicano studies at the University of California at Berkeley. Presently, she serves as an artist-in-residence at BRAVA! for Women in the Arts, where she teaches writing for performance. Moraga's theater and poetry have been anthologized in numerous literary publications both in the United States and Mexico.

MAJOR WORKS AND THEMES

Moraga's work embodies her Chicana feminist lesbian experience and identities. Major themes in her work include issues of ethnic and sexual sovereignty, indigenous women's issues, immigrant rights, health care, domestic violence, and the dominance of Catholicism in Chicano culture.

Moraga's original writing voice was first expressed through her poetry. *Loving in the War Years* is a collection of poems, journal entries, prose pieces, and essays that poignantly critiques Chicana racial-sexual oppression. Moraga's joint investigation of female sexuality and identity politics was unprecedented in that it brought lesbianism to the attention of mainstream Chicanos. She summarizes her politicization:

When I finally lifted the lid to my lesbianism, a profound connection with my mother reawakened in me. It wasn't until I acknowledged and confronted my own lesbianism in the flesh, that my heartfelt identification with and empathy for my mother's oppression—due to being poor, uneducated, and Chicana—was realized. My lesbianism is the avenue through which I have learned the most about silence and oppression, and it continues to be the most tactile reminder to me that we are not free human beings. (52)

The sexuality of Mexican/Chicana women in general, lesbianism in particular, as well as rape and violence against women, are recurring themes in her work. She asserts that "sex has always been part of the question of freedom. The freedom to want passionately" (v).

Her three plays all have central female characters who personify Chicana sisterhood, sexual desire, self-determination, and resistance to Chicano machismo and white patriarchy. "The woman who defies her role as subservient to her husband, father, brother, or son by taking control of her own sexual destiny is purported to be a 'traitor to her race' " (113). In *Giving up the Ghost*, Moraga "explores the ways in which both lesbian and heterosexual Chicanas' sense of self as sexual beings has been affected by their culture's definition of masculinity and femininity" (Yarbro-Bejarano, "Chicano Literature" 144). Moraga's female characters illustrate the complexities of women's relationships in Chicano culture. Ultimately, the salvation and liberation of Chicanas are realized through Chicana sisterhood—women loving women as sisters, mothers/daughters, and lovers.

Shadow of a Man underscores the potentially destructive love-hate relationship between daughter and mother, personified in her characters Leticia and Hortensia. In one scene, Leticia rebels against her mother by willfully losing her virginity. Leticia explains to her mother, "I wanted it to be worthless, Mama . . . not for me to be worthless, but to know that my worth had nothing to do with it." The young Chicana character Cerezita in Moraga's third play, *Heroes and Saints*, dramatizes Chicanas' struggle for autonomy and freedom. Confined to a wheelchair because of a severe birth defect caused by pesticide exposure to her farmworker mother, Cerezita has no body; she has only a head. Cerezita is a visionary who not only dreams and writes about her own liberation, but also of her people: *La Raza*.

Cherrìe Moraga's status as an outsider (mixed-blood, lesbian, intellectual of working-class origins, and feminist cultural nationalist) has thoroughly informed her work. A fundamental task in her work has been to seek a recuperation of language, reunion with family, and the retribalization of her people.

CRITICAL RECEPTION

Writing as openly lesbian has, on one hand, opened up a very receptive and eager audience to Moraga, and at the same time, it has completely eliminated access to certain other communities such as "traditional Chicanos." Conversely, she has been well received by gay and lesbian readers. *Lambda Book Report: A Contemporary Review of Gay and Lesbian Literature* listed Moraga among the fifty most influential people in gay and lesbian literature in the past decade; and listed *This Bridge Called My Back* among the top banner books in the 1980s (March/April 1991). *This Bridge Called My Back* won the Before Columbus Foundation American Book Award in 1986.

Cuentos: Stories by Latinas, co-edited by Moraga, was the first collection of stories by Latina feminists in the United States. *Cuentos* is a precursor to anthologies by Chicana/Latina lesbians who now write as openly lesbian. In her review of *Cuentos*, Chicana feminist Ana Castillo comments: "The age of the silenced Latina/Chicana has come to an end. . . . The book resounds with the exhilarated breath of the degagged" (135). *This Bridge* and *Cuentos* have become standard texts in women's studies courses.

After several years of play writing and the premiere of *Giving up the Ghost*, Moraga finds that heterosexism and homophobia remain formidable barriers to getting her plays produced in Chicano theater. Ironically, it wasn't until her play *Shadow of a Man* (as yet unpublished) gained mainstream recognition that Chicano theater directors began expressing interest in her plays. Commenting on the impact of Cherríe Moraga's plays, Chicana feminist critic Yvonne Yarbro-Bejarano writes, "In taking the theme of sexuality and the perspective of the Chicana lesbian to the stage, Moraga has broken a silence which has lasted over twenty years in the contemporary Chicano theater movement" ("Cherríe Moraga's *Giving Up the Ghost*" 113). The premiere of *Shadow of a Man* in 1990 established Moraga as a serious playwright in both Chicano and mainstream theater. *Shadow of a Man* won the Fund for New American Plays Award, a project of the John F. Kennedy Center for Performing Arts.

BIBLIOGRAPHY

Works by Cherríe Moraga
Books

Loving in the War Years: (lo que nunca pasò por sus labios). Boston: South End, 1983.
Giving up the Ghost: Teatro in Two Acts. Los Angeles: West End, 1986.
A Collection of Three Plays by Cherríe Moraga: Giving Up the Ghost, Shadow of a Man, Heroes and Saints. Albuquerque: West End Press, 1993.
The Last Generation. Boston: South End Press, 1993.
Shadow of a Man. Albuquerque: West End Press, 1993.

Play Productions

Giving Up the Ghost, San Francisco, Theater Rhinoceros, February 10, 1989.
Coatlicue's Call [performance piece], San Francisco, Theater Artuad, October 25, 1990.

Shadow of a Man, San Francisco, Eureka Theater, November 10, 1990.
Heroes and Saints, San Francisco, Mission Theater, April 4, 1992.

Other Works

This Bridge Called My Back: Writings by Radical Women of Color. Ed. Moraga and
Gloria Anzaldúa, with a preface by Moraga. Watertown, MA: Peresphone, 1981.
Cuentos: Stories by Latinas. Ed. Moraga, Alma Gòmez and Mariana Romo-Carmona.
New York: Kitchen Table: Women of Color, 1983.
Esta puente, mi espalda: voces de mujeres tercermundistas en los Estados Unidos. Ed.
Moraga and Ana Castillo, with a preface by Moraga. San Francisco: Ism, 1988.
"The Saving of America: A Chicana Lesbian Response to the Quincentennial" (unpub-
lished). [Parts of this essay originally appeared in "Entre Nosotras: A Personal
Response to the 13th International Lesbian and Gay Conference in Acapulco."
Outlook 4:3 (Winter 1992).], 56–57.
Shadow of a Man. Shattering the Myths. Ed. Denise Chávez. Houston: Arte Publico,
1992.

Studies of Cherrìe Moraga

Alarcòn, Norma. "Interview with Cherrìe Moraga." *Third Woman* 3, nos. 1 and 2 (1986):
127–34.
———. "Making Familia from Scratch: Split Subjectivities in the Work of Helena Maria
Viramontes and Cherrìe Moraga." *Chicana Creativity and Criticism: Charting
New Frontiers in American Literature*. Ed. Maria Hererra-Sobek and Helena Maria
Viramontes. Houston: Arte Publico, 1988. 147–59.
Castillo, Ana. "Cuentos Review." *Third Woman* 3, nos. 1 and 2 (1986): 135.
Quintanales, Mirtha N. "Loving in the War Years: An Interview with Cherrìe Moraga."
off our backs (Jan. 1985): 12–13.
Saldivar, Ramon. "Gender and Difference in Rios, Cisneros, and Moraga." *Chicano
Narrative: The Dialectics of Difference*. Madison: University of Wisconsin Press,
1990.
Umpierre, Luz Maria. "With Cherrìe Moraga." *Americas Review* 14 (Summer 1986):
54–67.
Yarbro-Bejarano, Yvonne. "Cherrìe Moraga's *Giving Up the Ghost*: The Representation
of Female Desire." *Third Woman* 3, nos. 1 and 2 (1986): 113–20.
———. "Chicano Literature: From a Chicana Feminist Perspective." *Chicana Creativity
and Criticism: Charting New Frontiers in American Literature*. Houston: Arte
Publico, 1988. 144.
———. "Deconstructing the Lesbian Body: Cherrìe Moraga's *Loving in the War Years*."
Chicana Lesbians: The Girls Our Mothers Warned Us About. Ed. Carla Trujillo.
Berkeley: Third Woman Press, 1991. 143–55.

ROBIN MORGAN (1941–   )
Blanche Wiesen Cook

BIOGRAPHY

Child star, feminist activist, award-winning poet, journalist, novelist, editor-in-chief of *Ms.* magazine, Robin Morgan has devoted her great wit, energy, and vision to the empowerment of women worldwide. A leader of "this wave" of the contemporary feminist movement, she has spent most of her adult life opposing war, poverty, racism, sexism, homophobia, and violence in every guise. Her emphases as an activist and writer changed over time, and for over twenty years, Robin Morgan's passionate commitment to women has influenced and enhanced virtually every movement for women's rights and empowerment in the United States and internationally. Her two classic anthologies, *Sisterhood Is Powerful* (1970) and *Sisterhood Is Global* (1984), remain required reading for activists and students of feminism globally.

Born on January 29, 1941, in Lake Worth, Florida, Robin Morgan first achieved fame as the child star who played Dagmar in the vastly popular 1950s television series "Mama." But she always knew she wanted to be a writer. Even earlier, during a party fund-raiser for UNICEF (then the United Nations International Children's Emergency Fund), when Robin was perhaps four, perhaps six, and the star of her own radio program on WOR, "The Little Robin Morgan Show," Eleanor Roosevelt asked her what she wanted to do when she grew up. Robin, much to her stage-mother's chagrin, replied immediately and forcefully: "I am going to be a writer." Eleanor Roosevelt responded: "You will then be a writer: You can do anything you really want to do" (personal conversation).

After graduating with honors from the Wetter School in Mount Vernon, New York, in 1956, Robin was privately tutored in the United States and Europe between 1956 and 1959. She studied literature and classics at Columbia University and took poetry workshops with Louise Bogan, Babette Deutsch, and Mark Van Doren.

During the 1960s, Robin Morgan opposed the war in Vietnam, participated in the struggle against segregation and for civil rights, was active with CORE (Congress of Racial Equality) and became a member of the first women's caucus of SNCC (Student Nonviolent Coordinating Committee), associated with the militant Left, decided revolution was about feminism, divorced the Left, helped found the Women's International Terrorist Conspiracy from Hell (WITCH) and the New York Radical Women, which organized the first Miss America protest in Atlantic City in 1968—a demonstration which inaugurated the grass-roots movements that blossomed into the contemporary wave of feminism during the 1970s.

Also in 1968, Morgan publicly "came out" in the *New York Times*. Her son Blake Morgan (Pitchford) was born in 1969 and is now a talented and acclaimed musician. Although Morgan and her husband Kenneth Pitchford, a founder of Gay Liberation Front (GLF—the group that did Stonewall), continued to struggle through their marriage until 1983, women occupied the core of her heart and became the essence of her work. Since 1984, she has been involved in a transnational relationship with Marilyn J. Waring, a goat farmer, author, economist, and former member of New Zealand's parliament.

Between 1968 and 1992, Morgan wrote countless articles, and over thirteen books—most of them published internationally and translated into eight languages. She has lectured at every major university in North America, and throughout Europe, Central America, the Caribbean, New Zealand, and Australia. She has been awarded the National Endowment for the Arts Prize in Poetry (1979), the Front Page Award for Distinguished Journalism (1981), the Woman of the Year Award (1990) from the Feminist Majority Foundation, and an honorary doctorate in humane letters by the University of Connecticut at Storrs (1992).

MAJOR WORKS AND THEMES

Controversial and provocative, direct and radical, Robin Morgan's best and most enduring works are frequently autobiographical and reflect her life's journey—often bumpy, always passionate. In 1969, she became part of the Women's RAT collective, which took over the male-dominated underground newspaper and attempted to transform it. As part of that effort, she published her classic "Goodbye to All That," which represented her permanent farewell to Left political orthodoxy and alliances with male supremacists. With a six-month-old baby and a mainstream job as an editor, Morgan began to contemplate her collection *Sisterhood Is Powerful*. When orthodox leftist women at RAT decried feminism as bourgeois, Morgan moved on. There was no turning back. In her new collection, *The Word of a Woman: Feminist Dispatches 1968–1992* (Norton, 1992), Morgan reprints the essay and describes her intellectual journey.

In another essay, "The Politics of Silence," Morgan notes that class and culture played their part:

As a European American, a white, apostate Jew who has lived most of her life in New York, . . . I acknowledge that my style tends to dramatize events, exaggerate states of being, and delight in conversation for its own sake, almost as an art form. . . . My tools as an artist are words—with all the inherent dangers thereof. A lifelong vocation addressing the silence of the unknowable reader. (170, 189)

In 1973 Morgan keynoted the Los Angeles Lesbian Feminist Conference, with a widely quoted and much acclaimed address: "Lesbianism and Feminism: Synonyms or Contradictions?" That speech analyzed the contours of all that divided or united women, in and out of the women's movement, and presented Morgan's most precise statement of her own position and vision. Later published in her collection *Going Too Far* (1977), it remains a classic and generative challenge for the future of the women's movement to get beyond the stereotypes that keep us separated and apart. Having been "straight-baited, dyke-baited, red-baited, violence-baited, mother-baited, and artist-baited," Morgan had the "scars" to discuss with significant authority the lesbian-straight split among feminists. She recalled her "very first consciousness-raising" meeting, where she described herself as bisexual: "Every woman in the room moved, almost imperceptibly, an inch or so away from me." Morgan dealt directly with the need to define oneself clearly, and to create words and new vision to deal with the backlash against radical feminism, and lesbianism, that had begun within the feminist community as early as 1970:

I am a woman. I am a feminist, a radical feminist, yea, a militant feminist. I am a witch. I identify as a lesbian because I love the People of Women and certain individual women with my life's blood. Yes, I live with a man. . . . Yes, I am a mother. . . . The man is a faggot-effeminist, and we are together the biological as well as the nurturant parents of our child. This confuses a lot of people—it not infrequently confuses us. But there it is. Most of all, "I am a monster—and I am proud." (174)

The last line is from the title poem of Morgan's first book of poetry, *Monster* (1972). One turns to Morgan's vivid and lyrical poetry for her earliest references to her love for women. In *Monster*, Morgan dedicated "Lesbian Poem" "to those who turned immediately from the contents page to this poem." There she introduces us to Joan of Orleans' great love, Haiviette, "with whom Joan lived, loved, slept." And, she tells us, scholar Margaret Murray, author of *The Witch-Cult in Western Europe*, has found evidence also that "Joan was Wica, after all."

It is Morgan's love for women, her commitment to facing the difficulties of loving women, for getting to the edge of danger where eroticism resides and enjoying the flowers of that love, that one finds most keenly in her poetry, from *Monster* to *Lady of the Beasts*, to *Depth Perception: New Poems and a Masque*. In 1990, Norton published *Upstairs in the Garden: Selected and New Poems*.

In her most autobiographical work, her first novel, *Dry Your Smile* (1987), Morgan explores her relationships with women, the complexities and contradictions of family love and rage, marriage and freedom, the haunting pulls of mother love, jealousy and possession, and her first really major love affair with a woman. The frontispiece, a Caribbean proverb, prepares the reader: "When a woman loves a woman, it is the blood of the mothers speaking."

Morgan's most recent novel, an enchanting prose-poem, *The Mer-Child: A Legend for Children and Other Adults*, is a parable of loneliness in the face of bigotry, misunderstanding, and exclusion. But love beyond difference prevails and endures; and every child should receive a copy, for hope, for the future.

The need to move beyond racism, beyond bigotry, beyond all those atrocities that violently or passively divide us and distort our culture, that sense of a hopeful future beyond hate or misunderstanding has impelled Robin Morgan to help found several institutions for feminist change, including the Sisterhood Is Global Institute, the Feminist Women's Health Network, the National Network of Rape Crisis Centers, and the Battered Women's Refuge Network. Morgan's powerful writings have reflected her dedication to a non-violent and feminist future: *The Anatomy of Freedom: Feminism, Physics, and Global Politics* (1982) and most notably *The Demon Lover* (1989).

Morgan's *The Demon Lover: On the Sexuality of Terrorism* is an investigation of male violence, out of the context of her own experience and research. In part, Morgan set out to purge her own past in a courageous confrontation with her youthful self. Terrorists are half in love with death, and when Morgan discovered her great love for women, she decided that she did not "want to die, after all" (217). She rejected "all revolutions that long for catastrophe," for a revolution that would create "women as a global political force" (243).

In this, her most powerful prose book, written out of anguish and love, Robin Morgan presents an absorbing and fervently feminist analysis of terrorism, from the Americas, to the Middle East, to Asia and Africa. The demon lover destroys what he would create: subjugation cannot be liberation. Violence in the streets; violence in the sheets. It is no accident that in the United States a woman is battered every fifteen seconds by her significant other.

Dedicated to absolute pacifism, Morgan has ardent love for justice and women. She calls for a "politics of ecstasy" on behalf of love and survival. On most issues her wit and verve are delightful; her scholarship vast. Morgan wants justice and an end to torture and political imprisonment. Why, she asks, are Alejandrina Torres (sentenced to thirty-five years), Susan Rosenberg (sentenced to fifty-eight years), and Sylvia Baraldine (isolated, and suffering with cancer) still in prison?

Morgan concludes with an appeal for women to move beyond terror, toward transformation and action. Silence is consent. Morgan's passionate intensity makes the giant step from personal liberation to revolutionary global politics sound easy—to see the connectedness in all things; to work with other women to celebrate and honor this life and the living of it, in all its fragile, transient beauty.

CRITICAL RECEPTION

Robin Morgan's various works have been critically acclaimed in a wide spectrum of the media and reprinted abroad, in various feminist and mainstream journals. Indeed as one of the editors of the first *Ms.* magazine, and now editor-in-chief of the new no-advertising international *Ms.*, Morgan has helped to create the U.S.'s most important feminist literary magazines.

BIBLIOGRAPHY

Works by Robin Morgan

Poetry

Monster. New York: Random House, 1972.
Lady of the Beasts. New York: Random House, 1976.
Death Benefits. Port Townsend, WA: Copper Canyon Press, 1981.
Depth Perception: New Poems and a Masque. New York: Doubleday, 1982.
Upstairs in the Garden: Selected and New Poems, 1966–1988. New York: W. W. Norton, 1990.

Fiction

Dry Your Smile. New York: Doubleday, 1987.
The Mer-Child: A Legend for Children and Other Adults. New York: Feminist Press, 1991.

Non-Fiction

The New Woman: An Anthology, co-edited. New York: Bobbs-Merrill, 1969.
Sisterhood Is Powerful: An Anthology of Writings from the Women's Liberation Movement. New York: Random House, 1970.
Going Too Far. New York: Random House, 1977.
The Anatomy of Freedom: Feminism, Physics, and Global Politics. New York: Doubleday, 1982.
Sisterhood Is Global: The International Women's Movement Anthology. New York: Doubleday/Anchor, 1984.
The Demon Lover: On the Sexuality of Terrorism. New York: W. W. Norton, 1989
The Word of a Woman: New and Selected Essays. New York: W. W. Norton, 1992.

Selected Studies of Robin Morgan

Altman, Meryl. *Women's Review of Books* (October 1990): 16.
Becker, Alida. "Mask over Masks." *New York Times Book Review* September 27, 1987: 16.
Dick, Leslie. "The Orphans' Refusal." *New Statesman* (April 1988): 27.
Eaglen, A. B. *Library Journal* October 15, 1976: 2180.
Foster, Sallie L. *Library Journal* November 15, 1982: 160.
Hacker, Andrew. *New York Times Book Review* January 27, 1985: 12.

Kaveney, Roz. *New Statesman* June 23, 1989: 40.

Parini, Jay. *Poetry* (August 1977): 293.

————. *Times Literary Supplement* November 12, 1982: 1251.

Robinson, Paul. *Psychology Today* (January 1983): 15.

Rubin, Merle. *Christian Science Monitor* June 7, 1989: 12.

Stuttaford, Genevieve. Review of *The Demon Lover*. *Publishers Weekly* December 23, 1988: 72.

Walt, Vivienne. *Nation* March 2, 1985: 248.

Weinberg, Joanna K. *New York Times Book Review* April 30, 1989: 17.

EILEEN MYLES (1949–   )
Debra Weinstein

BIOGRAPHY

Eileen Myles was born on December 9, 1949, in Cambridge, Massachusetts. Her father was a mail carrier at Harvard Yard. After graduating in 1971 from the University of Massachusetts in Boston, she traveled the world. When she returned, she began graduate school at Queens College but dropped out. Shortly thereafter, she enrolled in the free writing workshop at St. Mark's Church, where she studied with Ted Berrigan and Alice Notley. At twenty-four, she decided to make writing her life's work, and she has been, in her own words, "unemployed" ever since.

New York City became Myles's poetry stomping ground. She did her first poetry reading at CBGB's, New York's prototypical punk club, in 1974, and "came out" as a poet three years later when she read love poems (which she later collected in her book *Sappho's Boat*) at St. Mark's Church. In 1977, unable to publish her own work, Myles began *dodgems*, her own literary magazine, where she published many well-known writers. In 1979, Myles got a job working as the assistant to the poet James Schuyler, who became her mentor and friend. Schuyler's aesthetic, which calls for out-of-the-closet poetry written in "a voice conversational and prosaic, yet capable of rising to moments of exaltation," informs her work (Selman 170).

Eileen Myles has published poems in such journals as *CUZ*, *Ploughshares*, *Bomb*, *New Directions*, *Paris Review*, *Partisan Review*, *Between C & D*, *Kenyon Review*, *Outlook*, and *City Lights*. Her poems have been anthologized in *The Best American Poetry, 1988* and *Gay and Lesbian Poetry in Our Time*. Two of her plays have been produced at PS 122 in New York City, and she has toured nationally and internationally giving performances of her writing. Two collections of her stories, *Bread and Water* and *1969*, were published by Hanuman. Her collection of poetry *Not Me* was nominated for a Lambda Book Award.

From 1984 to 1986, Myles served as artistic director of the Poetry Project at St. Mark's Church. She has been a fellow of the MacDowell Colony, has been awarded an NEA (National Endowment for the Arts) Inter-Arts grant, and has been the recipient of the New York State Creative Artist's Public Services grant. In 1992, she was the first lesbian poet to announce her candidacy for president of the United States. She writes on literature and visual arts for the *Village Voice* and *Art in America*.

MAJOR WORKS AND THEMES

Eileen Myles is as American as Gertrude Stein. She is the voice of every working-class lesbian who ever desired to have been born a Kennedy. Her poems are both expansive and inward. They expand to tell all matters of the universe but are aphoristic in design. They are often written in two- or three-word lines that run down the page like a ribbon. This is because Myles writes her poems in little notebooks, usually on the subway, crouching in her seat so no one can see over her shoulder.

In Eileen Myles's poetry, we see the tension between the private life and the public place. She is the big booming voice of the common woman calling the sleeping Americans to action, reminding us that we live in a society which is "home of the business man and home of the rich artist" ("An American Poem," *Not Me* 16). But Myles is also the private voice of the lover, reminding each of us that "somewhere everyone is naked, just a little bit" ("Twentieth Century Dinosaur," *Not Me* 59).

Myles's fiction is also informed by her keen eye and sensual delight in the world. In her non-stop, frenetic style she writes of "baseball hat and truck country . . . where men are all men" (*Bread and Water* 63) and women are all lesbians. She writes about speeding on amphetamines, drinking oneself senseless, sleeping with women, and about the hopelessness of a working-class life in America.

Myles's working-class sensibility informs all of her work. She believes that her writing is part of the oral tradition in literature and this belief is partly responsible for her unpretentious, unliterary, conversational tone. She says, "In a working class background, the person who is taken seriously is the one who can speak the best. Someone who talks well has more power than the writer in her tower. My goal is to write work that my mother will want to listen to" (unless otherwise noted, all quotations are from personal communication with the author).

Her 1992 write-in candidacy for the president of the United States is, no doubt, a natural consequence of a lifetime of oral strategizing. As presidential candidate, she has been interviewed by the media and has drawn attention to the under-representation of women and gays in the United States. She has been vocal about the need for alternative forms of birth control, "especially lesbian sex," which Myles says "is something I wish more women in public life would be open about.'' A political activist, she has been arrested for protesting for the rights of all women.

CRITICAL RECEPTION

Eileen Myles has had a difficult time gaining acceptance as a gay writer. Internalized homophobia in the gay community has until recently prevented her from gaining greater visibility. In 1981, for example, a renowned gay and lesbian bookstore in New York City would not stock her book *A Fresh Young Voice from the Plains* because it did not have enough ''gay'' content. Because she was initially integrated into the ''New York School'' poetry community (a community of writers that includes John Ashbery, Barbara Guest, Frank O'Hara, and Jimmy Schuyler, among others), she has had to struggle to gain acceptance in lesbian circles. She says, ''The interesting thing about being a gay poet is that if you don't come up through the lesbian circle, you don't get defined as a lesbian poet, so your work often misses the audience it was meant for.''

Critical reception for her books has been quite positive. The issue of her sexuality is often handled in a matter-of-fact way. In the *Village Voice*, C. Carr writes, ''Eileen Myles . . . values her differentness. As a poet, bohemian, lesbian, she becomes the heroic anti-hero of her poems'' (29). Often critics are more interested in her influences and affinities than in her subject matter. Writing for *Outweek*, James Conrad compares her to Walt Whitman, for ''she indulges in a kind of ecstasy in herself as poet, explorer, woman and lover'' (60). Robyn Selman says in the *Kenyon Review* that Myles ''is rather easily located within a feminist tradition, picking up on the work of Anne Waldman, Judy Grahn and Susan Griffin'' (168). In a review of her performance in *Leaving New York*, she was described by Albert Williams as a ''street scene Sappho'' (43).

Liz Kotz wrote in *Artweek* that Myles ''is to me one of the most compelling recorders of contemporary lesbian life in all its sexiness and pain, its gritty realities and wry humor'' (13). Indeed. Eileen Myles is a multifaceted, multitalented artist, who, given another decade or two, just might be our president.

BIBLIOGRAPHY

Works by Eileen Myles

Books

The Irony of the Leash. New York: Jim Brodey Books, 1978.
A Fresh Young Voice from the Plains. New York: Power Mad, 1981.
Sappho's Boat. Los Angeles: Little Caesar, 1982.
Bread and Water. New York: Hanuman Books, 1987.
1969. New York: Hanuman Books, 1989.
Not Me. New York: Semiotext(e), 1991.

Works in Anthologies

"The Nude Bombadier." *Fresh Paint, An Anthology of Younger New York Poets*. Ed. Michael Slater and Yuki Hartman. New York: Ailanthus Press, 1977. 1.

"New York," "Polemy." *Coming Attractions: An Anthology of Poets in Their 20s*. Ed. Dennis Cooper. Los Angeles: Little Caesar, 1981. 102–6.

"Down," "Medium Poem," "Poetry Reading," "My Cheap Lifestyle," "On the Death of Robert Lowell," and "Greedy Seasons." *Uplate: American Poetry Since 1970*. Ed. Andrei Codrescu. New York: 4 Walls 8 Windows, 1987. 343–46.

"A Woman Like Me." *Gay and Lesbian Poetry in Our Time*. Ed. Joan Larkin and Carl Morse. New York: St. Martin's, 1988. 275.

"At Last." *Poets for Life: Seventy-Six Poets Respond to AIDS*. Ed. Michael Klein. New York: Crown, 1989. 188.

"Public Television." *The Best American Poetry, 1988*. Ed. John Ashbery. New York: Macmillan/Collier, 1989. 138.

Studies of Eileen Myles

Bosveld, Jane. "Poetry in Short." *Ms*. (Sept. 1982): 94.

Carr, C. "Spies Like Us." *Village Voice Literary Supplement* (June 1991): 29.

Conrad, James. "Without Me, You're Nothing." *Outweek* May 8, 1991: 60.

Killian, Kevin. "Not Me." *Small Press Traffic* (Spring-Summer 1991): 8.

Kotz, Liz. Review. *Artweek* March 29, 1990: 13.

Scholnick, Michael. "Similitude in Dissimilitude." *Poetry Project Newsletter* (January 1983): 4.

Schulman, Sarah. "It Could Be Verse." *Interview* (Dec. 1990): 48.

Selman, Robyn. "Everything Has Its Place." *Kenyon Review* (Spring 1992): 167–71.

Williams, Albert. Review. *Chicago Reader* May 31, 1991: 43.

JOAN NESTLE (1940–   )
Susan Rochman

BIOGRAPHY

Joan Nestle was born on May 12, 1940, in New York City. She was raised by her mother, Regina Nestle; her father died before she was born. From a young age Nestle was aware of her sexual attraction to other women, and she came out as a femme in the 1950s—an era and a sexual identity that have consistently informed her political activism and her writing.

In 1957, Nestle graduated from Martin Van Buren High School in Queens. She then attended Queens College in Flushing, New York, where she was graduated in 1963 with a B.A. in English. Nestle obtained a master's degree in English from New York University in 1968 and spent the following two years as a doctoral candidate in English, completing all work except for her dissertation.

During the late 1950s and through the 1960s, Nestle was part of a thriving bar community in Greenwich Village, New York. This experience, which involved weekly encounters with police and vice squad members, became the inspiration for much of her later writing. While in college, Nestle became involved with the civil rights movement and the Congress of Racial Equality (CORE). She went to the South in 1965 to assist in the voter registration drive and joined in the civil rights march from Selma to Montgomery. Nestle became active in the feminist movement in 1971 through her participation in lesbian groups such as the Lesbian Liberation Committee. But joining with women and creating a woman-identified environment was not new, it was instead a more public and publicized extension of a struggle for equal rights she had confronted in the lesbian bars of Greenwich Village.

In 1972, Nestle helped establish the Gay Academic Union, an organization formed to speak to and for gays and lesbians on college campuses. There she met other lesbians who, in the face of a rapidly changing lesbian culture, were interested in documenting lesbian existence prior to the feminist movement. In

1973, these women founded the Lesbian Herstory Archives, housed in a small room in Nestle's apartment. The archives grew to contain thousands of books, letters, private journals, and photographs. They sprawled from one room to the next in Nestle's home, until they were moved in 1992 to a three-story house in Park Slope, Brooklyn, their permanent location.

For Nestle, literature and history are intimately connected. "I see literature as the expression of history and history as a form of literature," Nestle explains (unless otherwise noted, quotations are from personal communication, January 1992). Her interest in these two areas is reflected in her work as a writing instructor in the SEEK (Search for Enlightened and Elevated Knowledge) program at Queens College, where she has taught since 1966. The focus of her course is a memoirs project, an assignment that provides students with the opportunity to document and give life to their individual histories.

Nestle began writing political essays about butch-femme relationships, poetry, and pornography in 1978, when she was diagnosed with a chronic illness. Since then, she says, when times are hard the one thing that has always been able to pull her through has been her writing. Over the past decade, Nestle's writing has appeared in a wide range of feminist and lesbian publications, from the political and cultural *Big Apple Dyke (B.A.D.) News, Body Politic, Common Lives/Lesbian Lives, Conditions, Gay Community News, Heresies, Lesbian Connection, off our backs, 13th Moon* and *Sinister Wisdom*, to the lesbian porn magazines *Bad Attitude* and *On Our Backs*.

Nestle has spoken about lesbian history, censorship, and sexuality at over 200 college campuses and at numerous conferences and forums. She is on the advisory boards of *Out/Look National Gay and Lesbian Quarterly Bridges*, a feminist Jewish journal, the National Council of Jewish Women Resource Center, and Three Dollar Bill Theater Company.

In all of her endeavors, Nestle has confronted common lesbian and feminist assumptions about lesbian culture and history. "As a woman, as a Lesbian, as a Jew, I know that much of what I call history others will not," Nestle writes. "But answering that challenge of exclusion is the work of a lifetime" (*A Restricted Country* 10).

MAJOR WORKS AND THEMES

"The women's movement understood the need for a profound breaking of boundaries when it embraced the slogan 'the personal is political.' I would like to carry it one step further: if the personal is political, the more personal is historical" (*A Restricted Country* 10). Joan Nestle's expansion of this feminist credo is emblematic of the ways in which she has used her writing to create a lesbian history that is infused with the diversity of the lesbian community and inclusive of the women who have been moved into the margins of the dominant feminist discourse.

Nestle's book *A Restricted Country*, published in 1987, is a collection of twenty-eight political essays, autobiographical writings, and pornographic love stories that she began writing in 1978. Her writing proudly presents all of who she is: Jewish, femme, feminist, lesbian. She describes how her body—strong, defiant, and sexual—provided her with the ability to take part in and to define history, and how it became a living marker for others' definitions: deviant, outcast, other.

In the title essay, Nestle describes her family's trip in 1956 to the Shining Star Guest Ranch in Arizona, a resort they soon discovered denied access to Jewish people. Her family was accepted at a nearby Jewish dude ranch, but they were still outsiders: a working-class family, a single mother. On a horseback ride near the end of their week's stay, Nestle was confronted by real estate signs proclaiming the land as the most restricted country in Arizona—a euphemism for no Jews allowed.

This theme of who or what is permissible, of borders and boundaries, outsider and other, marks much of Nestle's work. Writing about these restrictions is an act of transgression, transforming what is deemed personal, private, or "wrong" into a history that is public, honest, and affirming. Nestle's writing is informed by a historically specific lesbian identity, but it is more than autobiography; individual remembrance becomes the collective history of political divisions, discrimination, lesbian passion, and butch-femme sexuality. "History will betray us if we betray it," writes Nestle. "If we do not learn the language of each other's historical truths, if we do not grow aware of the places where life has been stolen, our histories and our lives will be selfish things" (*A Restricted Country* 186).

Many of Nestle's political essays document the history of butch-femme relationships. She explores the complexities of these relationships and the contradictions inherent in a feminist theory that discredits and maligns butch and femme lesbians, women who redefined womanhood based on their own experience. Nestle argues that butch-femme relationships are not imitating or perpetuating heterosexual relationships but are demonstrating a distinctly lesbian way of being, pushing at the boundaries of sexuality, and making a "complex erotic statement."

Nestle describes her own experiences of being labeled "patriarchal" and "male-identified" by other lesbians and feminists for being a femme who enjoys wearing lipstick, and who sees clothing and makeup as a personal exploration of sexuality as well as a means of engaging in an erotic exchange with other lesbians. And she describes the power that some feminists have misunderstood or been unable to see. "Fems are women who have made choices, but we need to be able to read between the cultural lines to appreciate their strength," writes Nestle. "Lesbians should be the mistresses of discrepancies, knowing that resistance lies in the change of context" ("The Fem Question" 236).

While many women have found support and validation for their own experiences in Nestle's writing, others have attempted to silence her voice. For example, what is now one of Nestle's most quoted and discussed pieces, "Esther's Story"—about a one-night stand Nestle had with a passing woman, a woman who looked like a man to the straight world—almost went unpublished when a woman working for the typesetter used by *Big Apple Dyke News* termed it "offensive."

In writing about her mother, Regina, in "Two Women: Regina Nestle, 1910–1978, and Her Daughter, Joan," and "My Mother Liked to Fuck," Nestle uses her mother's experiences to question certain feminist assumptions about heterosexuality and sexual pleasure. Regina, a single mother, was a bookkeeper and sometimes prostitute. She had affairs with her bosses and took money from their offices to make ends meet. But Nestle refuses to write about her mother as the victim of male power or heterosexuality. Instead, she writes of the strength she gained from her mother's refusal to be denied her right to be sexual and from her mother's ability to work the system the best way she knew how.

Following the publication of *A Restricted Country*, Nestle co-edited with Naomi Holoch *Women on Women: An Anthology of American Lesbian Short Fiction*, published in 1990. Nestle's goal in assembling this collection of stories, she says, was to provide lesbians with the opportunity "to see their lives in a different way." Thus *Women on Women*, like *A Restricted Country*, illustrates Nestle's belief that "women's lives are our deepest text" ("The Fem Question" 239).

CRITICAL RECEPTION

Despite the controversy that has surrounded pornography and sexuality in the feminist movement, Nestle's *A Restricted Country* was highly praised in the feminist and lesbian press. In the *National Women's Studies Association Journal*, Bettina Aptheker describes *A Restricted Country* as "beautifully crafted," adding, "Her images are vivid, her language clear and tough, her feelings palpable" (722). Other reviews have termed Nestle's book "provocative," "passionate," "brave," "brilliant," "audacious," and "a work of exquisite honesty and strength."

The American Book Association (ABA) awarded *A Restricted Country* the 1988 Gay Book Award. A reviewer in *Booklist*, the publication of the ABA, called Nestle's writing "limpid, graceful, yet rhetorically impressive," noting, "the autobiographical essays are extraordinarily clear-sighted and moving; the attacks on the feminist anti-porn movement are full of political and humane wisdom; and the erotic sketches . . . are steamy and ardently affectionate . . . [a]ltogether an amazing book" (517).

Nestle's essays that describe and document butch-femme relationships and identities have greatly benefited the lesbian and gay community as well as other historians and scholars. Her work is quoted and referenced in articles in a wide range of scholarly journals including *Quarterly Review of Film*, *Modern Drama*, and *Theatre Journal*.

BIBLIOGRAPHY

Works by Joan Nestle

"The Fem Question." *Pleasure and Danger: Exploring Female Sexuality*. Ed. Carole Vance. Boston, London, Melbourne, and Henley: Routledge and Kegan Paul, 1984. 232.

"The Gift of Taking." *On Our Backs* Winter 1984. 20.

"A Change of Life." *Bad Attitude* Winter 1985. 10.

A Restricted Country. Ithaca, NY: Firebrand Books, 1987. Contains essays and stories previously published in a wide range of lesbian and feminist publications.

Women on Women: An Anthology of American Lesbian Short Fiction. Ed. Joan Nestle and Naomi Holoch. New York: New American Library, 1990.

The Persistent Desire: A Femme-Butch Reader. Ed. Joan Nestle. Boston: Alyson Publications, 1992.

Women on Women II: An Anthology of American Lesbian Short Fiction. Ed. Joan Nestle and Naomi Holoch. New York: New American Library, forthcoming, 1993.

Sisters/Brothers: An Anthology of Writings on Lesbians and Gay Men. Ed. Joan Nestle and John Preston. forthcoming.

Studies of Joan Nestle

Aptheker, Bettina. "Review: *A Restricted Country*." *National Women's Studies Association Journal* 1 (Summer 1989): 722.

Constantine, Lynne. "Liberation—With a Memory." *Belles Lettres* (July-August 1988): 17.

Gordon, Rebecca. "Flouting and Flaunting." *Women's Review of Books* (April 1988): 15.

Kulp, Denise. "*A Restricted Country*." *off our backs* (February 1988): 19.

Minkowitz, Donna. "Hot Damn: Review of *Women on Women*." *Village Voice* (June 26, 1990): 72.

Olson, Ray. Review. *Booklist* 84 (November 15, 1987): 517.

LESLÉA NEWMAN (1955–   )
Robin Bernstein

BIOGRAPHY

"The first thing I ever got published was a poem in *Seventeen* magazine, and I thought my career was made. That is still the most money I've ever gotten for a single poem in my life." (Unless otherwise noted, all quotations are from personal communication with the author.)

Lesléa Newman wrote only poetry until she was twenty-seven. Born in Brighton Beach, a Jewish section of Brooklyn, she attended the University of Vermont as an undergraduate, then studied poetry at the Naropa Institute as Allen Ginsberg's apprentice. With Ginsberg's help, Newman's first chapbook, *Just Looking for My Shoes*, was published by Back Door Press in 1980.

After Naropa, Newman entered a master's program at Boston University, but she hated the competitiveness she encountered there. Depressed and coping with an eating disorder, she dropped out after one semester.

From Boston Newman moved to New York City, where she "did the starving artist bit." After a year of "counting cockroaches," she moved to Northampton, Massachusetts, at age twenty-seven.

"Everything broke for me," she says. "I came out, which was 97 percent of the problem all along. I started reading women's literature; I couldn't read enough. Women were writing about what happens in their kitchens, in their bedrooms, in the streets. My eyes were opened and I started writing again. Still, mostly poetry."

She was teaching day care to support herself, but then her contract was not renewed. "I went to a psychic and I said, 'What kind of job should I look for?' And she said, 'Don't look for a job; go home and do your work.' And I knew exactly what she meant. I came home, and I wrote the first 20 pages of *Good Enough to Eat*."

Newman was also in an accident, from which she received a settlement, which became, in her words, "the grant I had always waited for." The settlement supported her through the eight months it took to write *Good Enough to Eat*, her first novel. She sent the manuscript to Firebrand Books, and they called her in a week: they wanted to publish it.

Her next book, a collection of poetry entitled *Love Me Like You Mean It*, was published by HerBooks in 1987. "At that point," she says, "I had written a novel and two books of poetry, and I realized there was something in-between. That, of course, was short stories."

Newman wrote the nine short stories that comprise the collection *A Letter to Harvey Milk* to explore "the two identities of being a lesbian and being Jewish: how they fit together and how they don't, and how to live in both worlds, which is something I still struggle with."

During this time, Newman was also supporting herself by teaching writing workshops. She started teaching a single workshop in 1983, and this class stemmed into different groups for poetry and prose. Soon she was leading writing workshops focusing on such varied subjects as body image, family, and the nitty-gritty of getting published. Since 1987, Newman has supported herself solely by writing and teaching writing workshops.

One day in 1987, a woman stopped Newman on the street and asked her to write a children's book for kids with two mothers. Newman responded with *Heather Has Two Mommies*. This picture book was the first ever to depict a family in which two women choose to have a child together.

Despite its uniqueness, no one wanted to publish it. After deciding to publish it herself, Newman sent out a fund-raising letter requesting donations. Donors of $10 or more, she said, would receive a copy of the book when published. The response was tremendous, and Newman received over $4,000, most of it in $10 and $20 donations. After the book was published and warmly received, Alyson Publications picked it up in 1989 for its new line of children's books, Alyson Wonderland. Also in 1989, Newman and her lifetime companion, Mary, held their commitment ceremony.

Newman has published widely in lesbian magazines and lesbian anthologies, but she also hopes someday to reach a "wider" audience. "I think the reason I've been published so much is because I am a lesbian and there is a lesbian press. My books have gotten a lot of attention in that world, and I'm very grateful for that. I certainly don't want to give that up . . . I just want to expand on it."

MAJOR WORKS AND THEMES

In Lesléa Newman's work, *theme* often springs from and merges with *identity*. For example, her characters are mostly Jews, and Jewishness figures prominently in her writing. Yet it would be awkward to call Jewishness a *theme* in Newman's work. Jewishness is, rather, the center from which Lesléa Newman writes, a major shaper of her vision. Yes, sometimes she writes *about* being Jewish, but more often she *writes Jewishly*.

This distinction is best illustrated in *A Letter to Harvey Milk*, Newman's first collection of short stories. All the main characters are Jewish lesbians, yet some stories, such as "The Gift" and "One *Shabbos* Evening," are clearly about being Jewish, while others, such as "Something Shiny" and "The Best Revenge," carry Jewishness more as a backdrop.

This gentle shifting from foreground to background, from theme to outlook, extends into Newman's other identities. Incest and other forms of sexual abuse are persistent visitors in her writing; again, sometimes they are the focus, as in "Secrets," the title story of her second collection of short fiction. Other times, incest is a vague, ominous presence, as in "Sunday Afternoon," from *A Letter to Harvey Milk*. Still other times, incest figures in characters' pasts, as in "The Best Revenge," also from *Harvey Milk*.

Newman has dealt with incest most directly in "Rage," a seventeen-page poem found in her most recent volume of poetry, *Sweet Dark Places*. "Rage" was also produced as a play by Gay Performances Company in New York.

Perhaps the most obvious recurrent subject-cluster in Newman's writing is eating/body image/food/eating diseases. Her only non-fiction work, *SomeBody to Love*, is a healing guide "for every woman who has ever looked at herself in the mirror and responded to her reflection with anything less than pure joy" (3). Based on her writing workshop, "What Are You Eating/What's Eating You?," this book contains forty-two writing exercises designed to help women connect with feelings about food, eating, and body image. It also includes an anthology of women's writing about these issues.

Belinda's Bouquet, Newman's third children's book, deals with the body image of a fat girl. After being teased, Belinda decides to go on a diet. An encounter with a lesbian couple (mothers of Belinda's friend, Daniel), however, convinces her that she's beautiful and important just as she is.

Good Enough to Eat is an agonizing (yet hilarious) novel about Liza Goldberg, a twenty-five-year-old bulimic. This book is shocking, almost embarrassing in its honesty. Liza berates herself, obsesses about food and her weight, gives herself enemas, binges, and purges, and all this is described in minute detail. Halfway through the book, Liza begins to come out, and this is also painful. She jokes viciously about lesbianism, all the while savoring the power of the word. These scenes are difficult to read, but certainly no more so than her other self-hating antics.

Eventually, Liza connects with other lesbians, many of whom also have issues with food. Slowly, she reaches toward health and self-love, toward a sane relationship with food and an honest sexuality. Sexuality and food are intertwined in this book, as are the dual healings.

Sexuality is a constant and joyful presence in all of Newman's work. Perhaps her most delicious sex scene appears in "A True Story (Whether You Believe It or Not)," from the collection *Secrets*. This story is told by Zoey B. Jackson, a self-described "proper old-fashioned stone-bulldyke that doesn't flip for nobody" (166). Zoey joined the fire department as a gift to herself for her fortieth birthday, and also to console herself after her lover, who had grown frustrated with small-town life, moved to San Francisco.

Then, out of nowhere, a beautiful woman with dozens of bracelets appears; what follows is perhaps one of the best sex scenes in modern lesbian literature. For the first time, Zoey allows herself to be made love to. In the morning, the woman is gone, leaving one of her bracelets. Knowing she'll never see the woman again, Zoey begins to feel the isolation that was always there, the isolation of being a lesbian in a small town. She begins to dream of moving to San Francisco.

Change, and the bravery it requires, is another theme in Newman's work. The best example of this is found in "Flashback," a short story in *A Letter to Harvey Milk*. In this story, Sharon, a young Jewish lesbian, is obsessed with the Holocaust. When President Reagan honors SS graves, calling the Nazis "as much victims of the Holocaust as . . . Jews," and Sharon sees a swastika drawn in dirt on a truck, she is pushed over the edge and becomes convinced the Holocaust is happening all over again. She goes into hiding in her apartment, not eating (for she's sure the food is poisoned), using the toilet only once a day, and not answering the phone. Soon her friend, Abbie, another Jewish lesbian, comes to find Sharon. When Sharon doesn't answer the door, Abbie writes her a note, inviting Sharon to a birthday party.

Sharon takes the note as code, but she's not sure how to decipher it. "She came up with three possibilities: 1. Abbie was organizing a meeting for women who wanted to work in the resistance; 2. Abbie was rounding up Jewish Lesbians in exchange for her own life; or 3. Abbie and everyone else were completely unaware of what was going on" (141).

The birthday party could be a deathtrap, but, Sharon decides,

I'll go to them. . . . Even if it means being tortured and killed, even if it is a trick and Abbie has betrayed us all, I've got to go. Even if only one of us lives long enough to tell the story, that will be enough. (143)

This is the most extreme example, but the desire to take control over fear and make courageous decisions is found often in Newman's work. "The Dating Game," in *Secrets*, honors the courage it requires to ask someone for a date. And in "Retreat," from the same volume, a woman finds the courage to break a vow of silence in a meditation retreat, in order to defend herself from unwanted advances.

Perhaps the most prevalent theme in Newman's writing is hope. Not all her works feature neat or happy endings, but there is almost always a sense of life continuing, of the possibility for growth, of the potential for happiness.

CRITICAL RECEPTION

Lesléa Newman has received very few bland reviews: people seem either to love her writing or to hate it. *Good Enough to Eat*, for example, was hailed in *off our backs* as "the best coming out story in recent lesbian literature" (20), but was called "simplistic" in *Belles Lettres* (32). The stories in *A Letter to Harvey Milk* were characterized as "distinctly and ethnically Jewish" in the *Lambda Rising Book Report*, but "stereotypical" (11) and "superficial" in *Dare* (8).

Response to her poetry has been more uniform: reviewers have simply raved. Terri Jewell, writing in *Bay Windows*, described *Love Me Like You Mean It* as "poetry you give your lover as a gift or share with strangers during the most common times of your day. . . . I am convinced Newman could write about fish emulsion and make it poignant" (17). Joan [no last name] in *Common Lives/Lesbian Lives* wrote, "She uses forms and formal devices . . . with great deftness. Every poem fits its body" (117).

Newman has received the most attention for her children's books. As the first picture book to depict a lesbian couple choosing to have a baby together, *Heather Has Two Mommies* received mention in the *Philadelphia Inquirer*, *Newsweek*, and the *New York Times*. Most of *Heather*'s reviews were overwhelmingly positive and enthusiastic; the book filled an enormous gap in children's literature. Some reviewers, however, criticized *Heather* as really being for adults, not children.

Whomever it's for, *Heather Has Two Mommies* continues to sell very well. In 1990, it was nominated for the Lambda Literary Award in the Children's Book Category.

Newman's other literary awards include a Poets and Writers Grant in 1991 and a commendation in the National Poetry Competition in 1988. In 1987, she was a second-place finalist in the Raymond Carver Short Story Competition, and in 1989, she received a Massachusetts Artist Fellowship Award in Poetry.

BIBLIOGRAPHY

Works by Lesléa Newman

Just Looking for My Shoes. Seattle, WA: Back Door Press, 1980.
Good Enough to Eat. Ithaca, NY: Firebrand Books, 1986; London: Sheba Feminist Publishers, 1986.
Love Me Like You Mean It. Santa Cruz, CA: HerBooks, 1987.
A Letter to Harvey Milk. Ithaca, NY: Firebrand Books, 1988.
Heather Has Two Mommies. Northampton, MA: In Other Words, 1989; Boston: Alyson Publications, 1990.
Secrets. Norwich, VT: New Victoria, 1990.
Belinda's Bouquet. Boston: Alyson Publications, 1991.
Gloria Goes to Gay Pride. Boston: Alyson Publications, 1991.
SomeBody to Love: A Guide to Loving the Body You Have. Chicago: Third Side Press, 1991.
Sweet Dark Places. Santa Cruz, CA: HerBooks, 1991.
In Every Laugh a Tear. Norwich, VT: New Victoria, 1992.

Works Edited

Bubbe Meisehs by Shayneh Maidelehs: An Anthology of Poetry by Jewish Granddaughters about Our Grandmothers. Santa Cruz, CA: HerBooks, 1989.

Films

A Letter to Harvey Milk. Produced and directed by Yariv Kohn. York University, Canada, 1990.

Plays

After All We've Been Through. Women in Performance, Durham, NC, April 1989. Portland Women's Theatre Co., Portland, OR, April 1989. Between the Acts, Lexington, KY, February 1990.
Rage. Gay Performances Company, New York, NY, 1991.

Studies of Lesléa Newman

Dryden, Sherre. Rev. of *Letter to Harvey Milk. Dare* Aug. 19, 1988: 8.
Greenspan, Judy. *"A Letter to Harvey Milk* by Lesléa Newman." *Lambda Rising Book Report* 1, no. 5: 11.
Jewell, Terri. Rev. of *Love Me Like You Mean It. Bay Windows* (July 1988): 17, 19.
Joan [no last name]. Rev. of *Love Me Like You Mean It. Common Lives/Lesbian Lives* 26 (Spring 1988): 117.
Rev. of *Good Enough to Eat. Belles Lettres* (March/April 1987): 32.
"Women's Lives in Review." *off our backs.* (Oct. 1987): 20.

ELISABETH NONAS (1949–   )
Judith V. Branzburg

BIOGRAPHY

Elisabeth Nonas was born in New York City in 1949 to a Latvian-German-Jewish family. She spent her formative years in New York City and entered Vassar in 1967. During her junior year, she had her first lesbian experience. She never looked back.

Nonas graduated from Vassar in 1971 with a degree in English. In 1973, after working at a variety of jobs, she enrolled at the New York University (NYU) Graduate Institute of Film and Television. Her short film *Mother to Dinner*, which she adapted (from a story of the same title by Tess Slessinger), produced, directed, and edited, won the 1976 award for the Best Graduate Film at the NYU Film Festival. *Mother to Dinner* was also a finalist in the Student Academy Awards.

After receiving her M.F.A., Nonas moved to Los Angeles to enter the film industry. Her first screenplay, a coming-out story, did not sell. After pitching a number of ideas that left her uninspired and unemployed, Nonas decided to write from her own experience again. The resulting teleplay, the story of a family coming to terms with the mother's terminal illness (Nonas's mother died when Elisabeth was twenty), eventually became "Ask Me No Questions," an episode of "True Confessions," a syndicated TV drama.

In the meantime, Nonas had become involved in gay and lesbian politics in Los Angeles. She was particularly active in the successful battle against the Briggs Amendment (1978), which would have forbidden any mention, positive or negative, of homosexuality in California public schools. Nonas continued her involvement after the Briggs battle, and from 1983 to 1986, she served on the board of MECLA, Municipal Elections Committee of Los Angeles, a bipartisan gay and lesbian lobbying group.

Around 1982, Nonas's lover, Carole Topalian, a photographer, suggested that

Elisabeth, frustrated with the market requirements of Hollywood screenwriting, write a novel of lesbian life. Three and half years later, Nonas's first novel, *For Keeps*, was completed and published by Naiad Press. By 1988, Nonas had decided to devote herself full-time to novel writing. Her second novel, *A Roomful of Women*, was published in 1990, also by Naiad Press. She is currently at work on her third novel, tentatively titled *Staying Home*.

Nonas has also taught writing at Valley College in Los Angeles and at the University of California at Los Angeles (UCLA) Extension. At UCLA, she has been a pioneer, developing and teaching the first ever lesbian and gay fiction writing class offered by the Extension Writing Program and organizing and moderating UCLA's continuing lesbian and gay writers' salon. Nonas continues to teach in the Extension Writing Program. She also writes for the *Advocate*, the national gay and lesbian newspaper, specializing in articles about lesbian and gay families.

Nonas is a member of PEN Center USA West and the Los Angeles Gay and Lesbian Writers Circle.

In 1983, Nonas and her lover Carole, after being together for two years, had a public commitment ceremony. They are currently living near Los Angeles.

MAJOR WORKS AND THEMES

Nonas's two published novels, *For Keeps* (1985) and *A Roomful of Women* (1990), are particularly notable for their realistic depiction of the lives of highly motivated, professional, educated, unapologetic lesbians living in the America of the eighties. For Nonas's characters, homosexuality is not a major issue. Their lesbianism is a given. At issue in Nonas's work is the way lesbians make relationships and the interplay of the families lesbians are raised in and those they create themselves.

In her first novel, *For Keeps*, Nonas examines these issues by exploring the aftermath of a breakup of a relationship against the backdrop of family illness. The novel is divided into three parts that allow the reader to follow the protagonist through various stages of recovery from loss to maturation.

In the first section, the protagonist, Kate, a young, white, successful Hollywood screenwriter, deals with the breakup of her relationship with Anne by searching for an idealized True Love. Kate becomes superficially involved with a few women, enjoying the sex (as does the reader in some highly erotic sex scenes), but she is puzzled about how to make a substantial emotional connection. Finally, at dinner at a friend's house, Kate meets Lauren. Lauren is the only one of the women who offers the potential for a serious, lasting relationship. That "she was a possibility Kate was not willing to explore" (52) reveals to Kate her fundamental inability to make a serious attachment.

By following Kate through this emotional and sexual odyssey, Nonas exposes with great sympathy the confusion of lust and love that often comes in the aftermath of a breakup. Just as importantly, Nonas uses Kate's predicament to show that we survive our difficult times with the help of our friends. That lesbians, within their own communities, create their own families, is one of Nonas's major themes. Kate's friends are her family. They are supportive, sensitive, honest, and sometimes irritating. Further, Nonas uses Kate's friends to show the reader something of the range of relational options lesbians avail themselves of: Eve has "a house and children and a life" and an eight-year relationship; Emily is doing fine on her own, dating a lot and being uninterested in settling down with one woman; Claire has recently broken up after a long-term relationship; and, in New York, Sarah, an old friend, is a former lesbian, now straight and considering children. Significant also is that all these lesbians are successful career women in highly competitive fields, from law to film editing. They are not apologetic or confused about being lesbians or about being successful at what they have chosen to do. Such characterizations are salutary.

Nonas also wants to show that having lesbian families does not negate the importance of the families one is raised in. In *For Keeps*, Kate is called to New York to visit her Aunt Alice, who is dying of cancer. Visiting Alice, Kate's last link to her mother who died when Kate was nineteen, forces Kate to acknowledge her sorrow and finish mourning for her mother. If we are not able to work through issues with our childhood families, Nonas tells us, we will not be able to form strong, lasting relationships among ourselves. In this particular case, Nonas's point is that if we are not able to accept the possibility of loss, whether the loss of a lover or a parent, we will not be able to accept the possibility of love.

Nonas's second novel, *A Room Full of Women*, continues and expands the themes of family and relationships. The novel focuses on two characters, Blair and Natalie, with a supporting cast of their friends, again a group of white, professionally successful lesbians living in Los Angeles. Through an examination of Blair's and Natalie's lives at the near forty/forty crisis point, Nonas is able to explore the difficulties of commitment, the importance of family, and the range of lesbian life.

Blair, an attractive, successful package designer in her thirties, exemplifies the lesbian who is eternally single and playing around. She is the lesbian who uses the collapse of other relationships to justify her cynicism about and distance from commitment. But Nonas understands that such cynicism is often a defense, and through Blair's development, she reveals another nuance of the difficulty of loving.

As in *For Keeps*, reconciliation with the mother is necessary before any kind of commitment can be made. But in *A Room Full of Women*, Nonas uses Blair's relationship with her mother not simply to explore issues of loss, but to point out the destructive effects of homophobia on familial and lesbian relationships. The novel recalls how four years earlier, Blair's once-close relationship with her mother, Constance, had collapsed into one of estrangement and silence after Constance's refusal to accept Blair's lesbianism. Now, Constance has suffered a stroke and is near death. Blair visits her comatose mother and pours out her anger, her pride in being a lesbian, and finally, her love for her mother. Only with this cleansing and declaration of love for her mother can Blair return to Los Angeles and even consider the possibility of commitment.

However, Nonas is concerned with more than single women finding love and commitment. She also offers insight into the challenges involved in keeping long-term relationships long term through her portrayal of Natalie Bazarian's mid-life crisis. Natalie, one of Blair's friends, is a highly successful, highly pressured real estate attorney who has been "married" to Annie, a video editor, for ten years. Their relationship is held up in the lesbian community as a model of love and stability. But all is not well with Natalie, whose discontent is brought to a crisis point by her infatuation with Maggie, a young law student working for Natalie as an intern. Natalie's sometimes harrowing journey away from Annie to some image of a new life mirrors the experience of many women caught up in the daily grind of living. Nonas warns the reader, through Natalie, that the solution to problems of identity, meaning, and work does not necessarily lie in a rejection of the past and in the arms of another woman. Women would do best, Nonas suggests, to take the more difficult path and to examine the self more closely to salvage what has been loving and good rather than to sacrifice it.

It is important to note that Nonas's characters in *A Room Full of Women* depend on their lesbian friends for companionship and support in good times and bad. Both Natalie and Annie survive their most critical moments through the sustaining power of the love of their friends.

The lesbians of the eighties and nineties are in the midst of building a new culture for themselves. Involved in this culture building are both new and old concepts of family, relationships, and love. Involved also is the art that lesbians produce that both reflects and enlarges upon lesbian daily life. Through reading novels such as Elisabeth Nonas's, whose centers are lesbians' everyday lives, we recognize ourselves and, in that recognition, know ourselves better.

CRITICAL RECEPTION

Both *For Keeps* and *A Room Full of Women* were widely reviewed in the gay and lesbian press. They also received some attention in mainstream literature and cultural guides and publications. For the most part, the critical appraisal of *For Keeps* was positive, with praise coming for the novel's readability, its realistic sense of contemporary lesbian life, and its erotic sex scenes. Reviewers were especially impressed that Nonas was able to offer new insight into what was basically the old story of the search for true love. On the other hand, a number of critics complained that the novel was superficial and the characters too white, wealthy, and successful to be representative of lesbians.

The critical response to *A Room Full of Women* was more uniformly and enthusiastically positive. While some complaints about wealth and superficiality persisted, most reviewers avidly praised Nonas for her realistic presentation of contemporary lesbian life, calling the novel incisive, moving, and bold. A number of critics also called the novel well-crafted and praised Nonas's crisp writing style.

BIBLIOGRAPHY

Works by Elisabeth Nonas

Mother to Dinner (motion picture). 1976.
For Keeps. Tallahassee, FL: Naiad Press, 1985.
"Ask Me No Questions" (teleplay). "True Confessions." Syndicated, 1988.
A Room Full of Women. Tallahassee, FL: Naiad Press, 1990.
"Family Outings: Lesbians Creating Family." *Advocate* 9 Oct. 1991: 62–64.
Staying Home. Tallahassee, FL: Naiad Press. Forthcoming, 1993.

KAREN LEE OSBORNE (1954–)
Jennifer M. Isbell

BIOGRAPHY

Karen Lee Osborne was born June 19, 1954, in Washington, D.C., the youngest of five children. Her family lived in Fairfax, Virginia, until 1960, when they moved to Manatee County (Sarasota-Bradenton), Florida. As early as the third grade Karen was writing poems and long short stories and was encouraged by her teachers.

Her interest in journalism began in elementary school as well. During those years and continuing through high school, she founded small underground newspapers and became a skilled photographer. She persuaded the high school principal to build a darkroom for the school publications and selected the equipment. Her photographs appeared in the yearbook and in the school paper, of which she was the editor. Osborne has commented that her early experience as a journalist and photographer helped prepare her to become a fiction writer by developing her eye for images.

One teacher Osborne has cited as having been particularly influential was Joe Berta Bullock, a journalism instructor at Manatee High School. Of Bullock, Osborne writes, "She was differently abled and taught all of us that nothing stood in our way if we worked hard and kept rising to meet challenges" (personal communication with the author, 1992). With instructors like Bullock having influenced Osborne's outlook, it is easy to understand the depth of her seemingly simple philosophy. As she remarked in a recent interview with Dianna Delling in the *Chicago Reader*, "Life is too short to cooperate in your own oppression."

In addition to her journalism work at school, Osborne wrote a weekly column for the Bradenton *Herald*, where she interned in the darkroom and also published a number of feature articles. In another extracurricular project, Osborne co-directed a short film on drug abuse for a contest and won a small prize.

Osborne graduated from the University of Florida with high honors in 1975, earning her B.S. in journalism. She then continued her education at the University of Denver, earning both M.A. and Ph.D. degrees in English. While at Denver, she was a teaching fellow and a member of the Graduate Writing Program. From 1979 to 1981, she was an instructor of English at Stetson University in Deland, Florida. During this time, an interest in providing opportunities for emerging poets led her to co-found and become editor of a small press specializing in poetry chapbooks. Moonsquilt Press is still viable and fulfilling Osborne's vision in Florida, where it is being operated by its co-founder, Michael Hettich.

From 1981 to 1985, Osborne was an assistant professor of English at Illinois Wesleyan University. A rather rare and dramatic opportunity came to Osborne in 1985, when she was selected for a Fulbright Senior Lectureship in American Literature at Tbilisi State University in (then Soviet) Tbilisi, Georgia. Along with the enriching experience as an educator, Osborne was struck with a deeper appreciation of her own freedom. As she said in the *Chicago Reader* interview, "You've got to be willing to use the freedom when you have it."

Returning to the States in 1986, Osborne was persuaded by a close male friend to move to Chicago, where she now lives. Since 1986, she has taught English and creative writing at Columbia College, where she is an assistant professor of English. Osborne's continuing interest in assisting developing writers led her in 1990 to found City Stoop Press. City Stoop has become a vehicle for such works as *West Side Stories*, an anthology of short fiction coming out of Chicago's long-neglected though culturally rich West Side. Osborne's third novel, a sequel to *Hawkwings*, is scheduled for publication by Third Side Press in 1993.

MAJOR WORKS AND THEMES

A major theme that runs through Osborne's works is reconciliation. It might be said that Osborne finds her own voice in careful, respectful observation of others, be they writers, poets, artists, or her own fictional characters, and in approaching any writing she does about them without assuming that embellishments and exaggerations on her own part are needed. The results are photographically crisp portraits of people, art and events which, through Osborne's words, are allowed their authenticity. This affords her readers a multidimensional sense of her subjects so that readers' own reactions may be clear.

Osborne's first novel, *Carlyle Simpson*, published in 1986 by Academy Chicago, won two book awards and garnered praises from the *New York Times Book Review* and *Publishers Weekly*. It is a story told from the point of view of a sixty-five-year-old heterosexual man whose best friend has died. The angry Carlyle is a semi-retired building contractor who drinks too much and despises tourists, trailer parks, and shoddy home construction. He is a frustrated perfectionist in a world of imperfect human beings who do imperfect work. As a favor to a friend, he builds one last house, and in the course of its construction, Carlyle's anger reaches a crescendo that affects his family, his workers, and his friends.

As with all of Osborne's characters, Carlyle is drawn with graphic clarity and acute psychological insight. Though he is not the most likable person, Osborne shows herself a first-rate author by depicting his character and his story with such precision that the reader becomes understanding of, and interested in, Carlyle's plight.

The reconciliation for Carlyle is in going on with his life after Duffy, his best friend, dies. The universality of this theme, and the artistry with which it is handled, place Osborne's first novel at a level that won her recognition as a fine, promising young writer.

Osborne's second novel, *Hawkwings*, published by Third Side Press in 1991, is her first lesbian novel. In a recent interview Osborne speaks of her "coming out," as it were, as a novelist in this genre. "Writing a lesbian novel was a new thing for me, and I think it's a healthy and almost inevitable thing," she says. "The character Emily is not me, but she's pretty close. Closer to me than I would ever have dared to write before. It took me a while to feel the sense of permission to do that" (*Chicago Reader*).

Reconciliation, grief, recovery, and starting again are the themes Osborne handles in *Hawkwings*, in which the main character, Emily, is grieving the loss of her best friend, George, to AIDS, recovering from a recent breakup with a young woman named Bonnie, and starting a relationship with mysterious, beautiful Catherine. When Paul, another friend dying of AIDS, asks Emily to find and relay a message to his former lover, she finds herself trying to help him make amends and move on with his life, while making choices about her own. Emily finds a way to live with her values, to say directly what she wants and needs from her lover, and to accept her sensitive side with dignity and humility. The cautious but tantalizing relationship with Catherine unfolds with a reminder to us all of the power of our words, our bodies, and our ability to choose and defend what we want.

Osborne brings to lesbian fiction the response expressed by many to the self-help directives, like the inward-spiralling, spartan lifestyle in which relationships are considered a luxury, rather than a necessity to personal growth. Her character, Emily, calls herself "a romantic in rebellion," and Osborne uses this attribute to show the solidarity among lesbians that is founded on love and cooperation. True to her art, the characters in *Hawkwings* are multidimensional and come to life in vivid descriptions. While *Carlyle Simpson* is set in the sticky, St. Augustine–choked yards of Florida, *Hawkwings* is set in Chicago, the city in which Osborne lives and works. Her love of the city is easy to see as her characters move along Halsted and Roscoe, eat at the Chicago Diner, dance at Paris, and march in the Pride Parade. With the opening up of setting in her second novel, and the move from a character like Carlyle to those who embrace life and love, even in the face of loss, it comes as no surprise that Osborne also reveals her talent in capturing erotic lesbian sex scenes with taste and finesse.

CRITICAL RECEPTION

Both of Karen Lee Osborne's novels have been highly praised, with *Carlyle Simpson* being recognized in several major newspapers and periodicals. *Hawkwings* has received excellent reviews in several gay and lesbian newspapers and was a finalist for the American Library Association's Gay/Lesbian Book Award. While different audiences tend to read and review the two books, the enthusiastic reception and praise are evident from all. It is a mistake to identify Osborne solely as an author of lesbian fiction, and a mistake for heterosexual readers not to read the lesbian fiction she is writing. Dianna Delling's Sept. 20, 1991 interview in the *Chicago Reader* quotes Osborne: "Why shouldn't straight people read lesbian novels? I'm not a straight man, and yet somehow I read novels by Faulkner and enjoy them."

In 1987, *Carlyle Simpson* won first prize from the Friends of American Writers and another award from the Chicago Foundation for Literature, presented by the Friends of Literature. On October 10, 1986, Burton Raffel in the *Rocky Mountain News* calls *Carlyle* "masterful, delightful story-telling." Jerry Nemanic, in the December 30, 1987, *Chicago Tribune*, writes, "*Carlyle Simpson* is not only an excellent first novel, it is . . . one of the best novels of this year." *Publishers Weekly* also reviewed *Carlyle* and reported in its August 22, 1986, edition, "In her carefully wrought first novel, Osborne draws a powerful psychological portrait," a comment that is echoed in the praise given by Elizabeth Lacovara in the October 13, 1986, *Washington Times*: "Miss Osborne has produced a deft and poignant psychological study of a complicated man."

Hawkwings, as reviewed by Barbara Emrys in the August 23, 1991, *Seattle Gay News*, "is about people forgiving themselves for their needs." Emrys calls the novel "an excruciatingly accurate portrait of hopeful vulnerability." Tami Parr, in the November-December 1991 issue of *New Directions for Women*, describes it as "a sensitively written narrative about people you can imagine as your friends." Of the erotic scenes in *Hawkwings*, novelist Lee Lynch in the September-October 1991 *Lambda Book Report*, writes, "[The scenes] are all the more convincing because they depict not just passion, but a swinging and sliding away from each other, back, away again. . . . *Hawkwings* is, finally, about learning to fly."

The short stories of Karen Lee Osborne, appearing in *Naming the Daytime Moon: Stories and Poems by Chicago Women*, as well as the recently published *New Chicago Stories*, are being enjoyed by an ever-increasing audience. One of her stories, "Getting What You Came For," is the basis for a thirty-minute color feature film directed by Doreen Bartoni.

BIBLIOGRAPHY

Works by Karen Lee Osborne

"The Kick." *Denver Quarterly*. Summer 1977.

"Father's Shadowy Legacy." *Floridian* (St. Petersburg *Times* magazine). June 13, 1982.

"Dreams of a Starving Woman." *Transpersion* Summer 1983.

"Level, Plumb and Square." *Karamu* Fall 1983.

"Wednesday." *Sing Heavenly Muse!* 8 (Fall 1983).

"I Am Not Always Nice." *Conditions* 11–12 (Summer 1985): 36–54.

Carlyle Simpson. Chicago: Academy Chicago, 1986.

"Egan's Tennis Shoes." *Other Voices* Fall 1986.

"All This Facility of Travel." *Naming the Daytime Moon: Stories and Poems by Chicago Women*. Chicago: Feminist Writers Guild, 1987.

"Getting What You Came For." *Evergreen Chronicles* 6:1 (Winter 1990/Spring 1991). Rpt. in *New Chicago Stories*. Chicago: City Stoop Press, 1990.

Hawkwings. Chicago: Third Side Press, 1991.

"Survival." Forthcoming in *Common Lives/Lesbian Lives*

PAT PARKER (1944–1989)

Ayofemi S. Folayan and Stephanie Byrd

BIOGRAPHY

Known as a black lesbian feminist poet, Pat Parker was born a premature infant with pneumonia on January 20, 1944, in Houston, Texas, where she was consigned to an incubator for nearly three months. She was the youngest of four daughters whose father, Buster Cooks, moved them from the public housing projects to the suburbs of Houston and encouraged them to escape on the freedom train of education. Married to playwright Ed Bullins, Parker began crafting poetry to avoid his relentless criticism and devaluing of her prose work.

Parker moved to the Oakland, California, area in the early seventies. She served as medical coordinator of the Oakland Feminist Women's Health Center from 1978 to 1987, when she retired to devote more time to her writing. Under her wise administration, the clinic expanded from a single site offering family planning and abortion services, to six clinics offering expanded services such as a sperm bank and second trimester abortions. Her political activism drew her into the Black Panther party in the sixties and the Black Women's Revolutionary Council in the seventies. She was an important force in the development of the Women's Press Collective in Oakland.

Parker traveled extensively around the country to college campuses and women's bookstores, performing her poetry and building bridges with other lesbians, particularly other black lesbians, whom she invited to join her in performance of her signature work, "Movement in Black." Parker played softball and Ms. PacMan as relentlessly as she crusaded for justice in the world. She died from cancer on June 17, 1989, and is survived by her partner, Marty Dunham, and her daughters Cassidy Brown and Anastasia Dunham-Parker.

MAJOR WORKS AND THEMES

While Parker's three early works have lapsed out of print, many of those poems are included in her signature collection *Movement in Black*. The book is divided into four sections. The first is "Married." The very first poem in the collection is "Goat Child," the epic autobiographical piece that chronicles the many times the young child and young woman was battered by her encounters with a working-class family, a racist school system, and a sexist marriage that all failed to recognize the genius/poet/woman who would later emerge. The poems in this first section are raw, exposing the pain of giving up a daughter for adoption, of realizing the hypocrisy of smooth-talking men, of the rage her marriage engendered and her ultimate decision to leave.

In the section entitled "Liberation Fronts," Parker addresses issues such as racism in the feminist community, violence against women, and the presence of Nazis on a college campus. She was not afraid to challenge even those within the gay and lesbian community who colluded with their oppressors in "Where Will You Be?" The final poem in this section is "Movement in Black," a call and response choral poem in the style of southern black preachers that catalogues the many heroines of black history, from slavery to the present.

From alcoholism to homophobia, Parker switches with equal ease from tender descriptions of her lover to sardonic self-deprecation in the third section of the book, "Being Gay." In "My Lover Is a Woman," Parker reveals how the pain of her family's homophobia and the memories of early racism splinter the warm bonds between herself and her white, blonde-haired lover. She challenges the heterosexist assumptions of "The Straight Folks Who Don't Mind Gays But Wish They Weren't So BLATANT."

The final section of *Movement in Black* is noteworthy for the inclusion of the title poem of one of Parker's earlier books, "Womanslaughter," a poem that chronicles the brutal murder of her sister Shirley by her former husband and the trial that followed. Outraged by the failure of the police and the justice system to protect her sister, Parker took this poem to the International Tribunal on Crimes against Women, convened in Brussels in 1976, as a statement of her commitment to do more than just mourn her sister's death. While her grief and rage are transparent to the reader, it is an eloquent example of Parker's genius that this poem is the mainstay of a section entitled "Love Poems."

Parker's final volume of poetry, *Jonestown & Other Madness*, is a collection of longer poems that focus critical attention on events from the headlines with the probing intensity of a magnifying glass reflecting rays of summer sun. The title poem, "Jonestown," asserts without any doubt that "Black folks do not commit suicide," while pondering the reality of more than nine hundred people dying in the Guyana settlement named for a charismatic religious leader who attracted most of his followers from the northern California bay area that Parker called home for nearly twenty years. "One Thanksgiving Day" ponders the pursuit of justice in the case of a black woman named Priscilla Ford who drove into a crowd of pedestrians in Reno, Nevada, on that holiday and killed six of them. Parker delivered a startling indictment of the larger social reality that allowed the murder of black youths in Atlanta in "Georgia, Georgia, Georgia on my Mind." Nor was Parker afraid to tackle the controversial topic of carving a swastika on a woman's shoulder during an S/M encounter, which was the subject of "Bar Conversation."

While these probing questions keep Parker's political attitudes prominent, the poems in *Jonestown & Other Madness* are also woven together with the tender threads of love poems for Parker's friend Blackberri and her lover Marty, as well as the stunning achievement of "Legacy," a poem written to her younger daughter and celebrating the generations of courage and strength passed from Parker's own grandparents to her child.

CRITICAL RECEPTION

Pat Parker has been described as a visionary, a preacher, and a pedagogue. Critics, however, have failed to see how Parker tried to integrate all that she was into her work. The very nature of Parker's narrative poems springs from her "race education" in Texas and the oral traditions of African-American people who supplemented this education with stories that have gone unwritten.

In her early book *Pit Stop*, Parker used repetition and the form of call and response with the idea of weaving together all of what she saw and felt. The reader perceives Parker's vision and comes to learn and believe that separation is an ideological construction. This same message is carried into *Womanslaughter* and reaches its pinnacle in *Movement in Black*.

It is because of her use of orality and didacticism that non-feminist and non-lesbian and gay criticism tends to view her work as more political and less artistic. Gerald Barrax found Parker's "preachiness" to be a weakness when compared with the work of Dudley Randall and Naomi Madgett (254–62). Barrax, however, is ignoring the universality of Parker's themes when he distances her from her heterosexual poetic counterparts. Parker was aware of the voice she presented on the page, and as that voice matured and grew in stature, her narrative style began to lose some of its preachiness, and Parker found a new and sharper landscape in which to explore her visions, as exemplified in *Jonestown & Other Madness*.

While the poem "Jonestown" is the weakest in the book according to Terri Jewell (38), it serves as a central point from which the rest of the poems radiate. In "One Thanksgiving Day" and "Love Isn't," Parker continues to explore the necessity of society coming to terms with its own multifacetedness. Although lesbian in identity, Parker refuses to allow this identity to overwhelm her work and constantly points to the paths that lead to the multiplicity of identity in black lesbian women. As Priscilla Ford commits homicide, the reader sees that this act is intricately connected to Jim Jones and the debacle in Guyana in 1978.

Pat Parker worked both on the page and off the page to create a place for all people, black and white, women and men. By employing an old African-American tradition of oratory in the narrative poem, Parker gave action to language as well as a road to new ideas of being. The tragedy, of course, is that her star burned too briefly; the metamorphosis began in 1971 and ended in 1989.

BIBLIOGRAPHY

Works by Pat Parker

Child of Myself. Oakland, CA: Shameless Hussy Press, 1972; Oakland, CA: Women's Press Collective, 1974.

Pit Stop. Oakland, CA: Women's Press Collective, 1974.

Womanslaughter. Oakland, CA: Diana Press, 1978.

Movement in Black. Oakland, CA: Diana Press, 1978; Freedom, CA: Crossing Press, 1983; Ithaca, NY: Firebrand Books, 1989.

Jonestown & Other Madness. Ithaca, NY: Firebrand Books, 1985.

Works in Anthologies

The Anthology. Noh Directions Press, 1968.

Dices or Black Bones; Black Voices of the Seventies. Ed. Adam David Miller. Boston: Houghton Mifflin, 1971.

Mark in Time: Portraits & Poetry/S.F. San Francisco: Glide Publications, 1971.

Best Friends 2. Albuquerque: University of New Mexico Press, 1972.

Woman to Woman. Oakland, CA: Women's Press Collective, 1974.

Amazon Poetry. Ed. Joan Larkin & Elly Bulkin. New York: Out and Out Press, 1975.

Crimes against Women. Ed. Diane E. H. Russell and Nicole Van de Ven. Millbrae, CA: Les Femmes, 1976.

Poetry from Violence. Auburn, WA: Lighthouse, 1976.

True to Life Adventure Stories, vol. 1. Ed. Judy Grahn. Oakland, CA: Diana Press, 1978.

Conditions Five. Ed. Lorraine Bethel and Barbara Smith. New York: Conditions, 1979.

The Lesbian Path. Ed. Margaret Cruikshank. Angel Press, 1980.

Lesbian Poetry. Ed. Elly Bulkin and Joan Larkin. Watertown, MA: Persephone Press, 1981.

This Bridge Called My Back. Ed. Cherrìe Moraga and Gloria Anzaldúa. Watertown, MA: Persephone Press, 1981.

Home Girls. Ed. Barbara Smith. Latham, NY: Kitchen Table: Women of Color Press, 1983.

I Never Told Anyone. Ed. Ellen Bass and Louise Thornton. New York: Harper and Row, 1983.

Record Albums

Any Woman's Blues, anthology. Unitarian Service Committee, 1975.

Where Would I Be Without You?: The Poetry of Pat Parker and Judy Grahn. Olivia Records, 1976.

Lesbian Concentrate, anthology. Olivia Records, 1977.

Studies of Pat Parker

Annas, Pamela. "A Poetry of Survival: Unnaming and Renaming in the Poetry of Audre Lorde, Pat Parker, Sylvia Plath and Adrienne Rich." *Colby Library Quarterly* 18 (March 1982): 9–25.

Barrax, Gerald. "Six Poets: From Poetry to Verse." *Callaloo* 9 (Winter 1986): 248–69.

Beemyn, Brett. "Bibliography of Works by and about Pat Parker (1944–1989)." *Sage* 6:1 (Summer 1989).

Birtha, Becky. "Speaking Out Loudly before the Madness." *off our backs* (November 1985): 17.

Clarke, Cheryl. Rev. of *Movement in Black: The Collected Poetry of Pat Parker, 1961– 1978. Conditions Six* 2 (Summer 1980): 217–25.

Culpepper, Emily. *Gay Community News* (September 3, 1989): 8.

Folayan, Ayofemi. "Gifts of a Mentor." *Gay Community News* (September 3, 1989): 9.

Ford, Donis. *Calyx* 10 (Summer 1986): 83–84.

Jewell, Terri. *Body Politic* 118 (September 1985): 37–38.

Kowalewski, Jean. "Edward the Dyke: Parker the Poet," *Body Politic* 64 (June/July 1980): 36.

Kuras, Pat. "Pat Parker: Poet as Preacher." *Gay Community News Book Review Supplement* October 26, 1985: 1.

off our backs (December 1978): 13–14.

Oktenberg, Adrian. "A Quartet of Voices." *Woman's Review of Books* 3 (April 1986): 17–19.

Smith, Barbara. "Naming the Unnameable: The Poetry of Pat Parker." *Conditions Three* 1 (Spring 1978): 99–103.

Smith, Barbara, and Beverly Smith. "The Varied Voices of Black Women." *Sojourner* 4:2 (October 1978): 5, 21.

Walker, Donna. *Black/Out* 1 (Summer 1986): 23–24.

MINNIE BRUCE PRATT (1946–   )
Louise Kawada

BIOGRAPHY

Minnie Bruce Pratt was born September 12, 1946, in Selma, Alabama, and grew up in nearby Centreville. An only child, raised in a family that valued politeness and Protestantism, Pratt met all expectations. She earned good grades, read the Bible daily, and attended church three times a week. As she later admitted, however, "I was a very good child, but I speculated about being a rebel" (*Rebellion* 11).

Speculation began to be translated into action when Pratt, at age twenty, married Marvin E. Weaver II, a poet and a Roman Catholic. Their first son, Ransom (named after one of the Fugitive poets), was born in 1968, the same year Pratt was graduated from the University of Alabama and awarded three prestigious fellowships: a Title IV–NEA, a Woodrow Wilson, and a Fulbright. In 1969, Pratt gave birth to their second son, Ben, while she was a graduate student in English at the University of North Carolina at Chapel Hill. Here she earned a Ph.D. in 1979 in Renaissance and seventeenth-century English literature.

Pratt was by this point divorced (in 1976) and had been refused custody of her children, because in another transgression of limits, she had begun a lesbian relationship. At this time, too, Pratt had embarked on her "second education" and was learning to organize grass-roots level action with other women to counter sexism, racism, and other forms of oppression. During this period, she taught at traditionally all-black colleges in North Carolina and helped to edit and publish *Feminary* (1978–1983), a southern journal for lesbians.

In June 1981, Pratt began a relationship with the photographer Joan E. Biren. Pratt is at present a member of the Graduate Faculty at the Union Institute (Cincinnati) and has taught several courses in the Women's Studies Program at the University of Maryland at College Park.

MAJOR WORKS AND THEMES

Forthright, even insistent in her identity as a lesbian writer, Minnie Bruce Pratt describes in her essays and poetry the stages of her growth and transformation. Her writings inscribe a journey toward self-possession, starting out in a geography unmarked and often hostile, where memory must be mined for spirit sustenance; and an accepted place to carry on one's living without concealment or compromise is still the outline of projected desire.

Pratt began her career as a poet with the publication of a chapbook, *The Sound of One Fork*. The themes of these early poems—lesbian identity and desire, racial segregation and its horrors, male domination and violence—are ones that she has continued to address, and the poems are written in a style that we now associate with Pratt—at once lucid and lyrical, sensuously evocative, and unabashedly direct.

The same themes receive a fuller development in Pratt's first full-length volume of poetry, *We Say We Love Each Other*. In these poems, whose settings might be the pine woods and red clay of Alabama or an apartment on Capitol Hill, Pratt is working on who she has been and where she is now in relation to others. With this concern for place, small wonder that the three long poems positioned as structural supports in the volume should be titled "Reading Maps." Landscape here is vision and identity, and map reading is an exercise in epistemology and self-understanding. In "Reading Maps: One," Pratt describes a landscape of violence, murder, and rape, along with memories of her husband shoving her out the door and literally displacing her, "while he took control"(7). Pratt admits here to an almost overwhelming sense of self-effacement:

> . . . For weeks I could not think
> what to put in the white spaces on the application blank,
> years of never knowing where I was,
> years of marriage when he drove and I tried
> to read the map, to see my body in relation
> to the space around me, to find it on the diagram: (5)

Through meeting with other women (and reading maps to find their homes), Pratt begins to regain a sense of self. She starts to dream beyond her immediate needs and imagine a special place of safety and harmony. A realist in temperament, Pratt grounds her imaginings in actual places and people; and, typically, she locates the visionary in a lesbian love relationship:

> . . . Sometimes I sleep
> with a lover, my bed an island in the water of the night.
> *With my hand between her breasts, near her heart,*
> *I dream of a place, green, flourishing, where we*
> *live safe.* (8)

In this volume, Pratt also begins to catalogue the cumulative power of women in their various guises: witch, mad woman, wise woman, mother. She searches for these sources of deep power among her relatives and friends, from history, her psyche, or the street. These figures range from the mythical—the Gorgons and a Celtic figure, Maighread Ni Lachainn, a mother of twelve, whom men buried "face down in the dirt, a witch and a poet" ("Waulking Song: One" 15) to the more common magicians of the everyday: the midwives, those who raise children, the black woman in D.C. who set pinwheels whirling on her front lawn, Pratt herself who gardens and can see the earth as "full of possibilities, acts of love not yet performed" (75). Pratt also celebrates Joan E. Biren for her photographs (a magical medium) of lesbian culture:

> . . . the years you've made the world
> rearrange itself around the fact of *lesbian*: the years
>
> you've made photographs that show the moment, limber
> as light, when we walk from present into future, the change
> that follows us like a shadow across the ground, unnoticed . . . (71)

In the final poem of the volume, Pratt turns to a political activist and writer a generation ahead of her, Barbara Deming, for advice on "how to find a place without sorrow" (95). Deming had to struggle with her own attempts to deny her lesbianism, a painful struggle that found its eventual release:

> She cast the secret of her love, finally, into a pool of silence,
> a listening circle of women. Released, dizzy, her body
> flew open. She unlocked herself in a new place with the others.   (96)

Stylistically, *We Say We Love Each Other* displays Pratt's characteristic directness but also a concern for poetic form that often enhances the speaking voice. "Wings," for example, is a shaped poem in the form of winged maple seeds that describes the lover's absence and anticipated return. Several other poems suggest the sonnet form in their fourteen-line length. One of them, "First Year," appropriates Elizabeth Barrett Browning's obsession with counting and the ways of love. The sonnet celebrates Pratt's first anniversary with her lover and begins:

> Or if we count by nights: a hundred and one,
> some as fabulous as a fairy tale, the rare kisses,
> the what we did with our tongues, the adventures at hand,
> the rough soft passage through cliffs of our bodies.   (50)

These lines, like many others in the volume, begin to tell the untellable and inscribe a lesbian erotics, here in the formal context of a tradition of heterosexual love poetry. The literary allusions in the poem and the punning sense of humor bespeak a level of comfort and assurance that would have been impossible in an earlier era, an utterance as fabulous as anything in an Arabian Nights tale.

Pratt's next book of poetry, *Crime against Nature*, takes its title and its narrative substance from a civil statute declaring same-sex love a crime. The statute rendered Pratt an unfit mother, who at the time of her divorce could not petition for the custody of her sons, then ages six and seven. If Pratt worked to hone a poetic style and craft in her earlier books, she undertakes nothing less than a honing of self in this volume. In "Poem for my Sons," a prologue poem, she makes this effort clear:

> I had to make a future, willful, voluble,
> lascivious, a thinker, a long walker,
> unstruck transgressor, furious, shouting,
> voluptuous, a lover, a smeller of blood,
> milk, a woman mean as she can be some nights,
> existence I could pray to, capable of
> poetry.   (13)

Perhaps the most striking feature of these poems is the emotional range and the chronicle of growth they display from anguish and fear, to guilt and rage, and finally to a sense of celebration beyond mere survival. In these poems, Pratt faces her own pain, rendered literally palpable, as she recalls what it was like to touch and hold her children. Pratt describes in "Shame" her feelings of guilt for having chosen the seemingly selfish pleasure of her own love and desire over the needs of her children:

> The past repeats in fragments: What I
> see is everybody watching, me included,
> as a selfish woman leaves her children,
> two small boys hardly more than babies.   (45)

Guilt eventually gives way to an acknowledgment of how "they've grown up, survived, no suicides" (47). The poem then moves toward wholeness, love, and celebration. Her sons, now old enough to travel alone and talk politics, accept Pratt's lover. The poem concludes with the four of them walking along a lake's edge watching ice break up in early spring. "It was a comedy, a happy ending, pleasure" (50), Pratt says simply, and that spirit with its uplifting sense of freedom and empowerment informs the remaining poems in the volume.

Other poems in *Crime against Nature* bear witness against the suppression of women's rights, the erasure of black identity, the warmongering impulse that fed conflict in Vietnam, Grenada, Lebanon. With her newly articulated strength, Pratt can fend off questions, such as "What do your children think of you" (62) or *"But how could that happen to someone with a Ph.D.?"* (67). Pratt's rage is palpable in these poems, by no means the polite undertone of controlled anger. There is toughness and a sense of triumph here, for Pratt has refused to evade or conceal her identity as a lesbian—"to pass"—and thereby smooth the course of her acceptance. The closing image of the final and title poem fairly boasts this personal and public victory:

> ... In the end my children visit me
> as I am. But I didn't write this story until now when
> they are too old for either law or father to seize
> or prevent from hearing my words, or from watching
> as I advance in the scandalous ancient way of women:
> our assault on enemies, walking forward, skirts lifted,
> to show the silent mouth, the terrible power, our secret.　(120)

Pratt expands upon the same thematic concerns in her recent essay collection, *Rebellion: Essays 1980–1991*. Some of the pieces collected here explore political issues, such as anti-Semitism, lesbian-gay protest over the Bowers vs. Hardwick decision (1986), and Senator Jesse Helms and the harassment of certain writers (Pratt among them). Pratt also builds on personal perspectives and describes her childhood, the books she read, the friends she had, some of whom she later learned were lesbian. She speculates on these missed connections and "*exactly* how we had been kept from ourselves and each other" (42).

Rebellion contains Pratt's well-known essay "Identity: Skin Blood Heart," first published as part of *Yours in Struggle* (1984). In this autobiographical essay, Pratt recounts how her coming out as a lesbian in North Carolina showed her the oppression, fear, and self-denial others felt as victims of racism and anti-Semitism. She describes how she learned of blacks there, who had organized themselves politically during the nineteenth century. She also learns of the area's "nourishing Jewish culture" (45), the huge anti-Vietnam rallies held there, the lesbians stationed at Ft. Bragg, the Lumbee Indians who in the 1950s broke up Klan rallies held to warn them to "keep their place" (45). With newly informed insight, she sees the town as a place of "so many resistances" (46), and it is this dialectic between the oppressive design of place-keeping and the visionary hope of place-making that informs much of her work.

A pivotal essay, "My Mother's Question," appears midway through the collection, describing how Pratt and her mother, a social worker, witness the effects of poverty and discrimination on others—usually women. Pratt presents a keen analysis of her own "unearned privilege" as someone who was white, married, a mother, but how that privilege was taken back because of her lesbian identity. Perhaps the most remarkable quality of the essay, though, and the reason that it is pivotal, is that Pratt finds and is able to articulate the union she now feels with her mother. As she comments:

That afternoon I saw how much she had given me, her sorrow and despair, the care of her attention, and her hidden passion. By her life she challenged me to work with more than words or theory, to learn from her strengths and her mistakes. She showed me the stubbornness with which she faced the daily needs of poor women in the county; despite isolation and inadequate information, she went on trying to figure out how things could change, if only in some small way. (118)

Pratt has come home in this essay and found a deep center for the writing, teaching, and political organizing she will no doubt continue to do. Having acknowledged a source of her own empowerment, Pratt turns her focus in the remaining essays on the idea of power itself—its uses, abuses, curtailment, or extension—power to withhold and uphold, or simply, and most profoundly, power to be oneself, uncompromisingly. In her closing essay, written as the ground war in Iraq was beginning, Pratt analyzes the military and the backlash militarism of conservative Senator Jesse Helms:

The drum beats beside me, against war, against power-over-others. I watch the hands of the drummers. I have seen how we have held our lives up, bloody and beautiful, in the grim face of assaults on us, held out to others our lives in poetry, in art, showing the possibility, how we imagined another way to live. (235)

This is her prayer and her power, this the possibility she would offer to us all.

CRITICAL RECEPTION

Minnie Bruce Pratt has received a number of awards for her poetry and has generally been well reviewed by both mainstream and alternative publications. Her work has not as yet received much critical attention in the academic press. Reviewers commend Pratt for her directness and acknowledge that she is helping to revitalize the American poetic tradition with a newfound emphasis on ethics and politics combined with an open eroticism and sensuality. Adrienne Rich contrasts Pratt's poetry of sensuality and political passion—this "dynamic un-settling poetry"—with the neo-formalism now in favor with the poetry estab-lishment. Mary Ann Daly remarks that "the Southern renaissance has not died out, but simply has changed hands" (14). Reviewers are in agreement that Pratt's contributions both in poetry and in prose can effect a radical reclamation of the power of the word.

Pratt began to receive a measure of the attention she so richly deserves when *Crime against Nature* was named the Lamont Poetry Selection in 1989 by the Academy of American Poets. John Hollander and James Merrill officiated at the ceremony and expressed obvious discomfiture during Pratt's acceptance speech in which she spoke openly of her life as a lesbian. In 1990, Pratt received a Creative Writing Fellowship from the National Endowment for the Arts (NEA). At that time, Helms specifically attacked the work of Pratt, Chrystos, and Audre Lorde as obscene (all had received NEA grants) and called for an end to this "misuse" of taxpayers' money. Pratt, along with Chrystos and Lorde, was awarded the Lillian Hellman–Dashiell Hammett Award as "targets of right-wing forces'' from the Fund for Free Expression (1991), and Pratt also received the American Library Association's Gay and Lesbian Book Award in 1991 for *Crime against Nature*.

BIBLIOGRAPHY

Works by Minnie Bruce Pratt

The Sound of One Fork. Durham, NC: Night Heron Press, 1981. (out of print.)
Yours in Struggle: Three Feminist Perspectives on Anti-Semitism and Racism. Co-authored with Elly Bulkin and Barbara Smith. Brooklyn, NY: Long Haul Press, 1984. Ithaca, NY: Firebrand Books, 1988.
We Say We Love Each Other. Ithaca, NY: Firebrand Books, 1992. First published by Spinsters/Aunt Lute, 1985.
Crime against Nature. Ithaca, NY: Firebrand Books, 1990.
Rebellion: Essays 1980–1991. Ithaca, NY: Firebrand Books, 1991.

Studies of Minnie Bruce Pratt

Clausen, Jan. "Still Inverting History." *Women's Review of Books* (July 1990): 12–13.
Daly, Mary Ann. Review of *We Say We Love Each Other*. *Washington Blade* 7 March 1986, 14.
deVries, Rachel Guido. "Loss and Power." *Belles Lettres* (Spring 1990): 7.
Gordon, Leonore. "Tongues of Ice." *American Poetry Review* (April-May 1991): 21.
Henry, Alice. "Racism and Anti-Semitism in the Women's Movement." *off our backs* (Aug.-Sept. 1984): 3–4.
Innes, Charlotte. "Questioning Out Loud." *Lambda Book Report* (Jan.-Feb. 1992): 19–20.
La Bonte, Richard. Review of *Rebellion*. *Advocate* 3 December 1991, 85.
McKnight, J. "Explaining in a Way People Can Hear." *Gay Community News* 13 May 1990, 8.
Marks, J. "Toward the Oracle of Ourselves" (interview). *Lambda Book Report* (Feb. 1990): 6.
Muske, Carol. "Sons, Lovers, Immigrant Souls." *New York Times Book Review* 27 Jan. 1991: sec. 7, p. 20.
Oktenberg, Adrian. "A Quartet of Voices." *Women's Review of Books* (April 1986): 17–19.
Rich, Adrienne. "Sliding Stone from the Cave's Mouth." *American Poetry Review* (Sept.-Oct. 1990): 11–17.
Selman, Robyn. "*Crime against Nature* by Minnie Bruce Pratt." *Village Voice Literary Supplement* (April 1990): 7.

MARGARET RANDALL (1936–   )
Trisha Franzen

BIOGRAPHY

Margaret Randall was born in New York City in 1936, the first of three children of John and Elinor Randall. When Margaret was eleven, her family moved to Albuquerque, New Mexico. She attended public schools there while her father taught music and her mother worked as a translator. After high school, Margaret attended the University of New Mexico.

In 1955, Margaret Randall left Albuquerque, the hometown to which she would not return for twenty-nine years. After traveling in Europe with her first husband, Randall settled in New York City. Here, in one of the centers of the beat movement, Randall began her career as a writer. After divorcing and becoming a single mother by choice, Randall took her son to Mexico City, settling there in 1961. From 1962 to 1969, she edited *El Corno Emplumado/The Plumed Horn*, a bilingual literary quarterly, at different times with Harvey Wolin, Sergio Mondragon, and Robert Cohen. Randall married Mondragon, had two daughters with him, Sarah and Ximena, and took on Mexican citizenship. In 1968, through the journal, Randall was identified as publicly supporting the demands of the Mexican student movement and protesting the massacre at the Plaza of Tlateolco. In 1969, Randall divorced Mondragon, had her third daughter, Ana, with Robert Cohen, and unsuccessfully attempted to regain her U.S. citizenship. Soon afterwards, as a result of the repression following the student movement, Randall was forced underground. With her four children and Cohen, Randall moved to Cuba, where she lived for the next ten years.

In Cuba, Randall worked for six years for the Cuban Book Institute and then as a free-lance journalist and writer. In Cuba, she became a photographer and an oral historian. Influenced by the reemergence of the women's movement, Randall began to focus her work increasingly on women, studying and writing about the lives and struggles of Cuban, Chilean, Peruvian, Vietnamese, and

Nicaraguan women. Through her books and her speaking tours, Randall became an important source for making these women's voices accessible to English-language audiences. In 1980, Randall moved to Nicaragua, where she lived with her two younger daughters for three and a half years, continuing her work as an oral historian, photographer, and journalist.

In 1984, she returned to the United States and married poet Floyce Alexander. She began teaching women's studies and American studies at the University of New Mexico. In 1985, Randall, whose family had petitioned the Immigration and Naturalization Service (INS) for permanent resident status on her behalf, was denied this status under the McCarthy-era McCarren-Walters Act. She was given thirty days to leave the country.

The New York–based Center for Constitutional Rights took on Randall's case. Supporters of Randall and the First Amendment founded defense committees across the United States and PEN, the international writers organization, joined her challenge. This struggle continued on various levels for over four years. A synopsis of this case can be found in Randall's *Coming Home: Peace without Complacency*. During this time, she continued to teach at the University of New Mexico as well as at Trinity College, Hartford, Connecticut; Macalester College, St. Paul, Minnesota; and the University of Delaware. She also began to give readings and lectures throughout the United States and to speak about her case and similar ones challenging the McCarren-Walters Act. In July 1989, without confronting the ideological exclusion issues in this case, the INS Board of Immigration Appeals resolved her suit by deciding that she is and had always been a U.S. citizen and should never have been subjected to deportation hearings.

In the midst of this political struggle, Randall came to claim her lesbian identity, although she had to remain closeted or risk providing additional grounds for deportation. With the resolution of the case, Randall was free to "come out" in her writings and teachings. In addition to incorporating her experiences as a lesbian into her work, Randall has spoken and written as an incest survivor. She currently lives in Albuquerque with her lover of six years.

MAJOR WORKS AND THEMES

"We must teach ourselves how to use language powerfully; only then will its reclaimed and highly charged memory enable us to create ourselves into the world of equality and justice we so urgently need," Randall writes in *Walking to the Edge*. Art and politics, the personal and political, are intertwined in Margaret Randall's substantial and diverse body of work. While Americans generally attribute the identifying of the personal as political with the second wave of the women's movement, Randall's persistence in joining art and politics, combining activism and creativity, speaks from her years as an artist/activist in Latin America. In contrast to the United States, where the political content of art is often denied, in these other Americas artists do not hold their work apart from their culture's social and political struggles. In Randall's writings it is clear that she does not simply see an apolitical literature as a luxury some cannot yet afford; she sees herself contributing to a people's culture, sees that art at its best conveys the texture of daily life and is part of the daily lives, the celebrations and the struggles, of all people.

This theme not only is consistent in the content of Randall's writings, which trace U.S. cultural change from the beats through feminism and global movements from socialist revolutions through the ending of the cold war, but also is apparent in the forms and methods of her works. While Randall has consistently contributed her voice to the body of women's poetry and, since 1989, to that of lesbian poets (in thirty-three years she has published twenty-one books of poetry), she has also brought other people's voices, especially women's, to us through her translations and oral histories. In her essays, she provides an analysis informed by her living and working in other cultures. Overall, she has played a significant role in providing the tools for building the connections and cross-cultural understandings that are essential for a global women's movement.

As a resident of Cuba, Randall was in a special position to bring the stories of Cuban women to the U.S. reader. As a result, her first work of oral history, *Cuban Women Now* (1974), was widely used, particularly in women's studies courses. From revolutionary leaders to students and teachers, mothers and daughters, the women in this volume give us a sense of the various experiences of women within Cuban society. Similarly, *Sandino's Daughters* (1981) offers a view of the struggles of Nicaraguan women within the larger revolutionary movement. While this work chronicles how women built their roles in these movements, how they defined themselves and their issues, it also raises the consideration of how changes for women are maintained in the formation of governments. Randall has just completed the oral histories of Nicaraguan women to continue the explorations begun in *Sandino's Daughters*.

Almost as companions to these works are *Breaking the Silences: Twentieth Century Poetry by Cuban Women* (1982), *Risking a Somersault in the Air: Conversations with Nicaraguan Writers* (1984), and Randall's translations of Nicaraguan Writer Daisy Zamora's poetry (in press, 1992). In these books, Randall presents the English-language audience with additional material for understanding the lives and literature of these Latin American writers; she brings us their voices, both their poetry and their views on the place of their art in their lives. Through these works Randall argues against the isolation of the arts and the artist.

Randall gives us no less for herself. We have her poetry, her essays, and her photographs. In *Coming Home: Peace without Complacency* (1990), she combines these three forms to celebrate her immigration victory. Each contributes a different perspective to our understanding of Margaret Randall as a woman, an artist, and an activist. Just as she does not allow us to forget that Cuban women are poets as well as workers as well as mothers and lovers, she will not allow us to separate her heart from her mind from her body, from the ideals she loves from the people she loves from the actions she will resist.

Margaret Randall has been and continues to be a tireless writer and activist. Not only has she given us invaluable sources for viewing the lives of women writers, workers, and activists, but as a whole her works are a statement of feminist theory. Randall's theory is, just as her art is, grounded in politics, in action, in resistance, and in everyday life.

CRITICAL RECEPTION

The critical response to the works of Margaret Randall is evidence of the difficulty this culture has acknowledging the artist-activist. The press she has received since her return to the United States has focused almost exclusively on her struggle with the INS. She is another in the long line of writers including Gabriel García Márquez, Graham Greene, Hortensia Buzzi de Allende, Dennis Brutus, and Ernesto Cardenal that the INS has tried to exclude from the United States on the basis of the political ideas expressed in their writings. Consequently, many people know Randall more as a political radical than as a literary artist. Seldom is her work discussed in literary journals or the mainstream press.

BIBLIOGRAPHY

Works by Margaret Randall

Poetry

Giant of Tears. New York: Tejon Press, 1959.
Ecstasy Is a Number. New York: Tejon Press, 1961.
Poems of the Glass. Cleveland, OH: Renegade Press, 1964.
Small Sounds from the Bass Fiddle. Albuquerque: Duende Press, 1964.
October. Mexico City: El Corno Emplumado Press, 1965.
Getting Rid of Blue Plastic. Bombay, India: Dialogue Press, 1967.
So Many Rooms Has a House But One Roof. New York: New Rivers Press, 1967.
Twenty-five Stages of My Spine. New Rochelle, NY: Elizabeth Press, 1967.
Water I Slip into at Night. Mexico City: El Corno Emplumado Press, 1967.
Part of the Solution. New York: New Directions Publishers, 1972; Lima, Peru: Editorial Causachun/Coleccion Poesia, 1973.
Day's Coming! Los Angeles: privately printed, 1973.
With These Hands. Vancouver, B.C., Canada: New Star Books, 1974.
All My Used Parts, Shackles, Fuel, Tenderness, and Stars. Kansas City, MO: New Letters, 1977.
Carlota: Poems and Prose from Havana. Vancouver, B.C., Canada: New Star Books, 1977.
We. New York: Smyrna Press, 1978.
A Poetry of Resistance. Toronto: Participatory Research Group, 1983.
Risking a Somersault in the Air: Conversations with Nicaraguan Writers. San Francisco: Solidarity Publishers, 1984.
Albuquerque: Coming Back to the USA. Vancouver, B.C., Canada: New Star Books, 1986.

The Coming Home Poems. East Haven, CT: LongRiver Books, 1986.
This Is about Incest. Ithaca, NY: Firebrand Books, 1987.
Memory Says Yes. Willimantic, CT: Curbstone Press, 1988.
Dancing with the Doe. Albuquerque: West End Press, 1992.

Essays

Cuban Women Twenty Years Later. New York: Smyrna Press, 1980.
"We Have the Capacity, the Imagination, and the Will: Milu Vargas Speaks about Nicaraguan Women." [pamphlet] Toronto: Participatory Research Group, 1983.
Testimonios. Toronto: Participatory Research Group, 1985.
The Shape of Red: Insider/Outsider Reflections. With Ruth Hubbard. Pittsburgh: Cleis Press, 1988.
Coming Home: Peace without Complacency. Albuquerque: West End Press, 1990.
Walking to the Edge: Essays of Resistance. Boston: South End Press, 1991.
Gathering Rage: The Failure of Twentieth Century Revolutions to Develop a Feminist Agenda. New York: Monthly Review Press, 1992.
The Old Cedar Bar. Nevada City, CA: Gateways, 1992.

Translations

Let's Go! (selection of poems by Guatemalan poet Otto-Rene Castillo). London: Cape-Golliard, 1970; reissued Willimantic, CT: Curbstone Press, 1984.
This Great People Has Said "Enough!" and Has Begun to Move! (poetry and prose from Latin America). San Francisco: People's Press, 1972.
These Living Songs/Estos cantos habitados (poetry by fifteen young Cuban poets). Fort Collins, CO: Colorado State University Press, 1978.
Breaking the Silences—Twentieth Century Poetry by Cuban Women. Vancouver, B.C., Canada: Pulp Press, 1982.
Carlos. The Dawn Is No Longer beyond Our Reach (a long prose poem by Tomas Borge Martinez). Vancouver, B.C., Canada: New Star Books, 1984.
Clean Flight: Selected Poems (poetry by Daisy Zamora). Translated by Elinor Randall and Margaret Randall. Willimantic, CT: Curbstone Press, 1993.

Studies of Margaret Randall

Chevigny, Bell. "Interview with Margaret Randall." *Ms.* June 1986.
"Conversando con Margaret Randall." *Araucaria de Chile* 24 (1983), n. pag.
Crawford, John, and Patricia Smith. "Margaret Randall." *This Is about Vision—Interviews with Writers of the Southwest.* Albuquerque: University of New Mexico Press, 1990. 71–81.
Greenberg, Alvin. "The Sense of the Risk of the Coming Together." *Minnesota Review* 6:2 (1966), 166–68.
Hijar, Alberto. "La fotografia como arma." *Plural* 9:2a (July 1980).
Kessler, Stephen. "A Complicated Homecoming." *Santa Cruz Express* October 24, 1985: 10.
"Margaret Randall: no soy una feminista radical." *FEM* 1:1 October/December 1976, n. pag.
Nathan, Debbie. "Adjustment of Status: The Trail of Margaret Randall." *Women and*

Other Aliens: Essays from the U.S.-Mexican Border. El Paso, Texas: Cinco Puntos Press, 1991. 90–108.

Rivers, Pamela Canyon. "Un encuentro con Margaret Randall." *Conceptions Southwest* 9:1 (Spring 1986): 33–40.

Semeiks, Joanna G. "Margaret Randall: Reticent Revolutionary." *American Notes and Queries* 16 (1977).

Volpendesta, David. "Margaret Randall vs. the Thought Police." *Poetry Flash* (December 1985): 6–13.

Walton, Marcus. "She Wants to Come Home." *Impact Magazine Albuquerque Journal.* 4:13 (January 14, 1986): 4–11.

ADRIENNE RICH (1929–   )
Diane McPherson

BIOGRAPHY

Adrienne Cecile Rich was born on May 16, 1929, in Baltimore, Maryland. Her mother, Helen Elizabeth Jones, was a pianist; her father, Arnold Rice Rich, was a physician, at the time of her birth working as a teacher and researcher at Johns Hopkins Medical School. She was educated at home until the fourth grade, by her mother; her father encouraged and directed her ambitions as a reader and as a writer. In 1951, she graduated *cum laude* from Radcliffe College; that same year her first collection of poems, *A Change of World*, was chosen by W. H. Auden to win the Yale Series of Younger Poets Award.

In 1953, Rich married Alfred H. Conrad, an economist then teaching at Harvard; between 1955 and 1959 she gave birth to three sons. She also continued to write and publish poetry. By 1966 she had begun teaching as well; she conducted poetry workshops at the YM-YWHA Poetry Center in New York City from 1966 to 1967. She was a visiting lecturer at Swarthmore College from 1967 to 1969 and an adjunct lecturer at Columbia University, Graduate School for the Arts, during the same period. From 1968 to 1975, she taught at City College of the City University of New York, first as a lecturer in the SEEK English program and later as an instructor in the creative writing program and as an assistant professor of English. Between 1972 and 1986 she also held positions at Brandeis University, Bryn Mawr College, Rutgers University, Cornell University, and at Scripps College and Pacific Oaks College in California. Since 1986 she has been professor of English and feminist studies at Stanford University. From 1981 to 1983 she served as co-editor of the lesbian-feminist journal *Sinister Wisdom*. Since 1952 her poetry has won her such awards as two Guggenheim Fellowships, in 1952 and 1961; the Ridgely Torrence Memorial Award of the Poetry Society of America in 1955; and the Grace Thayer Bradley Award of the Friends of Literature (Chicago) in 1956. Rich was named Phi Beta

Kappa poet by the College of William and Mary in 1960, by Swarthmore College in 1965, and by Harvard University in 1966. She was awarded the Litt.D. from Wheaton College in 1967 and from Smith College in 1979; the Eunice Tietjens Memorial Prize of *Poetry* magazine in 1968; the Shelley Memorial Award of the Poetry Society of America in 1971; the National Book Award in 1974 for *Diving into the Wreck: Poems, 1971–1972*; the National Book Critics Circle Award in Poetry nomination in 1978 for *The Dream of a Common Language: Poems, 1974–1977*; and the Ruth Lilly Poetry Prize by the Modern Poetry Association and the American Council for the Arts in 1986. In 1981, she was awarded the Fund for Human Dignity Award by the National Gay Task Force. She is currently at work on a fourth collection of essays.

These dates and events, the factual information about Adrienne Rich, constitute public knowledge: that which we all—writers, educators, students of literature, straight women and lesbians—believe we are entitled to know about any writer still living, teaching, and working. Are we entitled to more? One of the most vexing problems of the 1980s and early 1990s has been the extent to which literary criticism has inched its way toward biography; the question is especially problematic in a format that expressly identifies all the included writers as lesbian. Since the 1963 publication of *Snapshots of a Daughter-in-Law: Poems, 1954–1962*, Rich has written in a woman's voice and foregrounded women's experiences, a deliberate refusal of the "universality" (Rich has called this a "white male voice") the academy expects of the modern poet—at considerable risk to her reputation as a poet. Since 1970, according to her foreword to *Blood, Bread, and Poetry*, she has identified as a radical feminist—an equally risky public stance. Her lesbianism has been public knowledge for nearly as long: in a personal letter to the author, dated January 11, 1992, she says "I have been very visible as a lesbian, in and out of my work, for almost twenty years." In essays, monographs, reviews, and public addresses, discussing her feminist politics and offering insights into the institutions of motherhood and compulsory heterosexuality, she has included, along with political analysis, something of herself, of her own personal struggles. The reader who wishes to know the woman can, I think, encounter her there. Read "When We Dead Awaken: Writing as Re-Vision" in *On Lies, Secrets, and Silence*; in it, the poet, a young mother, her first book of poems already gathering critical acclaim, wonders whether she is "ungrateful, insatiable, perhaps a monster . . . a failed woman and a failed poet" (42). because she can't find a balance between the creative imagination and the traditional expectations of her as a woman. Read "Split at the Root: An Essay on Jewish Identity" from *Blood, Bread, and Poetry* for Rich's description of her education, viewed through the lens of identity politics. A generosity of spirit underwrites these essays, an exemplary honesty; they are distinguished by the courageous act of naming all of her disparate (and often risky) identities, and by the more courageous act of owning her own blindness, her own racism, her own anti-Semitism; of deriving, from her own unfinished journey, a critical vision of women's precarious position in culture with the power to inform, and, hopefully, to mobilize, all of us.

MAJOR WORKS AND THEMES

Rachel Blau DuPlessis, in her essay "The Critique of Consciousness and Myth in Levertov, Rich, and Rukeyser" (reprinted in *Shakespeare's Sisters*), identifies Rich's "Snapshots of a Daughter-in-Law" as "an outstanding poem" representing the "critique of consciousness, analyzing the mental and cultural structures that have formed women and inspecting their strategies of response" (284). This feminist "critique of consciousness," which Rich shares with her two contemporaries, is a significant and recurrent theme in both her poetry and prose.

The reader searching for other major themes is fortunate to have Rich's three collections of essays, *Of Woman Born* (1976), *On Lies, Secrets, and Silence* (1979), and *Blood, Bread, and Poetry* (1986), which serve as compendia of the thematic concerns of her poems, and which map the process of refinement and change in Rich's ideas. In her "New Introduction" to the tenth anniversary edition of *Of Woman Born*, Rich claims that on its first appearance the book was "both praised and attacked" because of its innovative combination of "personal testimony mingled with research, and theory which derived from both" (x). The book was also one of the earliest theoretical texts to concentrate on motherhood. Both of these ideas, approaching theoretical understanding by examining personal experience and analyzing women's experience in feminist terms, continue to underwrite much of Rich's work, as does the related theme of the sisterhood of all women. Another theme is defining patriarchy, which is linked in Rich's work with refusal of the myths and images that idealize women. Rich mentions another ongoing idea in her "New Introduction," that writing is a "continuous process"; "this book," she says, "is the work of one woman who has continued to learn, reflect, act, and write" (xxxv).

The second collection, *On Lies, Secrets, and Silence*, extends and adds to these early themes. In these essays, too, Rich uses her own history to illustrate, and to develop, theory; some of them are now basic texts for women's studies and lesbian studies courses. "It is the Lesbian in Us," a paper originally delivered in December of 1976 at the Modern Language Association (MLA) convention, begins to advance her idea of "the lesbian in all women," by which she means not merely the woman who "goes to bed" with women but the creative force, derived from female energy, that can drive "the woman who refuses to obey, who has said 'no' to the fathers" (202). Another essay, perhaps her most widely read, "When We Dead Awaken: Writing as Re-Vision" was also delivered at the MLA, in 1971; in it she provides a model of what "a radical critique of literature, feminist in its impulse" (35) might look like; once again she combines the personal, including a feminist re-reading of her own early poetry, with the theoretical.

By her own account, much of what the young Rich knew about the craft of poetry, she learned at home, from her father, a reader of poetry. She recalls, in "Split at the Root": "he criticized my poems for faulty technique and gave me books on rhyme and meter and form" (113). However, Rich looks back on her early mastery of form, praised by Auden in his introduction to her earliest book of poems, *A Change of World*, as being part of a "strategy" that conferred distance and manageability on otherwise unmanageable materials (and masked their emergent subversiveness). And even in this earliest publication, one can discern, beneath the surface formalism, tensions, strains, faultlines developing where the break with universality will eventually occur, and themes traceable through the whole of Rich's career as a poet. In "Aunt Jennifer's Tigers," the soul-killing oppression ("the massive weight of uncle's wedding band") of patriarchal institutions on a woman's imagination. The first traces of a compassionate inquiry by one woman into another woman's life.

Another theme, in hindsight clearly linked to her later overt lesbian themes, emerges as early as her second book of poetry, *The Diamond Cutters*. The sense of a woman's estrangement and skepticism within the traditional heterosexual romance, as expressed in "Living in Sin," might be identified as falling within "the lesbian continuum," a phrase Rich uses in her essay "Compulsory Heterosexuality and Lesbian Existence" to describe a range of "woman-identified experiences." The heroine of the poem, her eyes temporarily unblinded, is "jeered by the minor demons": dust, grime, the beetle watching from the dishware shelf. Though she is able, with some effort, to talk herself back into love by the end of the day, it is with the certainty that she will be awakened from the dream again soon.

By the appearance of *Snapshots of a Daughter-in-Law* (1963), Rich had begun to write deliberately from a woman's perspective; she had also abandoned much of the formalism of her earlier works. In one of her most frequently quoted essays, "When We Dead Awaken: Writing as Re-Vision," she called the title poem of *Snapshots*, which was written over two years (from 1958 to 1960), "an extraordinary relief to write" (45), because, in writing it, she abandoned the constriction of the "universal" voice. While the poem seems to Rich "too literary, too dependent on allusion" (45), it also previews many of her later themes: impatience, anger, sisterhood coexistent with women's persistent mistrust of each other, women's "sinecure" in the male-centered universe where our value rests in our "overpraised" indolence, slattern thought, and mediocrity.

Leaflets (1969) further develops Rich's theme of sisterhood. In poems like "Charleston in the Eighteen-Sixties," "For a Russian Poet," and "Poem of Women," she translates, retells history in a woman's voice. In "5:30 A.M." and "Abnegation" she encodes sisterhood and the precarious situation of women who refuse to dull the pain (or manage the knowledge) of their situation with either drugs or myth, in the image of the red fox, linking woman and fox in their "foreboding, foreboding" that despite their "miracle escapes" the "dull-jawed, onrushing killer," truth, "will have our skins at last." At the same time

Rich is already turning away from what Craig Werner has called "cultural solipsism," the tendency to consider only one's own group (cultural, racial, gender, national) as being "real," a tendency Rich identifies as one of the most pernicious attitudes of patriarchy. In "When We Dead Awaken," she calls "Orion," also included in *Leaflets*, "a poem of reconnection with a part of myself I had felt I was losing—the active principle, the energetic imagination" (45); within "Orion" this "active principle" is embodied in the "fierce half-brother" the narrative persona takes back.

Many of the poems in *The Will to Change: Poems, 1968–1970* attest to Rich's continuing commitment to move away from "cultural solipsism" and to employ that "energetic imagination" in making what are often difficult and demanding connections. These are poems of resistance: to mythic representations, to historical misrepresentations, to literature, to language, to love. In "Planetarium," the poetic persona turns her attention from the skies, which are full of "Galaxies of women," imagined female shapes ("A woman in the shape of a monster / a monster in the shape of a woman") to the forgotten woman, sister of the remembered astronomer, "and others" like her, the forgotten women whose contributions to history can only be read between the lines of history. "The Burning of Books Instead of Children," prefaced by a quote from Daniel Berrigan ("I was in danger of verbalizing my moral impulses out of existence"), records the poet's struggle to compose what may well be "useless" books in what she knows is "the oppressor's language."

Alicia Ostriker, in *Stealing the Language*, calls the title poem from *Diving into the Wreck* Rich's "major quest poem" (109); she remarks that while in much of Western male literature, "descent into water signifies danger or death, consistently associated with the feminine," in the work of women poets like Rich "the image of water comes to mean security instead of dread. It is alien, and yet it is home" (109). Publication of this volume marked Rich's definitive break with a poetic tradition in which she could no longer believe; her subsequent books carry her farther from that tradition, toward the woman-centered world from which she writes to this day.

CRITICAL RECEPTION

In a letter to the author, Adrienne Rich pointed out that the most controversial aspect of her work (not coincidentally, it was the aspect least often treated in early reviews by a mostly male critical establishment) was not her lesbianism, but her insistence on writing from a woman-centered perspective:

Long before I could write as a lesbian I was writing as a woman, in a period when to do so was believed to opt for the non-universal, the minor, even the trivial. That seemed to me, in the fifties and early sixties, without a political movement around me, truly dangerous and difficult.

Rich's first book of poetry could hardly have had a more auspicious reception: recognition by Auden, publication in the Yale Series of Younger Poets awards. The four books that followed were also well received, carefully read, and praised, by male poets of no small reputation. In his carefully composed foreword to *A Change of World*, Auden invokes Eliot's well-known precepts, articulated in "Tradition and the Individual Talent," that "the more perfect the artist, the more completely separate in him will be the man who suffers and the mind which creates" (Eliot 54). In Rich's earliest poems Auden recognizes not only her poems' "family tree" (he discerns the influences of Frost and Yeats) but her "craftsmanship . . . evidence of a capacity for detachment from the self and its emotions without which no art is possible" (Cooper 211). However, in nominating Rich to a place in this male tradition of poets, what Auden finds occasion to praise in Rich seems curious: "a modesty not so common at that age, which disclaims any extraordinary vision" (210). From the feminist perspective of the 1990s, one cringes at the patronizing undertone: Auden is saying that this is a young woman who knows her place.

Five years later, Donald Hall, a poet contemporary with Rich, favorably reviewed *The Diamond Cutters* in *Poetry 87* (February 1956). Comparing Rich's second collection of poems to *A Change of World*, Hall calls the earlier book "sometimes tame, and even a little smug about its ability to keep experience away from the door" (212). In *The Diamond Cutters*, Hall says, "the wolf is inside," and Hall approves; "precision and frequent profundity characterize the best of her verse" (212), he says. Hall does issue a caution: this young poet requires "a diet of dissatisfaction" to bring forth her best work. He challenges her "to find things she cannot with all her skill do, and then try to do them" (213).

Philip Booth, another of Rich's contemporaries, reviewed *Snapshots of a Daughter-in-Law*, again favorably, in the *Christian Science Monitor*, January 3, 1963. While some of Booth's language in praise of the book, that it is "demandingly quiet in its tones and persuasively selfless in its fictions" (215), is reminiscent of Auden's foreword, he is not put off by what Rich herself sees as the female-centeredness of the poems. Booth says that "it is ourselves we most see in the candid focus of her many poems about women" (215). What Booth's generous praise indicates is that Rich has not quite abandoned that caution she recalls in "When We Dead Awaken," that "poetry should be 'universal,' which meant, of course, nonfemale" (44). He describes as her subject "the commonplaces of human experience seen from such uncommonly candid angles that even her most domestic images are raised to the nth power of universal implication" (216).

After the publication of *Snapshots of a Daughter-in-Law*, however, critics began to describe Rich's work in more negative terms, as she herself recalls in "Blood, Bread, and Poetry": "I was told, in print, that this book was 'bitter,' 'personal'; that I had sacrificed the sweetly flowing measures of my earlier books for a ragged line and a coarsened voice" (180). It is the presence of the political in these poems, Rich suggests, that alienated the critics. And although her subsequent books have been reviewed positively and often sensitively, in some of those reviews the critic's response to individual poems is paired with what seems a determined blindness to her woman-centered images and ideology.

John Ashberry's review of Rich's next book, *Necessities of Life*, which appeared in the *New York Herald Tribune Book Week*, September 4, 1966, is apparently a positive review, both praising the new poems and connecting Rich to a female poetic tradition. Rich has "made progress since those schoolgirlish days" of "At a Bach Concert"; now, says Ashberry, "she emerges as a kind of Emily Dickinson of the suburbs, bleakly eyeing the pullulation and pollution around her" (217). The virile language with which he praises these poems, however, would hardly do for Dickinson, and seems awkward in regard to Rich: "In this hard and sinewy new poetry she has mastered the art of tacking between alternative resolutions of the poem's tension and of leaving the reader at the right moment, just as meaning is dawning" (218).

Denis Donoghue, reviewing *Leaflets*, reads the poems as reflections of the 1960s, "a bad time for those Americans who would like to be quiet" (219), but somehow misses, in his mention of "5:30 A.M." and "Abnegation," Rich's evocation of endangered sisterhood in the figure of the fox: female, menstruating, self-preserving, and single-mindedly pursued for the clarity of her vision. David Kalstone, reviewing *The Will to Change*, is likewise sensitive to Rich's project of linking the personal and the political; he is generous in his praise of the book's "determination," its "watchful honesty." "Her method," he says, "is courageous and radical in intention" (225). But Kalstone's review, too, carefully overlooks the explicitly female consciousness beginning to emerge in these poems. He reads "Planetarium," for instance, as a poem in praise of "the early astronomers," ignoring the presence of "Caroline Herschel, astronomer, sister of William" and failing to notice that "others" refers not to other "early astronomers" but to the anonymous sisterhood of unrecognized "sisters" of astronomers.

The gratitude one feels, as a feminist, in reading Cheryl Walker's review of *Diving into the Wreck*, published in *The Nation*, October 3, 1973, is prompted by such increasingly puzzling omissions. Walker prefaces her discussion of Rich's poems with a description of the feminist innovation Rich was to use to such advantage in her essays: that "queer and wonderful phenomenon" of combining insightful and intelligent readings of literature with speaking from the perspective of the woman writer's own life about the difficulty of producing literature in which one speaks as a woman. Walker also highlights a phenomenon familiar in male reviews of women poets when she describes Robert Boyers's *Salmagundi* (Spring/Summer 1973) article; Boyers "managed to discuss Rich's work at length without ever dealing with the importance of feminism for this poet" (227). In addition, Walker makes other observations lacking thus far in critical readings of Rich, taking her insights from things Rich herself has said: "that she would like to write poetry which could be useful to women"; that "the figure, the 'I,' which recurs in these poems, both is and is not Adrienne Rich." Finally, Walker makes clear that "the personal" in Rich's poems does not mean "the private" at all, but the political. The book, she claims, is "another valuable book to add to the community of works about women's developing consciousness" (230); she cautions, however, that like other works of this community, its "dark, tentative atmosphere of exploration" (230) will result in Rich's exclusion from serious critical consideration.

It would be naive to assume that ensuing critical treatment of Rich's work might split along gender lines as the insights of feminist (and lesbian) criticism accumulated and were disseminated. That this was not the case is illustrated in critiques of Rich's next works. In Rosemary Tonks's review of *Diving Into the Wreck*, appearing in the *New York Review of Books*, October 4, 1973, what Walker feared has already begun to come true; Tonks faults Rich's newest book for "an out-of-date modernness" in which she fails to recognize a feminist sensibility; instead, she claims that Rich has "taken on too much, and the imagination is exhausted by the effort required to familiarize itself with all the burdens of the modern world" (234).

Margaret Atwood, reviewing the same book in the *New York Times Book Review* of December 30, 1973, has a more positive reaction. She describes feeling, when she heard Rich read from the book, "as though the top of my head was being attacked, sometimes with an ice pick, sometimes with a blunter instrument: a hatchet or a hammer" (238). But if Atwood's review is positive, it is cautiously so. "It would be easy," she says, to classify Rich as "just another vocal Women's Libber, substituting polemic for poetry, simplistic messages for complex meanings" (238). Atwood does not do this, and yet the specter of the dismissal she evokes lingers in the restraint with which she praises some of the work: the poems are most convincing "when they resist the temptation to sloganize, when they don't preach at me" (240).

What is apparent in readings of Rich's later work is that such disagreement as occurs has as a subtext the writer's attitude toward feminism. Ruth Whitman's admiring review of *Poems: Selected and New, 1950–1974* in *Harvard Magazine*, July-August 1975, sees in Rich's evolution as a poet a pattern of the history of women's transformation: "from careful traditional obedience (that was Auden's description of her) to cosmic awareness" (242). Eleanor Wilner's review of the same book, in *American Poetry Review*, March/April 1975, also centers on Rich's transformation; she concentrates on the transformation of female, from Aunt Jennifer's "unlived life" in the earliest of Rich's poems, to "the meeting of sophisticated artistry and the primal volcanic energy of underground material, set in motion by fire" in *Diving into the Wreck*. In the newest poems, Wilner finds other female images, some new, some which Rich returns to: knots, scars, the separation of women into mother and monster, and a movement beyond that separation to "the moment when the attrition begins to end, when the circles of guilt begin to open" (261), in Rich's poem "The Alleged Murderess Walking in her Cell," in which recognition of her sisterhood with the monster allows the mother to forgive herself.

Rima Shore, reviewing *Twenty-One Love Poems*, in *Conditions: One*, April 1977, finally uses the name lesbian for those poems, in connection with "the theme of choice." Shore's review also articulates the connections between Rich's choice of loving women and her choice of addressing a reader who is a woman through her poems; "from the very beginning" of these love poems "the poet has spoken of her lover and her poetry in a single breath" (270).

Hayden Carruth's review of *The Dream of a Common Language*, published in *Harper's*, November 1978, refers to Rich's "recent polemical writing" in *Of Woman Born*, to which he compares the poems; although he discerns "minor points of irrationality, even hysteria" in *Of Woman Born*, he describes Rich's poems as "fine, assured, calm . . . *reasonable*" (271). Carruth's review is generous in explaining that it is "the present condition of society" that pressures the poet into "adopting an antimale, frankly sexist posture" (273). He is equally generous in allowing the polemic's importance to the poetry (combining "traditional poetic resources with continual personal experiment" is, he says, "exactly the combination that has always produced the strongest literature" [272]). However, like critics before him, Carruth privileges those aspects of the poems that can be called "universal": "the genuinely literate sentences woven into genuinely poetic measures . . . the easy, perfectly assimilated classical allusion" and "the details—here the female mountain and flower—turned into generalized insights of humane value" (272).

Poet Olga Broumas, who also reviewed *The Dream of a Common Language* in *Chrysalis*, no. 6 (1978), calls the book, "the most difficult, complex, demanding of Rich's work" (274). Although it has been prepared for by Rich's previous poetry and prose, Broumas experiences *The Dream of a Common Language* as "a shock I've found difficult to recover from" (275). For Broumas, "Twenty-One Love Poems," reprinted from its original edition, forms "the core of the book"; however, although she is generous in her praise of the book (it is not only "heroic," but "a redefinition *of* the heroic" [274]), Broumas does not use the word *lesbian* in describing these poems. Nor does she acknowledge that they are about love between women; such an omission, like other critics' failure to mention feminist concerns in earlier reviews, has the ultimate effect of undermining the positive nature of the review with the disquieting implication that "lesbian" and "heroic" are not words that can coexist.

BIBLIOGRAPHY

Works by Adrienne Rich

Poetry

A Change of World. New Haven: Yale University Press, 1951.
The Diamond Cutters and Other Poems. New York: Harper & Brothers, 1955.

Snapshots of a Daughter-in-Law: Poems, 1954–1962. New York: Harper & Row, 1963;
    New York: Norton, 1967; London: Chatto & Windus, 1970.
Necessities of Life: Poems, 1962–1965. New York: Norton, 1966.
Selected Poems. London: Chatto & Windus, 1967.
Leaflets: Poems, 1965–1968. New York: Norton, 1969; London: Chatto & Windus, 1972.
The Will to Change: Poems, 1968–1970. New York: Norton, 1971; London: Chatto &
    Windus, 1973.
Diving into the Wreck: Poems, 1971–1972. New York: Norton, 1973.
Poems: Selected and New, 1950–1974. New York: Norton, 1975.
Twenty-One Love Poems. Emeryville, CA: Effie's Press, 1976.
The Dream of a Common Language: Poems, 1974–1977. New York: Norton, 1978.
A Wild Patience Has Taken Me This Far: Poems, 1978–1981. New York: Norton, 1981.
Sources. Woodside, CA: Heyeck Press, 1983.
The Fact of a Doorframe: Poems Selected and New, 1950–1984. New York: Norton,
    1984.
Your Native Land, Your Life: Poems. New York: Norton, 1986.

Prose

Of Woman Born: Motherhood as Experience and Institution. New York: Norton, 1976.
Women and Honor: Some Notes on Lying (monograph). Pittsburgh: Motheroot Publi-
    cations, 1977. Repr. in *On Lies, Secrets and Silence*. 185–94.
On Lies, Secrets, and Silence: Selected Prose, 1966–1978. New York: Norton, 1979.
Blood, Bread, and Poetry: Selected Prose, 1979–1986. New York: Norton, 1986.

Plays

Ariadne: A Play in Three Acts and Poems. Baltimore: J. H. Furst, 1939.
Not I, But Death, A Play in One Act. Baltimore: J. H. Furst, 1941.

Studies of Adrienne Rich

Addelson, Kathryn Pyne. "Words and Lives: On 'Compulsory Heterosexuality and Les-
    bian Existence'—Defining the Issues." *Signs: Journal of Women in Culture and
    Society* 7 (Autumn 1981): 187–99.
Arnup, Katherine. "Adrienne Rich: Poet, Mother, Lesbian Feminist, Visionary." *At-
    lantis: A Women's Studies Journal* 8.1 (1982): 97–110.
Ashberry, John. "Tradition and Talent." *New York Herald Tribune Book Week* 4 Sep-
    tember 1966: 2. Reprinted In *Reading Adrienne Rich: Reviews and Re-Visions,
    1951–81*. Ed. Jane Roberta Cooper. Ann Arbor: University of Michigan Press,
    1984. 217–18.
Atwood, Margaret. "Review of *Diving into the Wreck*." *New York Times Book Review*
    December 30, 1973: 1–2. Reprinted in *Reading Adrienne Rich: Reviews and Re-
    Visions, 1951–81*. Ed. Jane Roberta Cooper. Ann Arbor: University of Michigan
    Press, 1984. 238–41.
Bennett, Paula. *My Life a Loaded Gun: Female Creativity and Feminist Poetics*. Boston:
    Beacon, 1986.
Booth, Philip. "Rethinking the World." *Christian Science Monitor* January 3, 1963: 15.
    Reading Adrienne Rich: Reviews and Re-Visions, 1951–81. Ed. Jane Roberta
    Cooper. Ann Arbor: University of Michigan Press, 1984. 215–16.

Broumas, Olga. "Review of *The Dream of a Common Language.*" *Chrysalis* 6 (1978): 109–13. Reprinted in *Reading Adrienne Rich: Reviews and Re-Visions, 1951–81.* Ed. Jane Roberta Cooper. Ann Arbor: University of Michigan Press, 1984. 274–86.

Carruth, Hayden. "Excellence in Poetry." *Harpers* (November 1978): 81–88. Reprinted in *Reading Adrienne Rich: Reviews and Re-Visions, 1951–81.* Ed. Jane Roberta Cooper. Ann Arbor: University of Michigan Press, 1984, 271–73.

Carruthers, Mary J. "The Re-Vision of the Muse: Adrienne Rich, Audre Lorde, Judy Grahn, Olga Broumas." *Hudson Review* 36.2 (1983): 293–322.

Chenoy, Polly N. " 'Writing These Words in the Woods': A Study of the Poetry of Adrienne Rich." *Studies in American Literature: Essays in Honour of William Mulder.* Ed. Jagdish Chander and Narinder S. Pradhan. Delhi: Oxford University Press, 1976. 194–211.

Christ, Carol P. "Homesick for a Woman, for Ourselves: Adrienne Rich." *Diving Deep and Surfacing: Women Writers and Spiritual Quest.* Boston: Beacon, 1980. 75–96.

Cooper, Jane Roberta, ed. *Reading Adrienne Rich: Reviews and Re-Visions, 1951–81.* Ann Arbor: University of Michigan Press, 1984.

Donoghue, Denis. "Review of *Leaflets: Poems 1965–1968.*" *New York Review of Books* May 7, 1970: 7. Reprinted in *Reading Adrienne Rich: Reviews and Re-Visions, 1951–81.* Ed. Jane Roberta Cooper. Ann Arbor: University of Michigan Press, 1984. 219–20.

DuPlessis, Rachel Blau. "The Critique of Consciousness and Myth in Levertov, Rich, and Rukeyser." *Shakespeare's Sisters: Feminist Essays on Women Poets.* Ed. Sandra M. Gilbert and Susan Gubar. Bloomington: Indiana University Press, 1979. 280–300.

Eliot, T. S. "Tradition and the Individual Talent." *The Sacred Wood.* London: Methuen, 1920.

Erkkila, Betsy. "Dickinson and Rich: Toward a Theory of Female Poetic Influence." *American Literature* 56.4 (1984): 541–59.

Flowers, Betty S. "The 'I' in Adrienne Rich: Individuation and the Androgyne Archetype." *Theory and Practice of Feminist Literary Criticism.* Ed. Gabriela Mora and Karen S. Van Hooft. Ypsilanti, MI: Bilingual, 1982. 14–35.

Friedman, Susan Stanford. " 'I go where I love': An Intertextual Study of H.D. and Adrienne Rich." *Signs: A Journal of Women in Culture and Society* 9.2 (1983): 228–45.

Gelpi, Albert. "Two Ways of Spelling It Out: An Archetypal-Feminist Reading of H.D.'s *Trilogy* and Adrienne Rich's *Sources.*" *Southern Review* 26.2 (1990): 266–84.

Gelpi, Barbara Charlesworth, and Albert Gelpi, eds. *Adrienne Rich's Poetry: Texts of the Poems, the Poet on Her Work, Reviews and Criticism.* New York: W. W. Norton, 1975.

Gould, Jean. *Modern American Women Poets.* New York: Dodd, Mead, 1984.

Hall, Donald. "A Diet of Dissatisfaction." *Poetry* 87 (February 1956): 299–302. Reprinted in *Reading Adrienne Rich: Reviews and Re-Visions. 1951–81.* Ed. Jane Roberta Cooper. Ann Arbor: University of Michigan Press, 1984. 212–14.

Harris, Victoria Frenkel. "Scribe, Inscription, Inscribed: Sexuality in the Poetry of Robert Bly and Adrienne Rich." *Discontented Discourses: Feminism/Textual Interven-*

tion/Psychoanalysis. Ed. Marleen S. Barr, and Richard Feldstein. Urbana: University of Illinois Press, 1989. 117–37.

Herzog, Anne. "Adrienne Rich and the Discourse of Decolonization." *Centennial Review* 33.3 (1989): 258–77.

Juhasz, Suzanne. "The Feminist Poet: Alta and Adrienne Rich." *Naked and Fiery Forms: Modern American Poetry by Women, A New Tradition*. New York: Harper-Colophon, 1976. 177–204.

Kahn, Coppelia. "Excavating 'Those Dim Minoan Regions': Maternal Subtexts in Patriarchal Literature." *Diacritics* 12.2 (1982): 32–41.

Kalstone, David. "Adrienne Rich: Face to Face." *Five Temperaments: Elizabeth Bishop, Robert Lowell, James Merrill, Adrienne Rich, and John Ashbery*. New York: Oxford University Press, 1977. 129–69.

——. "Review of *The Will to Change: Poems 1968–1970*." *New York Times Book Review* May 23, 1971: 31–32. Reprinted in *Reading Adrienne Rich: Reviews and Re-Visions, 1951–81*. Ed. Jane Roberta Cooper. Ann Arbor: University of Michigan Press, 1984. 221–25.

Kennard, Jean E. "Ourself behind Ourself: A Theory for Lesbian Readers." *Gender and Reading: Essays on Readers, Texts, and Contexts*. Ed. Elizabeth A. Flynn and Patrocinio P. Schweickart. Baltimore: Johns Hopkins University Press, 1986. 63–80.

Keyes, Claire. *The Aesthetics of Power: The Poetry of Adrienne Rich*. Athens: University of Georgia Press, 1986.

McDaniel, Judith. *Reconstituting the World: The Poetry and Vision of Adrienne Rich*. Argyle, NY: Spinsters Ink, 1978.

Martin, Wendy. *An American Triptych: Anne Bradstreet, Emily Dickinson, Adrienne Rich*. Chapel Hill: University of North Carolina, Press, 1984.

Matson, Suzanne. "Talking to Our Father: The Political and Mythical Appropriations of Adrienne Rich and Sharon Olds." *American Poetry Review* 18.6 (1989): 35–41.

Middlebrook, Diane Wood. "Three Mirrors Reflecting Women: Poetry of Sylvia Plath, Anne Sexton, and Adrienne Rich." *Worlds into Words: Understanding Modern Poets*. New York: Norton, 1978. 65–95.

Mieszkowski, Gretchen. "No Longer 'by a miracle, a twin': Helen Vendler's Reviews of Adrienne Rich's Recent Poetry." *South Central Review: The Journal of the South, Central Modern Language Association* 5.2 (1988): 72–86.

Miller, Nancy K. "Changing the Subject: Authorship, Writing, and the Reader." *Feminist Studies: Critical Studies*. Ed. Teresa de Lauretis. Bloomington: Indiana University Press, 1986. 102–20.

Nowik, Nan. "Mixing Art and Politics: The Writings of Adrienne Rich, Marge Piercy, and Alice Walker." *Centennial Review* 30.2 (1986): 208–18.

Ostriker, Alicia Suskin. *Stealing the Language: The Emergence of Women's Poetry in America*. Boston: Beacon, 1986.

Schweickart, Patrocinio P. "Reading Ourselves: Toward a Feminist Theory of Reading." *Gender and Reading: Essays on Readers, Texts, and Contexts*. Ed. Elizabeth A. Flynn and Patrocinio P. Schweickart. Baltimore: Johns Hopkins University Press, 1986. 31–62.

Shore, Rima. "To Move Openly Together/In the Pull of Gravity." *Conditions: One* 1 (April 1977): 113–18. Reprinted in *Reading Adrienne Rich: Reviews and Re-*

Visions, 1951–81. Ed. Jane Roberta Cooper. Ann Arbor: University of Michigan Press, 1984. 263–70.

Slowick, Mary. "The Friction of the Mind: The Early Poetry of Adrienne Rich." *Massachusetts Review* 25.1 (1984): 142–60.

Stimpson, Catharine. "Adrienne Rich and Lesbian/Feminist Poetry." *Parnassus* (Spring/Summer/Fall/Winter 1985): 249–68.

Stout, Janis. "Breaking Out: The Journey of the American Woman Poet." *North Dakota Quarterly* 56.1 (1988): 40–53.

Strine, Mary S. "The Politics of Asking Women's Questions: Voice and Value in the Poetry of Adrienne Rich." *Text and Performance Quarterly* 9.1 (1989): 24–41.

Tonks, Rosemary. "Cutting the Marble." *New York Times Review of Books* October 4, 1973: 8–10. Reprinted in *Reading Adrienne Rich: Reviews and Re-Visions, 1951–81*. Ed. Jane Roberta Cooper. Ann Arbor: University of Michigan Press, 1984. 232–37.

Vendler, Helen. "Adrienne Rich." *Part of Nature, Part of Us: Modern American Poets*. Cambridge: Harvard University Press, 1980.

Walker, Cheryl. "Trying to Save the Skein." *Nation* October 3, 1973: 346–49. Reprinted in *Reading Adrienne Rich: Reviews and Re-Visions, 1951–81*. Ed. Jane Roberta Cooper. Ann Arbor: University of Michigan Press, 1984. 226–31.

Werner, Craig. *Adrienne Rich: The Poet and Her Critics*. Chicago: American Library Association, 1988.

Whitman, Ruth. "Three Women Poets." *Harvard Magazine* (July/August 1975): 66–67. Reprinted in *Reading Adrienne Rich: Reviews and Re-Visions, 1951–81*. Ed. Jane Roberta Cooper. Ann Arbor: University of Michigan Press, 1984. 242–43.

Wilner, Eleanor. "This Accurate Dreamer." *American Poetry Review* (March/April 1975): 4–7. Reprinted in *Reading Adrienne Rich: Reviews and Re-Visions, 1951–81*. Ed. Jane Roberta Cooper. Ann Arbor: University of Michigan Press, 1984. 244–62.

Zita, Jacquelyn N. "Historical Amnesia and the Lesbian Continuum: On 'Compulsory Heterosexuality and Lesbian Existence'—Defining the Issues." *Signs* (Autumn 1981): 172–87.

RUTHANN ROBSON (1956–   )
Jorjet Harper

BIOGRAPHY

Ruthann Robson was born June 27, 1956, the only child of white working-class parents. She left high school and went to college on an early acceptance program at Ramapo College in Mahwah, New Jersey, in the early 1970s at a time when, she says, "it was an experimental college with a political spectrum ranging from anarchist to marxist/feminist." (Unless otherwise noted, all quotations are from personal communication with the author.) She graduated three years later, in 1976, with a major in philosophy, minor in Asian studies. At this time she also received her high school diploma (GED)—making her the first person in her family to graduate from high school.

Robson attended a year of graduate school in philosophy at the University of South Carolina at Columbia. During her college and graduate school years, Robson worked as a waitress and a bartender, and in factories, in retail sales, and in book sales to support herself. She began looking around for other avenues for her future. "I thought I would need to make a living, and philosophy wasn't going to be a way I could do that," she recalls.

The idea to be a lawyer came to her in an almost sideways manner: some other students she was living with at the time were going to take the LSAT (Law School Admission Test), and that gave her the idea to take it too. "I thought law might be interesting to do. Being an attorney would be a good job to have, and I would always have a job. And that would give me time to write and the money to write," says Robson.

In fact, she did quite well on the exam—well enough to be offered a number of scholarships to law schools. She chose Stetson College of Law in St. Petersburg, Florida, and went there on a scholarship in 1977—continuing to work all the while at a variety of low-paying jobs. She graduated from Stetson with honors in 1979.

After passing the bar, Robson made her home in Florida for the next thirteen years, working for federal judges, practicing poverty law, and teaching. "I've never worked for a law firm or a corporation. I've represented people that I didn't like, but I've never had to represent someone I didn't want to represent," she says.

Robson says she has always considered herself a lesbian. She came out "by reading books and by watching people—watching women be women. Seeing that it was possible. I think the reason I like books and literature is because I think it has, not necessarily the potential to change people—though that might be true—but the potential to present them with options that they may or may not be able to articulate for themselves. Before you make a choice you have to know or to see that such a choice is possible."

Robson had been writing stories and poems since childhood. It was during her years in Florida that her work began to appear in a number of lesbian and feminist periodicals. It was also during this time, in 1984, that she gave birth to her son, Larkin.

Robson's first collection of short stories, *Eye of a Hurricane*, was published by Firebrand in 1989. In 1990, the book won the prestigious Ferro-Grumley Award for Lesbian Fiction.

Robson moved to California to attend the University of California at Berkeley School of Law (Boalt Hall), receiving a Ll.M. (Master of Law) degree in 1989 for a project on lesbian legal theory. Robson now teaches at CUNY (the City University of New York) Law School. It is, Robson says, "one of the few progressive law schools in the United States." Among the subjects she teaches are Feminist Jurisprudence and Sexuality and the Law.

In 1991, Robson's next collection of stories, *Cecile*, appeared. In 1992 Robson's training in law, her longtime love of writing, and her lesbianism were able to merge in a very direct way in *Lesbian (Out)law*, nonfiction essays about lesbians and the law. Both are also published by Firebrand.

MAJOR WORKS AND THEMES

Ruthann Robson considers herself a "second-generation" lesbian writer—that is, one who is no longer obliged to write "coming out stories" or "gay and proud" stories. "I can't imagine not being a lesbian, so it's hard to say how it's influenced me. Just like I can't imagine not being a writer. I haven't had to write coming out stories, because they were already out there. I don't think I've ever written anything where someone comes out. And I don't have to write that 'we're as great as everybody else.' I'm one of the first people to benefit from the work that other lesbian writers have done."

Robson's prose writing is often highly poetic and multilevelled. Most of her earliest works, published in journals, would be labeled poetry, though they blur and sometimes dissolve the line between poetry and prose. Robson would more likely define them as fiction-theory: "Sometimes they're prose, sometimes poetry, usually in sections. They're less explicitly narrative or lyrical and more about theory or ideas,'' she explains. Her literary form has been highly influenced by the work of some Canadian lesbian writers, including Nicole Brossard.

Robson is a writer who is interested in ideas. Breaking out of set structures—whether imposed by mainstream patriarchal culture or by lesbian culture—to find one's own definitions and create one's own identity as a lesbian is a recurring theme in her fiction.

Robson's first book, *Eye of a Hurricane*, looks at lesbian lives from quirky, imaginative vantages. A lesbian college professor with a penchant for shoplifting who is in a "fervently non-monogamous" relationship. A "sexual pluralist" lesbian vegetarian "freelance housecleaner." A lesbian prostitute who becomes an aerobics teacher on a Greek island. A lesbian mother who manages a 7-Eleven and has "an address book full of women she's left" because, she tells them all, she's "incapable of commitment to adult humans." The teenage daughter of a lesbian lawyer whose mother is in jail for refusing to turn the girl over to her father after he won custody.

All thirteen of the stories in the collection are written in the present tense, and often in the first person. Through the immediacy of the narrators' voices and the often abrupt actions, the effect Robson creates is one of great emotional suspensions—distances the characters themselves can't bridge. At the same time, some of Robson's characters view themselves with affable humor and an acute sense of the unbridled nature of circumstance.

Robson's second book, *Cecile*, is also a collection of stories, but these are all about the same characters—the unnamed narrator, her lover Cecile, and their son Colby. The narrator—Colby's biological mother—who has a history of sexual experiments and exploits, is so deeply in love with Cecile that when she looks in a mirror now, she sees Cecile's face. "I have looked at Cecile so hard and so long that any other face, even my own, is foreign. And I have touched her and stroked her so soft and so long that any other body, even my own, would be peculiar. I guess that's monogamy." Through the observations, descriptions, feelings, and memories of the narrator, we follow this family from Florida to the West Coast to New York, as Robson charts the small seismic shifts in their relationship.

In *Cecile*, the lesbian identities and politics of Cecile and her lover are givens, and Robson's focus is squarely on the quotidian. "What I wanted to do was write about the stuff about daily life," Robson says. "But it's also not supposed to be mundane, not 'oh, isn't this great, lesbians are like everybody else.' It's about everyday political struggles, and the struggle to make a living, to have a halfway decent life, and do halfway decent things."

Robson deliberately constructed *Cecile* as a set of short stories rather than as a novel; she didn't want to create "a plot with a climax where something happens, and then it's resolved—which is the way I understand the traditional novel. That's explicitly what I didn't want to do. The point was to show people without a big crisis. How people can shape their own lives. That sometimes we're shaped by crisis, and sometimes we're shaped by all the little things that happen.''

Robson's exploration of lesbian identity extended into nonfiction with the 1992 publication of *Lesbian (Out)law*, in which she examines the ways in which the law does and does not define and serve lesbian realities. While there are books treating gay legal issues that may contain a cursory treatment of lesbian concerns, *Lesbian (Out)law* is the first work ever written to directly focus on lesbians and the law.

Some of the essays are reworkings of papers first published in law journals in which Robson has researched lesbian legal history, and began developing a lesbian legal theory. She was motivated to write *Lesbian (Out)law* because she was disturbed by the way lesbians ''take legal concepts and try to either fit themselves into them or use them against each other.''

A dense and carefully argued work that is at the same time very readable, the book is subtitled *Survival under the Rule of Law*. Robson argues for an awareness of when the law serves the interests of lesbians and when it does not, a ''resistance to the law's domestication,'' and presents an analysis of how legal concepts shape lesbian thinking. Her goal is not only to get lesbians to cast a more critical eye on the law in their daily lives, but to begin to build a lesbian theoretical perspective on the law.

Robson presents a historical framework for her discussion, based on her research. She shows that, contrary to popular notions that gay men but not lesbians have a history of legal persecution, the law has not ignored or been benign toward lesbians.

''Some books say there's no such thing as lesbian legal history, that men have been persecuted and women haven't, and that's just not true,'' she says. ''European and American historical evidence on lesbians—though they were not named as such—shows them being prosecuted and executed. If a woman is executed for making love to another woman, I think that's good enough to call her lesbian.''

The bulk of *Lesbian (Out)law* focuses on contemporary legal concepts as they relate to lesbians—such as the concept of ''privacy.''

''We want to be able to say that our sexuality is no one's business, and we want to be out of every closet. We can be convinced that such desires are contradictory if we accept what is often called the public/private split enforced by the rule of law,'' she writes *(Out)Law* 64). Robson continually posits lesbian survival rather than adherence to law as the determining factor in her analysis. ''The tension between the private and the public is a tension maintained by the rule of law. When we put lesbians at the center, it is not that this tension disappears; rather, it no longer makes sense. Our sexuality does not belong to the public sphere or the private one. It belongs only to us'' *(Out/Law* 76).

Robson discusses specific cases—the Hardwick opinion, the fight of Karen Thompson for guardianship of Sharon Kowalsky, the Perry Watkins case—in her arguments. In a discussion of lesbian sexuality and the law, she brings her point vividly to life by excerpting erotic passages from Judith McDaniel's novel *Just Say Yes* to illustrate how and where lesbian sex is outlawed and confined—and ultimately defined—by legal strictures.

Robson also continues to write fiction.

CRITICAL RECEPTION

When *Eye of a Hurricane* was published by Firebrand in 1989, it inspired a flurry of favorable reviews in the gay and lesbian and feminist press. In 1990, the book was not only a Lambda Literary Award nominee in the "lesbian debut" category; it also garnered Robson the prestigious Ferro-Grumley Award for "an outstanding work of fiction on lesbian life published by an American author."

Hurricane appeared at a time when many readers were beginning to tire of "cheerleader" novels about lesbianism—especially simplistic, preachy ones—and reviewers sat up and took notice.

"Robson refuses to write about what women's lives should be like; she writes instead about what they are like," says Katherine Sturtevant in *Lesbian Contradiction*, calling *Hurricane* a book with "a refreshing variety of unique, credible characters with interesting histories"(18).

Patricia R. Schwartz, writing in *Bay Windows*, has a similar reaction: "What makes these stories virtually unique in the canon of lesbian, feminist writing is that they seem to be about life as the author has discovered it to be, the raw grit of what is, rather than as some lavender-tinged visionary would want it to be."

Robson, says Schwartz, makes no apologies for anyone, especially in the area of sexuality. "These stories are not explications of why someone has the sexuality she has; simply, each woman or man she writes about IS. How refreshing in a fictional genre often hamstrung with rhetoric and rigidity about what it's acceptable to write about."

Hurricane is also appreciated for its emotional restraint. "[Robson] refuses to reveal the emotion that other authors splash around so freely. She manages to move us with what she leaves unsaid; with understatement and painful silence," says Sturtevant. "This is nowhere as true as in Robson's skilled descriptions of the frequent sexual encounters of her characters, which are more often detached and alienated than tender and integrated. The women in Robson's stories are frequently strong; they are survivors. But their survival has been costly. They have not left their pain behind"(18).

Writing for the *Women's Review of Books*, Marge Piercy, who calls Robson "a remarkable poet," says the stories contained in *Hurricane* "comprise a strong and fresh contribution to current women's literature. The voice varies but the overseeing eye has an uncompromising, clear and unapologetic feminist perspective that informs the stories and the language. The focus on women is unhesitatingly and extremely honest. The author is as interested in how we exploit and damage each other in our society as in how we form strong bonds of love and friendship and solidarity'' (22).

Robson's craft is also lauded by Schwartz. "Her ability to underscore plot and characterization with theme and symbol is a lovely thing to experience,'' said Schwartz. "Place, character, story-line, language all meld into wholes as rare as perfect shells found along the tide line."

The only "problem" *Hurricane*'s stories presents for Schwartz is the "relentlessness of a vision of people as simply NOT nice." Robson's focus, as Schwartz perceives it, "[leaves her] with a bit of a chill at the heart of humanity."

Cecile's reception was a bit more bumpy, but on the whole it has also been praised. *Publishers Weekly* calls *Cecile* an "intelligent, lively volume," and praises Robson's writing as "spare and graceful, with wonderfully original sparks of sarcasm and wit ('the land looks burnt, as if by an encounter with a terrible hairdresser') sprinkled liberally throughout."

Marie Kuda, writing in *Booklist*, calls Robson "a fine writer, skillful at conjuring the atmosphere of surviving in occupied territory. She makes the reader share her characters' anger, their sense of the seeming futility of their battle, and their refusal to relinquish hope."

After the unqualified praise for *Hurricane*'s starkly honest and eclectic visions, a few reviewers see *Cecile* as cozily domesticated. *Library Journal* describes the narrator and Cecile as "a modern-day Ozzie and Harriet coparenting a boy named Colby." That reviewer approved. "Though caught up in the round of daily concerns, they are not naive or bland but likeable, even quirky."

Ultimately, the review continues, the beauty of these stories "is their very ordinariness: they show a family unit of two women and their son in circumstances that aren't very different from those of any other family." *Library Journal* recommends the book for public libraries, "especially where patrons share these characters' concerns."

Novelists reviewing *Cecile* found different things to like and dislike. Lesléa Newman, in her review for *Lambda Book Report*, says that "without being didactic, *Cecile* explores hard topics." But Newman, who has written gay-positive books for children, wants to hear more from the couple's child Colby—in his own voice. Although she is "utterly impressed with Robson's style, craft, and complete control of language," she finds the first-person narrative "unrelenting," that it "very often reels off from the storyline into a sometimes too long internal monologue, consisting of memories, philosophies, and worldly observations. The book is saved by the fact that these transgressions are, more often than not, extremely interesting and original" (31).

Sarah Schulman, reviewing *Cecile* in the *Advocate,* has almost the opposite reaction to the book's internal monologues: "Cecile gets back into gear when Robson starts to expose her protagonist's past. By exploring loneliness, self-destruction, and previous lovers, Robson lays bare the admissions and confessions that cannot easily coexist with the nice domesticity pictured here" (101).

Schulman believes that "Robson gets caught in the dilemma that every fiction writer pioneering new territory must deal with. Does documenting taboo or marginalized lives dictate the use of 'positive images' only, or can the author also employ a full range of human conflict and expression?'' (101). This is an interesting comment in light of the fact that Robson's earlier book was especially noted for breaking out of exactly this ''positive image'' dilemma. Schulman nevertheless sees *Cecile* as a ''breakthrough book about lesbian parenting'' (101).

At this writing, Robson's book of essays, *Lesbian (Out)law*, has just been published, and reviews are not yet available. And as is often the case with ground-breaking books in previously unexplored areas such as lesbian theory, the full extent of its value and influence may not be appreciated for several years to come.

BIBLIOGRAPHY

Works by Ruthann Robson

Poetry

Robson's poetry has appeared in many feminist, lesbian, and lesbian/gay periodicals, including *Common Lives/Lesbian Lives*; *Calyx*; *Kalliope*; *Sinister Wisdom*; *Conditions*; *Room of One's Own*; *Trivia*; and *Out/Look*; and in anthologies such as *Early Ripening: American Women's Poetry Now* (edited by Marge Piercy).

Fiction

Eye of a Hurricane, Stories by Ruthann Robson. Ithaca, NY: Firebrand Books, 1989.
Cecile, Stories by Ruthann Robson. Ithaca, NY: Firebrand Books, 1991.

Theory/Non-Fiction

Lesbian (Out)law: Survival Under the Rule of Law. Ithaca, NY: Firebrand Books, 1992.

Studies of Ruthann Robson

Harper, Jorjet. ''Lives That Look Like Rain.'' *Lambda Book Report* (Oct/Nov. 1989): 10.
———. ''Writer on the Move.'' *Lambda Book Report* (June 1990): 11.
Kuda, Marie. *Booklist* November 15, 1991, n. pag.
Newman, Lesléa. ''Colby and Company: At Least the Cheese Wasn't Muenster.'' *Lambda Book Report* (November 1991): 31.
Nussbaum, Lisa. *Library Journal* (December 1991).
Piercy, Marge. ''Daily life, daily struggle.'' *Women's Review of Books* (May 1990): 22.
Publisher's Weekly. Rev. of *Cecile*. September 27, 1991.
Schulman, Sarah. ''Mother Times Two.'' *Advocate* December 3, 1991: 101.
Schwartz, P. R. ''P.C. or not P.C.'' *Bay Windows* July 1990: n. pag.
Sturtevant, Katherine. ''Unspoken Secrets—And a Talking Mango Tree.'' *Lesbian Connection* Spring 1990: 18.

ALEIDA RODRÍGUEZ (1953–   )
Elizabeth Beverly

BIOGRAPHY

Aleida Rodríguez was born on a kitchen table in Güines, a small town south of Havana, Cuba, six years before the revolution. At the age of nine she was sent, via Operation Peter Pan, to live with a Presbyterian minister's family in Illinois where, for two years, she awaited the arrival of her parents. As she recalls: "Because I had been forbidden the use of Spanish—in order to help me 'adapt'— I could not communicate with my parents when they arrived" (unless otherwise noted, quotations are from personal communication with the author). Three years later, she moved with her parents to Los Angeles.

Except for a single year of drama study at the Boston Conservatory of Music after high school, Aleida Rodríguez has lived in Los Angeles for the past twenty-five years. Returning to Los Angeles at age twenty, she began publishing poems and living openly as a lesbian. At California State University, Los Angeles, she studied creative writing with Henri Coulette and worked on the college literary magazine. Further publication followed in local magazines. With the meeting of Jacqueline de Angelis came the decision to start a literary magazine of their own, *rara avis* (1978–1984) and a press, Books of a Feather (1980–1984).

Although she has also published prose, Aleida Rodríguez considers herself a poet. Her poems have appeared in numerous periodicals and anthologies and have been collected in a yet-to-be-published manuscript, *The Geography of Light*. She has been active in the Los Angeles community working as a poet with schoolchildren as well as with women in the AIDS unit of the California Institution for Women at Frontera. She also works as a free-lance editor.

MAJOR WORKS AND THEMES

Aleida Rodríguez states, "I think the first thing I really knew about myself was that I was a lesbian." This knowledge came in Cuba, in Spanish, long before her exile from motherland and mother tongue, long before her awareness of herself as a person of color. Yet all three elements—her lesbianism, her condition of exile, the awareness of ethnicity in a racist society—have contributed to the sense of isolation and "otherness" that is foundational to her poetry. Long before she became a poet, Aleida Rodríguez knew herself to be an observer, waiting to see how the world would reveal itself to her.

Her early work often emphasizes the isolation of the poetic "I." In the autobiographical prose work "Sequences" (1981), the recollection of childhood sexual abuse threatens to strand her in a tortured sleeplessness, but finally the safety of the lover's body cradles her to sleep. The poem "The Ubiquitous Mirrored Ball" (1980) follows the simple narrative line of an evening spent in a disco with a long-term lover and introduces the element of the "I" as watcher, who is originally stranded from the lover and cannot emotionally join her until together they see and evaluate the crowd. This act of conjoined vision as the expression of love is an early suggestion of the instrumental role that vision will play in her work.

Although the earlier poetry contains a body of work on Cuba ("Little Cuba Stories" and "Exploraciones" 1982), some of it in Spanish, the emphasis in this work is on the accuracy of visual memory, the eye's insistence on the need to review, if not revise, its past. Even in this earlier work, the act of writing poetry is the act of bearing witness to that which is known because it has been seen.

In this manner Aleida Rodríguez's art is intensely personal, although not "confessional" or "taboo-violating," since to be so would be to acknowledge the primacy of the social norms that create taboos and require confessions. She is much too occupied with the accurate record of her own vision to concentrate on the power of normative values.

In "It Was in the Fifth Grade That I Learned the Word *Simultaneous*" (1992), the poet waits while her lover informs the lover's mother of their lesbian relationship. While this poem could threaten to occupy very familiar terrain—the shocked mother, the waiting poet—it refuses to be simple, for as soon as the poet imagines her lover uttering the word *lesbian*, the poet knows that the mother will see only a bed; she will be unable to keep herself from seeing it. This bed, "looming larger" than the reality of "two singles pushed together," will occupy all maternal consciousness, will strand the mother and the daughter, as well as the poet, in a moment of complete isolation. The word *simultaneous* alone is not sufficient to bring them together.

As the poet knows, the eyes will have their way and will tug the mind and the heart along with them. Vision, in this sense, is radically erotic, for the eyes, even those of the mind, are irresistibly drawn to that which they must see. In Aleida Rodríguez's erotics of vision, the emphasis is not on the sexualized body driven by a genital urgency, but on the resonant body brought to awareness through the agency of sight. The eyes are not tempted by the culturally engendered "penetrating gaze," but rather they manifest a patience and forbearance.

When the eyes wait, the world can glow like a "Dutch landscape," and rounded clouds can offer themselves to the poet like "so many fat biscuits" ("Landscape," forthcoming, *Kenyon Review*).

Aleida Rodríguez understands that the attending eye may appear to be simply passive, particularly to a physically active other ("The Raven and the Hummingbird," unpublished; "Moving to Allesandro," 1977). The danger for the watcher is that being mis-seen may lead to violation. In "Interior with Figures" (unpublished), an erotically drowsing woman, holding an apple, is lost in reverie. Her immobility may be "lovely," but to the other woman in the poem, she looks like a "vacant house"; in a rush of motion the second woman "grabs the apple, takes a bite." She makes the usual Western mistake of equating stillness with inaction, and her ensuing irritation leads to an eruptive act. Although Aleida Rodríguez trusts that the larger natural world—trees, shrubs, birds—will not make this mistake, still it is human companionship, even with its attendant risks, that the poet craves ("Open," 1984).

Such companionship is possible only through the agency of shared sight. It is not literal compassion, the ability to *feel with*, that determines the capacity to love, but the ability to *see with*, even when the sight may be haunting or devastating ("Still Life: *June 16, 1987*, Oil on Board," unpublished). Only the merging eye can transcend the limits of flesh and time. Aleida Rodríguez's growing oeuvre, with its instrumental blending of image and language, places her in the ranks of such contemporary poets as Jorie Graham, the late James Schuyler, and even John Ashbery.

CRITICAL RECEPTION

Aleida Rodríguez's most notable reception has been expressed in the form of grants and awards. She won a National Endowment for the Arts Creative Writing Fellowship in 1982. She also received the 1983 Women of Promise Award from the National Feminist Writers' Guild. In 1992, she was awarded a California Arts Council Grant as well as a residency at Cottages at Hedgebrook on Whidbey Island, Washington.

BIBLIOGRAPHY

Works by Aleida Rodríguez

"Moving to Allesandro." *Bachy*. Ed. Leland Hickman. Los Angeles: Papa Bach Books, 1977.
"The Ubiquitous Mirrored Ball." *Beyond Baroque 802*. Ed. George Drury Smith. Venice, CA: Beyond Baroque Foundation, 1980. 44.
"Sequences." *Lesbian Fiction: An Anthology.* Ed. Elly Bulkin. Watertown, MA: Persephone Press, 1981. 132–37.
"Exploraciones: Bronchitis: The Rosario Beach House." *Fiesta in Aztlan*. Ed. Toni Empringham. Santa Barbara, CA: Capra Press, 1982. 27–33.

"Little Cuba Stories, I, II, III, IV." *13th Moon.* Ed. Marilyn Hacker. New York: 13th Moon, 1982. 25–26.

"It Was in the Fifth Grade." Published in the program of the Lesbians of Color Conference, Malibu, CA, 1983.

"Open," "Epiphany," "I've Got Something Personal against the Bomb," and "Letter to the Editor." *Southern California Women Writers and Artists.* Ed. Jacqueline de Angelis. Los Angeles: Books of a Feather, 1984. 55–58.

"Peter on the Run." *Chester H. Jones Foundation Winners.* Ed. Diane Wakoski. Cleveland, OH: Chester H. Jones Foundation, 1984. 36.

"Breaking Loose," "Epiphany," "Little Cuba Stories, II," and "We Are Intimate." *Poetry Loves Poetry.* Ed. William Mohr. Los Angeles: Momentum Press, 1985.

"Epiphany" and "Island of the Living." *An Ear to the Ground: Anthology of Contemporary American Poetry.* Ed. Marie Harris and Kathleen Aguero. Athens, GA: Georgia University Press, 1989. 239–50.

"This Here Life." Ed. Kathleen Aguero and Ruth Lepson. *Sojourner* 15:11 (July 1990): 32.

"My Face in the Faces of Others." *Indivisible.* Ed. Terry Wolverton and Robert Drake. New York: Plume Books/New American Library, 1991. 235–38.

"The Surreal Answer the World Hands You." *Blood Whispers: L.A. Writers on AIDS.* Ed. Terry Wolverton. Los Angeles: Silverton Books and the Gay and Lesbian Community Services Center, 1991. 82–83.

"Landscape." *Kenyon Review.* Ed. Marilyn Hacker. Forthcoming, 1994.

"Interior with Figures," "The Raven and the Hummingbird," and "Still Life: *June 16, 1987,* Oil on Board." *The Geography of Light.* (unpublished manuscript).

MARIANA ROMO-CARMONA
(1952–   )
Juanita Ramos

BIOGRAPHY

Mariana Romo-Carmona, the daughter of two working-class Chilean artists, was born in Santiago de Chile, Chile, in 1952. As a child, Romo-Carmona felt enriched by the artistic influences of her parents and other family members. This influence was reflected early on, and by the age of twelve, Romo-Carmona became a narrator of a children's radio program. By then, Romo-Carmona's family had moved to the oasis town of Calama.

When she was fourteen, her parents and their two daughters immigrated to the United States. Living in a part of Connecticut that had no visible Latina(o) community, Romo-Carmona's family experienced discrimination, and she experienced extreme isolation from her culture.

At nineteen, Romo-Carmona married a North American white male with whom she had a son in 1974. Soon after the birth of her son, and while she was still living with her husband, Romo-Carmona came out as a lesbian. Her coming out led to her losing custody of her son when he was two years old. She spent the next nine years in court battles to secure reasonable visitation rights, which never entirely materialized. When she was finally granted overnight visitation rights in 1982, it was with the condition that "the plaintiff will not expose Christian [her son] to organized gay rights political activities during visitation" ("Una Madre" 191).

While still living in Connecticut, Romo-Carmona produced "There Is Another Alternative," the only openly lesbian feminist radio program in the state at the time. The program discussed both lesbian and gay issues and issues relevant to the Connecticut Latina(o) community.

In 1980, Romo-Carmona moved to Boston to be closer to her son. In Boston, Romo-Carmona met Latina lesbian activists and reclaimed her Latina identity. She worked with the Latina Lesbian Collective to organize Boston's First Latina

Women's Conference in 1981 and contributed to the lesbian of color section of *The New Our Bodies Our Selves.*

Early in 1981, Romo-Carmona became a member of Kitchen Table: Women of Color Press, and in 1984, she moved to New York City, where the press was located. Her move was also motivated by the existence of a larger community of lesbians of color in New York City and by her relationship with her lover of eight years, June Chan. While in New York City, she was a consulting editor for *Companeras: Latina Lesbian (An Anthology)*, a co-founder of the Latina Lesbian History Project, a co-founder of Las "Buenas Amigas," Latina Lesbian Group, and a member of the People of Color Lesbian and Gay Steering Committee. She has appeared on several radio and television programs in Boston, Miami, and New York City speaking about the plight of lesbian mothers and Latina lesbians. Since 1988, she has been on the editorial collective of *Conditions.*

Romo-Carmona is currently working on a collection of poetry and fiction entitled *Speaking Like an Immigrant*, as well as on a novel and a collection of long fiction pieces. In 1991, in recognition of her writing, she received an Astraea National Lesbian Foundation Lesbian Fiction Award. In 1992, Romo-Carmona received a letter from her son's stepmother informing her that their family, and hence, her seventeen-year-son Christian, had moved to Louisville, Kentucky.

MAJOR WORKS AND THEMES

Mariana Romo-Carmona's work includes fiction, non-fiction, and poetry. Her themes cover a wide range of subjects. In "La virgen en el desierto," which appears in *Cuentos* (95–104), Romo-Carmona writes about the people, the culture, and the landscape of the Chilean desert as well as the oppressive conditions encountered by the poor. The story is told through the eyes of a twelve-year-old girl who travels from town to town with her mother, who organizes art fairs. This story reveals Romo-Carmona's fascination with the desert, which figures prominently in her short stories about Chile.

In *Compañeras*, Romo-Carmona demonstrates how multifaceted her writing is. In the short story "Gabriela" (105–15), originally written in Spanish, a fifteen-year-old girl tells us how she falls in love with another girl and "comes out" as a lesbian while on vacation in the Chilean mountains. In "Una Madre" (185–93), Romo-Carmona uses narrative and journal entries to communicate the pain involved in losing custody of her son and the manner in which their relationship has been affected as a result. In the introduction to the anthology, Romo-Carmona speaks of the racism Latinas face from Anglos and of the heterosexism of both the Latina(o) and Anglo communities:

For those of us who live in the U.S., our Latin identification is crucial. The pride in ourselves is what allows us to confront and survive the various forms of discrimination we face when dealing with the white North Americans who, by no means, see it to their advantage to regard us as equals in "their" society. However, when we turn to our families for support, we often find that we can only get it if we are willing to repress our lesbian selves. (xxv)

Her poem "Abuelita en Chile" (8) tells us about Romo-Carmona's special relationship with her grandmother and also draws a parallel between the violence people face in the United States and that perpetrated by the Pinochet dictatorship in Chile. In "Piece de Resistance," Romo-Carmona documents how a group of women got together in Boston and placed seven sculptures representing parts of a woman's body in sites where women had been raped.

Romo-Carmona's unpublished manuscript, *Speaking Like an Immigrant*, is a collection of poetry and fiction. The book includes both new and previously published material. One of the short stories, entitled "2280," is particularly exciting because it is one of the first, if not the first, Latina lesbian science fiction pieces.

Romo-Carmona writes in both Spanish and English. Her memories of life in Chile are written in Spanish and sometimes translated by her into English. When writing about her experiences in the United States, she generally uses English.

CRITICAL RECEPTION

Cuentos: Stories by Latinas, of which Romo-Carmona is co-editor with Alma Gomez and Cherrìe Moraga, was hailed as a ground-breaking work because it was "perhaps the first anthology exclusively dedicated to recounting the experiences of Hispanic women both in the United States and in their lands of origin" (Thomases 13). Its major aims, according to Romo-Carmona, were to connect "with Latin American women on issues of oppression, and [to reach] a bilingual population in this country." The anthology is also one of the first books to include the voices of both heterosexual women and Latina lesbians who are open about their lesbianism.

In a review of *Compañeras: Latina Lesbians* for *Gay Community News*, Vanessa Nemeth states, "One of my favorite pieces in the whole book is, 'Gabriela,' by Mariana Romo-Carmona." She states that Romo-Carmona's way of story-telling makes the reader wish she were the main character: "You could just die thinking of your favorite girl when you were 15 or 16 . . . it's so romantic. I can totally transport myself back to that age and feel that way" (8–9). One of Romo-Carmona's strengths as a short story writer is her ability to allow the reader to transport herself or himself to the time and place she is describing.

BIBLIOGRAPHY

Works by Mariana Romo-Carmona

"Poem for My Grandfather." Appeared as "Esta mañana" in *El Sur*, Concepcion, Chile (September 9, 1979): 5.

"Piece de Resistance." *Fight Back! Feminist Resistance to Male Violence*. Ed. Frederique delaCoste and Felice Newman. Pittsburgh: Cleis Press, 1981. 209–11.

"Story for Hallows." *Sojourner* Oct. 1982.

Co-editor with Alma Gomez and Cherríe Moraga of *Cuentos: Stories by Latinas*. New York: Kitchen Table Press, 1983.

"Late to Work." *Sojourner* April 1984.

"Problems and Pride for Gay Parents." *Gay Community News* (August 1984): 7.

"Women of Color Speak from Blood." *Gay Community News* (February 1985): 4.

"Introduction," "Gabriela," and "Una Madre." *Compañeras: Latina Lesbians: An Anthology*. Ed. Juanita Ramos. New York: Latina Lesbian History Project, 1987. xx-xxix, 105–15, and 185–93.

"Abuelita en Chile." *Womenews* 9:3 (March 1988): 8.

"Gabriela." *Conditions 15* (1988): 9.

"Encuentro de Lesbianas en Costa Rico." *Womenews*. 11:6 (June 1990): 1, 8.

"2280." *Conditions 17*. (1990): 89.

Queer City: The Portable Lower East Side. New York: Portable Lower East Side, 1992. Edited by Kurt Hollander. Guest editors: Harold McNeil Robinson, Mariana Romo-Carmona, Ira Silverberg, and Jacqueline Woodson.

Romo-Carmona's work has also appeared in *Colorlife Magazine*.

MURIEL RUKEYSER (1913–1980)
Eloise Klein Healy

BIOGRAPHY

Muriel Rukeyser was born in New York City on December 13, 1913, and died there February 12, 1980. She was the daughter of Lawrence B. Rukeyser, a construction engineer, and Myra (Lyons) Rukeyser, a homemaker and book-keeper. Her parents were Jewish and Muriel attended a religious school, but the household bore no marks of Jewish culture in Rukeyser's early childhood. After her mother grew interested in religion, Muriel accompanied her to temple every Saturday. Although Rukeyser had a comfortable existence among maids and servants, she was learning about the life on the streets from her playmates. Her mother was always afraid her behavior would endanger her. Ultimately, she would be disinherited by her father because she rejected the narrow confines of his worldview.

Rukeyser attended Vassar College, where she was the literary editor of the leftist *Student Review*. It was for this magazine that she went to Alabama to cover the trial of the Scottsboro Boys, nine African-American youths who had been accused of raping two white girls. Rukeyser was arrested for talking to African-American journalists who were also covering the story; during her short jail stay she contracted typhoid fever. Her lifelong commitment to social justice, so evident in her poem "The Trial" and in her writing over five decades, was shaped by her understanding of social inequities. Rukeyser was among the earliest to elucidate the kinds of concerns now taken for granted in "political" poetry.

Her first book, *Theory of Flight*, reflected her interest in science, technology, and film editing (which she studied with Helen Van Dongen). She won the Yale Younger Poets Award for this volume, which sets forth themes that formed the heart of her career in poetry. Like Whitman, she believed that it is necessary for poets to be engaged in society and that the natural speaking voice of the poet is an oracular one. She also gave evidence of choosing to struggle with large issues. Unlike many poets of her day, she did not adopt a tone of alienation. *Theory of Flight* was meant to counter the dejected stance of T. S. Eliot and his followers with a representation of the individual's power to change the world.

In 1936, Rukeyser found herself in Spain the first day the civil war broke out. She was evacuated to England, but a man she was in love with, Otto Boch, was later killed fighting for the Loyalist forces. Her involvement in the Spanish cause made her more of an internationalist than many of her fellow poets. That same year, she traveled to West Virginia to investigate the deaths of miners preparing for a hydroelectric plant. Although aware of the danger, the plant's owners sent workers to certain death "dry mining" silica. Rukeyser, in *U.S. 1*, capitalized on the ironic situation of miners engaged in a giant power project yet having no power of their own.

In 1943, Rukeyser took a job in the poster division at the Office of War Information, but she and other artists soon quit when their ideas were rejected because of their political content. She moved to San Francisco in 1945 and taught at the California Labor School. She married Glynn Collins, a painter, but the marriage was annulled after a few months.

Subsequently, Rukeyser had one son, (William) Laurie Rukeyser, born out of wedlock in 1947. That same year, an anonymous benefactor left Muriel a yearly allowance, which she forfeited when she started teaching at Sarah Lawrence in 1954. From 1948 on she was raising a child by herself. In *The Gates*, she writes about how this affected her development as a poet.

Rukeyser also wrote three biographies—*Willard Gibbs* (1942), *One Life*, about Wendell Lewis Willkie (1957), and *The Traces of Thomas Hariot* (1971)—again, using a non-conventional approach. Her intention was to incorporate a mythic dimension, and she used many techniques from her poetry in chronicling the lives of people much like herself—independent thinkers who demonstrated a wide range of social concerns.

In 1964, she suffered her first stroke but continued to write and lead a vigorous life. In the 1970s, she was active in the anti-Vietnam War movement, traveling to Hanoi to protest American involvement. She called this war a failure of human imagination. She also protested the threatened execution of South Korean poet Kim Chi-Ha by going to Seoul to seek his release. Reflecting her lifelong interest in science and technology, she helped establish the Exploratorium, an interactive museum in San Francisco.

Rukeyser was embraced by a new generation of women writers in the feminist movement, for both her poetry and her political activism. A well-known women's anthology, *No More Masks! An Anthology of Poems by Women* (ed. Florence House and Ellen Bass, Garden City, NY: Anchor Press, 1973), takes its title from "The Poem As Mask." Like several other women writers of her generation, she was known to have had relationships with women but did not directly claim a lesbian identity in her work. Her later poetry can definitely be viewed as woman-identified, particularly in *The Speed of Darkness*. Rukeyser had accepted an invitation to speak at the "Lesbians in Literature" panel of the Modern

Language Association in 1978, but her health prevented her from doing so. She died in New York City in 1980.

MAJOR WORKS AND THEMES

The primary vision in Rukeyser's work is the social responsibility of the poet to speak, to record inequities, and to bridge opposites. She championed science, for she believed it shared, with art, a common promise for humanity. She had Whitman's grounding in the ordinary and a belief in a progressive science, making her a visionary of a sort other than the mystical. Rukeyser's intent was to drive deeper into life and its complexity, not to stand removed or above it.

Her first book, *Theory of Flight*, announces her natural exuberance and her belief in the possibility of change. Rukeyser imbues the language of the machine with human meaning. Her work abounds in technical details (she had taken flying lessons) and expresses a desire for human connection. She also forges an identification with those suffering injustice.

Although her work was often compared to W. H. Auden's, there is little similarity. Rukeyser was never attracted to formalism in poetry. She was instinctively attuned to the cinematic, to journalistic techniques, and to the vigor of direct speech.

Also, Rukeyser never expressed pessimism about life or the value of poetry as many of her contemporaries did, caught in wars or between wars. Likewise, she did not accept all of the 1930s Marxist ideology, and her colleagues on the Left criticized her for not being ''politically correct.'' The FBI, however, considered her a communist and collected a 178-page dossier on her and her family.

Rukeyser was interested in how romantic love is constructed so as to turn people inward instead of outward to embrace the world (''Sundays, They Sleep Late''). Essentially, she felt the same about poetry and its audience as she did about the erotic. Poetry is both an emotional and an imaginative experience, created simultaneously by the poet and the reader, demanding a total engagement and response. Poetry should lead in to the most human part of us and out to the world—likewise, love.

A Turning Wind, completed just as Poland was falling to Hitler in 1939, enlarges upon Rukeyser's belief that the poetic imagination must be engaged in social causes, especially in a broken world. *Wake Island* focuses on war as a central feature of human experience in this century. *Beast in View*, published during World War II, again connects individual and broad social concerns. ''Ajanta,'' named after the sacred caves of India, was Rukeyser's answer to the withdrawal from social causes of her contemporaries. Her interior landscape offered images of integration and possibility. ''Wreath of Women'' praises three women for their choice to be real individuals and not gauzy grown-up girls. She identifics here as woman, American, and Jew—and for this she says she must speak (''Bubble of Air'').

Childbirth and motherhood enter her work in *The Green Wave*, a collection that also includes translations from Octavio Paz, a poet Rukeyser identified with for his political and artistic ideals.

The Life of Poetry, written as a series of lectures in the 1940s, should be read in conjunction with all of Rukeyser's work. Uniformly well-received, this book sets out Rukeyser's theories about poetry's place in culture, especially in a time of crisis. In *Body of Waking* and *Waterlily Fire: Poems 1935–1962*, her work centers even more on the body and a more musical poetry emerges. *The Orgy*, like much of her work, was widely derided for being too excessive and widely praised for being experimental and new.

The Speed of Darkness, *Breaking Open*, and *The Gates* are characterized by a condensation of imagery and a shortening of lines. Again, the themes of the child, of growth, of the need for social engagement are primary, especially in her long poem about Kim Chi-Ha. For Rukeyser, speech itself was imprisoned in the person of a jailed poet. Her energy is clarified in this work, directed at the largest view of human need for expression against totalitarian promotion of war and censorship.

Rukeyser's work warned against the small, the static, the polarized, the overly perfected. Her argument was for dynamism, directness, and change.

CRITICAL RECEPTION

The critical reception of her work has always been mixed. What some considered bardic and visionary in *Theory of Flight* (W. R. Benet, *Saturday Review of Literature*) others held to be didactic posturing (Thomas Stumpf, *Carolina Quarterly*). Louise Bogan carried on what seems to be a vendetta against Rukeyser's work (*New Yorker*). Bogan was troubled by whether or not Rukeyser wrote as a woman poet should write; in fact, many of Rukeyser's detractors attacked her for what would have been praised in a male poet (Michael Roberts reviewing *Theory of Flight* in *Spectator*).

Unfortunately for Rukeyser, her poetry and her beliefs about it did not fit the tenets of the New Criticism, which began to make its influence widely felt in the 1940s. Her poetry, lacking in irony and polished surfaces, brought down the wrath of many. Randall Jarrell, writing in *Poetry and the Age* (1953), said "she works with a random melodramatic hand, and with rather unfortunate models and standards."

The split in the reception given her work always reflected political attitudes as much as critical approaches. But current appraisals of her poetry and her experimental biographies are more generous in their measure of her skill and talent. (See, for example, Anne Stephenson, "With Head and Heart," *New York Times Book Review*, February 11, 1979: 12–13.) Virginia R. Terris in the *American Poetry Review* adds that Rukeyser is a poet whose work must be understood cumulatively. Likewise, her writing about sexuality must be placed in the context of her time in that her work anticipates the poetry of more overtly lesbian writers. We might describe her situation using the poet Judy Grahn's words, "I am the wall at the lip of the water" (*The Common Woman Poems* 98). Though no complete study of her life and work exists as yet, feminist and lesbian poets have adopted her methods, her engaged stance, and her attitude, expressed in these highly charged lines from "Kathe Kollwitz":

> What would happen if one woman told the truth about her life?
> The world would split open.

HONORS AND AWARDS

Rukeyser was the recipient of the following honors and awards: the Yale Younger Poets Award in 1935; the Oscar Blumental Prize in 1940; the first Harriet Monroe Poetry Award in 1941; and a grant from the American Academy of Arts and Letters and the National Institute of Arts and Letters in 1942. She received a Guggenheim Fellowship in 1943, an honorary doctorate in literature from Rutgers University in 1961, and the Eunice Tietjens Memorial Prize in 1962. Rukeyser was also voted president of PEN American Center in 1975, and in 1977, she won the Copernicus Prize and the Shelley Prize for Poetry.

BIBLIOGRAPHY

Works by Muriel Rukeyser

Poetry

Theory of Flight. New Haven: Yale University Press, 1935.
Mediterranean. Writers and Artists Committee, Medical Bureau to Aid Spanish Democracy, 1938.
U.S. 1. New York: Covici, Friede, 1938.
A Turning Wind: Poems. New York: Viking Press, 1939.
The Soul and Body of John Brown. privately printed, 1940.
Wake Island. New York: Doubleday, 1942.
Beast in View. New York: Doubleday, 1944.
The Green Wave. New York: Doubleday, 1948.
Elegies. New York: New Directions Press, 1949.
Orpheus. San Francisco: Centaur Press, 1949.
Selected Poems. New York: New Directions Press, 1951.
Body of Waking. New York: Harper, 1958.
Waterlily Fire: Poems 1935–1962. New York: Macmillan, 1962.
The Outer Banks. Santa Barbara: Unicorn Press, 1967.
The Speed of Darkness. New York: Random House, 1968.
Mazes. New York: Simon and Schuster, 1970
29 Poems. London: Rapp and Whiting, 1972.
Breaking Open: New Poems. New York: Random House, 1973.
The Gates: Poems. New York: McGraw-Hill, 1976.
The Collected Poems of Muriel Rukeyser. New York: McGraw-Hill, 1978.

Biography

Willard Gibbs. New York: Doubleday, 1942.
One Life. New York: Simon and Schuster, 1957.
The Traces of Thomas Hariot. New York: Random House, 1971.

Children's Books

Come Back, Paul. New York: Harper, 1955.
I Go Out. New York: Harper, 1962.
Bubbles. Ed. Donald Barr. New York: Harcourt, 1967.
More Night. New York: Harper, 1981.

Unpublished Plays

"The Middle of the Air," produced in Iowa City, Iowa, 1945.
"The Colors of the Day," produced in Poughkeepsie, N.Y., 1961.
"Houdini," produced in Lenox, Mass., 1973.

Translator

(From the Spanish; with others) Paz, Octavio. *Selected Poems of Octavio Paz.* Bloomington: Indiana University Press, 1963; rev. ed. *Early Poems 1935–55.* New York: New Directions Press, 1973.
Paz, Octavio. *Sun Stone.* New York: New Directions Press, 1963.
(With Leif Sjoeberg) Eckeloef, Gunnar. *Selected Poems of Gunnar Eckeloef.* New York: Twayne Publishers, 1967.
Ekeloef, Gunnar. *Three Poems.* Lawrence, KS: T. Williams, 1967.
Brecht, Bertolt. *Uncle Eddie's Moustache.* (unpublished).
(With Sjoeberg) Ekeloef, Gunnar. *A Molna Elegy: Metamorphoses.* 2 vols. New York: Unicorn Press, 1984.

Other

The Life of Poetry. New York: Current Books, 1949.
The Orgy (a three-day journal). New York: Coward, 1965.
The Poetry and Voice of Muriel Rukeyser (recordings). Caedmon, 1977.

Studies of Muriel Rukeyser

Benet, W. R. Rev. of *Theory of Flight. Saturday Review of Literature* December 7, 1935.
Bogan, Louise. *Selected Criticism: Prose, Poetry.* New York: The Noonday Press. 1955.
Brinnin, John M. "Muriel Rukeyser: The Social Poet and the Problem of Communication." *Poetry* 61 (January 1943): 554–75.
Daniels, Kate, and Richard Jones, eds. *Poetry East* 16 & 17 (Spring/Summer 1985), double issue on Muriel Rukeyser.
Gregory, Horace, and Marya Zaturenska. *A History of American Poetry 1900–1940.* New York: Harcourt, Brace, 1946.
Jarrell, Randall. *Poetry and the Age.* New York: Knopf-Vintage, 1953. 148.
Kertesz, Louise. *The Poetic Vision of Muriel Rukeyser.* Foreword by Kenneth Rexroth. Baton Rouge: Louisiana State University Press, 1980.

Murphy, Rosalie. *Contemporary Poets of the English Language*. New York: St. Martin's Press, 1970.

Rexroth, Kenneth. *American Poetry in the Twentieth Century*. New York: Herder and Herder, 1971.

Roberts, Michael. Rev. of *Theory of Flight*. *Spectator* May 1, 1936.

Rosenthal, M. L. "Muriel Rukeyser: The Longer Poems." James Laughlin, ed. *New Directions in Prose and Poetry*, 14 (1953): 202–29.

Stumpf, Thomas. (untitled) *The Carolina Quarterly* (Spring 1974): 101–2.

Terris, Virginia R. "Muriel Rukeyser: A Retrospective." *American Poetry Review* 3 (May/June 1974): 10–15.

JANE RULE (1931–   )
Ann Klauda

BIOGRAPHY

Jane Rule was born in March of 1931 in Plainfield, New Jersey. She grew up in the American midwest and California and graduated from Mills College in Oakland. She moved to Canada in 1956 to teach at the University of British Columbia in Vancouver. A Canadian citizen, Rule has said, "Since I didn't really have roots in any specific place in the States, my commitment to a nation is really much clearer as a Canadian" (Crean 11).

While teaching at Massachusetts' Concord Academy in 1954, Rule met Helen Sonthoff, who was to be her life partner. In 1976, after twenty years of writing and teaching in Vancouver, they moved to Galiano Island, off the coast of British Columbia, where they live today.

Rule knew at age sixteen that she wanted to be a writer. Her career spans three decades: her first book, a novel, was published in 1964 and her last, also a novel, was published in 1989. She has since "retired" from writing, partially because of her health (she has had osteoarthritis since her mid-forties) but largely because she has said what she had to say. "Sure there will always be the fish that got away," she told Susan Crean in 1991, "but I have written what I wanted."

All of Rule's books are in print. Her American publisher is the Naiad Press, a lesbian-feminist press in Florida.

MAJOR WORKS AND THEMES

Jane Rule has published seven novels, three collections of short stories, and three collections of essays (*Outlander* includes both short stories and essays). All of them concern lesbian life to some extent, although lesbian life is far from their only concern. Jane Rule is a writer who is frankly and openly lesbian but whose writing—whose fiction, particularly—suggests a perspective formed by far more than simply her lesbianism. In her essay "Lesbian and Writer," Rule writes: "I am a politically involved lesbian, and I am a writer. I do not see the two as mutually exclusive; neither do I see them as inextricably bound together. Yet one of those two conflicting views is held by most people who read my work" (*A Hot-Eyed Moderate* 42).

Rule has no time for preconceived, politically mandated notions about her writing. In her essay "For the Critic of What Isn't There," Rule says, quite rightly, "I can serve no one's life experience and imagination but my own" (*A Hot-Eyed Moderate* 56). She explains herself fully in a 1984 interview:

It does seem to be that literature is about what *is* . . . and a lot of people in the movement would like literature to be about what ought to be or what we'd like it to be. So, you know, I do write about happy lesbians and I also write about unhappy lesbians, I write about very competent gay men and I write about gay men who kill themselves, because I think we have a great range of experiences, as anybody else does, and I think we're also people under pressure. So a gay character can give a kind of deeper vibration of those social pressures than perhaps some heterosexuals. (Goldsmith 1)

Rule refuses to subscribe to or be directed by any party line:

Though I have no difficulty with the labels "woman," "feminist," "lesbian," they don't encompass my concerns as a novelist where I am often required to produce points of view quite different from my own. I do have trouble with the view that only auto-biography is authentic, that any attempt to represent views other than one's own is politically incorrect. . . . Though I understand the hunger of lesbians for better images of themselves in print, I don't feel obligated to serve that hunger. My obligation is to my own vision of reality, which does include many bright, strong and loving people of all sorts. I can be irritated with, disapprove of, even rage against some of my characters; but I don't write about people I don't care about and basically respect. My political obligations are more those of a citizen. (*Women's Review of Books*, July 1989, 29)

A common characteristic of Rule's novels is that they involve several main characters, rather than a single protagonist around whom the story revolves. In a 1984 interview, Rule said that she tries

to concentrate on relationships and community. . . . I think those are the things that I write about most. [My books are] about voluntary community, because I think most of us have moved away from our families. Not just gay people, I mean everyone. And I'm fascinated with the kinds of support groups we build around ourselves to make a community. (Goldsmith I).

Unlike many writers who are also lesbian, Rule is sexually inclusive in her fiction. That is, she is as interested in her heterosexual and male characters as she is in the many lesbians who people her work; those characters are no less real than the lesbians. A reviewer remarked in the *Washington Blade* (April 7,

1989) that "men are legitimate characters and are not routinely depicted as antagonists" (Jablonski 21). In none of Rule's novels, and in very few of her short stories, are lesbians treated as women apart from humanity's mainstream.

Rule is also inclusive when it comes to age: she writes about men, women, and children of all ages, with equal compassion and insight. Her many portraits of the aging bring to life a sector of the population that is frequently ignored, discounted, or presented in stereotypical terms. Rule's older women, particularly, are wise or ornery or sexual or depressed or all of the above, but they are no less real than the younger people she writes about.

Though she sees humankind as basically social, Rule also believes in the necessity of solitude. Many of her characters choose to be alone, or they choose quiet lives with one other. Rule has said,

None of my characters is ever totally sustained by the community. I don't think anybody ever is. I think there are times when you feel really involved with and sustained by your community, but—maybe this is partly the statement of an artist, too—you spend an awful lot of time alone. . . . Communities can provide false senses of security, as families can. (Goldsmith 1)

The Novels

Jane Rule's first novel, *Desert of the Heart*, was published in 1964 by Macmillan of Canada, an act Rule characterizes as "very courageous" considering the book's openly lesbian theme. It is probably her best-known work, thanks to *Desert Hearts*, the mainstream film made from it by Donna Deitch in 1985. (The very sexy film is a cult favorite among American lesbians; it provoked the sale of 20,000 copies of the book in the three months following its release.) Set in Reno, Nevada, during the summer of 1958, *Desert of the Heart* is the story of the romance between Kay, a young "change apron" who works in a casino, and Evelyn, an older (although less worldly) professor in the process of ending her chilly marriage.

It was six years before Rule's second novel, *This Is Not for You* (1970), was published by the Naiad Press in Florida. Perhaps her least accessible (and most literary) novel, *This Is Not for You* recalls Radclyffe Hall's *The Well of Loneliness* in its comparative obliqueness and in its protagonist's presumptuous rejection of lesbian life on behalf of her beloved. Beginning with the sentence "This is not a letter," it is in fact a long, lovely, literary—if angst-ridden—letter from Kate to Esther.

Against the Season (1971) followed close on the heels of *This Is Not for You*, and it could hardly be a more different book. Rule examines for the first time the importance of the communities we create for ourselves. Among the characters who move in and out of each other's lives are Amelia, an elderly woman coming to terms with her dead sister—and with her own cancer—as she reads her sister's diaries; Agate, unmarried, pregnant, and keeping house for Amelia; and Dina and Rosemary, an unmatched lesbian pair whose vast differences heighten their mutual sexual attraction.

The characters in *The Young in One Another's Arms* (1977) live together in a Vancouver rooming house presided over by Ruth and her beloved mother-in-law, Clara. (A character named Ruth in love with her mother-in-law inevitably recalls the biblical Book of Ruth, and in fact there are other parallels.) Ruth's house is a haven for society's outcasts, including a string of American draft evaders. Ruth must decide what to do—or what not to do—about her family of misfits when the house is slated for demolition.

Contract with the World (1980) consists of six portraits, each presented from a different point of view. The subjects' lives are interwoven in what are really six overlapping short stories. All the characters, most of whom are artists, appear in all six segments, but each character is individually memorable. *Contract with the World* contains some of Rule's most frankly erotic writing in the segment "Alma Writing," which consists of journal entries written by a newly out lesbian. Alma is divorced from the self-consciously macho Mike and is in love with Roxanne, an artist whose medium is sound. (Mike and Roxanne take their turns on center stage in the segments "Mike Hanging" and "Roxanne Recording.")

In *Memory Board* (1987), Rule portrays an aging lesbian couple with sharp poignancy yet with an utter lack of sentimentality. The title refers literally to a clipboard that takes the place of Constance's failing memory, on which Diana, whose mind is sound but whose physical health is declining, records each day's activities (from "Get dressed" to "Go to bed"). Into their cozy, solitary life comes David, Diana's estranged twin, who wants to make up for a lifetime apart and be once again part of Diana's world, as he was in childhood. Rule alternates Diana's point of view with David's.

In Rule's last novel, *After the Fire* (1989), she revisits her themes of living well and dying well, community and solitude, and family into which we are born versus family we choose. Set on an unnamed island a ferry ride from Vancouver, the novel's opening scene is a midnight house fire beyond the capabilities of the volunteer fire department. We meet the major characters: Karen Tasuki, half-Canadian and half-Japanese, who has come to the island to heal wounds caused by the breakup of an eight-year relationship; Henrietta Hawkins, the island matriarch whose life is anchored by frequent trips to a nursing home in Vancouver to visit the husband who no longer recognizes her, and Red Smith, a young woman who cleans the homes of the island's "ladies" and rejects all attempts to make her conform.

After the Fire is unique in Rule's oeuvre in that all the main characters are women. One is tempted to make something of this passionately inclusive author choosing to write only about women in this, her last work of fiction. (One suspects, however, that Rule would scoff at this tendency.)

The Short Stories

Jane Rule's short stories are snapshots of the themes she develops more fully in her novels. In "Inside the Easter Egg," an essay about Marian Engel, she writes, "Characters in short stories are more like friends you drop in on, whose histories you know only in arbitrary anecdotes and quirky facts, than like the family you live with as you also live with characters in a novel'' (*A Hot-Eyed Moderate* 27).

In a 1989 interview, Rule admitted a somewhat whimsical approach to publishing short stories: ''I don't write that many short stories, and, when I do, I put them in a drawer, and if someone asks for a short story I look in the file. When there are enough short stories I bring them out as a book'' (Ruebottom 6).

The first and last stories in *Theme for Diverse Instruments* (1975), ''In the Basement of the House'' and ''In the Attic of the House,'' show how two women's views of their own lesbianism are formed by watching other members of two very different households—one watching from a basement, the other from the attic.

The title story of *Outlander* (1981) concerns a woman who saves herself from an alcoholic breakdown and rebuilds her life and self-respect in small-town New Hampshire. ''The Killer Dyke and the Lady'' explores that endlessly fascinating—and uniquely lesbian—topic, butch/femme (or white collar/blue collar, or martini/beer). ''A Perfectly Nice Man'' somehow makes credible the improbable scenario of a pair of lesbians, who share an ex-husband, having dinner with their ex-husband's third wife.

The story from which *Inland Passage* (1985) takes its title is shamelessly and gloriously romantic: two strangers, women in their forties, are assigned to the same cramped stateroom for a three-day steamer cruise, with predictable results. ''His Nor Hers'' is the coming-out story of a just-divorced woman who discovers too late that in her conventional marriage, she'd had her cake and been able to eat it as well.

The Essays

Jane Rule's essays are marvels of clear thinking and open-mindedness. They invariably illuminate and inform. One is left believing Rule's subjects lucky that they interested her. In *Lesbian Images* (1975) Rule writes:

[It is] not intended to be a comprehensive literary or cultural history of lesbians. It is, rather, a common reader—or not so uncommon reader—a statement of my own attitudes toward lesbian experience as measured against the images made by other women writers in their work and/or lives. . . . The reality of lesbian experience transcends all theories about it.

With its copious endnotes and thorough index, *Lesbian Images* includes scholarly discussions of lesbian writers from Radclyffe Hall and Gertrude Stein to May Sarton and Maureen Duffy. Two introductory essays, ''Myth and Morality, Sources of Law and Prejudice'' and ''From Sin to Sickness,'' provide a concise overview of how male and female homosexuality has been regarded throughout history.

Essays constitute the last third of Rule's *Outlander* (1981). All having to do with lesbianism in some way, they feature provocative titles like "Private Parts and Public Figures" (in which she reviews three biographies that purport to address the lesbianism of their subjects) and "Fucking Pariahs on the Schoolroom Shelf" (in which she contemplates how violence is more acceptable than sex as a subject matter for young readers). And while Rule is always convincing, she is never more so than on the subject of "politically correct" lesbianism, as in "With All Due Respect."

The expectation that she (or anyone else) conform to a mandated definition of correctness is among the subjects of Rule's latest collection of essays, *A Hot-Eyed Moderate* (1985). She addresses such diverse and volatile subjects as cross-dressing ("Drag"), pornography ("Censorship"), AIDS ("An Act of God"), and the trend toward regarding ethnic inclusiveness as a desirable quality of fiction ("The Affirmative Action Novel"). This volume also includes eleven essays on writing and publishing, and several pieces that are more memoir than essay. Rule is eminently readable as she remembers her young self and her encounters with Jessamyn West ("The 4th of July, 1954") and W. H. Auden (" 'Silly Like Us,' A Recollection").

CRITICAL RECEPTION

Because of her endurance (almost three decades) and prolificity, Jane Rule's reputation is quite that of a grande dame of lesbian literature. She has come a long way since *Desert of the Heart* shocked and titillated the reading public (and simultaneously slaked the thirst and wet the whistles of a vast, hidden lesbian audience).

In the introduction to *Lesbian Images* (1975), Rule cites some of the frankly homophobic comments that characterized the reception of *Desert of the Heart* in 1964: "Miss Rule's writing has a kind of perverted good taste about it." "I learned a lot more about Lesbians than I care to know." One reviewer studied Rule's jacket photo and wondered "how such a nice looking woman could ever have chosen so distasteful a subject."

Criticism of Rule's work has changed dramatically over the years, making those early comments about *Desert of the Heart* seem positively quaint. A reviewer wrote in April 1989:

Friendly critics have described Rule's style as having substance and insight; as being witty and intellectual. Others have found it somewhat sentimental and serviceable and question her lack of third world female characters. Perhaps the best description of Rule's style is to say that she is "literary." A reader looking for pat Gay or Lesbian themes will not find what he or she is seeking in her novels. Rather, Rule's art is one of exploration of the relationships among people in various types of communities, regardless of gender or sexual orientation. (Jablonski 21)

Rule has received negative criticism for her essentially assimilationist—that is, non-separatist—view of lesbian life. In her book *Sisters & Strangers: An Introduction to Contemporary Feminist Fiction*, Patricia Duncker describes Rule's presentation of lesbians as equal, if minority, citizens in a basically heterosexual world as old-fashioned and defensive.

Jane Rule has received numerous awards for her writing. In 1978, the Canadian Authors' Association named *The Young in One Another's Arms* best novel of the year, and "Joy" (from *Inland Passage*) best short story of the year. That year she also received the Literature Award from the Gay Academic Union. In 1983, Rule received the award of merit from the Fund for Human Dignity.

BIBLIOGRAPHY

Works by Jane Rule

Desert of the Heart (Novel). Tallahassee, FL: Naiad Press, 1964.
This Is Not for You (Novel). Tallahassee, FL: Naiad Press, 1970.
Against the Season (Novel). Tallahassee, FL: Naiad Press, 1971.
Lesbian Images (Essays). Freedom, CA: Crossing Press, 1975.
Theme for Diverse Instruments (Short stories). Tallahassee, FL: Naiad Press, 1975.
The Young in One Another's Arms (Novel). Tallahassee, FL: Naiad Press, 1977.
Contract with the World (Novel). Tallahassee, FL: Naiad Press, 1980.
Outlander (Short stories and essays). Tallahassee, FL: Naiad Press, 1981.
A Hot-Eyed Moderate (Essays). Tallahassee, FL: Naiad Press, 1985.
Inland Passage (Short stories). Tallahassee, FL: Naiad Press, 1985.
Memory Board (Novel). Tallahassee, FL: Naiad Press, 1987.
After the Fire (Novel). Tallahassee, FL: Naiad Press, 1989.

Studies of Jane Rule

Andrews, Audrey. "Rule Fails to Equal Genre's Best" (Review of *Inland Passage*). *Calgary Herald* February 2, 1986: C7.
Baker, Janet. "Jane Rule's Fiction" (Review of *Inland Passage*). *Atlantic Provinces Book Review* 13:2 (May-June 1986): 2.
Bradbury, Patricia. "Passages Ruled by the Heart" (Review of *Inland Passage*). *Quill & Quire* 51:11 (November 1985): 25.
Crean, Susan. "Divining Jane Rule: A Profile of Progress." *B.C. Bookworld* (Summer 1991): 11.
Duncker, Patricia. *Sisters & Strangers: An Introduction to Contemporary Feminist Fiction* (in Chapter 6: Writing Lesbian, 186–189). Oxford, UK and Cambridge, MA: Blackwell Publishers, 1989.
Giustini, Dean. "Gay Games and What Festival???" *Angles* (June 1990): 8–9.
Goldsmith, Larry. "Jane Rule." *Gay Community News* November 17, 1984: 1–2, 11.
Hill, Douglas. "Honesty and Respect for an International Author" (Review of *A Hot-Eyed Moderate*). *Globe & Mail* May 3, 1986, n. pag.
Jablonski, Noel. "Lesbian Literature's Golden Rule." *Washington Blade* April 7, 1989: 21.

Michaud, Janice. "Rule's Views of Life, Literature Clouded by Her Homosexuality" (Review of *A Hot-Eyed Moderate*). *Calgary Herald* April 27, 1986: D10.

O'Grady, Jane. "Imprecise Intertwinings" (Review of *This Is Not For You*). *Times Literary Supplement* June 26, 1987: 698.

Review of *Outlander*. *Kirkus Reviews* March 1, 1981.

Roof, Judith. *A Lure of Knowledge: Lesbian Sexuality and Theory* (in Chapter 2: *This Is Not for You*: The Sexuality of Mothering, 92–118). New York: Columbia University Press, 1991.

Ruebottom, Anne. "A Harmonious Balance: Jane Rule Talks about Her Life as a Writer on Galiano Island." *XS* (A Supplement to *XTRA! Magazine*) (November 1989): 1, 6.

Surguy, Phil. "Laughing on the Outside." *Books in Canada* 16:9 (December 1987): 4–5.

Williams, Dianna J. "Dousing the Flames Does Not Extinguish the Embers" (Review of *After the Fire*). *Washington Blade* September 8, 1989: 31.

Women's Review of Books 6:10–11 (July 1989): 23–29.

KATE RUSHIN (1951–)

Evelynn M. Hammonds

BIOGRAPHY

Kate Rushin (given name Donna K.) was born on July 7, 1951, in Syracuse, New York. Shortly after her birth, her parents, Frank D. Rushin, an electroplater, and her mother, B. Elizabeth Williams Rushin, a social worker, moved to Camden, New Jersey. At the age of ten, after her mother's death, Kate went to live with her grandparents, Addie O. and George E. Williams, Sr., in the predominantly black town of Lawnside, New Jersey. By the time she entered Haddon Heights High School she had already developed an interest in poetry. When she was twelve, her aunts gave her two poetry books for Christmas. The first was a collection edited by Arna Bontemps and Langston Hughes, *Poetry of the Negro,* and the second was *Best Loved Poems of the American People.* These two books opened up the world of poetry to her, especially the poetry of African-American writers. She began to memorize and recite poems from these two collections and in high school began writing poetry. Rushin submitted poems to her school's literary magazine and had her first poems published in the local newspaper, the Camden *Courier-Post.*

Rushin entered Oberlin College in 1969, majoring in communications and theater. During her college years, she was very involved with an experimental black theater group that allowed her to present her poems for the first time to live audiences. Upon graduation in 1973, Rushin returned to New Jersey. In 1977, she was awarded a Fine Arts Work Center Fellowship in Provincetown, Massachusetts, followed by a 1978–80 residency at the Cummington Community of the Arts in Cummington, Massachusetts. Since 1982, Rushin has lived in Cambridge, Massachusetts. She was poet-in-residence at South Boston High School for three years. In 1978, she was an Artists' Foundation Poetry Fellow and a finalist for the same award in 1985. From 1982 to 1992, she has been a member of the New Words Bookstore Collective.

Kate Rushin has been a frequent and popular speaker at poetry and cultural events in Boston and Cambridge and nationally, giving numerous lectures at universities and colleges in the area and around the country. In addition to her teaching and lecturing, Rushin has written several reviews and essays on African-American film and culture for *Sojourner: The Women's Forum* and *Gay Community News*. She has taught writing at Curry College and women's studies at the University of Massachusetts at Boston and MIT (Massachusetts Institute of Technology).

Kate Rushin's poetry has appeared in a number of anthologies, literary magazines, and women's studies journals. Undoubtedly, her poem "The Bridge Poem" has received the most attention. Most recently her poem "Family Tree" was published in the anthology *Double Stitch: Black Women Write about Mothers and Daughters* (Beacon Press, 1991). In the fall of 1992, Kate Rushin entered the M.F.A. program in creative writing at Brown University. Her first book of poetry, *The Black Back-Ups,* is to be published in 1993 by Firebrand Books.

MAJOR WORKS AND THEMES

Beginning with her first exposure to the poetry of Langston Hughes and Gwendolyn Brooks, Kate Rushin was, even as an adolescent, deeply drawn to the poetry that she calls "people poetry." This poetry, as exemplified by Hughes's work, had a particular down-to-earth quality that reflected the lives and speech of the ordinary African-American people that she saw around her in the small black town in New Jersey where she grew up. The use of chanting, rhyming, and repetition, so often found in the sermons of the ministers in the Methodist and African Methodist Episcopal churches Rushin attended, fueled her interest in representing the language and stories of these people in her poetry.

Rushin came of age during the heyday of the black arts movement. She was very influenced by the vibrancy of the work of some of the most visible and widely published writers in this group, The Last Poets, Imamu Baraka, Carolyn Rodgers, and, in particular, Nikki Giovanni. She melded their use of free verse and emphasis on oral presentation into her own narrative style.

Rushin's work received the greatest attention with the publication of her poem "The Bridge Poem" in the ground-breaking anthology *This Bridge Called My Back: Writings by Radical Women of Color*. Although, according to Rushin, the poem was not written expressly for the anthology, it has come to represent for many readers, critics, scholars, and theorists, the essential statement of the theme of the book. Since its publication in 1981, *Bridge* has been one of the most widely used texts in women's studies courses in the United States. It is considered to be one of the primary texts of the second wave of the U.S. women's movement particularly because it provides women of color a forum through which to challenge the very foundation of the movement. Rushin's poem opens the book, and its conversational, yet forceful tone sets the context for the essays that follow it. As critic Norma Alarcon noted, Rushin's poem exposes the shattered hopes that women of color had for the feminist movement. The speaker's refusal to play "bridge," an enablement to others as well as to self, is the acceptance of defeat at the hand of political groups whose self-definition follows the view of self as unitary, capable of being defined by a single "theme." Furthermore, "The Bridge Poem" vividly evokes the commonality of experience in the women's movement for women of color who consistently found themselves relegated to the position of translators while being forced to deny the cost of such an effort. In the poem, according to Alarcon in "The Theoretical Subject(s) of *This Bridge . . . ,*" the speaker's perception that the "self" is multiple gives emphasis to the relationality between one's selves and those of others as an ongoing process of struggle, effort, and tension (in Gloria Anzaldúa's *Making Face, Making Soul,* San Francisco: Aunt Lute, 1990, 365). Thus Rushin's poem was transformed by the context of appearing as the opening to *Bridge,* from expressing the singular experience of the poet to expressing the collective rage of women of color.

As in "The Bridge Poem," much of Rushin's work attempts to portray the ways in which African-American women are disempowered in U.S. society. In the poems "The Black Back-Ups" and "The Tired Poem: Last Letter from a Typical Unemployed Black Professional Woman," Rushin describes two of the archetypal roles that African-American women have had to play in this culture, the backup singer and the strong black woman. In "Black Back-Ups," she begins by describing the familiar black female singer, singing backup to innumerable famous white male and female singers. The poem shifts from this image of the backup singer to all the black women who, as domestics, housekeepers, and cooks, kept white families afloat, from the background. In "The Tired Poem," Rushin contrasts this image of the backup to the black professional woman assaulted by black men who declare, "Dear you were born to suffer." In both poems, Rushin captures a recognizable black female voice and experience.

In this same vein, Rushin's poems that address specifically lesbian themes attempt to locate black lesbians within the larger African-American community. Rushin brings the reader into her own experience of recognizing that "Wanita is her girlfriend," thus emphasizing that black women who are lesbians live in and are part of the African-American community. Rushin's poems, with their very personal narrative style, most often succeed in making the reader and the listener participate in the observations of a specific, yet not overly so, black female, lesbian experience. Rushin's poems speak in the voice of the generation of black women born in the 1950s, who came of age in the sixties and seventies when notions of gender, sexuality, family, community, and connection to an identifiable black sensibility were much clearer, grounded in the everyday life of African-American neighborhoods.

CRITICAL RECEPTION

Judging from the fellowships and prizes awarded to her, the large number of poetry readings she is invited to give, and the wide variety of journals publishing her work, it is clear that Kate Rushin is a highly regarded poet. To date, however, there has been no critical writing on her work. The expectation is that such review will be forthcoming after the publication of her first book in 1993.

HONORS AND AWARDS

Kate Rushin was the recipient of the Grolier Poetry Prize in 1988. She was the first African-American woman to receive this award. She was also the recipient of the 1989 Amelia Earhart Award, given by the Greater Boston Lesbian/ Gay Political Alliance.

BIBLIOGRAPHY

Works by Kate Rushin

"The Bridge Poem." *This Bridge Called My Back: Writings by Radical Women of Color.* Ed. Cherrìe Moraga and Gloria Anzaldúa. Watertown, MA: Persephone Press, 1981; 2nd ed. Latham, NY: Kitchen Table Press, 1983. xxi. Also in *New Worlds of Literature*, ed. Jerome Beaty and J. Paul Hunter (New York: Norton, 1989, 695) and *Gay and Lesbian Poetry in Our Time: An Anthology*, ed. Carl Morse and Joan Larkin (New York: St. Martin's Press, 1988, 350).

"The Black Back-Ups," "The Tired Poem: Last Letter from a Typical Unemployed Black Professional Woman," and "The Black Goddess." *Home Girls: A Black Feminist Anthology.* Ed. Barbara Smith. New York: Kitchen Table Press, 1983. 160, 255, 328.

"Family Tree." *Sojourner* January 1983. Also in *Double Stitch: Black Women Write about Mothers and Daughters.* Ed. Patricia Bell-Scott et al. Boston: Beacon Press, 1991. 11.

"Living in My Head" and "The Bricklayer." *Women's Review of Books* 1:2 (Nov. 1983): 15.

"Comparative History." *Sojourner* March 1984: 8. Also in *Callaloo* Spring 1989: 290.

"In Answer to the Question," "Lizzie's Girl: It's the Saturday Morning Before School Starts," "Making Way for Sister," and "It Was in Ibadan." *The Grolier Poetry Prize.* Ed. Louisa Solano. Cambridge, MA: Ellen La Forge Memorial Poetry Foundation, 1988. 8–13.

"Syracuse: By Night in Transit," "The Invisible Woman," "In Answer to the Question: Have You Ever Considered Suicide?" and "It's the Saturday Morning Before School Starts" *Sojourner* Oct. 1988: 12.

"Double Dutch Song" and "The Rapper." *Origins*, vol. 2. New York: Teachers Writers Union, 1989. 73, 158.

"Kaighns Ave., Camden, New Jersey." *Black/Out, The Magazine of the National Coalition of Black Lesbians and Gays* 2:2 (Summer 1989): 9.

"Why I Like to Go Places," and "The Black Back-Ups." *An Ear to the Ground: An Anthology of Contemporary American Poetry.* Ed. Marie Harris and Kathleen Aguero. Athens: University of Georgia Press, 1989. 251–56.

"In Answer to the Question: Have You Ever Considered Suicide?" *The Black Women's Health Book.* Ed. Evelyn C. White. Seattle, WA: Seal Press, 1990. 3.

"The Tired Poem: Last Letter from a Typical Unemployed Black Professional Woman" and "The Black Back-Ups." *Literature and Society: An Introduction to Fiction, Poetry, Drama, and Non-Fiction*. Ed. Pamela Annas and Robert Rosen. New York: Prentice-Hall, 1990. 552, 787.

"The Black Back-Ups." *The Jazz Poetry Anthology*. Ed. Sasha Feinstein and Yusef Kimunyakaa. Bloomington: Indiana University Press, 1991. 179–82.

"Rosa Revisited," adult ed.," "Have You Seen Them?" "Home," "The Ancestors," and "Sunday. After Church." *Radical Teacher* 42 (1992): 22, 27.

JOANNA RUSS (1937–)
J. Caissa Willmer

BIOGRAPHY

Joanna Russ knew at the age of eleven that she was a lesbian, but by the age of sixteen, she had been convinced by her mother and the prevailing wisdom of society that it was just a stage and that her duty was to become a *real* woman and to serve men. She has said that she had no true sexual identity for close to twenty-five years, and that by the end of graduate school, "I no longer had problems with 'feelings about women'; I felt nothing about anybody" ("Not for Years but for Decades" 158). Nevertheless, she married, in 1963, "a short, gentle, retiring pleasant man and worked very hard at sex, which I loathed" (158).

In 1967 she made what she called "the first genuine decision of my adult life and left my husband" (160). Then when "feminism had burst over all of us I stopped loving men ('it's too difficult') and in a burst of inspiration, dreamed up the absolutely novel idea of loving women" (160). This led to a wrenching and releasing insight: "If this is possible, anything is possible" (*The Female Man* 208)—an understanding that informs the most powerful of her writings.

Joanna Russ was born in the Bronx on February 22, 1937, into a secular Jewish family. She has called herself a convinced and serious, even passionate atheist. She was a very bright and bookish child. Exceptionally apt at science, she was accepted at the Bronx High School of Science in the first class to admit women students, but, she says, "family insanity" prevented her going. In spite of that, she "ended my four years somewhere else by becoming one of the top ten Westinghouse Science Talent Search winners in the country, for growing fungi that looked beautiful but made my mother hysterical because I stored them in the refrigerator" (Ellison 270).

She graduated from Cornell in 1957, where she had majored in English, studying with Vladimir Nabokov, among others, and coming away feeling that she had received a splendid technical training but had been nearly killed as a human being. She has recalled, in an unpublished paper, an experience where a story that she wrote about the pains of being a wallflower at a high school dance was found "funny but trivial," whereas another story—which must have been written in a torrent of satiric, reactive rage—was highly praised. It was "about rape, a fight in a bar, and a woman who was thrown down and 'taken' brutally by her husband on the floor she was scrubbing just after she'd come out of the hospital for the excision of a coccyxal cyst (the odors of which were described at length). . . . The story ended, 'That night their idiot child was conceived.' " She concludes:

I ended my college career convinced that I knew nothing of real life, that high school dances weren't important (though I had suffered horribly at them), and that Great Literature lay in a realm I could never enter because as sure as God made little green sophomores, I was never going to a fist fight in a bar, piss in a urinal, buy a whore, fight bulls, hunt whales, or rape my wife. ("Creating Positive Images of Women: A Writer's Perspective," paper presented at the Women and Literature Forum of the Midwestern Modern Language Association, St. Louis; 1975 2; quoted in Friend 154).

Joanna Russ earned an M.F.A. from the Yale University School of Drama in 1960, but she turned to writing science fiction. Then she began "writing adventure stories about a woman in which the woman won. It was one of the hardest things I ever did in my life. These are stories about a sword-and-sorcery heroine called Alyx, and before writing the first I spent about two weeks in front of my typewriter shaking and thinking of how I'd be stoned in the streets, accused of penis envy, and so on (after that it is obligatory to commit suicide, of course)" (Hacker 71).

She has won numerous awards for her fiction: her short story "When It Changed" won the 1972 Nebula Award of the Science Fiction Writers of America; the story "Souls" won the Hugo Award of the World Science Fiction Convention, as well as a Nebula Award, in 1983; she was granted a National Endowment for the Humanities Younger Humanist Fellowship in 1974–1975; her novel *The Female Man* was reprinted in the Science Fiction Hall of Fame series in 1986 and was also reprinted by Beacon Press as a modern classic in 1987, and this is only a sampling of the honors that have come her way.

She is currently a professor of English at the University of Washington, Seattle.

MAJOR WORKS AND THEMES

Joanna Russ is a science fiction writer and critic of formidable capacities— intellectual, stylistic, and analytic. Her first published science fiction story, "Nor Custom Stale," came out in 1959, and she is considered to be one of the New Wave of science fiction writers—including Ursula K. LeGuin, Samuel Delany,

Thomas Disch, Roger Zelazny, and Marion Zimmer Bradley—who appeared in the early sixties and seventies and who brought a new social, sexual, political, and literary sensibility to the writing of speculative fiction.

In the hands of Joanna Russ, science fiction becomes a means of confronting the issues in contemporary society that cause pain and dislocation and lack of fulfillment—especially among women. Her work is a complex and challenging critique of patriarchy, the Western capitalist system, and finally of heterosexism. It is deliberately didactic. She has lessons to teach and visions to project of utopias or dystopias—potential futures derived from the extensions of some of the best and many of the worst of present society's tendencies and impulses. In short, ideas are central to her work—ideas presented with dynamic narrative skill, challenging shifts of style and language, strong characterization, and vivid evocation of setting. She is a polemicist who is also a writer's writer.

A lesbian feminist, she has characterized herself as being on the Lavender Left, and frank sexuality—diverse and various—is a frequent current in her fiction. Apart from one novel, *On Strike against God*, Joanna Russ's fiction does not deal with lesbian issues per se. Her early work—the Alyx short stories, *Picnic on Paradise*, and *And Chaos Died*—was heterosexually oriented. Some lesbian critics would also say that Whileaway, the all-woman society Russ has created in *The Female Man*, does not deal with lesbian issues because lesbian issues arise from being "other," from being on the margins of heterosexual society.

Writing from a radical feminist position, however, Russ demonstrates time and again that gender roles are social conventions, not biological imperatives. She also maintains that a feminist work must have at least two women working and/or fighting together, or one helping to liberate or empower the other. A prevailing theme in Russ's work is *the rescue of the female child*—a rescue, however, in which the mentor also learns much from the child.

The Two of Them plays out that theme on two levels. Irene Waskiewicz, restless daughter of a middle-class family of the 1960s, who finds her life options severely limited, wangles her way into an apprenticeship with an agent of the mysterious interplanetary Trans Temporal Authority. Her mentor and trainer, Ernst Neuman, also becomes her partner and lover. They are sent on a routine assignment to a planet called Ka'abah, whose surface is too hot to support life, but whose people have carved out an underground milieu. At first Ka'abah's society appears to be a parody of Islamic mores, with the men free to come and go as they please but the women immured in harems, their only preoccupation being to keep themselves beautiful for their husbands and to train their daughters to be beautiful and compliant for future husbands.

It soon becomes apparent that this is a marvelously bizarre re-creation of Levittown, U.S.A. The women are bored out of their minds and are kept under control with tranquilizers. If they show any signs of intellectual vigor, they are labeled crazy and disciplined into mindless conformity. One who had wanted to be a poet has had books and writing materials taken from her and been locked in a remote room—deliberate shades of Charlotte Perkins Gilman's "Yellow Wallpaper."

Irene steps beyond the bounds of her mission when she determines to rescue young Zubedeh—a girl child and a poet—from inevitable stultification and spiritual death. In the process, Irene comes to realize that although she had escaped the limiting fate that her early upbringing had in store for her, and that although she has learned to live by her wits and her weapons and to range over a sizable interplanetary universe, she is still subject to the approval and permission of Ernst. Finally, in order to free both herself and Zubedeh, she must murder Ernst.

The process of liberation or empowerment often derives from the female protagonist's acquiring the capacity and the willingness to maim and/or kill. Asked about this, Russ wrote:

[A]nger is absolutely essential to any kind of coming to feminist (or any other kind of) consciousness. And I do think that women have got to kill that figure of a man which occupies the central territory of partriarchy and install themselves in that space. And after all, while we're on the subject, how many killings are there in *The Female Man* and *The Two of Them* compared with men's murders of women in so many many movies and books and so on? Few. And all taken seriously. (Personal communication with the author)

Russ rages at the constraints and limitations that have been placed on women and women's potential especially, but also on the whole of society, by the controlling and jealous forces of hierarchal patriarchal culture. By some miracle of spirit, Joanna Russ lards that rage with chunks of hilarious playfulness and with blasts or jabs of an antic humor that is in turn acerbic and witty, cuttingly banal, and outrageously farcical—but the laughter she provokes is always the other side of anger.

Russ is also preoccupied, though, with creating alternative worlds in which she explores the fruitful possibilities inherent in egalitarian and cooperative social processes as opposed to hierarchal and competitive systems. Within those positive worlds, sexuality is spontaneous, free, and diverse, while technology plays a benign and liberating role, modeled on the workings of a nature that is learned from and never exploited.

Countering the utopian visions, however, are portrayals of hideous potential futures that might evolve from current patriarchal modes—from the cynical escalation of the war between the sexes, from the spiritual and sensual bankruptcy of a rigid heterosexuality, and from the continued manipulation and control of the mass of people by a greedy and power-hungry few.

Along with the liberating potential that Russ sees for women when they touch into their lesbianism and find they can live without men is the nagging suspicion that it may be impossible to build a truly egalitarian and cooperative two-gendered society.

These themes are clearly apparent in *The Female Man*, Russ's third novel—

her tour de force and a classic of contemporary feminist speculative fiction. A complex and highly idiosyncratic work, it does not have an easily summarized plot. Four protagonists—Janet, Jeannine, Joanna, and Jael—are genetically identical, but inhabit parallel time frames—one present, one past, and two in the future. The women come together in 1969—the year that Russ began to write the piece—and together they intimate the infinite variety of everywoman's possibilities.

Janet comes from Whileaway—an egalitarian, all-woman future society (potential in the present) that has learned to reproduce through the merging of ova. She is self-determining, highly resourceful, and quite capable of throwing an importunate man across a room without compunction.

Jeannine has been summoned from an America still deep in the Depression, but one where World War II never occurred. She has been made to see herself as only half realized unless she marries, but the men in her life fill her with a dreary despondency.

Joanna, who is and is not the author, inhabits that early coming-to-feminist consciousness of the late 1960s, but is still thoroughly ensnared in the need to please the man or to prove herself by thinking like a man. It is her reality, however, that is rent by a lesbian encounter that reveals the social possibilities inherent outside of patriarchy.

Jael represents the extreme development of antagonism between the sexes. In her world, men and women occupy separate continents, and are in a perpetual state of war.

And Chaos Died once again juxtaposes worlds that are possible projections of our own. In the first, the inhabitants have exquisitely developed powers of extrasensory perception by means of which they have wrought a high level of technology—in the healing and genetic arts, for instance, and in teleportation and communication—that derives from exquisite sensitivity to natural processes. The society is agrarian, cooperative, and egalitarian.

Onto this planet crashes a spaceship from earth carrying a brutal commanding officer and Jai Vedh, a homosexual, presumably a fashion designer, who is blind to all except outward form, color, and design. His education in inward seeing forms the fundamental movement of the novel, which has been hailed as a brilliant technical evocation of what it might be like to experience the world as a telepath.

When Russ was writing this novel, she perceived homosexuality as a disease—Jai-Vedh's homosexuality is "cured" when he falls in love with the woman, Evne, who teaches him about "psionic" powers. With the publication of *The Female Man*, which was her next novel, Russ had clearly suffered a conversion.

We Who Are About To is also about a spaceship crash, but this time onto an uninhabited and uncharted planet. The passengers, five women and three men who have no hope of rescue, set to with the determination to survive and build a colony. All the passengers, that is, but one. The protagonist—a youngish woman, a musicologist and one-time social activist—sees only a reassertion of patriarchal modes of social construction. She and the other women who are young enough will be expected to become breeders of the next generation, and she refuses to be part of it. When it becomes clear that the others are prepared to force her—to in effect enslave and rape her—she kills all but one whom she provokes into suicide, and the greater part of the novel consists of a monologue and meditation on her life, her civilization, and her dying. This has been called an archetype of the anti-formula novel that turns reader expectations—derived from the *Swiss Family Robinson* convention—on their heads.

On Strike against God is a coming-out novel. It is a personal, if not confessional work—judging from the parallels one finds to Russ's life and echoes of material in "Not for Years but for Decades," Russ's work is a contribution to *The Original Coming Out Stories*. The protagonist Esther, like Joanna in *The Female Man*, is struggling to maintain a professional foothold and a sense of personal identity in a man's world. She is an English professor in her late thirties, and she finds herself falling in love with a female student, Jean. When Jean accepts her advances, Esther suffers a moment of revelation—as did Joanna in *The Female Man*—that the world is full of possibilities not yet dreamed of.

Russ has great fun describing the fumbling first lovemaking between the two who don't quite know how lesbians go about it. There is a reversal of the rescued child motif, as Jean proves far more able to cope with the shock and doubts that accompany their cataclysmic discovery about themselves, and it is Jean who completes their transformation by acquiring a shotgun and teaching Esther how to shoot. They make themselves ready—physically and emotionally—to kill the man if they must.

The story "The Mystery of the Young Gentleman" in *Extra (Ordinary) People* is a lesbian romp. It takes place in the late nineteenth century aboard a transatlantic steamship. An elegant young man who is handy with a knife, a derringer, and a pack of cards—is not a man at all. S/he is traveling with a fifteen-year-old hoyden from the slums of Barcelona, whom s/he calls her niece. When a fellow passenger, a doctor with a salacious interest in deviance, begins to suspect that the young gentleman is not what he would seem, the young gentleman takes a wicked and witty revenge on him in order to force him into silence.

Extra (Ordinary) People, *The Hidden Side of the Moon*, and *The Zanzibar Cat* are short story collections that demonstrate, in ways that the novels cannot, the extraordinary range of Russ's knowledge of literary convention and tradition and her remarkable chameleon capacity for assuming a variety of forms and modes to suit a host of intellectual purposes. She is a protean stylist with a multitude of messages.

CRITICAL RECEPTION

As Samuel Delany, a prominent science fiction critic and writer who is also gay, has noted, Joanna Russ's writing—especially the novels—give "some readers great pleasure and others great distress" (98). He says that her work is a "touchstone" (96) for the field of science fiction, that she is "a contemporary writer working at the highest level of rhetorical risk'' (99), and that he ''is struck by the interplay of aesthetic and social intelligence on page after page'' (100).

Russ is humorless and bitter to some, marvelously witty and provocative of belly laughs to others. She has frequently been taken to task—mainly by male critics—for her anger and for her female characters' eruptions of violence against men. Rachel Blau DuPlessis, on the other hand, says Russ's anger is ''cathartic, healing, and it fuses the fragments of women's consciousness'' (7), and Marge Piercy says that *The Two of Them* is ''violent and cozy at once, a very female work'' (''Shining Daughters'' 14).

The Female Man was characterized by one male reviewer as ''a long, clever, sometimes amusing, more times exasperating finger-waving discourse on The Female'' (Baird Searles, ''Four Heroines in Search of a Novel,'' *Village Voice*, January 20, 1975, 39), while DuPlessis finds *The Female Man* ''a dazzling montage of jump cuts and manifestos'' and ''as devastating and witty as [Virginia Woolf's] *Orlando*, which is its spiritual foremother'' (5).

BIBLIOGRAPHY

Works by Joanna Russ

Novels

Picnic on Paradise. New York: Ace Books, 1968.
And Chaos Died. New York: Ace Books, 1970.
The Female Man. New York: Bantam, 1975; Boston: Beacon Press, 1986.
We Who Are About To. New York: Dell Books, 1977.
Kittatinny: A Tale of Magic. New York: Daughters, 1978.
The Two of Them. New York: Putnam-Berkley, 1978.
On Strike against God. New York: Out and Out Books, 1980.
Extra (Ordinary) People. New York: St. Martin's Press, 1984.

Story Collections

The Adventures of Alyx. New York: Pocket Books, 1983.
The Zanzibar Cat. Sauk City, WI: Arkham House, 1983.
The Hidden Side of the Moon. New York: St. Martin's Press, 1987.

Non-fiction Books

How to Suppress Women's Writing. Austin: University of Texas Press, 1983.
Magic Mommas, Trembling Sisters, Puritans and Perverts: Feminist Essays by Joanna Russ. Trumansburg, NY: Crossing Press, 1985.

Essays

''The Image of Women in Science Fiction.'' *Images of Women in Fiction: Feminist Perspectives*. Ed. Susan Koppelman Cornillon. Bowling Green, OH: Bowling Green State University Popular Press, 1972. 79–94.
''What Can a Heroine Do? or Why Women Can't Write.'' *Images of Women in Fiction:*

Feminist Perspectives. Ed. Susan Koppelman Cornillon. Bowling Green, OH: Bowling Green University Popular Press, 1972. 3–20.

"On Setting." *Those Who Can: A Science Fiction Reader*. Ed. Robin Scott Wilson. New York: New American Library, 1973. 149–54.

"Alien Monsters." *Turning Points*. Ed. Damon Knight. New York: Harper & Row, 1977. 132–43.

"SF and Technology as Mystification." *Science Fiction Studies* 5 (1978): 250–60.

"Recent Feminist Utopias." *Future Females: A Critical Anthology*. Ed. Marleen Barr. Bowling Green, OH: Bowling Green State University Popular Press, 1981. 71–85.

"Reflections on Science Fiction." An interview in *Building Feminist Theory: Essays from Quest, a Feminist Quarterly*, New York and London: Longman, 1981. 243–50.

Introduction. *Uranian Worlds: A Reader's Guide to Alternative Sexuality in Science Fiction and Fantasy*; by Eric Garber and Lyn Paleo. Boston: G. K. Hall, 1983. xxi–xxiv.

"*Amor Vincit Foeminam*: The Battle of the Sexes in Science Fiction." *Gender Studies: New Directions in Feminist Criticism*. Ed. Judith Spector. Bowling Green, OH: Bowling Green State University Popular Press, 1986. 234–49.

"Not for Years but for Decades." *The Original Coming Out Stories*. Ed. Julia Penelope and Susan J. Wolfe. Freedom, CA: Crossing Press, 1989. 153–68.

Studies of Joanna Russ

Barr, Marleen. "Permissive, Unspectacular, a Little Baffling: Sex and the Single Feminist Utopian Quasi-tribesperson." *Erotic Universe: Sexuality and Fantastic Literature*. Ed. Donald Palumbo. New York: Greenwood Press, 1986. 185–96.

Bartkowski, Frances. *Feminist Utopias*, Chapter 2, The Kinship Web. Lincoln, Nebraska: University of Nebraska Press, 1989.

Clark, Michael. "The Future of History: Violence and the Feminine in Contemporary Science Fiction." *American Studies in Transition*. Ed. David E. Nye and Christen Kold Thomsen. Odense, Denmark: Odense University Press, 1985. 235–58.

Decarnin, Camilla. "Future Sex: Science Fiction Writer Joanna Russ." *Advocate* December 10, 1981: 25–27.

Delany, Samuel R. "Orders of Chaos: The Science Fiction of Joanna Russ." *Women Worldwalkers: New Dimensions of Science Fiction and Fantasy*. Ed. Jane B. Weedman. Lubbock, Texas: Texas Tech Press, 1985. 95–123.

DuPlessis, Rachel Blau. "The Feminist Apologues of Lessing, Piercy, and Russ." *Frontiers* IV, no. 1 (Spring 1979): 1–8.

Ellison, Harlan. Introduction to Joanna Russ, "When It Changed." *Again, Dangerous Visions*. Ed. Harlan Ellison. New York: New American Library, 1972. 266–71.

Friend, Beverly. "Virgin Territory: The Bonds and Boundaries of Women in Science Fiction." *Many Futures Many Worlds: Theme and Form in Science Fiction*. Ed. Thomas D. Clareson. Kent, OH: Kent State University Press, 1977. 140–63.

Garber, Eric, and Lyn Paleo. *Uranian Worlds: A Reader's Guide to Alternative Sexuality in Science Fiction and Fantasy*. Boston: G. K. Hall, 1983. 115–19.

Goldfarb, Diana. "Joanna Russ' Feminist Science Fiction." *Sojourner* (July 1979): 5, 26.

Gomez, Jewelle. "Meeting the Aliens." Review of *The Zanzibar Cat* and *Extra (Ordinary) People*. *Women's Review of Books* (February 1985): 11.

Hacker, Marilyn. "Science Fiction and Feminism: The Work of Joanna Russ." *Chrysalis*, no. 4 (1977): 67–79.

Howard, June. "Widening the Dialogue on Feminist Science Fiction." *Feminist Re-Visions: What Has Been and Might Be*. Ed. Vivian Patraka and Louise A. Tilly. Ann Arbor, MI: Womens Studies Program, University of Michigan, 1983. 66–96.

Huckle, Patricia. "Women in Utopias." *The Utopian Vision: Seven Essays on the Quincentennial of Sir Thomas More*. Ed. E. D. S. Sullivan. San Diego: San Diego State University Press, 1983. 115–36.

Johnson, Charles. "A Dialogue: Samuel Delany and Joanna Russ on Science Fiction." *Callalloo* 7 (Fall 1984): 27–35.

Landon, Brooks. "Eve at the End of the World: Sexuality and the Reversal of Expectations in Novels by Joanna Russ, Angela Carter, and Thomas Berger." *Erotic Universe: Sexuality and Fantastic Literature*. Ed. Donald Palumbo. New York: Greenwood Press, 1986. 61–74.

Law, Richard. "Science Fiction Women: Victims, Rebels, Heroes." *Patterns of the Fantastic*. Ed. Donald M. Hassler. Merces Island, WA: Starmont House, 1983. 11–20.

Pearson, Carol. "Women's Fantasies and Feminist Utopias." *Frontiers: A Journal of Women Studies* 2, no. 3 (Fall 1977): 50–61.

Piercy, Marge. "From Where I Work." *American Poetry Review* (May/June 1977): 37–39.

———. "Shining Daughters." *Sojourner* (October 1978): 14.

Rosinsky, Natalie M. "A Female Man? The 'Medusan' Humor of Joanna Russ." *Extrapolation* 23, no. 1 (Spring 1982): 31–36.

Scholes, Robert. "A Footnote to Russ's 'Recent Feminist Utopias.' " *Future Females: A Critical Anthology*. Ed. Marleen Barr. Bowling Green, OH: Bowling Green State University Press, 1981. 86–87.

Searles, Baird. "Four Heroines in Search of a Novel." *The Village Voice* January 20, 1975: 39.

Shinn, Thelma J. "Worlds of Words and Swords: Suzette Haden Elgin and Joanna Russ at Work." *Women Worldwalkers: New Dimensions of Science Fiction and Fantasy*. Ed. Jane B. Weedman. Lubbock, TX: Texas Tech Press, 1985. 207–22.

Spector, Judith. "The Functions of Sexuality in the Science Fiction of Russ, Piercy, and Le Guin." *Erotic Universe: Sexuality and Fantastic Literature*. Ed. Donald Palumbo. New York: Greenwood Press, 1986. 197–207.

Spencer, Kathleen L. "Rescuing the Female Child: The Fiction of Joanna Russ." *Science Fiction Studies* 17 (1990): 167–87.

Walker, Nancy A. *A Very Serious Thing: Women's Humor and American Culture*. Minneapolis: University of Minnesota Press, 1988.

———. *Feminist Alternatives*. Jackson and London: University Press of Mississippi, 1990.

Walker, Paul. "Joanna Russ." *Speaking of Science Fiction: The Paul Walker Interviews*. Ed. Paul Walker. Oradell, NJ: Luna Publication, 1978. 243–52.

Warrick, Patricia S. *The Cybernetic Imagination in Science Fiction*, Chapter 4, An Aesthetic and an Approach. Cambridge, MA: MIT Press, 1980. 80–89.

BARBARA RUTH (1946–   )
Adrienne Lauby

BIOGRAPHY

> "When I was born
> The doctor had to ask
> What race
> Shall I put on
> The birth certificate?"

(*Past, Present and Future Passions* 21)

Barbara Ruth's Jewish mother and Potowatomee/Blackfoot/German father did their best to raise her as a white Christian. "My parents think / Forgetting will protect them / 'It was all so long ago' / 'That's not the way we live now' " (*Passions* 28). In the small midwestern towns where she grew up, Ruth always felt queer, even before she fell in love with a girl at age seven. Since childhood she has written poems "as an act / of resistance / of defiance" (*Passions* 2) and as a way of explaining herself, to the world, and to herself.

Ruth's schoolteacher parents maintained silence on crucial issues of family identity but encouraged her writing, directing her toward conventional forms and subject matter. Ruth had a difficult childhood, marked by conflicts and rebellions. When she was fifteen she refused to go to pep rallies because she thought they promoted nationalism. At sixteen she ran away from home to participate in the 1963 March on Washington. She has continued to struggle for social justice, in isolation and in community.

Leaving home at seventeen, Ruth immersed herself in the civil rights and hippie movements. She wrote, "On Haight Street, 1967, I felt / Like Van Gogh just come to Paris" (*Passions* 75). She attended several colleges where she was out as a bisexual. A relationship with a lesbian heroin addict resulted in her being "scared straight" (unless otherwise noted, all quotations are from personal communication with the author). She married, graduated from college, and earned two advanced degrees. In 1973, within the context of the women's movement, she divorced and came out as a lesbian-feminist. From 1969 to 1975, she performed and published extensively under the name Barbara Lipschutz.

In the mid–1970s she was active in DYKETACTICS!, an anarchist action group in Philadelphia. "I am the womon who always / Talks back to hecklers, / Carries a knife in her hand at night / Never lets anything / Just / Go / By" (*Passions* 189). In the late 1970s she toured the United States with her lover, Kathy Fire (a songwriter and musician), performing original music and poetry in lesbian bookstores, coffeehouses, and other venues.

Ruth settled in San Diego and became the local coordinator of California Poets in the Schools. She also taught with the program, an experience that remains "the most satisfying work for pay of my life."

In 1983, Ruth moved to Berkeley and shortly thereafter became disabled. Her environmental illness and associated disabilities have resulted in both physical and cognitive limitations, necessitating changes in all aspects of her life, including her writing. Access, in all its permutations, is a primary focus of her work. Her "inspiration and sustenance come primarily from other disabled lesbians."

MAJOR WORKS AND THEMES

Barbara Ruth's work, an "ongoing attempt to make sense through my writing of what has happened to me," reveals and expands themes central to three decades of the U.S. lesbian-feminist movement. In early work, she protested the use of male pronouns and nouns as generic terms, then she went on to challenge presumptions of heterosexuality, whiteness, class privilege and, most recently, the able-bodied view of reality. Throughout she questioned the use of false universals, finding them inaccurate to her own reality.

Past, Present and Future Passions, a two-hundred-page collection of poems that span fifteen years, not only presents these themes but exemplifies her wide-ranging interests and her commitment to the lesbian community. Her theoretical work, often found in reviews, reflects her anarchist concerns for individual freedom and mutual responsibility. She also has a small body of satire that pokes fun at heterosexual presumption and lesbian-feminist orthodoxy.

Throughout her career, Ruth has concerned herself with issues of accessibility. Like many lesbian writers of the early 1970s, Ruth developed a style that "would make my work comprehensible to my communities." These lesbian, disabled, Jewish, Native American, and leftist communities include many people who are not academic or literature oriented. Consequently, Barbara Ruth "writes poetry the way a story teller tells tales, in a way that is direct and accessible, . . . [with] subtlety and craft" (jodi 23). Her novel *A Different Kind of Prom* addresses issues of lesbian teens in a style and vocabulary familiar to them.

Another recurring theme, that of multiple identities, is central in Ruth's novel

The Book of Marie. The viewpoint character, a biracial child rejected by her parents, finds a home in her psychic abilities as she forges a lesbian identity and creates a non-biological family.

One of Ruth's favorite forms is the biographical narrative poem. These portraits celebrate the complexity of women's actual lives, both famous and otherwise. In her essay "Piece de Resistance," Ruth writes about disabled women like Helen Keller, whose leftist politics are not widely known, and about leftist women like Harriet Tubman, Emma Goldman, and Alejandrina Torres, whose disabilities are not often acknowledged.

Ruth often writes about passing, the necessity and costs of the choice to pass, and the subtle ways in which conformity and blending-in occur as habit, as responses to shame and fear. In "I go to work in drag," she discusses what is hidden in conventional classrooms, for the children as well as the teacher. In "Yiddishkeit," she claims a language her mother claims to have forgotten.

Resistance to injustice and the maintenance of integrity recur often in Ruth's work. Since she became disabled, orthodoxy is often presented as the Western medical system, and her resistance (and wounding) takes place in hospitals. In "Machu Picchu," she contrasts early dreams of fast-paced international activism with the sacrifice of her sex organs in "welfare hospitals in four different counties." She affirms the value of resistance wherever it occurs, noting in "Noncompliant" the importance of controlling her medical decisions. Using the language of political struggle, she interacts with bureaucracies to "take what I need." But she does not limit her challenge to Western medicine. In "The Remedy" she lists a series of possible remedies which include lesbians living in fully accessible cities and yurts (Mongolian tent houses) "with time enough to dream."

Nature appears in Ruth's work as an instructive, often humorous force. In "Whales Never Worry about Getting Fat," she contrasts a fanciful oceanic life with contemporary society, and in "Geology Lab," her rocks are "Impervious to all / My learned vivisection" (*Passions* 86).

Ruth's lesbian identity is primary to her work. She writes in detail about her erotic life and asks that these and other of her works be shared only with women.

Unfortunately, many records of Barbara Ruth's work were lost when her home was pesticided without warning in 1991. Some may eventually be recovered through indexing of various publications. Her short stories have appeared in *Black Maria, Both Sides Now, Common Lives/Lesbian Lives, Everywoman, Ladder,* and *Nitty Gritty.* Individual poems appeared in *Albatross, Chomo-Uri, Common Lives/Lesbian Lives, Focus, Hikane, off our backs, Poetry Now, Second Wave, Sinister Wisdom, WomanSpirit, Women: A Journal of Liberation, Shameless Hussy Review, Feminary, Big Mama Rag, Country Women, Higginson Journal of Poetry,* and other small press publications. Articles, including satires, appeared in *Centerfold, Lesbian Voices, RT, Radiance, Dykes, Disability and Stuff, Hera, Hikane, The Reader,* and *The Second Wave.* The year and a half

Ruth spent touring the United States (1977–78) is chronicled by articles in *Lesbian Tide* and *Philadelphia Gay News*.

Ruth also produced and edited one issue of a periodical called *Out/Inside: A Women's Newsjournal Focusing on Lesbian Prisoners* (Spring 1989). She wrote several articles for the issue.

CRITICAL RECEPTION

Since 1973, Barbara Ruth has regularly read her poetry at special events and extended readings. Popular with both lovers of poetry and less literary women, she is a favorite of lesbian and disabled organizers. Her early collection, *From the Belly of the Beast*, reflected the excitement of the seventies, "that curious blend of women-loving / man-hating lesbian feminist energy" (Friedman 16).

Her 1987 collection, *Past, Present and Future Passions*, reflects fifteen years of growth and experience. It garnered seven extended reviews in major lesbian-feminist publications and was widely recommended by readers.

Most reviewers of this collection identified with Ruth as a disabled lesbian and found strength in her self-portrayal as a writer: "She clarifies the devastating limitations of environmental illness and articulates relentless skepticism about western medicine" (Lieberman 11). Carrie Dearborn headlined her review "A Gift to the Disabled Lesbian Library" and praised Ruth's "plain honesty" (8). She credited the poem "Anesthesia" with empowering her to name an operation she endured while in a coma as rape. Raven said the poems helped her to fight a "one-dimensional" self-image as a "body with her aches, fatigue and runny nose" (5).

Rebecca Ridgely placed the autobiographical nature of the book in a wider context, noting that "inventing oneself is something all Lesbians have to do, fighting a lifelong war against countless kinds of denial" (118). She especially praised poems that create a disabled lesbian identity, noting their "uncharted territory . . . [where] the only answers are personal, close to the heart, close to the bone" (119). Ridgely makes special note of Ruth's language, the "clarity" of her writing in these ground-breaking areas, "the clear, precisely chosen words [which] say directly what needs to be said and subtly evoke secondary meanings" (119).

Many reviewers expressed appreciation for the extensive afternotes that define words, credit sources, and chronicle changes in poems because of Ruth's changes in life experience and political awareness.

As a result of her illness, Ruth now significantly limits her public appearances. She performed in the San Francisco Bay Area during the late 1980s with MotherTongue Readers' Theater, Wry Crips Disabled Women's Theater, and the Jewish Lesbian Writers Group.

BIBLIOGRAPHY

Works by Barbara Ruth

Contractions. (As Barbara Lipschutz.) Pittsburgh: Know, 1974 (out of print).

From the Belly of the Beast. Ware, MA: Four Zoas, 1976 (out of print).

The Politics of Relationships. New York: Seven Woods, 1979.

"In My Disabled Women's Group." *With Wings: An Anthology of Literature by and about Women with Disabilities*. Ed. Marsha Saxton and Florence Howe. New York: Feminist Press, 1987. 32–33, 81.

Past, Present and Future Passions. Oakland: Ruth, 1987. Available through HerBooks, P.O. Box 7467, Santa Cruz, CA 94061.

"I Write." *Disabled Calligraphy*. Ed. Cheryl Marie Wade, Beverly Slapin, and Elaine Belkind. Berkeley: Kids, 1988. 2, 45, 66.

"Familial Amnesia." *Naming the Waves*. Ed. Christian McEwen. Freedom, CA: Crossing Press, 1989.

"Hidden," "Anesthesia," and "Song of the Woman with Rope in Her Hair." *Close to the Truth: An Anthology Featuring the Creative Works of Women and Men with Disabilities*. Ed. Cheryl Marie Wade. Berkeley: Kids, 1989. 18–19, 50.

"Piece de Resistance." *Hikane: The Capable Woman* 3 (1989): 20.

"The Eskimos." *Making Face, Making Soul/Haciendo Caras: Creative and Critical Perspectives of Contemporary Women of Color*. Ed. Gloria Anzaldúa. San Francisco: Aunt Lute, 1990. 191.

"Ursula, My Love." *Cats (and Their Dykes)*. Ed. Irene Reti and Shoney Sien. Santa Cruz, CA: HerBooks, 1991. 45.

"Playing Roles." *The Persistent Desire: A Femme-Butch Reader*. Ed. Joan Nestle. Boston: Alyson, 1992. 45.

"The Remedy." *Hikane: The Capable Woman* 8 (1992): 10.

The Book of Marie. Unpublished novel.

A Different Kind of Prom. Unpublished novel.

"Homeless" and "Unsafe Surgery and Other Risky Business." *Canaries in the Mines*. Ed. Toni Fitzpatrick.

Studies of Barbara Ruth

Dearborn, Carrie. "A Gift to the Disabled Lesbian Library." *Gay Community News* (Oct. 1–7, 1989): 8.

Friedman, Laurie. Review of *From the Belly of the Beast*. *Albatross* (Winter 1978): 16–17.

jodi. Review of *Past, Present and Future Passions*. *Hikane* 1:4 (Spring 1990): 23.

Karon, Sara. Review of *Past, Present and Future Passions*. *Dykes, Disability and Stuff* 1:4 (Spring 1989): 11.

Lauby, Adrienne. Review of *Past, Present and Future Passions*. *off our backs* (May 1988): 16.

Lieberman, Meryl [pseud., Santa Fe]. Review of *Past, Present and Future Passions.* *Lesbian Connection* (July/August 1989): 11–12.

Raven. "Disability and Survival." *Lesbian Contradiction* (Spring 1989): 5.

Ridgely, Rebecca [pseud. of Rebecca Ripley]. Review of *Past, Present and Future Passions. Sinister Wisdom* 25 (Summer/Fall 1988): 117–20.

CANYON SAM (1956–   )
Mona Oikawa

BIOGRAPHY

Writer, activist, performance artist, teacher, and founding sister of the Asian/Pacific lesbian movement, Canyon Sam was born Gail Caroline Sam on April 11, 1956, in San Francisco. A third-generation Chinese American, she is the only daughter and middle child in a family of three children. Growing up in San Francisco's racially mixed Richmond district, Sam felt torn between her parents' conservative, family-oriented Chinese American expectations and the dynamic, revolutionary possibilities offered by the Bay Area in the 1960s and 1970s. Her political and creative work has since demonstrated how she resolved this "crisis of identity," integrating differing parts of her cultural formation through passionate spiritual vision and powerful expression.

A graduate of Lowell High School and an honor student at the University of California at Berkeley, Sam received a National Endowment for the Arts scholarship after her freshman year to study movement and performance with dance pioneer Anna Halprin. Delighted to find other Asian artists, she also studied with the Asian American Theater workshop of the American Conservatory Theater. In 1974, in her sophomore year, she abandoned her academic training at Berkeley. She came out as a lesbian and left the Bay Area, traveling to Hawaii, the Pacific Northwest, and Europe, and briefly attending Warnborough College in Oxford, England.

"Coming out as a radical lesbian feminist . . . provided me with a foundation . . . for understanding the world and its forces in political terms" (*Kanemoto* 1984). It was while living on women's land in Oregon that the inspiration for the name Canyon came to her in a dream. Renaming herself was an important act in her defining of self.

Sam moved back to San Francisco in 1977, at the height of the Anita Bryant anti-gay uproar and the statewide campaign to ban gay teachers from California schools. Seeing the political necessity of organizing Asian women as an autonomous and visible presence in the larger lesbian/gay movement, she founded the first group of Asian-Pacific lesbians in the United States. In 1979, she co-founded Unbound Feet, a performing ensemble of Chinese American writers. Following the demise of Unbound Feet in 1981, she performed solo readings and began to publish her work.

A major turning point in Sam's life occurred in 1986 with her first trip to Asia, in which she journeyed to China, Tibet, India, Nepal, and Pakistan. She spent several months in Tibet and Tibetan areas of India and Nepal, discovering both the rich, spiritual tradition of Tibet and the cultural devastation wreaked upon the country by the occupying Chinese government. Deeply influenced politically, spiritually, and artistically by her travels and her study of Buddhism, upon her return to the States in 1987, she devoted much of her political organizing and writing talents to support the Tibetan cause. Her work on behalf of Tibetan nuns is powerfully documented in her solo performance theater piece "The Dissident," which she performed along with her other one-woman play, "Taxi Karma," to wide acclaim across the United States in 1992.

Sam has worked in the skilled trades to support herself, primarily as an electrical contractor. She has also taught writing in the Women's Studies Department of San Francisco State University. Her current projects include a third play, the theme of which intersects gay/lesbian and Chinese-American cultures, a book-length autobiographical work, and an oral history project by Tibetan women.

MAJOR WORKS AND THEMES

Canyon Sam is an accomplished writer of fiction, drama, essays, and journalistic articles. In her work the boundaries between fiction and non-fiction are blurred; such literary distinctions are arbitrary, particularly as applied to the work of women of color, where autobiographical storytelling and oral traditions often inform the structure and content of written genres.

Sam's poetry and short stories have been published in primarily lesbian-feminist publications. Publishing since 1981 establishes her as a forerunner in creating an Asian lesbian literature in the United States. Her writing, interwoven with themes of race, culture, and identity, has challenged the white-dominated definitions of "lesbian literature," expanded our vision of community, and provided affirming Asian women-loving images for a generation of Asian-Pacific lesbians coming to voice in the 1980s and 1990s.

Sam's writing is largely autobiographical. A consistent theme in her work is the multifaceted experience of identity. Race and culture are always constructs in her writing, ordinary and real in her expression of memory and self-discovery, part of her journey through her Chinese-American past and present.

Politics are often understated in her works of fiction; her narratives on race, gender, and sexuality are written with gentle irony rather than with didacticism.

Humor is a technique that she skillfully uses to make a point, connecting the reader to a meeting place of identification and empathy with the characters of her stories.

Sam's characters inhabit a world of women, where men are marginal or non-existent. Although the word *lesbian* is seldom used in her fiction, her Chinese-American lesbian sensibility provides the steady subcutaneous text beneath the bare poetically layered detail of the everyday. It is only in her post-Asia writing that men begin to appear. This change reflects the larger, less separatist political world of which she has begun to write.

Sam handcrafts each word in her stories, etching finely detailed portraits of life and its characters, establishing an immediate sense of time and place. This is densely layered writing. Imagination is captured in the moment of her imagery; her skillful use of metaphor heightens sharp prose to dramatic clarity.

Sam's writing career began in 1979. In collaboration with the women of Unbound Feet, from 1979 to 1981, she authored and performed four short satires, including "Assimilate" (1981).

Her first publication was a poem entitled "The Visit" (1981), followed quickly by "On Hayfever in America" (1982).

Sam's poem "For Victoria" (1982) is a tribute to activist Victoria Mercado, a close associate of Angela Davis, murdered in May 1982. With this work, she inscribes what has become a signature of her writing style and content: sharp, clear, moving, political women-loving words.

The publication of "Untitled" (1984) marked Sam's transition from writing poetry and satirical vignettes to writing short fiction. This shift to the narrative short story form gave her room to expand her creative voice and nurture her talent for descriptive prose. It also established her as a writer articulating the complex issues of race and identity in what was at the time a largely white-constructed world of lesbian literature.

"Untitled" depicts Sam's childhood and her realization at the age of nine that she must choose her own direction through her "painfully conflicted and confused" (69) identity as a Chinese-American girl living in a white-dominated culture. That this insight—being conscious not only of her "identity crisis" but also her need to choose her own path—came so early in her development, foreshadowed the reflective and self-actualizing spirit with which she has approached her life and her work.

"Leaf Peeking in Vermont" (1984) was Sam's first publication in an anthology of lesbian short fiction. In this first-person narrative, the author's light-hearted desire to explore New England turns into a journey in which she discovers a reactionary conservative moralism in the region taught to her in school as "America, its root and its heart" (95). The breathtaking fall beauty she so exquisitely describes is the frame for her "sobering" unmasking of the superficial pictorial myths of history textbooks. This frightening recognition of insularity and racism creeps up on the protagonist, first in the imposing presence of the obnoxious woman traveler who sits beside her and holds forth on her stereotypical knowledge of "orientals," and later, it is drawn more chillingly in descriptions of book burning and other destructive moralizing rituals. Her stark discovery raises questions about the fragility of safety for feminists, especially for women of color, who travel outside their progressive communities.

In 1987, Sam began chronicling her journey through Asia in essays and short stories. Her autobiographical stories, "Women at Kokonor" (1988) and "Stories from Asia: Lhasa" (1988), paint landscapes from Tibet and from the China of her ancestral past. Typically, these journeys are inhabited by women whose strong and loving portraits are indelibly drawn in Sam's unique poetic style.

Written ten years before its publication, "Heavy to the Touch" (1988) deals with the frightening and complex issue of self-defense in a world of violent crimes against women. The theme of alienation found in this story is also the basis for "People Like This" (1988), Sam's second publication in a major feminist anthology. Exact and skillful characterizations quickly establish the setting where the simple act of buying stamps becomes a bureaucratic nightmare. The tension is created in her portrayal of the obtuse rigidity of a white postal worker and her refusal to trust a woman of color in an ordinary business transaction. This short story demonstrates Sam's ability to convey the dynamics of interracial power and to show that people of color can experience the imposition of powerlessness on a daily basis.

"The Gathering Time" (1988), although less autobiographical in content, is thematically related to Sam's discovery of her Chinese heritage. In this beautifully descriptive third-person narrative, a daughter travels to meet the mother she had never known, the woman her father abandoned in war-torn China. The anticipation of the mother-daughter reunion moves the reader to recognize how finding the truths of our histories serves as a metaphor for self-discovery and healing.

Sam's "Sapphire" is a major example of her growing contribution to lesbian literature. Published in the best-selling lesbian anthology *Lesbian Love Stories*, her contribution underscores an increasing sophistication as a short story writer. This humorous, sensitive tale captures a recently out Asian lesbian's back-to-the-Oregon-women's-land experience and her unexpected meeting with the legendary Sapphire, "the first other Asian lesbian I'd ever met" (267). Sam deftly portrays the disappointment in this encounter as one of the amusing ironies that occur when our political expectations, our yearnings for "instant rapport" as "common loaves in an army of lovers" (267), conflict with the real jealousies and histories intertwined between players in our scenes of "Lesbian Drama."

In "Emei Shan," Sam describes the landscape and the travelers encountered by a woman climbing to the peak of the Emei Mountain. After a two-day journey, she discovers she has miscalculated by a day her date of departure. She must descend the mountain within a twelve-hour period in order to catch her connecting bus. The grueling descent at breakneck speed is written in sparse, rhythmic prose. Once again, Sam's work is brilliantly suggestive of themes of identity and gender, as the intrepid mountain climber meets the people of her foreparents' homeland, understanding only few and fleeting words of the Mandarin dialect spoken to her. Fear and suspicion of her unlikely fellow traveler, a male porter, is captured in her feminist musing, "Are men not men all over the world?" (27). But mistrust fades to joyful thanks when she bids farewell to her anonymous guide, reaching her destination in time.

Documenting Tibet's struggle to gain religious and political independence from the repressive Chinese regime has become an urgent theme in Sam's current writing. "Conversation with a Spiritual Friend" records her audience with His Holiness the Dalai Lama. In this moving memoir, Sam weaves a story, central to which is the truth of the decimation of the Tibetan people, "the worst genocide since World War II" (176). Deeply political words create loving, humorous impressions of the Tibetan spiritual leader and a respect for the Buddhist philosophy that inspires both his people and the author to continue to fight for justice.

The richness of Sam's craft lies in the kernel of autobiography she plants in each work and her giftedness in reaping a larger social history by the end of the story's telling. Creating language that gives testimony to truths as she lives them has produced fine and moving writing. Her continued contribution to lesbian literature, through the sharing of her vision, is anticipated in the years to come.

CRITICAL RECEPTION

Over a decade of reading and performing her work in the San Francisco Bay Area has solidified Sam's basis of support in her home community. In 1982, Kim Marshall, in *Poetry Flash*, praised a public reading of her work as "an inspiration for all women" and "wonderful" (11). Reviewing *New Lesbian Writing*, Adele Prandini highlighted Sam's "Leaf Peeking in Vermont" as demonstrating a "special talent which creates so strong a picture . . . more like watching a mental movie than reading a book" (22).

The Asian-Pacific lesbian community has long been appreciative of Sam's creative contributions. In reviewing her recent dramatic works, "Taxi Karma" and "The Dissident," for *Phoenix Rising: The Asian/Pacifica Sister Newsletter*, Teri Ng wrote, "Canyon has not only (again) affirmed that she is an established and effective writer, but also a powerful performance artist" (4).

National public acclaim of her writing and dramatic abilities in the 1992 production of "Taxi Karma" and "The Dissident" signal long overdue mainstream recognition of Sam's creative talent. Evelyn McDonnell in the *Village Voice* touted her as "a master storyteller" (110). The *San Francisco Examiner* praised her "storyteller's eye for telling detail" (Rosenberg C–11). The *Boston Globe* called her work "riveting, heartbreaking" (Robinson 25). Award-winning theater critic Kate Bornstein wrote, "Sam's work does not directly deal with her lesbianism but rather reflects her experience of being on the 'other side' of a dominant culture" (25). Bornstein concludes her laudatory comments: "[Canyon Sam's] genius lies in her ability to inspire through storytelling" (25).

HONORS AND AWARDS

In 1974, as part of the Minority Leadership in the Arts Training Program, Canyon Sam was awarded a National Endowment for the Arts Scholarship. She was honored for her activism in the lesbian/gay movement in San Francisco when she was invited to serve as honorary emcee of the San Francisco Lesbian/ Gay Parade in 1982, earning the distinction of being the first Asian-American emcee in the history of the parade. She is the grandmother of the national Asian/ Pacific Lesbian (APL) community, having organized the first APL group in the United States. Her writing and performance projects have won grants from the Zellerbach Family Fund, the Columbia Foundation, and the Franklin Furnace Fund/New York State Council on the Arts.

BIBLIOGRAPHY

Works by Canyon Sam

"Assimilate." *Vortex: A Journal of Art and Culture* 8 (1981): 6.
"The Visit." *On Parade* (June 1981): 27.
"For Victoria." *Coming Up!* (July 1982): 2.
"On Hayfever in America." *Coming Up!* (Jan. 1982): 12.
"Leaf Peeking in Vermont." *New Lesbian Writing*. Ed. Margaret Cruikshank. San Francisco: Grey Fox Press, 1984. 92–95.
"Untitled." *Common Lives/Lesbian Lives* 11 (Spring 1984): 67–71.
"Big Event." *Phoenix Rising: Asian Women's Newsletter* (Mar. 1988): 6–7.
"The Gathering Time." *Conditions* 15 (Dec. 1988): 97–107.
"Heavy to the Touch." *Hurricane Alice: A Feminist Quarterly* (Spring 1988): 3.
"People Like This." *Unholy Alliances: New Women's Fiction*. Ed. Louise Rafkin. Pittsburgh and San Francisco: Cleis Press, 1988. 89–93.
"Stories from Asia: Lhasa." *Mama Bears News & Notes* 5.2 (Apr. 1988): 12.
"Women at Kokonor." *Coming Up!* (Feb. 1988): 15.
"Emei Shan." *Finding Courage*. Ed. Irene Zahava. Freedom, CA: Crossing Press, 1989. 18–28.
"Sapphire." *Lesbian Love Stories*. Ed. Irene Zahava. Freedom, CA: Crossing Press, 1989. 261–68.
"Conversation with a Spiritual Friend." *Seattle Review* 13.1 (Summer 1990): 173–84.
"The Dissident." Unpublished play, 1991.
"Taxi Karma." Unpublished play, 1991.

Studies of Canyon Sam

Baetz, Ruth. "Canyon Sam." *Lesbian Crossroads*. New York: Naiad Press, 1980. 50–56.
Bornstein, Kate. "What's in a Name?" *Bay Area Reporter* 22.4 (Jan. 23, 1992): 25, 30.
Kanemoto, Lisa. *We Are*. San Francisco: Outreach Press, 1984.

502 Contemporary Lesbian Writers of the United States

Kim, Elaine. "Electrician: Canyon Sam." *With Silk Wings: Asian American Women at Work*. San Francisco: Asian Women United of California, 1983. 92.

McDonnell, Evelyn. "Caught Between Cultures: The Next Wave in Asian American Performance Art." *Village Voice* 37.12 (Mar. 24, 1992): 108, 110.

Marshall, Kim. "Simmering Stew." *Poetry Flash* 117 (Dec. 1982): 10–11.

Ng, Teri. "Interview: Canyon Sam." *Phoenix Rising: The Asian/Pacifica Sisters Newsletter* 37 (Jan./Feb. 1992): 4–5.

Prandini, Adele. "Local Anthology: *New Lesbian Writing*." *Bay Area Reporter* (Nov. 28, 1985): 22.

Robinson, John. "A Salute to Minorities Within Minorities." *Boston Globe* (April 21, 1992). 25.

Rosenberg, Scott. "Canyon Sam Runs Deep in Monologues on Tibet." *San Francisco Examiner* (Feb. 21, 1992). C–11.

Turoff, Randy. "Canyon Sam." *San Francisco Bay Times* 13.10 (Feb. 13, 1992). 32.

SAPPHIRE (1950–   )
Terri L. Jewell

BIOGRAPHY

Sapphire (Ramona Lofton) was born on August 4, 1950, in Fort Ord, an army base near Monterey, California. Her mother, from Philadelphia, and her father, son of a Texas sharecropper, met in the army in the 1940s and married. One of four children, Sapphire lived on and off army bases until she was thirteen: "The army was a means for poor and working-class blacks to escape the desperate poverty of the 1930s" (unless otherwise noted, quotations are from personal communication with the author). Such a nomadic existence discouraged development of roots and an extended family. Sapphire was usually the only black among poor whites in the schools she attended.

In 1963, Sapphire's father retired from the army and went to Europe while her mother kept the children in South Philadelphia. Her parents separated soon afterwards, and the children were sent to live with their father in Los Angeles, California.

Sapphire dropped out of high school at age sixteen or seventeen and learned the ways of the streets. At age twenty-one, she hitchhiked to San Francisco, where she hoped to reconstruct her life. Her first job was as an operator for the telephone company. She attended San Francisco City College in 1973 and began her studies in pre-medicine ("so that I could be of use to black people"). Despite excellent grades, she soon lost interest in the pre-med curriculum and turned to dancing and the performing arts. She transferred to a private college, then left it and California to pursue her career in New York City. By this time, she was doing some writing, but the performing arts were her main interest.

In the spring of 1977, Sapphire was published for the first time in *Azalea: A Magazine by and for Third World Lesbians*, one of the first literary magazines of its kind in the country. She soon joined the collective. During that same year, Sapphire initiated NAPS with Aida Mansuer and Irare Sabasu. This was the first known black lesbian performing group in the country. She returned to college to graduate *cum laude* from the City University of New York in 1983. She earned her bachelor of fine arts degree from the Davis Center for the Performing Arts.

Sapphire produced several performance pieces in New York City: "Gold Ringed Warrior with a Feather Shield" in the late 1970s; "Nile Blues" in the early 1980s; "Unknown Female Voices" in the mid–1980s; and "Are You Ready to Rock?" in 1990. In 1990, Sapphire made a conscious decision to cease performing and to concentrate on writing. Presently, she is a full-time teacher in a literary program in the Bronx.

MAJOR WORKS AND THEMES

In addition to the performance works mentioned previously, Sapphire has self-published one volume of poetry entitled *Meditations on the Rainbow*. During the National Black Writers Conference held in Brooklyn, New York, in March 1988, guest writers concurred that the business at hand for any black writer is to address the concerns of race and of African-American life in this country. To deter from this focus, they said, would be to lie. Sapphire, black lesbian feminist, has published her work in the lesbian/gay presses for over a decade. Not only has she been consistent in examining the issues that affect her own urban experiences and herstory, but she has used the full nuance of her cultural voice as a black woman who loves women. The thematic thread throughout all her work is an exploration of violence against women, including incest, racism, sexism, and heterosexism.

Meditation on the Rainbow reads like one long stream-of-consciousness poem that is broken up into sections of color. Sapphire says about the title of her book, "I was home alone one New Year's Eve night and lit a lot of different colored candles. I looked at the candles and began to write. When I read the poems around the city, they got a great reception and I was encouraged to publish them."

Sapphire uses clear, vivid language that impacts the reader line by line. Her imagery is immediate, written to be read out loud, as much of the black poetry from the 1960s was written, true to African-American oral tradition. In "Yellow," she makes a point of addressing black lesbian invisibility as well as nuclear waste dumping in Africa, the proliferation of drugs in black communities, and soul-draining materialism. She asks readers to be unafraid in analyzing their own world and in instigating change. The "Red" poem arises from Sapphire's gift as a performance poet and best derives its meaning and flavor when articulated by a strong vocalist. In this piece, red is passion, birth, pain, power, and rejuvenation.

In the section "Black," Sapphire ruminates on the Black woman's responsibility and the need to seize every chance to act toward societal and world metamorphosis. "Black," then, lends voice to the omnipotence of African-American women by using the symbolism of that color that is all colors, and, in essence, all possibilities. Sapphire juxtaposes a fat, black woman as birth-mother of the universe with herself and all other black women as birth-mothers to themselves—whole, healthy, and fulfilled.

The rallying cry in "Lavender" not only strikes a chord for connectedness among lesbians and gays, but also recognizes the dangerous and paralyzing realities of internalized homophobia, classism, and petit bourgeois opportunism. Nevertheless, Sapphire, as in all the pieces in *Meditations on the Rainbow*, ends on a note of hope and triumph. "White" continues the call for perseverance for justice as does "Green," which draws from the firm human instinct to live.

The strongest segment of Sapphire's book is the last, "Blue." Not only is it a blues poem, but it is a testimonial to a black lesbian's legacy. This sweet-sour segment tells of blueswoman Big Mama Thorton's love of women, white capitalism of black musics, and the potency of a woman's love and sexuality. Sapphire succeeds not only in exposing the sheer folly of racism in this country but in crystalizing the many flavors of sensuality among women.

At present, Sapphire is working on a collection of her poetry and prose.

CRITICAL RECEPTION

Sapphire, in her modesty, feels her work has received no critical reception. "I do not believe my work has been critically received because it is difficult to gauge whether audiences are responding to me as a performer or as a writer." Nevertheless, her highly controversial poetry has been not only reported to Scotland Yard's Obscene Publications Squad because it "celebrated her sexuality" (*South London Press*, June 15, 1990, 3), but "circulated in the White House and quickly became a campaign issue" among National Endowment for the Arts critics (*Sunday Washington Post*, March 1, 1992, p. G1). Sapphire's work provides "a shocking but clear and passionate window to the issues of AIDS, adult education, abuse, brutal crime, and the city," wrote Jacolia Monette of the *Mirror* (Lakeland College, February 21, 1992, p. 1). When one looked beyond the shock value of her language and imagery, one "found that it was indeed a vital part of the image of life she presented us."

BIBLIOGRAPHY

Works by Sapphire

"Nile Blues." *Common Lives/Lesbian Lives: A Lesbian Quarterly* 8 (Summer 1983): 52–55.
Meditations on the Rainbow. New York: Crystal Banana Press, 1987.
"The Refrigerator Story." *Sinister Wisdom* 31 (Winter 1987): 96.
"Eat." *Women on Women*. Ed. Joan Nestle and Naomi Holoch. New York: Plume, 1990. 45–46.
"Crooked Man." In *Loving in Fear: An Anthology of Lesbian and Gay Survivors of Childhood Sexual Abuse*. Toronto: Queer Press, 1991.

"Wild Thing." *Queer City The Portable Lower East Side*. Ed. Kurt Hollander. Guest
     editors: Harold McNeil Robinson, Mariana Romo-Carmona, Ira Silverberg, and
     Jacqueline Woodson. New York: Portable Lower East Side, 1992. 41–46.
"American Dreams." *City Lights Review* 5 (1992): 130–36.
"boys love baseball." *Brooklyn Review* 9 (1992): 32–34.
"Violet '86." *Loss of the Ground-Note: Women Writing about the Loss of Their Mothers*.
     Ed. J. Vozenilek. Los Angeles: Clothespin Fever Press, 1992.

MAY SARTON (1912–)
Nancy Seale Osborne

BIOGRAPHY

Eleanore Marie Sarton began her extraordinary life on May 3, 1912, the eve of World War I, in a small country home in Wondelgem, Belgium. At the age of eighty, she now lives at Wild Knoll on the rocky Atlantic coast in York, Maine. She considered her parents remarkable friends, choosing to write a chapter about each of them in *A World of Light: Portraits and Celebrations*. Mabel Elwes Sarton, as described by Sarton in her introduction to her mother's correspondence, *Letters to May*, was an excellent cook, gardener, painter, designer of furniture and textiles, teacher of applied design, and photographer. "Through my mother I witnessed extreme awareness of all forms of beauty, and extreme sensitivity to human beings and human relationships" (*World of Light* 20). Her father, George Sarton, the noted historian of science, was in the habit of spending the half hour before dinner reading Arabic, Greek, or Latin. She remembers the family "listening to music . . . travelling to Europe . . . spending a year in Beirut, [and] going to Uppsala" for her father to receive an honorary doctorate (*Letters to May* xi).

In the autumn of 1914, the Sarton family fled Belgium as refugees, for England, Mabel Sarton's homeland. The chaos of war mobilization orders and ringing church bells in the little village of Wondelgem is vividly described in *I Knew a Phoenix*. The three arrived in Washington, D.C., in 1916, and George Sarton set about learning English and finding a job. His part-time position at Harvard, along with Mabel Sarton's design firm, Belgart, allowed them to move to Cambridge, Massachusetts, in 1918. The money from her mother's silk and wool embroidered designs paid May's school bills, sent her to camp, and helped, in no small way, to support the family.

The young May attended Shady Hill School, a progressive cooperative school in Cambridge, coming to love poetry through the guidance of one of her teachers,

Agnes Hocking. Accompanying her parents on a year's sabbatical leave in Belgium when she was twelve years of age, she studied at the Institut Belge de Culture Française. After graduation from the Shady Hill School in 1926, she completed her formal education at the High and Latin School in Cambridge.

At seventeen, most girls of her milieu were heading for college. Sarton chose instead to join Eva Le Gallienne's Civic Repertory Theatre in New York. She subsequently founded a small company of her own, the Associated Actors" Theatre, which disbanded after their third season. Sarton became a writer, taught writing at both Harvard and Wellesley, and began publishing in four genres: poetry, novel, memoirs, and journal.

The lecture circuit beckoned her when her father bought her a new Mercury convertible, allowing her to explore, among other vistas, New Orleans, the Texas plains, and the pinon-dotted Sangre de Cristo Mountains in Santa Fe. Mabel Sarton died in 1950; George Sarton in 1956. The author's remembrance of her parents has suffused her writing throughout her life. In a recent interview, Sarton spoke of the rich environment of her parents' home. "I miss them terribly because I miss the conversation," she declared (Straw 34).

Plant Dreaming Deep is dedicated to Sarton's partner Judy, with whom she lived for fifteen years, "who believed in the adventure from the start," as they discovered a new home together, a New Hampshire eighteenth-century farmhouse with five fireplaces and thirty acres of land bounded by a brook. May Sarton had at last found a home for the four pieces of Flemish furniture that had survived World War I and remained with her parents throughout their life.

By the time *Journal of a Solitude* was written, Sarton was alone. *As We Are Now* expresses her anguish, as both Judy and Sarton's faithful gardner, Perley Cole, were "suffering from the change to a new place" (*Journal* 21), a nursing home. At the close of the journal, she has found "a stretch of wild woodland, rocky coast, meadows running down to the sea as in Cornwall . . . on the shore line of Maine" (*Journal* 143).

MAJOR WORKS AND THEMES

Carolyn G. Heilbrun suggests that there are four ways to write a woman's life: she may tell her own story through autobiographical writing; she may write her life in the form of fiction; a biographer may write her life; or she may "write her own life in advance of living it, unconsciously and without recognizing or naming the process" (11). A full-fledged biography on May Sarton has not yet emerged; Margot Peters has been chosen by Sarton to do the definitive biography.

Sarton's nine non-fiction journals, from *I Knew a Phoenix* to *May Sarton: A Self Portrait*, are autobiographical; threaded through each are the prosaic aspects of her days as well as the rich background of her childhood, her early years in which poetry became a first language, her parents, and her loves and muses over the years. Both the Sarton fiction (nineteen novels, from *The Single Hound* to *The Education of Harriet Hatfield*) and poetry (sixteen volumes, from *Encounter in April* to *Letters from Maine*) have autobiography as cornerstones. Instead of writing a life "in advance of living it," Heilbrun proposes that Sarton, recognizing that anger, despair and pain were not to be detailed in "the old genre of female autobiography" (12), concealed these emotions in *Plant Dreaming Deep*. Five years later, in *Journal of a Solitude*, Sarton acknowledged rage as a necessary avenue to take control over her life. Because of Sarton's honesty in a deliberate retelling of the record of her anger, Heilbrun recognizes *Journal* as "the watershed in women's autobiography" (13).

"The fear of homosexuality is so great that it took courage to write *Mrs. Stevens [Hears the Mermaids Singing]* "(*Journal* 91–92). Sarton is aware that she would have been unable to write a novel about a "woman homosexual" (she did not use the word *lesbian* at this time) if her parents had still been alive, if she had had a regular job, or if she had not already written several novels concerned with marriage and with family life. In *Journal*, Sarton and her friend, Judy, celebrate a friendship of nearly thirty years. A love affair with "X" is valued at its beginning as "a long hymn of praise" (*Journal* 159). Sarton hopes for the time for tolerance, patience, and understanding between herself and "X," to "bridge the gaps between our personalities and temperaments, even between our values . . . and the *Gestalt* of our lives" (*Journal* 159).

May Sarton's earlier poetry is written in the masculine voice because she envisioned her poet self as masculine. Within the last decade, both gender and language have changed in her writing. Recently in an interview, in response to Deborah Straw's question about "the new genre, lesbian books," Sarton replies, "Don't forget when I was growing up, you simply couldn't come out as a lesbian. And you had to conquer in yourself a great deal of self-doubt, of wondering if it was a morally viable life" (Straw 37). Expressing a desire to be in a "first-rate" anthology, Sarton concedes that she is now in lesbian anthologies. "The woman living alone has given me a kind of *raison d'etre* from the critical point of view" (37). And as Sarton approached the age of eighty, she had faithfully written about its approach: "Gestalt at Sixty," a poem from *A Durable Fire*: "I am always a lover here / Seized and shaken by love"; *At Seventy: A Journal*: "Letters! The other day my letters to Judy came to me. So I am pulled hither and thither these days, rich days, where the past floods into the present" (284); and *After the Stroke: A Journal*: "Friday, January 2 . . . There are to be tremendously high tides . . . I'm glad I'm up here on the Wild Knoll for which the house was named" (235).

A last "theme" of Sarton's work, accompanying the themes of anger, homosexuality, "the woman alone," and aging, is evidenced by her social conscience. Throughout her journals and memoirs, she maintains a vigorous interest in the state of the world. Complex, heartbreaking issues surrounding homelessness, war, poverty and global desolation suffuse her writings. Her poem "The Tortured," as timely as Amnesty International's latest report, was published in a 1972 peace anthology, *Enough of Dying! Voices for Peace* (Boyle 293).

CRITICAL RECEPTION

Carolyn G. Heilbrun's words were written about Sarton's memoirs, but the same could be said of Sarton's entire oeuvre:

Throughout all the memoirs Sarton feels, as who does not feel when they have worked as long and honorably as she, that she has been insufficiently loved and appreciated. I do not speak of a petty person seeking empty reassurance and emptier public acclaim. Hers is the sudden chill of doubt reserved for those have been unusually courageous, unusually generous, unusually overlooked . . . she has been remarkably unlucky in her reviewers, especially in the powerful *New York Times*. (Heilbrun 51).

Heilbrun asserts that she celebrates Sarton's memoirs, most especially *Plant Dreaming Deep*, because in this volume, Sarton pledges that women may live lives "both solitary and triumphant."

A *New York Times* review by Doris Grumbach, one exception to Heilbrun's statement, asserts that May Sarton's life "has been a long, fruitful, often valuable struggle with her muse, achieved amid the solitary terrors and pleasures of a single life. She has dealt with every aspect of the female existence, with every kind of love" (4).

A recent online search of *Dissertation Abstracts* revealed eleven doctoral dissertations about and including May Sarton. Two of these are Mary Kirk Deshazer's "*The Woman Poet and Her Muse: Sources and Images of Female Creativity in the Poetry of H. D., Louise Bogan, May Sarton and Adrienne Rich*" (University of Oregon Ph.D., 1982) and Christine Margaret Flug's "*The Journey Inward: An Examination of the Non-Fictional Prose of May Sarton*" (Harvard University Ph.D., 1986).

Contemporary critical review of Sarton's work endures in conference presentations and feminist publications. New generations of academic and community women are re-visioning the extensive, magnificent body of work of May Sarton.

WORKS CITED

Boyle, Kay, and Justine Van Gundy. *Enough of Dying! Voices for Peace*. New York: Dell, 1972.

Grumbach, Doris "May Sarton: Modern Marriage." Review of *Crucial Conversations*. *New York Times Book Review*, 27 April 1975: 4.

Heilbrun, Carolyn G. *Writing a Woman's Life*. New York: W. W. Norton, 1988.

Straw, Deborah. "Belles Lettres Interview." *Belles Lettres: A Review of Books by Women* 6.2 (Winter 1991): 34–37.

BIBLIOGRAPHY

Works by May Sarton

Poetry

Encounter in April. Boston: Houghton Mifflin, 1937.
Inner Landscape. Boston: Houghton Mifflin, 1938.
The Lion and the Rose. New York: Rinehart, 1948.
The Land of Silence and Other Poems. New York: Rinehart, 1953.
In Time Like Air: New Poems. New York: Rinehart, 1958.
Cloud, Stone, Sun, Vine: Poems Selected and New. New York: W. W. Norton, 1961.
A Private Mythology. New York: W. W. Norton, 1966.
As Does New Hampshire. Peterboro, NH: Richard R. Smith, 1967.
A Grain of Mustard Seed: New Poems. New York: W. W. Norton, 1971.
A Durable Fire. New York: W. W. Norton, 1972.
Collected Poems, 1930–1973. New York: W. W. Norton, 1974.
Selected Poems of May Sarton, edited and with an introduction by Serena Sue Hilsinger
    and Lois Brynes. New York: W. W. Norton, 1978.
Halfway to Silence. New York: W. W. Norton, 1980.
Letters from Maine: New Poems. New York: W. W. Norton, 1984.
A Winter Garland: New Poems by May Sarton. Concord, NH: William B. Ewert, 1982.
    Limited edition, one hundred eighty-six copies. Designed and with a wood en-
    graving by Michael McCurdy.
The Silence Now: New and Uncollected Earlier Poems. New York: W. W. Norton, 1988.

Novels

The Single Hound. Boston: Houghton Mifflin, 1938.
The Bridge of Years. New York: W. W. Norton, 1946.
Shadow of a Man. Toronto: Rinehart, 1950.
A Shower of Summer Days. New York: W. W. Norton, 1952.
Faithful Are the Wounds. New York: W. W. Norton, 1955.
Joanna and Ulysses. New York: W. W. Norton; Toronto: Clarke, Irwin, 1955.
The Birth of a Grandfather. New York: Rinehart; Toronto: Clarke, Irwin, 1957.
The Fur Person. New York: W. W. Norton; Toronto: George J. McLeod, 1957.
The Small Room. New York: W. W. Norton, 1961.
Mrs. Stevens Hears the Mermaids Singing. New York: W. W. Norton, 1965.
Miss Pickthorn and Mr. Hare. New York: W. W. Norton, 1966.
The Poet and the Donkey. New York: W. W. Norton, 1969.
Kinds of Love. New York: W. W. Norton, 1970.
As We Are Now. New York: W. W. Norton, 1973.
Crucial Conversations. New York: W. W. Norton, 1975.
A Reckoning. New York: W. W. Norton, 1978.
Anger. New York: W. W. Norton, 1982.
The Magnificent Spinster. New York: W. W. Norton, 1985.
The Education of Harriet Hatfield. New York: W. W. Norton, 1989.

Journals/Memoirs

I Knew a Phoenix. New York: W. W. Norton, 1959.
Plant Dreaming Deep. New York: W. W. Norton, 1968.
Journal of a Solitude. New York: W. W. Norton, 1973.
A World of Light. New York: W. W. Norton, 1976.
The House by the Sea. New York: W. W. Norton, 1977.
Recovering: A Journal. New York: W. W. Norton, 1980.
At Seventy: A Journal. New York: W. W. Norton, 1984.
After the Stroke: A Journal. New York: W. W. Norton, 1988.

Essays and Other Writings

"The Rewards of Living a Solitary Life." *New York Times*, 8 April 1974: 35.
Writings on Writing. Orono, ME: Puckerbrush Press, 1980.

Anthology

Daziel, Bradford Dudley, ed. *Sarton Selected: An Anthology of the Journals, Novels, and Poetry of May Sarton*. New York: W. W. Norton, 1991.

Letters

Sarton, Eleanor Mabel. *Letters to May*. Orono, ME: Puckerbrush Press, 1986. Fifty letters selected by May Sarton.

For Children

Punch's Secret. New York: Harper and Row, 1974.
A Walk Through the Woods. New York: Harper and Row, 1976.

Studies of May Sarton

Blouin, Lenora P. *May Sarton: A Bibliography*. Metuchen, NJ: Scarecrow Press, 1978.
Code, Lorraine. "Persons and Others." *Power, Gender, and Values*. Ed. Judith Genova. Edmonton, Alberta, Canada: Academic Printing and Publishing, 1987.
Gaskill, Gayle. "The Mystery of the Mother and the Muse in May Sarton's *Mrs. Stevens Hears the Mermaids Singing*." *Notes on Modern American Literature* 8.1 (1984): n. pag.
Heilbrun, Carolyn G. "May Sarton's Memoirs," *May Sarton Woman Poet*. Ed. Constance Hunting. Orono, ME: National Poetry Foundation, Inc., at University of Maine at Orono, 1982. 43–52.
Hunting, Constance, ed. *May Sarton: Woman and Poet*. Orono, ME: National Poetry Foundation, Inc., at University of Maine at Orono, 1982.
Innes, Charlotte. "Sarton Becomes Herself: Or Does She? A Writer Distilled." *Lambda Book Report: A Review of Contemporary Gay and Lesbian Literature* 2.11 (1991): 22–23.
May Sarton: A Self-Portrait. Marita Simpson and Martha Wheelock. New York: W. W. Norton, 1982. A companion to the Ishtar Film, made by filmmakers Simpson and Wheelock.
Robitaille, Stephen, and Bill Suchy. *May Sarton: Writing in the Upward Years*. Video-

cassette, 1991. Distributed by Terra Nova Films, 9848 South Winchester Avenue, Chicago, IL 60643.

Sibley, Agnes. *May Sarton*. New York: Twayne, 1972.

Springer, Marlene. "As We Shall Be: May Sarton and Aging." *Frontiers* 5.2 (1981): 46–49.

Stone, Deborah. "In Love with Solitude." *Yankee* September 1976: 92–95 + .

Time for Being: May Sarton, Poet and Novelist. Tape 5 of the series *Shaping a Fulfilling Life, Part 2*. Dodson Gray Roundtable Conferences for Professional Women, Four Linden Square, Wellesley, MA 02181. 1978 Conference for Professional Women: Managing Lifespace.

World of Light: A Portrait of May Sarton. 16mm, 30 minute documentary color film. Ishtar, 305 East 11th Street, New York, NY 10003. (212) 477–3702.

SARAH SCHULMAN (1958–   )
Victoria Stagg Elliott

BIOGRAPHY

Sarah Schulman, both Jewish and a New Yorker to the core, was born in Greenwich Village and grew up around Manhattan with a brother and a sister, both of whom also grew up to be writers.

As a child, she was often read to from books such as *Goodnight, Moon* and *Where the Wild Things Are*. As she grew, she read books on her own like *Harriet the Spy* and *The Pushcart Wars*. Schulman said in a personal interview that the discovery of *The Diary of Anne Frank* was very important to her.

After attending Hunter High, a New York public high school, Schulman attended the University of Chicago, where she got her first taste of writing by publishing a couple of articles in the university newspaper, *The Chicago Maroon*. She also became involved in a women's group, one of her earliest political involvements. Schulman said, "There were two women's groups on campus. One was straight. One was gay, but I was in the straight one."

She then moved back to New York, settling on the lower east side. She studied under Audre Lorde at Hunter College and eventually received her degree from Empire State College.

After returning to New York, she waitressed, wrote for *Womanews*, a New York City feminist newspaper, and published over seventy articles in feminist, gay, and progressive publications. Out of her experiences at *Womanews*, she produced *The Sophie Horowitz Story*, a mystery published in 1984.

That book was followed by *Girls, Visions, and Everything* in 1986 and *After Delores* in 1988.

Her most recent novel, *People in Trouble*, published early in 1991, is certainly the most controversial of her books and deals with ACT-UP (AIDS Coalition to Unleash Power), the AIDS crisis, and the effects of the epidemic on people's lives. Her book *Empathy* was released late in 1992, and she has already begun work on her sixth novel, which will be called *Rat Bohemia*.

While Schulman doesn't plan to write another mystery in the style of *The Sophie Horowitz Story*, she does plan to continue writing fiction, a vocation she describes as "addictive."

Schulman has lived on New York's lower east side for the past eleven years and has been a member of ACT-UP since 1987.

MAJOR WORKS AND THEMES

"I follow in the tradition of Jewish neurotic writers," Sarah Schulman remarked in a personal interview. While Jewishness is never the central theme in any of Schulman's novels, it is always present even when she tries to erase it. An ever-present theme is politics, even when the characters are not directly involved with organizations or even read the feminist newspaper. The stories, all gritty and urban, tackle violence, fear, and love. And even the most serious stories are told with a fine dry wit.

Schulman's protagonists are ordinary women. The don't run corporations. They aren't pretending to be Dyke 007. They are not idealistic, and they suffer broken hearts.

Schulman's first book, *The Sophie Horowitz Story*, is her only mystery novel and the one with the most emphasis on being Jewish. Sophie, the title character, is a writer for *Feminist News*, a fictional New York newspaper. She spends her time looking for Germaine Covington and Laura Wolfe, two notorious feminists; chasing down good cheesecake; working sixty hours a week; bathing with her weekend lover; and falling in love with a straight woman. And while all this is going on, she has to worry about Women Against Bad Things, a radical group that always protests other feminist groups.

Some of the most humorous moments in the book are when Sophie's imagination runs wild. At one point she is afraid that the FBI, the police, and everybody else is after her. Schulman injects with a quick wit:

First, I'd hitch to Montreal, a wedding band on my left hand for protection. I'd say my husband is in the service. The truckers would tell me their army stories. Then, I'd hop a tanker for Europe where I would spend the rest of my life under an assumed name. I tried out aliases: Emma Goldman. No, too obvious . . . Emma Goldstein. (53–54)

Schulman's 1986 novel, *Girls, Visions, and Everything*, features Lila Futuransky, a dyke on the go. She dates, has sex, performs in theater, and generally wanders about. She is a woman without a past. Her future is uncertain; it is neither bleak nor promising. While Sophie Horowitz's Jewishness is a major part of her character, Lila's Jewishness takes a back seat to her lesbianism.

In order to completely take away the main character's Jewishness in *After Delores*, Schulman leaves her unnamed. We know that she is a waitress and that her lover, Delores, dumped her for a yuppie. In an interview in *Visibilities, The Lesbian Magazine* in early 1989, Schulman explained the narrator's anonymity. "The narrator is unnamed because taking away her name took away her ethnicity. . . . I couldn't write the Jewish character without being really funny. I didn't want to be that funny this time. . . . Later people told me it was funny anyway. It's deadpan humor."

After Delores is a departure from Schulman's other three books. It is by far the funniest and the most non-conventional of her works. When discussing Coco Flores, the unnamed protagonist's good and dependable friend, Schulman writes,

If everybody's got a best friend, I guess she's mine. She's always been a good talker, but she learned to listen since she started working as a beautician. We met when she was managing an all-girl punk band called Useless Phlegm. Their name accurately described both their music and their personalities. When Coco suggested changing it to Warm Spit, they fired her. (59)

Another novel, *People in Trouble*, is about the AIDS crisis in New York and is told from three distinct, yet intertwined, views. Molly is a lesbian working at a movie theater box office a few days a week and living in a rent-controlled apartment. Kate, a successful painter, is her lover. Kate, however, is married to Pete, a lighting designer.

The most fascinating aspect of this novel's characters is not their quirky personalities but their responses to the crisis and each other even though they are not directly affected by AIDS. They are just completely surrounded by it. They run in and out of each other's circles, they radicalize each other, and they piss each other off.

Schulman's characters rarely leave New York's lower east side, which sometimes creates an insular feeling as in *Girls, Visions, and Everything* or an alone-in-a-crowd feeling as in *People in Trouble*. But the most important aspect of her fiction is the psychological drama played out as characters grow and change.

CRITICAL RECEPTION

Schulman started receiving attention from the press with the publication of *After Delores*, her first commercially published work.

Since then she has made some definite inroads into mainstream publishing—*People in Trouble* was even reviewed by *Mademoiselle*—but not all the responses have been positive, and sometimes the reception has been downright chilly.

Feminist Review, in its summer 1990 issue, charged: "If you think that killing is sometimes justified, in fact necessary, then it will be possible to enjoy this book for the energy and excitement of its writing" (119–21). Linda Simple, who wrote the article, reported that Schulman's writing was good, but that she preferred *The Dog Collar Murders* by Barbara Wilson because of its investigation of political concerns.

While *After Delores* only started to stir up trouble, *People in Trouble* was almost a full-fledged controversy. Critically, the book was well received. Politically, however, because the novel encourages lesbians and gays to work together to fight the AIDS crisis, Schulman has been accused of sexism, homophobia, and ''lesbian incorrectness.''

''*People in Trouble* is an emotional call to action'' reported *Nation* in its May 21, 1990, issue (715–16). On that level and on a literary level, the book works very well. The controversy probably comes from the fact that the book is too much of a challenge to people who have attempted to ignore the AIDS crisis or to just wish it away.

BIBLIOGRAPHY

Works by Sarah Schulman

The Sophie Horowitz Story. Tallahassee, FL: Naiad Press, 1984.
Girls, Visions, and Everything. Seattle: Seal Press, 1986.
After Delores. New York: Plume Books, 1988.
People in Trouble. New York: Plume Books, 1991.

Studies of Sarah Schulman

Conversation With Sarah Schulman. *Visibilities, The Lesbian Magazine* 3 (January/February 1989): 8–11.
Simple, Linda. Book Review: *After Delores*. *Feminist Review* 35 (Summer 1990): 119–21.
Book Review: *People in Trouble*. *Mademoiselle* 96 (March 1990): 112.
Book Review: *People in Trouble*. *Nation* 250 (May 21, 1990): 715–16.
Straight Shots. *Mother Jones* 15 (July/August 1990): 14.

PATRICIA ROTH SCHWARTZ
(1946–)
Jenney Milner

BIOGRAPHY

Patricia Roth Schwartz was born on October 12, 1946, in Charleston, West Virginia. Her mother, Virginia Austin Roth, a housewife, was from a lower-middle-class background of Scots-English descent. Her father, Rexford Frazier Roth, was an insurance executive from a working-class background and was of Waldensian-Moravian-Scots-Irish descent. A sister, Susan Austin Roth, was born in 1950. The family lived in Charleston and Wheeling, West Virginia, until they moved to Los Angeles in 1959, and then to West Hartford, Connecticut, in 1961.

Schwartz's first published work was a poem in *American Girl* magazine in 1963. In 1968, she received a B.A. in English composition, *magna cum laude*, from Mount Holyoke College, and in 1970, an M.A. in English literature from Trinity College. During this time, her experiences of discrimination as a woman trying to find meaningful work led her into the women's movement. Volunteer work for the Hartford Region YWCA (Young Women's Christian Association) evolved into a full-time position as director of Women's Issues.

During these watershed years, Schwartz began to question her sexual identity and came out as a lesbian in 1975. In the fall of 1976, she left the YWCA, her husband of eight and a half years, Joel L. Schwartz (who remains a friend), and a woman lover of less than a year. She went to live alone for the first time and began to write more seriously, attempting fiction as well as poetry. A feminist writing workshop led by poet Joan Shapiro broke a writing silence dating from college.

In 1978, after a job in community college administration, she returned to graduate school, attending Antioch/New England, to earn a degree in counseling psychology. An internship on a pediatric ward with terminally ill children was an influential experience, deepening her sense of spirituality which was already enhanced by involvement with women's groups exploring feminist and goddess-inspired ritual. During this time, Schwartz also joined the Blue Spruce Poets, a feminist writers' group founded by Shapiro, and she helped form the Calliope Feminist Theatre, which used improvisational humor as a vehicle for feminist issues.

Schwartz received her counseling degree in 1980 and began a private practice, which eventually specialized in incest survivors and adult children from dysfunctional families. Her critical writing was widely published, especially by Boston's gay and lesbian newspaper, *Bay Windows*. She also penned a humorous column for that paper and has since served as the women's poetry editor. When three of Schwartz's short stories were accepted for publication within a short span of time, she began to write fiction much more seriously. She attended the Feminist Women's Writing Workshops in New York each summer between 1985 and 1987. She also participated in Joan Larkin's workshop at Blueberry Cove, Maine, where she became a member of the newly formed Fly by Night writers' group.

In 1991, Schwartz relocated to central New York to fulfill a dream of creating an organic herb farm. Schwartz is now a part-time college instuctor, part-time therapist, and owner of Weeping Willow Farm/Heartshome Herbals.

MAJOR WORKS AND THEMES

In 1978, the Blue Spruce Poets brought out Schwartz's book of poetry, *Hungers*, as part of a collective publishing effort funded by Aetna Life. In *Hungers*, Schwartz disengages from the "congenial cell" of her marriage and reveals her burgeoning, often bitterly terminated, passions for women. The hungers depicted in these often-autobiographical poems are exorbitant and unfulfilled; the poet rails against the failures, traps, and abuses of love in a system that makes love impossible because "We cannot experience desire without anger: / we wear wounds" ("Choices"). Yet for Schwartz, playfulness and awe remain abundant, even in sorrow; frequently the memory of truncated joy is sustained by an electrified jumble of all the senses, making her words buzz with pleasure: "stringing our days together like fat, / wooden beads in primary colors." And she is buoyed by common miracles: the imagination, passion in winter ("my body a radiant object / in a polar zone"), and hope.

In 1989, Schwartz captured a place in the literary landscape with the publication of *The Names of the Moons of Mars* (New Victoria), which won the 1990 Lambda Literary Award for the category "lesbian debut." In this volume of short fiction, Schwartz's narratives are constructed of concise dialogue, minute observations of the surroundings, and biting humor. Characters frequently deny or run away from their troubles, but they ultimately confront the problem with determination and spunk. Anne, a lesbian feminist lawyer in the opening story, "Feather," expresses this pervasive theme. "Any one of us can only run so far so long. Eventually we've got to turn and face what we're running from." In

"Keys," a survivor of childhood sexual abuse flees her home and her newly surfaced memories. She quits the "other self who was capable of feeling" and drives in a frenzy from Massachusetts to Florida. There she discovers, interspersed with garish stretches of shopping malls, enclaves of fragile but persevering species like the Key deer, whose footprint at birth is the size of a thumbnail. Rare ecosystems where "other kinds of growth become possible" become both a metaphor and an inspiration for Sally's transformation from denial and flight to self-acceptance.

Several of Schwartz's finest stories are vivid depictions of dysfunctional families. In the title piece, Anna moves in with her retired parents after Bradford, her second husband, leaves town with her jogging partner. Schwartz's fluid prose is a wide-angle lens that carefully locates its subjects within the "green brilliance" of the suburbs. The physical architecture is a precisely drawn reflection of the emotional terrain: "Ma" spends the day in her bathroom "getting ready," while Anna's father George holes up in his "decked out" garage, which he calls "Piazza Giorgio." The kitsch and unintended camp of middle-class U.S. life provides a darkly humorous backdrop for Schwartz's dissection of tense family relationships. The remarkable denouement of this story features the return of Sheila, the jogging partner, who abandons Bradford to rejoin Anna for more exercise and business ventures.

Schwartz's sympathetic portraits often skirt the stereotypical images of lesbians and emphasize instead the creative way that women—straight and lesbian—craft relationships with other women. Marty proclaims her love of women in "Intensive Care" ("I calm myself . . . with soothing fantasies of women," she declares), yet in the story her sexual identity remains ambiguous. "Spinsters" relates the adventures of a provincial actress who tries to build a career in New York City; she grows increasingly close to her friend Amanda, who concedes she's not a lesbian, yet announces cheerily that "some of us were meant to be spinsters, plain and simple. Why fight it?"

The lives and concerns of out lesbians are also richly explored. Schwartz's subjects are as varied as the epic drama and coming-out story of "Jesse," a working-class teenager who emerges successfully from an abusive childhood; the politicization of an older lesbian couple when some young dykes move in next door ("It's like unearthing an alien civilization," says Eleanor, the protagonist, "one that you know you've been part of . . . somehow"); and the struggle of a woman whose friend is dying of cancer. In this delicate story, "Bodies," the narrator shuttles grumpily between her persistently empathic lover and the health club, where she leaves nasty notes in the suggestion box (" 'Why don't bodies last forever?' I wrote on my paper today. 'Why aren't you lobbying for more funding for things like AIDS and cancer and the heartbreak of psoriasis?' "). Schwartz's dazzling moments of humor transform this story into an uplifting one.

In 1993, New Victoria will publish a volume of humor by Schwartz, compiled in part from columns she published in *Bay Windows*. Schwartz is currently writing a novel and working on a new collection of humor about rural life.

CRITICAL RECEPTION

The Names of the Moons of Mars has been widely and universally acclaimed in the feminist and lesbian/gay press from Boston to Australia. Reviewers have emphasized Schwartz's craft. The *Gay Community News* critic Nan Donald writes that "Schwartz clearly revels in language" and that potentially heavy-handed "issues like poverty, class privilege, elitism, and 'activism as narcotic' are deftly woven into the fabric of the whole."(13). Philip Gambone, the reviewer in Boston's gay and lesbian weekly, *Bay Windows*, comments that "her prose style can be colloquial or lyric, direct or intricate, spontaneous or carefully modulated"(16). Liz Galst in the *Women's Review of Books* praises Schwartz's "spunky, visual" fiction and "vital, talky stories [that] bring life to the difficult choices the characters make and illuminate the world that constricts them" (11).

Reviewers have also been impressed by Schwartz's versatility and her insistence on tackling issues that both encompass and transcend the lesbian community. In an unusual decision for a gay paper, *Bay Windows* assigned *The Names of the Moons of Mars* to a man for review; he asserts in his article that "in the best stories . . . the deep concerns of lesbians, of women, become concerns for us all. 'What is all the pain for?' the narrator asks in the final paragraph of 'Bodies.' . . . This brave, imaginative, deft, and moving book explores that question for all of us." In *Gay Community News*, the reviewer commends Schwartz for exploring straight characters and themes as ably as lesbian ones. In addition, this reviewer writes, "Unlike many lesbian authors who keep biological families invisible, or at the best one-dimensional, Schwartz focuses a keen eye on parents and other relations" (13).

New American Writing, in conjunction with the United States Information Agency's Book Program, included *The Names of the Moons of Mars* in its 1990 international book exhibit. The exhibit represented the best of the small presses in the United States. In published interviews, Schwartz has outspokenly challenged the ghettoization of lesbian literature and has said "I want *everyone* to read my book!" However, as a proudly lesbian-feminist book from a small lesbian press, *The Names of the Moons of Mars* has received no attention from mainstream critics.

BIBLIOGRAPHY

Works by Patricia Roth Schwartz

Hungers. South Windsor, CT: Blue Spruce Press, 1978.
The Names of the Moons of Mars. Norwich, VT: New Victoria Publishers, 1989.

Studies of Patricia Roth Schwartz

Barnes, Noreen C. "Reality for Women Uncovered" *Bay Area Reporter* July 27, 1989.

Donald, Nan. "Broken Hearts, Messed Up Families, and New Beginnings." *Gay Community News* December 17–23, 1989. 13.

Galst, Liz. "Everyday Lesbians." *Women's Review of Books* (January 1990). 11.

Gambone, Philip. "Anthems Away." *Bay Windows* (Aug. 10, 1989). 16–17.

O'Sullivan, Kimberly. Review of *The Names of the Moons of Mars. Campaign Australia.* November 1990.

Scott, Suzanne. Review of *The Names of the Moons of Mars. Belles Lettres* 4:4 (Summer). 22.

Vine, Elynor, Review of *The Names of the Moons of Mars. Visibilities* (March/April 1990). 22.

SANDRA SCOPPETTONE
(1936–   )
Elizabeth E. Reed

BIOGRAPHY

Sandra Scoppettone stands out from the ranks of contemporary writers in many respects and especially through the portrayal of her new lesbian detective, Lauren Laurano. *Everything You Have Is Mine* (1991), the first in this series, is also a first in the annals of lesbian detective fiction: it has a mainstream publisher, Little, Brown and Company. The detective bears other similarities to the author besides success in a mainstream-dominated profession, although some of the biographical discrepancies are more interesting than the parallels, such as the fact that Scoppettone did not attend college and did not train with the FBI. For Scoppettone, the facts of her biography include that she was born in Morristown, New Jersey, grew up in South Orange, went to live in New York City at eighteen, and began to support herself as a writer. She has written twelve novels, of which three mysteries appeared under the pseudonym Jack Early (one winning the Shamus Award), and two addressed the issues of gay and lesbian identity to a young adult audience. In addition, she is a playwright and scriptwriter and a founding member of Sisters in Crime.

Perhaps the most significant biographical facts are available to the reader of Sandra Scoppettone because of her candid responses in interviews. Without her claiming to see herself as a role model, there are implications in what she has revealed that she is willing to make use of her life experience in this way. Scoppettone has been out as a writer since 1954. Her book jackets let us know that she lives with writer Linda Crawford, upon whom Lauren Laurano's partner, Kip Adams, is clearly based. A recovering alcoholic with nineteen years of sobriety, the only child of an alcoholic mother who once accompanied her to a gay bar to see what it was like, Sandra Scoppettone continues to explore those experiences that her life has given to her with the same compassion with which she observes her New York neighborhood. Her internal exploration has been equally intensive. After writing three novels that dealt with incest, she discovered that she, too, was an incest survivor.

MAJOR WORKS AND THEMES

Two of Scoppettone's published works (and the forthcoming *I'll Be Leaving You Always*) contain explicit themes of lesbian self-identity in a heterosexually oriented setting that runs the gamut from heterosexism to homophobia. In *Everything You Have Is Mine*, hopeful notes are found in the strength of the community of friends that supports, or, at times, tolerates the time-honored single-mindedness of Lauren's profession. Scoppettone's genius lies in her ability to construct a murder mystery plot and then to surround it with social commentary.

The alienation of the female detective characterizes detective fiction in general, whether gay or straight, and probably derives from the old, sexist image of the American hero popularized by television in the fifties. Scoppettone has instead gone back to an earlier tradition, that of the couple who ferociously love each other (i.e., Nick and Nora Charles), except that Kip does not participate in the sleuthing, only in the loving. But of the list of characters who precede Lauren (and whose ghosts she summons), none provides a model of living fully in the world in which one also earns a living. And nowhere else in this more recent branch of the detective novel can we find a description of sexual satisfaction between two women who have been lovers for eleven years.

Scoppettone's inclusion of sex as an unselfconscious and integral part of a lesbian relationship goes back to her 1976 young adult novel, *Happy Endings Are All Alike,* and her frank treatment of homosexuality (in this case male) precedes that by four years. *Trying Hard To Hear You* (1974) was named an ALA (American Library Association) Best Book for Young Adults despite the controversy it caused. With her usual deftness for first lines, Scoppettone begins *Happy Endings*: ''Even though Jaret Tyler had no guilt or shame about her love affair with Peggy Danziger she knew there were plenty of people in this world who would put it down.'' The range of responses in Gardener's Point, as in the New York City Lauren Laurano inhabits, is wide and, sadly, believable. The mind of the rapist is presented to us through unidentified journal entries long before we can connect them to the plot, a highly effective structure that would appear again in the 1985 *Razzamatazz.* The discomfort of Jaret's mother Kay is introduced to us on page one, whereas we wait, uneasily, to learn what both fathers think. The adults in this story do not find language adequate to communicate their love or their fear. It would be wonderful to say that the absence of wholehearted acceptance by even loving adults is now dated, but that is not true in most households where lesbians are struggling to come out. What has changed since 1978, however, is the prospect of a childless future, so that thankfully young women now do not have to ask their parents what Jaret does: ''Does it bother you that you'll never have any grandchildren from me?'' (198).

CRITICAL RECEPTION

Everything You Have Is Mine was widely and positively received, including appearances in Herbert Mitgang's column from the daily *New York Times* reprinted in newspapers across the country. Scoppettone sees the *Times* as having legitimized the book, particularly by referring to her handling of the lesbian relationship as romantic. This review, she adds, "is a big moment for *us*" (Lassell 93). Many reviewers applauded the relationship between Lauren and Kip, as well as the cameo portraits of other lesbian and gay members of their circle. Some appeared less comfortable than others with how to describe this new detective, and a common occurrence is the use of "also a lesbian" or "also gay" at the end of a list of other attributes. Mitgang calls Laurano a "feisty Manhattan lesbian," and several reviewers provide her sexual identity right off. Alix Madrigal, writing for the *San Francisco Chronicle*, refers to the two as "happily coupled" and as a "lesbian version of Nick and Nora Charles . . . but sexier, more tender and more down to earth" (9). Dan Gillmor, in the *Detroit Free Press*, refers to "love in this book" without regard to the sexual identities of the various groups of characters. No one, however, notes the fact that the private investigator (and narrator) herself repeatedly calls this relationship a "marriage." *American Woman* magazine has the only known review that neglects to mention lesbianism, although *Mystery News* seems to have used the ambiguous name of Lauren's "lover" as a way of avoiding the issue. Of the few articles that placed the book within lesbian literature, only Susanna J. Sturgis raised the question of problems it shares with "most" contemporary lesbian fiction; notably that the women are "drop-dead gorgeous—at forty-something— and their sex lives are scintillating—after 11 years in a committed relationship" (16).

Happy Endings Are All Alike received the fewest reviews of any of Sandra Scoppettone's novels. All the reviews address the lesbian relationship that is the book's raison d'être, and perhaps the most surprising applause came from *Catholic Library World*'s anonymous reviewer, who wrote: "[*Happy Endings Are All Alike* is] a candid novel about a very controversial subject, lesbianism. The author handles the topic delicately, yet, frankly. She does not back down on moral values but faces the issue in such a manner that it could lead to an intelligent, unbiased discussion" (117). A more comprehensive understanding of the novel's scope, however, appeared in *The Lion and the Unicorn* in Geraldine DeLuca's piece entitled "Taking True Risks: Controversial Issues in New Young Adult Novels." DeLuca addresses the homophobia of those "who feel threatened by homosexuality or who achieve a vapid sense of superiority, regardless of the emptiness of their own lives, by virtue of feeling 'normal' " and recognizes that in the midst of this "sensing where one's happiness actually lies, and being willing to struggle for it, is by far the braver and wiser choice" (129–30).

BIBLIOGRAPHY

Works by Sandra Scoppettone

Suzuki Beane. New York: Harper & Row, 1961.
Trying Hard To Hear You. New York: Harper & Row, 1974; New York: Bantam, 1976.
The Late Great Me. New York: G. P. Putnam's, 1976; New York: Bantam, 1977.
Some Unknown Person. New York: G. P. Putnam's, 1977; New York: Bantam, 1978.
Happy Endings Are All Alike. New York: Harper & Row, 1978; New York: Dell, 1979.
Such Nice People. New York: G. P. Putnam's, 1980; New York: Fawcett Crest, 1981.
Long Time Between Kisses. New York: Harper & Row, 1982; New York: Bantam, 1984.
Innocent Bystanders. New York: New American Library, 1983; New York: Signet, 1984.
Playing Murder. New York: Harper & Row, 1985; New York: Harper Keypoint, 1987.
Everything You Have Is Mine. Boston: Little, Brown, 1991.
I'll Be Leaving You Always. Boston: Little, Brown, 1992.

Works by Jack Early (Pseudonym of Scoppettone)

A Creative Kind of Killer. New York: Franklin Watts, 1985; New York: Ballantine, 1985.
Razzamatazz. New York: Franklin Watts, 1985; New York: Paperjacks, 1986.
Donato and Daughter. New York: Dutton, 1988; New York: Signet, 1969.

Studies of Sandra Scoppettone

"Books and Periodicals." *Wilson Library Bulletin* (April 1991): 105.
DeLuca, Geraldine. "Taking True Risks: Controversial Issues in New Young Adult Novels." *The Lion and the Unicorn* 3, no. 2 (Winter 1979–80): 125–48.
"*Everything You Have Is Mine*." *Mystery News* (March/April 1991): n. pag.
Gillmor, Dan. "Browsing." *Detroit Free Press* (May 1, 1991): sec. D3.
"*Happy Endings Are All Alike*." *Catholic Library World* 50, no. 3 (October 1978): 117.
Lassell, Michael. "Murder She Writes." *Advocate* (July 2, 1991): 93.
Madrigal, Alix. "A Very 90's Detective." *San Francisco Chronicle Review* (March 31, 1991): 9.
McQuade, Molly. "Books." *American Woman* (July/August 1991): 65.
Mitgang, Herbert. "Feminist Detectives, One Familiar, One New." *New York Times* (May 6, 1991): C19.
Sturgis, Susanna J. "Laptop, Vampire Aid Women Sleuths." *Martha's Vineyard Times* (June 6, 1991): 16.

SUSAN SHERMAN (1939–   )
Joellen Hiltbrand

BIOGRAPHY

Susan Sherman was born in Philadelphia on July 10, 1939, and was raised in Los Angeles by her mother, a first-generation Jewish American, and her step-father, a Russian Jewish immigrant. In 1957, Sherman moved to Berkeley, California, to attend the University of California, where she was introduced to the world of poetry, jazz music, and political activism (she participated in the House Un-American Activities Committee demonstrations). In 1960 she was awarded the university poetry prize, the Emily Chamberlein Cook Poetry Award, and she received her B.A. in English and philosophy in 1961.

After graduating from college, Sherman moved to New York City. She was active in the poetry scene at the Deux Mégots, and later at Le Metro, where she helped co-ordinate readings. She was poetry editor and wrote theater criticism for the *Village Voice* and had nine plays produced off-off-Broadway. She taught at the experimental Free School of New York and the Alternate University. She received her M.A. in philosophy from Hunter College in 1967 and traveled to Cuba to attend the Cultural Conference in Havana in 1968, a trip that profoundly influenced her life and work. She returned to Cuba a year later for an extended stay. Sherman has also traveled to Chile (1972) and Nicaragua (1983).

Sherman was editor of *IKON* magazine from 1965 to 1969, when it ceased publication, and became editor again when it resumed publication in 1982. She also coordinates IKON cultural and educational presentations.

She has been, and continues to be, actively involved in many political struggles, including those for women's liberation, gay and lesbian rights, the Central American peace movement, and anti-racism and anti-apartheid struggles.

Sherman teaches philosophy and an elective course titled "Creativity and Social Change" at Parsons School of Design. She has been a writer-in-residence and was involved in Poets in the Schools in New York from 1974 to 1979.

Sherman's awards include a New York Foundation for the Arts Poetry Fellowship (1990), a Creative Artists Public Service Grant for Poetry (1976–1977), and editor's awards from the New York State Council on the Arts (1986) and the Coordinating Committee of Literary Magazines (1985). She served as a juror on the Maryland State Council on the Arts Poetry Panel (1990–1991) and the Delaware State Council on the Arts Poetry & Non-Fiction Panels (1989–1990).

MAJOR WORKS AND THEMES

Trained in poetry and philosophy, Susan Sherman uses both disciplines, combined with her political commitment to change, to investigate definitions of concepts: What is community? What is love? How is it expressed? What values shape our worlds? What are the possibilities of change, of relationship, of poetry?

Sherman's voice is firmly placed in the world. She sees not only an interrelationship of people, but an interrelationship of movements, a world in which we are all connected. Her poems and essays reflect her understanding of European philosophical traditions such as Marxism and phenomenology, namely, the emphasis on human interconnectedness and on change as the result of internal struggle. In the content of her work, as well as in the structure of that work on the page, she emphasizes process, the struggle to connect words with meaning and to connect, with words, to other human beings.

For Sherman, poetry, lesbian relationships, and political involvement are all part of revolution and change. They are creative forces within a linguistic, political world that obscures and falsely and arbitrarily defines our human experience.

Her books, *Areas of Silence* (1963), *Women Poems, Love Poems* (1975), *Shango de Ima: A Yoruba Mystery Play* (1970), *With Anger/With Love* (1974), *The Color of the Heart: Writing from Struggle & Change 1959–1990* (1990), as well as the collaborative collection *We Stand Our Ground: Three Women, Their Vision, Their Poems* (1988, written with Kimiko Hahn and Gale Jackson), investigate what it means to love, to connect, to change, in our interconnected and largely falsely defined world.

Women Poems, Love Poems was published in 1975 by Two & Two Press and contains illustrations by Chilean artist Maria Luisa Senoret. The fourteen love poems echo with Sherman's relationships with women. The poems deal with the themes of connection and loss: our memories of those we love, the intangible presence of a lover, even long after she's gone. Poems such as "Chatter" and "A Poem" struggle with the very nature of poetry, the process of stringing together individual words and imbuing them with meaning, a process that never fully embodies the depth of human feeling.

"Love Poem 12/16/71" discusses another major theme of Sherman's work, namely, how one defines and places oneself in the world. Sherman writes that her poetry is at her core and informs her reaching out to individuals and the world. She describes herself as wanting endlessly to feel and to investigate what she calls that question "that is our lives."

Shango de Ima: A Yoruba Mystery Play was written by Cuban playwright Pepe Carril. The Spanish version was first presented by the Teatro Guinol, Consigo Nacional de Culture in Havana, Cuba. Sherman's English adaptation of the play was first presented by the La Mama Dance Drama Theatre, on January 1, 1970. The play is a written version of various Yoruba legends about the orisha Shango, and it reflects Cuba's rich Afro-Cuban heritage.

Sherman saw the play produced in Cuba in 1968 and wrote the English adaptation in 1970. Her preface to *Shango*, in which she writes about her experiences in Cuba, reflects her developing artistic and political sensibility. To speak about one aspect of a poem separate from the others, she claims, is to only partially explain the poem. Similarly, she explains, to describe Cuba with words obscures and diminishes the unity of the whole. The revolution, she writes, is about people, people creating as individuals and as groups, so that their separate creations can become one great work. Cuba, as poetry, as interrelated community, is whole and can be dealt with "with anger and with love."

With Anger/With Love, obviously, is a continuation of Sherman's investigation of poetics and politics. Throughout this book, Sherman struggles to find a way to articulate her innermost feelings in words, a process akin to fitting an ocean into a river bed. Her poems are full of questions.

Lesbian relationships are prominent in *With Anger/With Love*. In "Ten Years After," Sherman writes that she is "haunted" by everyone she has known or will know. She writes that she is "driven" by love. In "Lilith of the Wildwood, of the Fair Places," she embraces Eve, the outlaw, the identity she has been taught to hate and to fear, and comes to trust the knowledge contained within her body. "Love Poem/For a Capricorn" describes how Sherman approaches her lover: with all her years, her experiences, her emotional and material possessions. "How a Face Changes" describes the process by which strangers become familiar, loved, the people who occupy our days. Contrarily, "Second Thought" speaks of the movement of lovers from present into the ever-increasing frame of the past, a theme that continues in "Areas of Silence." Lovers' faces become hazy, their worlds unfamiliar. Typically, the poems in this book *connect*: the past, present, and future; one woman to another; one culture to another.

The two prose pieces in *With Anger/With Love* resound with Sherman's interrelated themes of creativity, change, language, and philosophy. In "Creativity & Change," Sherman, citing Marx, writes that the transformational nature of creativity brings about change. She links factual history to ideas to form the base for individual and community action. The words *creativity* and *change* denote relationship, ongoing process. Culture and art are inseparable from the whole of human daily existence. "The Language of Art" is an essay in which Sherman discusses dialectical philosophy and its search for the relationship between things such as experience and thought.

We Stand Our Ground is a collaborative work written by Sherman, Kimiko

Hahn, and Gale Jackson. The book opens with a section entitled "Three Voices Together: A Collage," a conversation among the women made up of letters, discussions, and taped conversations recorded between July and October 1987. In this section, Sherman writes about her origins, by which she means not only her birthplace or familiar origins, but everything that has moved or defined her. She writes in more detail about her family's class background and Judaism, her political and poetic beginnings. She discusses her search for meaning in her poetry, the way she connects personal, political and philosophical concerns in her work. The motivation to collaborate with people from different cultures, races, class backgrounds—the fight against isolation and artificial limitations—informs much of her discussion in this section.

We Stand Our Ground also contains poetry by the three authors. In "What I Want," Sherman longs to be free of her unending need for love, free of her constant observation of the world, but concludes the poem with the knowledge that she is bound to work for change, bound to hold and be held. "Morning Poem" expresses Sherman's struggles with time, which is both our enemy and our friend, and the ways we continue in our life cycles, only to find ourselves changed and yet the same. "Opening Stanzas" discusses the small and seemingly inconsequential details one remembers about past lovers. "A Small Question" is a poem of directives: Sherman tells the reader not to look for her in any extraordinary symbol such as the sun and the ocean. She is ordinary, present, and as she states in the last line, she still believes in love.

The Color of the Heart is a collection of Sherman's prose, poetry, and essays from 1959 to 1990. Grouped in six sections, the topics range from her early cultural, sexual, and political experiences during her undergraduate years, to trips to Central America and Cuba, ideological division within the women's movement in the 1970s, identity and sexuality, Laconian psychoanalysis, and the effects of deconstruction on politics and art.

The section entitled "Sexuality and Identity" consists of eight poems and an essay, "Women, Identity, Sexuality: A Re-examination," edited from a talk presented at a feminist conference in France in 1982. The poems draw upon Sherman's themes of loss, change, and yearning, and on her struggles with language to express meaning.

In the essay, Sherman claims that any discussion of identity must include an examination of the relationship of an individual to her background, to her community, and to history. She writes, "What people we choose to surround ourselves with is one of the most important choices we make. And no less important is whether that choice is ours to make" (127). Sherman writes that as long as women's struggles are defined in terms of sexuality (the war between the sexes, reproductive rights, lesbianism as an issue of sexual choice), women will continue to exist within a sexually defined context, a context that obscures the roles of class and race in our relationships to each other and to the world at large.

Sherman cites the 1970 Radicalesbians essay "The Woman-Identified Woman" for its emphasis on primary relationships between women, relationships not needing male validation or approval in order to exist. Asserting the need for women to work in conjunction with other revolutionary movements, she cautions white lesbians to pay heed to the much-needed energy and leadership of strong communities of women of color within the feminist community. She cautions white lesbians to learn from their own struggles with the feminist movement and not to make divisive mistakes. The feminist and lesbian movement must be strong, but flexible enough to change as times warrant, "remembering that a change in labels, in outward form, is meaningless unless it grows from a change in attitude and is accompanied by . . . a radical alteration in our way of existing in the world" (136).

CRITICAL RECEPTION

Susan Sherman's work has been respected for the risks she takes and for the breadth of her political/emotional vision. Although her work has been reviewed in various newspapers and journals, the lesbian content of her work is mentioned peripherally in most of the reviews. Jan Clausen, however, in her review of *With Anger/With Love* and *Women Poems, Love Poems* ("That Question That Is Our Lives," 1977) speaks of Sherman's lesbianism and her political vision as the two facts basic to her work. Clausen writes that Sherman's work challenges the reader's conceptions of political and lesbian poetry. In her discussion of Sherman's love poetry, Clausen mentions her sensuous natural imagery and states: "She is particularly successful at conveying the feeling of identification—at times almost of fusion with the lover—which is perhaps peculiar to lesbian relationships" (71). Clausen praises Sherman's ability to illustrate the connection between her political and love poetry, as well as the connection between her writing life and her life out in the world. She writes: "There is something extraordinary about Susan Sherman's clear vision: passionately desiring freedom, she knows the extent to which she is unfree . . . hers is a thoroughly human courage" (76).

Margaret Randall, in her introduction to *Color of the Heart*, praises Sherman's ability to convey the "fullness of her wisdom and her spirit" (15) in several genres. Randall states that Sherman is a visionary, a writer who insists on taking risks in her life and in her work. She praises Sherman's true, lived commitment to diversity and change, a commitment carried on before those ideas were popular or widely shared.

Sherman's work, Randall asserts, is not separate from her daily life, a life "only half over, but . . . lived thus far to its limits" (11). Hers is a life lived not only in the joy of discovery but also in the questions raised by doubt and fear, questions for which there are not always ready answers. "This is personal and political/cultural history in the deepest sense" (12).

Rachel Guido deVries, in reviewing *We Stand Our Ground*, praises the political vision and urgency of the work. Citing the writers' strong sense of their cultural/ethnic origins, she describes the process of creating a home built out of language and insights that reveal our "otherness." Bobbye Ortiz's review of the same book cites Sherman's ability to convey a wide range of interrelated personal and political experiences. She notes the themes of the passage of time and the loss of lovers and friends, in short the passage of life itself ("Voices Blend" 18). Carol Seajay calls the essays in *The Color of the Heart* "historical, analytical, intensely personal, provocative, and controversial" (99).

BIBLIOGRAPHY

Works by Susan Sherman

Areas of Silence. New York: Hespiridian Press/Hardware Poets Theatre, 1963.
Trans. Preface. *Shango de Ima: A Yoruba Mystery Play*. By Pepe Carril. Garden City: Doubleday & Company, 1971.
With Anger/With Love: Selections: Poems & Prose (1963–1972). Amherst: Mulch Press, 1974.
Women Poems, Love Poems. New York: Two & Two Press, 1975.
We Stand Our Ground: Three Women, Their Vision, Their Poems. With Kimiko Hahn and Gale Jackson. New York: IKON, 1988.
The Color of the Heart: Writing from Struggle & Change, 1959–1990. Willimantic: Curbstone Press, 1990.

Studies of Susan Sherman

Bernikow, Louise. "Out of the Bell Jar." *New Times* 29 October 1976; 46–54.
Clausen, Jan. "That Question That Is Our Lives: The Poetry of Susan Sherman." *Conditions* 1 (April 1977): 66–76.
Davis, Susan E. "Susan Sherman Fuses Art & Politics." *New Directions for Women* March/April 1991: 23.
———. Rev. of *The Color of the Heart: Writing from Struggle & Change, 1959–1990*. *New Directions for Women* March/April 1991: 23.
deVries, Rachel Guido "Making the Beautiful Real." Rev. of *We Stand Our Ground: Three Women, Their Visions, Their Poems*. *Belles Lettres* 4:3 (Spring 1989).
Knauer, Lisa Maya. "A Conversation with Susan Sherman: 'The Color of the Heart' " (includes new poems). *Contact/II* 10, nos. 62–64 (Fall 1991/Spring 1992): 30–40.
McKenna, Shelia. "Manhattan Profile." *New York Newsday* 7 Aug. 1990: 22.
Miller, Beverly. Rev. of *The Color of the Heart: Writing from Struggle & Change, 1959–1990*. *Library Journal* 11 Aug. 1990.
Ortiz, Bobbye. "Voices Blend." Rev. of *We Stand Our Ground: Three Women, Their Vision, Their Poems*. *New Directions for Women* Sept.-Oct. 1989: 18.
Randall, Margaret. Introduction. *The Color of the Heart: Writing from Struggle & Change, 1959–1990*. Willimantic: Curbstone Press, 1990. 7–15.
Reyna, Bessy. Interview with Susan Sherman. *Curbstone Ink* (Spring 1991): 1.
Seajay, Carol. Rev. of *The Color of the Heart: Writing from Struggle & Change, 1959–1990*. *Feminist Bookstore News* 13:3 (Sept.-Oct. 1990): 99.

Sorgen, Carol. "Fleeting Glances." Rev. of *The Color of the Heart: Writing from Struggle & Change, 1959–1990*. *Baltimore Sun* 15 Oct. 1990: A7.

Rev. of *We Stand Our Ground: Three Women, Their Vision, Their Poems*. *Booklist* 7 Sept. 1988: 29.

Rev. of *The Color of the Heart: Writing from Struggle & Change, 1959–1990*. *Book Watch/Midwest Book Review* 11:11 (Nov. 1990).

Rev. of *The Color of the Heart: Writing from Struggle & Change, 1959–1990*. *People's Culture* 2:1 (Sept. 1990): 22.

Rev. of *The Color of the Heart: Writing from Struggle & Change, 1959–1990*. *Publishers Weekly* 237:27 6 July 1990.

SHEILA ORTIZ TAYLOR
(1939–   )
Jeane Harris

BIOGRAPHY

Sheila Ortiz Taylor was born September 25, 1939, in Los Angeles, California, to John Santray Taylor, whom Taylor has described as a "tap dancer, lawyer, sailor, and dream maker," and Juanita Loretta Taylor, who, according to Taylor, was a "Yo-yo painter" (*Faultline* ix). Along with her older sister Sandra, Ortiz Taylor grew up in Los Angeles "participating in barrio culture" (personal letter from Ortiz Taylor, Dec. 26, 1991). Through her mother's family, "thirteen children presided over by [a] Mexican-American grandmother" (*Faultline* ix), Ortiz Taylor benefited from a culturally diverse upbringing that has enriched her life and her fiction.

After completing elementary and junior high school, she attended John Marshall High School, where she wrote poetry and worked on the school paper. One year into her coursework at UCLA (University of California at Los Angeles), Ortiz Taylor married John Leonard Clendenning and moved to Iowa City, Iowa, where she worked full-time at the Hospital School for Handicapped Children and as a secretary in the Physics Department at the University of Iowa. On her return to Los Angeles in 1960, she again enrolled at UCLA and was awarded the Mabel Wilson Richards Fellowship. After transferring to California State University in Northridge, Ortiz Taylor was named Outstanding Student of Language and Literature. She graduated *magna cum laude* in 1963 with a bachelor's degree in English and a minor in Spanish.

The following year Ortiz Taylor completed her master's degree in English at UCLA and moved to Middletown, Connecticut, where her first daughter, Andrea Bo, was born in 1965. During her master's work she had begun compiling a bibliography on Emily Dickinson, which she continued to work on during her stay in Connecticut. Returning to southern California in 1965, she resumed teaching at Cal State, and in 1966, she gave birth to her second daughter, Jessica

Ann. In 1968, Kent State University Press published her bibliography on Dickinson.

Ortiz Taylor taught English at the college level in California; later on, in Massachusetts, she wrote the draft of her first novel, *Harley*, which remains unpublished. In 1971, Ortiz Taylor again moved back to southern California and entered the Ph.D program in English at UCLA, where she was the recipient of several fellowships. Divorced in 1972, she earned her Ph.D. in English the following year. Ortiz Taylor joined the English Department at Florida State University in Tallahassee in 1973, where she is now a professor of English. She teaches courses on creative writing, women's studies, and the novel. In addition to her three novels and one book of poetry, Ortiz Taylor has written scholarly articles and reviews for such journals as *Journal of Narrative Technique*, *Eighteenth Century Studies*, *College Composition and Communication*, and *Studies in the Humanities*. Currently at work on her autobiography and a murder mystery, Ortiz Taylor lives in Tallahassee with her partner.

MAJOR WORKS AND THEMES

Ortiz Taylor's major works include three novels and a book of poetry, all published by Naiad Press. Her relationship with Naiad seemed fated from the outset. She moved to Tallahassee in 1973, long before Naiad arrived in 1981. After Naiad arrived, friends of Ortiz Taylor began telling Naiad publisher Barbara Grier about *Faultline*, and eventually Grier ordered Taylor to "send the damn thing over" (Chestnut 8). Grier accepted the manuscript, and in 1982 Ortiz Taylor's first novel, *Faultline*, was published.

Faultline features Arden Benbow, a lesbian mother of six children whose household is comprised of her children, her lover, Alice Wicks, her live-in babysitter, a dog, and three hundred rabbits. The plot ostensibly concerns Arden's battle with her ex-husband, Malthus, for custody of their children. Each chapter is told by a different character, creating a rich, multivoiced narrative that demonstrates Ortiz Taylor's talent for characterization. Among the voices the reader hears are those of Wilson Topaz, the live-in babysitter, who describes himself as "black, gay and six foot three in my stocking feet" (21); Arden's lover, Alice; her ex-husband, Malthus; Ben Griffin, Arden's "feed man"; Muncey, from Muncey's Old English Sheepdog Farms; Homer Rice, an orderly in the rest home where Arden's Aunt Violet lives; Ruby Red, of Ruby's Campground and Trailer Park; and Alison Honey, a cook for Raven Carbonara, Caterers, San Francisco. In addition to the different voices, Ortiz Taylor also includes letters and portions of a diary in the text. The effect of this myriad of voices is a decentering of the authority that usually resides with the first- or third-person narrator and a subversion of conventional literary structure.

In addition, *Faultline* shows the limited, restricted nature of marriage and the traditional nuclear family. Both Arden and Alice speak of the emptiness of their respective marriages; after talking to her husband on the phone, Alice feels "as if I had been visited by a flying saucer in some remote and desolate field'' (101). One of Ortiz Taylor's greatest accomplishments in *Faultline* is exploring alternative, unconventional ways of constructing the text and redefining the nature of family.

That *Faultline* (and its sequel, *Southbound*) reflects many of Ortiz Taylor's own experiences is evident. She has admitted that ''there are many similarities between herself and Arden'' (Ryals). Both graduate from UCLA with degrees in literature, both accept teaching jobs from schools in Florida, both are mothers, and both have ties through their mothers to Chicano culture.

Ortiz Taylor's second novel, *Spring Forward/Fall Back* (1985), also employs an unconventional structure in that it utilizes what Ortiz Taylor explains as ''coincidental action, two people living their lives at the same time and having no knowledge of each other'' (Stearns). *Spring Forward/Fall Back* is the story of two women, Elizabeth Rivers and Marcie Tyson, who are worlds apart in terms of age and experience. When the novel opens, Elizabeth is seventeen years old and lives on Catalina Island. Just out of high school, Elizabeth is bored and restless with her uneventful life on Santa Catalina Island; she wants to go to college. Marcie, twenty-nine, is lonely and disillusioned with her marriage to a philandering husband, Buck. When the paths of the two women finally converge ten years later in a gay bar called the Daily Planet, both have been through long-term relationships with women.

Ortiz Taylor's interest in exploring the positive dynamics of a lesbian family of friends is also evident in *Spring Forward/Fall Back*. Elizabeth Rivers's family consists of her mother, Olive, who toils as a waitress in the Sea Gull Cafe, and her mother's boyfriend, Leon Feeny, an overbearing oaf with wandering hands. Elizabeth is befriended by a schoolmate's mother, Chris Broadwin, who is a lesbian, and through Chris, Elizabeth becomes acquainted with the small circle of lesbians and gays on the island. Through her relationships with these wise men and women, Elizabeth learns the true meaning of family.

Marcie Tyson finds her family of friends in her relationships with the men and women at the Daily Planet. In a pivotal scene, Marcie leaves her mother-in-law's house, where she and Buck have been living, and moves into her own house, which she has purchased with money left to her by her mother. The house is in immediate need of repair, and when Marcie is at her loneliest and ready to despair, the Daily Planet Emergency Salvation Crew, regulars at the Daily Planet, show up with their toolboxes and a keg of beer to rescue her.

Neither Elizabeth nor Marcie finds true happiness in the conventional nuclear family. Ortiz Taylor demonstrates that lesbian families are especially suited to nurturing children and empowering women by liberating them from rigid role-playing.

In *Southbound* (1990), the sequel to *Faultline*, Ortiz Taylor returns to the adventures of the Arden Benbow family. In this novel, Arden finally graduates from UCLA with her Ph.D. and is faced with the task of finding a job—a process that brings her into conflict with just about everyone in the novel. Her ex-husband,

Malthus, who is engaged to a twenty-four-year-old woman, threatens another custody battle, and Arden's lover, Alice, who has just been offered a vice-presidency in the company she works for, is uncertain about moving to Florida, where Arden has been offered a job.

Unlike *Faultline*, *Southbound* does not employ multiple narrators, but the same kind of improbable, bizarre events that occur in *Faultline* also happen in *Southbound*. Arden drives a powder-blue hearse across the country, attends the Modern Language Association convention where she is mistaken for a Tupperware saleswoman, breaks her leg putting on panty hose, and becomes embroiled in a drug deal. And, like *Faultline*, *Southbound* draws much of its strength and energy from Arden's memories of the Chicana women on her mother's side of the family. The presence of these warm, wise, strong women infuses the novel with a rich, multicultural perspective.

Ortiz Taylor's other contribution to lesbian literature is her book of poetry, *Slow Dancing at Miss Polly's* (1989). In this collection Ortiz Taylor writes about family, coming out as a lesbian, relationships, and love. Many poems in the first section, "Album," concern Ortiz Taylor's family, and again her Chicano heritage enriches her work. One poem, "Marker," is a poignant account of the death of her mother. Part 2, "Dyke Patrol," chronicles the evolution of the writer's lesbian identity, capturing the joyful, yet sometimes painful, nature of her choice. Part 3, "Sunday Morning," contains the poem "Southern Exposure," in which Ortiz Taylor uses the metaphor of building a house for the careful labor involved in building a relationship.

CRITICAL RECEPTION

Sheila Ortiz Taylor has received nearly unanimous praise from critics for her works. *Faultline* was selected as Book of the Year by the *Weekly News* in 1982 with Jesse Monteagudo calling it "the best lesbian novel since *Rubyfruit Jungle*" (26). *Dustbooks* also selected *Faultline* as a Small Press Book Club Selection. Jane Rule, esteemed lesbian novelist, claimed that Taylor's first novel "introduces . . . an authoritative voice" (40). Jane Troxell of *Lambda Book Report* called Ortiz Taylor "a gifted storyteller" and *Southbound* "an admirable book" (25). In her review of *Southbound* in the *Florida Flambeau*, Mary Jane Ryals asserted that "it is not a literary stretch to mention Taylor in the same breath as Rita Mae Brown." Critics almost universally applaud Taylor's unique humor and wit; one critic ventured that "*Faultline* is to gay wit what the San Andreas Fault is to rock formations" (Monteagudo 1982: 26).

In addition, Juan Bruce-Nova, a professor of Spanish and Chicano literature at the University of California at Irvine, has written and delivered papers about Ortiz Taylor in an academic setting. His 1991 article, "Sheila Ortiz Taylor's *Faultline*: A Third-Woman Utopia," examines Taylor's novel rhetorically, looking particularly at her unique place in the Chicano canon. Finally, Bonnie Zimmerman's 1990 *The Safe Sea of Women* discusses two of Ortiz Taylor's novels, *Faultline* and *Spring Forward/Fall Back*.

BIBLIOGRAPHY

Works by Sheila Ortiz Taylor

"Cocktail Hour." *Eclipse* 2 (1963): 29.

"Vaudeville." *Eclipse* 2 (1963): 29.

Emily Dickinson: A Bibliography, 1850–1966. Kent, OH: Kent State University Press, 1968.

"Emily Dickinson: Annual Bibliography for 1972." *Emily Dickinson Bulletin* (May 1973): 187–90.

"Emily Dickinson: Annual Bibliography for 1973." *Emily Dickinson Bulletin* 26 (1974): 93–101.

"Emily Dickinson: Annual Bibliography for 1974." *Emily Dickinson Bulletin* 28 (1975): 107–11.

"Emily Dickinson: Annual Bibliography for 1975." *Emily Dickinson Bulletin* 30 (1976): 55–65.

"Episodic Structure and the Picaresque Novel." *Journal of Narrative Technique* 7 (1977): 218–25.

"A Friend of the Family." *Focus* (Sept./Oct. 1981): 23–25.

"With Friends Like These." *Lesbian Voices* 4 (Aug. 1981): 18–24.

"An Excerpt from *Faultline*." *Christopher Street* 5, no. 11 (1982): 40–45.

Faultline. Tallahassee, FL: Naiad Press, 1982. British edition: Women's Press, 1982. German edition: Subrosa Frauenverlag, 1983. Greek edition: Daedalus, 1984. Italian edition: Estro, 1985. Spanish edition: Horas y Horas, 1991.

Spring Forward/Fall Back. Tallahassee: Naiad Press, 1985.

"Dyke Patrol." *Common Lives* 24 (Fall 1987): 27–28.

"The Author to Her Former Husband, etc." *Appalachee Quarterly* 28 (Spring 1988): 37–38.

"Midlife Love." *Broomstick* 10, no. 3 (May/June 1988): 18.

"Siendo Equales Todas Las Cosas." *Antologia Retrospectiva del Cuento Chicano.* Comp. Juan Bruce-Nova. Mexico, D.F.: Consejo Nacional de Poblacion, 1988. 161–70.

"Marker." *North of Wakulla.* Ed. M. J. Ryals and D. Decker. Tallahassee, FL: Anhinga Press, 1989. 21–23.

"Rearview Mirror." *New Visions: Fiction by Florida Writers.* Ed. Omar Castaneda et al. Orlando, FL: Arbiter Press, 1989.

Slow Dancing at Miss Polly's. Tallahassee, FL: Naiad Press, 1989.

Southbound. Tallahassee, FL: Naiad Press, 1990.

Studies of Sheila Ortiz Taylor

Bruce-Novoa, Juan. "Sheila Ortiz Taylor's *Faultline*: A Third-Woman Utopia." *Confluencia; Revista Hispanica de Cultura y Literature* 6, no. 2 (Spring 1991): 75–87.

Chestnut, Cathy. "Workshop Points Writers to Publication." *Florida Flambeau* (January 25, 1989): 8.

Monteagudo, Jesse. "Book Nook." *Weekly News* 17 (November 17, 1982): 26.

———. "Book Nook." *Weekly News* (March 20, 1991): 4.

Rule, Jane. "Arden, Alive and Five Hundred Rabbits." *Body Politic* (Jan./Feb. 1982): 40.

Ryals, Mary Jane. "Southbound Is Delightful Journey." *Tallahassee Democrat* (April 7, 1991): n. pag.

Stearns, Jamie. "Local Novelist Talks about Time, Teaching and Feminism." *Florida Flambeau* (October 3, 1985): n. pag.

Troxell, Jane, "Winds of Change: Shaky Times Hit Faultline 2." *Lambda Book Report* (Jan./Feb. 1991): 25.

Zimmerman, Bonnie. *The Safe Sea of Women*. New York: Beacon Press, 1990.

NANCY TODER (1948–   )
Loralee MacPike

Loralee MacPike

BIOGRAPHY

Nancy Toder was born in New York City on June 1, 1948, the youngest child of Emanuel and Florence Toder. She attended the prestigious Bronx High School of Science and then took a bachelor's degree in psychology from the University of Buffalo and a Ph.D. in clinical psychology from the University of California at Los Angeles (UCLA), as well as advanced study at the Newport Psychoanalytic Institute. She currently practices psychotherapy and psychoanalysis in Beverly Hills, California, with a specialty in lesbian therapy, both couples and individuals. Although she published a few poems while she was in graduate school, the novel *Choices* is Toder's only major work of literature.

MAJOR WORKS AND THEMES

Because Toder was attracted to girls and women from childhood, and because her life work is helping lesbians clarify their identities and values, it is not surprising that in *Choices* she focuses on the issue of lesbian identity. Toder had not intended to write a novel at all; *Choices* was originally a screenplay "born out of fury." One day in 1978 a colleague asked her to read a screenplay written by a straight man about a lesbian couple. Called "Passion," the screenplay was, for Toder, devoid of both passion and lesbian sensibility: its central character left her woman lover for a man. Recognizing that there was nothing available to counter this view of lesbians, Toder wrote her own screenplay to counter this male vision of lesbianism that she knew was wrong. Then she spent 1979 taking that screenplay around the industry. She garnered several responses, all unhelpful: vitriolic attacks from closeted lesbians, positive responses from straight women who still wouldn't touch it because it would have a negative effect on their careers, and support from straight men who nonetheless didn't feel there was a market for it. And so the screenplay languished (personal interview, January 1992).

But out of that screenplay, the novel *Choices* was born. In it, Toder says that she tried to create a world for and of women, centered on bonds between women and on a wide range of possibilities for women beyond the traditional roles of "feminine" and "masculine." It took a year of non-stop writing to complete, and it has been a steady lesbian best-seller since Persephone Press published it in 1980. When Persephone went out of business, Alyson picked the novel up in 1984 and reports average annual sales of nearly 5,000 copies through 1991. The novel's large and continuing readership attests to its ability to engage succeeding generations of lesbians seeking meaning in their fiction. And it engages them through an enduringly felt search for the roots of lesbian affection combined with an astute presentation of ongoing political concerns. Toder's lesbian sensibility, educated by her professional training and experience, has created a work that seems almost timelessly to re-echo essential lesbian questions and feelings.

Choices is the story of Sandy Stein. It begins when she leaves home for college and ends when she is a successful therapist in her mid-thirties. (In this it follows Toder's own life path.) In college, Sandy rooms with Jenny Chase. Initially unaware of the nature of her feelings, Sandy assumes they are "just friends"—*close* friends—until that first kiss, so familiar and evocative to all of us that it is virtually archetypal in teen coming-out fiction. For a year or so they are ardent lovers, aware of the need to hide from others but frank (with that frankness only the very young can feel) about their mutual enjoyment of one another. All too soon, however, Jenny begins to succumb to the enculturated fears and shame that the idea of women loving women arouses. She "becomes" heterosexual and brutally deserts Sandy emotionally. In reaction, Sandy briefly dates and is sexual with one of the most pleasant, non-dominating young men in twentieth-century fiction. But she is less able that Jenny to deny her nature, and so she tells Mike the truth about her sexual affections and then leaves to create a lesbian life.

The second half of the novel takes place some fifteen years later. Sandy has completed her Ph.D. at UCLA and is a practicing therapist just in the process of becoming politically active as a lesbian within her profession. She and her partner, Shelly, have established a loving, supportive, sensual, and conflicted relationship. At a professional conference in Hawaii, Sandy again meets Jenny, who is married and deep in denial of the meaning of her past with Sandy. After several days, Shelly joins Sandy, and the three women probe through uncertainties to reach varying levels of understanding and acceptance of their lesbian selves and their life choices. Predictably, Jenny remains unresolved; she begins to admit her attraction to women, and she gratifies Sandy's unfulfilled yearning for acknowledgment of their love by rather dramatically saving Sandy from a jellyfish bite, but she remains unwilling to relinquish heterosexual privilege. Her own need for validation finally filled, Sandy is better able to assess the strengths, rather than the weaknesses, of her relationship with Shelly. The final image of

Shelly and Sandy standing together facing a still-confused Jenny leaves the reader with a portrait of genuine lesbian identity.

Choices also raises a broad range of political issues. The 1978 California ballot issue (the Briggs amendment) proposing to remove all lesbians and gays from public service, particularly classroom teaching, is discussed by a group of lesbians representing a spectrum of opinion, from willingness to face jail sentences to a naive belief that such oppression could never happen in America. Toder draws analogies to Nazi Germany and the internment of Japanese-Americans during World War II in her effort to historicize the campaign against homosexuals. The issue of bisexuality is briefly addressed, with Sandy deciding that it's a refuge for lesbians afraid to risk a full commitment to honoring their true sexuality. Jenny's questioning of her sexual orientation and its relation to her identity as a human being allows Toder to present the age-old question about the relative "masculinity" or "femininity" of lesbians.

Through Jenny's internalized homophobia, Toder is able to dramatize the fear that others may be judging one on one's sexual orientation (Toder uses the word *preference*). Through hostile questioning by one of the attendees at Sandy's conference panel, Toder presents the oft-attempted dismissal of legitimate lesbian and gay issues as "political whims," ideologizing, or mere activism. And through Sandy's continuing attraction to Jenny, Toder is even able to slip in a psychologically current analysis of lesbians' attractions to straight women. In trying to puzzle out why some women embrace and others deny their love for women, Sandy delves into the definition of lesbian identity itself. There's a nice bit of lesbian guided imagery and a lengthy lesbian group therapy session to round out the lesbian psychological content. Even apparently trivial issues, such as dress and hairstyle and manner of walking, become topics of concern, discussion, and, therefore, political awareness, as Toder develops her ultimate confrontation between Jenny's fearful homophobia and Sandy's psychologically grounded, healthy acceptance.

Although she is considerably more enlightened, graceful, and perceptive than most mortal women, Sandy isn't a perfect heroine by any means. Particularly when she meets Jenny in Hawaii, she is wracked with doubts about the nature and meaning of her contradictory responses. Jealousy, fantasy, cultural conditioning, a need for superiority, a perverse desire to forcibly show Jenny the thrills she must be missing with a man—all these natural emotions sweep over Sandy. But Toder never lets Sandy deviate very far from her self-chosen politically correct path of understanding, compassion, and lesbian sensibility. While such virtue makes her a difficult woman to emulate, it is also what makes her such an enduring lesbian heroine. She models for readers healthy ways to deal with the choices that a self-chosen lesbian identity presents. Sandy works through the expectable doubts about whether she will "choose" to spend her life with women; she is realistic about what she can expect from Shelly; and she consciously selects appropriate outlets for anger. On the other hand, Jenny worries about wrinkles and fears that strangers will think she's a lesbian just because she's at a lesbian bar. The issues and valuations are clear-cut, and so when at the end Jenny relents and acknowledges her early love for Sandy, Sandy is satisfied and can at last move beyond her need for that validation.

It is thus no wonder that *Choices* has continued to be a model of lesbian identity to a whole generation of lesbians faced with similar choices. Its impeccable politics and admirable heroine make it a classic of lesbian literature.

CRITICAL RECEPTION

Choices was reviewed in the lesbian and gay press when it first appeared in 1980, but, as with most review of lesbian fiction, these reviews are not available to the general public and have not been indexed in mainstream review indexes. Until the inception of the *Women's Review of Books*, there has been no mainstream review coverage of lesbian novels. Following the Persephone publication, Toder did an extended reading and lecture tour of the East Coast, speaking in Washington, D.C., in Boston, at Yale, and at the Women's Salon in New York City. She appeared on the "New England Morning" show and was interviewed by East Coast radio stations. The 1984 Alyson re-issue was reviewed in Los Angeles–based *Lesbian News*. The best indication of the continued favorable reception of *Choices* is its continuing sales record.

BIBLIOGRAPHY

Work by Nancy Toder

Choices. San Francisco: Persephone Press, 1980; Boston: Alyson Publications, 1984.

KITTY TSUI (1952–   )

Ryn L. Edwards

BIOGRAPHY

Kitty (Kit Fan) Tsui (pronounced "Sway") was born on September 4, 1952, the year of the Dragon, in Kowloon, Hong Kong. Her name, Kit Fan, translates to Fragrant Purity. She was the first of four children born to her Chinese parents, of whom she chooses to have "no memory" (personal conversation with Tsui, March 1992). Her maternal grandmother, Kwan Ying Lin, a famous Chinese operatic star who toured the United States during the 1920s and 1930s, raised her in Hong Kong during her early years. When she was five years old she was sent to Liverpool, England, to live with her parents, where her father was the first Chinese captain hired by a British shipping firm, the Blue Funnel Line. When Tsui was ten, her entire family returned to Hong Kong when her father took on a directorship of a nautical training school, and in 1968, when she was fifteen, they emigrated to San Francisco after her father gained an executive position at the Port of Oakland. Her aunt and grandmother had emigrated earlier. Tsui writes of her family, "[I remember] silence. My grandma, parents, siblings and members of our extended family sitting down to dinner. And silence. No conversation or laughter. Just the sound of soup spoons and chopsticks against the rice bowls" (*Lesbian Philosophies and Cultures* 49). And in recollecting her childhood, Tsui writes:

In Hong Kong when I was growing up I heard all around me mothers shouting in exasperation at their children: "*Say nui, mow yung, ngai say.*" Dead Girl, no use, you dead. And "*ngai ge sai yun tow!*" Your dead head.

We were not just called bad girls or naughty brats. We were called dead girls. What a way to begin life! Hearing myself called dead girl so many times I was sure I was a dead girl, meaningless, useless, worthless. In addition to this, I was always told what I couldn't do, what I couldn't say, what I couldn't be. I could dream but I could never be.(50)

Tsui ran away from her parents and her traditional Chinese upbringing at the age of sixteen, took a job in a hospital kitchen, and put herself through college, earning her degree in creative writing from San Francisco State University in 1975.

Friendly with alcohol from high school, Tsui struggled with rejection in every aspect of her life. At the same time, however, her desire to be heard enabled her to be strong. In 1971, she helped create Third World Women Communications collective, which published the heralded anthology *Third World Women* (1972). In her coming out as a lesbian at the age of twenty-one, Tsui began fervently to record and research her grandmother's stories, to build a bridge between her culture and her love of women. Kwan Ying Lin, her grandmother, was a role model, a woman who had lived with another operatic woman for ten years while raising her children and touring as a professional actress. Much of her spirit, in fact, lives in Tsui's writings.

As Tsui continued her research, her activism expanded. She became involved with Unbound Feet, a writers group of six Asian-American women in San Francisco in 1979. Shortly thereafter, the group split over whether politics was essential to their writings, and the political element became Unbound Feet Three, formed by Tsui and two other women, which has since disbanded. Although her first book, *The Words of a Woman Who Breathes Fire*, was published in 1983, Tsui feels that bouts with alcohol and drug abuse slowed her own progress as a writer (personal conversation with Tsui, April 1992). She attributes the fact that her work is heavily anthologized to her constant fight to be included because, as she says, "color is viewed as a black and white (sometimes Hispanic) issue." "It's hard to be a successful and prolific writer when one has to struggle and fight to be visible, to be included. It's doubly hard to be a writer, an Asian American and a lesbian in a vacuum" (personal correspondence from Tsui, June 1992). Being such a fighter and an outspoken woman has likely contributed to the fact that interviews with Tsui are much sought after by the San Francisco and Chicago lesbian and Asian communities, where they are featured in numerous newspapers, weeklies, and magazines, particularly the *Advocate*, *Plexus*, and *Chicago Outlines*. Several videos and one Canadian film have also featured interviews with Tsui (*The Third Sex*, film by Margaret Wescott, Canada, 1992; *Framing Lesbian Fashion*, video directed by Karen Everett, USA, 1992; *Women of Gold*, video directed by Eileen Lee and Marilyn Abbink, USA, 1990).

Athleticism has been a source of strength for Tsui; with it, she has been able to disengage from her alcoholism and drug abuse twice in her life. She is a solid swimmer and runner, and in the early 1980s, she took up body building to regain control of her life. The First Gay Olympic Games of 1982 inspired Tsui to enter competitive body building, and she competed in the Gay Olympic Games II and III, winning a bronze medal in 1986 and a gold medal in 1990, both in the physique competition. During this time, she also became a vocal advocate of lesbian sadomasochism and has been featured on the cover and in the pages of *On Our Backs* (Summer 1988, Nov./Dec. 1990).

Tsui has lived in San Francisco for the past twenty-three years. She is presently residing in Chicago, where she is working on her first novel. Tsui is a free-lance journalist. She writes a column, "Leathertalk Top to Bottom," for *Chicago Nightlines*. She has written for numerous publications including the *Advocate*, *Bay Area Reporter*, *Sentinel*, *San Francisco Bay Guardian*, *Bay Times*, *On Our Backs*, *off our backs*, *Plexus*, *East/West*, *City Arts Magazine*, *New Phoenix Rising*, and *Chicago Outlines*.

MAJOR WORKS AND THEMES

The themes that have been central to Kitty Tsui's life are those central to her poems and short prose: her love and admiration of women/self, the cultural/ human subtle and barbaric oppression experienced by Chinese immigrants in the United States, and aspects of her Chinese and American heritage that inform/ transform her lesbianism. Her writing has intent and purpose as it is characterized by an astute sense of conversation, the power of rooted emotion, and an eye for neglected irony.

Tsui's works appear primarily in anthologies and journals, with the exception of a collection of poetry and short prose, *The Words of a Woman Who Breathes Fire*, published in 1983 by Spinsters Ink. This work is dedicated to Tsui's maternal grandmother, who died in 1979. It considers the cultural discord, isolation, and unrecognized citizenship/personhood of the Chinese immigrant in America, her grandmother's renown and warrior spirit, the strength of being lesbian, violence against women, and alcoholism; from all of which is gained a great voice of empowerment, celebration, anger, and activism. One poem about her grandmother, "Chinatown Talking Story," has been published in several anthologies, including *Early Ripening* (1985), edited by Marge Piercy.

Tsui also has re-created a set of myths and adventure tales about "crane woman" and "dragon woman," two of which have been published in a series of books edited by Irene Zahava. In "Why the Sea Is Salty" (1986, in *Hear the Silence*) and "Why the Milky Way Is Milky" (1989, in *Lesbian Love Stories*), we are told stories that embody the love between women and the wisdom and harmony learned from nature. Tsui is more explicit about lovemaking in the effectively short "One Night Stand," published in the Lambda Literary Award– winning book, *Intricate Passions* (1989), edited by Tee Corinne.

Tsui is autobiographical in "Breaking Silence, Making Waves and Loving Ourselves," published in *Lesbian Philosophies and Cultures* (1990), edited by Jeffner Allen. Here she describes her alienation within Chinese culture, her coming out as a lesbian, her rejection by family (except her grandmother), and her alcoholism. Tsui takes this set of circumstances and shows how she learned to love herself and how she turned her oppression into power through uniting and building with other Asian Americans. Moreover, she shows how we can all empower ourselves to resist or to change conditions that create our poverty, our oppression, our silence.

CRITICAL RECEPTION

Critical review of Tsui's work has been exceedingly limited because her work appears largely in anthologies and journals. Because most of the anthologies and some of the journals have been published by lesbian or feminist presses, they are not found in every bookstore. Her book *The Words of a Woman Who Breathes Fire* was published in San Francisco by Spinsters Ink, and like most of her work, it has been reviewed only in lesbian/gay and Asian-American news/arts publications. Both Pat Califia (*The Advocate*, 1983) and Audrey E. Lockwood (*Feminist Forum* (Japan), Vol. V(11) Nov. 1983) reviewed Tsui's book favorably, emphasizing her skill in capturing the realities of Chinese life in America and her personal and direct means of showing homophobia, racism, and sexism in day-to-day living. Tsui's contribution to a set of 1979 special issues of *Bridge: An Asian American Perspective* journal, which addressed Asian-American women, was part of a critical review by Barbara Noda in *Conditions* (Vol. 6, 1980, 203–211). Noda acknowledges Tsui's vision of strength gained from reaffirmation of the Chinese and the lesbian spirit, yet she appears to chastise Tsui for her exclusion of her homophobic family from her life/vision. Noda apparently empathizes with the difficulties of being a mother of a lesbian in a strange land, rather than understanding the family's talent for isolating Tsui, which is the experience through which Tsui constructs her perspective. Tsui's talent as a writer can perhaps be better assessed by the fact that most reviews of anthologies that include Tsui's writing usually mention her contributions in citing the quality of the anthology.

HONORS AND AWARDS

In 1969, Tsui was first place winner of a poetry contest sponsored by Friends of the Public Library and the Poetry Center, San Francisco State University. In 1980, she was a finalist in the National Women's Playwriting Competition, sponsored by the One Act Theater Company, San Francisco.

BIBLIOGRAPHY

Works by Kitty Tsui

Third World Women. (K. Tsui, coeditor). San Francisco: Third World Communications Press, 1972.

The Words of a Woman Who Breathes Fire. New York and San Francisco: Spinsters Ink, 1983.

Tsui's work also appears in the following anthologies:

Odes to Bill Sorro: Poetry from Both Sides of the Pacific. Japan: Fukuoka Press, 1974.

In Common. Ed. Jeffrey Chan. New York: Harcourt Brace Jovanovich, 1975.

In Touch. Ed. Jeffrey Chan. New York: Harcourt Brace Jovanovich, 1975.

"Kapendewa . . . " and "For My Spirit, In Love and Out of Love." *Time to Greez!*

Incantations from the Third World. Ed. Janice Mirikitani. San Francisco: Glide Publications, 1975. 50–51.

"Poa Poa is Living Breathing Light." *Lesbian Fiction.* Ed. Elly Bulkin. Watertown, MA: Persephone Press, 1981. 168–74.

"The Words of a Woman Who Breathes Fire: One." *Lesbian Poetry.* Ed. Elly Bulkin and Joan Larkin. Watertown, MA: Persephone Press, 1981. 244.

"In Training." *Out from Under: Sober Dykes and Our Friends.* Ed. Jean Swallow. San Francisco: Spinsters Ink, 1983. 34–43.

"It's In the Name" and "Chinatown Talking Story." *Breaking Silence: An Anthology of Contemporary Asian American Poets.* Ed. Joseph Bruchac. Greenfield Center, NY: Greenfield Review Press, 1983. 262–68.

"It's In the Name." *The Second Seasonal Political Palate.* Ed. Bloodroot Collective. Bridgeport, CT: Sanguinaria Publishing, 1984. 167.

"Why the Sea Is Salty." *Hear the Silence.* Ed. Irene Zahava. New York: Crossing Press, 1986. 56–72.

"Don't Call Me Sir, Call Me Strong," "From Red Rock Canyon, Summer 1977: (IV) The Vision," and "Chinatown Talking Story." *Early Ripening: American Women's Poetry Now.* Ed. Marge Piercy. London: Pandora Press, 1987. 236–40.

"A Chinese Banquet." *Gay and Lesbian Poetry in Our Time.* Ed. Carl Morse and Joan Larkin. New York: St. Martin's Press, 1988. 373–74.

"Chinatown Talking Story." *Making Waves: An Anthology of Writings by and about Asian American Women.* Ed. Asian Women United of California. Boston: Beacon Press, 1989. 132–33.

"Don't Let Them Chip Away at Our Language." *An Ear to the Ground: Anthology of Contemporary American Poetry.* Ed. Marie Harris and Kathleen Aguero. Athens, GA: University of Georgia Press, 1989. 286–88.

"One Night Stand." *Intricate Passions.* Ed. Tee Corinne. Austin, TX: Banned Books, 1989. 110–13.

"Solitary Pleasure." *Finding Courage: Writings by Women.* Ed. Irene Zahava. Freedom, CA: Crossing Press, 1989. 217–29.

"Why the Milky Way Is Milky." *Lesbian Love Stories.* Ed. Irene Zahava. Freedom, CA: Crossing Press, 1989. 285–97.

"Breaking Silence, Making Waves and Loving Ourselves: The Politics of Coming Out and Coming Home." *Lesbian Philosophies and Cultures.* Ed. Jeffner Allen. Albany, NY: State University of New York Press, 1990. 49–61

"Who Says We Don't Talk About Sex?" *The Persistent Desire: A Femme-Butch Reader.* Ed. Joan Nestle. Boston, MA: Alyson Publications, 1992. 385–87.

LUZ MARÍA UMPIERRE-HERRERA (1947–)

Nancy Vosburg

BIOGRAPHY

Luzma Umpierre is a Puerto Rican poet, scholar, critic, teacher, and minority activist—and not necessarily in that order. Born and raised in a working-class neighborhood of Santurce, Puerto Rico, Umpierre has resided in the United States since 1974. Although she was her parents' only child, Umpierre spent her first four years in the large household of her father's sister, all of whom were dependent on her parents. Her father eventually found a larger house within the neighborhood where the entire family, including her parents, two aunts, an uncle, eight cousins, and her grandmother, could live together. This early circumstance has led Umpierre to reflect occasionally on her "two mothers." Responding to the great sacrifices made by her parents to send her to an upper-class private school in San Juan—her first encounter with class discrimination—Umpierre distinguished herself academically to such a degree that she was awarded several scholarships (among them the Puerto Rican Senate Scholarship and the Chase Manhattan Bank Scholarship) to attend the all-women Universidad del Sagrado Corazón in her hometown. Popular among her peers, she was class president, editor of the student newspaper, and president of the Disciplinary Tribunal. Upon completing her B.A. in Spanish in 1970, she was awarded the "Santa Teresa Medal" for highest cumulative grade point average in her field and graduated *cum laude*. Her academic profile earned her a scholarship to study law at the Universidad Católica de Ponce. After a year at Ponce, she transferred to the law school in Río Piedras, where she continued to work toward a law degree while venturing into the teaching profession as head of the Spanish Department at the Academia María Reina.

In 1974, a semester shy of her law degree, Umpierre decided to pursue doctoral studies in Latin American literature at Bryn Mawr College in Pennsylvania. Reflecting on that decision, Umpierre cites two reasons for wanting to leave

Puerto Rico: on the one hand, she needed to break away from her father's authoritarian presence, and on the other, she had begun to experience harassment at the Academia María Reina because of her lesbian identity. Umpierre recalls how "extraordinarily supportive" her parents were when the issue of her sexuality was raised. Her mother for years resorted to coded language (she referred to the gay and lesbian community as "la cofradía") to inquire after Umpierre's friends. Her father was relatively silent on the subject, but always accepted Umpierre's friends and lovers quite graciously.

Umpierre's years at Bryn Mawr were not completely liberating, however. There she encountered both the subtle racism that pervades U.S. society, and, more specifically, the class discrimination rampant in many American academic institutions, where Puerto Rican Spanish is considered substandard. Although she was named director of the Spanish House, and was awarded teaching and graduate assistantships, the constant confrontations with racism and classism took their toll. It was during that period that Umpierre published her first poems and received her initial recognition as a poet, winning an Honorable Mention from International Publications (IP) in 1976 for her poem "El trabajo escrito," and IP's First Prize in Poetry the following year for "Ghetto." In keeping with her ground-breaking spirit, in 1978, Umpierre defended the first doctoral dissertation on Puerto Rican literature in the hundred-year history of Bryn Mawr. Umpierre's first published collection of poetry, *Una puertorriqueña en Penna* (1979), was written while she was a student at Bryn Mawr. In Umpierre's words, these poems constitute a response to "all sorts of issues dealing with race, national origin, class, and my 'place' within the new environment" (Martínez, "An Interview" 10).

After a one-year visiting lectureship at Immaculata College in Pennsylvania, Umpierre accepted a tenure-track position at Rutgers University. Prior to receiving tenure, she was awarded several research grants from Rutgers and the prestigious National Research Council/Ford Foundation Postdoctoral Fellowship in 1981–82, which enabled her to pursue studies in literary theory at the University of Kansas. Umpierre was actively engaged in both scholarly and creative writing, publishing her second collection of poetry, *En el país de las maravillas* (1982); two books on Puerto Rican literature, *Ideología y novela en Puerto Rico* (1983) and *Nuevas approximaciones críticas a la literatura puertorriqueña contemporánea* (1983); and numerous scholarly articles, interviews, book reviews, and poems.

Umpierre's distinguished scholarly, academic, and creative activity seemed to presage an easy tenure decision in 1984, but such was not the case. Umpierre speaks candidly about the misunderstandings and personal rancors, many of which she attributes to racism and homophobia, that escalated within the department during the year that her tenure was to be decided. The Rutgers administration eventually stepped in, and not only was she granted tenure, but the tenure procedure was changed to prevent future discrimination. Although Umpierre was the first Puerto Rican woman to be granted tenure in the Spanish

Department at Rutgers (New Brunswick), her problems with Rutgers were not over.

After receiving tenure, and after publishing her third collection of poetry, . . . *Y otras desgracias/And Other Misfortunes* . . . (1985), Umpierre became active in organizing a group of women of color in a class action discrimination suit against Rutgers, which of course only enhanced her image as a "troublemaker." Yet on the professional front, she was awarded in 1986 a second postdoctoral fellowship from the New Jersey State Department of Education to study university administration. Her credentials firmly established, Umpierre applied to become chair of Puerto Rican Studies, a program that was to be completely reorganized as Caribbean Studies. Umpierre was among the final three contenders for the position, but the first offer went to a male candidate. When he rejected the offer, a second search was opened, and in 1987 another male candidate was hired. Umpierre responded to the irregularities in the procedure by filing an EEOC (Equal Employment Opportunity Commission) complaint.

Also in 1987 Umpierre published her fourth collection of poetry, *The Margarita Poems*. In her prologue to the collection, Umpierre writes that the poems, all composed between 1985 and 1986, responded to her need to speak " 'lo que nunca pasó por mis labios,' that which I had not uttered, and which was being used as a tool in my oppression by others, murmured behind closed doors. . . . What I needed to verbalize is the fact that I am, among many other things, a Lesbian'' (1). Deeply affected by the loss of her mother that same year, Umpierre gave a reading, in her mother's memory, of *The Margarita Poems* to a standing-room-only crowd at Rutgers, despite the university's attempts to cancel the reading.

The legal battle that ensued from March through December of 1988 because of Umpierre's EEOC complaint is a bizarre chapter in her life. On Umpierre's birthday (October 15) she was informed by her lawyer that the university was seeking to "detenure" her for "insubordination" because she refused to submit to psychiatric evaluations ordered by the administration. Forced by the circumstances to comply with the procedure, she submitted to three separate evaluators, who reached the predictable conclusion—that Umpierre was a "non-typical Hispanic woman." She was finally reinstated in January of 1989, but her campus offices, which she never again used, were moved out of the Spanish Department. In keeping with her principles, Umpierre conducted her office hours in her car in the parking lot for the remainder of that academic year.

In 1989, Umpierre was named professor and chair of the Modern Languages and Intercultural Studies Department at Western Kentucky University in Bowling Green. The Women's Alliance at Western Kentucky named her Woman of the Year in 1990, the same year she was awarded a Lifetime Achievement Award by the Coalition of Lesbian and Gay Organizations in New Jersey. The second edition of *En el país de las maravillas* was published in 1990. Umpierre spent the summer of 1991 at Pennsylvania State University as a distinguished scholar in residence in the Women's Studies Program. In the fall of 1991, Umpierre was named professor and chair of the Spanish Department at SUNY (State University of New York) at Brockport, a position she describes as particularly rewarding because, since the Rochester area has the second highest percentage of Puerto Rican residents in the United States, she has more personal contact with students from her country. Nevertheless, her attempts to open up the curriculum to minority studies, particularly gay and lesbian and Puerto Rican studies, have met with much resistance from within her department.

In addition to her stellar scholarly and creative activity, Umpierre has served on several distinguished panels, including the National Endowment for the Humanities, the U.S. Department of Education, the National Graduate Fellows Program, the National Research Council, and the Delegate Assembly of the Modern Languages Association. She also has served on the editorial board of the *Americas Review* and as guest editor of a special issue of *Third Woman*, as a reader/consultant for both the *Latin American Theater Review* and the *National Women's Studies Association Journal*, as chair of numerous sessions on Hispanic Women Writers, and as keynote speaker at several conferences. Umpierre has received numerous institutional and national research and travel grants. She continues to speak out for incorporating more gay and lesbian studies into the academic curriculum, and works to secure easier access to publishers on behalf of women, ethnic minorities, and gay and lesbian writers.

MAJOR WORKS AND THEMES

Umpierre's first experiences in the United States and her confrontations with racial discrimination (she considers herself a "woman of color"), cultural bigotry, and socioeconomic class hierarchies while a student at Bryn Mawr College are the material of her first published collection of poems, *Una puertorriqueña en Penna* (A Puerto Rican in Penna [wordplay on English "Pennsylvania" and Spanish "suffering"], 1979). The poems, all but one of which were subsequently incorporated into her second collection, *En el país de las maravillas* (In Wonderland, 1982, 1990), are a series of self-portraits that situate the poet in the Anglo-Saxon cultural milieu. They represent her resistance to an elitist Hispanist view within academia that scorns her native Puerto Rican culture and language as "substandard," and society's attempts to define/contain/control her identity, and that of other Puerto Ricans, through the creation of an exotic consumer product labeled "Goya." As is evidenced in the title, Umpierre's linguistic province is "Spanglish," and her poetry thrives on phonetic and semantic wordplays reflecting an irreverent adaptation to the dominant culture that is both scathingly critical and ironically humorous. Bryn Mawr, for example, is transformed into "Bring Mal" in the collection's poetic universe, Gringolandia. Her highly creative code switching exalts a cultural identity rich in its duality while affirming her rejection of dominant stereotypes and pretensions. *En el país de las maravillas* is composed of three books, "Exodo" (Exodus), "Jueces" (Judges), and "Lamentaciones de Luz María" (Luz Maria's Lamentations). The new poems in the collection move beyond Umpierre's private Gringolandia at Bryn Mawr as she embraces the U.S. Puerto Rican community, in general, and other Hispanic women, in particular. While criticizing the discrimination against Latinos/as in the United States, she also confronts the traditional myths about women generated within the Hispanic community that serve as a tool of oppression. Other poems reflect nostalgically on the lost island, contrasting her sunny and sea-splashed homeland to the cold and snowy environment that has become her new home. As the poet struggles with her ambivalence toward "presence" and "absence," refusing to let go of her cultural identity, a new and empowering sense of self-identity based on the duality of "here" and "there" emerges.

. . . *Y otras desgracias/And Other Misfortunes* . . . (1985) is a landmark in Umpierre's development as a poet. She employs humorous code switching and phonetic wordplay to cut through patriarchal oppression, authoritarian dogma, hypocrisy, and racism, exposing a world of social and political injustice, as Nancy Mandlove underscores in her introduction to the collection. For Mandlove, the theme of creation and destruction is the central and most powerful feature of the work, not only in its social and political dimension, but more importantly in the personal development of the poet (Introduction to . . . *Y otras desgracias* xi). The assault on traditional ideologies, present in her previous collection, is now reinforced by a lucid feminist consciousness that allows the poet to begin to create a new female archetype as old myths are humorously pulverized. English predominates in Part One, "Mishaps," while Spanish is the predominant language of Part Two, "Poemas Malogrados" (Ill-fated Poems).

Yet it is not until her fourth collection, *The Margarita Poems* (1987), that Umpierre's powerful and empowering lesbian identity clearly emerges, and when it does, it is lusty, sensual, erotic, and self-affirming. Responding to the need to speak what others were saying behind closed doors, to wrest from her oppressors that which had become their tool, the poet seeks out her lesbian muse and identifies it in an act of liberation that she invites others to share. And in so doing, she recognizes that her true homeland is not the island on which she was raised, but rather a new island. As she celebrates her individual liberation, she recognizes the nurturing and empowering support of other women, paying tribute to her literary foremothers and sisters and reaching out to all women, sisters and "margaritas" all.

Throughout Umpierre's collections, there runs a single unifying theme that is as much political as personal: the will to combat imperialistic and patriarchal oppression in order to create new ways to envision humankind.

CRITICAL RECEPTION

While Umpierre is considered by many of her critics to be one of the foremost "Latina lesbian" poets, this label in itself reflects the kind of discrimination that she confronts in the reception of her creative works: because of her gender, ethnicity, and sexual preference, she has generally been marginalized from the major U.S. poetry journals and anthologies. And within the Hispanic community, widespread recognition of Umpierre as a poet has also been slow to come— discrimination against women, particularly "non-traditional Hispanic women," has been a constant obstacle. Arte Público, for example, the leading publisher of (until recently mostly male) Hispanic writers in the United States, turned down her request for the first and second editions of *En el país*, and excluded her from its *Bibliography of Latino Literature in the United States.*

As is evident from the bibliography of critical studies on her poetry, most of Umpierre's critics are Hispanic women and/or gays and lesbians, who are quick to point out the importance of her poetry within the realm of women's and minority studies. But Umpierre has much to say about the human condition, and until her poems reach the broader society she examines and critiques, her success as a poet will continue to be attenuated. It is interesting to note that her scholarly and academic work has begun to fuse almost imperceptibly with her creative impulse as she now engages almost exclusively in "homocriticism" of Caribbean literature. More importantly, Umpierre has appeared as guest lecturer and guest writer at several major literary conferences throughout the United States, where her denunciation of the "mainstream mentality" has begun to reach the larger audience she addresses in her poetry, coinciding with the move within the American academic milieu to recognize and reflect the diversity of our multicultural society. This augurs well for a poet dedicated to creating alternative modes of perception and valuation in her struggle to reaffirm human rights.

BIBLIOGRAPHY

Works by Luz María Umpierre-Herrera

Una puertorriqueña en Penna. San Juan, PR: Masters, 1979.
En el país de las maravillas. Prologue by Eliana Rivero. Bloomington, IN: Third Woman Press, 1982. 2nd ed. Berkeley: New Earth Publications, 1990.
. . . Y otras desgracias/And Other Misfortunes. . . . Introduction by Nancy Mandlove. Bloomington: Third Woman Press, 1985.
The Margarita Poems. Prologues by Julia Alvarez, Roger Platizky and Carlos Rodríguez. Bloomington: Third Woman Press, 1987.

Studies of Luz María Umpierre-Herrera

Agosín, Marjorie. "The Margarita Poems." *Sojourner* (June 1988): 40.
Alarcón, Norma. "Latina Writers in the United States." *Spanish American Women Writers*. Ed. Diane Marting. New York: Greenwood Press, 1990.
Alvarado, Ana María. "En el país de las maravillas" by Luz María Umpierre (review). *Chasqui: Revista de Literatura Latinoamericana* 15, 1 (1985): 90–92.
Azize Vargas, Yamila. "A Commentary on the Works of Three Puerto Rican Women Poets in New York." Trans. Sonia Crespo Vega. *Breaking Boundaries: Latina*

Writings and Critical Readings. Ed. Asunción Horno-Delgado et al. Amherst: University of Massachusetts Press, 1989. 146–65.

———. "Poetas puertorriqueñas en Nueva York." *Cupey: Revista de la Universidad Metropolitana* 4, 1 (Jan.-June 1987): 17–24.

Fernández-Olmos, Margarite. "From the Metropolis: Puerto Rican Women Poets and the Immigration Experience." *Third Woman* 1, 2 (1982): 40–51.

———. "En la metrópoli: el exilio, la emigración y la poesía de escritoras puertorriqueñas en Nueva York." *Sobre la literatura puertorriqueña de aquí y de allá*. Santo Domingo, DR: Alfa y Omega, 1989. 83–104.

Horno-Delgado, Asunción. "Señores, don't leibol mi, please!!: *ya soy Luz María Umpierre*." Trans. Janet N. Gold. *Breaking Boundaries: Latina Writings and Critical Readings*. Ed. Asunción Horno-Delgado et al. Amherst: University of Massachusetts Press, 1989. 136–45.

Martínez, Elena M. "An Interview with Luz María Umpierre." *Christopher Street* 163 (1991): 9–10.

———. "Luz María Umpierre: A Lesbian Puerto Rican Writer in America." *Christopher Street* 163 (1991): 7–8.

Ortíz, Ana Terri. "The Generous Poetry of Luz María Umpierre and Chrystos." *Gay Community News* (4–10 September 1988): 7 and 14.

Pérez-Erdelyi, Mireya. "And Other Misfortunes" by Luz María Umpierre (review). *Revista Iberoamericana* 53, 140 (1987): 736–38.

———. "Interview with Luz María Umpierre, Puerto-Rican Poetess." *Chasqui: Revista de Literatura Latinoamericana* 16, 2–3 (November 1987): 61–68.

Phillips, Elda María. "Luz María Umpierre-Herrera—Bilingual Poet in Wonderland." *Verbena* (Fall/Winter 1984): 11–13.

Platizky, Roger. " 'Y otras desgracias/ . . . And Other Misfortunes.' " *Frontiers* 10, 3 (1989): 85–87.

Rodríguez, Carlos. "The Margarita Poems." *Linden Lane Magazine* 9, 1–2 (Jan.-Mar. 1990): 23.

Rose, William. "La tensión bilingüe en un poema de Luz María Umpierre." *Alcance: Revista literaria* 1, 2 (1983): 2–3.

Roses, Loraine Elena. "New Critical Approaches to Contemporary Puerto-Rican Literature" by Luz María Umpierre (review). *Chasqui: Revista de Literatura Latinoamericana* 14, 2–3 (1985): 65–66.

Torres, Lourdes. "A Passionate Muse." *Conditions* 15 (1988): 157–60.

CHEA VILLANUEVA (1952–   )
Alice Y. Hom

BIOGRAPHY

Chea Villanueva was born on May 13, 1952, in Philadelphia, Pennsylvania, of Filipino (her father) and Irish (her mother) heritage. When Villanueva was ten, her mother died, which left her father, a working-class Filipino immigrant, the responsibility of taking care of her with the help of her two older sisters. Her childhood consisted of being a tough tomboy in a poor, working-class white and Latino neighborhood, where she was beat up and teased constantly because of her dress and biraciality. Villanueva's father molded his daughter ''into the son that he wanted'' (*ALOEC Newsletter*, 1983), so he taught her to fight in order take care of herself. Wearing her short hair slicked back and boys' clothing and being called ''chink,'' ''nigger,'' and ''spic'' caused her ''to forget who I was really.'' Kissing girls since the age of six, Villanueva knew she had an identity problem with sexuality and race, which is one of the themes in her writing.

Villanueva was in and out of reform schools during her teenage years, rebelling against any type of authority. Pregnant and forced to marry because, she said, ''I wanted my family to like me,'' Villanueva left her husband after six months. (Unless otherwise indicated, all quotations are from personal communication with the author.) She lost custody of her baby daughter because of her lesbianism. Although Villanueva has secretly seen her daughter in the past, her second oldest sister, who has custody and disapproves of lesbianism, has forbidden their meetings; Villanueva has not seen or talked to her daughter for four years.

Growing up with African-American and Latino friends in North Philadelphia informs and reflects much of her writing, which she began as a song lyricist during her teens. Villanueva worked nights to obtain a GED (general equivalency diploma), studied journalism for a year at Temple University, and graduated with honors as a registered medical assistant. During her seven-year stay in New York, Villanueva met and discussed writing with her favorite authors, such as

Joan Nestle, Jessica Hagedorn, Hattie Gosset, and Sapphire. During this time, she came in contact with other Asian-Pacific lesbians and has incorporated her multiple identities as a mixed heritage Asian-Pacific lesbian into her work. Experiences with other lesbian and/or ethnic writers have deepened her desire to continue her craft. However, surviving as a writer was hard in New York, so she moved back to Philadelphia for a few years before her current residency in San Francisco, the home of her partner, Theresa Thadani.

Villanueva works as a medical assistant at a blood bank in San Francisco. With a year of nursing under her belt, she plans to pursue a degree in nursing because of the difficulty in writing as a full-time career. She has remained in close contact with Asian-Pacific lesbian groups, especially Asian Pacifica Sisters in San Francisco and Asian Lesbians of the East Coast (ALOEC) in New York. Villanueva is currently working on the last book of her *Girlfriends* trilogy, *The House of Wilnona Will*. She is also working on an upcoming novel and giving readings in local bookstores.

MAJOR WORKS AND THEMES

Among lesbian writers, there are few Asian-Pacific lesbians (or lesbians of color, for that matter) represented. Villanueva is one of the few Asian-Pacific lesbian writers who have taken a strong stand in articulating the lives and experiences of lesbians of color. Much of Villanueva's work revolves around the issues of race and sexuality, eroticism and sexual agency (these women desire rather than are objects of desire) for lesbians of color. Her works have appeared in a variety of publications, including *Asian Lesbians of the East Coast Newsletter*, *Big Apple Dyke (B.A.D.) News*, *Taking Control Reproductive Rights Newsletter*, and *Ang Katipunan*, a newsmagazine of the Union of Democratic Filipinos.

Her poetry and fiction highlight the erotic, sensual experiences of lesbians. Villanueva's works reflect her identity as a multiracial lesbian of a working-class background. She began her writing career with poetry, focusing on lesbian love. Her verses range from short and economical poems depicting sexual attraction between women to longer poems commenting on colonization of the Philippines. They also address issues of class, gender, and race, as evidenced in "Factory Girls," which talks about the Filipina women forced to sell their bodies in the "free trade zone."

In accordance with her poetry, Villanueva's short stories resonate with issues of friendship, love, and sex between women of color. "Friends," about two lesbians of color, speaks to the lives of working-class women, and "Philly Gumbo" portrays the daily routine of lesbians on the make, playing roles, switching girlfriends, and losing loves. Her other stories reveal a deep sense of innocence about childhood and sexuality. Her pre-Stonewall life experiences echo within her tales, as seen in the excerpts from her upcoming novel *In the Shadows of Love*. These excerpts reflect the different stages a girl goes through while finding love and sexual awakening with another girl. Her writings speak to forbidden love and to the joy of experimenting with kissing and petting other girls. The intense feelings of love and happiness, mingled with the bittersweet breakup when her girlfriend leaves her for a boy, affect the reader, especially since the experience of a first love with a best friend is common for lesbians.

Villanueva's two novels in the *Girlfriends* trilogy follow in the vein of her short stories and poetry, but with an added twist of comedy to the sex, fun, and games. The novels deal with the continuing saga of the wild escapades and woolly happenings of Miz Pearly Does and her cohorts. The two novels are in the form of imaginary and real letters (received by the author), which are written and exchanged between Asian-American and African-American characters. Both novels have an aura of real people's lives because they are based on her real-life friends and acquaintances. Villanueva's writings span a continuum of life experiences that help us to be aware of our "herstory" as lesbians. She speaks about lives that are rarely heard in mainstream society, much less in white lesbian communities.

CRITICAL RECEPTION

Villanueva's work has been received favorably by her audience. Readers admire her ability to capture the foibles and follies of lesbian sexual escapades. Her success has mainly been by word-of-mouth praise in the various cities in which she has lived. Yet, in a few places, her novels have been banned in feminist bookstores because of the explicit sexual content as well as her lack of white lesbian characters. A feminist bookstore in the South declined to stock Villanueva's books because of their explicitly erotic nature. During the first printing of her first book, a lesbian publisher made some mistakes in the printing. The publisher tried to correct the grammar and misspellings, which were in context in the novel. Another example of misguided comments from a lesbian publisher, asking Villanueva to cut out the dildo scenes and to make the lead character monogamous, forced her to self-publish her second novel.

In personal communication with the author, Villanueva remarked that there are some white lesbians who do not understand her syntax and delivery style during her readings because her slang is very working class and written in Black dialect. Furthermore, her characters are all lesbians of color. She has, in fact, received the most enthusiastic and favorable comments from lesbians of color. Villanueva has captured the culture, style, and slang of these African-American, Latina, and Asian-Pacific lesbians because she has lived among them most of her life. The lack of reviews of Villanueva's work can be attributed not only to the homophobia of mainstream publications but also to the racism in lesbian publications. The fact that a lesbian publisher specifically asked her to add white lesbians and cut out the dildo scenes reflects a kind of censorship within the ranks of lesbian writing.

BIBLIOGRAPHY

Works by Chea Villanueva

Fiction

Girlfriends (no. 1 in the Girlfriends Trilogy). New York: Outlaw Press, 1987.
"Philly Gumbo." *Common Lives/Lesbian Lives* 27 (Summer 1988): 5–12.
The Chinagirls (no. 2 in Girlfriends Trilogy). Lezzies on the Move Publications, May 1991 (self-published).
"Friends." *Riding Desire: An Anthology of Erotic Writing*. Austin: Banned Books, 1991. 88–92.
"In the Shadows of Love." *The Persistent Desire: A Femme-Butch Anthology*. Ed. Joan Nestle. Boston: Alyson Publications, 1992. 220–24.

Poetry

"Despair," "Episode of My Dream Sequence," and "Magic Evening." *Matrix* (Washington) May 1983: 7.
"The Web Is Cast." *South Street Star* (Philadelphia) October 27, 1983: 7.
"On Rice, Pesos, and Children" and "Dream Sequence." *Asian Lesbians of the East Coast (ALOEC) Newsletter* 1 February 1984: 28, 32–33.
"Butch Blues." *Feminary* 15 (Summer 1985): 4.
"Factory Girls." *Making Waves: An Anthology of Writings by and about Asian American Women*. Boston: Beacon Press, 1990. 295–96.
"The Things I Never Told You."*The Poetry of Sex: Lesbians Write the Erotic*. Ed. Tee Corinne. Austin: Banned Books, 1992. 120.

Studies of Chea Villanueva

Faulkner, Valerie N. "Current Lesbian History." *Au Courant* March 25, 1991: 12–13.
Hom, Alice Y. Review of *Chinagirls*. *Phoenix Rising* 37 (January/February 1992): 5–6.
Kim, Lorrie. "China Girls." *Philadelphia Gay News* June 14–20, 1991: 12–13.
———. "The Wild Bunch" (Review of *Chinagirls*). *Advocate* June 18, 1991: 81.
Shilpa, Mehta. "Villanueva: An Involved Asian Lesbian Activist." *Philadelphia Gay News* March 31–April 6, 1989: 4, 15.

JESS WELLS (1955–   )
Kim Ainis

BIOGRAPHY

There was only one period in Jess Wells's life when she did not want to be a writer, she wanted to be a lawyer. But she discovered that "after about six months of not having a typewriter under my fingers I couldn't stand it anymore." (All quotations are from conversations with the author in May 1992.) Wells relates that her mother confirms this long-standing desire to create stories. Her mother recalls that when Wells was a young child she used to sit behind the sofa with her Raggedy Ann dolls and tell stories all day. One day she emerged from behind the sofa and said, " 'Gee, mom, I wish they could talk for themselves. This is hard work."

Jess Wells was born January 21, 1955, in Jackson, Michigan, a town of about 45,000 people. Her parents were printers who started their own printing company. The middle child of three siblings, she describes herself as a "heavily frustrated troublemaker" in a controlling environment.

Wells decided not to be a lawyer because she was afraid of becoming "one giant pinstripe." Instead of attending law school, she traveled in Europe for three years. Her turning point in committing herself to writing occurred on a train. She thought to herself that if she were totally free, she could get on a train going in the opposite direction whose destination was unknown and see what happened. She got off her train and did just that. Then she thought, "If I am that free, what do I want to do with my life?" She decided to write.

Wells's self-definition as a writer only slightly preceded her coming out as a lesbian in 1980. When she returned from Europe, she moved to San Francisco to be in a vital gay and lesbian culture. Living in San Francisco gave her freedom as a lesbian and as a lesbian writer. She feels "devoted to writing about lesbians and lesbian culture."

Jess Wells has been with her partner, Sharon, whom she calls her "wife," since 1984. She feels "blessed" to have entered Sharon's tight-knit family and to have two adult stepdaughters and a new grandchild.

MAJOR WORKS AND THEMES

Jess Wells's early work was influenced by magical realists such as Gabriel García Márquez and Salman Rushdie. Her earliest published writings are a piece of experimental history, *A Herstory of Prostitution in Western Europe* (1978), and two volumes of experimental fiction, *Run* (1981) and *The Sharda Stories* (1982).

Her next three works, *The Dress, The Cry and A Shirt with No Seams* (1984), *The Dress/The Sharda Stories* (1986), and *Two Willow Chairs* (1987), are volumes of structured short stories. *AfterShocks* (1992) is her first novel.

Some of Wells's major themes include erotica, butch-femme roles, issues of identity and the way different identities inform one another, family, and dysfunctionalism. The psychological and emotional development of characters underlies most of her work.

Wells is considered one of the earliest and best writers of lesbian erotica even though she has published only four erotic stories: "The Succubus," "The Dress," "A Visit to the Seamstress," and "Morning Girls."

She is enamored with the butch-femme theme and has explored it erotically and psychologically. She believes that butch and femme are "metaphors for part of the mythology, cultural icons if you will, of our community.... I rarely meet a couple that doesn't embody that duality, some aspect of it. That's a given throughout almost all cultures—gay culture, straight culture."

Her story "The Dress" erotically explores edges of butch and femme identities. It was the first piece to herald "femme-drag." The main character, a "spikey-dyke" butch, tries on a sexy gown and has an erotic, drag experience. She wonders why she loves this dress and she ruminates over her perceptions of roles. "This is a dress I wouldn't even have thought of wearing when I was straight. But now it's safe. My lover isn't going to think me incompetent if I dress a little femme-y, I think, fingering the strange layers hanging off my waist. Now it's possible to embrace . . . well, more of my . . . beauty. And this dress is the hidden side of me." Wells captures the liberation so many lesbians feel in being lesbian while at the same time playing with the tensions of butch and femme within a person, within a relationship, and, by implication, within the lesbian community.

Wells' characters are not reduced to a generic "femme" or "butch." She is interested in "how cultures are illuminated by places the cultures overlap." Butch and femme characters intersect with their various historical periods, regions, class identities, and ages.

For example, "Nore and Zelda" is a richly textured story set in the early 1900s. The central character, Nore, having worked as a field hand on a farm since she was adopted as a child by the family, grows big and muscular. When she becomes painfully aware that she doesn't fit in, being fully accepted by neither the men nor the women, she flees to Chicago. She soon meets, and is drawn to and accepted by, Zelda and her friends. They too don't quite fit in since many are suffragettes and all are gay and lesbian.

Through her new friends, Nore is introduced to "passing," the gay world, and herself. Again Wells explores the appeal and boundaries of roles as the reader sees that although Nore was able to find fulfilling work in a print shop by "passing" as a man, she is uncomfortable with not being able to be herself—a strong woman.

Class is another theme explored in "Nore and Zelda" and in other works by Wells. Wells explains, "Class is important to me. I'm only marginally middle class, I don't come from intelligentsia, I don't have a higher degree, I have no intention of getting one. I identify a lot with working-class life. My lover is working class."

Much of Wells's fiction, especially *AfterShocks*, examines the multifaceted theme of family. She delves into issues related to both family of origin and the families and communities lesbians create. Skillfully and often poignantly, Wells explores the complexity of parent-child relationships from the point of view of both. Like butch and femme, "family" does not have just one definition.

In "Two Willow Chairs," Beetle, a young lesbian, reminisces over the photographs of her favorite aunt and her aunt's female lover. Beetle was largely raised by these aunts, who were the role models that most lesbians wish they had. She is willing to accept their authority since they carried "the weight of maturity *and* the righteousness of twenty years of lesbian lifestyle behind them" (19). She remembers the rituals revolving around their everyday lives, including the visits that always began in the two willow chairs in their backyard. In a quite short story, Wells manages to capture the love, the struggle, the joy, and the sorrow in the relationships of the three women.

Gretchen, the main character of "Solstice," is a woman dealing with her past and present relationship with her mother as she attempts to understand her need to mother her adult stepchildren.

"A Favorite Haunt" traces the relationship of "a couple of working-class dykes" by following selected celebrations at an expensive French restaurant from their first birthday celebration together to their fifteenth anniversary. The reader not only sees their relationship evolve but watches them establish a close community of family and friends. Critic Nedhera Landers (1987) aptly wrote, "No story has ever felt so bittersweet and real to me as this one" (19).

AfterShocks, Wells' first novel, probes multiple layers of family by exploring the families of origin and the current families (or lack thereof) of many characters. The birth, death, and rebirth of individuals, relationships, and families movingly intersect and interact within the novel. Family, in fact, is one of Wells' subthemes, particularly the causes and impact of dysfunctionalism on the individual and family. Part of the disturbance in her own family arose from her mother's alcoholism. Wells considers the last two books and *The Common Price of Passion* (a novel in process as of 1992) to be a "three-step process in my healing." Many of the stories in *Two Willow Chairs* explore the pain of dysfunctionalism. *AfterShocks* addresses the consequences of growing up in a family like that. The main character in *The Common Price of Passion* realizes that the only way to make a choice is by being her own person. Only then can she escape the fate of becoming like her parents.

In *AfterShocks*, Well's most complex exploration of dysfunctionalism, Trout is a motherless child whose father gradually went mad. By the age of ten, she is taking care of herself and her father. The reader discovers that Trout associates lack of control with tragedy. It is only when her city and home are destroyed by an earthquake and all her elaborate systems of control can no longer protect her that she comes to learn that controlling prevents her from trusting, and it is only by trusting that love can occur. Her lover, Patricia, confronts what it means not to have Trout taking care of everything and learns to find strength within herself. The book's other characters are also forced to look anew at their lives when the earthquake disrupts the patterns they have settled into.

Wells' novel and stories are not primarily "coming out" stories. Rather, they record and illumine the various facets of the lives of women who are already living as lesbians. She thinks that lesbians are "not a sexual preference or orientation. . . . We're a culture and always have been."

Wells suggests that lesbian writers "come from behind" partly because in the 1960s and 1970s lesbians were shut out of universities. Furthermore, she says,

We're a community that has needed to get the word out, and has been so vilified that we needed positive pictures of ourselves. . . . I know some writers who felt impinged upon, they couldn't write the complexity, the dark sides of our relationships because the community wanted happy pictures only. If you take the happy picture phenomenon and being cut off from traditional education, you get a literature that's a little less polished.

I think we're coming out of that now and have been in the last five years. . . . I think we have the potential for writing much better stuff than has been seen in decades and decades, really high quality, revolutionary—in the sense of literature, not in the sense of politics necessarily—because what we have to say based on our political understanding and the kind of culture we have, is so profound in terms of what it challenges in society and the boundaries that are broken. . . . We are women who are not necessarily as truncated by patriarchy as I would think straight women are, and at the same time we are closer to that whole wellspring of emotional work, so that the stuff we are going to be putting out in the next ten to twenty years will be astounding.

CRITICAL RECEPTION

Like many lesbian writers, Jess Wells has not achieved widespread recognition in the heterosexual or academic worlds. She is also not well known among lesbians. Fortunately, since *AfterShocks* was published by a larger press with more money and energy for promotion, she will probably become better known. Despite her still limited recognition, she has been anthologized in eleven books and reviews have been consistently favorable.

Reviewers have commented on Wells' ability to create compelling characters that capture the language and lives of lesbians. The *Common Lives/Lesbian Lives* Collective wrote, "Jess Wells' characters are real lesbians, not the cardboard kind, they come alive in great variety through conversation, dialogue, dramatic spoken interaction. You're never distanced from a scene: the speech of women draws you in. It's her skill in capturing the truths of lesbians talking that gives her work much of its intensity and presence" (Dust jacket, *Two Willow Chairs*). Sarah Schulman, a highly regarded lesbian writer, concurs. "Jess Wells recreates and interprets the fragmented rhythms and subtle textures that make up the secret language of lesbians" (Dust jacket, *Two Willow Chairs*).

Irene Zahava perhaps best summed up Jess Wells' writing: "She is a visionary writer who has both feet firmly planted in reality" (Dust jacket, *AfterShocks*).

BIBLIOGRAPHY

Works by Jess Wells

Run. San Francisco: Library B Books, 1981.
A Herstory of Prostitution in Western Europe. Oakland: Shameless Hussy Press, 1982.
The Sharda Stories. San Francisco: Library B Books, 1982.
The Dress, The Cry and A Shirt with No Seams. San Francisco: Library B Books, 1984, 1985.
The Dress/The Sharda Stories. rev. San Francisco: Library B Books, 1986.
Two Willow Chairs. San Francisco: Library B Books, 1987.
"Visit to the Seamstress." *On Our Backs, 5th Anniversary Issue: The Best of OOB Writers* (September-October 1989): 20–22, 42–45.
AfterShocks. Chicago: Third Side Press, 1992.

Studies of Jess Wells

Barnes, Noreen C. "Fearless Novelist: An Interview with Jess Wells." *Bay Area Reporter* 2:24 (June 11, 1992): 38–39.
———. "Surviving the Tremors." *Bay Area Reporter* 2:24 (June 11, 1992): 38.
Fox Rogers, Susan. "How to Survive Natural Disaster: An Earthquake Brings Out the Best in Jess Wells' New Novel." *Lambda Book Report* (May/June 1992): 26.
Hamilton, Jennifer. "New Arrivals." *Mama Bears News and Notes* (October-November 1987): 20.
Kuda, Marie. "*AfterShocks*." *Booklist* May 15, 1992.
Landers, Nedhera. "Do Femmes Really Have More Fun?" *Chicago Outlines* 1:25 (November 19, 1987): 19.

Lynch, Lee. "Writing against the Odds." *Washington Blade* (May 29, 1992): 53.
Merriam, Eve. "The Graying of Literature." *Ms.* 2:5 (March-April 1992): 58–60.
Micha of Lona, Dona. "Short Stories Represent Our Agonies and Our Strengths." *Seattle Gay News* 14:46 (November 27, 1987).

BARBARA WILSON (1950–   )
Jane Troxell

BIOGRAPHY

Barbara Wilson was born in 1950 in Long Beach, California, a granddaughter of Swedish and Irish immigrants, and a daughter of an accounting instructor and a Sunday school teacher. The author of over ten books, she also runs a successful publishing house, Seal Press. Wilson's first mystery, *Murder in the Collective* (Seal Press, 1984), is often credited with starting the current wave of lesbian-feminist mystery writing.

Wilson's values as a writer and publisher can be traced to her mixed class background. Her father believed poverty lay around every corner, while her mother taught her children the upwardly mobile values she learned in her religious Michigan hometown. This mix, as well as her childhood in a working-class neighborhood in Long Beach, helped make Wilson a hard worker, an astute businesswoman, and a thoughtful writer. Although she didn't learn to read until she was seven, she knew when she was eight that she wanted to be a writer. Sadly, her mother, who had always encouraged her daughter's creativity, died when Wilson was twelve.

Majoring in philosophy at a California college in the late 1960s, Wilson soon tired of academia and decided she should see the world instead. She went to a university in Spain for a year, and traveled to Morocco, Portugal, and Norway. Wilson worked in many jobs around the world before settling on her life's career in 1976. She "worked on assembly lines and at fast-food counters, managed a souvenir shop and washed dishes on a ship.... [She] sold encyclopedias in Arizona, taught English in Spain, and took care of children in Norway" ("My Work" 230). One biographical sketch credits Wilson with having held twenty-three different jobs before settling in Seattle, Washington, in 1974.

Two years later, Wilson and Rachel da Silva founded Seal Press with just over a hundred dollars. They ran the press, then a collective, out of a garage in its first years. Wilson says that she and da Silva taught themselves "to do everything from book packing to selling rights, from designing books to promoting them" ("My Work" 230). It was in 1984, when Seal Press published Wilson's first murder mystery, that she was finally able to quit her other job at a local hospital.

Even while working other full-time jobs and running a small press, Wilson wrote. Her first books included a children's story and two collections of short fiction. Wilson's own experiences at a leftist printshop collective informed both her 1982 novel *Ambitious Women* (Spinsters Ink) and 1984's *Murder in the Collective* (Seal Press), the first in the Pam Nilsen series. In 1983, Seal Press published Wilson's *Walking on the Moon: Six Stories and a Novella*.

The second Pam Nilsen mystery, *Sisters of the Road* (Seal Press, 1986), was the product of Wilson's research into teenage prostitution and a stay in Portland, Oregon, with poet Judith Barrington and publisher Ruth Gundle. Gundle's own Eighth Mountain Press published Wilson's 1988 novel, *Cows and Horses*, which remains that press's best-selling title. That same year, Seal brought out a collection of its prolific publisher's short stories, *Miss Venezuela*. Wilson wrote the third Pam Nilsen book, *The Dog Collar Murders* (1989), in England, where she was then living. Wilson also finished the 1990 mystery, *Gaudí Afternoon* (Seal Press), in London.

It was in Norway that Wilson came upon another phase of writing, that of translation. In the mid–1980s, she translated the works of Norwegian writers Ebba Haslund and Cora Sandel, an award-winning venture. Wilson then started the Women in Translation imprint of Seal in order to bring the work of international feminist writers to the English-speaking market. Her own books have been translated and published in many languages.

Over the years, Wilson has been widely represented in lesbian and feminist anthologies, including *Lesbian Love Stories* (Crossing Press, 1989), *Reader, I Murdered Him* (St. Martin's Press, 1989), *An Intimate Wilderness* (Eighth Mountain Press, 1991), *A Woman's Eye*, edited by Sara Paretsky (Delacorte Press, 1991), among others. In 1985, she herself co-edited the fiction anthology *The Things That Divide Us* (Seal Press). Today, Wilson lives on Lake Union in Seattle, where she devotes most of her energy to her writing.

MAJOR WORKS AND THEMES

The lesbian themes in Barbara Wilson's work would be difficult to overlook. Writes the author in "My Work," "Perhaps because I have been an explicit feminist and lesbian almost as long as I have been publishing, the lesbian-feminist content of my writing has never been ignored. In my Pam Nilsen mysteries, especially, I marked out my territory: the lesbian and leftist culture" (228). Her overtly political concerns inform all of Wilson's work, which explores, among other themes, violence against women, lesbian lives, and issues of race and class.

Wilson's first Pam Nilsen mystery, *Murder in the Collective*, opened the floodgates of lesbian-feminist mystery writing. Wilson's politically conscious amateur detective presented a popular forum for tackling lesbian-feminist issues. In *Murder in the Collective*, Pam Nilsen not only solves a murder but comes out as a lesbian, ponders her and others' racism, learns of government atrocities in the Philippines, and contemplates class disparity via her wealthy girlfriend. Despite the charged content, the book succeeded both as a mystery and as a feminist dialogue, inspiring many other lesbian writers to try the same.

Because Pam is young, eager to work on her politics, and surrounded by leftist thinkers, Wilson's best known works are wrought with political themes. Pam Nilsen is a character at odds with the sociopolitical reality before her, and it is her internal debate that drives the first-person narrative common to the whole series. *Murder in the Collective* explores the dynamics of collectives, as well as the role of women in undeveloped countries. In the second Nilsen work, *Sisters of the Road*, Pam reconciles her conflicting feelings about prostitution before completing her search for the murderer of a teenage prostitute. In *The Dog Collar Murders*, Pam contemplates the S/M and pornography debates.

Violence against women is a common Wilson theme. In *Sisters of the Road*, Pam uncovers Seattle's world of teenage prostitution in which young girls are forced to stay in the business, dependent on pimps and clients who abuse them. Pam is raped near the end of the book, the heroine giving a painful first-person account of the rape and its aftermath. Incest also figures in, as a young prostitute on the run had been sexually abused by her father. In *The Dog Collar Murders*, two lesbians become murder victims of internalized homophobia.

Class issues figure throughout Wilson's fiction. Pam Nilsen comes from a middle-class background yet works in a collective. Her lover, Hadley, on the other hand, is filthy rich yet denies her wealth because she is embarrassed by its entitlement and power. The protagonists in Wilson's feminist working-class novel, *Ambitious Women*, represent struggles different from Pam and Hadley's, while other Wilson characters fall all over the class spectrum. While many lesbian writers seem to prefer professional protagonists or to try to downplay their characters' work lives, Wilson grounds her characters in their work, exploring economic status and its effects by juxtaposing characters from different back-grounds.

Lesbian politics also play a major role in the Nilsen series. Through three books, readers witness the heroine's coming out and subsequent development as a lesbian. Pam discovers her lesbianism through the usual channels: she falls in love. "I couldn't say I'd always been a lesbian," Pam states. "Some of it definitely had to do with Hadley" (134). Wilson breaks with lesbian fiction's usually romantic ideals at the end of *Murder in the Collective*. The two lovers hardly ride off into the sunset: Hadley dumps Pam, who is left alone in *Sisters* to explore her newfound sexuality. She has a few casual, fumbled affairs, learning that lesbianism does not mean uncomplicated love and sex. In *Dog Collar Murders*, Pam goes outside the boundaries of her own head to explore lesbian sexuality. A weekend conference on lesbian sexuality, S/M, and pornography opens Pam's eyes to lesbian sexual politics.

Sexuality is explored on a more personal level in Wilson's *Cows and Horses*. The novel begins at the end of Bet and Norah's ten-year relationship, with Bet seeking to fill her emptiness through an affair. Wilson not only explores the butch-femme dichotomy (Bet's new lover is butch and her opposite in many ways) but also connects lesbian sexuality with more than just sex. Bet's sexuality is not cut off from her thoughts and actions but is integral to her identity, in the same way that Wilson's sex writing here is not removed from the narrative but is central to the story.

Wilson left Pam Nilsen behind in 1990 to introduce a new lesbian detective, Cassandra Reilly, in *Gaudí Afternoon*. Older, more sophisticated, and more comfortable with her lesbianism than Pam, Cassandra offers Wilson a chance to explore political themes on a different level. Here, Wilson confronts the issues of gender and transsexualism, parenting and custody rights, and lesbian relationships between women who are long past coming out. Set in Barcelona, *Gaudí* displays Wilson's international scope and interest in global feminism.

Wilson's early work—short story collections and one novel—introduced her special trademarks of political acuity, humor, and her passion for lesbian-feminist ideals. (While Wilson's short stories present a vital young author, the books have gone out of print and won't be discussed in detail here. However, her best short stories from the period were collected in 1988's *Miss Venezuela*.) These trademarks have remained constant throughout her impressive career.

CRITICAL RECEPTION

Barbara Wilson's refusal to compromise her politics has dictated her critical reception. Wilson summarizes her experience: "My books have long been 'seen' in terms of their political and sexual content. . . . The headline might read 'Too Much Sex, Not Enough Mystery,' but the reviewer does deal with the lesbian characters. Of course this means that sometimes my books don't get reviewed, but it also ensures that when they are, women as lesbians will be there" ("My Work" 228). Mainstream reviews, when they are published, recognize Wilson has much to say about women's lives. Lesbian and feminist critics, on the other hand, hail Wilson as one of the leading lesbian-feminist writers of her time.

Lesbian readers knew right away what Wilson, already an acclaimed short story writer and novelist, was offering with *Murder in the Collective*. *Lammas' Little Review* stated, "Since the essence of the mystery novel is the exploration of motives, ulterior and otherwise, the feminist writer is free to range far beyond political platitudes and into the complexities of what it means to live our politics. . . . *Murder in the Collective* is an intriguing mystery . . . and a political novel that doesn't preach. That's a tough combination to beat" (Fall 1984). Wilson wasn't the first feminist mystery writer, but she was most successful at it. Echoed

Sojourner, "*Murder in the Collective* succeeds where others have failed" (December 1984, 35).

Even non-gay papers noticed. *The Listener*, out of London, where the Women's press published *Murder in the Collective*, confirmed, "Despite [the book's] load of noble intentions, this is a really good thriller: murder in a Seattle collective printshop, feuding with the Lesbian typesetters, new love for the narrator, and a kind of pocket guide to U.S. female radicalism over the past decade" (January 10, 1985). Another Londoner, a gentleman, stated, "I've come away with a greater understanding of lesbianism than I'd have got from a hundred worthy studies. . . . Barbara Wilson is currently occupying my Best Thriller of 1984 slot" (Durrant's, October 18, 1984).

With *Sisters of the Road*, Wilson began to garner more press reviews from mainstream outlets, with coverage in *Over My Dead Body!* computer bulletin board service, the *Seattle Post-Intelligencer*, and even *Screw*. She still enjoys attention in the more liberal review outlets, such as the *Village Voice, Booklist, Publishers Weekly*, and *Bloomsbury Review*, which declared, "Wilson has profound things to say about women, how they relate to each other as friends and lovers, and how they understand themselves in an age that offers a range of options."

By *The Dog Collar Murders*, lesbians saw a new Wilson mystery as a major event. *Sojourner* declared at the time, "Wilson's work has created one of the most interesting detectives in the genre today. . . . Pam Nilsen isn't so sure she wants to—or should—help the lawmen" (March 1989).

The tale of Wilson's new sleuth from 1990's *Gaudí Afternoon*, Cassandra Reilly, was no less well received, and caught the eye of mainstream reviewers. The *Baltimore Sun* wrote, "Wilson's a sharp and amusing writer who propels her *Gaudí Afternoon* along with dash and verve and a sort of enlightened intelligence" (January 8, 1991, E1). The *Bloomsbury Review* added, "As in good mystery fiction, the reader delights in being fooled, again and again" (June 1991). Lesbian and gay media agreed; the *San Francisco Bay Times* trumpeted Wilson the "Queen of Lesbian Mystery" (January 1991).

Gaudí Afternoon recently won the British Crime Writers Award for "best crime novel set in continental Europe," as well the 1990 Lambda Literary Award for Lesbian Mystery.

BIBLIOGRAPHY

Works by Barbara Wilson

Ambitious Women. Seattle: Seal Press, 1981; Albany, NY: Spinsters Ink, 1982.
Thin Ice and Other Stories. Seattle: Seal Press, 1981.
Walking on the Moon. Seattle: Seal Press, 1983.
Murder in the Collective. Seattle: Seal Press, 1984.
Sisters of the Road. Seattle: Seal Press, 1986.

Cows and Horses. Portland, OR: Eighth Mountain Press, 1988.

Miss Venezuela. Seattle: Seal Press, 1988.

The Dog Collar Murders. Seattle: Seal Press, 1989.

Gaudí Afternoon. Seattle: Seal Press, 1990.

"My Work." *Inversions*. Ed. Betsy Warland. Vancouver, B.C., Canada: Press Gang, 1991. 227–36.

Studies of Barbara Wilson

Brownworth, Victoria. "Making the Personal Political." *Outweek* January 9, 1991: 68–70.

Thomas, June. "Title." *off our backs* January 1990: 10–11.

MARY WINGS (1949–   )
Ellen Lewin

Mary Wings, mystery writer and community historian, was born Mary Geller in 1949 in Chicago. Her father was a furniture designer and manufacturer; her mother, a graphic designer and painter. She has a younger brother, John. Her father's only partially realized artistic ambitions formed a dominant aspect of the atmosphere in the family's upper-middle-class suburban home. Wings remembers his reciting poetry at dinner and affecting what she describes as "a nineteenth century depressive" style, Byronesque, vain, and tragic. In contrast, she recalls her mother as presenting a cheerful demeanor, apparently consciously balancing the depressive episodes of her father.

While the Gellers' home was conventional in most ways, they differed from other families around them in having adopted the Baha'i religion. Wings traces her later fascination with mystical religion (a Rajneesh-like movement in *She Came in a Flash* and Catholicism in *Divine Victim*) to her early feelings of jealousy of those who had more romantic and mystical religious experiences. Baha'i was austere and rational, lacking almost totally in ritual or ceremony of any kind, and it failed to ignite any spiritual sparks in Mary.

Wings attended Shimer College in Illinois and later studied ceramics at the Museum Art School in Portland, Oregon. But until she became involved in the women's movement in the early 1970s, she had difficulty finding a way to mobilize her creative energies.

Wings describes her discovery of women's liberation and, shortly thereafter, her coming out as a lesbian, as classic conversion experiences. She was living in Portland in 1971, and like many other women involved in women's consciousness-raising groups, read *Notes from the Second Year*. The underground publication of essays and manifestos by radical feminists convinced her immediately that she was a lesbian, and she went about reorganizing her life within the lesbian-feminist community. Her involvement in the often bitter controversies of the radical feminist world was the direct stimulus for her *Come Out Comix* (1973) (and for subsequent ventures in this genre, *Dyke Shorts* [1980] and *Are Your Highs Getting You Down?* [1979]), which she wrote in response to cartoonist Trina Robbins' earlier satire of radical lesbians.

Come Out Comix established Wings as a figure in the radical lesbian cultural scene. She also entered the world of women's music during this period, playing the banjo with Robin Flower and Woody Simmons in a band called Robin, Woody and Wings, and working as a studio musician. Her studio work led to appearances on albums with Woody Simmons, Robin Flower, Willie Tyson, and Cassie Culver. By the mid–1970s, Wings had moved with the band to the San Francisco Bay Area, where she worked at various odd jobs and eventually dropped out of the band. Feeling dissatisfied with the circumscribed world of lesbian feminism in the Bay Area, she moved to the Netherlands in 1980, remaining there for most of seven years before returning to San Francisco in 1987, after the publication of her first novel.

Once Wings had reestablished herself in San Francisco, she became involved both in the San Francisco Gay and Lesbian History Project and Frameline, which organizes and supports the annual San Francisco Lesbian and Gay Film Festival. She also studied theater set design at San Francisco State University, studies that allowed her to bring together her visual sense with her interest in narrative. Her work with the History Project led her and fellow community historian Eric Garber to produce a lecture-slide-video presentation on Greta Garbo, "Greta Garbo: A Woman of Affairs." The show has appeared frequently around the San Francisco Bay Area and has been presented at the Directors' Guild in Los Angeles, as well as at lesbian/gay film festivals in London, Turin, Rome, Melbourne, Amsterdam, and Chicago.

MAJOR WORKS AND THEMES

Wings describes her years in the Netherlands as a period of increasing isolation from her own cultural roots. Though she finally became fluent in Dutch, she found herself suffering from "language loneliness," a state in which her command of Dutch was imperfect at the same time that she feared that her competence in English was beginning to decline. After reading a Lawrence Sanders mystery, she told herself that she could do better, and more or less to entertain herself, she began to write a novel one evening.

Looking back now, Wings remarks that she didn't know anything formal about the craft of writing fiction. She simply began to write at the typewriter, making up for the lack of a premeditated plot with details recalled from her years in the women's movement in the United States. After completing twenty-six pages in one night, Wings showed what she had written to her friend, Wendy Chapkis, who was a professional writer. She was amazed, she now recalls, when Wendy asked, "What happens next?" This was Wings's first realization that she had a gift for writing suspense, a discovery that led to the publication of *She Came Too Late*, first published in England in 1986. *She Came Too Late* appeared in the United States in 1988.

In *She Came Too Late*, Wings introduced her lesbian detective, Emma Victor, a volunteer at a Women's Hotline. After a mysterious call from a woman in trouble, Emma becomes involved in a murder and the murky politics of a feminist health clinic, all filtered through the complications of attractions to various women she meets while trying to solve the mystery. Emma Victor's lesbianism is taken for granted, her erotic weaknesses familiar and authentic.

Wings quickly followed her first novel with a second featuring Emma Victor, *She Came in a Flash* (published in England in 1988, in the United States in 1989). By the time of the second book, Emma had moved from Boston to the San Francisco area, paralleling Wings's own return to California. In this second novel, Emma does battle with trendy lesbian musicians, a Rajneesh-like cult, and a cast of slightly worn veterans of the women's movement. Again, her heroine solves the mystery, though not without detours into flirtations with unworthy but compelling lesbian characters. As in the first novel, Emma despairs of finding a lover she can stay with; both books are energized by Emma's struggles with imperfection and impermanence.

Wings describes her first two novels as grounded in the ambivalence of her main character, Emma Victor, and as posing questions rather than answering them, a departure, she feels, from the more doctrinaire stance of her earlier *Come Out Comix*. The books avoid ''happy talk'' about lesbianism; rather they examine the protagonist's lesbian relationships in contexts that are basically flawed and that swing dramatically from elation to distress. Emma is always confronting breaking up, rather than settling down for life; she asks why people fall in love and whether falling in love is fundamentally dangerous. The answers she finds to all of these questions are mired in ambiguity, definite only in their ambivalence.

Wings's books are rich in descriptive detail of the scenes Emma traverses—the women's health movement, lesbian parties, the women's music scene, mystical cults—her writing far more engaged in setting scenes and establishing the voice of her protagonist than in controlling plot elements. Her writing is strong in that it feels intuitive and immediate; as a writer she trusts herself and her reactions to her characters so much that the details of plot are almost superfluous. Her models, Raymond Chandler, Patrick McGrath, and Toni Morrison (especially in *The Bluest Eye*), are all writers whose strength is in the voice of their narrators rather than in the sequences of a story line.

Wings's third novel, *Divine Victim*, will be published in 1993 in England and the United States. This book brings in a new female protagonist, an American academic who has worked in Europe, drawing on Wings's own experiences during her years in the Netherlands. For *Divine Victim*, she carried out extensive research on Catholic mysticism, on nuns and convents, and on art history, involving the reader again not solely in the plot, but in the evocation of scenes and emotions. As before, her central character is looking for love, but seems doomed to succeed only with a woman who doesn't really interest her. Instead, she remains intensely committed to a past failed relationship, as her memories of this relationship become central figures in the story. The book is less an exercise in *noir* detective writing, as her first two books were, than an effort that shifts between mystery, ghost story, and gothic, defeating the reader's desire to control the action. Like her earlier books, *Divine Victim* is replete with contemporary cultural references, including images that call to mind *Silence of the Lambs*, Camille Paglia, and Daphne du Maurier's *Rebecca*.

Wings is now at work on a fourth novel with the working title *Too Thin to Be Believed*. This book will be situated in a treatment center for anorectics, and will bring contemporary debates about eating disorders and faddish, highly profitable, treatments for both obesity and anorexia into perspective. The narrative will be more complex than that in her previous works, using the voices of an anorectic patient and a woman police officer investigating a crime. She intends the book as a commentary on the various self-improvement movements gaining rapid acceptance in American medicine, and a critique of simplistic feminist models of eating disorders and related problems. The ambiguities and uncertainties of women's experience with food will be major themes in the book.

Wings describes herself as an enthusiastic researcher, who enjoys the process of digging up "background" material for her books as much as she does writing them. She immerses herself in reading and interviews when preparing a book, and often does on-the-scene fieldwork to get a feel for the atmospheres she plans to describe. She is aware of writing for a select audience of six or seven friends; just as completion of her first book was aided by the encouragement of one friend, she feels that she continues to write in order to entertain a close circle of readers.

Wings has also published a number of short stories. Her story "Kill the Man for Me" appeared in *A Woman's Eye*, a collection of mystery fiction by women edited by Sara Paretsky. Another story, "Mars Bar," appeared in *Out/Look* magazine. She has worked on film treatments for both of these stories for MayaVision, a production company based in London, and on *The Making of Queen Christina*, work to be based on her historical research on Greta Garbo.

CRITICAL RECEPTION

Critics who have responded to Mary Wings's work have associated her writing with the more well known efforts of Sara Paretsky and Sue Grafton, using the term "genre bending" to point out the adept movement in the work of all of these authors between the familiar hard-boiled detective novel and sensitive social commentary. Though only Wings is a lesbian author whose protagonist is a lesbian, all of these writers deprecate traditional expectations of the feminine while not quite letting their characters totally identify with the macho heroes of Raymond Chandler and Dashiell Hammett.

Mary Wings's work has received its most significant critical reception in Great Britain. Her first book, *She Came Too Late*, was on the London City Limits Bestseller List for seven weeks and was voted Best Novel of the Year in the 1986 Reader's Poll. The *New Statesman*'s Nick Kimberley called it "a brisk, cynical thriller which . . . pits individual integrity against an inflexibly corrupt system"(16). The *Women's Review* described Wings's writing as "spare, witty prose . . . almost as hard boiled as the boys' but soft centred," and said that the book presents an "unsentimental, but committed portrait of a cross-section of the Women's Movement under siege" (11).

The book also attracted attention in the United States. A review in the *Women's Review of Books* characterized Wings as "the wittiest of the current lesbian detective writers, as well as the one with the most affinity for the bizarre" (20). Emma Victor, of *She Came Too Late*, is "the quintessential woman of the eighties, the pilgrim who got some experience and became a tourist" (20). Reviewers were quick to praise Wings's treatment of lesbianism as both sensitive and realistic. R. Ruby Rich, writing in the *Village Voice*, said that Wings "sticks to a resolutely lesbian-feminist perspective that doesn't flinch from satirizing '80s foibles as precisely as an Alison Bechdel dykes-to-watch-out-for cartoon" (19).

She Came in a Flash also appeared on the City Limits Alternative Bestseller List in London, where reviewers called it "fast-moving and refreshing" (10). In the United States, *Gay Community News* reviewer Liz Galst called Emma Victor "a dick I could get used to" (12). Galst says that neurotic and wacky, Emma "fits in well with the absurdist world around her" (12). *Elle*'s reviewer not only praised Wings's "way with a one-liner," but found Emma Victor's lesbianism an intriguing twist on detective traditions. Victor is a new-style femme fatale, directing her wiles toward other women, and leading into "some steamy couplings" (13).

Wings's short fiction has also begun to attract attention. A review of "Kill the Man for Me" in the *Women's Review of Books* praised the story as offering "the most accomplished sleight-of-hand in the book [*A Woman's Eye*] informed by rigorous politics" (9) and singles out the author's deftness in managing two different narrators and points of view in a fourteen-page story.

BIBLIOGRAPHY

Works by Mary Wings

She Came Too Late. London: Women's Press, 1986; Freedom, CA: Crossing Press, 1988.
She Came in a Flash. London: Women's Press, 1988; New York: New American Library, 1989.
"Mars Bar." *Out/Look* (Summer 1990): 32–35.
"Kill the Man for Me." *A Woman's Eye*. Ed. Sara Paretsky. New York: Delacorte Press, 1991. 235–49.

Divine Victim. London: Women's Press, 1992; New York: New American Library, forthcoming.
(Translations of Mary Wings's works have appeared in Dutch, German, Japanese, and Spanish.)

Studies of Mary Wings

Galst, Liz. "A Girl after My Own Heart." *Gay Community News* 1989: 12–13.
Howell, John. "Genre Bending." *Elle* (December 1990): 160, 162.
Kimberley, Nick. "Body Politic." *New Statesman* 6 June 1986.
Johnston, Sheila. "Mary Wings." *Women's Review* (May 1986): 11.
Marlowe, Jane C. "Writing: *She Came Too Late*." *Spare Rib* (June 1988): 28.
Munk, Erika. "Deadly Delights." *Women's Review of Books* 9 (February 1992): 8–9.
Paris, Sherri. "In a World They Never Made." *Women's Review of Books* (July 1988): 20.
Rich, R. Ruby. "The Lady Dicks." *Village Voice* 9 May 1989: 19.

TERRY WOLVERTON (1954–   )
Susan Silton

BIOGRAPHY

Terry Wolverton was born on August 23, 1954, in Cape Canaveral, Florida, into a working-class family. When she was just over one year old, her parents divorced, and her mother took her to Detroit, where they lived with Wolverton's maternal grandparents, while her mother supported herself as a secretary. Wolverton credits her grandmother for her love of literature and her ambition from an early age to be a writer.

When Wolverton was five, her mother remarried. Alcoholism soon came to dominate family life, and Wolverton endured sexual abuse by her stepfather. She attended Cass Technical High School in Detroit, majoring in performing arts and graduating in 1972. While there she received awards in acting and in oral interpretation of literature.

Wolverton was deeply influenced by events of the sixties, including the civil rights and anti-war movements, the Detroit riots, and the assassinations of Martin Luther King and John F. Kennedy. Such events caused Wolverton to question the accepted social values of the time and ultimately to turn to a countercultural point of view. At seventeen, she began an involvement with drugs that lasted until 1983.

Wolverton spent her first year of college at the University of Detroit, where she majored in theater and psychology and began her activism in the women's movement. She moved to Canada in 1973 and majored in theater, psychology, and women's studies at the University of Toronto, where she co-founded the Toronto Feminist Theatre Troupe. It was also in Toronto that she came out as a lesbian. A psychological breakdown brought her back to Detroit in 1974, where she worked as a waitress. In the summer of 1975, she attended Sagaris (an independent institute for the study of feminist political theory) in Lyndonville, Vermont. Later in 1975, she enrolled in Thomas Jefferson College, an alternative college in western Michigan. She graduated there with a bachelor of philosophy degree (equivalent to bachelor of arts), with academic emphasis in theater, women's studies, and creative writing. In western Michigan she also founded Scarlet Women, a radical theater troupe.

In 1976, Wolverton moved to Los Angeles to attend the Feminist Studio Workshop at the Woman's Building. During the course of this two-year art program, she self-published a book of poetry, *Blue Moon*, and shifted her emphasis from theater to performance art. Over the next several years, she created ten full-length performance art works, including writing or co-writing the texts. These were produced in Los Angeles, San Diego, and New York, and included *An Oral Herstory of Lesbianism* (created with twelve other performers under Wolverton's direction), *In Silence Secrets Turns to Lies/Secrets Shared Become Sacred Truth* (a solo work focusing on Wolverton's incest experience), and *Me and My Shadow* (a solo performance piece about the intersection of racism and sexism). In 1986, Wolverton retired from performance art in order to concentrate full-time on her writing career.

Between 1977 and 1984, Wolverton shared a romantic relationship with poet Bia Lowe, and each served as inspiration and support for the other's creative endeavors.

Wolverton's thirteen-year association with the Woman's Building included initiating and organizing numerous cross-disciplinary projects, such as the Lesbian Art Project, the Great American Lesbian Art Show (GALAS), the Incest Awareness Project, and a White Women's Anti-Racism Consciousness Raising Group. She also worked as the organization's development director and eventually became its executive director.

Since 1972, Wolverton has operated a management consulting business specializing in non-profit organizations, small businesses, and individuals. She has also taught creative writing since 1977 at the Woman's Building, Connexxus Women's Center, the Gay and Lesbian Community Services Center, and UCLA (University of California at Los Angeles) Extension. In addition, she has produced and exhibited audio, video, and installation art.

She has edited three anthologies, has received six artist-in-residence grants for literature and performance from the California Arts Council, and has been awarded an Individual Artists Grant from the City of Los Angeles Cultural Affairs Department.

Currently, Wolverton shares her life in Los Angeles with artist Susan Silton and attributes her increased artistic productivity to the support from that relationship.

MAJOR WORKS AND THEMES

Multidimensional and charged with raw energy, Terry Wolverton's work spans many forms, including dramatic scripts, poetry, fiction, essays, journalism, and art criticism. While each form provides her with a different voice, there is a thread of rigorous honesty that weaves through all of her work.

Wolverton's dramatic scripts often explore issues of identity and coming to terms with one's past, particularly in relationship to others. The text for her 1979 performance, *In Silence Secrets Turn to Lies/Secrets Shared Become Sacred Truth*, examines early incest experiences with her stepfather as the catalyst not only for self-evaluation, but for transformation. The collaboratively created *An Oral Herstory of Lesbianism* (1979) looks at the multiplicity of lesbian identities. *Ya Got Class, Real Class* (1980) and *Me and My Shadow* (1984) explore class difference and racism, respectively. And her full-length play, *A Merry Little Christmas*, deals with the emotional aftermath of growing up in an alcoholic family. In Kitty, the daughter of alcoholic Buddy, Wolverton has created an anti-heroine as a dramatic edge. Even though she is the victim of Buddy's alcoholic behavior, she is brittle while Buddy is charming and sympathetic. Victimization does not ennoble Wolverton's characters; rather, it provides the necessary tension for self-reflection.

Poetry is most often autobiographical for Wolverton, highly image- and sound-based, and risk-taking in its exploration of painful emotional experiences. This is clearly evident in her most recent collection of poetry, *Black Slip* (1992). The collection spans past and present with piquancy, often utilizing everyday settings for an even sharper emotional edge. In "Gin," Wolverton matches daughter against mother in what seems like a simple card game, but the ritual plays out in unbearable emptiness. In "Black Slip," it's not so much a love that is lost, but the shell of love, seen "draped on the back of the door." Fragility of love and the bittersweetness of commitment, as seen in a myriad of lesbian relationships, are constant poetic themes. "Anniversary" places two lovers on a metaphoric high wire, and in "For my writing students who are HIV+" she confronts the imminent loss.

In her fiction, Wolverton often examines the psychological dynamics between people, particularly what is left unspoken. One of the most telling examples of this probing style is "A Whisper in the Veins." On his way back to Los Angeles from a business trip, Greg visits his seventy-one-year old mother, with the intention of telling her that he is HIV-positive. Instead the story digs deep into the loving but limited relationship between mother and son, as they sit and play cards to avoid their typically awkward interaction. In reverie Greg remembers his childhood and adulthood, thinks about "all the ways we are known to each other, all the ways in which we are unknown."

In the story "Pretty Women: A Lesbian Fable," two women, vastly different on the surface, come together in a refreshingly romantic fashion, while the story explores the psychological tension between love and lust, beauty and ugliness, facade and reality.

Since 1988, Wolverton has been writing a novel, *The Labrys Reunion*, which explores the impact of feminism on a group of women from two different generations: one active in the sixties and seventies, and one just now coming of age in the nineties. The book explores the mutual disappointments these generations feel in one another and suggests that the future of the women's movement may rest on their resolution.

Finally, in her essays, Wolverton frequently conveys a nostalgic sense of place. This form allows her to hold onto what is real, to grasp the past in an effort to save it for future reference. In a catalogue essay for the Los Angeles exhibit *Insistent Landscapes* in 1990, she writes, "The landscape is not what it used to be, and yet it lives on, pulsing inside of us like a stream alive and bubbling underground. Something within us refuses to forget those earliest lessons, those visions etched onto our eyelids and soaked into our skin."

CRITICAL RECEPTION

To a large extent, Wolverton's literary work has not received critical discussion, perhaps because much of her work has been published as individual stories and poems. Her performance art pieces have been extensively reviewed and often highlight her willingness to tackle painful and controversial subject matter. There do exist interviews where Wolverton discusses her creative intents and strategies, although these tend to be focused primarily on her performance works.

HONORS AND AWARDS

Among Wolverton's numerous awards are a Vesta Award in Literature by the Woman's Building in 1991, a Lesbian Rights Award by the Southern California Women for Understanding in 1986, a Merit Award for a video of "Me and My Shadow" at the JVC Tokyo Video Festival in 1984, and a Gay and Lesbian Academic Union award for contributions to the fine arts in 1981.

BIBLIOGRAPHY

Works by Terry Wolverton

Books

Blue Moon. Los Angeles: Women's Graphic Center and Terry Wolverton, 1977.
Harbinger: Poetry and Fiction by Los Angeles Writers. Co-edited with Benjamin Weissman. Los Angeles: Los Angeles Festival and Beyond Baroque, 1990.
Blood Whispers: L.A. Writers on AIDS. Ed. Terry Wolverton. Los Angeles: Silverton Books and the Gay and Lesbian Community Services Center, 1991.
Indivisible: Short Fiction by West Coast Gay and Lesbian Writers. Co-edited with Robert Drake. New York: Plume Fiction, 1991.
Black Slip. Los Angeles: Clothespin Fever Press, 1992.

Selected Anthologies

"In Silence Secrets Turn to Lies/Secrets Shared Become Sacred Truth," performance text. *Voice in the Night: Women Speaking about Incest*. Ed Toni McNaron and Yarrow Morgan. Minneapolis: Cleis Press, 1982. 49–56.

"Pretty Women." *Indivisible*. Ed Terry Wolverton and Robert Drake. New York: Plume Fiction, 1991. 223–29.

Selected Periodicals

"An Oral Herstory of Lesbianism," excerpts from performance text, *Sinister Wisdom* 12 (Winter 1980): 61–66.

"Ya Got Class, Real Class," performance text. *Heresies* 18 (1986): 88–93.

"Black Slip," poem. *Jacaranda Review* 3:2 (Fall/Winter 1988): 134–35.

"A Whisper in the Veins," short fiction. *Glimmer Train Stories* 4 (Fall 1992): 25–37.

Studies of Terry Wolverton

Beckman, Laurel and Kathleen Sorensen. "Power and the Power Over—A Conversation with Terry Wolverton." *Lucky* 2 (1989).

Burnham, Linda Frye. "An Oral Herstory of Lesbianism." *High Performance* 2:4 (Winter 1979–1980): 17–25.

George, Lynell. "Terry Wolverton." *L.A. Style* (September 1990): 196.

Hachim, Samir. "Creating a Context of Facades and Feminism." *Advocate* (July 7, 1983): 55–56.

Lowe, Bia. "Theater as Community Ritual." *Heresies* 17 (1984): 48–49.

JACQUELINE WOODSON
(1963–   )
Catherine Saalfield

BIOGRAPHY

Jacqueline Woodson was born on February 12, 1963, in Columbus, Ohio, into an extended family of Jehovah's Witnesses. Her parents were divorced two months later, at which point she, her older brother, and sister moved to Greenville, South Carolina, to live with their mother's mother. In time for first grade, Woodson and her siblings caught up with her mother in Brooklyn, New York, where she met her baby brother and failed her first ever spelling test. From then on, however, she was always an outstanding English student who never focused on math or geography, thus confounding the teachers with her specialized confidence, ability, and wit.

In fifth grade, Woodson won a poetry contest with a poem called "Tribute to Martin Luther King," and was called into the principal's office and accused of plagiarizing. Yes, the first six lines—"Black brothers, / black sisters, / all of them were great, / no fear, / no fright, / but a willingness to fight . . . "— had been copied from a poem her older sister, a seventh grader, had written. But not the rest: "In fine big houses lived the whites and in little old shacks lived the blacks. One of them was Martin with a heart of gold, not like white bigots with hearts colder than cold. He fought for peace and freedom too. He fought for me and probably you." Her teacher suggested she change the line from "like white bigots" to "like some white bigots," which Woodson didn't approve of, but recalls as her first experience with revisions.

Woodson displayed her cavalier attitude toward sex and sexuality from early on, passing notes which read "My Pussy" to Michael in second grade. In third grade, a classmate, Charles, took his penis out, and even though she didn't see it, Woodson told Mrs. Moskowitz that she had and Charles was expelled. Her first crush was on a girl named Alina, also a Jehovah's Witness, who had new breasts and would torture Woodson by asking if she was still flat chested, which she was. When she turned fourteen, her girlfriends began dating boys, and Woodson doctored her intricate love letters by changing the name at the top to that of a boy.

Woodson came out in a creative writing class taught by a bisexual man her sophomore year at Adelphi University in Garden City, New York, where she pledged Alpha Kappa Alpha sorority despite its inherently heterosexist sensibility. She went on to earn her B.A. in English in 1985. After college, she began working as an editorial assistant at a children's book packaging company called Kirchoff/Wohlberg, where she met her future agent who, at the time, suggested she turn a trade book blurb into a novel. Her first children's book, *Last Summer with Maizon*, emerged from that initial contact. After a writing class at the New School for Social Research in 1987, she sold *Maizon* to Delacorte and decided to stop working full-time and free-lance, word processing for rent money. She also spent a short time in East Harlem doing drama therapy with ten- to seventeen-year-old runaways and homeless kids, talking about AIDS and giving them safer sex information.

By the time she was awarded her first fellowship (1990) at the MacDowell Colony in Peterborough, New Hampshire, Woodson had sold a trilogy, which included *Last Summer with Maizon*, *Maizon at Blue Hill* and a third, as yet untitled book. She had also been contracted to write *The Dear One*. She currently lives in Brooklyn, following her residency (1991–1992) at the Fine Arts Work Center in Provincetown, Massachusetts. As she completes the last book in the *Maizon* trilogy, Woodson has begun writing adult essays, a screenplay, and a novel. Her most recent work, *From the Notebooks of MelaninSun*, is the first book for young adults with a lesbian theme to be published by Scholastic.

MAJOR WORKS AND THEMES

Writing for children, Jacqueline Woodson has maintained the integrity of her characters' complicated lives. Children's books, even if penned by lesbians, rarely embrace issues of lesbian sexuality, either a child's blossoming interests or lesbian and gay issues in the adult world. The few examples of children's books with lesbians in them end in the stereotypical way: with suicide or with boyfriends. Of course, there are pop psych books put out by small presses about kids growing up with lesbian and/or gay parents. Never condescending or simple, however, Woodson's books weave a myriad of themes together, always structured by female networks of best friends, grandmothers, mothers and their friends, and neighbors. Developing sexualities and female bonds are fluid and plentiful.

The Dear One (1991) follows a middle-class, suburbanite adolescent, Afeni, through a season with her mother's college friend's daughter, Rebecca, who has come to spend the last three months of her pregnancy in Afeni's home. Afeni, a loner, doesn't want street-smart Rebecca, who has a boyfriend and a big belly, to disrupt her very comfortable solitude. The fierce, well-scripted dialogue between the girls evolves into a sharing relationship with which Woodson tackles issues like alcoholism, death, divorce, class conflicts in the African-American community, lesbianism, adoption, and mental illness.

Woodson combines many "big issues" in one book, and she deals with them directly and easily. The warm, honest, and loving stories are no less "realistic" for their complexity, but draw on the most layered influences of each character's experience. For example, nothing is forced with respect to lesbianism in *The Dear One*. Feni's and Rebecca's mothers were college pals, along with Bernadette, who is now in a long-term relationship with a woman named Marion. Feni has grown up with what Rebecca calls "dites," and they are a natural thread in her fabric of life. Termed "ironic" in reviews, the lesbian couple "seems to be intact while the straight couples have divorced and suffered."

Woodson's new young adult novel, *From the Notebooks of MelaninSun*, focuses on the struggles of a short, twelve-year-old boy with quirky hobbies and fascinations, who is coming of age while taking care of his single mother. When she becomes involved with a white woman, MelaninSun faces lesbianism in the context of a multicultural community. Casually gleaning evidence from her own experiences, Woodson infuses all of her books with the issues of friendship, the nurturing of the gifted black child, independence, depression, death, divorce, racism, self-discovery, and cross-race and cross-class relationships.

The ambitious author wants to get the same messages across to adults that she imparts to children. Since grown-ups rarely read children's books, she is working on her first adult novel, *Writing My Name on Water*, in which the main character is a lesbian. At the same time, she is completing a collection of related short stories, *Autobiography of a Family Photo*, which captures four siblings exploring sexuality and violence through best friends, incest, fantasy, television, secrets, and white people.

CRITICAL RECEPTION

Jacqueline Woodson's work has been critically acclaimed in the *New York Times*, *Newsday*, and various children's and trade book magazines. The *Times* review of *Last Summer with Maizon* notes that "Ms. Woodson writes with a sure understanding of the thoughts of young people, offering a poetic, eloquent narrative that is not simply a story of nearly adolescent children, but a mature exploration of grown-up issues." A *Newsday* reviewer wrote of *The Dear One*, "[Woodson] has a keen ear for 'teenspeak,' and her dialogue is so delightful and real that I laughed while I eavesdropped—and felt real pain at times" (16–17). Frequently, the author is invited to speak at schools nationwide, and she has received hundreds of enthusiastic and thoughtful thank-you letters from the students.

Woodson has read poetry and short stories to packed audiences in New York's Mosaic Books Reading Series, Strathmore Arts Center's Writing Women/Fighting Women Reading Series, New York's Lesbian and Gay Community Services

Center's In Our Own Write Series, and in the New Writers Series at Judith's Room Bookstore in New York City. In 1991, she served both as the fiction editor of the anthology *Other Countries II—Sojourner: A Chronicle of Living, Black Gay Men Respond to AIDS*, and on the editorial board of the Portable Lower East Side—*Queer City*.

BIBLIOGRAPHY

Works by Jacqueline Woodson

"The Company of Friends." *Common Lives Quarterly* (Spring 1987).
"Consumption." *Common Lives Quarterly* (Fall 1987).
"Causes." *Out/Look* (Fall 1989). Anthologized in *Women on Women*. Ed. Joan Nestle. New York: New American Library, 1990.
"Idella's Child, Tyler." *Conditions* 17 (1990).
Last Summer with Maizon. New York: Delacorte, 1990.
Martin Luther King, Jr. New York: Silver Press, 1990.
The Dear One. New York: Delacorte, 1991.
"Growing Up Black and Gay among Good Christian Peoples." *Belle Lettres* (Spring 1991).
Maizon at Blue Hill. New York: Delacorte, 1992.
Between Madison and Palmetto. New York: Delacorte, forthcoming.
Autobiography of a Family Photo. New York: Dutton, forthcoming.
From the Notebooks of MelaninSun. New York: Scholastic, forthcoming.
I Hadn't Meant to Tell You This. New York: Delacorte, forthcoming.

Studies of Jacqueline Woodson

Brailsford, Karen. Review of *Last Summer with Maizon*. *New York Times Book Review* (July 29, 1990).
Chiappinelli, S. Robert. "Author Reaches Out to Children." *Providence Journal* May 9, 1991.
E.F. Review of *The Dear One*. *Horn Book Magazine* (November/December 1991).
Lawrence, Beverly Hall. "Sister from the City." *New York Newsday* November 3, 1991.
Moore, Hazel S. Review of *The Dear One*. *Voice of Youth Advocates* (October 1991).

APPENDIX A:
PUBLISHERS OF LESBIAN WRITERS

While many mainstream and university presses publish some lesbian and gay books, the following publishers have consistently shown their commitment to lesbian publication.

Alyson Publications
40 Plympton Street
Boston, MA 02118
(617) 542–5676

Aunt Lute Foundation
P.O.Box 410687
223 Mississippi Street
San Francisco, CA 94141
(415) 558–9655

Banned Books
c/o Edward-William Publishing Co.
P.O. Box 33280, #292
Austin, TX 78764
(512) 282–8044

Calyx Books
P.O. Box B
Corvallis, OR 97339
(503) 753–9394

Cleis Press
P.O. Box 8933
Pittsburgh, PA 15221
(412) 937–1555

Clothespin Fever Press
10393 Spur Court
La Mesa, CA 91941
(619) 660–2242

The Crossing Press
P.O. Box 1048
Freedom, CA 95019
(408) 722–0711
(Formerly Trumansburg, NY)

Eighth Mountain Press
624 Southeast 29th Avenue
Portland, OR 97214
(503) 236–9862

The Feminist Press at the City University
    of New York
311 East 94th Street
New York, NY 10128
(212) 360–5790

Firebrand Books
141 The Commons
Ithaca, NY 14850
(607) 272–0000

Frog in the Well
P.O. Box 170052
San Francisco, CA 94117
(415) 431–2113

HerBooks
P.O. Box 7467
Santa Cruz, CA 95061
(408) 425–7493

Ism Press
P.O. Box 12447
San Francisco, CA 94306

Kitchen Table: Women of Color Press
P.O. Box 908
Latham, NY 12110
(518) 434–2057

Lace Publications, Inc.
P.O. Box 10037
Denver, CO 80210
(303) 355–9136

Naiad Press, Inc.
P.O. Box 10543
Tallahassee, FL 32302
(904) 539–5965

New Victoria Publishers
P.O. Box 27
Norwich, VT 05055
(802) 649–5297

Onlywomen Press
38 Mount Pleasant
London, England WC1X OAP
01–837–0596

Press Gang
603 Powell Street
Vancouver, British Columbia
Canada V6A 1H2
(604) 253–2537

The Publishing Triangle
P.O. Box 114
Prince Street Station
New York, NY 10012

Seal Press
3131 Western Avenue, No. 410
Seattle, WA 98121
(206) 283–7844

Shameless Hussy Press
P.O. Box 5540
Berkeley, CA 94705
(415) 548–7800

Sidewalk Revolution Press
P.O. Box 9062
Pittsburgh, PA 15224
(412) 361–8927

Silverleaf Press
P.O. Box 70189
Seattle, WA 98107

Spinsters Book Company
P.O. Box 410687
223 Mississippi Street
San Francisco, CA 94141
(415) 558–9655

Third Woman Press
Chicano Studies
Dwinelle Hall 3404
University of California
Berkeley, CA 94720

Timely Books
4040 Mountain Creek Road, #1304
Chattanooga, TN 37415
(615) 875–9447

Tough Dove Press
P.O. Box 184
Willits, CA 95490

Violet Ink
307 West State Street
Ithaca, NY 14850
(607) 273–2325

Volcano Press
P.O. Box 270
Volcano, CA 95689
(209) 296–3445

Wild Violet Publishing
P.O. Box 1311
Hamilton, MT 59840
(406) 363-2696

Woman in the Moon (WIM) Publications
3601 Crowell Road, #100
Turlock, CA 95380
(209) 667-0966

Womyn's Braille Press, Inc.
P.O. Box 8475
Minneapolis, MN 55408
(612) 822-0549

Word Weavers
P.O. Box 8742
Minneapolis, MN 55408

Also of interest: Largest U.S. Bookstore Specializing in Out-of-Print Gay/Lesbian Books

Elysian Fields Booksellers
80-50 Baxter Avenue, Suite 339
Elmhurst, NY 11373
(718) 424-2789

APPENDIX B:
SELECTED PERIODICALS AND JOURNALS OF INTEREST TO READERS OF LESBIAN WRITINGS

Aché: A Journal for Black Lesbians
P.O. Box 6071
Albany, CA 94706
(510) 849–2819

The Advocate
Liberation Publications, Inc.
P.O. Box 4371
Los Angeles, CA 90078

Alternative Press Index
P.O. Box 33109
Baltimore, MD 21218

Amazon Times
P.O. Box 135
Owings Mills, MD 21117

Atalanta
P.O. Box 5502
Atlanta, GA 30307
(404) 378–9769

Backbone
P.O. Box 95315
Seattle, WA 98145

Bad Attitude
P.O. Box 110
Cambridge, MA 02139
(617) 395–4849

Bay Windows
1523 Washington Street
Boston, MA 02118
(617) 266–5973

Belles Lettres
11151 Captain's Walk Court
North Potomac, MD 20878
(301) 294–0278

Black Lace
P.O. Box 83912
Los Angeles, CA 90083
(213) 410–0808

Black/Out: The Quarterly Magazine of
  the National Coalition of Black
  Lesbians and Gays
930 F Street, N.W. #514
Washington, DC 20004

BLK: The National Black Lesbian and
   Gay Magazine
Box 83912
Los Angeles, CA 90083
(213) 410–0808

Bridges: A Journal for Jewish Feminists
   and Our Friends
P.O. Box 18437
Seattle, WA 98118
(206) 721–5008

Calyx: A Journal of Art and Literature by
   Women
P.O. Box B
Corvallis, OR 97339
(503) 753–9384

Common Lives/Lesbian Lives
P.O. Box 1553
Iowa City, IA 52244

Conditions
P.O. Box 56
Van Brunt Station
Brooklyn, NY 11221
(718) 788–8654

Connexions: An International Women's
   Quarterly
4228 Telegraph Avenue
Oakland, CA 94609
(415) 654–6725

Deneuve
FRS Enterprises
2336 Market Street, #15
San Francisco, CA 94114
(415) 863–6538

Diversity: The Lesbian Rag
P.O. Box 66106
Station F
Vancouver, British Columbia
Canada V4N 5L4
(604) 872–3026

Dykes, Disability and Stuff
P.O. Box 8773
Madison, WI 53714

Entre Nous: Between Us
P.O. Box 70933
Sunnyvale, CA 94086
(408) 246–1117

Equal Time
711 West Lake Street, #505
Minneapolis, MN 55408
(612) 823–3836

Gay Community News
62 Berkeley Street
Boston, MA 02116
(617) 426–4469

Golden Threads
P.O. Box 3177
Burlington, VT 05401

Hag Rag: Intergalactic Lesbian Feminist
   Press
P.O. Box 93243
Milwaukee, WI 53203
(414) 372–3330

Heresies
P.O. Box 1306
Canal Street Station
New York, NY 10013

I Know You Know
5435 North Tacoma Avenue
Indianapolis, IN 46220

IKON
P.O. Box 1355
Stuyvesant Station
New York, NY 10009

Journal of Homosexuality
Haworth Press
12 W. 32nd Street
New York, NY 10001

Lambda Book Report
1625 Connecticut Avenue N.W.
Washington, DC 20009
(202) 462–7924

Lambda Update
132 W. 43rd. Street
New York, NY 10036

Lesbian Connection
Elsie Publishing Institute
P.O. Box 811
East Lansing, MI 48826
(517) 371–5257

Lesbian Contradiction: A Journal of
    Irreverent Feminism
584 Castro Street, #263
San Francisco, CA 94114

Lesbian Ethics
P.O. Box 4723
Albuquerque, NM 87196

Lesbian Herstory Archives News
P.O. Box 1258
New York, NY 10116

The Lesbian News
P.O. Box 1430
Twenty-Nine Palms, CA 92277

LGSN: Lesbian and Gay Studies
    Newsletter
Gay and Lesbian Caucus for the Modern
    Languages
Margaret Morrison, Editor
Department of English
P.O. Box 3721
North Carolina Wesleyan College
Rocky Mount, NC 27804

Maize, A Lesbian Country Magazine
P.O. Box 130
Serafina, NM 87569

Mom's Apple Pie
P.O. Box 21567
Seattle, WA 98111

New Directions for Women
108 West Palisade Avenue
Englewood, NJ 07631
(201) 568–0226

NWSA Journal
English Department
University of New Hampshire
Durham, NH 03824

off our backs
2423 18th Street, N.W.
Washington, DC 20009
(202) 234–8072

On Our Backs
526 Castro Street
San Francisco, CA 94114
(415) 861–4723

Outlines
3059 North Southport
Chicago, IL 60657
(312) 871–7610

Out/Look: National Lesbian and Gay
    Quarterly
2940 16th Street, #319
San Francisco, CA 94103
(415) 626–7929

Outweek Magazine
159 West 25th Street
New York, NY 10010
(212) 337–1200

Parents and Friends of Lesbians and Gays
    Newsletter
P.O. Box 15711
Philadelphia, PA 19103

San Francisco Bay Area Gay and Lesbian
    History Society Newsletter
P.O. Box 2107
San Francisco, CA 94126

Signs: Journal of Women in Culture and
    Society
Center for Advanced Feminist Studies
495 Ford Hall
University of Minnesota
Minneapolis, MN 55455
(612) 626–1826

Sinister Wisdom
P.O. Box 3252
Berkeley, CA 94703

Sojourner: The Women's Forum
42 Seaverns Avenue
Jamaica Plain, MA 02130
(617) 524–0415

13th Moon: A Feminist Literary
  Magazine
English Department
SUNY-Albany
Albany, NY 12222
(518) 442–4181

Trivia, A Journal of Ideas
P.O. Box 606
N. Amherst, MA 01059
(413) 367–2254

Visibilities: The Lesbian Magazine
P.O. Box 1258
Peter Stuyvesant Station
New York, NY 10009
(212) 473–4635

The Women's Review of Books
Center for Research on Women
Wellesley College
106 Central Street
Wellesley, MA 02181
(617) 283–2087

BIBLIOGRAPHY: SELECTED NON-FICTION ON LESBIAN ISSUES
Compiled by Ellen Kline

Abbott, Sidney, and Barbara Love. *Sappho Was a Right-On Woman: A Liberated View of Lesbianism*. 1972. New York: Stein & Day, 1985.

Adair, Nancy, and Casey Adair, eds. *Word Is Out: Stories of Some of Our Lives*. San Francisco: New Glide Publications, 1978.

Adelman, Marcy. *Long Time Passing: Lives of Older Lesbians*. Boston: Alyson Publications, 1986.

Allen, Jeffner. *Lesbian Philosophy: Explorations*. Palo Alto, CA: Institute of Lesbian Studies, 1986.

———, ed. *Lesbian Philosophies and Cultures*. Albany: State University of New York Press, 1990.

Alpert, Harriet, ed. *We Are Everywhere: Writings about Lesbian Parents*. Trumansburg, NY: Crossing Press, 1988.

Alyson, Sasha, ed. *Young, Gay, and Proud!* 2nd ed. Boston: Alyson Publications, 1985.

Anderson, Bonnie S., and Judith P. Zinsser. *A History of Their Own*. vol. 1. New York: Harper & Row, 1988.

Anzaldúa, Gloria, ed. *Borderlands/La Frontera: The New Mestiza*. San Francisco: Spinsters/Aunt Lute, 1987.

Atkinson, Ti-Grace. *Amazon Odyssey*. New York: Links Books, 1974.

Aurora. *Lesbian Love Signs: An Astrological Guide for Women Loving Women*. Freedom, CA: Crossing Press, 1991.

Baetz, Ruth, ed. *Lesbian Crossroads: Personal Stories of Lesbian Struggles and Triumphs*. William Morrow, 1980. Tallahassee, FL: Naiad Press, 1988.

Balka, Christie, and Andy Rose, eds. *Twice Blessed: On Being Lesbian, Gay, and Jewish*. Boston: Beacon Press, 1989.

Barrett, Martha Barron. *Invisible Lives: The Loving Alternative of Millions of Women*. William Morrow, 1989. New York: HarperCollins, 1990.

Barrington, Judith, ed. *An Intimate Wilderness: Lesbian Writers on Sexuality*. Portland, OR: Eighth Mountain Press, 1991.

Beck, Evelyn Torton, ed. *Nice Jewish Girls: A Lesbian Anthology*. rev. ed. Persephone Press, 1982. Boston: Beacon Press, 1989.

Becker, Carol. *Unbroken Ties: Lesbian Ex-Lovers*. Boston: Alyson Publications, 1988.

Berzon, Betty. *Permanent Partners: Building Gay & Lesbian Relationships That Last*. Dutton, 1988. New York: New American Library, 1990.

———, ed. *Positively Gay*. rev. ed. Los Angeles: Mediamax Assoc., 1984.

Birkby, Phyllis, et al. *Amazon Expedition: A Lesbian Feminist Anthology*. Albion, CA: Times Change Press, 1973.

Boffin, Theresa, and Jean Fraser, eds. *Stolen Glances: Lesbians Take Photographs*. London: Pandora Press, 1991.

Borhek, Mary V. *Coming Out to Parents: A Two-Way Survival Guide for Lesbians and Gay Men and Their Parents*. New York: Pilgrim Press, 1983.

Boston Lesbian Psychologies Collective, eds. *Lesbian Psychologies: Exploration and Challenges*. Chicago: University of Illinois Press, 1987.

Bozett, Frederick W., ed. *Gay and Lesbian Parents*. Westport, CT: Greenwood Press, 1987.

Bright, Susie. *Susie Bright's Lesbian Sex World*. Pittsburgh: Cleis Press, 1990.

———. *Susie Bright's Sexual Reality: A Virtual Sex World Reader*. Pittsburgh: Cleis Press, 1992.

Brody, Michal. *Are We There Yet? A Continuing History of 'Lavender Woman': A Chicago Lesbian Newspaper, 1971–1976*. Iowa City: Aunt Lute Books, 1985.

Brooks, Virginia R. *Minority Stress and Lesbian Women*. Lexington, MA: Lexington Books, 1981.

Bulkin, Elly. *Enter Password: Recovery. Re-enter Password*. Albany, NY: Turtle Books, 1990.

Bunch, Charloltte. *Passionate Politics: Feminist Theory in Action*. New York: St. Martin's Press, 1987.

Butler, Becky, ed. *Ceremonies of the Heart: Celebrating Lesbian Unions*. Seattle: Seal Press, 1990.

Butler, Sandra, and Barbara Rosenblum. *Cancer in Two Voices*. San Francisco: Spinsters Book Co., 1991.

Cade, Cathy. *A Lesbian Photo Album: The Lives of Seven Lesbian Feminists*. Oakland, CA: Waterwoman Books, 1987.

Califia, Pat. *Lesbian Sadomasochism Safety Manual*. Austin, TX: Lace Publications, 1990.

———. *Sapphistry: The Book of Lesbian Sexuality*. 3rd rev. ed. Tallahassee, FL: Naiad Press, 1988.

Cant, Bob, and Susan Hemmings, eds. *Radical Records: Thirty Years of Lesbian and Gay History, 1957–1987*. London: Routledge, Chapman, & Hall, 1988.

Cavin, Susan. *Lesbian Origins*. rev. ed. San Francisco: Ism Press, 1985.

Cheney, Joyce. *Lesbian Land*. Minneapolis: Word Weavers, 1985.

Clardy, Andrea Fleck. *Words to the Wise: A Writer's Guide to Feminist and Lesbian Periodicals & Publishers*. 3rd rev. ed., updated and expanded. Ithaca, NY: Firebrand Books, 1990.

Clunis, D. Merilee, and G. Dorsey Green. *Lesbian Couples*. Seattle: Seal Press, 1988.

Cooper, Baba. *Over the Hill: Reflections on Ageism Between Women*. Freedom, CA: Crossing Press, 1988.

Cornwell, Anita. *Black Lesbian in White America*. Tallahassee, FL: Naiad Press, 1983.

Corrine, Tee. *Cunt Coloring Book*. 1975. pub. as *Labia Flowers* by Naiad Press, forthcoming as *Cunt Coloring Book* from Last Gasp.

————. *Women Who Loved Women*. Ashland, OR: Pearlchild, 1984.

Covina, Gina, and Laurel Galana, eds. *The Lesbian Reader: An Amazon Quarterly Anthology*. Oakland, CA: Amazon Press, 1975.

Cruikshank, Margaret, ed. *The Lesbian Path: 37 Lesbian Writers Share Their Personal Experiences, Viewpoints, Traumas and Joys*. rev. ed. 1980. San Francisco: Grey Fox Press, 1985.

————, ed. *Lesbian Studies: Present and Future*. Old Westbury, NY: Feminist Press, 1982.

Curb, Rosemary, and Nancy Manahan, eds. *Lesbian Nuns: Breaking Silence*. Tallahassee, FL: Naiad Press, 1985. New York: Warner Books, 1986.

Curry, Hayden, and Denis Clifford. *A Legal Guide for Lesbian and Gay Couples*. 5th ed. Berkeley, CA: Nolo Press, 1989.

Darty, Trudy, and Sandee Potter, eds. *Women-Identified Women*. Palo Alto, CA: Mayfield, 1984.

D'Emilio, John. *Sexual Politics, Sexual Communities: The Making of a Homosexual Minority in the United States, 1940–1970*. Chicago: University of Chicago Press, 1984.

Dicksion, Rhonda. *Lesbian Survival Manual*. Tallahassee, FL: Naiad Press, 1990.

Douglas, Carol Anne, ed. *Love and Politics: Radical Feminist and Lesbian Theories*. San Francisco: Ism Press, 1990.

Downing, Christine. *Myths and Mysteries of Same-Sex Love*. New York: Continuum, 1991.

Duberman, Martin B., Martha Vicinus, and George Chauncey, Jr., eds. *Hidden from History: Reclaiming the Gay and Lesbian Past*. New York: New American Library, 1989.

Ettnore, E. M. *Lesbians, Women and Society*. London: Routledge & Kegan Paul, 1980.

Faderman, Lillian. *Odd Girls and Twilight Lovers: A History of Lesbian Life in Twentieth-Century America*. New York: Columbia University Press, 1991. New York: Penguin USA, 1992.

————. *Surpassing the Love of Men: Romantic Friendship and Love Between Women from the Renaissance to the Present*. New York: William Morrow, 1981.

Fairchild, Betty, and Nancy Hayward. *Now That You Know: What Every Parent Should Know about Homosexuality*. San Diego: Harcourt Brace Jovanovich, 1989.

Falk, Ruth. *Women Loving: A Journey Toward Becoming an Independent Woman*. New York: Random House, 1975.

Fletcher, Lynne Yamaguchi, and Adrien Saks. *Lavender Lists: New Lists about Lesbian and Gay Culture, History, and Personalities*. Boston: Alyson Publications, 1990.

Foster, Jeannette H. *Sex Variant Women in Literature*. 1956. Oakland, CA: Diana Press, 1975. Tallahassee, FL: Naiad Press, 1985.

Freedman, Estelle B., Barbara C. Gelphi, Susan L. Johnson, and Kathleen M. Weston, eds. *The Lesbian Issue: Essays from 'Signs.'* Chicago: University of Chicago Press, 1985.

Freedman, Marcia. *Exile in the Promised Land: A Memoir*. Ithaca, NY: Firebrand Books, 1990.

Frye, Marilyn. *The Politics of Reality: Essays in Feminist Theory*. Freedom, CA: Crossing Press, 1983.

————. *Willful Virgin: Essays in Feminism, 1976–1992*. Freedom, CA: Crossing Press, 1992.

Galana, Laurel, and Gina Covina, eds. *The New Lesbians: Interviews with Women across the U.S. and Canada.* Berkeley, CA: Moon Books, 1977.

Gibbs, Joan, and Sara Bennett, eds. *Top Ranking: A Collection of Articles on Racism and Classism in the Lesbian Community.* New York: February 3rd Press, 1980.

Gidlow, Elsa. *Ask No Man Pardon: The Philosophical Significance of Being a Lesbian.* Mill Valley, CA: Druid Heights Books, n.d.

Gough, Cal, and Ellen Greenblatt, eds. *Gay and Lesbian Library Service.* Jefferson, NC: McFarland, 1990.

Grace, Della. *Love Bites.* London: Gay Men's Press, 1991.

Grahn, Judy. *Another Mother Tongue: Gay Words, Gay Worlds.* Boston: Beacon Press, 1990.

————. *The Highest Apple: Sappho and the Lesbian Poetic Tradition.* San Francisco: Spinsters/Aunt Lute, 1985.

————. *Really Reading Gertrude Stein: A Selected Anthology with Essays.* Freedom, CA: Crossing Press, 1989.

Grier, Barbara. *Lesbiana: Book Reviews from "The Ladder," 1966–1972.* Tallahassee FL: Naiad Press, 1976.

Grier, Barbara, Jan Watson, and Robin Jordan. *The Lesbian in Literature: A Bibliography.* 3rd ed. Tallahassee, FL: Naiad Press, 1981.

Griffin, Carolyn Welch. *Beyond Acceptance: Parents of Lesbians and Gays Talk about Their Experiences.* Englewood Cliffs, NJ: Prentice-Hall, 1986. New York: St. Martin's Press, 1990.

Hall, Marny. *The Lavender Couch: A Consumer's Guide to Psychotherapy for Lesbians and Gay Men.* Boston: Alyson Publications, 1985.

Handscombe, Gillian, and Jackie Forster. *Rocking the Cradle: Lesbian Mothers, A Challenge in Family Living.* Boston: Alyson Publications, 1982.

Harris, Simon, ed. *Lesbian and Gay Issues in the English Classroom: The Importance of Being Honest.* Bristol, PA: Taylor & Francis, 1990.

Hepburn, Cuca, and Bonnie Gutierrez. *Alive and Well: A Lesbian Health Guide.* Freedom, CA: Crossing Press, 1988.

Hertz, Jennifer, and Martha Ertman. *Lesbian Queries: The Book of Lesbian Questions.* Tallahassee, FL: Naiad Press, 1990.

Hoagland, Sarah Lucia. *Lesbian Ethics: Toward New Value.* Palo Alto, CA: Institute for Lesbian Studies, 1988.

Hoagland, Sarah Lucia, and Julia Penelope, eds. *For Lesbians Only: A Separatist Anthology.* London: Onlywomen Press, 1988.

Hobby, Elaine, and Chris White, eds. *What Lesbians Do in Books.* London: Women's Press, 1991.

Holmes, Sarah, ed. *Testimonies: A Collection of Lesbian Coming Out Stories.* Boston: Alyson Publications, 1988.

Hunter, Nan D., Sherryl E. Michaelson, and Thomas B. Stoddard. *The Rights of Lesbians and Gay Men: The Basic ACLU Guide to a Gay Person's Rights.* 3rd ed., rev. and updated. Carbondale, IL: Southern Illinois University Press, 1992.

Hutchins, Loraine, and Lani Kaahumanu, eds. *Bi Any Other Name.* Boston: Alyson Publications, 1991.

Jay, Karla, and Allen Young, eds. *Lavender Culture: The Perceptive Voices of Outspoken Lesbians and Gay Men.* New York: Jove/Harcourt Brace, 1979.

————. *After You're Out: Personal Experiences of Gay Men and Lesbian Women.* New York: Links Books, 1975.

———. *Out of the Closets: Voices of Gay Liberation.* New York: Douglas/Links, 1972.

Jay, Karla, and Joanne Glasgow, eds. *Lesbian Texts and Contexts: Radical Revisions.* New York: New York University Press, 1990.

JEB (Joan E. Biren). *Eye to Eye: Portraits of Lesbians: Photographs.* Tallahassee, FL: Naiad Press, 1979.

———. *Making a Way.* Washington, DC: Glad Hag Books, 1987.

Jo, Bev, Linda Strega, and Ruston. *Dykes-Loving-Dykes.* Oakland, CA: Battleaxe, 1990.

Johnson, Susan E. *Staying Power: Long Term Lesbian Couples.* Tallahassee, FL: Naiad Press, 1991.

Johnston, Jill. *Lesbian Nation: The Feminist Solution.* New York: Simon & Schuster, 1973.

Katz, Jonathan. *Gay American History: Lesbians and Gay Men in the U.S.A.* New York: Harper & Row, 1976.

———. *Gay/Lesbian Almanac: A New Documentary.* New York: Harper & Row, 1983.

Kehoe, Monika. *Lesbians in Literature and History.* New York: Harrington Park Press, 1986.

———. *Aspects of Lesbianism.* New York: Hawthorne, 1986.

———. *Historic, Literary, and Erotic Aspects of Lesbianism.* New York: Harrington Park Press, 1986.

———. *Lesbians Over 60 Speak for Themselves.* New York: Haworth Press, 1989.

Kennedy, Elizabeth Lapovsky, and Madeline Davis. *Boots of Leather, Slippers of Gold: The History of a Lesbian Community.* London: Routledge, Chapman & Hall, 1993.

Kitzinger, Celia. *The Social Construction of Lesbianism.* London: Sage Publications, 1987.

Klaich, Dolores. *Woman + Woman: Attitudes towards Lesbianism.* New York: William Morrow, 1974. Tallahassee, FL: Naiad Press, 1989.

Koertge, Noretta, ed. *Philosophy and Homosexuality.* New York: Harrington Park Press, 1984.

Krieger, Susan. *The Mirror Dance: Identity in a Women's Community.* Philadelphia: Temple University Press, 1983.

Lanning, Lee, and Vernette Hart. *Ripening: An Almanac of Lesbian Lore and Vision.* Minneapolis: Word Weavers, 1981.

Lesbian Lives: Biographies of Women from the Ladder. Oakland, CA: Diana Press, 1976.

Lewis, Sasha Gregory. *Sunday's Women: A Report on Lesbian Life Today.* Boston: Beacon Press, 1979.

Likosky, Stephan, ed. *Coming Out: An Anthology of International Gay and Lesbian Writings.* New York: Pantheon, 1992.

Lilly, Mark, ed. *Lesbian and Gay Writing: An Anthology of Critical Essays.* Philadelphia: Temple University Press, 1990.

Lobel, Kerry, ed. *Naming the Violence: Speaking Out about Lesbian Battering.* Seattle: Seal Press, 1986.

Lorde, Audre. *A Burst of Light: Essays.* Ithaca, NY: Firebrand Books, 1988.

———. *I Am Your Sister: Black Women Organizing across Sexualities.* New York: Kitchen Table: Women of Color Press, 1986. (pamphlet)

———. *Sister/Outsider: Essays and Speeches.* Trumansburg, NY: Crossing Press, 1984.

———. *Uses of the Erotic: The Erotic as Power.* Brooklyn: Out & Out Books, 1978. Freedom, CA: Crossing Press., n.d. (pamphlet)

————. *Zami: A New Spelling of My Name*. Watertown, MA: Persephone Press, 1982. Trumansburg, NY: Crossing Press, 1982.

Loulan, JoAnn. *The Lesbian Erotic Dance: Butch, Femme, Androgyny, and Other Rhythms*. San Francisco: Spinsters Book Co., 1990.

————. *Lesbian Sex*. San Francisco: Spinsters Ink, 1985.

————. *Lesbian Passion: Loving Ourselves and Each Other*. San Francisco: Spinsters/ Aunt Lute, 1987.

Macdonald, Barbara. *Look Me in the Eye*. San Francisco: Spinster's Ink, 1983.

McConnell-Celi, Sue. *Lesbians and Gays in Education: Twenty-First Century Challenge*. Austin, TX: Banned Books, 1991.

McNaron, Toni, ed. *I Dwell in Possibility: A Memoir*. New York: Feminist Press, 1992.

MacPike, Loralee, ed. *There's Something I've Been Meaning to Tell You: An Anthology about Lesbians and Gay Men Coming Out to Their Children*. Tallahassee, FL: Naiad Press, 1989.

Maggiore, Dolores J. *Lesbianism: An Annotated Bibliography and Guide to the Literature, 1976–1986*. Metuchen, NJ: Scarecrow Press, 1988.

Martin, Del, and Phyllis Lyon. *Lesbian/Woman*. San Francisco: Glide, 1972. New York: Bantam Books, 1983. rev. and enlarged as *Lesbian/Woman*. Volcano, CA: Volcano Press, 1991.

Meese, Elizabeth. *(Sem)Erotics; Theorizing Lesbian: Writing*. New York: New York University Press, 1992.

Minton, Henry, ed. *Gay and Lesbian Studies: The Emergence of a Discipline*. New York: Haworth Press, 1992.

Moraga, Cherrìe. *Loving in the War Years: Lo que Nunca Pasó por sus Labios*. Boston: South End Press, 1983.

Moraga, Cherrìe, and Gloria Anzaldúa, eds. *This Bridge Called My Back: Writings by Radical Women of Color*. 2nd ed. Watertown, MA: Persephone Press, 1981. New York: Kitchen Table: Woman of Color Press, 1983.

Moses, Alice E. *Identity Management in Lesbian Women*. New York: Praeger, 1978.

Muller, Ann. *Parents Matter: Parents' Relationships with Lesbian Daughters and Gay Sons*. Tallahassee, FL: Naiad Press, 1987.

Murphy, Marilyn. *Are You Girls Traveling Alone?: Adventures in Lesbianic Logic*. Los Angeles: Clothespin Fever Press, 1991.

Myron, Nancy, and Charlotte Bunch, eds. *Lesbianism and the Women's Movement*. Baltimore: Diana Press, 1975.

Nestle, Joan. *A Restricted Country*. Ithaca, NY: Firebrand Books, 1987.

Nestle, Joan, ed. *The Persistent Desire: A Femme-Butch Reader*. Boston: Alyson Publications, 1992.

Nieman, Linda. *Boomer: Railroad Memories*. Pittsburgh: Cleis Press, 1991.

The Nomadic Sisters. *Loving Women*. Sonora, CA: Nomadic Sisters, 1975.

Parmeter, Sarah-Hope, and Irene Reti, eds. *The Lesbian in the Classroom: Writings by Lesbian Teachers*. Santa Cruz, CA: HerBooks, 1988.

Patton, Cindy, and Janis Kelly. *Making It: A Woman's Guide to Sex in the Age of AIDS*. 3rd ed., rev. and updated. Ithaca, NY: Firebrand Books, 1990, 1987. (English/ Spanish) Spanish trans. by Papusa Molina.

Penelope, Julia. *Call Me Lesbian: Lesbian Lives, Lesbian Theory*. Freedom, CA: Crossing Press, 1992.

Penelope, Julia, and Sarah Valentine, eds. *Finding the Lesbians: Personal Accounts from Around the World*. Freedom, CA: Crossing Press, 1990.

Penelope, Julia, and Susan J. Wolfe, eds. *The Coming Out Stories*. Watertown, MA: Persephone Press, 1980. rev. and expanded as *The Original Coming Out Stories*. 2nd ed. Freedom, CA: Crossing Press, 1989.

Pharr, Suzanne. *Homophobia: A Weapon of Sexism*. Inverness, CA: Chardon Press, 1988.

Phelan, Shane. *Identity Politics: Lesbian Feminism and the Limits of Community*. Philadelphia: Temple University Press, 1989.

Pies, Cheri. *Considering Parenthood*. 2nd ed., upd. San Francisco: Spinsters/Aunt Lute, 1988.

Pollack, Sandra, and Jeanne Vaughn, eds. *Politics of the Heart: A Lesbian Parenting Anthology*. Ithaca, NY: Firebrand Books, 1987.

Ponse, Barbara. *Identities in the Lesbian World: The Social Construction of Self*. Westport, CT: Greenwood Press, 1978.

Potter, Alice H. *How to Be a Lesbian with Class*. Ft. Lauderdale, FL: Ashley Books, 1989.

Potter, Claire, comp. and ed. *The Lesbian Periodicals Index*. Tallahassee, FL: Naiad Press, 1986.

Pratt, Minnie Bruce. *Rebellion: Essays 1980–1991*. Ithaca, NY: Firebrand Books, 1991.

Rafkin, Louise, ed. *Different Daughters: A Book by Mothers of Lesbians*. Pittsburgh: Cleis Press, 1987.

———. *Different Mothers: Sons and Daughters of Lesbians Talk about Their Lives*. Pittsburgh: Cleis Press, 1990.

———. *Queer and Pleasant Danger: Writing Out My Life*. Pittsburgh: Cleis Press, 1992.

Ramos, Juanita, comp. and ed. *Compañeras, Latina Lesbians: An Anthology*. New York: Latina Lesbian History Project, 1987.

Rich, Adrienne. *Blood, Bread, and Poetry: Selected Prose, 1979–1985*. New York: W. W. Norton, 1986.

———. *Compulsory Heterosexuality and Lesbian Existence*. Freedom, CA: Crossing Press, 1980 (pamphlet).

———. *Of Woman Born: Motherhood as Experience and Institution*. New York: Bantam Books, 1977.

———. *On Lies, Secrets, and Silence: Selected Prose, 1966–1978*. New York: W. W. Norton, 1979.

Richards, Dell. *Lesbian Lists: A Look at Lesbian Culture, History, and Personalities*. Boston: Alyson Publications, 1990.

Richardson, Diane. *Women and AIDS*. London: Methuen, 1988.

Roberts, J. R., comp. *Black Lesbians: An Annotated Bibliography*. Tallahassee, FL: Naiad Press, 1981.

Robson, Ruthann. *Lesbian (Out)law: Survival Under the Rule of Law*. Ithaca, NY: Firebrand Books, 1991.

Roscoe, Will, ed. *Living the Spirit: A Gay American Indian Anthology*. New York: St. Martin's Press, 1989.

Rothblum, Esther D., and Ellen Cole. *Lesbianism: Affirming Nontraditional Roles*. New York: Haworth Press, 1988.

———. *Loving Boldly: Issues Facing Lesbians*. New York: Harrington Park Press, 1988.

Rule, Jane. *A Hot-Eyed Moderate*. Tallahassee, FL: Naiad Press, 1985. Toronto: Lester & Orpen Dennys, 1986.

————. *Lesbian Images*. 1975. Trumansburg, NY: Crossing Press, 1982.

Russ, Joanna. *Magic Mommas, Trembling Sisters, Puritans and Perverts: Feminist Essays*. Trumansburg, NY: Crossing Press, 1985.

Samois Collective, eds. *Coming to Power: Writing and Graphics on Lesbian S/M*. Boston: Alyson Publications, 1982.

Sang, Barbara, Joyce Warshow, and Adrienne J. Smith, eds. *Lesbians at Midlife: The Creative Transition*. San Francisco: Spinsters Book Co., 1991.

Sausser, Gail. *Lesbian Etiquette: Humorous Essays*. Trumansburg, NY: Crossing Press, 1986.

————. *More Lesbian Etiquette*. Freedom, CA: Crossing Press, 1990.

Schulenberg, Joy. *Gay Parenting: A Complete Guide for Gay Men and Lesbians with Children*. Garden City, NY: Anchor/Doubleday, 1985.

Segrest, Mab. *My Mama's Dead Squirrel: Lesbian Essays on Southern Culture*. Intro. by Adrienne Rich. Ithaca, NY: Firebrand Books, 1985.

Silvera, Makeda, ed. *Piece of My Heart: A Lesbian of Color Anthology*. Toronto: Sister Vision Press, 1991.

Sisley, Emily L., and Bertha Harris. *The Joy of Lesbian Sex*. New York: Simon & Schuster, 1977.

Smith, Barbara, ed. *Home Girls: A Black Feminist Anthology*. New York: Kitchen Table: Woman of Color Press, 1983.

Smyth, Cherry. *Lesbians Talk Queer Nations*. London: Scarlet Press, 1992.

Stewart, Susan, in collaboration with Persimmon Blackbridge and Lizard Jones. *Drawing the Line: Kiss and Tell*. Vancouver: Press Gang Publishers, 1991.

Stockton, Christine Heron. *Lesbian Letters*. San Francisco: Heron Press, 1986.

Stoddard, Thomas B., et al. *The Rights of Gay People*. rev. ed. New York: Bantam Books, 1983.

Swallow, Jean, ed. *Out from Under: Sober Dykes and Our Friends*. San Francisco: Spinster's Ink, 1983.

Tanner, Donna M. *The Lesbian Couple*. Lexington, MA: Lexington Books, 1978.

Trujillo, Carla. *Chicana Lesbians: The Girls Our Mothers Warned Us About*. Berkeley, CA: Third Woman Press, 1991.

Umans, Meg, ed. *Like Coming Home: Coming-Out Letters*. Austin, TX: Banned Books, 1988.

Van Deurs, Kady. *The Notebooks That Emma Gave Me: The Autobiography of a Lesbian*. self-published, 1978.

Van Dyke, Annette. *The Search for a Woman-Centered Spirituality*. New York: New York University Press, 1992.

Vida, Ginny, ed. *Our Right to Love: A Lesbian Resource Book*. Englewood Cliffs, NJ: Prentice-Hall, 1978.

Warland, Betsy, ed. *InVersions: Writing by Dykes, Queers, and Lesbians*. Vancouver: Press Gang, 1991.

Weise, Elizabeth Reba, ed. *Closer to Home: Bisexuality and Feminism*. Seattle: Seal Press, 1992.

Weiss, Andrea, and Greta Schiller. *Before Stonewall: The Making of a Gay and Lesbian Community*. Tallahassee, FL: Naiad Press, 1988.

West, Celeste. *A Lesbian Love Advisor: The Sweet and Savory Arts of Lesbian Courtship*. Pittsburgh: Cleis Press, 1989.

Wittig, Monique. *The Lesbian Body.* Trans. David Le Vay. 1973. New York: William
    Morrow, 1975. New York: Avon, 1976. Boston: Beacon Press, 1986.
————. *The Straight Mind and Other Essays.* Boston: Beacon Press, 1992.
Wolf, Deborah Goleman. *The Lesbian Community.* rev. ed. Berkeley, CA: University
    of California Press, 1980.
Wolff, Charlotte. *Love Between Women.* 2nd ed. London: Duckworth, 1973.
Young, Tracy. *Women Who Love Women.* New York: Pocket Books, 1977.
Zimmerman, Bonnie. *The Safe Sea of Women: Lesbian Fiction, 1969–1989.* Boston:
    Beacon Press, 1990.
Zipter, Yvonne. *Diamonds Are a Dyke's Best Friend: Reflections, Reminiscences, &
    Reports from the Field on the Lesbian National Pastime.* Ithaca, NY: Firebrand
    Books, 1988.

INDEX

To enhance the usefulness of this book as a bibliographical source book, works are included even if they are merely mentioned; in those cases the work appears with the author's name but no page number

ABOUT THE EDITORS AND CONTRIBUTORS

BARBARA ADAMS helped found the Writing Program at Ithaca College where she teaches composition, journalism, and arts criticism and directs a computer-based writing initiative. She is a regional theater critic and a photographer; her images can be seen on the covers of *Lesbian Love Stories,* vols. 1 and 2.

KIM AINIS is the founder and Director of The Reading Center, where she teaches reading to children and adults. Her poetry has appeared in *Naming the Daytime Mood: Stories and Poems by Chicago Women* (1987) and in a performance entitled *Queer Stories* (1992) produced by Zebra Crossing Theatre.

DONNA ALLEGRA is an African-Caribbean-American writer of poetry, fiction, essays, and cultural journalism. She has published in feminist and lesbian publications and all her work assumes a lesbian audience.

DOROTHY ALLISON teaches writing classes in the San Francisco Bay Area. She is currently working on her second novel.

NUALA ARCHER has recently taught at Yale University and is now teaching and directing the Poetry Center at Cleveland State University.

BRYN AUSTIN is the Managing Editor of *The Advocate*, the national gay and lesbian newsmagazine. She has written a number of articles on the media and underground publishing.

ROBIN BECKER is the author of *Giacometti's Dog* (University of Pittsburgh Press, 1990). She teaches in the writing program at Massachusetts Institute of Technology and serves as the Poetry Editor for *The Women's Review of Books*.

ROBIN BERNSTEIN is a twenty-three-year-old Brooklynite. Her writing has appeared in *Common Lives/Lesbian Lives,* the *Philadelphia Gay News, Bay Windows*, and other periodicals as well as in three anthologies. She is a graduate of the High School of Performing Arts in New York City.

ELIZABETH BEVERLY is a poet, playwright, and ethnographer living in Portland, Oregon. She is currently working on a novel about anthropology in rural West Africa.

SHARON D. BOYLE received her B.A. and M.A. in English literature from Ohio University in Athens, Ohio. She teaches composition, literature, and creative writing at Mohawk Valley Community College in Utica, New York. She has published in *Kansas English*, *The Ohio Journal of English Language Arts*, and *Teaching English in the Two-Year College*.

JUDITH V. BRANZBURG teaches writing and literature at Pasadena City College, Pasadena, California. She writes reviews for the *Los Angeles Lesbian News* and other publications. She received her Ph.D. in literature from the University of Massachusetts at Amherst in 1983 with specialties in American studies, women's studies, and the literature of ''minorities.'' She is working on her first novel.

TONI P. BROWN is an African-American lesbian writer of poetry and short fiction. Her work has appeared in *Sinister Wisdom* (#31, #47), *Common Lives/Lesbian Lives* (#6, #33), and *The Poetry of Sex: Lesbians Write the Erotic*.

KATE BURNS is in a Ph.D. program in literature at the University of California at San Diego, where she is continuing her studies in lesbian literature and lesbian-feminist literary theory.

STEPHANIE BYRD lives in upstate New York. She is a published poet and writer whose work has appeared in *Sojourner*, *Black Books Bulletin*, *American Voice*, and *The Kenyon Review*.

GLYNIS CARR is an Assistant Professor of English at Bucknell University, where she teaches U.S. literature and feminist theory. She is editor of the *Bucknell Review* special issue on feminist theory (Fall 1992) and has published on Zora Neale Hurston, Virginia Woolf, Fannie Hurst, and women's folklore. Her work in progress concerns U.S. women's fiction about interracial friendship.

KATE CARTER is a poet and a sculptor who lives in North Eastham, Massachusetts. She is the recipient of an Ohio Arts Council Fellowship in Poetry. Most recently her work has been published in *The Cosmos Review*.

JUDY CHEN is a hapa Chinese lesbian. She seeks to document, encourage, and explore cutting-edge creative work by Asian and Pacific Islander woman-identified women. She writes for a Seattle Asian newspaper on women's art and activism and works as a clerical/information and referral aide.

BLANCHE WIESEN COOK is a historian, journalist, activist, and Professor of History at John Jay College and the Graduate Center of the City University of New York. She is the author of *Eleanor Roosevelt, The Declassified Eisenhower*, and *Crystal Eastman: On Women and Revolution*, among other books. Her articles include ''Female Support Networks and Political Activism'' and

"Women Alone Stir My Imagination: Lesbianism in the Cultural Tradition." She is currently Vice-President of the American Historical Association.

ROSEMARY KEEFE CURB is Professor of English and Women's Studies and Coordinator of the Women's Studies Program at Rollins College in Florida. She has articles on lesbian and other political women playwrights in *Theatre Journal*, *MELUS Journal*, *Chrysalis*, and in books of literary and drama criticism. She is co-editor of *Lesbian Nuns: Breaking Silence*.

RITA B. DANDRIDGE is Professor of English and Foreign Languages at Norfolk State University where she teaches women's studies, multiethnic fiction, and African-American literature. Her publications include *Ann Allen Shockley: An Annotated Primary and Secondary Bibliography* (Greenwood Press, 1987) and *Black Women's Blues; A Literary Anthology, 1934–1988* (1992).

NANCY DEAN is Professor Emerita in English Literature from Hunter College, where she taught Chaucer, medieval studies, women's studies, and creative writing. She has been writing plays since 1983. Her novel *Anna's Country* (1981) was published under the name Elizabeth Lang.

LINDA DUNNE teaches at the New School of Social Research and is director of the Adult B.A. Program. She is currently working on a study of deformity and deviance in the narrative fiction of American women writers from the late-nineteenth to the mid-twentieth centuries.

BEVA EASTMAN is Associate Professor of Mathematics at William Paterson College, Wayne, New Jersey. Her article "Women, Computers, and Social Change" appeared in *Computers for Social Change and Community Organizing* (1991). She has received several grants on the use of technology in mathematics.

RYN L. EDWARDS is Professor and Chair of Biology at Kenyon College, where she also teaches women's studies. As an active radical feminist and lesbian separatist, she has been a strong force in shaping women's future at Kenyon, which was a male bastion until 1969.

VICTORIA STAGG ELLIOTT is a senior in rhetoric at the University of Illinois at Urbana–Champaign. She is working on a recent oral history of Eastern Europe, numerous magazine articles, and several photo projects. She has been published in *The Daily Illini*, *The National Book Collector's Journal*, *The Paper Salad Journal*, and *Passport: A Student Traveller's Guide*.

TUCKER PAMELLA FARLEY began teaching lesbian studies courses in the mid–1970s. She has lectured and published articles on Virginia Woolf, lesbian literature theory, and twentieth-century American literature. She teaches feminist literary theory at Brooklyn College, City University of New York.

AYOFEMI S. FOLAYAN is a writer of fiction and journalism, a theatrical director, a performance artist, and a community activist. She lives in Los Angeles, where she is at work on her second novel.

TRISHA FRANZEN is Director of the Women's Center and Women's Studies concentration at Albion College. Her doctoral dissertation from the University of New Mexico was entitled "Spinsters and Lesbians: Autonomous Women and Institutionalized Heterosexuality 1890–1920 and 1940–1980." She has taught women's studies at the State University of New York at Buffalo, the University of New Mexico, and Colby College.

SUZANNE GARDINIER is the author of *Usahn: Ten Poems and a Story* (1990) and a book-length poem, *The New World*. Her work has appeared in *IKON*, *The New Yorker*, *Parnassus*, *The Women's Review of Books*, and many other journals. She lives in Sag Harbor, New York.

GINNIE GODDARD is a free-lance writer and video producer specializing in corporate management training programs. She also writes monologues for women.

JEWELLE L. GOMEZ is the author of two collections of poetry and a novel, *The Gilda Stories* (1991). She is originally from Boston and has lived in New York City since 1971. She is the Director of the Literature Program for the New York State Council on the Arts.

RUTH GUNDLE is the publisher and editor of the Eighth Mountain Press, which publishes literature and quality non-fiction by women writers.

EVELYNN M. HAMMONDS is an Assistant Professor at the Massachusetts Institute of Technology. She has contributed numerous articles and reviews on Black women writers.

JORJET HARPER has been the arts and entertainment editor for Chicago's lesbian and gay newsmonthly, *Outlines*, and book editor for *Windy City Times*. Her work has appeared in over thirty journals and magazines. She writes a syndicated lesbian humor column, Lesbomania, and is working on a full-length comic novel.

JEANE HARRIS is an Associate Professor of English and Director of Freshman Composition at Arkansas State University. She is the author of two novels, *Black Iris* (1991) and *Delia Ironfood* (1992). She has also published articles on Willa Cather.

ELOISE KLEIN HEALY has published four books of poetry, *Building Some Changes*, *A Packet Beating Like a Heart*, *Ordinary Wisdom*, and *Artemis in Echo Park* (1991). *Artemis* was nominated for the Lambda Book Award. She teaches writing, women's studies, and gay/lesbian studies.

LISA L. HIGGINS is a Ph.D. candidate in folklore and rhetoric at the University of Missouri at Columbia.

JOELLEN HILTBRAND writes poetry, fiction, and non-fiction and is working on a book of essays, *She Thinks Who She Is*, which will discuss a neighborhood in Brooklyn during the 1960s and 1970s.

ROBERTA HOBSON is an M.A. candidate in history at San Diego State University. Her co-authored essay "Helen Kezia Hunt" will appear in *American National Biography*; her co-authored "Putting Pen to Paper" will appear in *Getting Published (Even) in Graduate School*. Her essay on Helen Hunt Jackson will appear in *Women of the West*. Her thesis is entitled "Murders and Crimes of Passion Committed by San Diegan Women (1880–1910)."

JOY HOLLAND attended Edinburgh University. After teaching in France and Moscow she began a career in publishing and book distribution. In 1986 she moved to the United States, where she completed a Ph.D. in comparative literature at Brandeis University. She currently writes poems and articles and is revising her dissertation for publication.

ALICE Y. HOM is a second-generation Chinese American. Her M.A. thesis from the University of California at Los Angeles was entitled "Family Matters: A Historical Study of the Asian Pacific Lesbian Network." She has a Rockefeller grant for "American Generations: The Asian Pacific Program" at UCLA, where she will continue her research on Asian Pacific Islander lesbians and gay men, specifically focusing on parents' issues with their lesbian or gay children.

JENNIFER M. ISBELL is a creative writing major at California State University at Long Beach. She has written award-winning essays and published reviews.

TERRI L. JEWELL is a Black poet and free-lance writer whose work appears widely. Her book *The Black Women's Gumbo Ya-Ya: Quotations and Other Words* will be released late in 1993.

LOUISE KAWADA holds a Ph.D. in English from the University of Chicago and is a founding member of the Alliance of Independent Scholars. She compiled and edited *The Apocalypse Anthology* and has published articles in *The Walt Whitman Review*, *Papers on Language and Literature*, and *Sexual Practice, Textual Theory*. She was recently appointed Assistant Professor of Critical Studies at the Massachusetts College of Art.

ANNE B. KEATING is a Ph.D. candidate in American Studies at the University of Maryland at College Park. She teaches American intellectual history and writing at New York University. She is currently working on her dissertation, "The Farm: Kate Millett's Feminist Utopia, 1978–1990."

KENDALL is a lesbian performer, author, and scholar who toured the U.S. feminist theater circuit in 1980, earned a Ph.D in drama in 1986, and chaired the theater department at Smith College, 1990–1992. She edited an anthology of eighteenth-century women's plays, *Love and Thunder* (1988) and is currently writing a novel. She continues to publish poems, short stories, and essays.

ANN KLAUDA edits fiction manuscripts for Naiad Press and has written feature articles and book reviews for *The Advocate* and *Equal Time*. She also writes and edits software manuals for a medical office services company.

ELLEN KLINE lives in Ithaca, New York, where she and two partners run Borealis, an independent alternative bookstore.

DENISE D. KNIGHT is an Assistant Professor of nineteenth-century American literature at the State University of New York at Cortland. Her publications include *Cotton Mather's Verse in English* (1989) and *The Yellow Wall-Paper and Selected Stories of Charlotte Perkins Gilman* (1993). She has recently completed work on a critical edition of Gilman's personal diaries. Other areas of scholarly interest include nineteenth-century women writers and autobiography.

SUSAN KRAUSE teaches writing at Lehman College in the Bronx. She is fiction editor of *One Meadway* and lives in Mount Vernon, New York.

MICHELLE KWINTNER lives in Ithaca, New York, where she is a graduate student at Cornell University and teaches Latin.

CAROLYN KYLER is an Assistant Professor of English at Washington and Jefferson College. Her current research interests focus on politics and the family in American literature.

ADRIENNE LAUBY is a lesbian writer of fiction and poetry and a longtime feminist. She recently received an M.A. in English and is working on a novel about lesbian punks.

LESLIE LAWRENCE is a recipient of a Massachusetts Artists Foundation Fellowship and a National Endowment for the Arts Fellowship. Her work has appeared in *The Massachusetts Review, The Colorado Review*, *Sojourner*, and *The Women's Review of Books* and has been anthologized in *Feeding the Hungry Heart*, *Women on Women*, and *Daily Fare* (forthcoming). She teaches writing at Simmons College.

ELLEN LEWIN has taught women's studies and anthropology since the early 1970s, most recently at the University of California at Berkeley. She is the author of *Lesbian Mothers: Accounts of Gender in American Culture* (1993).

ANNA LIVIA is the author of the lesbian novels *Relatively Norma, Accommodation Offered, Bulldozer Rising*, and *Minimax*; the collections of short stories *Incidents Involving Warmth* and *Incidents Involving Mirth*; and a translation of "the best of Natalie Clifford Barney" entitled *A Perilous Advantage*.

CAMILLE D. LOYA is completing her J.D. at Loyola Law School in Los Angeles. Her interests are in public policy as it affects people of color and children. She worked in the UCLA Women's Studies Program and at the UCLA Chicano Studies Research Center.

DIANE LUNDE is an Assistant Professor of English at Wilson College in Pennsylvania, where she also teaches women's studies. She received her M.A. degree from the University of London and her D.A. from the State University of New York at Albany, where she received a Distinguished Doctoral Dissertation

Award. She has published in *13th Moon, Mildred, Visions, St. Andrews Review, Sycamore Review, Poetry Northwest,* and other journals.

DIANE McPHERSON is a lesbian fiction writer and critic who teaches in the writing program at Ithaca College. She earned an M.F.A. in creative writing in 1984 and a Ph.D. in women's literature in 1990, both from Cornell University.

LORALEE MacPIKE is Professor of English at California State University at San Bernardino. She is the author of *Dostoevsky's Dickens* and the anthology *There's Something I've Been Meaning to Tell You* (1989) about lesbian and gay parents coming out to their children. Since 1985 she has been review editor of *Lesbian News.*

S. MARI MADYUN earned her B.A. in philosophy and French at Howard University in 1988 and has studied at the University of Sorbonne. She presently resides in New York City and is working on "Women's Voices Around the World," a compilation of research about women storytellers in Africa, Asia, and South America.

REBECCA MARK is an Assistant Professor of American Literature at Tulane University. She has written several articles on gay pedagogy and edited an edition of Gertrude's Stein's *Licking Belly.* Her book *Dragon's Blood: A Feminist Intertexuality in Eudora Welty's "The Golden Apples"* was published in 1993. She is currently working on *The Killing of Sister Femme,* which explores mass media images of butch-femme sexuality.

BARBARA DALE MAY is an Associate Professor of Romance Languages at the University of Oregon. She has written articles on contemporary Spanish women writers in American, Spanish, and Latin American journals and is the author of *El dilema de la nostalgia en la poesía de Alberti.*

DEBORAH T. MEEM is an Associate Professor of English and Women's Studies at the University of Cincinnati, where she teaches courses in literature, writing, and lesbian studies.

JENNEY MILNER is a manuscript editor at a biology journal and co-edits the book review section of *Sojourner.* She is active within the Jewish community in opposing Israel's occupation of the West Bank and Gaza Strip.

HELENA LOUISE MONTGOMERY was born in 1949 in Roxbury, Massachusetts. Since 1989 she has made Atlanta, Georgia, her home. She is currently working on her first novel.

LISA MOORE teaches English and women's studies at the University of Texas at Austin. She is currently working on a book about representations of sex between women in English prose of the eighteenth and early nineteenth centuries.

MADELINE R. MOORE is Associate Professor of English literature at the University of California at Santa Cruz. She has published *The Short Season*

Between Two Silences, a critical biography of Virginia Woolf, and is under contract to edit, annotate, and write a critical introduction to *Orlando*. Her first novel, *The Red Rocking Horse*, takes place in Paris. She is working on a second novel, *Whitney's Antigone*, a retelling of the Antigone story set in Louisiana in the 1950s, and on *Thirty-One Women Artists: An(other) Tradition*, an examination of the first international gathering of women artists in New York in 1943. *As You Desire* won the Spinsters Ink 1992 first prize for fiction by lesbians and was published in April 1993.

LINDA L. NELSON is a free-lance writer, editor, and Production Manager for *The Village Voice*. She was co-editor of *Trivia, A Journal of Ideas* from 1986 to 1991. Her short fiction, critical essays, and poetry have been anthologized and have appeared in *The Village Voice*, *Out/Look*, and *The Native*. She is currently at work on a lesbian road novel.

MONA OIKAWA is a Sansei (third-generation Japanese Canadian) lesbian writer and editor who lives in Toronto. She is a doctoral student in feminist studies at the Ontario Institute for Studies in Education. Her poetry, short stories, and essays have been anthologized in the United States and Canada, and she is currently working on a collection of her work.

NANCY SEALE OSBORNE is a reference librarian, certified archivist, and women's studies faculty member at the State University of New York at Oswego. Her interests are curriculum development and transformation, library access for diverse populations, and humor in classroom and reference transactions. She reviews for *Choice* and *Women Library Workers Journal*, has published in *Research Strategies: A Journal of Library Concepts and Instruction*, and has co-edited, with Barbara Gerber, the "Crossing the Mainstream: Lesbian Perspectives" issue of *The Creative Woman*.

PENNY PERKINS is a writer and activist. She received an M.A. in English from SUNY at Albany. Her fiction has been published in *Queer City: The Portable Lower East Side* and *The Gulf War: Many Perspectives*.

LUVENIA PINSON is a Black lesbian. A grants writer for the NYC Human Resources Administration, she is a former member of the Harlem Writers Guild and the Frederick Douglass Creative Arts Center, and a current member of Writer's Voice and NYU's screen writers course. In 1987, she helped publish the magazine *The Other Black Woman: The Black Lesbian*. Most recently she is a founding member of and contributor to *Colorlife*, a new magazine addressing the issues of lesbians, gays, and two-spirited people of color, and a member of the lesbian collective that publishes the newsletter *Radical Chick*.

SANDRA POLLACK is Professor of Humanities and Women's Studies at Tompkins Cortland Community College in upstate New York. She is co-editor (with Charlotte Bunch) of *Learning Our Way: Essays in Feminist Education* (1984) and co-editor (with Jeanne Vaughn) of *Politics of the Heart: A Lesbian Parenting*

Anthology (1987). She is currently working on a documentary film of labor educator Alice H. Cook.

MARY S. POLLOCK is an Associate Professor of English at Stetson University. She has published articles on women's music and Victorian women's literature.

JUANITA RAMOS is a Black Puerto Rican lesbian-feminist socialist, editor of the anthology *Compañeras: Latina Lesbians*, and co-founder of the Latina Lesbian History Project. She is an Assistant Professor of Sociology at SUNY Binghamton.

ELIZABETH RANDOLPH is a poet and writer. She is on the Board of Directors of the Astraea National Lesbian Action Foundation and works with Circle of Voices, organizing the first annual Women of Color music festival in the eastern United States. Her dream is to compile a collection of biographies that tell the stories of "not-so-famous" Black women who have made a difference in their communities.

ELIZABETH E. REED received her Ph.D. from Cornell University in 1974. She is a psychotherapist active in gay affirmative politics and staff development for AIDS caregivers. She is a founding member of the Alternative Spiritual Community, a place to celebrate diversity and to honor all loving relationships.

SUSAN ROCHMAN is a free-lance writer based in Ithaca, New York. Her works have appeared in *The Advocate*, *Gay Community News*, and *The Progressive,* and in the anthologies *Loss of the Ground Note: Women Writing about the Loss of Their Mother* and *Work of Mouth 2*.

JUNE V. ROOK lives in New York City and works as a typesetter. She was Associate Editor of *13th Moon* from 1976 to 1978. She was co-recipient, with Ellen Marie Bissert, of a Fels Award for editing a piece on the concrete poet Amelia Etlinger.

CATHERINE SAALFIELD writes on independent film and video, AIDS, and various lesbian and gay issues. She is the Project Coordinator and co-facilitator of Media Network's community-based "Seeing Through AIDS Media Workshops" in New York City. In 1991, she and Jacqueline Woodson co-directed *Among Good Christian Peoples*, based on Woodson's essay of the same title.

PATRICIA ROTH SCHWARTZ is a writer of short fiction, poetry, non-fiction, and reviews. She serves on the board of the Feminist Women's Writing Workshops. Currently she teaches at the community college level.

CYNTHIA SECOR is Director of HERS Mid-America, at the University of Denver. She directs the Summer Institute for Women in Higher Education Administration at Bryn Mawr College and the Management Institute for Women in Higher Education. Currently she is writing a study of Gertrude Stein's prose narratives.

JOCELYN SHEPPARD received an M.L.S. and a Ph.D. in English from the State University of New York at Buffalo. She is a librarian at Bethany College, West Virginia, and is the co-author of *The Bibliography of Contemporary American Fiction, 1945–1988: An Annotated Checklist* (1989).

SUSAN SHERMAN is a poet, essayist, playwright, and editor of *IKON* magazine. Her most recent books are *The Color of the Heart: Writings from Struggle and Change, 1959–1990* and *We Stand Our Ground: Three Women, Their Vision, Their Poems* in collaboration with Kimiko Hahn and Gale Jackson.

SUSAN SILTON is a visual artist, designer, and writer residing in Los Angeles. Her work has been exhibited at the California Museum of Photography/Riverside, Beyond Baroque Gallery, Los Angeles Contemporary Exhibitions, Daniel Saxon Gallery, and the Armory Center for the Arts in Pasadena. She has won numerous awards for her graphic design work. Her writing has appeared in *Blood Whispers: L.A. Writers on AIDS*.

SHARON SILVAS is publisher of *Colorado Woman News, Inc.,* a monthly feminist newsmagazine. She is a writer, journalist, and photographer and does a great deal of public speaking on feminist issues.

JANE TROXELL regularly reviews books and interviews authors for *The Advocate*, *The Washington Blade,* and other outlets. She is senior editor of *Lambda Book Report* and director of the annual Lambda Literary Awards program. A long-time Washington, D.C., resident, she has begun a first novel, *Murder at Half-Court*.

KITTY TSUI is an author, athlete, and community activist. She has won bronze and gold medals in physique at Gay Games II and III. She writes "Leathertalk Top to Bottom," the midwest's first leather column, for *Chicago Nightlines*. As a model she has been on the cover of *The Advocate, On Our Backs,* and *The Village Voice*.

ELAINE MARIA UPTON is on the faculty at the University of Maryland– College Park, where she teaches African-American literature and literature by women of color. She writes poetry and also is working on women writers, especially poets, of the African diaspora.

ANNETTE VAN DYKE is Director and Assistant Professor of Women's Studies at Denison University. She is the author of *The Search for a Woman-Centered Spirituality*. She has published articles on Native American women writers in *Lesbian Texts and Contexts*, *Multi-Ethnic Literature of the United States*, *Studies in American Indian Literatures*, the *National Women's Studies Association Journal*, and *Hurricane Alice*.

NANCY VOSBURG is an Assistant Professor of Spanish at Stetson University. Her Ph.D. dissertation from the University of Iowa was on the works of Esther Tusquets. She has recently co-edited a collection of critical essays on Catalan writer Mercè Rodoreda and is working on a manuscript exploring multiple states of exile in relation to Spanish women writers of the post–civil war period.

SKYE WARD is an Afrafemcentric lesbian activist residing in Oakland, California. She is an original core group member of *Aché*, a national journal for lesbians of African descent. She continues to serve on the Board of Directors for the Aché project.

MARY C. WARE is Assistant to the Dean of Professional Studies and a Professor of Education at the State University of New York at Cortland. She received her Ph.D. from Syracuse University, and her work, predominantly on women and computing, has been published in numerous scholarly journals.

ELIZABETH M. WAVLE is head of Technical Services at Elmira College's Gannett-Tripp Library. She also serves as the Coordinator of Women's Studies and is the author of "A Gay and Lesbian Core Collection," which appeared in *Choice: Current Reviews for College Libraries* (July/August 1991).

DEBRA WEINSTEIN has been a fellow of the MacDowell Colony and Yaddo. Her poems have appeared in *Tikkun*, *The Portable Lower East Side*, *Outweek*, *Christopher Street*, *The James White Review*, *Common Lives/Lesbian Lives*, and *Open House: New Gay and Lesbian Poets*.

CYNTHIA WERTHAMER is an English instructor, poet, and academic administrator. She holds an M.Phil. in nineteenth- and twentieth-century English and American literature from Oxford University. She has authored a book on *The Canterbury Tales* as well as many articles for *Ms.*, *New Directions for Women*, and other publications. She was the recipient of a Woodrow Wilson residential fellowship in poetry writing.

MARIE-ELISE WHEATWIND has an M.A. in English from the University of California at Berkeley. She has been awarded two literature fellowships from the California Arts Council and a PEN syndicated fiction prize. Her work has appeared in numerous anthologies, including *Chicana Lesbians: The Girls Our Mothers Warned Us About* (1991) and *She Who Was Lost Is Remembered* (1992).

EM L. WHITE is an educated, working-class Native American lesbian who lives in Ithaca, New York. She has a B.A. from SUNY Regents in Albany in Liberal Arts and is currently attending Cornell University. She writes short stories and works as an editor. Her interests are in American women's history, particularly the Civil War period.

J. CAISSA WILLMER is a writer, free-lance journalist, and editor, sometime playwright and poet, who lives in Cortland, New York.

TERRY WOLVERTON is a writer of fiction, poetry, essays, and drama, the co-editor of *Harbinger: Poetry and Fiction by Los Angeles Writers* and *Indivisible: Short Fiction by West Coast Gay and Lesbian Writers* (Plume Fiction). She has published a book of poetry, *Black Slip* (1992), and is currently at work on her first novel, *The Labrys Reunion*.